The Gospel of Matthew

A Commentary by
Michael Mullins

the columba press

First published in 2007 by
the columba press
55A Spruce Avenue, Stillorgan Industrial Park,
Blackrock, Co Dublin

Cover by Bill Bolger
Origination by The Columba Press
Printed in Ireland by ColourBooks Ltd, Dublin

ISBN 978 1 85607 591 6

Acknowledgements
Scripture quotations are taken from The New Revised Standard
Version, copyright (c) 1989, by the Division of Christian Education of
the National Council of the Churches of Christ in the United States of
America. Used by permission.

Contents

Preface

The gospels do not give us a single monochrome picture of Jesus. Each gospel has its own rich perspectives as it tells the story of Jesus in changing times and differing circumstances. Matthew's gospel tells the story of Jesus to a mixed group of Jews and Gentiles at a very difficult time. On the one hand, there was the problem of growing tension between Rabbinic Judaism and the Jewish Christian movement. On the other hand, there was the growth in numbers of Gentile members in the church and the Jewish Christians' fear of losing sight of their roots and their Jewish identity. Matthew assures his Jewish Christian audience that Jesus is the authentic interpreter of the Torah as he calls for 'the greater righteousness'. He assures them also that they can experience in Christ and his church the presence of God and the forgiveness of sins, two of the major functions of the temple and its atoning rituals, the loss of which had been a devastating blow to the Jewish people.

By using the history of Israel as a paradigm or archetypal experience, Matthew aligns the story of Jesus and his followers with the literary, historical and theological perspectives of Israel's religious inheritance. At the same time, he deals with the fact that his church, now including many Gentiles, is facing a whole new and uncertain future in the Gentile world. The need to adapt is crucial. Significantly, he points to Jesus' comment on the wise scribe who stands out as a model of the kingdom. Such a scribe is at one and the same time rooted in God's work in history and open to God's new initiative in the present and future: 'Every scribe who has become a disciple of the kingdom of heaven is like a householder who brings out of his treasury things new and old' (Mt 13:53).

I offer this commentary on St Matthew's Gospel at a time when many people are taking a serious interest in the scriptures and looking for reading material to deepen their spiritual understanding of the inspired word and broaden their knowledge of biblical scholarship. I offer it as an aid for students of theology and as a guide for serious readers in the hope that it will deepen their spiritual and theological insight, and bring them to an initial level of academic competence. I offer it also to those many preachers who wish to

11

underpin their preaching with serious reading and to the many people who practise *lectio divina* and other forms of spiritual reading. No prior technical knowledge of biblical scholarship is assumed and I explain technical terms and translate important Greek and Hebrew words and expressions as we meet them. Since the general reader may wish to read the book in stages, and the student may wish to consult or revise a particular section, there is an element of recapitulation throughout. For the same reasons, I refer to books and articles in the notes relating to each section, in addition to the bibliography at the end of the book.

I owe a debt of gratitude to many scholars who have written on St Matthew's Gospel and related texts and whose contributions greatly influenced my understanding and approach. Their contributions will be obvious from the quotations and notes.

My thanks are due to my colleagues in St Patrick's College, Maynooth, to Frs Seamus O'Connell and Brendan McConvery CSSR in the Scripture Department for their support and encouragement, and to Frs Thomas Norris, Oliver Treanor, Padraic Corkery and Edmond Cullinan for reading and making helpful suggestions on sections of the text.

My thanks extend in a special way to Seán O Boyle and the staff of The Columba Press for their encouragement and for their professional competence in bringing this book to its readers.

Michael Mullins.
St Patrick's College,
Maynooth.
Feast of St Benedict,
Patron of Europe
11 July 2007

Introduction

1. THE WRITTEN GOSPELS

The gospels of Matthew, Mark, Luke and John are first and foremost gospels, *euaggelia*, 'good news' in narrative form, the literary genre which early on in the life of the church became the preferred paradigm by which to communicate the mystery of Christ. The writing of the gospels was the third stage in the handing on of the gospel or 'good news'. It represents the transition from oral, liturgical and epistolary proclamation and instruction to written gospel. The first stage was the historical ministry of Jesus in which his person, words, actions, death and resurrection impacted on the original witnesses. The second stage in handing on the traditions about Jesus consisted of a sustained period of oral and epistolary instruction, mission preaching, theological reflection and liturgical celebration, all carried out in the light of the resurrection and outpouring of the Spirit. The third stage was the committing to the written gospel form of the tradition(s) thus built up, reflected on in the light of the Old Testament and applied to pastoral situations over a considerable period of time.

Though the written gospels drew on earlier traditions, they are not simply a series of units loosely strung together like beads on a string, even though the sayings, parables, miracle stories, pronouncement stories, controversies and other elements already existed in the oral tradition. Each gospel is a meaningful whole. The elements are arranged in an overall pattern like the panes of a stained glass window or the pieces of a mosaic which are arranged together to present a single overall picture. Each section of a gospel is therefore understood in the context of the whole work.

The gospels tell the story of Jesus within the framework of a 'biographical sketch'. There is no evidence, in fact it is most unlikely, that anyone went around with Jesus writing down an eyewitness account of his words and deeds so the 'biographical sketch' is largely a created framework for relating the remembered and interpreted story of Jesus. The post-resurrection insights, experiences and problems of the church communities play a major part in shaping the telling. Reflection on the Old Testament also plays a major part as it enables understanding and provides a dictionary of religious language, categories and literary genres for the task of writing the gospels.

How original and how influenced by the contemporary literary genre of a *bios* or 'biographical sketch' was the proclamation and explanation of the good news in narrative form? There were many examples of biographical writing in the Greco-Roman and Jewish worlds on which the evangelists could have drawn, although they were very different to our twenty-first century understanding of biography. They were not comprehensive, detailed 'objective' or uninterpreted accounts related in strict chronological order. They did not speculate on inner motivation and engage in psychological analysis. They focused on the typical characteristics, teaching and actions of the protagonist and had a clearly defined didactic character and purpose. They worked on the assumption that actions reveal good or bad character and emphasised the necessary consistency between values expressed in word and carried out in deed. They focused on the broad framework of a public life between birth and death. They arranged the material around memorable episodes and gathered teaching together in themes. Noble ancestry and birth in high society or honourable birth in obscure circumstances combined with heroic or honourable death crowning a life's achievement were of particular importance in a *bios*. Of particular importance also was the outcome of one's life, especially in leaving behind a body of teaching and a following of disciples and admirers to be guardians of one's legacy. The beginning (*archê*), the flowering (*akmê*) and the final end or outcome (*telos*) of such a life were important points around which to organise the material for a *bios*. Usually Hellenistic biography focused on 'ideal' or single dimension characters. Plutarch followed a process of *synkrisis*, a comparison and contrast between different people's lives. The Roman writers Sallust, Suetonius and Tacitus differed from this Hellenistic genre of *bios* as they focused more on complicated character descriptions and events. They could be quite critical and at times bitingly cynical of their subjects.

Within the Jewish world there was the tradition of the prophetic writings, produced by the disciples and schools of the prophets, but apart from the story of Jeremiah the prophetic writings for the most part show little interest in the biographical details of the prophets themselves. In New Testament times Philo wrote biographical sketches of the Patriarchs in which he associated each individual

with a particular virtue. He wrote on Joseph as a model politician.
His two books on Moses focused respectively on Moses as leader
and Moses as lawgiver.[1]

The gospels and the' bios' genre

The question must now be asked: 'How do the gospels relate to the
bios genre?' Rudolf Bultmann, and others following his lead, saw in
the gospels an original Christian creation entirely at the service of
the faith, cult and pastoral concerns arising from and illustrating
the Christian *kerygma* with little or no connection to such secular
biography.[2] The *kerygma*, a Greek term meaning a 'public proclamation' by the *kêryx*, the herald or town/city crier, refers to the public
proclamation of the victory of God in the life, death and resurrection of Jesus and, by extension, it refers to the influence of the public
proclamation on the written word.

The earliest preaching seems to have been presented around a
'two point proclamation (*kerygma*)', reflected in the sermons in the
Acts of the Apostles, which could be summed up as: 'You (or they)
put Jesus to death, but God raised him up.' The speeches of Peter at
Pentecost, in the Portico of Solomon, to the council following the
healing of the cripple and in the house of Cornelius are built around
this two-point proclamation (Acts 2:23f; 3:13f; 4:10; 5:30f; 10:39f). So
also is the speech of Paul in Antioch (13:28-30). This proclamation is
the bedrock on which New Testament theology builds.

Building on the 'two point' proclamation, the language of rejection, betrayal, handing over, envy, murder, and so on, accrue to the
first point (' You/they put Jesus to death') while the language of
raising up, vindication, victory, glory, exaltation to the right hand
of God and the establishment of the crucified one as Lord and
Christ, accrue to the second ('God raised him up').

Resulting from the proclamation of the victory manifest in the
Father's vindication of Jesus, the first Christians came to realise that
'in his name', that is, in the life, death and resurrection of Jesus, God
has given us salvation. There follows, therefore, the call to repent
and to be baptised in the name of Jesus Christ for the forgiveness of
sins and the reception of the Holy Spirit. Forgiveness of sins, not the

---

1. *De Josepho, De Mosis.*
2. R. Bultmann, *History of the Synoptic Tradition*, translated by John
Marsh, Oxford: Basil Blackwell, 1968.

destruction of the sinner, and not only the cancellation of past wrongs but the promise of new life in the Spirit, are offered to those who repent and are baptised in the name of Jesus Christ.

When Paul wrote to the Corinthians, the 'two point proclamation' that he had received as tradition and was in turn handing on, was furnished with an interpretation explaining the salvific nature of Jesus' death, 'for our sins'. It also emphasised that Jesus' death and resurrection were in accordance with the scriptures (that is, in fulfilment of God's plan). In addition two 'apologetic' points are in evidence. He was buried, so he was truly dead. He appeared to witnesses, so he was truly risen. Paul wrote:

> For I handed on to you as of first importance what I in turn had received: that Christ died for our sins in accordance with the scriptures, and that he was buried, and that he was raised on the third day in accordance with the scriptures, and that he appeared ... (1 Cor 15:3f).

For Paul and other New Testament writers, the term 'good news' was particularly apt for the offer of salvation revealed in the life, death and resurrection of Jesus Christ. He used the term *euaggelion*, 'good news' more than sixty times both as a proclamation and a theological synthesis of the revelation and salvation brought about through the life, death and resurrection of Jesus Christ. In the Old Testament the equivalent Hebrew term for good news, *bsr*, was used especially in the Psalms and in Deutero-Isaiah with special reference to the gracious act of God in effecting the return of the exiled or scattered people to Zion, the ending of punishment and promise of new beginnings. The proclamation of the *kerygma* was regularly prefaced, as in the examples quoted from the Acts, with a summary of 'salvation history' showing how God prepared the people over a long period of time for the coming of the Christ/Messiah.

The gospels are a presentation of the origins of this good news in the ministry of Jesus. They present the messenger of the good news, announce the good news, portray Jesus as the embodiment of that good news and proclaims Jesus the Risen Lord as the vindication by God of the good news. This is a very different task to that of writing history in the conventional sense, whether according to ancient or modern norms of historiography. For this reason Bultmann and his followers saw in the gospels an original Christian creation entirely at the service of the faith, cult and pastoral concerns arising from and illustrating the Christian *kerygma*, the proclamation of the good news, with little or no connection to such secular biography.

Contrary to Bultmann, however, it must be said that even though there is a very clear distinctiveness about the gospels, they reflect some of the trends of the Hellenistic *bios* in so far as they endeavour to capture the essentials of the ideal character and teaching of Jesus and present it in a general 'biographical sketch' or loose overall framework of his life, dealing with the origins of his person and mission, the flowering of his public life and the outcome of his endeavours. Furthermore, this *bios* genre can be adapted relatively easily to cater for the theological and pastoral concerns of the evangelists.

However, in agreement with Bultmann it must be stated that the gospels are very distinctive and differ in a number of essential aspects from the Hellenistic *bios* or Roman *vita*. They are theological productions and not just interesting or entertaining accounts of great, good, interesting or wicked persons who for some reason should be remembered by future generations as heroes or villains from the past. The gospels are narratives about a person whom the writers believe to be alive and active after his execution and death.[3] They are designed to spell out in narrative genre the identity between the crucified and risen one, that is, between Jesus of Nazareth and the Christ living at the heart of the primitive Christian communities. They are narratives about someone whose words and deeds, whose life and death, whose earthly life and glorified presence are as relevant to the reader or hearer today as they were to the characters in the story and the original intended audience/readership. The gospels, therefore, should be seen as a special type or sub-genre of the broader *bios* genre, a *bios Iêsou*.

Not alone did the ancient writers conform to the norms of a literary genre but the readership/audience[4] had definite expectations in approaching a *bios*. Warren Carter in his recent study, *Matthew: Storyteller, Interpreter, Evangelist*, devotes a large portion of his book

---

3. C. Focant, *L'Évangile selon Marc*, Commentaire biblique: Nouveau Testament 2, Les Éditions du Cerf, Paris, 2004, 30.

4. Manuscripts were extremely rare and therefore most people would not have access to the manuscript but would hear it read in the assembly. For this reason the skills of public speaking and the use of rhetorical techniques used in public address continue to be of influence after the transition to writing the story of Jesus in biographical form.

to the authorial audience (the intended audience that can be reconstructed from an examination of the text) in an endeavour to bring the modern audience as close as possible to an understanding of the background and expectations of the audience for whom the gospel was originally intended.[5] He quotes the works of C. Talbert and R. A. Burridge in reconstructing the expectations of such an audience, before giving his own summary. He points out that according to C. Talbert the authorial audience expected to find in a *bios* a pattern to copy, a correction of false information about the master or founding figure to ensure a true image, an exposing of a false teacher, a legitimation of the authentic teaching and tradition after the demise of the master or founder figure and the provision of the key for interpreting his teaching.[6] According to R. A. Burridge there are seven possible functions of the *bios*. These he describes as eliciting praise, providing a model, informing, entertaining, preserving memory, instructing and providing material for debate and argument.[7] Having considered these, Warren Carter then gives his own succinct summary:

> The ancient audience thus expects a biography to present the figure's teaching and life as a possible model for its own living. The paradigmatic actions and words of the hero legitimate or discredit important cultural and community values and practices. Biographies function to shape identity and guide the audience's way of life.[8]

A gospel is not, therefore, just an interesting story about a great person of the past. Neither is it an academic theological treatise. It is the committing to writing of a narrative born from the faith-filled vision, theological perspective and pastoral concerns of the evange-

5. W. Carter, *Matthew: Storyteller, Interpreter, Evangelist*, Peabody, Mass: Hendrickson, 2004.

6. C. Talbert, *What Is a Gospel? The Genre of the Canonical Gospels*, Philadelphia: Fortress, 1977, 92-98.

7. R.A. Burridge, *What Are the Gospels? A Comparison with Graeco-Roman Biography*, Society for New Testament Studies Monograph Series 70. Cambridge: Cambridge University Press, 1992. See also, Aune, D., 'Greco-Roman Biography' in *Greco-Roman Literature and the New Testament: Selected Forms and Genres*, Society of Biblical Literature Sources for Biblical Study 21, ed. D. Aune, Atlanta: Scholars Press, 1988.

8. W. Carter, *op. cit.* 41.

list. The purpose of the evangelist in creating the narrative is not just informative. It is also performative and transformative because it aims to secure, influence or transform the lives of the readers or listeners by engaging them in the story of Jesus and calling them to be his disciples. Warren Carter sums up the matter very well:

> In reading Matthew's gospel, the authorial audience expects to find legitimation for its identity and way of life, its past and future in relation to Jesus ... Matthew is an ancient biography or story, which functions as a vehicle for proclamation about Jesus. Though it contains historically accurate material, this gospel proclaims the significance of Jesus for the purpose of shaping the identity and lifestyle of a particular community of faith ... the author uses the genre of an ancient biography to express his theological and pastoral concerns. The recognition of this genre denotes a set of expectations that guide the authorial audience in its reading. The audience in turn expects a biography to portray its hero's life in a way that shapes its own identity and lifestyle.[9]

2. AUTHORSHIP, DATE AND PLACE OF COMPOSITION.[10]

A. THE AUTHORSHIP OF THE GOSPEL

The anonymous early Christian document known as the *Gospel According to Matthew* was written by a Christian so steeped in Jewish tradition that most commentators believe that the author was almost certainly a Jewish Christian. The gospel does not identify its author and the author makes no specific claim in the work to be an eyewitness of the events recorded. The ascription to Matthew came later. One naturally asks: 'Who was the Matthew in question and why was the work ascribed to him?' Is this the Matthew who figures in the lists of the Twelve (Mt 10:3; Mk 3:18; Lk 6:15)? Is he the tax collector whose call to discipleship is described in Mt 9:9? If so, how does he relate to the tax collector Levi in the parallel passage in Mk 2:4 and Lk 5:27? These questions are not answered directly within the gospel so one has to rely on what can be gleaned from external witness.

---

9. W. Carter, *op. cit.*, 41,42.
10. The earliest extant manuscripts of Matthew are papyri fragments from the late second or third centuries, and the fourth and fifth century Sinaiticus, Alexandrinus and Vaticanus codices.

External Witness

The first explicit references to Matthew as author of the gospel are found in Irenaeus (c. 180AD). Writing at the height of the Gnostic crisis, Irenaeus was very anxious to establish the apostolic credentials of the four gospels.[11] He considered Matthew to be the tax collector called to be a disciple and appointed one of the Twelve, and he considered John to be the son of Zebedee, one of the Twelve. He described Mark as 'the interpreter of Peter' and Luke as 'the friend of Paul'. He said Matthew wrote while Peter and Paul were actively involved in Rome (i.e. in the sixties of the first century).

Eusebius of Caesarea (c. 260-340AD) quotes Papias (c. 60-130) who was bishop of Hierapolis as saying that Matthew compiled (*synetaxato*, put in order) the *logia* (sayings or oracles) of the Lord in the Hebrew language (dialect) and each one translated (interpreted) them as well as he could.[12] Speaking of the origins of the gospel of Mark, Eusebius quotes Papias' source as John the Presbyter. Could he be the original source of the Matthew tradition also? Maybe. But it remains only speculation. By *logia* did he mean a catena of single sayings or an organised body of teaching, and did it have a narrative framework? Speaking of the gospel of Mark, Eusebius uses the expression *kyriaka logia* in relation to what he has called 'those things which were spoken and done by the Lord'. This use of *logia* for the *res gestae* of the Lord would seem to point to the possibility of a broader use of the term *logia*. This would concur with the traditional view that Matthew wrote a gospel, some kind of structured narrative 'in the Hebrew language/dialect' which has not survived. This Papias tradition also lies behind the statement of Augustine that 'Mark walks in Matthew's footsteps and abridges him.'[13]

Eusebius also quotes Origen's commentary on Matthew in which he states that the gospel of Matthew was the first to be composed, that it was composed in the Hebrew language and that it was composed for believers from Judaism.[14] What is meant by 'the Hebrew language (or dialect)'? Does it mean Hebrew, at the time a scholarly language no longer spoken or understood by the ordinary

---

11. *Adversus haereses*, 3.1.1, quoted by Eusebius in *Historia Ecclesiastica*, 5.8.2.
12. *Historia. Eccleiastica*, 3.39.16
13. *De Consensu Evangelistarum*, 1.2.4.
14. *Hist. Eccles.*, 6.25.4

Jewish people, or does it mean 'the spoken language of the Hebrews' which in fact was Aramaic? Scholars generally believe that Aramaic is the language in question. However, they remain somewhat unsure of, and have many questions about the accuracy of the Papias-Eusebius tradition.

Keeping in mind the paucity of any really incontestable inform-ation, one must still ask how the association of the Greek gospel with Matthew arose. Even if he is not the one who actually wrote the canonical gospel in the Greek language, he may have had a relation-ship with the community in which and for which the gospel was written. Did the community owe its initial conversion to him? Was he the apostolic patron of the community? Did the community see itself as the guardian of his apostolic witness as it handed on his gospel and, through its evangelist, commit it to writing? Any of these relationships, however tenuous, could be sufficient to associ-ate the gospel with Matthew the Apostle and for the memory of such an association to survive in the tradition. One can only specul-ate on these questions due to lack of specific information.

It is of some significance that traditionally Matthew's gospel is placed first in the canonical order in almost all New Testament texts. From early on it required a premier status among the gospels. This may well be because of its rich catechetical potential, its perceived focus on church order and discipline and its influence in the liturgy where, for example, Matthew's version of the Beatitudes and the Lord's Prayer became the standard.[15] It may also reflect a residual awareness of a connection with an apostolic figure

If one accepts the fact that there was an Aramaic Matthew one is left with serious questions about its relationship to Greek Matthew, which, from its Greek style and usage does not appear to be a close translation of an Aramaic (or Hebrew) document. Furthermore, modern scholarship has long been of the opinion that as the canoni-cal gospels now stand, canonical Greek Matthew is later than canonical Greek Mark. This opens up two very big questions. How does canonical Greek Matthew relate to the collection of sayings or primitive gospel (Aramaic Matthew?) referred to by Papias-Eusebius

---

15. There were some exceptions. J. Quinlan in 'The Gospel According to St Matthew' in *The New Catholic Encyclopedia* points to the order in the inscription from c. 440 in the Mausoleum of Galla Placidia near the church of San Vitale in Ravenna in which Matthew follows Mark.

and how does it relate to canonical Greek Mark ? An examination of these questions is beyond the scope of this present work.

B. THE DATE OF THE GOSPEL

Scholars generally regard Matthew's gospel as having been written in the eighties of the first century. There are possible but unacknowledged allusions or quotations from the gospel in 1 Peter 2:12 and 3:14 and in other documents such as the *Didachê* and the Letters of Ignatius in the early second century. The destruction of the temple is sufficiently in the past to allow the development of rabbinic, apocalyptic and Jewish Christian responses to reach a point of mutual tension. However, the separation does not yet appear to have been as clear-cut as the separation or expulsion from the synagogue evident in the gospel of John (cf. Jn 9:22). The intensity of Mt 23 has all the marks of a divided community still close enough to generate very heated and bitter 'in-house' rivalry and hostility. Scholars for these reasons tend to regard the gospel as having been written in the early eighties of the first century.

C. THE PLACE OF COMPOSITION

The implied audience (original intended readership) is obvious from a reading of the gospel. The overarching concerns of the gospel show that the author had in view an audience very largely, though not exclusively, made up of Jewish Christians. It is written with a large urban church in mind. It was obviously intended for a community living close to a large Jewish community with which it was in contention. The obvious concern about Gentiles points to a setting where there was also a considerable gentile population. Concerning the language, it can be said that the Greek of Matthew is good *Koinê* Greek, generally regarded as better than the Greek of Mark or Q.

Matthew is usually regarded as having been written in Syria, probably in Antioch, the capital of the Roman province of Syria, which was a large multi-ethnic, multicultural city, the third city of the Roman Empire, after Rome and Alexandria. Josephus witnesses to the presence of a large Jewish community in the city and throughout Syria.[16] The Acts of the Apostles and the Letter to the Galatians describe a significant Christian presence in Antioch. The Hellenist Jewish Christians fled there during the persecution, which

---

16. Josephus, *War*, 7:43.

followed the martyrdom of Stephen (Acts 11:18-19). Barnabas re-
cruited Paul to work with him there among the growing number of
Christians (Acts 11:25-26). Pointing to the development of an organised church is the fact that the names of the prophets and teachers in
Antioch are given and the church there was sufficiently established
and self-confident to send Barnabas and Saul (Paul) on a missionary
journey (Acts 13:1-3). From there the deputation went to Jerusalem
to discuss the matter of circumcision and observance of Jewish laws
and customs on the part of the Christians of pagan background
(Acts 15:2). It was there the followers were first called Christians
(Acts 11:26). It was there also that the dispute between Peter and
Paul, referred to in Galatians, took place (Gal 2:11-14). Antioch
would therefore fit the circumstances of the implied readers of
Matthew very well, with its established urban-based church with a
large Jewish membership and an increasing number of Gentile
members. Less likely, but other possible centres in Syria would have
been Edessa, or Damascus where there was a Christian community,
whither Paul was going with intentions of arresting the members,
and to whom he preached after his 'conversion' (Acts 9:1-25).

Palestine has also been suggested as a possible place of writing.
There were large urban areas with mixed populations and considerable Hellenist influence, particularly in places like Caesarea
Maritima and the ten Greek cities referred to as the Decapolis[17] and
even Galilee itself was referred to as 'Galilee of the Gentiles' because of its mixed population. However, Antioch in Syria remains
the most likely place of origin in the opinion of scholars.

3. SOURCES

There are three main sources or clearly identifiable bodies of material in the gospel, each of which was probably an amalgam of earlier
material.

A. THE MARKAN SOURCE

A majority of scholars today maintain that Greek Mark is the earliest of the canonical gospels and that Matthew and Luke used Mark
as a source. This opinion is based largely on the fact that the under-

---

17. The names of the ten cities were given by Pliny the Elder as
Damascus, Philadelphia, Raphana, Scythopolis, Gadara, Hippos, Dion,
Pella, Gerasa, and Canatha.

lying narratives of Matthew, Mark and Luke are strikingly similar and wherever all three are not in agreement in the order of events either Matthew or Luke usually agrees with the order in Mark. Therefore in the opinion of very many scholars, Mark is the underlying narrative from which the order in Matthew or Luke deviates at times. Of Mark's 661 verses 606 corresponding verses (approximately 92%) appear among Matthew's 1068 verses.[18]

Matthew put his own stamp on this material. In using sources it was commonplace for authors to employ a number of techniques such as abbreviation, correction, distillation, distribution, elaboration, and synthesis. Matthew's order of events in chapters 4-11 differs significantly from the order of corresponding events in Mk 1-6, though Luke follows the order in Mark. From chapter 12 on, the order in Matthew follows that in Mark. This appears to be because of Matthew's distribution of the miracle stories in Mt 8-9 in three triads with short commentaries, and his use of the material relating to the appointment of the Twelve in relation to his Mission Discourse in Mt 10.[19]

At times Matthew has an expanded version of the Mk/Mt tradition with short dialogues added in the healing stories and at times, especially in the miracle stories, a shorter version, eliminating secondary characters, circumstantial details, and descriptions of Jesus' emotions. Matthew also has a much more positive approach to the disciples and, where severe criticism of them appears in Mark, Matthew has either no criticism or a rather mild rebuke. Overall, scholars regard his Greek as an improvement on that of Mark.

It is possible in the light of their similarity and differences that both Mark and Matthew followed an established oral tradition or edited an earlier source. Whether Matthew is drawing on canonical Greek Mark or an earlier source on which Mark also relied, for convenience I will refer to the material common to Matthew and Mark as the Markan source/material.

---

18. This is a much higher proportion than the 350 verses of Mark (approximately 53%) that appear among Luke's 1149 verses.
19. See the recent study by A. M. O'Leary: *Matthew's Judaization of Mark: Examined in the Context of the Use of Sources in Graeco-Roman Antiquity*, New York/London, T&T Clark, 2006.

B. THE 'Q' SOURCE (*QUELLE*)

In addition to the main body of the narrative of Jesus' ministry which Matthew shares with Mark and Luke, there is a body of 235 very similar or even at times identical verses in Matthew and Luke which do not appear in Mark and which scholars refer to as Q (from the German term *Quelle*, meaning source). This sizeable body of material, which Matthew and Luke share and edit in their own individual way, consists mostly of sayings of Jesus, but also includes some sayings of the Baptist (Mt 3:5-10; Lk 3:7-9) and the accounts of the temptations in the desert (Mt 4:1-11; Lk 4:1-13). Scholars wonder if Q was simply a collection of sayings, like the Gospel of Thomas, the Book of Proverbs or the *Pirkê Aboth* (the 'sayings of the fathers'). Much has been written about the material ascribed to Q. It is difficult to ascertain the origins of the Q material and whether it represents one or many traditions. Furthermore, there has been a good deal of speculation on the community or communities in which the Q tradition(s) were transmitted, but much of it remains hypothesis. However, the designation Q is a useful way of referring to the verses common to Matthew and Luke and not present in Mark.

C. THE 'M' SOURCE / MATERIAL

In addition to the Mark and Q traditions there are 350 verses, which appear only in Matthew. This material, usually referred to as M, was probably assembled from different sources and edited by Matthew. It helps to give Matthew's gospel much of its distinctive character. It consists of the genealogy of Jesus (Mt 1:1-17), the Infancy Narrative (Mt 1:18-23), a number of parables (Mt 13:24-30, 36-50); significant sayings (e.g. Mt 3:13-17; 5:17-30; 6:1-8, 16-18; 7:6; 13:51-5), some elements in the Passion and Resurrection narratives such as the intervention of Pilate's wife at Jesus' trial (Mt 27:19), Pilate's washing of his hands (Mt 27:24), the guard on the tomb (Mt 27:62-66; 28:11-15), the women's encounter with Jesus at the tomb (Mt 28:9-10) and the final universal commissioning of the disciples on the mountain in Galilee (Mt 28:16-20).

D. THE EARLIER FUNCTION OF THE SOURCES

An important question about these 'sources' or bodies of traditional material can be raised here. How did they function and how did they relate to each other before they were incorporated into the gospel? Ulrich Luz, for example, makes an interesting suggestion in his recent book, *Studies in Matthew*, published in 2005:

> It can be shown, I think, that the Matthean community is rela-
> tively close to the environment of Q in sociological terms. It is
> virtually certain that the Sayings Source is strongly influenced
> by early Christian itinerant radicalism. Itinerant prophets of the
> ascended Lord founded settled communities, returned to visit
> them, wrote down Jesus traditions, collected them in a kind of
> notebook and transmitted them to the communities ... The
> Matthean community, then, appears strongly influenced in its
> sociological structure and its legal practice by the bearers of the
> Q traditions. This does not exclude the possibility of Matthew
> receiving significant theological impulses from the Gospel of
> Mark ... These impulses include the Son of God Christology, the
> miracles, the overall narrative design, the perspective of mission
> to the Gentiles and the judgment on Israel ... My assumption is
> that Mark's Gospel was an external influence on a community
> shaped by the traditions and Jewish Christian piety of the
> Sayings Source.[20]

Even if Matthew did not use canonical Greek Mark but that they both used and edited an earlier narrative (Aramaic Matthew or some similar document?), still the above comment of Luz makes a great deal of sense. The introduction of a narrative at a particular point brings its significant theological outlook and impulses into a community and shapes, expands and deepens its understanding while providing a narrative framework for the incorporation of ear-lier and more disparate materials.

What then of the M tradition? Scholars of the Two Source Hypothesis (Mk and Q) traditionally regarded M as a single coher-ent source providing the material not found in Mk or Q. In their opinion M was written in the 50s or 60s, possibly in Jerusalem, and concerned with obedience to the Law. That opinion no longer finds general acceptance. M is now seen as an amalgam of material. For example, Stephenson H. Brooks in his 1987 study *Matthew's Community: The Evidence of his special Sayings Source*, holds the posi-tion that M reflects material, not necessarily all written, from three

---

20. U. Luz, *Studies in Matthew*, Grand Rapids, Michigan/Cambridge, UK: Eerdmans, 2005, 8-9.

stages in the relationship of Matthew's community to the synagogue prior to 70AD, periods of inclusion, conflict and separation.[21]

Comments like those of Luz and Brooks just quoted point to the rich variety of preaching and teaching that took place in the pre-70 period. It is quite possible that Aramaic Matthew with its *logia* and a possible primitive narrative were not lost but simply absorbed into the developing traditions like those that are now referred to as Mark, Q or M during the early formation of the material.[22]

E. MATTHEW'S REDACTION

In addition to the material peculiar to Matthew, his own redaction of the traditions he shares with the other evangelists contributes significantly to the distinctive character of the gospel. The traditions about Jesus were not handed on, or finally redacted into the gospel genre, in a social, religious or political vacuum. The gospels of Matthew and John, for example, tell their story of Jesus in the aftermath of the terrible destruction of Jerusalem and the temple in 70AD. Both tell it to an audience / readership made up in large measure of Jewish Christian people who have suffered intensely from the war and its terrible outcome. They have suffered the human tragedy of the death and enslavement of many of their people. They have suffered the loss both of the temple with its atoning sacrifices and pilgrimage feasts and of the bonding symbolism of the mother city. They are now more than ever aware of the power and presence of the Roman conqueror. They also have suffered from the internal divisions that emerged among the Jews themselves as they strove to preserve their identity and way of life for a future without the traditional symbols of temple, city and land, which had hitherto given institutional expression to their ethnic and religious identity.

These internal divisions led to the alienation of the Christian Jews from the dominant group and to the stress, exclusion, pain and

---

21. S. H. Brooks, *Matthew's Community: The Evidence of His Special Sayings Material*, JSNT Sup 16, Sheffield: JSOT, 1987, 12-19. See also, for example, W. D. Davies and D. C. Allison in their three volume work, *A Critical and Exegetical Commentary on the Gospel According to Saint Matthew*, ICC, 3 Vols, Edinburgh: T&T Clark, 1998, 1991, 1997. These authors also hold the opinion that M is a symbol for a plurality of sources, vol 1, 121-127.

22. Similarly in the case of ' L', the material peculiar to Luke.

intimidation one feels when one is involved in a dispute with the power group in a society. This is particularly so when one feels that one still belongs to the group with which one is in serious conflict. Matthew's gospel represents a reaction to this situation and provides a severe criticism and polemic against those perceived to have caused the division.

By the time of John's gospel, a decade or so later, the lines have been clearly drawn and some of the heat has gone out of the discussion. The global expression 'the Jews' is used in John for the opponents, now seen as a separate group, whereas in Matthew the opponents are still a named group within Judaism, the scribes and Pharisees. K. Stendahl wrote of Matthew's gospel:

> It is clear that the most obvious polemic in this gospel is directed against 'the scribes and the Pharisees'. In Matthew these are neither the actual opponents of Jesus, nor are they general examples of haughty behaviour, as in Luke. They are the representatives of the synagogue 'across the street' in Matthew's community.[23]

The heat of internal division is felt very strongly in Matthew as the Jewish Christians fought to maintain their Jewish identity against the strict reformers who would have seen them as a suspect group reneging on their identity and tradition. It is still at the level of bitter sibling rivalry in Matthew, whereas in John it represents the separation of the group from the mother community. The movement from inclusion through conflict to eventual separation from their erstwhile synagogue is seen in a comparison of Matthew and John. To understand how such division, hostility and alienation came about, one needs to look to the aftermath of the war, which brought about the destruction of the city and temple.

4. THE AFTERMATH OF 70 AD

A. THE TRAGEDY

The Jewish historian, Josephus, describes the utter despair and disbelief that descended on the Jews on seeing their Sanctuary burned to ashes, their Holy City reduced to ruins and their people killed or

---

23. K. Stendahl, *The School of St Matthew and Its Use of the Old Testament*, Philadelphia: Fortress, 1968, xi.

taken into slavery.[24] For them the temple had been the dwelling place of God in their midst and its sacrifices and rituals provided the ongoing means of holiness, repentance and right relationship with God. What were the surviving Jews to do now that they were gone? What precedent had they to follow in such a calamity?

There was such a precedent and Josephus points out that it was remarkably obvious from the coincidence of date and circumstance:

> Grief might well be bitter for the destruction of the most won-
> derful edifice ever seen or heard of, both for its size and con-
> struction and for the lavish perfection of detail and the glory of
> its holy places; yet we find very real comfort in the thought that
> Fate is inexorable, not only towards living beings but also to-
> wards buildings and sites. We may wonder too at the exactness
> of the cycle of Fate: she kept, as I said, to the very month and day
> which centuries before had seen the Sanctuary burnt by the
> Babylonians.[25]

On that former occasion in 587BC the Jews were left to figure out how to understand their identity and re-interpret their religious ex-perience in a completely changed environment. They pondered on the reason for the destruction as they sought the means of survival. The deuteronomistic historian(s) in the editing of the Books of Joshua, Judges, Samuel and Kings traced the history of infidelity to the covenant and explained the destruction of the temple and the Exile from the Promised Land that followed as the result of 'doing what was displeasing to Yahweh', especially in the matter of idol-atry (cf 1 Kings 9:6-8).

In the wake of the collapse of the religious and civil institutions and the loss of the Promised Land in 587BC, it was the charismatic voice of the prophets that built on the one foundation that had not been destroyed – the promise of God to be covenant partner to the people. The prophet, known conventionally as Second Isaiah, based his message of hope for restoration on the belief that 'the word of our God endures forever' (Isa 40:8) and the exiled visionary, the priest-prophet Ezekiel, prophesying to the people promised new life to the scattered remnant of the nation (Ezek 37:1-4). Now, cent-uries later, history had repeated itself and after the destruction pro-

---

24. Josephus, *War*, Bk VI, iv, v., 323-325 .
25. Ibid.

voked by the Zealots and carried out by the Romans the people were again asking why it had happened and how they could continue their religious lives without the temple and its atoning sacrifices. Again they were asking what were the foundations that had not been destroyed. To this fundamental question there were three main lines of response, the Apocalyptic, the Rabbinic and the Jewish Christian. Sadly, former co-religionists now became rivals and bitter hostilities developed as each claimed to be the authentic voice continuing the Jewish identity, tradition and way of life.

B. THE APOCALYPTIC RESPONSE

After the destruction of temple and city two apocalyptic works, 4 Ezra and 2 Baruch, emerged. They were more or less contemporary with the later New Testament period of Matthew and John. Both followed the example of the Book of Daniel and presented their message in the form of a prophecy uttered during the sixth century Exile. The apocalyptic Book of Daniel was a reaction to the persecution of Antiochus IV, Epiphanes, when the Seleucid armies occupied the city and desecrated the temple with the profane image, 'the abomination of desolation' (168-164BC). The Book of Daniel prophesied the end of the persecution and the fall of the persecuting powers. It did so by presenting the history of persecuting dictatorships from the time of the Exile in 587 onwards in the guise of prophecy made beforehand. The books of 4 Ezra and 2 Baruch represent a similar response in the aftermath of 70AD. Lamenting the fate of Jerusalem, they asked how God could allow pagan Babylon to rejoice and holy Zion to be destroyed. Both works had to acknowledge the victory of the oppressor, but declared it ephemeral. God would have the last word and the final victory. Both books spoke of two worlds (ages), one passing away, the other to come when God's victory would be complete. Meanwhile strict obedience to the Torah and patience were called for as God was shortening the time until the Messiah would emerge to bring about the victory.

Reflecting on the loss of Jerusalem and the Temple with its atoning sacrifices, the author of 2 Baruch wrote about the enduring importance of the Law:

> For the shepherds of Israel have perished, and the lamps, which gave light, are extinguished, and the fountains from which we used to drink have withheld their streams. Now we have been

left in the darkness and in the thick forest and in the aridness of the desert ... Shepherds and lanterns and fountains came from the Law and when we go away, the Law will abide. If you, there-fore, look upon the Law and are intent upon wisdom, then the lamp will not be wanting and the shepherd will not give way and the fountain will not dry up (2 Bar 77:11, 13-16).

Matthew shares their apocalyptic view of the age to come and their emphasis on the Torah.

C. THE RABBINIC RESPONSE

The Temple service was now gone and with it the priestly caste had lost their social position and power base. The Sadducees, Zealots and Essenes were mortally weakened in the destruction. The Pharisees survived as the most powerful group and they set about reconstructing the religious life of the people. Prior to 70AD the Temple, the Torah and the Land held the different strands of Jewish society together and cemented their overall identity. Now only the Torah remained and so the Pharisees came into their own as the experts in Torah, seen broadly as the Law, the Prophets and the oral tradition built up around its observance.

Within the Pharisee movement it was the more liberal group in the tradition of the school of Hillel, rather than the more strict school of Shammai, that emerged in control. Their approach to scripture allowed them to adapt old laws and ways to new circum-stances, and their teaching on free will, judgement, life after death, retribution and recompense for suffering were ideal for the situa-tion that presented itself after the great suffering of 70AD. From the ruins of Jerusalem they removed their centre of learning and influ-ence to Jamnia (Jabneh) on the coastal plain south of Joppa (Jaffa). There under the guidance of Johanan ben Zakkai they initiated and successfully carried through their thoroughgoing spiritual, liturgi-cal, social and political reform, which was designed to renew the spirits of the people and to ensure their future identity.[26]

---

26. Some of the surviving priests probably threw in their lot with their former rivals, the Pharisees while others may have converted to Christ. Acts 6:7 tells how at an earlier stage 'a large group of priests had made their submission to the faith', probably a pointer to an ongoing soften-ing attitude towards Jesus and his followers among the priestly class as a whole.

Setting about their task, they looked back to the great rabbis and their schools for inspiration. Some two centuries earlier the famous Rabbi Simeon the Righteous, describing the foundations of their Jewish belief and way of life, had said: 'On three things does the age stand: on the Torah, on the temple service and on acts of piety.'[27] The temple service was now gone but Torah and acts of piety were indestructible and, building on these foundations, the Pharisees, under the guidance of outstanding figures like Rabbi Johanan ben Zakkai, gave the much needed leadership and hope to the survivors. When Rabbi Joshua lamented the destruction of the temple crying: 'Woe unto us that this, the place where the iniquities of Israel were atoned for, is laid waste!' Rabbi Johanan ben Zakkai replied: 'Be not grieved, my son. We have another atonement as effective as this ... acts of loving kindness, as it is said, "For I desire mercy (*hesed*) and not sacrifice".'(Hos 6:6)[28]

Just as the rabbi's reflections on Hosea 6:6 deepened his awareness of the importance of *hesed*, so too his awareness of the importance of ritual led him to organise a new calendar of feasts and festivals, centred now on the synagogue, and under the control of the Pharisees rather than the priests. Many of the priestly and temple functions were thus transferred to home and synagogue. In the absence of the temple and all it stood for, the synagogue (to be understood not just as the building but as the organised religious community which it housed for worship) now took on a whole new significance as the place where Jewish identity was focused and where religious life was nurtured.

Under the leadership of the Pharisees, the Jews thus redefined themselves along strict lines in a new situation. But the Pharisees had to overcome opposition from the survivors of the various other groups in order to have their reforms universally imposed. There were those who begged to differ, among them the Christian Jews. This led to alienation from the mother group and to the stress, exclusion, pain and intimidation one feels when one is involved in a dispute with the most powerful group in a society.

---

27. Translation from *Pirkê Avot* 1:2 by G. A. Yee, in *Jewish Feasts and the Gospel of John*, Zacchaeus Studies: New Testament, Delaware: Michael Glazier, Wilmington, 1989, 19.
28. Hos 6:6. *Avot de Rabbi Natan*, ch 6.

D. THE JEWISH CHRISTIAN RESPONSE

First of all it must be said that the Christian Jews had a good deal in common with the thinking of both the Apocalyptic and the Pharisaic/Rabbinic movements. Matthew's gospel shows the influence of apocalyptic thought in its emphasis on eschatology, the *parousia*, the coming in glory of the Son of Man, the end of the present age and the age to come. It shares also the concern of both the apocalyptic and rabbinic movements in its emphasis on living according to the Torah, but in the case of the Christians it is the Torah as interpreted authoritatively and authentically by Jesus who came 'not to destroy the Law and the Prophets but to fulfil them' (Mt 5:17). He declared that 'the one who infringes the least of the commandments and so teaches others will be considered least in the kingdom of heaven, and the one who teaches them and keeps them will be considered great in the kingdom of heaven' (Mt 5:19). His final words were: 'Teach them to observe all that I have commanded you' (28:20).

Furthermore, Matthew's portrayal of Jesus' attitude is very close to the sentiment of the great Rabbi ben Zakkai as they both cite Hosea's line: 'I desire mercy and not sacrifice' (Hos 6:6). Rabbi ben Zakkai cites it to illustrate how acts of mercy and loving kindness function as reparation for sin in the absence of the temple rituals, and Matthew cites it to highlight how Jesus in himself and his ministry replaces the atoning sacrifices of the temple, an attitude which is especially obvious in his dealings with tax collectors and sinners (Mt 9:13). Matthew uses this citation from Hosea again in showing how Jesus' compassionate presence and work outrank the role and functions of the sacred institutions of Sabbath and temple (Mt 12:7).

After the destruction of the temple and city in 587BC the deuteronomistic historians sought the reason for the destruction in the sin and disloyalty of the people and their leaders in 'doing what was displeasing to YHWH'. Matthew does something similar in his use of the parables of the wicked tenants of the vineyard (Mt 21:41, 43) and the wicked invitees to the wedding feast (Mt 22:2-14). The vineyard was a long established metaphor for Israel (Isa 5:1-7). The wicked tenants ill treated the messengers and killed the son when they came looking for the fruits of the vineyard. In reaction to their infidelity and murderous conduct, the owner 'will lease the vineyard to other tenants who will deliver the produce to him when the season arrives' and the kingdom of God will be taken from them and given to a people who will produce its fruit. The parable is really an allegory on the historical rejection of appointed messengers to Israel, culminating in the rejection of the son, followed by the mission to the Gentiles.

In the parable of the invitations to the wedding feast, also an established metaphor for the kingdom, Matthew (unlike Luke in the parallel passage in Lk 14:16-24) states that the host was a king and that the servants bringing the invitations were ill treated and killed and in reaction the king despatched his troops to destroy the murderers and burn their city. This parable also functions as an allegory on the rejection of the historical invitations by God and the ill treatment of the divinely appointed messengers resulting in punishment of the wicked and the destruction of their city. Both parables/allegories are like a potted history of Israel's ill treatment and rejection of the messengers sent by God, culminating in the rejection of the Son. Matthew's redaction of these parables, when taken together with his negative portrayal of Jerusalem and foreboding remarks about its destruction, 'Jerusalem that kills the prophets and stones those sent to you … your house will be left to you desolate' (Mt 23:37-39) points to the events of 70AD and the subsequent mission to the Gentiles.

Like the rest of the Jews, the Christian Jews also had lost the symbolism and bonding power of temple and city. It seems, however, that the Matthean community had not yet definitively left or been expelled from the synagogue. Such a move would represent a complete break with Judaism as such. They were rather in a transitional stage in which they experienced serious tension with the local synagogue(s), which resulted in the heated debate and tensions of an internal Jewish upheaval. That a serious disagreement has emerged is, however, obvious from the language used by Matthew when he speaks of 'their synagogues' (Mt 4:23; 9:35; 10:17; 12:9; 13:54) and 'the synagogue of hypocrites' (Mt 6:25; 23:6.34). These references could be understood as 'those other synagogues with which we are in serious disagreement'. The whole tone of the woes in Mt 23, however, shows a near breaking point. However, the observance of Sabbath, the emphasis on Torah and the fulfilment of the scriptures point to their not having abandoned their place within Judaism, but to their struggling to affirm their place in the face of a changing situation. John, on the other hand, speaks of 'the Jews' and 'the feasts of the Jews' and refers also to expulsion or fear of expulsion from the synagogue in a way that points to a much more complete break with the mother community.

As the Apocalyptists awaited the age to come and the Pharisees led the revival focused on the Torah and a comprehensive pro-gramme of Jewish religious life designed to replace the temple and the sacrificial system, how could these Jewish Christians maintain their Jewish tradition with its rich cultic life and at the same time ac-commodate their growing Gentile membership? They had to cope with two major difficulties: that of preserving their Jewish identity and heritage in spite of their strained relationship with the syna-gogue, and at the same time coping with increasing numbers of Gentiles in their community.

(a) Jewish Identity and Heritage
How could these Jewish Christians celebrate their heritage in the context of their faith in Jesus and their tensions with the (local) synagogue in the aftermath of 70AD? The destruction of the temple with its rituals, feasts and pilgrimages, brought home to them in a whole new way the realisation that in Jesus they had the presence of God and the saving work of redemption. Of himself Jesus says in the gospel: 'Something greater than the temple is here' (Mt 12:6). The temple signified for the Jews both the presence of God and the atoning sacrifices. Both elements are now to be found in Jesus. At the very beginning of the gospel, he is given two names that sum up the main functions of the lost temple. He is called Emmanuel, a name which means 'God is with us', replacing the Divine Presence in the temple, and he is given the personal name 'Jesus' (*Yeshua*) be-cause 'it is he who will save his people from their sins' thus replac-ing the atoning sacrifices of the temple (Mt 1:21-23).

Matthew saw the fulfilment of the hope of Israel in Jesus of Nazareth who came not to destroy but to fulfil the Law and the Prophets. The Matthean Jesus looks beyond social taboo as he eats with tax collectors and sinners, and beyond over-stringent interpre-tations of law when he defends the hungry disciples for plucking grain on the Sabbath. On both occasions Jesus quotes Hosea: 'For I desire mercy and not sacrifice.' (Hos 6:6; Mt 9:13; 12:7).[29] For Matthew who is greatly steeped in the tradition of the Torah Jesus was the Emmanuel, the presence of God among his people until the

---

29. Hos 6:6. *Avot de Rabbi Natan*, ch 6.

end of the world, the definitive interpreter of the Torah, the Son of
Man on earth who pronounces the forgiveness of sins and the glorious Son of Man who will return in glory on the clouds of heaven to
gather the elect into the kingdom.[30]

For Matthew Jesus is Emmanuel, God with us. Jesus promises
that he will be with the disciples whenever two or three are gathered in his name (Mt 18:20) and he will continue to be with them to
the end of the age as they fulfil their universal mission to make disciples of all nations and baptise in the name of the Father, and of the
Son and of the Holy Spirit (Mt 28:20).[31] In the gospels of Matthew
and John Christians tell their story of Jesus from this deepening of
theological perspective and from the standpoint of a group in tension with their erstwhile co-religionists and fellow citizens.[32]

As his community experiences opposition from the scribes and
Pharisees, Matthew goes on the offensive and highlights their shortcomings by way of focusing on a severe critique of them on the lips
of Jesus. He warns his followers that their righteousness must exceed that of the scribes and Pharisees (Mt 5:20) and his woes in Mt
23 recall the fiery condemnations of the prophets.

He also warns his disciples that they will suffer at the hands of
the Jewish authorities. 'They will scourge you in the synagogues'
(Mt 10:17). He warns of the rejection of their mission to Israel and
tells his apostles to shake the dust from their feet as they do when
leaving a pagan territory (Mt 10:14). Rather than Holy Zion,
Jerusalem is for Matthew the city that 'kills the prophets and stones
those sent to you' (Mt 23:37). It is the place where the political and
religious authorities schemed against Jesus at his birth and again at
his death.

---

30. For the Johannine reaction to the destruction of the temple, see M. L.
Coloe, *God Dwells With Us: Temple Symbolism in the Fourth Gospel*,
Collegeville: The Liturgical Press, Michael Glazier, 2001, 3.
31. For John the coming of the Spirit-Paraclete ensured that these temple and cultic symbols passed to the community wherein Father, Son
and Spirit dwell.
32. For John, steeped in the liturgical traditions of the temple rituals and
feasts, Jesus was in fact the definitive temple, altar and lamb of sacrifice.
He had fulfilled the promise of the feasts and had appropriated to himself the cultic symbols of bread, water, light and sacred space associated
with them.

(b) Jewish and Gentile

Another major factor was also at work when the gospel of Matthew was written. As more Gentiles entered Matthew's church, the Jewish members needed to be reassured of their Jewish identity and their ongoing links with their roots in the history of Israel. They may have feared a 'watering down' of identity as the Gentile numbers grew or they may have been accused of such watering down by their family or synagogue members. Fear of living in an undefined new situation in an increasingly Gentile world also played a part in their need for reassurance. In reaction to these concerns, the evangelist takes the greatest pains throughout the gospel to highlight the Jewish identity and character of Jesus and the unbroken spiritual heritage of Israel into which the Gentile members of the church have now been admitted, without detriment to the position or identity of the Jewish Christian members. This concern for showing the Jewish roots and identity of the Jewish Christian community is very much in evidence throughout the gospel, in spite of the harsh criticism of the Jewish religious leaders and authority figures.

First of all, Matthew is very careful to insist on the priority of the mission to Israel. He emphasises the nature of Jesus' original commission to the Twelve: 'Do not go among the Gentiles, nor enter into the city of the Samaritans, but go to the lost sheep of the House of Israel' (Mt 10:5-6). Later he describes the response of Jesus to the disciples when he was asked to heal the Canaanite woman's daughter: 'I have been sent only to the lost sheep of the House of Israel' and to the woman herself he says: 'It is not right to take the children's food and throw it to the house-dogs' (Mt 15:24, 26).

The genealogy of Jesus and the titles used to describe his identity and role root him and his ministry firmly in the ongoing history of God's chosen people. The fulfilment citations show Jesus' person and mission as the fulfilment of the promises, prophecies and expectations that emerged throughout their history. The use of the history of Israel with its major figures, momentous events and local associations as a paradigm for narrating the story of Jesus further highlights the Jewish roots and identity of Jesus and of the community for which Matthew is writing.

The attitude of Jesus to the Law and the Prophets which he has 'not come to destroy but to fulfil', his style of ethical/moral teaching which resembles the Jewish *halakah*, his emphasis on the authority of Moses ('the chair of Moses') and the acknowledgement of the teaching authority of the scribes and Pharisees (while at the same time severely criticising their failure to practise what they preached) show the unbroken chain of teaching authority. A core element of traditional prophetic teaching about the observance of the Law and the celebration of the cult is highlighted in the two uses, already mentioned, of the citation from Hosea: 'I desire mercy and not sacrifice' (Hos 6:6; Mt 9-13; 12:7).

Jewish customs are taken for granted and need not be explained. Jewish prayer styles and ritual actions are in evidence in the Lord's Prayer, in the multiplication of the loaves and at the Last Supper (Mt 6:9-13; 14:19;15:35; 26:26-28). Sabbath observance and ritual purity laws and customs are taken for granted though attitudes in their regard are criticised (Mt 12:1-14; 15:10-20). Jewish methods of interpretation are obvious as, for example, in the teaching about swearing (Mt 5:34-35; 23:16-22). The contemporary Jewish debates on divorce (Mt 5:31-32; 19:1-9), tribute to Caesar, resurrection of the dead, the discussion about the relative importance of various laws (Mt 22:15-40), all come to the fore and keep the story of Jesus rooted within contemporary Judaism.

By using Israel's history as a paradigm or archetypal experience Matthew aligns Jesus with the literary, historical and theological perspectives of Israel's history. At the same time he deals with the fact that his church, now including many Gentiles, is facing a whole new and uncertain future in the Gentile world. The need to adapt is crucial. Significantly he points to Jesus' comment on the good or wise scribe who stands out as a model of the kingdom, rooted in God's work in history and open to God's new initiative: 'Every scribe who has become a disciple of the kingdom of heaven is like a householder who brings out of his treasury things new and old' (Mt 13:53).

Jerome Murphy-O'Connor sums up the situation very neatly in his comment on Donald Senior's book, *Matthew*:

> The gospel was written for an early Christian community caught in a moment of profound transition, striving to remain faithful to its Jewish heritage and facing a new and uncertain future in the Gentile world.[33]

---

33. Comment ('blurb') on the back cover of D. Senior, *Matthew*, Abingdon Press, 1998.

5. INTERPRETING THE GOSPELS

DIFFERENT APPROACHES

Study of the gospels has gone through many stages and used many different approaches throughout history. People study the gospels for different reasons and from different perspectives. Some have primarily a historical interest in Jesus as the founder of the Christian faith, the world religious leader whom they follow and/or admire and a major figure in world history. Some have an interest in the theology or spiritual message of the various evangelists as they present the story of Jesus with different insights and from different perspectives. Others approach the gospels as great religious literature and study them according to the norms of literary criticism. Others approach them with an anthropological or sociological interest to see how the gospel view and values reflect and impact on the structures and value systems of various societies. All these approaches are complementary and each has its strengths. Together they lead to a very rich understanding of the gospels. Taken in isolation each approach has its strengths and obvious limitations.

Since the early days of the church the historical approach has been in evidence in efforts to harmonise the gospels, putting the various accounts together to fill out a life of Christ. This is a noble and understandable endeavour and it helps to put together a picture of the great historical figure of Jesus. It has been the inspiration for most artistic representations of Jesus and his contemporaries. However, it tended to regard the gospels simply as straightforward biographies of Jesus and the exercise can imply that each of the gospels is a defective biography, needing to be supplemented by information from the other three. This approach can easily neglect the integrity of each written gospel as a theological and literary whole. It can also take an over simplistic view of the gospels as uninterpreted chronicles. Since the Enlightenment, a corresponding approach has been taken, though in a different guise. The various *quests of the historical Jesus*, defined differently by those involved, have taken the focus off the gospels themselves in the search for the holy grail of a Jesus and his environment reconstructed from 'historical' data rather than a Jesus seen through the eyes of faith and the integral picture presented by each of the gospels.[34] As a result of the quest,

---

34. These two dimensions are conventionally referred to as the 'The Jesus of History' and 'The Christ of Faith'.

Source Criticism became very important as it sought the sources detectable within the gospel texts and others sources extraneous to the canonical gospels. Much energy has been spent seeking these sources, from secular writings, archaeological findings, and religious writings, including documents the early church regarded as lacking credibility, the so-called apocryphal documents. Mark's gospel was originally regarded as the most 'historical' gospel, an eyewitness account coming from Peter through Mark,[35] until it was rightly appreciated as a very theological and subtly literary document. Though a great deal was learned about Jesus and his times from these quests, no one agreed picture of the 'historical' Jesus has emerged. The *Historical-Critical Method* has given us a great deal of valuable information about Jesus and his world, preventing otherwise purely subjective or sectarian interpretations, but it can give a fragmented image of Jesus' person and mission, depending on the criteria and pre-suppositions of the individual scholar and the approach taken.

Form Criticism examines the literary forms in which the gospel material was cast during the process of oral transmission and investigates the social background in which they were developed. It turns the spotlight on the communities in which the traditions were nurtured and applied to community needs and expressed in community language and thought categories. Again much was learned from Form Criticism about the transmission process.

Interest in the theology or theologies of the evangelists resulted in *Redaction (editorial) Criticism*. Comparison of texts for purposes of discovering editorial work further sharpened awareness of the production process, particularly in comparative studies in the synoptic gospels and between the synoptics and John. The mind of the author discovered from these comparative studies became the dominant goal of research, a process of examination often running the risk of overlooking the independence of the final text as a work in itself. *Literary Criticism* declared the 'death of the author' and redressed the balance by insisting on the integrity of the work itself irrespective of its pre-history, the world behind the text and the mind of the author except in so far as it can be understood from the work itself.

---

35. This was an oversimplified understanding of the Papias tradition reported by Eusebius.

Therefore interest in the 'actual' author has given way to interest in the 'implied' author, that is, the 'author' as he/she can be deduced from the text, almost a personification of the text with its world-view, interests, agenda, body of information, literary skill etc. On the negative side, this approach can sometimes run the risk of forgetting the importance of history and tradition when dealing with a document that serves the purpose of engendering and transmitting the faith of a community ultimately rooted in a historical person and event outside the world of the individual text in question.

On the positive side, these various approaches have given great insight into the complexity of the process of transmission of the traditions and their final articulation in the literary genre of the written gospels. Perhaps the most positive result from seeing the shortcomings of various other approaches is the awareness of the importance of a return to focusing on the text itself as a theological and literary whole and an appreciation of the fact that it is a narrative, a story written to engage the reader as a person and not just in an academic context.

6. Literary Considerations

Putting the gospel traditions together into an overall *bios Iêsou* demanded not only access to the various sources but also the employment of literary technique in order to compose a story that would at one and the same time provide a vehicle for traditions about Jesus, convey a definite theological and pastoral outlook and meet the needs of the intended audience.

A. THE OUTLINE / *MACROSTRUCTURE* OF THE GOSPEL

At first glance, the reader is struck by the fact that between the Infancy and Passion Narratives the body of the gospel is arranged in a series of alternating blocks of narrative and discourse material. In contrast to Mark who portrays Jesus as powerful in word and deed and carries the reader along principally by the pace and dramatic effect of his narrative, Matthew, on the other hand, punctuates his narrative with the discourses which illustrate the powerful preaching of Jesus. He has arranged the gospel to facilitate the presentation of Jesus' teaching in five major edited discourses, each concluding with the comment, 'When Jesus had finished ...'(Mt 5-7, 10, 13, 18, 24-25). There are also two short, but key sermons, one of John the Baptist preparing for the imminent arrival of the kingdom

and the mission of Jesus to Israel (Mt 3:1-12), and the final sermon of
the Risen Christ to his disciples, inaugurating their mission to the
whole world (Mt 28:18-20). There are also two collections of sayings, which might be loosely classed as discourses. They are the collection of sayings following the Baptist's question in chapter 11 and
the collection of woes against the scribes and Pharisees in chapter
23. However, the latter two are woven into the narrative structure
in a way that the five major discourses are not. There is no doubt,
therefore, that in presenting such a volume of his teaching Matthew
wishes to portray Jesus as the teacher *par excellence*, a teacher in the
tradition of, but far surpassing, Moses.

Some commentators in the past focused almost entirely on the
five major discourses as the key to the overall structure of the
gospel. The most notable was B. W. Bacon in his book *Studies in
Matthew* published in 1930.[36] He saw in the five great discourses a
reflection of the Pentateuch with its five books and alternating narrative and discourse styles. He pointed out how each of the discourses ends with a similar statement pointing out that Jesus had
finished all he wanted to say. His approach cast Jesus firmly in the
mould of a new Moses giving a new Law.

Peter F. Ellis, like Bacon, also looked to the major discourses for
the purpose of constructing his macrostructure of the gospel.[37] In
his book, *Matthew: His Mind and his Message*, published in 1974, he
took a similar approach, seeing the discourses placed in a chiastic or
concentric arrangement and regarding the smaller sermon of John
(Mt 3:1-12) and the final discourse of Jesus (Mt 28:18-20) as part of
the overall concentric pattern.

He proposed a chiastic arrangement of the five major discourses
with chapter 13 as the pivot and the other discourses balancing each
other in length and similarity of theme, and all ending with a similar statement that Jesus had concluded what he wanted to say. The
narrative in each case built up to the discourse. He illustrated his
macrostructure with a diagram:

36. B. W. Bacon, *Studies in Matthew*, New York: Holt; London:
Constable, 1930.
37. P. F. Ellis, *Matthew: His Mind and His Message*, Collegeville: The
Liturgical Press, 1974, 12.

a. ch 1-4	*a*. ch 26-28
b. ch 5-7	*b*. ch 23-25
c. ch 8-9	*c*. ch19-22
d. ch10	*d*. ch18
e.ch 11-12	*e*. ch14-17
f. ch 13	

P. Ellis also regarded the two short discourses, the preaching of the Baptist inaugurating the mission of Jesus to Israel (Mt 3:8-12) and the final discourse of Jesus inaugurating the mission of his disciples to the world (Mt 28:18-20) as balancing each other. Furthermore he regarded the final discourse (Mt 28:18-20) as a key to Matthew's teaching. He stated:

> The little discourse is made to serve as a recapitulation of the central themes of the whole gospel: the authority of Jesus, the authority of the apostles, the mission of the apostles to disciplise all nations by teaching them to observe all that Jesus has commanded, and the promise of Jesus to be with his church till the end of time.[38]

He quotes D. W. Trilling's statement about this final discourse that 'The main themes ring out and are focused like rays through a lens.'[39]

J. P. Meier in his 1980 commentary on Matthew also emphasises the five major discourses:

> The public ministry is welded into five books, each book composed of first narrative and then discourse. Five great discourses, put together by Matthew, form the five pillars of the gospel ...[40]

Criticism of this 'discourse based' approach to the macro-structure of the gospel has been voiced by literary critics who maintain that it ignores the overall plot of the gospel, and in the case of Bacon's analysis that it reduces the Infancy and Passion Narratives to a preamble and epilogue. They point out that in addition to the very obvious insertion of the five major discourses there are other significant indications of editorial structuring of the narrative.

---

38. P. F. Ellis, ibid.19.
39. D. W. Trilling, *Das Wahre Israel, Studien zur Theologie des Matthäus Evangeliums*, Munich: Kosel-Verlag, 1964, 4.
40. J. P. Meier, *Matthew*, New Testament Message 3, Wilmington, Del: Glazier, 1980, xii.

J. D. Kingsbury in his book *Matthew: Structure, Christology, Kingdom*, published in 1975, drew attention to the fact that the phrase 'From that time Jesus began to ...' is used at two very important pivotal moments in the gospel.[41] At Mt 4:17 it is used to mark the beginning of Jesus' public ministry and at Mt 16:21 it is used again to mark the beginning of the section of the gospel which deals with his instruction about his forthcoming death and resurrection. This marks the gospel off into three major sections:

Mt 1:1- 4:16   Revealing the person of Jesus the Messiah
Mt 4:17-16:20   Public manifestation of Jesus the Messiah
Mt 16:21-28:20   The Suffering, Death and Resurrection of
                  Jesus the Messiah

Kingsbury accurately identified these pivotal points, but on their own they are inadequate as there are many more indicators of overall structure in the text.

Seymour Chatman, in *Story and Discourse* published in 1978, points out the importance of seeing a hierarchy of importance in the stories that make up the plot of a narrative.[42] Some stories are kernels or 'hinges' and others are satellites, the kernel and its satellites making up the various divisions of the gospel.[43] The kernels are essential to the plot. They advance the plot, emerge from and answer questions that arise from earlier kernels and look forward to subsequent ones. The satellites are dependent on the kernels. Francis J. Matera in his 1987 article 'The Plot of Matthew's Gospel'[44] and Warren Carter in his 1992 article 'Kernels and Narrative Blocks: The Structure of Matthew's Gospel'[45] build on this idea of kernels and satellites and, in his book *Matthew: Storyteller, Interpreter, Evangelist*, published in 2004, W. Carter suggests that the macrostructure for the gospel emerges from the following kernels from which the strings of satellites flow which make up the main sections of the gospel:

41. J. D. Kingsbury, *Matthew: Structure, Christology, and Kingdom*, Philadelphia: Fortress, 1975, 8.
42. S. Chatman, *Story and Discourse*, Ithaca: Cornell University Press, 1978.
43. Ibid., 53-56
44. F. J. Matera, 'The Plot of Matthew's Gospel', *Catholic Biblical Quarterly*, 49: 233-253, 1987.
45. W. Carter, *op. cit.*, and 'Kernels and Narrative Blocks: The Structure of Matthew's Gospel', *Catholic Biblical Quarterly* 54. 463-81. 1992.

a. Mt 1:18-25   The birth narrative
b. Mt 4:17-25   The inaugural summary at the beginning of the
                 public ministry
c. Mt 11:2-6   The question of John the Baptist
d. Mt 21:1-27   The triumphal entry into Jerusalem followed by
                 the cleansing of the temple and the questioning
                 of Jesus' authority for so doing
e. Mt 28:1-10   The women at the empty tomb

W. J. C. Weren in his 2006 article, 'The Macrostructure of Matthew's Gospel: A New Proposal'[46] argues against the approach of Bacon and Kingsbury on the grounds that their approach emphasises the caesuras and overlooks the relatively smooth flow of the story. One can identify three patterns in the travels undertaken by Jesus from the topographical data. Furthermore, the use of Matera's and Carter's distinction between kernels and satellites offer additional criteria. He suggests that kernels are better labelled as 'hinge texts' because they mark a turning point in the plot and have a double function. They are not only fleshed out in the subsequent pericopes but also refer back to the preceding block. It is especially these 'hinge texts' that underline the continuity of Matthew's narrative and should prevent us from focusing too much on alleged caesuras. Weren identifies the following pericopes as belonging to this category:

a. Mt 4,12-17   Jesus' withdrawal into Galilee after the arrest of
                 John
b. Mt 11:2-30   The question of the Baptist and the following
                 discussion
c. Mt16:13-28   The confession of Peter and the response of Jesus
d. Mt 21:1-17   The preparation for and triumphal entry into
                 Jerusalem and the cleansing of the temple
e. Mt 26:1-16   The fourth passion prediction, the scheming of
                 the authorities to arrest Jesus, Judas' offer to
                 facilitate their design and the anointing of Jesus
                 beforehand for his burial by the woman of
                 Bethany.

The awareness of 'hinge texts' or 'kernels' with 'strings of satel-

46. W. J. C . Weren, 'The Macrostructure of Matthew's Gospel: A New Proposal' , *Biblica* 87 (2006), 171-200.

lites' highlight the development of the narrative, like bridges between sections and stepping stones through the stream of narration.

The various contributions of scholars concerning the
macrostructure of the gospel alert this writer to the fact that there
are many indicators in the text, which can produce different, even
contending, results. Some of the indicators were already present in
the tradition(s) prior to Matthew's editing. The basic Mk/Mt narrative is a case in point, with its obvious indicators at the arrest of the
Baptist, the ministry in Galilee, the confession of Peter followed by
the first prediction of the Passion, the journey to Jerusalem, the
entry into and activity in Jerusalem and the Passion Narrative.

Arrangement of material in significant numerical patterns is
also a feature of Matthew's writing. The number five, possibly influenced by the five major books of the Pentateuch, is important.
His insertion of the five major discourses all ending with 'When
Jesus had finished …'(Mt 7-28; 11:1; 13:53; 19:1; 26-1) is an obvious
example of his 'imposition' on the older order. He also has five
major witnesses to Jesus' identity in the opening narrative, the
evangelist/narrator, the angel of the Lord, the magi, John the
Baptist and the voice from heaven (the Father) (Mt 1:1,20; 2:2; 3:11,
17). The Infancy Narrative consists of five stories with explicit biblical citations (Mt 1:23; 2:6, 15, 18, 23) and the teaching authority of
Jesus is illustrated with five antitheses beginning with: 'You have
heard that it was said but I say to you (Mt 5-21, 27, 33, 38, 43). The
third antithesis (Mt 5:31) follows a modified form, 'it was also said,'
and looks like an appendage to illustrate further the second antithesis, on adultery (Mt 5:27-30). If so, it appears there were originally
five antitheses.

Matthew's interest in gathering material in numerical arrangements is also obvious in his use of triads. He divides the genealogy
into three periods of fourteen generations. In the Infancy Narrative
he has three parallel angelic appearance accounts in which Joseph is
instructed to act in regard to the child and his mother. In the
Sermon on the Mount there are three examples of pious living
(almsgiving, fasting and prayer) (Mt 6:1-18) and three warnings
about judgement that round off the sermon (enter by the narrow
gate, watch out for false prophets and build on rock rather than
sand) (Mt 7:13-27). Mt 8-9 consists of three triads of miracle stories
with comments appended.

From what has been said, it is obvious that the gospel is poly-structural and that one needs to keep various considerations in mind as one sets about organising a commentary. I have a great deal of sympathy with the sentiment expressed by Wilfrid Harrington in his book, *Matthew: Sage Theologian*:

> I have become increasingly skeptical of scholarly plans of biblical writings, which purport to have discerned the literary map of a biblical author and provide the key that unlocks his purpose. Ironically, one finds that a convincingly attractive scheme is, very soon, blown apart by the next contender. Of course, some incontestable features will emerge. One cannot ignore that the five great discourses are distinctive of Matthew. One wonders if we should push far beyond that fact. In any case, I am content to work with a broad plan that does not appear to do violence to the gospel. I might even claim that it is, in the main, the route followed by most commentators.[47]

Keeping the various scholarly approaches in mind and referring to them from time to time, I too, am 'content to work with a broad plan that does not appear to do violence to the gospel.'

B. WRITING A STORY

Story, a narrative that engages the reader, is perhaps the best and most effective form of communication, and the reawakening in recent times of an appreciation of the power and impact of story for both the individual and the community has brought a whole new dimension to the study and interpretation of the gospels.

In this commentary I follow the narrative structure of the gospel, seeing it as a story, but keeping in mind that the story is set in a society, culture and time very different from our own. There are therefore many things that need explanation. The story is a vehicle for theology, christology, soteriology and eschatology and so attention has to be paid to these more theological issues. Attention must be paid also to the influence of the Old Testament in the formation and articulation of the narrative and to the concerns of the Christian community, which helped to shape it.

The story of Jesus in the gospels is really the outcome of three stories inexorably tied together. As the story of Jesus is told, the Old

---

47. W. J. Harrington, *Matthew, Sage Theologian: The Jesus of Matthew*, Dublin: The Columba Press, 1998, 11.

Testament story of God and the chosen people is re-echoed in allusion, quotation and festal celebration, and at the same time the story of the early Christian community shapes, and shines through the story of Jesus as it is told from the perspective and experience of the community.

Essential to any story are the narrator or storyteller, the plot, the characters, the settings and the various rhetorical techniques used to capture and maintain the interest of the reader or hearer. We look at each in turn.

(i) The Narrator

The person who tells the story is the narrator. The author uses the narrator to tell the story and to tell it in a particular way. Sometimes the narrator is a character within the story, actually telling the story, as is the case often in autobiography or in a novel or short story, in which case the vision and knowledge of the narrator are limited to those of that particular character and bounded by time, space and social location. More usually, and this is the case with the gospels, the narrator is not a character within the story but is more a rhetorical device for getting the story told, in which case it can be difficult at times to distinguish the roles of author and narrator. When the narrator is anonymous and not a character in the story, he or she tells the story from a partially or totally omniscient point of view, knowing more about the individual characters than they do themselves, not only describing their words and actions but exposing even their secret thoughts and motives. Obvious examples of such 'omniscience' on the part of the narrator are Jesus' reactions and quotations of scripture in the temptation accounts (Mt 4:1-11), his prayer in Gethsemane (Mt 26:39, 42, 45) and Pilate's awareness of the jealousy of the Jewish authorities in handing over Jesus (Mt 27:18). The use of fulfilment citations is another example of the narrator's 'omniscience' in regard to the overall divine plan of salvation. This ensures that the reader has privileged knowledge and an advantage over the characters in the story. The narrator may remain hidden behind the narrative or may become obvious from time to time by breaking into the narrative with an explanatory remark, as for example, about a foreign place, custom or turn of phrase. Whether hidden or seen and heard, the narrator ensures that the reader sees the narrative from his or her point of view. The gospel narrators are obviously Christians and see the story of Jesus from a believer's point of view. Imagine how different the story of Jesus would be if a narrator told it from the point of view of Caiaphas or Pilate or a spokesperson for the Pharisees and scribes! The narrator in Matthew's gospel tells the story from the point of view of a believer who is carefully guiding the reader to share that same belief.

After a period of oral transmission of the remembered stories about the life, work, teaching, death and resurrection of Jesus, the written gospels present the traditional material in an overall story or biographical sketch (*bios*). This change from oral preaching and teaching, which was probably very disjointed and fragmented, to the written medium using narrative technique had far reaching consequences for the story being transmitted. Unlike the catechist or preacher, the narrator of the *bios* is not delivering a lecture, or assembling notes for preaching. The narrator is telling a story.

Telling a story, be it fictional or historical, demands planning if meaning is to be conveyed and convincing. Three essential elements in such planning are plot, character and setting and all three are enhanced by techniques of style and arrangement. The author of fiction has unlimited scope to invent on all these counts, the only constraints being credibility within the chosen genre. Writing history, however, the author is constrained by the known historical events, characters and outcome, and writes within the conventional boundaries of historical writing at the time of composition. Matthew is not dealing with a fictional character, but with a real person whose life, death and resurrection has had a profound effect on human history. Furthermore Matthew wrote within living memory of the life of Jesus and possibly in and for a community where traditions about Jesus were well known. His narrative had to respect these historical parameters.

(ii) The Plot

The plot of a narrative is the ordered sequence of events, showing causality from one event to another, in an overall unified structure, moving towards a goal or end point and achieving emotional, psychological, moral, religious or artistic effects in the process, as more is being communicated than the bare storyline.[48] The plot is driven

---

48. Aristotle's *Poetics* 1450b–1451b, speaks of order, amplitude, unity and probable and necessary connection.

by the conflicts between belief and unbelief, understanding and misunderstanding, creation and relief of suspense, foreshadowing and fulfilment of events, inclusion and exclusion of persons, presence and absence of the kingdom. The reader's interest is engaged and sustained throughout by the suspense generated by these opposing forces.

The plot is the author's interpretation of the unfolding story. The plot is supported by action, characterisation and thought. The narrator makes sure the reader is kept up to date with the story as it unfolds, properly informed about the various characters' motivation and duly instructed about unfamiliar terms or practices. Furthermore, the narrator sees to it that the reader is led throughout the various twists and turns in the plot to identify with the desired goal of the story. The narrator also ensures that the reader takes the desired side in the various disputes. The plot is consistent both in the narrator's point of view and portrayal of characters. There is a unifying interconnection of all parts of the narrative achieved through the skilful use of literary techniques of repetition, arrangement of material, skilful use of connectives such as 'for', 'therefore', 'because' (*gar, oun, hoti*) which facilitate the sense of sequence and highlight cause and effect, and the temporal relationships such as *before, after, again, at that time*. The unity of the gospel is apparent in the integrity of the story it tells. Furthermore, its polemic against the scribes and Pharisees makes a powerful overall rhetorical impact.

(iii) The Characters

In a certain sense the characters and the plot are two sides of a coin. The characters are the agents of the plot, causing it to take shape and unfold as a result of their motives, words and actions. On the other hand the unfolding of the plot both reveals the characters and their motives and works on them to bring about change or confirm them in their motives or goals. The reader quickly sees in the character a determined force promoting or obstructing the overall goal of the narrative or an undecided and vacillating force awaiting further development and decision. In this way the reader may quickly come to identify with the character promoting the overall goal, adopt a hostile attitude to the character opposing the goal and form a psychological and emotional companionship with the undecided character in the hope of accompanying him or her to a favourable resolution. In this way the reader is drawn into the plot and may even find himself/ herself wondering with which character to identify, wishing to identify with a positive one but realising that an opposing or vacillating character may be a more accurate reflection of oneself.

The characters in a story are the 'creation' of the author and the narrator is 'omniscient' in their regard. The characters can reveal themselves in their actions and words or the narrator can tell the reader about them. Since characterisation enables the 'omniscient' narrator to expose the character to the reader more profoundly and thoroughly than a person is exposed in real life, the readers of the gospel will have a better vantage point for observing and understanding Jesus than his followers and opponents had, both during his historical ministry and in the story world of the narrative. This is the difference between a real live person and a character. Nobody fully understands another person. An author, however, creates a character around his/her own understanding. Jesus in each gospel is a creation of the post-resurrection faith and understanding of each of the evangelists.

Characters can be of two kinds. There are 'round' or 'autonomous' characters with traits and personalities, whose strengths and weaknesses, thoughts and emotions, are like mini-plots in themselves. They are complex in temperament and motivation, in ways unpredictable and capable of surprising the reader with unexpected actions or patterns of behaviour. Jesus, the protagonist, is a 'round' character whose humanity is not compromised by the fact that he is declared Son of God, empowered by the Spirit, prepared for by the Baptist and empowered with divine authority to establish the kingdom (reign) of heaven. He is gifted with prophetic knowledge and wisdom, a superb teacher, healer and forthright challenger of arrogance and self interest in institution and leadership. He is heir to the prophets and sages of Israel and a significant player in the contemporary religious landscape. He inspires loyalty, love, curiosity, opposition and hatred. Though empowered by the Spirit and with divine authority over evil spirits, sickness and even the elements, he does not compel acceptance and faith. He respects the freedom of the individual to respond to him or to reject him and as such exposes his vulnerability and lack of power and authority on the ' human' plain. He displays a whole range of human emotions and reactions. He shows great compassion towards the sick, the possessed and the outcast and towards the crowd who were 'like sheep without a shepherd'. He displays great courage in facing the wrath of the Jewish and Roman establishments and experiences repeated frustration with the unbelief of 'this generation'. Finally he is reduced to a state of distress in Gethsemane and to a sense of abandonment on the cross. He is challenged by disappointments and crises and appears at the end of his life to have been destroyed by forces hostile to him and his mission. This portrait of Jesus is quite different to the more one dimensional Hellenistic style portrait in John where Jesus, the pre-existent Word made flesh, comes into the world fully developed as a character and progresses from stage to stage in his life and ministry, always omniscient and always in control.

There are also 'flat' characters like Caiaphas or Pilate, whose function is not to be interesting in themselves but to fulfil a role in the narrative. They are personifications of a single trait, or functionaries carrying out a task.

There are also 'communal' characters constructed from identifiable groups such as the disciples, the women from Galilee, the adversaries, made up of various groupings of authority figures such as the chief priests and elders of the people, the Pharisees and Sadducees, the scribes and Pharisees, the crowd, those seeking help and healing and the demons representing a 'superior' power working to the detriment of the individuals they possess and to the destruction of the kingdom. These communal characters function in the narrative as characterisations of the forces of support, misunderstanding, failure, opposition, hope and division.

(iv) The Settings

For Matthew, as for all the evangelists, *place* is highly significant. First of all there is the biblical concept of the creation, comprising heaven, earth and underworld, wherein the drama takes place between God and the demonic forces. On the earthly level *place* signifies geographic location, socio-cultural, political and ethnic identity, hospitable or hostile territory and places of traditional religious significance. The *desert* was the place where God through the leadership of Moses formed a covenant people at Sinai from the band of Hebrew slaves whom he had led out of Egypt, and it was through the desert God promised to make a way and lead the exiles safely back from Babylon. The desert was the place where prophets went for inspiration and sinners for repentance. Groups in dispute with the religious and political establishment in Jerusalem, like the Essenes, the monastic community at Qumran, various Hasidim ('holy ones', hermits) found a home in the desert. It was where one depended totally on God. It was where wild beasts and evil spirits dwelt. Jesus' public life significantly begins in the context of the Baptist's activity in the desert, when he was sent by God as precursor to prepare the way of the Lord. In the desert at the Jordan, with all its significance of the place of crossing into the Promised Land and the beginning of a new life for the people, Jesus was baptised, the Spirit came upon him and the voice from heaven proclaimed him 'my Son the Beloved'. In the desert the Beloved Son was tested and the angels ministered to him. In the desert he fed Jew and Gentile prefiguring the Eucharist and the eschatological banquet in the kingdom.

The *mountain* was the traditional place of theophanies, where God was encountered and God's will was revealed. There Moses received the Law. There the covenant was made (Exod 19). On the mountain Elijah, the father figure of the classical prophets, heard the sound of the gentle breeze and wrapped his face in a mantle as the word of the Lord came to him (1 Kings 19:12). On the mountain Jesus proclaims that he has come to fulfil the Law and the Prophets as he delivers the Sermon on the Mount (Mt 5:17) and he brings the disciples to pray on a mountain and is transfigured before them in the company of Moses and Elijah (Mt 1:1-8). On the mountain in Galilee the Risen Christ commissions them to make disciples of all nations (Mt 28:16-20).

The *sea* was the place where the power of God was most spectacularly in evidence. The biblical accounts of creation and reflections on creation emphasise God's order on chaos and God's control of the forces of the deep. The sea was seen as the dwelling place of demons and monsters who could churn up the winds and waves and threaten the order of creation. The combination of agitated sea and darkness provide the setting for the terror of the disciples. Significantly Jesus showed how he has authority over the wind and waves. He saved the disciples from the raging sea and into that same sea the herd of pigs ran in terror as the demons took possession of them (Mt 8:32).

Public and private venues figure prominently in the narrative. Jesus carried on his public ministry in open spaces, desert places, synagogues, 'open' houses, and in the temple and public places in

Jerusalem. In these public places he preached, received the crowds, cured sick, exorcised the possessed and entered into controversy with his opponents. He withdrew with his disciples to instruct them further in private houses.

Galilee was the place where Jesus and the disciples were at home. There Jesus began his ministry, called his first disciples, preached his first sermons, healed and exorcised those who came to him for help. In Galilee the crowds flocked to him. Since Galilee was on the periphery of the 'Holy Land' and Jews lived there side by side with Gentiles, the Galileans were regarded with a certain amount of suspicion by the authorities in Jerusalem. Furthermore, in Roman eyes they were potential revolutionaries. From Galilee, Jesus had easy access to the neighbouring Gentile territory of Tyre and Sidon to the north, and the Decapolis to the east. Jews and Gentiles flocked to hear him and he fed them in the wilderness. In Galilee, Jesus also experienced rejection by his own family and the people in his native place, and the long hand of Jerusalem authority reached into Galilee to observe and criticise himself, his disciples and his mission. Jesus' final message to the disciples was that he would go before them into to Galilee and there they would see him just as he had told them (Mt 26:32; 28:8).

Between the ministry in Galilee and the ministry in Jerusalem, Jesus and his disciples are '*on the way*'. ' The way' is the geographic path leading to Jerusalem, but it is also, and more importantly, the way of the Son of Man and the disciples' way of following Jesus to his destiny in the city and on the cross. It is the setting for much of Jesus' teaching on the way of discipleship and its requirements of denial of self, service of others and suffering along with the Son of Man.

Jerusalem was the holy city, site of the temple, centre of religious power and influence. From here Jesus' first critics came into Galilee. In Jerusalem Jesus challenged the religious powers and institutions and prophesied the end of the temple and the end of the world, as we know it. On his approach to Jerusalem an enthusiastic crowd, proclaiming him as the one coming in the name of the Lord, received him. In Jerusalem he was arrested, abandoned by his disciples, tried by Jewish and Roman authorities, rejected by a mob of his own countrymen, and executed. The powers he challenged defeated him. But God triumphed over those powers and raised Jesus from the dead, to lead his disciples back into Galilee.

7. THEOLOGICAL CONSIDERATIONS

A. CHRISTOLOGY

The call to be his disciples, in Jesus' own time, in the time of the writing of the gospel, and in the present time of the actual reader, is intimately bound up with the question of Jesus' identity and the divine power authenticating his mission of salvation. The New Testament affirms in different ways the identity of Jesus as it proclaims the salvation brought about in his life, death and resurrection. The Letter to the Colossians states that: 'He is the image of the invisible God' (Col 1:15) and 'In him the fullness of God was pleased to dwell' (Col 1:19). The Johannine tradition affirms that: 'The Word became flesh and lived among us and we have gazed upon his glory' (Jn 1:14) and the Acts of the Apostles makes the point that: 'There is salvation in no one else, for there is no other name under heaven given among mortals, by which we must be saved' (Acts 4:12). Jesus is, therefore, not just the announcer of good news, he is the embodiment of the good news, which he announces. Paul speaks of him as 'our wisdom, our virtue, our holiness and our freedom' (1 Cor 1:30) and he describes the crucified Christ of his preaching as 'the power and the wisdom of God' (1 Cor 1:24).

Matthew (like the other evangelists) was faced with the task of incorporating these insights in a *bios Iêsou* that would speak to the church in his time. He did so largely through the use of the christological titles. These titles do not function independently but help to interpret each other and in so doing correct misunderstandings and false expectations that had grown up around the various titles. What Maurice Hogan wrote concerning the christological titles in Mark is equally perceptive and accurate in the case of Matthew:

> ... none of these (titles) can be properly understood apart from his narrative. For the christology is in the story, and it is through the story that we learn to interpret the titles.[49]

The reader meets these titles right from the first verse of the gospel and is given privileged information about Jesus' identity in the genealogy and in the Infancy, Baptism and Temptation Narratives where he is described as Messiah (Christ), Son of David, Son of Abraham, Emmanuel, Jesus ('the one will save his people

---

49. M. Hogan, *Seeking Jesus of Nazareth: An Introduction to the Christology of the Four Gospels*, The Columba Press, Dublin, 2001, 65.

from their sins'), Son of God, King of the Jews, Lord and Beloved
Son. From this privileged position, the reader sees the various characters in the gospel struggle with the questions, 'Who can this be?'
and 'Who do you/people say that I am?' However, in spite of the
privileged knowledge the reader is given from the beginning,
he/she is also challenged by these same questions in the context of
the unfolding, and often disturbing, events in the gospel.

Throughout the gospel the various titles appear in close association with each other, especially at the pivotal points in the narrative.
The opening verse of the gospel combines the titles 'Messiah
(Christ)', 'Son of David' and 'Son of Abraham' (Mt 1:1). A pivotal
point is reached in the middle of the narrative when Peter responds
to Jesus' question: 'Who do you say that I am?' with the profession:
'You are the Christ' combining it with 'The Son of the living God' (Mt
16:17). Peter's profession is followed shortly afterwards in the gospel
by Jesus' own description of the Son of Man coming in the glory of his
Father (Mt 16:27), and shortly afterwards again by the voice at the
transfiguration declaring him 'my Son, the Beloved' (Mt 17:5). Three
passion predictions follow Peter's profession of faith, in the second
and third of which Jesus refers to himself as the Son of Man (Mt 17:22;
20:18). At his Jewish trial, the high priest questions him in aggressive
fashion, putting him on oath to reveal 'if you are you the Christ, the
Son of God?'(Mt 26:63) and Jesus responds with a prophecy about the
Son of Man seated at the right hand of the Power and coming on the
clouds of heaven (Mt 23:64). Thus the high priest's question to Jesus
which combines the titles Messiah and Son of God, together with
Jesus' response about the Son of Man, again bring the three principal
titles together. The chief priests with the scribes and elders, in their
mockery of the crucified, bring together the titles King of Israel and
Son of God (Mt 27:42-44) again joining the messianic and Son of God
titles. The various titles will be examined further as they appear in the
gospel.

(i) Messiah/Christ
The opening verse of Matthew's gospel describes Jesus as Messiah
(*Christos* in Greek, Christ in English), a title that means 'The
Anointed One.' It had a long history in the Old Testament. It de-
notes a priest in the 'priestly' books of Leviticus and Numbers (Lev
4:3; 6:22; Num 3:3), a king in the 'royal' books of Samuel and in
Isaiah (1 Sam 16:6; 24:6; 26:11, 16, 23; 2 Sam 1:16; 19:21; Isa 45:1) and

from the time of Daniel it usually denotes a prince (Dan 9:25). 'Messiah' is a correct but on its own an inadequate title for Jesus. This is because there was no unanimously agreed understanding of the identity and role of the Messiah in Jesus' time. It was a 'catch-all' term for the 'one to come' who would fulfill hopes and expectations as different from each other as the coming of one to lead a violent revolution against the Romans and the coming of a prophet like Moses who would pronounce on such matters as whether the Samaritans belonged to the chosen people and whether or not their worship was valid (Jn 4:20-26). Even among the Qumran community different sets of expectations were current, resulting in the understanding that more than one figure might appear to fulfill the roles of a priestly, a political/royal/princely, and a prophetic Messiah.

The titles 'Son of David', 'King of the Jews' and 'King of Israel' are closely associated with the title Messiah. The expectation that the Messiah would be a descendant of David was common. Throughout the gospel, from the genealogy through the birth in Bethlehem, and throughout his ministry, Jesus is portrayed as Son of David, the shepherd-king, who is moved to compassion and responds to those who are ill, abandoned and are considered of little account, 'like sheep without a shepherd' (Mt 9:36).

The expectations about the 'Son of David' and 'the coming kingdom of our father David' led naturally to the idea of Jesus as king. For Pilate and the Roman soldiers who mocked Jesus the title 'king of the Jews' signified a political pretender to royal status (Mt 27:11, 29). For them the use of the title was a possible act of treason against Caesar. For the chief priests and scribes, however, the use of the term 'king of Israel' signified primarily a religious figure, the anointed agent of God who would free Israel from its enemies and establish the reign of God (Mt 27:42).

In combining the titles 'son of David' and 'son of Abraham' Matthew assures the Jewish Christians of their roots and ongoing position in the story of Israel through their Davidic Messiah, and also reassures them and their Gentile fellow members that both Jew and Gentile belong in the following of Jesus since the Messiah is also son of Abraham. The promise to Abraham that all nations would be blessed in his offspring had already been emphasised by Paul in the letters to the Galatians and Romans (Gen 12:1-9; 14:1-8; Gal 3:6-4:31; Rom 9:6-9). Matthew describes Jesus as son of Abraham and follows it with the story of the visit of the Magi, representatives of the Gentiles coming to pay homage to the Davidic King in Bethlehem (Mt 2:1-12), a gesture reminiscent of the biblical prophecies that the nations would come to pay homage in Jerusalem (Isa 2:2-5; 18:7; 45:14-17; 60:1-6; Mic 4:1-5; Ps 72:10-15) and foreshadowing the universal mission in Mt 28:19-20.

Jesus gives the title Messiah a whole new meaning in the discussion about the Messiah and the Son of David (Mt 22:41-46). He speaks of the Messiah as 'Lord', the term used as a circumlocution for 'God' in the Jewish custom of avoiding the pronunciation of the Divine Name *YHWH* and the post-resurrection designation of Jesus as Risen Lord by the Christian community. As Son of David the Messiah is in a special way Lord and Son of God (Ps 2:7; Mt 22:41-46).

(ii) Son of God

'Son of God' is very prominent as a title in Matthew. In fact it is the most important title in the gospel. It sums up the gospel's portrait of Jesus' close relationship with the Father.[50] The story of Jesus' birth (Mt 1:18-25) and the sojourn and return from Egypt (Mt 2:15) emphasise the reality of his sonship of God. The story builds up through the ministry, witness and baptism of John, through the 'opening of the heavens' and the coming of the Spirit on Jesus to the declaration by the voice from heaven: 'This is my Son, the Beloved' (Mt 3:16-17). That sonship is put to the test in the desert as the tempter begins two of the temptations with the challenging remark: 'If you are the Son of God ...' (Mt 4:3, 6). Right at the centre of the gospel, the voice from the cloud on the mountain of the transfiguration proclaims Jesus as 'My Beloved Son' (Mt 17:5). The two 'interventions' of God as a character in the gospel are, therefore, for the purpose of declaring Jesus the 'Beloved Son (of God)'. The charge of blasphemy brought against him by the religious authorities results from his claim to be the Son of God, a claim made in response to the high priest who asked him on oath to tell if he was the Christ, the Son of God (Mt 26:63). The gospel reaches its denouement when the heavens are darkened, the veil of the temple is torn in two and in a

50. In this the theologies of Matthew and John are very similar. Throughout the gospel God is usually referred to as 'Father', 'My Father', or 'Your Father', with 'in heaven' or 'heavenly' regularly used as a qualifier.

confession on human lips re-echoing the voice from heaven at the baptism and transfiguration, the centurion and the others (however they understood the title) standing guard over Jesus at his crucifixion said: 'Truly this man was the Son of God' (Mt 27:54). These examples show clearly the importance of the title 'Son of God' throughout the gospel.

In the Old Testament the title 'son of God' was used variously of the angels, the prophets, the king, the people of Israel, the righteous ones and those who received a special commission or blessing from God. Here in Matthew it is given a whole new level of meaning in keeping with Christian belief in the unique relationship of Jesus to the Father. It is emphasised in the Infancy Narrative, revealed at 'high points' in his life such as the Baptism and Transfiguration, and reflected on at moments during the ministry. Of particular significance is Jesus' description of his unique relationship with the Father and his role as revealer of the Father in Mt 11:25-30, a handful of verses that could be used as a summary of the Father-Son relationship as it appears throughout John's gospel. Finally he is vindicated as Son of God in his passion, death and resurrection.

The Son of God title is also closely associated with the role of the Servant. In fact the term *pais theou* can be translated as servant of God or son of God. At the eschatological sign of the rending of the heavens (Isa 63:19) and the coming of the Spirit upon him, the voice from heaven proclaims: 'This is my Son the Beloved, my favour rests on him' (Mt 3:17). Traditional designations of Son, Christ/Messiah and Servant are here combined and given a whole new meaning (Ps 2:7; Isa 42:1; 61:1).

The title son of God was also applied to the people and Matthew associates Jesus' experience with that of the people in the going into exile, the sojourn in Egypt and his return home, and in his sojourn and temptations in the desert where unlike the people in the desert wandering he does not succumb to the temptations but proves himself to be truly the Son of God (Mt 2:15; 4:1-11).

(iii) Son of Man

The title Son of Man occurs in the gospels in very different contexts, dealing with Jesus' earthly activity, with his suffering and death and with his future coming in glory. It is the most enigmatic of the titles applied to Jesus. In fact it is the title which he applies to himself in predicting the two very different outcomes to his life, in the immediate future his passion, death and resurrection and at the end of the age his return in glory.

In the Old Testament Ezekiel used the title 'son of man' of a human being or of humankind (Ezek 2:1; 3:1). Daniel used it of an apocalyptic figure 'like to a son of man' who will come 'with the clouds of heaven' and be given power, glory and the kingdom (Dan 7:13). In Daniel the figure is presented in representative terms (Dan 7:27), but he is also seen as an individual since he is awarded regal status and given a kingdom. In 1 Enoch and 4 Ezra the Son of Man appears as an eschatological judge and deliverer who will overthrow the wicked and vindicate the righteous (1 Enoch 46-53; 4 Ezra 13). These texts are important for the understanding in the early church of the future coming of Jesus as eschatological judge and vindicator, as evident in Matthew: 'You will see the Son of Man sitting at the right hand of the Power ...' (Mt 26:64 and / /s).

The Son of Man title is used to show the divine authority behind his earthly activity. It is used when Jesus claims two divine prerogatives, the power on earth to forgive sins (Mt 9:6) and lordship over the Sabbath (Mt 12:8). By way of contrast it is used of his having come not to be served but to serve and give his life as a ransom for many (Mt 20:28). In this he is portrayed as a model of humility and self-renunciation. His life is exemplary and his death salvific. Most commonly the title is used in connection with his approaching rejection, passion, death and resurrection when he will be 'handed over' in accordance with a divine plan in fulfilment of the scriptures (Mt 17:22; 20:18).

The Son of Man title is also used by Jesus of himself when speaking of his eschatological, apocalyptic 'coming in glory' when he will come 'in the glory of his Father with his angels' (Mt 16:27), in his warning that 'the Son of Man will come at an hour you do not expect' (Mt 24:44) and in his response to the High Priest's interrogation when he tells him that he will see 'the Son of Man seated at the right hand of the Power and coming on the clouds of heaven' (Mt 26:64).

(iv) Lord

Throughout the gospel Jesus is regularly addressed as 'Lord', a title reserved for God in the Old Testament where it is used as a circumlocution for *YHWH*. It is used of the glorified, risen Christ in the New Testament. In Matthew's gospel the title 'Lord' is the common way of addressing Jesus on the part of persons of faith. Jesus raised the understanding of Messiah, Son of David, to a new level by quoting Psalm 110:1 in which David addresses the Messiah as Lord (Mt 22:41-46).

B. JESUS, MOSES AND THE TORAH

All groups responding to the destruction of 70AD turned to the Torah as the remaining pillar of Judaism. The apocalyptic writers saw in the Torah the way forward from the crisis until the new age dawned. Fidelity to its prescriptions would guarantee them divine protection and favour as they waited patiently for the new age to come. The rabbinic response focused on the teaching of the great rabbis who had studied and produced the commentaries and reflections on the Torah. The Christian Jews saw in Jesus the authentic interpreter of the Law, putting him above Moses who received the Law on Sinai and on a par with the Divine Lawgiver: 'You have heard that it was said, but I say to you …' (Mt 5:21-48).

Jesus' teaching in Matthew is presented as a fulfilment of the Law and the Prophets (Mt 5:17). He calls for a righteousness that surpasses that of the scribes and the Pharisees (Mt 5:20). In the antitheses he pushes the prescriptions of the Torah to their logical conclusion in the case of divorce and oaths and looks behind the prescriptions to personal dispositions, motivation and interpersonal values in the case of murder and adultery (Mt 5:21-48). He plays a winning hand in the contemporary disputes about divorce (Mt 19:3-9) and Sabbath observance (Mt 12:1-8). He emphasises both the importance of traditional teaching and the necessity of new thinking, describing the scribe instructed (become a disciple) in the kingdom of heaven in terms of a householder who brings forth from his treasury things new and old (Mt 13:52). In the fraught post 70AD situation he is quite radical in presenting Jesus' call for love of enemies, turning the other cheek, going the extra mile and emphasising forgiveness (Mt 5:21-48; 18:21-35). Obedience to the Law and observance of covenantal obligations as interpreted by Jesus, summed up as doing the will of the Father in heaven (Mt 7:21), and acting in the spirit of compassion summed up in the prophetic statement: 'What I want is mercy not sacrifice' (Hos 6:6; Mt 9:13; 12:7) are the marks of the true disciple. One must practise what one preaches. Extolling the Law and parading status and authority as teachers of the law are not sufficient (Mt 22:2, 3).

The mighty figure and central role of Moses in the Old Testament provide a historical precedent, a literary model and a theological backdrop against which to portray Jesus as the new and definitive teacher of the Law. In addition to the emphasis on Jesus as the teacher *par excellence* and his authoritative and definitive interpretation of the Law, Jesus' entire story is told by Matthew with the outline of the Moses story in mind. His treatment of the threat to Jesus' life at his birth, his exile and return from Egypt (Mt 2:1-23), his fasting and temptations in the desert (Mt 4:11), his feeding of the multitude (Mt 15-32-39), his ascending the mountain to teach (Mt 5:1), his transfiguration on the mountain (Mt 17:1-8), his appointment and naming of the Twelve Apostles (Mt 10:1-4) and his final meeting on the mountain and sending of them into the whole world to make disciples of all nations (Mt 28:16-20) are all told with allusions to the story of Moses. A. M. O'Leary points out that:

> By focusing on the superiority of Jesus relative to Moses, Matthew does not diminish Moses. Rather, he uses the figure of Moses to amplify certain aspects of Jewish theology. He does so, ultimately, in order to amplify aspects of his Christology.[51]

C. JESUS, HISTORY AND THE KINGDOM

For Matthew Jesus is the pivotal figure in the history of Israel and of the world. Matthew's use of ten carefully edited fulfillment citations (Mt 1:23; 2:15,17-18,23; 4:14-16; 8:17; 12:17-21; 13:35; 21:4-5; 27:9), all deviating from the LXX, and only one of which arises out of the Mk/Mt narrative (Mt 21:4-5 // Mk 11:9-10),[52] shows how he saw clearly and carefully portrayed Jesus' ministry as the fulfilment of the prophecies and the promises made to Israel and how the history of Israel moved forward to a fulfilment in Christ.

The vindication of his whole life and death through the resurrection is a turning point in the history begun in Abraham. 'All the prophets and the Law prophesied until John' (Mt 11:13). Jesus and his ministry mark the ushering in of the kingdom of heaven. The restriction of his own ministry 'to the lost sheep of the house of Israel' (Mt 15:24) is but a first step. It is, however, an interim fulfilment. Matthew's description of apocalyptic events surrounding Jesus' death and resurrection, the earthquake, the opening of the tombs

---

51. A. M. O'Leary, *op. cit.*, 138.
52. Ibid., 136.

and appearance of the dead, open up a whole new period as they foreshadow the end of the present age and the arrival of the age to come (Mt 27:51-54). The vindication of the Son of God marks the beginning of the universal mission and points ahead to the final consummation, the age to come, the establishment of God's rule over all creation.

D. THE DISCIPLES IN MATTHEW

Matthew has a far more benign attitude to the disciples than Mark. Whereas Mark shows Jesus' exasperation with the disciples' 'little faith' and their almost complete lack of understanding, Matthew's Jesus regards their 'little faith' as incipient faith rather than lack of faith and he speaks of the disciples in a warm-hearted way, describing them as 'brothers' and 'little ones'. He insists on a fraternity of disciples in which honorific titles play no part. No one should be called 'rabbi' or 'father'. God alone is Father and all disciples are brothers (and sisters). The greatest is the one who serves and the one who humbles himself will be exalted (Mt 23:8-12). He prefers the title *mathêtês* (disciple, learner) and his final command is to make disciples (*mathêteusate*) of all nations (Mt 28:19). The disciples are, therefore, not only the historical disciples and companions of the earthly Jesus but models of all followers, and in a special way they are models for the intended readership/audience of the gospel. Peter plays a more prominent part in Matthew as leader, model and representative disciple.

8. APPROACHING THE GOSPEL

I write this commentary from the standpoint of one who sees the work as a whole, the text as it now stands. In dealing with sources, the 'historical' Jesus and the nature and composition of the communities in which the tradition was nurtured and transmitted, I do so only insofar as such information or speculation throws light on the text under examination and its place in the gospel as a whole. The author has shaped the final text from the sources, oral and written, at his disposal and in the process has produced a text that is a marriage of content and form. I refer to the other gospels not to 'fill out the gaps' in the story of Jesus, but to focus on the particular emphasis in Matthew's telling, or to further explain a detail in his text.

Furthermore, I see the gospel as an integral part of the whole canon of scripture, and consider exegesis as a science practised within the comprehensive view of the church. If one stands outside that comprehensive view one runs the risk of breaking up 'the indivisible unity of the figure of Christ'.[53] Hans Urs von Balthasar states it very clearly:

> Jesus' word can be understood by all, but only in the light of his testimony of being the Son of God does it become truly clear. Moreover, only in relation to his death and resurrection does it attain the fullness of its meaning: Jesus' entire being is one single Word. This perfect being becomes manifest only from the testimonials of faith … (which), all together, form a magnificent polyphony – not a pluralism in the contemporary sense … The more facets we can view, the better we can grasp the unity of the inspiration. The possessor of this inspiration is the church, the early charisma of which was to compose the New Testament and establish its canon. Only her eye of faith, guided by the Holy Spirit, could see the whole phenomenon of Jesus Christ.[54]

READING IN GREEK OR IN TRANSLATION

Ideally a serious study of any of the New Testament documents should be conducted from, and accompanied by, a reading of the Greek text. In reality, however, most students are still learning New Testament Greek and many general readers have little, if any, knowledge of the language. As every translation is but an approximation to the original it is advisable, therefore, to follow more than one translation when making a serious study of the text. Words and expressions are very important in Matthew and in translation they easily lose their impact and connotations. This is particularly true where a word group containing related noun, verb, adjective or adverb come from the same root, and are translated by very different words in English. In the commentary, I frequently use italics for such related words. I also use italics for recurring words of particular significance, and for the transliteration into the Roman alphabet of Greek and Hebrew words and expressions. This last group I introduce gradually and translate until they should be quite familiar to the reader.

---

53. H. U. von Balthasar, 'Theology and Aesthetic', *Communio*, 1 (1981), 65.
54. Ibid.

Chapter and Verse
It should also be kept in mind that the original Greek text was not divided into chapter and verse, not to mention neat divisions into paragraphs with supplied headings and subheadings as in some modern printed bibles. Chapter divisions were introduced into the bible by Stephen Langton, Archbishop of Canterbury 1207-28, and the verse divisions were made by the Parisian printer and publisher Robert Estienne for his 1551 Geneva edition of the New Testament. The chapter and verse divisions are very useful for referring to the text but they can be misleading at times if one wishes to follow the natural flow of the narrative.

IS MATTHEW ANTI-JEWISH (ANTI-SEMITIC)? A NOTE AND A WARNING
There is no denying the very regrettable fact that this gospel has been understood and used in an anti-Jewish (anti-Semitic) way. The 'woes' against the scribes and Pharisees in chapter 23 and the cry of the mob 'His blood be upon us and upon our children' (Mt 27:25) have been used as an excuse for prejudice and ill treatment of Jewish people over the centuries. This is a most unfortunate and completely inappropriate understanding of the gospel.

Taken in its own context in the first century, the polemical aspect of the gospel emerges from an internal Jewish debate and represents one side of a very heated argument. When compared to the writings of the prophets, it sits comfortably with their fiery sermons and condemnations of rulers, priests, and people. The polemics of Matthew follow the tradition of the polemics and woes of the prophets (Amos 5:18-20; 6:1-7; Mic 2:1-4; Isa 5:8-10, 11-14; 18-19, 20, 21, 22-24; 10:1-3; 28:1-4; 29:1-4; 30:1-3; 31:1-4; 45:9-10; Jer 13:27; 48:46; Ezek 16:23).

However, when they are taken out of that internal Jewish context and used by non-Jews against Jews they take on a very different character. All Christian preaching, teaching and artistic expression should be very vigilant on this account.

The Prologue:
The Origins of Jesus and His Mission
Mt 1:1-4:16

Introduction to the Prologue

The Prologue to the gospel consists of two parts. The first part, consisting of the Infancy Narrative (Mt 1:1 – 2:23) establishes the identity and role of Jesus and foreshadows the reception that he will receive from Jew and Gentile. The second part, consisting of the mission of the Baptist and the preparation of Jesus for his mission (Mt 3:1 – 4:16) confirms his identity and role already established in the Infancy Narrative and serves as an immediate preparation for the task ahead.

The first part, usually referred to as the Infancy Narrative (Mt 1:1 – 2:23), functions as a prologue or overture to the whole work. It serves to introduce the protagonist, Jesus of Nazareth, and to illustrate his centrality to the divine plan of salvation. It identifies him in terms of his human origins in the context of the history of the people of Israel by calling him son of David and son of Abraham and providing a genealogy back to Abraham. It identifies him also in terms of his divine origin as the one conceived by the Holy Spirit and therefore, by implication, Son of God. It places him in the divine plan of salvation by calling him (the) Christ and Emmanuel and by interpreting his name, Jesus (*Yeshua*, Joshua), as 'Saviour', explaining it in terms of 'the one who will save his people from their sins'.

The significance of his ministry in the overall plan of salvation history is spelled out not only in placing him at the arrival point of the genealogy and in the use of the christological titles, but also in the fulfilment (formula) citations, in the symbolically laden geographic references and in the Old Testament allusions and narrative parallels. All of these point to the fulfilment of a predetermined, consistent divine plan coming to fulfilment at the divinely appointed time. The Infancy Narrative illustrates both the continuity of God's plan and its discontinuities, showing in the exceptional circumstances of the birth of Jesus a new divine initiative within an overall continuity. Furthermore, the future acceptance, rejection and violent death of the protagonist are foreshadowed in the circumstances surrounding his birth and infancy.

The second part of the prologue (Mt 3:1 – 4:16) deals with the mission of John the Baptist to prepare the way of the Lord during which the identity and role of Jesus are publicly proclaimed by the Baptist, divinely confirmed at his baptism and then tested by Satan in the wilderness. When the mission of the Baptist is cut short by his arrest, Jesus returns to Galilee to begin his own mission to Israel.

The Prologue: Part I: The Infancy Narrative Mt 1-2

OUTLINE OF THE INFANCY NARRATIVE

1. Who, Whence and How?
Outline of Jesus' human and divine origins. Who Jesus is, where he comes from and how his coming takes place (Mt 1:1-25).

> A. Mt 1:1-1   Superscription/Title
> B. Mt 1:2-17   Genealogy
> C. Mt 1:18-25   The Birth of Jesus Christ

2. Whence and Whither
Reception by Jew and Gentile: The events and places in the account of Jesus' birth and infancy emphasise his identity and role and at the same time foreshadow his life and death (Mt 2:1-23).

> A. Mt 2:1-12   Magi + Herod; Reception by Jew and Gentile
> B. Mt 2:13-15   Flight into Egypt/Jesus' Exile
> C. Mt 2:16-2   Mourning in Ramah/Moses typology
> D. Mt 2:19-23   The Return from Egypt/Jesus' Exodus

1. WHO, WHENCE AND HOW MT 1:1-25

A. The Superscription/Title
'Book of the genealogy (or birth) of Jesus Christ son of David, son of Abraham' (Mt 1:1).

Book of the genealogy (or birth) of Jesus
The anonymous early Christian document which has been called since early Christian times *The Gospel according to Matthew* opens with the words *biblos geneseôs Iesou Christou huiou Daveid huiou Abraam.* The first question to be asked is: 'Do these words stand as a title over the whole book or are they referring only to the genealogy and birth of Jesus?' They have been variously translated

as '(The) book of the genealogy of Jesus Christ, son of David, son of Abraham' and '(The) record of the birth of Jesus Christ, son of David, son of Abraham.'[1]

These first words recall the words of the Book of Genesis (LXX), reflecting both the summary statement at the end of the first creation account in Gen 2:4: 'This is the book of the generation of heaven and earth when they came to be' (*hautê hê biblos geneseôs ouranou kai gês hote egeneto*), and the words of Gen 5:1: 'This is the book of the generation of human beings' (*hautê hê biblos geneseôs anthrôpôn*) which introduce 'the roll of Adam's descendants'. Matthew thus opens his gospel against the literary backdrop of Genesis, the first book of Moses and of the Bible as a whole which deals with the origins of creation, the origin and progress of humankind and of the tribes, and the origins and progress of sin. Through the use of genealogies, the Book of Genesis traces the progress of human history and the spread of sin, building up to the beginnings of 'salvation history' with the call of Abraham and the covenant God made with him. It then records the succession of generations who carried on the covenant and its promised future.

Given Matthew's rich and skilful use of the Old Testament, it is not surprising that he models the opening words of his gospel on these statements of cosmic creation and human beginnings in the Book of Genesis. How then should Matthew's *biblos geneseôs Iesou* be translated? Translating it as 'The book of the genealogy of Jesus Christ' is suggested by the fact that it traces the generations that lead up to the birth of Christ. Translating it as 'book of the birth of Jesus' also seems a good translation because the genealogy serves the purpose of building up to a climax in the account of the unusual circumstances surrounding the birth of Jesus. But, just as the Genesis account traces the origins and fortunes of the chosen people among all the peoples, so Matthew's gospel also goes beyond the initial event of the birth and infancy of Jesus to show the origins of the Jesus movement (the church) within Judaism and to foreshadow, in fact to command, its spread into the wider Gentile world in

---

1. In similar fashion the anonymous text which we call *The Gospel of Mark* identifies itself as 'The beginning of the Good News of Jesus Christ, Son of God', referring to the whole gospel which traces the origins of the good news in the life, ministry, death and resurrection of Jesus, believed in and followed by the people for whom the gospel was written.

the final words of Jesus in the gospel: 'Go, therefore make disciples of all nations' (Mt 28:19). In this it parallels the spread of humanity in Genesis, traced through the genealogies and fulfilling the command to 'be fruitful and multiply and fill the earth …' (Gen 1:28). Seeing a parallel with the genealogies and their function in Genesis, one could understand the 'book of the genealogy of Jesus' as referring to the entire history of salvation which is recorded in the genealogy and comes to fulfilment first of all in the birth of Jesus, then in his mission to the Jews and finally in his sending his apostles to carry his mission to the other nations. In this sense the opening words stand as a superscription or title above the entire gospel.

Christ (Messiah), son of David, son of Abraham

The opening verse, the superscription, adds three titles to the personal name, Jesus. He is described as Christ (Messiah), son of David and son of Abraham.

Christ (Messiah)[2]

'Christ/Messiah' is the first of the titles given to Jesus and it immediately puts him in a category of specially anointed people. As seen in the introduction, the title had a long history. Literally translated as 'the anointed one' it denotes a priest in the 'priestly' books of Leviticus and Numbers,[3] a king in the 'royal' books of Samuel and in Isaiah[4] and from the time of Daniel it usually denotes a prince.[5] By Jesus' time it was in use as a 'catch all' term for 'the one to come', the one who would bring about a change for the better in the spiritual and/or temporal fortunes of the people, an expectation that varied according to the needs and hopes of different religious and political groups. Matthew gives the title a definite accent and emphasis and it is complemented by the use of the other titles and fleshed out in the narrative. He is less hesitant about the title than Mark who wraps or even half sinks it in the Messianic Secret (the command to silence) to ensure it is not misunderstood.

---

2. *Christos* in Greek/*Messiah* in Hebrew.
3. Lev 4:3; 6:22; Num 3:3.
4. 1 Sam 16:6; 24:6; 26:11, 16, 23; 2 Sam 1:16; 19:21; Isa 45:1.
5. Dan 9:25.

Son of David

Matthew spells out the role of the Christ/Messiah in the opening verse in terms of his being 'son of David' and 'son of Abraham'. 'Son of David' highlights the pivotal role of David in salvation history and sets the Christ/Messiah in the context of the anointed one, a royal prince, in the line of David, whose role is very much that of a Christ/Messiah for the Jews, a fulfilment of the promise of a 'new David' to shepherd the flock of Israel (cf Ezek 34:23). The expectation that the Messiah would be descended from David is widely attested in the gospels (Lk 1:32, 33; 3:31; 18:35-43; Mt 1:1-17; 9:27; 20:29-34; Mk 22:46-52; Jn 7:42). Jesus even challenges what seems to have been a widespread but too narrow understanding of the identity and role of Messiah as son of David, and sets the title in the context of his identity as Lord (Mt 22:41-46; Mk 12:35-37; Lk 20:41-44).

Son of Abraham

The title or designation 'son of Abraham' sets the Christ/Messiah in the line of the Patriarch Abraham who was the ancestor of the people of Israel through Isaac but who was also the spiritual ancestor of universal humanity through God's promise to Abraham that he would be father of a multitude of nations (Gen 14:1-8) and that in his name (offspring) all nations would be blessed (Gen 12:1-9). In his letters to the Galatians and Romans Paul had already, prior to Matthew, emphasised this aspect of Abraham's significance as father of all believers through whom all the nations would be blessed (Gal 3:6-4:31; Rom 9:6-9). Following the destruction of Jerusalem and the temple in 70AD, as the divisions within Judaism emerged and the Christian Jews were accepting Gentiles into their movement, the spiritual fatherhood of Abraham, rather than his 'biological/ ethnic' fatherhood became very important. The gospels of Matthew, Luke and John emphasise this distinction (cf Mt 3:9; Lk 3:8; Jn 8:33-40). As son of Abraham, Jesus is very much a Christ/Messiah not only for Jews but also for all nations, for Jew and Gentile alike.

B. The Genealogy: Mt 1:2-17

a. Importance and use of genealogies

Genealogies in oriental cultures generally, and in the Bible in particular, were very important. They were used for establishing the right to kingship, priesthood, ownership of land, and membership of tribe or nation. They also provided a framework for recounting secular and salvation history. They were therefore more than archival records. They sketched the outline of significant events and personages. As in many cultures it is most likely that the biblical genealogies were originally oral recitations, fluid and variable in nature, and only at a later stage were they committed to writing and a fixed form. This is probably the case with the older genealogies in the Bible but it is obvious from the references to the reigns of the kings of Israel and Judah that historical records were kept prior to the Exile (1 Kings 11:41; 14:19, 29; 15:6, 7, 23, 31, 32; 16:14, 27; 1 Chron 29:29, 30 et al.) and after the Exile records were kept in the Jerusalem palace or temple archives, as is obvious from the references to such records (1 Chron 9:1; 2 Chron 12:15; 31:16; Ezra 2:59-62; 8:1; Neh 7:5, 64; 12:23f).

In the Old Testament there are important genealogies in Genesis, Exodus, Ruth, and both books of Chronicles.[6] In the New Testament, Matthew (1:1-17) and Luke (Lk 3:23-38) both have genealogies of Jesus' ancestors, though there are very significant differences between them.

Matthew's formula of the genealogy 'A begat B' follows the formula in the genealogy in Ruth 4:18-22. Luke, on the other hand, uses the formula 'A son of B, B son of C'. Matthew's genealogy moves forward in time from the famous ancestor to the protagonist in the story like Gen 5:1-23.[7] Luke's genealogy goes backwards from the protagonist to the famous ancestor. Matthew concentrates on the genealogy from Abraham to Jesus, Luke traces the generations from Jesus back to Adam and to God (Lk 3:23-38). Matthew divides

---

6. In Genesis there are a number of genealogies. The first lists the descendants of Cain down to Lamech (Gen 4:17-24) and it is followed by the list of the sons of Adam through Seth down to Enosh (Gen 4:25-26). There follow in turn a genealogy from Adam to the sons of Noah (Gen 5:1-32), a list of the descendants of Noah (Gen 10:1-32), a list of the descendants of Shem down to Abraham (Gen 11:10-32) and the final list in Genesis is that of the descendants of Jacob (Gen 46:8-27). A list of the descendants of Levi appears in Exod 6:16-25. Ruth 4:18-22 has a genealogy containing the list of the descendants of Perez down to David. 1 Chronicles 1-9 lists the descendants of Adam down to the descendents of Saul.

7. In this Matthew resembles Gen 5 where the story moves forward in time, tracing the progress of sin, from Adam to the story of Noah, the flood, and the new Noachian covenant and laws.

the genealogy into three neat divisions of fourteen generations reflecting a triple division of the history of Israel. Luke makes no such
divisions. Matthew gives the genealogy of Jesus as that of the royal
son of David. He uses material found in the genealogies in 1 Chron
1:28-42; 3:5-24 and Ruth 4:12-22 for the first two stages (Abraham to
David and David to the Exile) but the third stage does not correspond to any genealogical tables in the Old Testament, though
some of the persons mentioned figure in various narratives.[8]

Moving forward in time, the genealogy in Matthew marks the
three major stages in the history of salvation as it builds up to the
fulfilment of God's plan in the birth of the Son of God. It moves in
three stages from the call and first steps in faith taken by Abraham
(the covenant with Abraham and the promise made to him), to a
climax and turning point in David's accession to the throne and the
covenant with David. It then traces the period of the reigning Davidic
monarchy from the death of David to the disaster surrounding the
collapse of the Kingdom of David and the ending of the monarchy
at the time of the Exile to Babylon (587BC). The third period traces
the fortunes of the people from the Exile to the birth of the royal son
of David, the Christ / Messiah. Abraham, David and the Exile mark
three pivotal points involving new initiatives / beginnings in Israel's
history.

The formula of Matthew's genealogy 'A begat B' follows the formula in the genealogy in Ruth 4:18-22. The Greek term *egennêsen* is
the aorist of an active verb meaning 'to beget', 'to father' but translation into English often entails a periphrasis such as 'was the father
of', somewhat blunting the edge of the single Greek verb. There are,
however, some significant departures from, or rather, additions to,
the neat formula 'A begat B' in Matthew's genealogy. Jacob begat
Judah *and his brothers*, an addition that emphasises the inclusion, by
way of mentioning their eponymous ancestors, of all the tribes in
the history of the people of Israel, especially in the sojourn in Egypt.
Similarly, Josiah begat Jechoniah *and his brothers*, an addition to
show the extent of the people involved in the Exile. Jesse begat

8. Not only in the gospels but in the broader Jewish world of New
Testament times genealogies were in vogue, as seen from Jubilees (4:7-
33 and 8:5-9) which provides names for the wives of the Patriarchs who
are not named in the Old Testament and pseudo-Philo's *Biblical
Antiquities* which adds previously unknown names to the genealogies
of Gen 4-5 and 10-11.

David *the king*. The reference to 'the king' highlights the central role of the Davidic kingship in the history of the people. The references to the mothers in four cases (prior to the reference to the mother of Jesus) are also striking, because it departs from the formula and especially because it was not usual to include the mothers in genealogical tables. The significance of their inclusion is treated separately below. The most striking departure from the formula is the final reference: 'Jacob begat Joseph, husband of Mary, and of her was born Jesus who is called the Christ.' J. P. Meier makes the apt observation:

> The genealogy ... shows us Mt's basic approach to solving the relationship of the OT to Jesus. On the one hand, there is an underlying continuity, Mt even includes the psalmist Asaph and the prophet Amos among the kings of Judah to emphasise that Jesus is the fulfilment of all the scriptures. Yet, on the other hand, there is also a rupture as the final age breaks into Israel's history.[9]

D. J. Harrington, in summing up his treatment of the genealogy, makes an observation that will strike a chord with most readers:

> The genealogies of Jesus usually strike terror into the hearts of homilists and teachers. But once past the unfamiliar names it is possible to find in Mt 1:1-17 some important themes for actualisation: the roots of Jesus in the history of Israel, the surprising instruments that God uses, the peculiar assortment of people that make up the ancestors of Jesus (and the church in all ages), the tension between tradition and newness, the 'right' time as part of God's plan for salvation, etc.[10]

b. The peculiar assortment of people

A brief look at the personalities, so aptly described by D. J. Harrington as 'the peculiar assortment of people', and at the broad historical outline behind the genealogy highlights the multifaceted nature of salvation history which provides the backdrop for the story of Jesus as told and interpreted by Matthew.

---

9. J. P. Meier, *Matthew*, 5.
10. D. J. Harrington, *The Gospel of Matthew*, Sacra Pagina, 33.

i. From Abraham to David (cf 1 Chron 2:1-15; Ruth 4:12,18-22)

The first part of Matthew's genealogy begins with the history of the Patriarchs, Abraham, Isaac, Jacob, Judah and his brothers. These are the first generations in the history of salvation. The initiative of God in the story of the covenant with Abraham sets the history in motion. Abraham and Sarah, old in years and past the age of child-bearing, are given a son, Isaac, to be the bearer of the covenantal promise to Abraham that he would be the father of a multitude of nations and in his name all the nations would be blessed (Gen 12:3; 22:18). Isaac, weaker and somewhat overshadowed as a person in his own right because he was son of a more famous father and father of a more famous and scheming son, is the link with the renewed covenant with Jacob, renamed Israel after the struggle with the angel and the vision at Bethel (Gen 35:10). Jacob succeeded to the promise through the scheming of his mother and his own exploit-ation of the need of his brother Esau. 'Jacob begat Judah *and his brothers*' is an expansion on the 'A begat B' formula, most likely to highlight the involvement of the full range of tribes in the Egypt and Exodus experience.[11] Then Judah, one of the twelve sons of Jacob/Israel would have failed in his duty of ensuring the handing on of the line of the promise, had not his daughter-in-law Tamar taken the initiative and ensured the continuation of the line of the promises by trapping him into fathering the twins, Perez and Zerah.

Zerah was father of Hezron. The history of the sojourn in Egypt and the wandering in the desert before the conquest of the land is represented by Hezron, Aram,[12] Aminadab and Nashon of whom very little, if anything definite is known. Nashon was leader of the tribe of Judah in the desert (Num 2:3; 7:12, 13). Nashon was father of Salmon, the father of Boaz, the mother being Rahab, again a foreign woman who took the initiative in furthering God's plan and becom-ing associated with God's people. She was the prostitute in Jericho who sheltered the spies of Joshua and thus helped in the taking of the city, her family being spared in the process by the displaying of the red chord (Joshua 2:18).[13] Boaz begat Obed, Ruth being his

---

11. A similar expansion 'Josiah begat Jechoniah and his brothers' will occur at the time of the Exile, to involve them all in the Exile experience.
12. In the LXX he is named variously as Arran, Ram and Aram.
13. That Rahab of Joshua 2 is intended is sure, but there is no OT attesta-tion to her being mother of Boaz. There seems to be a shortening or omission between Rahab, Salmon and Boaz given the length of time in-volved.

mother. Ruth, advised by Naomi her mother-in-law, took the initiative and asserted her claim to his hand in marriage. She then became mother of his son, Obed, the father of Jesse, whose youngest
son, David, against all expectations was chosen by Samuel and
anointed king (1 Sam 16:1-13). He was king in Hebron for seven
years and then the northern tribes accepted him as king over all
Israel. He took Jerusalem, made it his military, civil, and religious
capital and reigned for another thirty-three years in Jerusalem, forty
years in all as king. Thus the genealogy so far gives a potted history
carefully arranged into fourteen generations of the unfolding plan
of God in building up to the establishment of the throne of David
and the covenant with David (2 Sam 7). It is certainly a collection of
'tales of the unexpected' where the initiative of God working in surprising circumstances leaves the reader with a sense of wonder. The
formula 'A begat B' is extended with the reference to the king,
indicating a climax and new departure. (A similar extension to the
formula will occur with the birth of Jesus *called Christ*.) There follows the account of the ruling house of David in the next (carefully
arranged) fourteen generations.

ii. From David to the Exile

David's adultery with Uriah's wife (Bathsheba), and his order to
have Uriah put in mortal danger in battle, resulting in his death,
was followed by the birth of a stillborn child, but the next child,
Solomon[14] lived and succeeded to the throne of David (2 Sam 11-12).
He was secured in his succession by the initiative of a woman, his
mother Bathsheba, (formerly) wife of Uriah the Hittite, who, together with Nathan the prophet, secured the succession from the ailing
David and foiled the usurper Adonijah (1 Kings1: 1-53). Solomon's
thousand women, seven hundred royal princesses and three hundred concubines, seriously compromised his religious fidelity. In
addition to this infidelity, his cutting across the traditional administrative prerogatives of the tribes and forced labour in the mines combined to cause the discontent which broke into open revolt after his
death and brought about the division of the kingdom, as Jeroboam
led away the northern tribes to form the northern kingdom, and
Rehoboam was left with the tribe of Judah, the southern kingdom

---

14. Luke traces the line of David through Nathan rather than through
Solomon.

centred on Jerusalem. A series of kings of Judah followed
Rehoboam, some faithful to YHWH, some not so. Abijah (913-
911BC) 'committed all the sins that his father did before him; his
heart was not true to the Lord his God like the heart of his father
David (1 Kings 15:3); Asaph (911-870BC)[15] 'did what was right in
the sight of the Lord as his father David had done (1 Kings 15:11);
Jehoshaphat (870-848BC) followed the good example of his father,
but the pagan places of worship, 'the high places', were not abolished and the people still offered sacrifice and incense on the high
places (1 Kings 22:41ff). Joram/Jehoram (848-841BC) did what is
displeasing to YHWH 'yet the Lord would not destroy Judah for the
sake of his servant David, since he had promised to give a lamp to
him and to his descendants forever' (2 Kings 8:16ff). There are three
kings missing at this point.[16] Next mentioned is Uzziah (781-740BC)
who 'did what was right in the sight of the Lord as his father
Amaziah had done' but the people still offered sacrifice and incense
on the high places (2 Kings 15:1ff). Jotham (740-736BC) also 'did
what was right in the sight of the Lord as his father had done' but
the people still offered sacrifice and incense on the high places (2
Kings 15:34ff). Ahaz (736-716) 'walked in the way of the kings of
Israel, even making his son to pass through fire, copying the shameful practices of the nations ... He offered sacrifices and incense on
the high places, on the hills and under every green tree' (2 Kings
16:1ff). He was challenged by Isaiah the prophet to seek a sign from
God in the context of the Syro-Ephraimite coalition when the tiny
kingdom of Judah was caught between the threats of the coalition

---

15. According to 1 Chron 3:10 his name was Asa (cf 1 Kings 15:9). J. P.
Meier, *Matthew*, 5, suggests that Mt includes the psalmist Asaph (Pss 50;
70-83; cf 1 Chron 16:5-37; 2 Chron 29:30) and the prophet Amos among
the kings of Judah to emphasise that Jesus is the fulfilment of all the
scriptures, including prophets and psalms. D. J. Harrington, *op., cit.,* 29,
n 10, does not agree.
16. There is a historical gap in the list of kings when compared to 1
Chron 3:1-12. The omission of Ahaziah, Joash and Amaziah between
Joram and Uzziah was probably done in the attempt to secure the overall number of fourteen, and these three may have been chosen for
exclusion because all three died by violence and, in addition, Joash was
not buried in the sepulchre of the kings (2 Chron 24:25). Maybe also his
relationship to the notorious Athaliah contributed to his exclusion.
Similarity between the names Ahaziah and Amaziah may also have
been a factor (2 Kings 11-14).

and the might of the all destroying Assyrian army. On that occasion
Isaiah prophesied that the child born of the maiden would be called
Emmanuel, meaning 'God is with us', a sign and promise for the
house of David that they would survive the crisis of impending destruction (2 Kings 16ff; Isa 7:10ff). The promised child was Hezekiah
(716-687BC), fathered or fostered and adopted by Ahaz who had
caused a son of his own to pass through fire. 'He (Hezekiah) did
what was right in the sight of the Lord just as his ancestor David
had done.' In fact he brought about one of the great reforms in the
history of the chosen people. He abolished the high places, broke
the pillars, cut down the sacred poles and smashed the bronze ser-
pent, reputedly made by Moses. 'He held fast to the Lord; he did
not depart from following him ...'(2 Kings 18-20). Manasseh (687-
642BC) did what was evil in the sight of the Lord following the
abominable practices of the nations ... He rebuilt the high places
that his father Hezekiah had destroyed and he set up altars to Baal.'
He shed innocent blood in such quantity that he flooded Jerusalem
from end to end. In response the prophets reported the judgement
that God 'will bring such evil upon Jerusalem and Judah as to make
the ears of everyone who hears it tingle ...'. Amos, probably correctly
called Amon/Ammon (cf 1 Chron 3:14; 2 Kings 21:18-26; 2 Chron
33:20-25) was the son of Manasseh according to 2 Kings (642-40). He
followed the ways of his father and did what was displeasing to
YHWH. He was murdered by his officers in the palace. He was followed by his son Josiah, the king who was praised above all others
in the record of the kings. He achieved a root and branch reform of
the Temple and cult, burned all the pagan cult objects and put an
end to the high places and their priests. 'No king before him had
turned to YHWH as he did with all his heart, all his soul, all his
strength, in perfect loyalty to the Law of Moses; nor was any king
like him seen again' (2 Kings 22). Matthew says Josiah was father of
Jechoniah and his brothers. In fact Josiah was father of Jehoahaz
and Jehoiakim[17] and Jehoiakim was father of Jechoniah.[18] Then
came the disaster of the Exile and the end of the actual reigning
house of David. Like the reference to Judah and his brothers the reference to Jechoniah and his brothers here is probably a way of
showing the widespread experience of the Exile.

17. Both reigned as king, as did their uncle Zedekiah.
18. Again the three were probably omitted to ensure the overall number
of fourteen generations.

As seen from the above sketch, the kings in the House of David were certainly a motley crew of saints and sinners. Though the disreputable element seems to have been very much in evidence, emphasised by the reforming zeal and judgemental editorial work of the deuteronomistic historian(s), the work of God moving forward the plan of salvation continued apace.

iii. From the Exile in Babylon to Jesus

This third group, from the Exile to Jesus Christ, differs completely from the list in Luke. It is possible that Matthew is following a royal line and Luke a line of natural descent. For the most part the persons mentioned in the third group are unknown in the Bible. Some observations can be made. Shealthiel was son of Jechoniah (1 Chron 3:17, 19) but he was not father of Zerubbabel, who was in fact son of Pedaiah, Shealthiel's brother. Abiud, the last person mentioned in the genealogy for whom there is Old Testament evidence does not figure in the list of Zerubbabel's children in the list in 1 Chron 3:19-20.

A very obvious difference between the genealogies in Matthew and Luke also occurs towards the end of the lists where Matthew names Jacob as the father of Joseph and Luke names Eli as his father.

There are in fact only thirteen 'begettings' in the third list. Some say this is because Jesus becomes Christ and so is to be counted as two begettings. Others think Matthew made a mistake and omitted one name.

iv. The women in the genealogy

The genealogy is striking in the fact that it includes the names of four women (prior to Mary mother of Jesus). Though the mothers of the patriarchs, judges and kings figure in the Old Testament narratives, they do not figure in the genealogical tables. Not only is the inclusion of mothers unusual here in Matthew's genealogy; it also breaks the smooth 'A begat B' pattern. It becomes even more striking when one looks at the actual characters, actions and situations involved. The women one would expect to see in the genealogy like Sarah, wife of Abraham and mother of Isaac, Rebecca, wife of Isaac and mother of Jacob and Esau, and Rachel, wife of Jacob and mother of Joseph and Benjamin do not appear. Instead one finds reference to Tamar, Rahab, Ruth and the wife of Uriah the Hittite (Bathsheba).

Tamar trapped and seduced her father-in-law Judah into a sexual union and bore him twins, when he failed to accept her as a wife for his third son (Gen 38). However, she is seen as righteous because Judah had in fact failed to act in accordance with the custom or law that eventually became enshrined in Deut 25:5-6 and is usually referred to as the Levirate Law. In her 'irregular action/liaison' she achieved justice for her late husband, a justice denied by his father who would have had her killed, had she not outwitted him. He was forced into admitting that: 'She is more righteous than I' (Gen 38:25-26).

Rahab is next mentioned. She was the prostitute in Jericho who gave hospitality to the spies of Joshua when they went to assess the position in the city prior to their advance (Joshua 2:1-24; 4:22-25). She threw in her lot, and that of her family, with the coming victors and accepted their God, acknowledging his mighty deeds on their behalf.

Ruth is next mentioned. She was a noble, upright woman, a widow who asserted her right to be taken in marriage by her cousin Boaz, asserting that right by finding the place where he lay, turning back the covering at his feet and lying there beside him as he slept, an action that can be interpreted in various ways from the simple action of lying at his feet to more serious sexual encounter (Ruth 3:1-15). Ruth was advised and abetted by her mother-in-law, Naomi, and together they brought about the happy outcome. W. J. Harrington puts it succinctly: 'Two admirable women do, gently, manipulate an admirable man.'[19]

Then comes the wife of Uriah (Bathsheba) who became wife of David after their adultery and David's scheming to have her husband killed in battle (2 Sam 11-12). It was through her determination that her son, Solomon, inherited the throne, promised by David, and in spite of the efforts of the usurper Adonijah and the threatened failure of the weakened and ailing David to secure it for him (1 Kings 1:1-53). Interestingly her name, Bathsheba is not given in the genealogy. Rather she is defined in terms of her marriage relationship to her first husband Uriah, a foreigner, a Hittite.

Why do these women figure in the story while outstanding women like Sarah, Rebecca, Rachel and other prominent women do not appear, though they were also wives and mothers in the direct line of the promises? Some scholars suggest that they are included to highlight the fact that, despite what one might expect, the 'irregular'

---

19. W. J. Harrington, *Matthew, Sage Theologian*, 33

nature of their behaviour and sexual/marital unions did not dis-
qualify them from the ancestral line of the Messiah, but rather ensured them of their position. This may have been a counter-argu-
ment to objections against believing that Jesus could be the Christ
because of rumours of something irregular about the circumstances
of his birth. There may be an element of truth in this understanding,[20] but the introductory verse of the gospel seems to give the key
to the primary meaning. Jesus is son of David, a Messiah for the
Jews, in fulfilment of Jewish expectations. But he is also ' son of
Abraham', a Messiah for the Gentiles, and significantly three of the
four women mentioned are definitely foreigners. Tamar was a
Canaanite, Rahab a Canaanite and Ruth a Moabitess. The fourth
woman, Bathsheba, was married to a Hittite, and significantly, as
seen already, her personal name is not given but she is identified by
way of reference to her marriage to the foreigner. This may or may
not point to her being a foreigner herself, but her identification with
a foreign husband emphasises a strong foreign element in her story.
All four were 'outsiders' who were taken into, or taken back into,
the house of Israel and became central to its story.[21] Each of them
took decisive action that ensured the continuation of the line of the
promises.

The presence of the women in the genealogy highlights the fact
that the history of salvation involved the active participation of Jew
and Gentile, male and female and persons in regular and irregular
unions and circumstances. These women took an initiative in a patriarchal and androcentric society and ensured the continuation of
the line of the promises and the unfolding of God's plan of salvation
at times when it appeared to be coming to a full stop. Significantly,
the genealogy comes to a climax with the fifth woman, found to be
with child conceived outside her contracted future marriage, but
hers is the strangest story of all for she 'conceived the child that was
in her by the Holy Spirit' (Mt 1:20).

---

20. cf Jn 8:41, where in a confrontation between Jesus and the crowd in
Jerusalem they say to him: 'We were not born of prostitution.' Was that
meant as a personal insult hinting at rumours about his birth or simply
a general remark about their being members of the chosen people?
21. It is also significant since a Jewish child takes its Jewish nationality
from its mother.

v. The Fourteen Generations

Having outlined the three periods with their continuity and discontinuity and their various characters, quirks, shocks and surprises, as illustrated above, the narrator then looks to the essential continuity of the divine plan and illustrates it by way of reference to the recurring pattern of fourteen generations. The number fourteen is obviously symbolic as it refers to three very different periods of time. From Abraham to David was about eight hundred years, from David to the Exile was about half that length, just over four hundred years, and from the Exile to Christ was between five and six hundred years. Speaking of the fourteen generations therefore is a symbolic approach that emphasises the continuity and coherence of the divine plan and the direction of salvation history.

Two different interpretations of the symbolism of the number fourteen are adopted by scholars, but they need not be mutually exclusive. One line of interpretation, known to scholars as *gematria*, takes into account the fact that in Hebrew the letters of the alphabet functioned also as numbers and so the letters of one's name could symbolically represent that person in numerical terms. The letters (consonants only) in the name David, *DWD* (David) when taken as numbers are 4+6+4, which added together make 14. The first fourteen generations show the build up to the kingdom of David, the second fourteen trace the genealogy of the occupants of the throne during the lifetime of the kingdom of David and the third fourteen outlines a genealogy of 'unknown' ancestors of the future royal son of David during the period between the collapse of the kingdom and the coming of the Messiah. Accepting this symbolism one sees how the person and kingdom of David were pivotal in the history of Israel. The genealogy in its three major divisions highlights the central role of David and of the throne, house and line of David. This line of interpretation looks at the arrangement of the generations focusing on the Davidic dimension.

The other line of interpretation, however, focuses more on the overall pattern and interprets the genealogy in keeping with the apocalyptic tradition, which would interpret the fourteen generations in terms of blocks of seven generations.[22] Since the time of

---

22. Apart from this apocalyptic use of the number seven Matthew has a penchant for the number seven, e.g. forgiving one's brother seven times, seventy seven times or seven times seventy times (Mt 18: 21f).

Daniel (mid-second century B.C.) the apocalyptic tradition saw the unfolding of God's plan in history in terms of 'weeks of years', that is, blocks of seven years. This is especially obvious in Daniel 9 which viewed history as divided into periods of seven years, or 'weeks of years' and describes a period of seventy weeks of years. Seven was the number of completion.[23] Seven times seven was the ultimate completion. Fourteen is 2 x 7 and seeing the genealogy in terms of three fourteens means that it is in fact 6 x 7, leaving the seventh seven as the completion of the historical process and the unfolding of the divine plan with the coming of the Christ.[24] A combination of both interpretations explains both the Davidic (3 x 14) and the apocalyptic (3 x 14 = 6 x 7) symbolism.

Summarising the genealogy

Taking into account all we have said about the genealogy, J. P. Meier's remark seems very apt when he states that the genealogies of Matthew and Luke are 'to be understood as theological statements, not biological reports'[25] and E. Schweizer comments in similar vein: 'Precisely because these genealogies are not meant as records of historical data, we must inquire all the more vigorously into what Matthew is trying to say.'[26] The genealogy shows the plan of God for salvation being worked out with Jew and Gentile, saint and sinner, male and female, in regular and irregular unions and circumstances. It shows an overarching continuity containing within itself a series of discontinuities, leading to the great discontinuity in the divine initiative in the virginal conception within the line of David, as the final age dawns and breaks into the evolving pattern of Israel's history.

D. Senior sums up:

Thus, far from being a lifeless list of names, the genealogy that inaugurates Matthew's story is saturated with his theological perspective. Jesus emerges from a history of Israel that originates in Abraham and unfolds with unexpected turns, finding

---

23. Multiplying a number by ten emphasised its magnitude, so Daniel's 'seventy weeks of years'.
24. For example, Peter is instructed to forgive in a saying of Jesus that could be translated as 'seventy times seven' or 'seventy seven times' (Mt 18:21-22).
25. J. P. Meier, *Matthew*, 3.
26. E. Schweizer, *The Good News According to Matthew*, 24.

its most expansive expression in the figure of King David (without forgetting his failure), experiencing the shattered hopes of
exile and the renewal of the return, and culminating in the advent of Jesus the Messiah. Through this genealogy, therefore,
Matthew alerts the reader to the gospel's understanding of history, one in which God fulfils the promises given to Israel in
often startling and unexpected ways.[27]

At the end of the genealogy the 'A begat B' pattern was very
abruptly changed to 'A, husband of B, and of her was born C' as one
reads: 'Joseph, the husband of Mary, and of her was born Jesus who
is called Christ' (Mt 1:16). The curiosity of the reader is naturally
aroused by this striking change of formula and prompts the question: 'Why this abrupt change?' The response to the reader's question was put on hold for a moment while Matthew drew attention
to the arrangement of the genealogy in three periods of fourteen
generations. Now the reader's question about the abrupt change of
formula is addressed.

c. The Birth of Jesus Christ Mt 1:18-25

Having been momentarily held in suspense while the narrator comments on the three periods of fourteen generations the reader now receives an answer to the question about why there is such a sudden
change of formula from 'A begat B', already repeated more than
forty times. The reader's question is addressed and the reason given
for the sudden change in formula, beginning with the words: 'This
is how the birth of Jesus the Messiah (Christ) took place' (Mt 1:18).[28]
The story that follows by way of explanation is one of discontinuity
illustrated by the divine initiative and the virginal conception, and
one of continuity illustrated by Joseph's action in adopting the child
into the royal line of David and into the history of Israel that stretches back to Abraham. It describes how the Son of God is also son of
Abraham and son of David. This highly theological account is the
first of three stories about angelic appearances to Joseph, which are
knit into the Infancy Narrative.

This story is the first of the ' kernels' or 'hinges' identified in the

---

27. D.Senior, *Matthew*, 39.
28. Some mss read ' the birth of the Messiah (Christ)', omitting the name
Jesus at this point.

analysis of S. Chatman, F. J. Matera and W. Carter.[29] It brings the movement of the genealogy to a climax and opens onto the succeeding narrative block of 'satellite' stories, which form the rest of the Infancy Narrative.

a. Child from the Holy Spirit

His mother Mary, betrothed to Joseph, before they came together was found with child from (the) Holy Spirit (Mt 1:18). Betrothal according to the Jewish custom of the time was, to all intents and purposes, already a marriage waiting to be consummated. The intended marriage was arranged by the parents, often while one or both parties to the marriage were quite young. The bridal price (dowry) was already paid. The contract was legally binding and subsequent sexual infidelity was seen in the same light as adultery. The marriage would be complete when the bride was brought with due ceremonial to the house of her husband.

In the case of Mary, she was betrothed but not yet taken to her future husband's house. She was found to be with child and therefore in apparent violation of the moral and legal obligations of the contract. Infidelity to the betrothal contract was seen in similar terms to infidelity in marriage and similar penalties were laid down in the Mosaic legislation. The Mosaic Law in Lev 20:10, 21 prescribed the death penalty for adultery, leaving the manner of execution open. Deut 22:21-22 specified stoning for a woman who could not show evidence of virginity. Deut 22:23-27 prescribed that a woman who was unfaithful during her betrothal should be brought to her father's house and stoned by the men of the city because of the disgrace she brought on her father's house. Stoning was meant to be carried out by the people, in the name of the people, and so a stoning often began with a representative laying on of hands on the one about to be stoned, signifying the involvement of the people in the rooting out of the evil in question.[30]

This law does not seem to have been enforced in Jesus' time and the 'injured party' seems to have had the option of dealing with the

---

29. See the discussion on the outline/macrostructure of the gospel in the introduction to this commentary.
30. Cf Deut 13:9-10 which prescribes a stoning for idolatry with the involvement of the people. After Jesus' time the Pharisees replaced stoning with strangulation as punishment for adultery.

matter privately (though in the case of the woman caught in adultery in Jn 7:53 – 8:11 the death penalty seems to have been a least a strong possibility). Joseph is described as *dikaios*, a just man, a pious Jew. Scholars have discussed at length what 'just man' means in this context.[31] Looking at the use of the adjective *dikaios* and the related noun *dikaiosunê* in the gospel, it is obvious that the adjective points to one who does the will of God and so facilitates God's plan for the inauguration of the kingdom. In practical terms this points to his being concerned to carry out his duty according to the Law.[32] The emphasis on his being *dikaios* seems to highlight the fact that the option of dealing with the matter privately was then an accepted practice and in contemplating it Joseph was not in violation of accepted custom. Being a just man he was aware of the requirements of the law but in choosing the other option he also showed the qualities of a pious Jew in displaying the much lauded biblical qualities of mercy and compassion, in keeping with the overall tenor of the gospel, a greater righteousness summed up in the citation from Hosea: 'What I want is mercy not sacrifice' (Hos 6:6; cf Mt 9:13; 12:7). He resolved to divorce her privately, and this would have required him to give the woman in question a statement of his intention to divorce her. Such a written statement fulfilled not only his obligation to the woman herself, but served as a guarantee to another future husband that the former husband or betrothed no longer had any rights according to the contract of promised or actual marriage. This, for example, would prevent disputes about dowries and property and prevented the former spouse from wanting to take her back as wife in the event of widowhood or another divorce (Deut 24:1-4).

'As he considered these things' Joseph would have been faced with a dilemma, not only between the strict observance of custom and law and the option of a private settlement, but also between his decision to divorce his betrothed / wife and his compassion for the divorced woman and her future child. The appearance of the angel of the Lord in a dream has the marks of an epiphany or divine encounter as the angel addresses Joseph with the exhortation not to

---

31. For a discussion of views see R. E. Brown, *The Birth of the Messiah*, 1977, 125-128.
32. In the genealogy, for example Judah and David were not upright men in their marital dealings and by implication, in God's plan, unlike Boaz who was exemplary.

fear to take Mary as his wife (*mê phobêthês*). Why would he fear to take her as wife? Is the reader meant to understand that Joseph suspected something supernatural in the conception of the child and so wondered how to align his own pre-arranged marriage with the situation? Not only is his decision not to expose his betrothed publicly confirmed by the angel of the Lord in a dream, but also he is told to reverse his decision to divorce her and to complete the marriage process, to take her into his home as wife and to name the child 'Jesus'. He is to make her his wife and to treat the child as his own, giving him a divinely designated name. Pointedly addressed by the angel of the Lord as 'son of David', Joseph is now instructed to bring the mother and child into the house and line of David. The name is not a name from his family line, but a name revealed to him by the 'angel of the Lord', the messenger of the One who is the real Father of the child.[33] The revealed name 'Jesus' is interpreted as a pointer to his mission: 'For he will save his people from their sins.'[34] Joseph identifies the divine origin of the command and responds immediately. This further confirms his standing as *dikaios*, a just man, a pious Jew who has the wisdom to discern the word of the Lord and where the work of the Lord is taking place and to respond accordingly.

The Holy Spirit

The discontinuity in the pattern of human begetting which takes place with the virginal conception signifies not just a 'miraculous birth' but also an eschatological event signified by the action of (the) Holy Spirit. The reference to (the) Holy Spirit here is like the reference to the Spirit bringing life and form to creation (Gen 1:2). As such, it reflects but surpasses the biblical stories of the miraculous births of Ishmael (Gen 16:1-16), Isaac (Gen 18:1-15; 17:15-22; 21:1-7), Samson (Judges 13:1-25) and Samuel (1 Sam: 9-20).[35] Furthermore, this eschatological outpouring of the creative activity of the Holy

---

33. The term 'angel of the Lord' signifies the messenger of the Lord and can be seen as a circumlocution to avoid directly predicating action on the part of the Lord.

34. For Matthew's intended readers Jesus fulfils the function of the atonement sacrifices of the temple.

35. Luke uses the annunciation and birth stories very subtly to assert the superiority of Jesus over the Baptist. In the story of the Baptist both parents are said to be beyond the age of having children, the first such

Spirit is totally different to mythological stories of 'sacred marriage' between a pagan god and a human mother, involving the 'sexual' activity of the gods of Greek mythology.

Jesus

The name 'Jesus' did not figure in Joseph's genealogy and its use further highlights the discontinuity and the new divine initiative in the plan of God, and emphasises the call to faith in the one so named. The angel of the Lord instructs Joseph: 'You will call his name Jesus' (Mt 1:21). His calling the child by the revealed name (Mt 1:25)[36] manifests his faith and obedience to the messenger/word of the Lord and illustrates further why he was called *dikaios*, a just man. Naming the child brings to completion the act of accepting the child and acknowledging his divine origin and purpose. The name 'Jesus' is interpreted in a new way as 'the one who saves the people from their sins'. This is a development of the Hebrew name *Yeshua*/Joshua which meant 'God helps/saves.' That Jesus will save his people from their sins is a major concern of the gospel as it sees him replacing the atonement rituals of the temple in the wake of its destruction.

b. The Formula/Fulfilment Citation Mt 1:23; Isa 7:14

The ten formula or fulfilment citations in Matthew, which are particularly in evidence in the Infancy Narrative, link the story of Jesus, and by implication the story of his followers, to the Old Testament, emphasising the continuity and consistency in God's work of salvation. They highlight the oneness of God's plan as they bring out the significance of Jesus' identity and mission. The hand of God, God's style, so to speak, is in evidence again as in the days of yore. The prophets and writers of old described how God

birth since Isaac. Jesus, on the other hand, is an even greater miracle, utterly unique in the history of God's mighty deeds. He is born of a virgin (Lk 1: 7, 18, 27, 34).
36. In Lk 1:31 Mary his mother is told to give the child his name and Luke says 'his name was called Jesus, the (name) called by the angel before his reception into the womb' (Lk 2:21). Mt 1:25 is translated as 'he called' because of the command to Joseph in Mt 1:21, other wise it could be translated as either 'he called' or 'she called.' The giving of the name usually took place on the eighth day after the birth when the male child was circumcised. It was given by either or both parents, as seen also in the case of John the Baptist (Lk 1:59).

worked in their day and predicted that God would always work in similar ways for his people. The broader Old Testament narrative supplied a model for telling and interpreting the story of Jesus. The citations are adapted to the context of the gospel as the evangelist sees a continuity or similarity with the work of God in the Old Testament. The prophets and sages of the Old Testament probably did not have a detailed vision of the future (like that which is some-times taught by biblical teachers and preachers) but the New Testament writers saw in the details of Jesus' life and mission/min-istry a fulfilment of prophecy in the sense of a continuity and con-sistency in God's work of salvation. New Testament narratives re-flect the great macronarrative of the Old Testament.

The citations were adapted to the context of the gospel and care-fully chosen and edited to bring out the significance of the stories being told and how they fit the overall plan of God. The citations in turn influenced the style, language or imagery used in the telling of the story itself. However, these stories, already established in the tradition were not created around an Old Testament text in midrashic fashion but rather the citations were chosen to bring out the significance of the stories already established in the tradition. This is borne out by the fact that they do not follow uniformly the Hebrew or LXX text but represent deliberate selection of unidenti-fied or conflated Old Testament traditions and editorial 'manipul-ation' to fit the stories being told.[37]

The virgin will conceive and give birth to a son (Mt 1:23; Isa 7:14)

This is the first of the fulfilment citations. It has been the subject of much debate since the early days of the Christian church[38] princi-pally because of the exact meaning the word *'almah* in the Hebrew text of Isaiah 7:14. The word *'almah* means a young woman of mar-riageable and childbearing age who may or may not still be a virgin. The Hebrew word used to signify a virgin would have been *bethu-lah*. However the LXX translates *'almah* with the Greek word

---

37. See R. E. Brown, *The Birth of the Messiah*, 96.
38. An early example of the discussion occurs in the works of Justin Martyr in his *Dialogue* with the Jew Trypho (early to mid second century AD). They discuss the meaning of *'alma* in *Dialogue lxvii* in which Trypho points out that *'almah* should not be translated 'virgin' but 'young girl'. In subsequent debates *neania*, 'young girl' was often sub-stituted for *parthenos* in the LXX in debates on the matter.

parthenos which means a virgin and it is in this sense that Matthew quotes it. A look at the context of Isa 7:14 and at the use of the citation by Matthew throws light on the situation.

Emmanuel

The original context of the 'prophecy' of Isa 7:14 focuses on the birth of a child whose birth and coming of age will be a sign of God's protecting presence among the people in a time of mortal peril. Both the forces of the all conquering Assyrians and the menacing Syro-Ephraimite coalition, which opposed them, threatened the very existence of the Kingdom of Judah and the House of David during the reign of Ahaz (735-715BC). Isaiah challenged the king, Ahaz, to seek a sign but when he refused Isaiah said God himself would give a sign. The promised birth and coming of age of the child was the sign that signified that God was with his people, hence the name Emmanuel, interpreted into Greek by Matthew as 'God is with us' (Isa 7:14). The Hebrew text of the prophet reads 'she will call …', the Greek LXX reads 'you will call …' and, interestingly, Matthew has 'they will call his name Emmanuel'. Again the 'manipulation' of the text is in evidence and very likely refers to the people who experience his saving presence among them as in a new temple. This further emphasises the point that the text was chosen to suit the already established story and to emphasise its meaning and it goes against the theory that the story was created as a midrashic exposition of the Isaian text. The name Emmanuel, given at his birth, foreshadows his promise that where two or three are gathered in his name he is present with them (Mt 18:20) and forms an inclusion with the final promise of Jesus to be with his followers as they make disciples of all nations till the end of the world (Mt 28:20).

The citation as used in Mt 1:23 signifies a virginal conception, not because of a misunding of the Isaian use of *'almah/parthenos*, nor because of a need to have a fulfilment of a misunderstood text, but because it highlights the meaning already contained in the story of Mary and Joseph. That story shows a new fulfilment of the Emmanuel prophecy in the birth of a child to a young woman, and the virginal conception is a further unexpected divine dimension to the fulfilment. The prophecy is doubly fulfilled as the virgin conceives and as the virgin gives birth. To emphasise the second aspect, 'the virgin gives birth' the statement that Joseph 'knew her not before she gave birth' is added. As it stands this neither implies nor denies subsequent sexual relations.

R. E. Brown sums up the position very succinctly in his comment on the citation and its interpreters:[39]

> If my remarks have pointed toward a rejection of a naïve or fundamentalist use of Old Testament prophecy, they also constitute a rejection of an overly simple liberal explanation of how the idea of the virginal conception of Jesus arose. It has been suggested that reflection on Isa 7:14 and on its prediction that a virgin would give birth gave rise to Christian belief in the virginal conception of Jesus. I am maintaining that there was nothing in the Jewish understanding of Isa 7:14 that would give rise to such a belief nor, *a fortiori,* to the idea of a begetting through the creative activity of the Holy Spirit, an idea found explicitly in both Matthew and Luke but not in Isa 7:14. At most, reflection on Isa 7:14 coloured the expression of an already existing Christian belief in the virginal conception of Jesus.

c. The Angelic Appearances to Joseph

This is the first of the three highly theological angelic, dream-based revelations which occur at three critical points in the Infancy Narrative in which Joseph, the husband of Mary, responds decisively to the command of the divine messenger in relation to an action to be undertaken on behalf of 'the child and his mother'. Dreams in the Old Testament were seen as vehicles of divine revelation, direction and wisdom. Not only his namesake Joseph who dreamed beforehand of his future elevation above his brothers (Gen 37:5-11) and who rose to prominence in Egypt on account of his ability to interpret Pharaoh's dreams (Gen 40-41), but also Abraham and Jacob had significant dreams dealing with their role in the future of the people (Gen 15:12; 28:10-19). Daniel also gained preferment because of his ability to interpret dreams (Dan 4:1-34). The psalmist acknowledges God's revelation in dreams as he addresses God who 'even at night directs my heart' (Ps 16:7).

These three Joseph stories, all told in similar fashion, are knit into the broader Infancy Narrative. R. E. Brown has pointed out how all the three stories follow a similar pattern:[40]

---

39. R. E. Brown, *The Birth of the Messiah,* 149.
40. R. E. Brown, *The Birth of the Messiah,* 108.

Pattern of the Angelic Appearances to Joseph.

a. Introduction: Resumptive clause connecting with what preceded (Gen. Participle):
1:20 'As he considered this ...'
2:13 'When they had gone away ...'
2:19 'When Herod died ...'

b. Behold (*idou*) an angel of the Lord appears to Joseph in a dream

c. The angel gives a command(s):
1:20 'Joseph, son of David, do not fear to take Mary your wife ...'
1:21 '... you will call his name Jesus'
2:13 'Get up; take the child and his mother and escape to Egypt and stay there until I tell you'
2:20 'Get up; take the child and his mother and go back to the land of Israel'

d. The angel offers a reason for the command (*gar*/for)
1:20 'for that which is begotten in her is of the Holy Spirit'
1:21 'for he will save his people from their sins'
2:13 'for Herod is going to search for the child to kill him'
2:20 'for those who were seeking the child's life are dead'

e. Joseph gets up and obeys: (*egertheis ... de*/and rising up ...)
1:24f 'When Joseph rose from sleeping, he did as the angel of the Lord had commanded him. He took his wife to his home, but he had no sexual relations with her before she had borne a son; and he called his name Jesus.'
2:14f 'So Joseph got up, took the child and his mother by night and went away to Egypt, where he stayed until the death of Herod.'
2:21 'So Joseph got up, took the child and his mother, and went back to the land of Israel.'

It is most likely that these angelic appearance stories constituted a Joseph tradition already known before the gospel was written in its present form. Joseph is the protagonist in the stories; the mother's role is passive, in contrast to Luke's account that is directly opposite, making the mother the protagonist in believing the word spoken to her and accepting the divine child. Matthew, on the other hand, has Joseph repeatedly acting on behalf of 'the child and his mother'

2. WHENCE AND WHITHER? RECEPTION BY JEW AND GENTILE MT 2:1-23

A. Herod and the Magi Mt 2:1-12

a. Born in Bethlehem of Judea: the Messiah, the Shepherd-King

Having placed Jesus in the context of the salvation history of the people of Israel from Abraham to his own time, and having shown how he was son of David and Son of God, Matthew now further emphasises his Davidic sonship by naming Bethlehem of Judea as the place of his birth.

Jesus' place of birth is mentioned in Mt 2:1 and again in Mt 2:6. In both places there is stress on the fact that it is Bethlehem in Judea/Judah, to distinguish it from Bethlehem in Galilee. This sets the birth of the son of David in the hometown of David. Luke in fact stresses the same point by speaking of 'the city of David, which is called Bethlehem' (Lk 2:4, 11). In Bethlehem David had been a shepherd and there he was chosen from the sons of Jesse and anointed king by Samuel (1 Sam 16:1-13). The place of his birth is very significant given the emphasis on the royal line of David, born in Bethlehem, great-grandson of Ruth and Boaz of Bethlehem, a royal line so much in evidence already in the genealogy. He is the Messiah, the shepherd-king, born in Bethlehem. The expectation of an ideal ruler in the line of David is the subject of Ezekiel's prophecy: 'I mean to raise up one shepherd, my servant David and to put him in charge of them and he will pasture them and be their shepherd. I Yahweh will be their God, and my servant David will be their ruler' (Ezek 34:23). Jesus is the promised new David, the shepherd-king, the eschatological good shepherd.

b. The days of Herod the King

Matthew sets Jesus' birth in the context of contemporary history and kingship, 'in the days of Herod the king' (37–4BC). In doing so he sets the scene for what follows. The reader senses that the apparently straightforward phrase 'in the days of Herod the King' is loaded with innuendo about the king, his background and his reign. Far from the traditional understanding of a divinely sanctioned and anointed line of kings charged with shepherding the flock of Israel, and further still from the prophetic expectation of a new David, a good shepherd, the Herod family had shown no mercy in their rise to power. A contrast of kingships is being introduced and the tension between them is about to begin. Herod and his royal house are very different from the messianic expectations of an ideal shepherd-king of Davidic descent. 'The caricature of corrupt power exemplified by Herod throws into relief the essentially different power that will characterise the Son of David.'[41] 'The days of Herod' were very dangerous days, particularly for any political rival within or without the family of Herod!

All lived in fear of his vengeance and would have rejoiced at his downfall. This led to his sense of insecurity among the people generally, which expressed itself in his construction of huge fortresses like the Antonia fortress beside the Jerusalem temple, the additional fortified buildings on Masada, and the massive Herodion fortress within sight of Bethlehem. He was insecure within his own royal house which was a hotbed of rumour and intrigue aimed at arousing his suspicions and jealousy and leading to the elimination of rivals following the spreading of malicious rumours. In this atmosphere Herod murdered several of his own family. He murdered one of his wives Mariamne (along with her mother and grandfather) due to rumours of political intrigue and marital infidelity, an action that haunted him for the rest of his days. He murdered his sons Aristobulus, Alexander, and, just a few days before his own death, he murdered a third son Antipater. Not surprisingly it was said that it was safer to be Herod's pig than his son, a remark attributed to the emperor Augustus (who may have been re-echoing a more widespread comment, playing on the Greek words *hus* (pig) and *huios* (son).[42]

Against such a background, very probably well known to the original readers, Matthew tells the story of the arrival of a group of gift-bearing magi from the east announcing the birth of a 'newborn king of the Jews', a child of whom Herod knew nothing. Furthermore the term 'king of the Jews' on Gentile lips would have had a very political connotation as the term 'king of Israel' was the more religious term used by the Jews. It was surely a match to set the tinder of insecurity and jealousy alight. The 'new-born King of the

41. D. R. Bauer, 'The Kingship of Jesus in the Matthean Infancy Narrative: A Literary Analysis', *CBQ* 57:306-323.
42. See R. E. Brown, *op. cit.*, 226.

Jews' would eventually make a very different impact as Son of David and die as 'King of the Jews' with the centurion and those guarding him confessing him to be the Son of God.

c. Magi bearing gifts

The coming of the magi is heralded in the story as a momentous event in salvation history and is introduced with the canonised expression for announcing such an event: 'Behold! (*idou*)' Even without the story of Herod the account of the coming of the magi would in itself be very significant as an example of prophetic fulfilment. The coming of Gentiles to Jerusalem to do homage already foreshadows the significance of Jesus as Christ, Son of Abraham, a Messiah for Gentiles as well as for Jews.

The artistry of Matthew is evident in the telling of the story. A procession of magi bearing precious gifts from the east would have been part of the contemporary royal scene in palaces and temples. Royalty and dignitaries came in procession to more powerful potentates to curry favour, seek protection or head off hostilities. Such processions combined aspects of a political embassy and a religious pilgrimage. Auspicious events such as the birth of a royal child, the dedication of a new city or temple, or the enthronement of a monarch would see such a procession of dignitaries from afar bearing gifts to a king and 'doing homage' to a god-king in a palace or to his god in the royal temple.[43]

d. They saw the star at its rising

The magi recognised the birth of the 'King of the Jews' in the star at its rising. Matthew's age would have been quite at home with the claim that a star rose to herald the birth of the King of the Jews and guided the magi-astrologers on their journey. R. E. Brown gives a number of examples to show how widespread the belief in signs and portents was in New Testament times.[44] Virgil reports that a star guided Aeneas to the place where Rome should be founded.[45] Josephus speaks of a star that stood over Jerusalem and of a comet,

---

43. R. E. Brown, *The Birth of the Messiah*, 174, gives an impressive list of such processions and embassies that may have fired the popular imagination around the time of Jesus and the New Testament.
44. Ibid., 170.
45. Virgil, *Aeneid*, ii 694

which continued for a year at the time of the fall of the city.[46] He expresses the belief of the time that 'God has a care for men and by all kinds of premonitory signs shows his people the way of salvation' – he relates this in particular to the Jewish belief that 'someone from their country would become ruler of the world'.[47]

The people of Israel had their own story òf a star and a magician who prophesied a famous birth in the future (Num 23-24). As the children of Israel who had emerged from their slavery in Egypt grew in number, strength and military might, the king of Moab, seeing their progress towards Moab, panicked and sent for Balaam a seer-magician and asked him to curse the children of Israel. Balaam refused to do so and instead issued a blessing/ prophecy: 'A star shall rise from Jacob and a sceptre[48] from Israel (Num 24:17). The star became a symbol of the expected leader as can be seen from the fact that the leader of the revolt against the Romans in the second century AD took the name Bar Kokhba, 'son of the star'. Seeing 'the star at its rising' in this 'theological' and symbolic context, and against the broader belief in the appearance of stars heralding major events and births, makes more sense than trying to ascertain an exact historical occurrence in the skies.[49]

e. All Jerusalem in turmoil

Matthew describes the foreign visitors as coming from the east to Herod's royal palace in Jerusalem. But they do not come to do homage to Herod or to a newborn son of his. They come to do homage to the newborn king of the Jews, of whom Herod has no knowledge! What a shock for Herod! However, the reaction to the news of a newborn king was not confined to Herod. Matthew portrays a united front against Jesus on the part of the Jews, people, priests and scholars, particularly in Jerusalem. Even though most of them would have been opposed to Herod and delighted to see his demise, they form a common front against the child, whether through insecurity, fear of reprisals, suspicion or gut level hostility. In this they foreshadow the reactions of the political and religious

---

46. Josephus, *War* VI v 3; #289
47. Josephus, *War* VI v 4: #310, 312.
48. The LXX reads '*anthrôpos ex Israêl*' 'man/human being from Israel' for 'sceptre'.
49. Such, for example, as the conjunction of Jupiter and Saturn in 7 BC.

leaders and the popular front at his triumphal entry into the city,[50] and during his arrest, trial and execution as King of the Jews. Jerusalem for Matthew, in spite his Jewish background, is the city of scheming, murderous intent and rejection of the Messiah.[51]

f. The nations come to Jerusalem

The magi represent the people of goodwill, those seeing the hand of God in the universe and reading the signs of the times. They represent those who will be open to the mission of the Christ/Messiah and his disciples. They come 'from the East.' There are arguments favouring both the Parthia/Persian realm and Arabia as the appropriate identification for 'the East' mentioned by Matthew.[52] However, Matthew was not so much interested in the details of their provenance as in the significance of their coming to offer gifts and homage to the newborn king.

Observing the proper course of salvation history, these Gentiles go to the Jews for instruction about messianic prophecy. However, the 'royal' authorities know nothing of his birth and the people of Jerusalem are alarmed at the news. Fulfilling a double function, the official scholars (the scribes) and the chief priests are consulted by Herod about the expected place of the Messiah's birth. They fulfil their professional function by producing the quotation (without any fulfilment introduction) which is a composite from the prophecy

---

50. Mt 21:10 says that the whole city was in turmoil at his triumphal entry, though a different verb is used.

51. This is in great contrast to Luke, a Gentile, who sees Jerusalem in positive light as the holy city where the great drama of redemption takes place. Luke opens and closes his gospel in the Jerusalem temple (Lk 1:8-25; 24:52f) and brings his infancy narrative and temptation accounts to their climax in Jerusalem (Lk 2:41-50; 4:9-12). He opens the Acts of the Apostles in Jerusalem, situates the Ascension there, gives the apostles the command to remain there until they receive the gift of God, which comes in the gift of the Holy Spirit at Pentecost. It is from there that the great journey of the Acts from Jerusalem to the ends of the earth begins. Luke shows preference even for the Semitic version of the name of the city *Ierousalêm* instead of the more Greek *Ierosoluma*, highlighting its place in salvation history. Such is the very great difference between Luke and Matthew in their approach to Jerusalem.

52. See R. E. Brown, *The Birth of the Messiah*, 607-613, for a comprehensive discussion on the Magi and the various suggested identifications of 'the east'.

of Micah and 2 Samuel: 'But you Bethlehem Ephrathah, least of the
clans of Judah, out of you will be born for me the one who is to rule
over Israel' (Mic 5:1, 3) and the proclamation of the tribes of Israel (2
Sam 5:2) at the anointing of David as king of Israel at Hebron: 'You
are the man who shall be shepherd of my people Israel' (2 Sam 5:2).
Matthew adds *oudamôs*, 'by no means'. They also fulfil the function
of colluding with Herod by putting their expertise in scripture at
the service of his malevolent intentions and investigations. They
foreshadow their own role as future enemies of Jesus and collaborators with the political authorities in his destruction.

In coming to Jerusalem and then offering homage and gifts to
the child, the magi fulfil the prophecies that proclaimed that the
nations would come to know the Lord, to worship him and learn his
law. Several Old Testament prophecies and allusions spring to
mind. The prophets Isaiah and Micah spoke of the nations coming
to 'the temple of the God of Jacob', to learn his law and bring it
throughout the nations, resulting in establishing the authority of
God over the nations, resulting in universal peace (Isa 2:2–5;
45:14–17; 60:1–6; 18:7; Mic 4:1-5). 'Offerings will be brought to
Yahweh Sabaoth on behalf of the tall and bronzed nation, on behalf
of the nation always feared, on behalf of the mighty and masterful
people in the country criss-crossed with rivers, to the place where
Yahweh Sabaoth dwells, on Mount Zion' (Isa 18:7). Deutero-Isaiah
speaks of the submission of 'the peasants of Egypt, the traders of
Cush and the tall men of Sheba' saying 'with you alone is God, and
he has no rival; there is no other God' (Isa 45:14-17). Trito-Isaiah
looks forward to the day when the exiles will return and 'the nations will come to your light and kings to your dawning brightness
… everyone in Sheba will come, bringing gold and incense' (Isa
60:1-6). The psalmist looks to the day when 'the kings of Sheba and
Seba will offer gifts; all kings will do him homage, all nations become his servants' (Ps 72:10–15). 'But from the furthest east to the
furthest west my name is honoured among the nations and everywhere a sacrifice of incense is offered to my name, and a pure offering too, since my name is honoured among the nations, says
Yahweh Sabaoth' (Mal 1:11). Against this rich background of
prophecies and allusions, Matthew's story of the foreigners coming
to pay homage and offer gifts in Jerusalem is extremely significant
and sets the scene for the universal mission which forms the climax

of the gospel story when the Risen Jesus commands the apostles to make disciples of all nations (Mt 28:19).

Because three gifts are mentioned, later tradition has assumed that there were three magi, and even supplied them with names.[53] Reference to the gift of gold is reminiscent of the gifts brought by the kings of Sheba and Seba in Psalm 72:10-15 and is probably the reason why later tradition transformed the magi into kings. Their interest in stars seems to point to their coming from Persia, while the gifts they bring would point to Arabia. The significance of their coming is the important point and the details serve to fill out the 'international' character of the embassy in line with biblical traditions. The gifts themselves were also subject to later interpretations, gold reflecting royal status, frankincense reflecting priestly office and myrrh signifying anointing, the anointing in Jesus' saving death, and also his anointing as Messiah/Christ (the anointed one).

g. They worship the child

Herod's hypocrisy matches his cunning as he sends the magi to Bethlehem to seek the child and to report to him so that he too can come and worship. The verb *proskyneô* signifies the attitude of worship due to God or a god-king. At this point the star reappears and directs them to the house where the child was, with Mary his mother. The focus now shifts to the child and his mother and the obeisance of the magi as they kneel to offer him gifts. The scene in itself is a fulfilment of the Old Testament prophecies of the coming of the nations to worship and offer gifts.

The magi story is now realigned with the Herod story by means of the angel of the Lord who warns them not to go back to Herod but to return home by another route. They are therefore in no way associated with Herod's subsequent actions.

Summarising the Herod and Magi Story

Probably the stories of Herod and of the Magi were originally distinct and are here skilfully joined by Matthew. The rejection by his own people and acceptance by the Gentiles are brought out in the two stories joined skilfully into a single narrative. Scholars point out that the joining of two originally separate stories is obvious from a few logical observations. Why did Herod not send some soldiers or his

---

53. Balthasar, Melchior and Gaspar.

trusted security police to inquire about the child or those promoting him? He was much too shrewd to rely on the report of a group of magi who were well disposed towards, and already even in awe of, the child and would surely have suspected Herod's discomfort or hostility and known his reputation. Furthermore, the star seems to serve two different functions. Firstly, at its rising it alerted the magi to the birth of 'the king of the Jews'. When the experts in scripture had directed them to Bethlehem, it stood over the house where the child and his mother were, a royal family and house unknown to his own people. The star did not go before them from the east all the way to Jerusalem, nor did it lead them to Bethlehem, as is often mistakenly represented in religious art, but finally pointed out the house where the baby and his mother were when they went to Bethlehem following the scriptures quoted to them. If it had led them from the east, why did it not lead them away from Herod's palace altogether and directly to the child and his mother? Theologically, two points had to be made. First of all, salvation is from the Jews and therefore the Gentiles had to observe the proper course and approach the Jews for instruction about messianic prophecy.[54] Secondly, it is only when the fulfilment of the prophecy goes unrecognised or rejected by his own people that the Gentiles are guided by an independent divine sign to 'the king of the Jews'. Here there is a foreshadowing of Jesus' mission which is first directed to Israel and then in the final scene in the gospel it is directed to all nations as Jesus commands his disciples to go into the whole world and make disciples of all nations, after the rejection of the mission by so many in Israel.

In summary, then, these stories introduce two major themes: on the one hand, the struggle between King Herod and the newborn 'King of the Jews', a struggle that is reminiscent of the story of Pharaoh's murderous attack on the Hebrew infants and the escape of the infant Moses, drawing a parallel between Jesus and Moses, the first of many such parallels in the gospel. On the other hand, there is the homage of the magi, reminiscent of the prophecies about the coming of the nations to worship and offer gifts in Jerusalem. Both themes also foreshadow the reactions to Jesus throughout his ministry and during his passion and death.

---

54. J. P. Meier, *Matthew*, 11.

Traditionally the church has celebrated the coming of the magi to Bethlehem to pay homage at the Feast of Epiphany. Most likely the influence of Ps 71 (72):10 with its reference to kings has been responsible for regarding the magi as kings, and in the West the three gifts they offered determined the idea of three kings. The church in the East has tended to speak of twelve magi and in the history of art two, three, four and eight magi have appeared.[55]

B. Flight into Egypt Mt 2:13-15

This is the second of the Joseph dream sequences and corresponds to the other two in form. This story of a wicked king trying to destroy the child at his birth and threatening many children in the process, recalls the circumstances surrounding the danger to the newborn Moses when the male Hebrew children in Egypt were under death sentence from a threatened Pharaoh (Exod 1:15–2:10). Literature contemporary with the New Testament further elaborated on the account in Exodus describing an angelic revelation to the father of Moses warning him of the danger to the child. Josephus gives an embellished account of the story in Exodus in which astrologers warn Pharaoh of the forthcoming birth of a liberator of the Hebrews and, when he reacts with his murderous edict, the father of Moses is warned in a dream.[56] The parallels with the magi seeing the star and coming to Herod informing him about the child destined to be king, his murderous reaction and the warning in a dream to the child's father are obvious. Jesus too had to be protected from the murderous intent of the king at his birth.

The history of the people is being re-enacted in Jesus' experience as a refugee in Egypt. Egypt was the traditional place of refuge. Jesus' flight into Egypt and his return recall first of all the journey of Jacob (Israel) and his sons, the ancestors of Israel, to Egypt when Joseph brought them there to escape the famine (Gen 45-47), and the subsequent return of the people in the Exodus from Egypt. Jesus and his mother take refuge in Egypt under the care of another Joseph who obeys the command of the angel of the Lord and remains there until instructed to return. When Solomon tried to kill Jeroboam he fled to Egypt and 'remained in Egypt until the death of Solomon' (1 Kings 11:40). In the time of Jeremiah when Uriah son of

---

55. 'Magi' in *The New Catholic Encyclopedia*, Vol 9, 1967.
56. Josephus, *Ant.* ii. 205ff., 210 ff., 254 ff.

Shemaiah prophesied in the same negative manner as Jeremiah against Jerusalem, King Jehoiakim and his ministers and officials decided to put him to death but he fled to Egypt for refuge (Jer 26:21).

Pharaoh and his agents wished to kill Moses again at a later stage in his life and he took flight from Egypt to Midian, and did not return until it was revealed to him that 'all those who sought his life were dead' (Exod 2:15; 4:19). 'So Moses took his wife and his son, and putting them on a donkey, started back for the land of Egypt' (cf Exod 4:20). Jesus will re-enact in his own life and experience these seminal moments of exile and return in the history of the people and in the life of Moses.

Even the reference to Joseph's escaping with the child and his mother to Egypt by night (*nyktos*) (Mt 2:14) resonates with the atmosphere of the night escape of the Hebrews from Egypt when the plague struck down the firstborn of the Egyptians at midnight and as they rose in the night to great lamentation Pharaoh summoned Moses and Aaron in the night and told them to lead the people out of Egypt (Exod 12:29-41).

From Egypt Jesus will return as in a new Exodus. The citation from Hosea 'Out of Egypt I have called my son', is introduced with the second fulfilment formula: 'This was to fulfil what the Lord had spoken through the prophet' (Mt 2:15; Hos 11:1). This is a high point in the Infancy Narrative as Jesus is given his most exalted title, a title which surpasses the original meaning in Hosea, and which will be put to the test in the narrative of the temptations in the desert when he is challenged with the words: 'If you are the Son of God ...'(Mt 4:3,5). It also serves to cast Jesus, the Son, in the role of the personified people of Israel as he recapitulates in himself the historic experience of the going down to Egypt and returning in the Exodus. It signifies a new beginning which will be further illustrated by the activity of the Baptist and the baptism of Jesus at the Jordan, followed by his sojourn in the desert (Mt 3-4; cf Exod 2-4). As the Israelites of old crossed the Jordan into the Promised Land, making a new life of covenanted relationship with God, so too Jesus will come to the Jordan and, embodying the people, will enter on their new life of repentance and preparation for the imminent arrival of the kingdom of heaven.

C. The Mourning in Ramah. Moses and Exile Typology Mt 1:16-18 (Jer 31:15; 1 Sam 10; Josh 8-10)

The Herod story continues with the command to massacre the children under the age of two years in Bethlehem and the surrounding area. Its comprehensive intent, 'all the male children in Bethlehem and in all the surrounding area', emphasises the vengeance of Herod and the universal experience of threat, which he provoked. Instead of saying whether or not the threat was carried out, and certainly not implying that God intended it by the use of the phrase 'in order to fulfil', the event is covered by the citation about the mourning of Rachel (Jer 31:15). Again an apparently straightforward story is used as a vehicle for emphasising a recurring biblical experience, that of the rejection of the prophet and his message, resulting in violence and the dispersal of the people.

Though not mentioned in Josephus or elsewhere, the violent reaction is in keeping with what is known of the character and previous actions of Herod. However, Josephus, the Jewish historian, is either ignorant or reticent about matters dealing with Jesus and the Christian movement. Furthermore, the massacre of children in a remote part of the empire by a regional ruler could easily escape or be of little interest to the Roman historians. It is in keeping with Herod's character and repeated actions in the face of a threat or the emergence of a rival. At the very least, it was a real threat to any infants he might suspect due to their family background or portents surrounding an important birth.

The citation from the Old Testament (Jer 31:15) describing the lamentation heard in Ramah recalls two of the bitterest experiences of Israel's history and symbolically associates them with the personal tragedy of Rachel. It recalls the lamentation of the people at the fall of the Northern Kingdom in 722/721BC when the Joseph tribes, Ephraim and Manasseh were taken into captivity by the Assyrians. The imagery is that of the matriarch, eponymous mother and grandmother to these tribes, lamenting in her tomb as the tribes, her children, are killed or taken away in captivity to a foreign land. The citation also recalls the fall of the Southern Kingdom to the Babylonians in 587/586BC when Jeremiah was held in chains at Ramah together with the prisoners from Jerusalem and Judah who were en route to exile in Babylon. Rachel again mourns the fate of her children, as she witnesses from her tomb the deportation of the children of Israel. On that occasion Jeremiah attempted symbolically to console the mother who has lost her children, promising a return from exile (Jer 31:15; 40:1).

The citation recalls also the personal tragedy of Rachel who died and was buried on the road to Ephrath, having given birth to a son to whom with her last breath she gave the name *ben-ôni*, 'son of my pain/sorrow'. Ephrath later became identified with Bethlehem, probably because of the movement of some of the tribe of Ephrathah, as seen in the verses from Micah already alluded to by Matthew: 'And you, Bethlehem-Ephrathah …'(Mic 5:1,3; cf Mt 2:6).

The imagery of a mourning Rachel is therefore as powerful as it is poignant. The story of Jacob (Israel) and his love for Rachel is one of the great love stories of the Bible and of ancient literature. Having fallen in love with her on first seeing her at the well, he worked for seven years for her hand in marriage but her father Laban tricked him into a marriage with her sister Leah. When he worked another seven years he received her hand. However, Leah, her handmaiden, and Rachel's handmaiden all had children for Jacob, but his true love, Rachel for a long time had none. Finally Joseph was born, and later Benjamin. The birth of Benjamin resulted in her death and as she died she called him Ben Oni, son of my sorrow/pain. She was buried at Ephrath, on the road to Bethlehem. Later Jacob changed the child's name to Benjamin, 'son of my good fortune' (Gen 29:1 – 30:24; 35:16-20). The death of the mother after her great anguish in labour provides a backdrop of poignant reality to the destructive nature of power-hunger and war, and its effects on the children brought into the world in the anguish of childbirth and its danger to the life of the mother. The mother Rachel representatively mourns the loss of the children these mothers brought into the world.[57]

The massacre of the children in Bethlehem and the surrounding

---

57. Ramah was on the route of the Exile. It lay in the territory of Benjamin about five miles north of Jerusalem, half way between Bethel and Ephrath. Ephrath/Ephrathah was both the name of a clan and of a place. It is the place where Benjamin was born and Rachel died and was buried (Gen 35:16, 19; 48:7). The identification of Ephrathah with Bethlehem in Gen 35:16, 19; 48:7 represents a later tradition placing her tomb at Bethlehem. Earlier tradition fixes her tomb at Ephrath, north of Jerusalem in the vicinity of Ramah (1 Sam 10:2). The identification of Ephrath with Bethlehem probably comes from the presence of the clan of Ephrath (a Judahite clan according to 1 Chron 2) in Bethlehem. Since the fourth century AD her tomb has been pointed out in Bethlehem.

area again causes the mothers to mourn. The message of the prophets in the north like Amos and Hosea, and in the south like Isaiah and Micah, had been ignored, resulting in the fall of the Northern Kingdom, and the warnings of Jeremiah before the fall of the Southern Kingdom were similarly ignored. Now in the gospel the story of Jesus is being told in the aftermath of the fall of Jerusalem, and this reference to the massacre and to the mourning of Rachel show how the violent consequences of the rejection of yet another of God's messengers had already started at the announcement of his birth.

D. Return from Egypt//Nazareth Mt 2:19-23 cf Isa 4:3; Judges 16:17

This is the third Joseph dream sequence and it follows the pattern of the other two. Again it is a story rich in biblical allusions. In the return from Egypt Jesus recapitulates in himself the foundation experience of Israel in the Exodus. His return also recalls the return of Moses from exile in Midian to lead the people from slavery in Egypt into freedom, 'when those who sought his life were dead' (Mt 1:20; Exod 4:19).

The story also builds up to the fulfilment citation: 'He shall be called a Nazarene (*Nazôraios*)' which focuses on Jesus' residing in, and being identified by way of reference to Nazareth. There are three strands of allusion in the citation. Jesus is identified several times in the New Testament by way of reference to his coming from Nazareth and, from early on, the followers of Jesus were called the Nazarenes. Secondly in using the term *Nazôraios*/Nazarene there is also a very likely pun on or allusion to the term *naziraios*/nazirite. The nazarite vow (Num 6:1-8) dedicated one to God, and obliged one to abstain from taking any wine or strong drink and from shaving one's hair. Samson tells Delilah of his nazirite vow in Judges 16:17 and John the Baptist is described as a nazirite in the annunciation of the angel to his father Zechariah (Lk 1:14). Thirdly, there is also a similarity with the Hebrew term *nesher* that means a branch or shoot of a tree. It is used of the Messiah/Christ by Isaiah: 'A shoot springs from the root of Jesse, a scion thrusts from his roots' (Isa 11:1), and Jeremiah utters the prophecy: 'I will raise a virtuous branch for David, who will reign as true king and be wise' (Jer 23:5). Since the citation is nowhere to be found in the Old Testament, and is introduced with the vague 'as spoken through the prophets', it is most likely that Matthew intends it to be a 'loose' citation rich in allusions to various texts.

Summary of the Infancy Narrative

Matthew and Luke wrote Infancy Narratives very different in style and content. However, they are in agreement on a number of basic facts. They agree in stating that Jesus was born in Bethlehem of Judea but was brought up in Nazareth. In both accounts his mother's name is Mary and his adoptive father Joseph. They were betrothed and before they came to live together Mary was found to be with child. Both accounts believe in the virginal conception. Both accounts emphasise the Davidic descent through Joseph. They seem to agree also that he was born in the days of Herod the King of Judea. In Matthew's account this is explicitly stated, and it can be inferred from Luke's narrative where the Baptist is but six months older than Jesus and Luke describes the annunciation of his birth to Zachariah as taking place in the days of King Herod of Judea (Lk 1:5).

Both narratives are highly theological and rich in biblical allusions. Some scholars see in the various stories the stylistic influence of *haggadic midrash*, though the stories are not, strictly speaking, *midrash* since *midrash* is a retelling and interpretation of an already established biblical story.

Matthew emphasises the role of Joseph, Luke that of Mary. For Matthew Joseph is the model pious Jew, 'a righteous/just man', who follows the Law with compassion and complies fully with the will of God. He stands at the beginning of this gospel which emphasises 'righteousness/justice' as a model of a righteous or just man. Both Matthew and Luke need to create a narrative to connect Jesus both to Bethlehem, his place of birth, and Nazareth, where he grew up. For this Luke tells the story of the census to bring the parents from Nazareth to Bethlehem, Matthew tells of the fear of Archelaus which caused them to settle in Galilee on their return from Egypt. Scholars speculate about the historical accuracy of both reasons since they seem so different. However, reality is usually more complicated and storytellers, in order to create a narrative link between important events or well known facts, choose or are obliged through lack of knowledge to rely on thin lines of narrative and simple explanations.

THE PROLOGUE PART 2: PREPARING THE WAY OF THE LORD
MT 3:1-4:16

The second part of the prologue (Mt 3:1-4:16) deals with the mission of John the Baptist to prepare the way of the Lord during which the identity and role of Jesus are publicly proclaimed by the Baptist, divinely confirmed at his baptism and then tested by Satan in the wilderness. When the mission of the Baptist is cut short by his arrest, Jesus returns to Galilee to begin his mission to Israel.[58]

Outline of Mt 3:1-4:16:
1 The Mission of John the Baptist (Mt 3:1-12)
    A. Call to Repentance / Prepare the Way
    B. Condemnation of the Pharisees and Sadducees
    C. Baptism in Water and Baptism in Holy Spirit (and fire)

2 Jesus Comes from Galilee (Mt 3:13-4:11)
    A. The Reaction of John
    B. The Baptism of Jesus
    C. The Testing in the desert
    D. Jesus returns to Galilee

1. THE MISSION OF JOHN THE BAPTIST MT 3:1-12

A. Call to Repentance/Prepare the Way
'*In those days John the Baptist came*[59] *in the desert of Judea, proclaiming: "Repent, for the Kingdom of heaven is close at hand".*' The narrator thus introduces the precursor with all the solemnity of an Old Testament prophet. Beginning with the biblically laden expression 'in those days', a description regularly used to introduce a new departure, a significant event or a birth (cf Judges 19:1; 1 Sam 28:1), the narrator goes on to announce that 'John the Baptist comes / appears (*paraginetai*)'.[60] In

---

58. From this point on in the gospel the parallels with Mark and Luke, and particularly with Mark, serve to highlight the distinctive insight and approach of the gospel.
59. Historic present tense serving the purpose of bringing the reader into the unfolding scene.
60. The sentence could be accurately paraphrased as 'At the appointed time John the Baptist appears ... '

his proclaiming (*kêryssôn*)[61] he is calling for repentance as a preparation because the kingdom of heaven is close at hand.

Whereas Mark describes John as preaching 'a baptism of repentance for the forgiveness of sins', Matthew reserves any mention of
the forgiveness of sins for the ministry of Jesus. Matthew firmly establishes the imminence of the kingdom as the motive for repentance.[62]

The Kingdom

'The kingdom of heaven' is Matthew's term for 'the kingdom of
God'. In using this term this he is respecting his Jewish members'
sensitivity about pronouncing the Divine Name. The other gospels
use the term ' kingdom of God'. It is difficult to give a clear definition of the kingdom of heaven (or kingdom of God), partly because
the term is used in different ways and partly because it is used for
its evocative power. It is very rare outside the synoptics where it is
found on the lips of John the Baptist and of Jesus. The two uses of
the term in the dialogue with Nicodemus are unusual in the
Johannine tradition (Jn 3:3, 5). The actual term is found only once in
the Old Testament (Wisdom10:10) and was not current in contemporary Judaism.

However, in the Old Testament and other Jewish writings, the
related idea 'God is King' is very frequently found in references to
God as Lord or primary agent in history, at its beginnings, throughout its unfolding course and in the predictions of the consummation
of creation and history when God's definitive reign will be established. This is obvious in the creation accounts, in the Exodus and
wandering narratives, in the royal and enthronement psalms and in
the eschatological writings of the prophets.

This concept of God as King is closely linked to the concept of
God as Shepherd of Israel who leads and cares for the flock, and it
underpins the concept of God's reign or kingdom as Jesus proclaims and seeks to establish it. Speaking of 'God's reign' emphasises
the fact of God's activity, while ' God's kingdom' tends to emphasise

---

61. 'Proclaiming' (*kêryssôn*) literally means announcing publicly like a
herald, a city/town crier (*kêryx*).
62. Mark, on the other hand, first calls for repentance, and the combined
quotation from Isaiah and Malachi about the way of the Lord seems for
Mark to include and 'absorb' the proclamation of the kingdom at this
point in the narrative (Mk 1:1-3).

the location or sphere of influence of that activity. Both dimensions are found in the gospels but the former is the more common. For those who are open to repenting and accepting the coming of the kingdom there must be an acceptance of the sovereignty of God over all things, an awareness of the providence of God in their lives and a hope for a sharing in the fullness of the kingdom in the fullness of time.

The kingdom is not a state or system brought about by good, religious, God-fearing people. It is 'God's project', a divine plan to which one must respond, and not a human programme, a fact emphasised by J. R. Donahue and D. J. Harrington:

> ... it is not easy to define the 'kingdom of God' because it is future in its fullness and transcendent in its origin. The kingdom is ultimately God's project ...[63]

They further point out that:

> The recovery of Jesus' vision of the Kingdom of God was one of the great achievements of theology in the twentieth century. And along with it comes the recognition that this demands a response that involves not only a change in attitude ('place your faith in the good news') but also a change of life ('repent'). Jesus is herald and agent, but the reign/kingdom belongs to God.[64]

Jesus was herald and agent of the kingdom but, as J. P. Meier states, in his study of the historical Jesus:

> The kingdom of God was simply Jesus' special and somewhat abstract way of speaking of God himself coming in power to manifest his definitive rule in the end time. God coming in power to rule in the end of time: that is the point of Jesus' phraseology.[65]

Since the fullness of the kingdom is in the future, there is an unfulfilled aspect to it in the here and now. This leads to a sense of secrecy, a mystery or plan of God as yet undisclosed, and a resulting tension between the known and unknown, the already revealed and as yet hidden. The future therefore has a strongly determining

---

63. J. R. Donahue and D. J. Harrington, *The Gospel of Mark*, Sacra Pagina, 72.
64. Ibid.
65. J. P. Meier, *A Marginal Jew*, Vol 2, 414.

influence on the present, setting the present 'given' nature of the kingdom in the greater eschatological perspective.

In the parabolic discourse Jesus will state: 'To you it has been given to know the mysteries of the kingdom ...'(Mt 13:10//Lk 8:9-10; cf Mk 4:11).[66] The mysteries of the kingdom are a gift of revelation. It is given to you to know, that is, to those open to receive and respond to them. They are described as mysteries, an unfolding plan of God, partly seen and partly hidden, partly present and partly in the future. Its presence issues in a challenge to respond here and now and its future beckons us to look beyond the here and now, beyond the world as we know it, to see all things in relation to their ending and reconstitution in the eschatological kingdom. This calls for a paradoxical outlook on life and the world with its established assessments and values.[67]

Bas van Iersel sums up the essential dimensions of the kingdom:

> It refers to a future event as yet unknown, as well as to a present reality one may already accept. In order to enter God's kingdom there are things in life you must do and other things you must leave undone, and in that sense it is intimately connected with the theme of ' the way'. The kingdom can be recognised but it is at the same time hidden. Likewise it is closely bound up with Jesus' presence and activity, his speaking and doing, and at the same time with the son of man who is to come when the end time, begun in Jesus, is one day fulfilled. So it is no accident that Jesus employs the language of parable, simile and metaphor when speaking about the kingdom of God.[68]

---

66. Mk 4:11 states 'To you has been given the mystery of the Kingdom of God.'
67. S. Légasse, L'évangile de Marc, (Italian Trans.), 222, describes the kingdom of God very succinctly: *senza perdere la sua dimensione futura e finale e senza evolversi, come altrove nel Nuovo Testamento, verso un Regno di Cristo, il Regno di Dio `e condizionato dal atto di seguire Gesù e la sua instaurazione definitiva e gloriosa coincide con la parusia ... Infine, come nozione sintetica, esso ingloba tutto l'opera di rinnovamento e di salvezza inaugurata da Cristo.*
68. Bas van Iersel, Reading Mark, 42. See B. T. Viviano, The Kingdom of God in History, Collegeville: The Liturgical Press, 1991 and B. J. Malina, The Social History of Jesus. The Kingdom of God in Mediterranean Perspective, Min: Fortress, 2001.

W. J. Harrington puts it very succinctly, emphasising the necessity of personal response to the arrival of the kingdom:

> The kingdom, though in its fullness still in the future, comes as a present offer, in actual gift, through the proclamation of the good news. But it arrives only on condition of the positive response of the hearer.[69]

Repent

To prepare for the kingdom John calls on the people to repent. The verb 'repent' and its related noun 'repentance' (*metanoeite/ metanoia*) are New Testament terms which signify a change of mind, heart, attitude and direction which takes place in the reassessment of one's life involving remorse for one's past and a new direction for one's future. They are more or less synonymous with the Greek word *epistrephein*, 'to turn around' which is the closest Greek term to the Hebrew word, *subh*, 'to turn back/return', a dominant term for repentance in the Old Testament. Turning round to face God in response and reconciliation, returning to God and making a new beginning are key concepts in the call to repentance. 'Repent' also captures the sense of the Hebrew *niham*, 'to be sorry'. Here in the gospel it represents the call back to God from the crooked paths on which one has strayed as the hearers are called on to prepare the way of the Lord, to make his paths straight. The call is made because of the imminence of the kingdom of heaven. First John, then Jesus proclaims its imminence and calls for repentance.

The desert

John proclaims his message *in the desert*. A new scenario is thus introduced. Already in the Infancy Narrative geographic links to the history and experience of Israel tied the infancy of Jesus to the paradigmatic story of the ancestors. Now the shift to the desert of Judea and the area around the Jordan again links the experience of Jesus to that paradigmatic history. The desert held a special place in the history and spirituality of the people. It was the place where Israel became God's chosen people through covenant, when God liberated them from the slavery of Egypt 'with mighty hand and outstretched arm, with great terror and with signs and wonders' (Deut 26:8) and where God continued to lead them through the desert as the Shepherd of Israel. It was also the place where they

69. W. J. Harrington, *Mark, Realistic Theologian*, 33.

were tested, where they grumbled, complained, hesitated and suffered punishment and purification as they were led to the Promised Land. Centuries later it was through the desert that God, in a new Exodus, would lead them back from the exile in Babylon, straightening the paths and making smooth the way.[70] The desert became the place where the devout and repentant would withdraw to be with God, rediscover their roots and remake their lives. Elijah repaired to the desert in crisis (1 Kings 19). The Essenes went there to found an ideal messianic community when they withdrew from the illegitimate religious authority in Jerusalem.

The desert was therefore the ideal spot for a group like the followers of the Baptist to assemble in their quest for new beginnings and for straightening the spiritual paths and making smooth the ways on which they walked in the journey of their lives. Jesus himself after his baptism is driven into the desert by the Spirit to be tested there by Satan. During the ministry of Jesus the desert will be the place where he will be moved to compassion to teach and feed the multitudes who come to the desert to be with him, to listen to him and to be healed by him. In doing so he will re-enact the caring and protecting activity of the Shepherd of Israel.

The Voice in the Desert / The way of the Lord

Matthew expressly applies the prophecy of (Deutero-) Isaiah to this activity of John and he identifies John as 'the voice crying out in the desert'. He writes: 'It was of him that the prophet Isaiah wrote: "a voice cries out in the desert"' (Isa 40:3).[71] In the Hebrew text of the Old Testament 'the way of the Lord' was seen in terms of a physical journey, a real physical path in the desert and the path was

---

70. For an examination of the influence of Deutero-Isaiah's concept of 'the way of the Lord' as a new Exodus, a new return under the care and protection of a shepherding and warrior God, see R. E. Watts, *Isaiah's New Exodus and Mark. Wissenschaftliche Untersuchungen zum Neuen Testament* 2. Reihe 88, Tubingen: J. C. B. Mohr (Paul Siebeck), 1997.

71. Unlike Mark, Matthew uses only the quotation from Isaiah and not a combination of quotations (Isa 40:3; Mal 3:1; Exod 23:20). Though the quotation in Mark is ascribed to Isaiah the first part of the quotation re-echoes the prophet Malachi's prophecy that God will send a messenger, identified as Elijah, before ' the great and terrible day of YHWH ' (Mal 3:1; 4:5).

described as the path of our God.[72] The imagery portrays God as the shepherd leading the people back from the exile in Babylon through the desert to their own land.[73]

Here in Matthew, and in the New Testament generally, the voice is 'the voice in the desert' and 'the way of the Lord' refers not to a physical path in the desert but to the way of Jesus, to God's way manifest in his life, death and resurrection for which the Baptist is preparing.[74] It is the way of discipleship in which Jesus will call his followers to share his destiny and walk with him on his divinely designated path. 'The way' becomes in his ministry 'the way to Jerusalem' which is 'the way of the Son of Man', Jesus' way to his passion, death and resurrection, and which is at the same time the context for a very significant portion of the teaching on 'the way of discipleship'. By the time of the writing of the Acts of the Apostles the term has become so established that Christians are referred to as people 'of the way' (Acts 9:2).

---

72. The MT has 'path in the desert'; the LXX and NT have 'voice in the desert'.

73. The synoptics and John follow the LXX 'voice in the desert' rather than 'path in the desert' but John's gospel takes an independent line from the synoptics when he conflates the two elements of the LXX, which read 'prepare the Lord's road, make straight God's path' into 'Make straight the Lord's path.' The synoptics have the two elements. The Qumran community used this text to explain their living, waiting, preparing and studying in the desert (I QS VIII 13-16). The synoptic narrators apply this text to John the Baptist but in John's gospel he applies it to himself in his response to the Jerusalem emissaries (Jn 1:23).

74. The term 'The way of the Lord' can be seen here both as 'the way of God' made manifest in Jesus or 'the way of (Jesus) the Lord'. The title 'Lord', *kyrios*, was used in the LXX as a translation of *adonai*, used in the Hebrew Bible as a substitute for *YHWH*, since the Jews regarded the name of God as too sacred to pronounce. The title *kyrios* became a standard title for the risen and glorified Christ in the early church. Referring to/addressing Jesus as Lord is a mark of the believer in Matthew's gospel so it is not out of place in the highly theological and christological prologue which includes the Infancy Narrative where he is shown to be Christ, Son of God, conceived by the Holy Spirit and in the inauguration of the ministry at the baptism where he is proclaimed Beloved Son by the voice from heaven, and invested with the Spirit. In Jerusalem at the end of his ministry Jesus will refer to the Messiah as Lord (Mt 22:41-46//Mk 12:35-37//Lk 20:41-44).

The Jordan

In choosing the Jordan as the site for ritual baptism and inauguration into his movement, John the Baptist chose a place rich in associations with Israel's past. Crossing the Jordan dry shod behind the ark which was carried in solemn procession into the promised land was a pivotal moment in the history of the chosen people as they entered into the land to live there as God's covenanted people (Josh 3-4). Baptising in the Jordan River therefore is rich in symbolism. It connotes a spiritual crossing of the Jordan and it recalls the new life and dedication originally required of the people as they emerged from the desert wandering, with its suffering and disaffection, to the joyous occupation of the land of milk and honey. On that historic occasion they promised faithfulness to the covenant relationship with the God who had led them from the slavery of Egypt to the Promised Land. John's followers now come to the Jordan to renew that promise. In this he is in line with the prophets who regularly called for repentance and for a return to the covenant way of life.

John and Elijah

John is the latest and final prophet in the former dispensation. 'All the prophets and the Law prophesied until John' (Mt 11:13). His dress and deportment recall those of the prophets and of Elijah in particular (Zech 13:4; 2 Kings 1: 8). His food consisted of locusts and wild honey. Locusts were one of the winged insects permitted in the Levitical code and featured in the Qumran diet (Lev11: 20-23; CD 12:14). Wild honey could be got from among the rocks, from trees and carcasses of animals (Deut 32:13; 1 Sam 14:25f; Judges 14:8f). The similarity to Elijah does not end with the description of John's clothes and diet. 'Preparing the way of the Lord' and announcing the coming of the 'stronger one' who will baptise in Holy Spirit and fire and preparing for the one coming after him re-echo very strongly the expected return of Elijah to usher in the Messianic time. The gospel will show how the similarity with Elijah continues as John is arrested and put to death by a latter-day Ahab tricked by a scheming latter-day Jezebel (cf 1 Kings 19; Mt 14:3-12//Mk 6:17-29//Lk 3:19-20). On the occasion of the Transfiguration Jesus will tell the inner group of apostles, Peter, James and John, that Elijah has already appeared and that they have treated him as they pleased, that is, his enemies have persecuted him. The narrator adds that the disciples knew he was referring to John (Mt 17:10-13).

The response of the crowds

The account of John's movement emphasises the 'universal' character of the response to his call to repentance. 'Jerusalem and all the Judean countryside and all the region around the Jordan went out to him' (Mt 3:6). This universal appeal on the part of the crowds in the context of the Baptist will be very characteristic of the response of the crowds to Jesus, particularly during his early ministry, changing only when a 'mob' in Jerusalem, under the instigation of a hostile authority, turn against him at the end. The people confess (*exomologoumenoi*) their sins. Confession of sins, in private and public, was reckoned as an important form of prayer/worship. This is obvious from the Old Testament, especially from the psalms (e.g. Ps 32, Ps 51). Josephus Flavius states that God is easily reconciled to those who 'confess and repent'.[75]

B. Condemnation of Pharisees and Sadducees Mt 3:7-10

When John sees some Pharisees and Sadducees coming for baptism he launches into an attack, calling them a 'brood of vipers', a term used for them later in the gospel by Jesus (Mt 12:34; 23:33). The combination of Pharisees and Sadducees is a generic term for a communal character representing some of the official forces that will oppose Jesus during his ministry.[76] Putting these two groups together, who were not on good terms with each other, is a way of showing the broad body of opposition.[77] The more usual grouping will be the scribes and Pharisees, since many of the scribes, professional biblical scholars and lawyers, were of the Pharisee party/movement. The Sadducees were more associated with the Jerusalem priestly class, the elders and the temple authority. In calling for the fruit that befits repentance, John uses apocalyptic, fiery language of the wrath that is to come. He warns that the axe is laid to the root of the

---

75. Ps 31(32):5; 37(38):18; 50(51):3-5; cf Lev 5:5; *The Prayer of Manasseh*; Josephus, *War*, 5.415; cf *Ant.*, 18:117.

76. Other generic terms for communal characters showing hostility are 'the scribes and Pharisees' and 'the chief priests and elders of the people'.

77. Mark achieves a similar effect by grouping the Pharisees and Herodians together (Mk 3:6).

tree that does not bear good fruit in order to cut it down and have it thrown into the fire (Mt 3:7f; cf Lk 3:7-14).[78] Their claim to be children of Abraham will be of no avail. He reminds them that God can raise up children to Abraham from the very stones, implying that if they wish to be children of Abraham they must live accordingly and not just claim physical descent from the Patriarch. This is very close to the argument of Jesus in John's gospel as he confronts the hostile Jerusalem crowds on the occasion of the Feast of Tabernacles (Jn 8:31-59). After speaking about the one coming after him, John will return to the note of apocalyptic judgement with his reference to the winnowing fan and the burning of the chaff (Mt 3:12).

C. Baptism in Water and Baptism in Holy Spirit (and Fire) (Mt 3:11-12)

John is preparing the way for the one coming after him and turns his attention to the nature of his own baptism and that of 'the one who is coming after me, the more powerful one, whose sandals I am not worthy to carry' (Mt 3:11).

The one who is coming

'The one who is coming' (*ho erchomenos*) is an established messianic designation. The apocalyptic tradition speaks of the one coming from among the followers, from behind, to take over the leadership. Here *erchomenos opisô mou*, 'coming after me' alerts the reader to such a coming one, a follower who will take over the leadership, confirmed by John as he identifies the 'coming one' in terms of 'the one stronger/more powerful than me' (*ischuroteros mou estin*). The designation 'stronger one' not only alerts the reader to the relative strengths of the Baptist and Jesus but also recalls the divine visitation in Deutero-Isaiah where God will come *meta ischyos*, 'with strength/in power', to shepherd his flock (Isa 40:10-11).

John's reference to the one whose sandals he is not worthy to carry (or untie) is common to all four gospels and Acts (Mt 3:11; Mk 1:8; Lk 3:16; Jn 1:27; Acts 13:25). A disciple was expected to do for a teacher what a slave did for his master, except tend to his feet/untie his shoes, as it was regarded as too demeaning. Rabbi Joshua ben Levi states: 'All services that a slave performs for his master a pupil

---

78. Mt 3:10-12; Lk 3: 7,9.18. These verses belong to the Q material, which scholars regard as a source for Matthew and Luke. This apocalyptic and moralising passage is missing in Mark (Mk 1:2-8).

should do for his teacher, with the exception of undoing his shoes.'[79] John is here proclaiming that 'he is no more than a slave whose task is to untie his master's sandal; and he feels unworthy even of that'.[80] The remark about the sandals may be a reminder to those who continued to see John as the messianic figure, that John himself was the first to deny any such role for himself.

Baptism in water for repentance

John's baptism is a baptism of repentance and it is sharply contrasted, by John himself, with the baptism in Holy Spirit and fire of the one coming after him (the reference to fire continues the apocalyptic tone of the attack on the Pharisees and Sadducees). His baptism is preparatory for the baptism/ministry of Jesus which John proclaimed in terms of the coming purification and judgement.

To appreciate the significance of the contrast between his baptism and the baptism in Holy Spirit and fire that radically surpasses his own baptism in water, John's baptism should be put in the context of the practice and understanding of baptism at the time.

John's baptism was a baptism of repentance accompanied by confessing of sins. John's baptism fits into a wider context as is evident, for example, from the baptismal rituals of the Qumran community with which he may have had contact or by whom he may have been in some way influenced. Given the fact that he conducted his ministry in an area close to the monastery at Qumran, it is quite possible that he was influenced in some measure by their asceticism, ceremonial practice and messianic expectation. Their Manual of Discipline is very definite, however, that mere washing cannot really make one clean. It can clean flesh, but only the submission of one's soul to God's ordinances can make one internally clean. It is only God who will finally purge all the acts of man and refine him by destroying every spirit of perversity in his flesh, cleansing him by a holy spirit and sprinkling upon him the spirit of truth like waters of purification to cleanse him.[81] The rite itself therefore was not seen as effecting forgiveness and purification and people could not use it to become like the holy ones. It was seen as an external expression of a sincere inner disposition of repentance.

---

79. *b.Ketubot* 96a.
80. W. J. Harrington, *John, Spiritual Theologian*, 32.
81. I QS 3:7-9; 4:20-22; I Q H 16:12; cf 7:6; 17:26; fragment 2:9, 3. The influence of Ezekiel is evident here (Ezek 36:25-27).

Josephus Flavius presents a similar view of John's baptism. He says that it was 'not to beg pardon for sins committed, but for the purification of the body, when the soul had previously been cleansed by right behaviour'.[82] This understanding highlights the preparatory nature of John's baptism and accentuates the contrast with the baptism of Jesus.[83]

Whatever the influences on him, John's practice of ritual baptism, as it stands here in the gospel, is unique to the Baptist in its broad scope and eschatological thrust.[84] It was not a repeating ritual, but had the character of a once-off definitive turning away from sin in expectation of the kingdom. John, however, emphasised the preparatory nature of his baptism and accentuated the contrast with the baptism by Jesus who would baptise in Holy Spirit and fire. A whole new era and a new baptism are about to be inaugurated with the rending of the heavens, the descent of the Spirit on Jesus and the voice from heaven proclaiming him 'My Son, the Beloved.'

John himself proclaimed the essential difference between his own baptism and that to be ministered by Jesus. He baptised with water but the one coming after him would baptise with the Holy Spirit (and fire) (Mt 3:11; Mk 1:8; Lk 3:16; Jn 1:26; cf Acts11: 16). This longer version in Mt 3:11 and Lk 3:16 which adds 'and fire' belongs to the Q tradition which has a generally punitive tone, promising judgement and wrath to come together with the purifying effects of fire. This apocalyptic note, coming so clearly through the Q tradition, was probably the dominant one historically in the preaching of the Baptist and explains why the merciful ministry of Jesus to sinners rather than the apocalyptic destruction of sin and sinner subsequently caused a problem which gave rise to the question of the Baptist: 'Are you he who is to come or shall we look for another?' (Mt 11:2f; Lk 7:18-20). The influence of Isaiah is seen in the combination of spirit and fire. The spirit (*ruah*) is presented in Isa 4:4 and 30:28 as a spirit of purification and judgement, in Isa 11:15 as a destructive spirit, in Isa 29:30 as a retributive spirit, and in Isa 32:15-17 as a spirit of blessing, prosperity and righteousness. The under-

---

82. Josephus, *Ant.*, 18:117.
83. Another possible influence may have been the process of proselyte baptism signifying the cleansing process of a Gentile before entering into the spiritual heritage of Israel.
84. J. P. Meier, *A Marginal Jew* 2, 53-55, sees John's baptism as quite original to John.

standing of the fire as one of punitive destruction is emphasised by
the fact that both Mt 3:11 and Lk 3:16 have the reference to fire, the
threat about the unfruitful tree being cast into the fire and the
metaphors of winnowing and destruction (Mt 3:10-12 and Lk 3:9,16-
17). The influence of the prophet Malachi (Mal 3:2f; 4:1) who spoke
of refining and destructive fire is evident in these verses as it is in
the baptismal ritual in the Qumran community according to I QS
4:21.

Baptism in Holy Spirit

Jesus' own baptism in the Jordan is a key to the new type of baptism he was to bring. Whereas the baptism of John was called a baptism for repentance (Mt 3:11) and could be graphically described as
an empty hand stretched out to God for forgiveness, the baptism of
Jesus, described as baptism in Holy Spirit (cf Acts 19:1ff), signifies
the beginning of a new era, a pivotal point in the economy of salvation, a guarantee of God's forgiveness of sins, a new and final initiative of God in Jesus.[85] The era of baptism as an empty hand
stretched out to God in repentance begging for the forgiveness of
sins is now passed. The rending of the heavens and the return of the
spirit 'quenched' since the days of the prophets, will initiate the
new era. The occasion of Jesus' baptism signals the beginning of the
eschatological time which will be marked by the healing work of
the Messiah above all in the forgiveness of sins.[86] This will be the
Baptism in Holy Spirit foretold by John.[87] Matthew is careful to re-
serve any reference to the forgiveness of sins to the ministry of
Jesus. He preached repentance in the light of the imminence of the
kingdom and the people confessed their sins. Mark, on the other
hand, says he preached repentance for the forgiveness of sins (Mt
3:2, 6; Mk 1:4).

---

85. Dunn, J. D. G., *Baptism in the Holy Spirit*, London, SCM Press, 1970,
16.
86. cf Acts 19:1-7 as a practical manifestation of the promised reality.
87. 'Baptism' can signify the beginning of a new life and a new state and
similarly 'Baptism in a Holy Spirit' signifies the beginning of a new
state, which involves a new and critical religious experience (cf Acts 1:5;
11:16). It can signify a crisis and decision about one's response to the
Messiah. Jesus himself used the metaphor of baptism for his impending
passion and death (Mk 10:38; Lk 12:50).

2. JESUS COMES FROM GALILEE MT 3:13-4:16

A. The Reaction of John Mt 3:13-15

Jesus comes out of Galilee to be baptised by John. The same solemn word, already used of the Baptist, *paraginetai*, 'he comes/ appears', is used to announce Jesus' entry into the story. He comes in a very deliberate way to John for baptism. John proclaims that it is he himself who should be baptised by Jesus, an action that would have effectively made him a follower of Jesus but Jesus insists on the divinely ordained plan. His first words in Matthew's gospel are: 'Let it be so for now for it is fitting to fulfil all righteousness.' Fulfilment of the divine plan, already taking place through the fulfilment of scripture as pointed out in the comment on the fulfilment citations, is his first duty. This is the bringing to completion of God's plan and facilitating the achievement of its purpose. It is the equivalent to the 'bringing to completion/perfection' of the will of the Father, in the language of John's gospel (Jn 5:36), a completion brought to perfection when the dying Jesus says *tetelestai*, it is completed (Jn 19:28, 30). The term righteousness/justice (*dikaiosunê*) is a recurring one in Matthew. First of all, *dikaiosunê* is the quality of God binding himself to the covenant through his fidelity in spite of sin and failure, and the corresponding demand on the people to respond to God with fidelity and proper ethical conduct before God and neighbour. There will be strong emphasis throughout the gospel on 'doing' righteousness, not just extolling or preaching it like the scribes and Pharisees. One's righteousness must exceed that of the scribes and Pharisees (Mt 5:20).

The New Testament generally is sensitive about the relative roles of John and Jesus. A lingering idea among some Jews that the Baptist was the Messiah, and a scruple on the part of the Christian community about an apparent subordination of Jesus to John due to his submission to John's baptism, seem to be behind all the accounts. Here in Matthew the clarification is made by way of a dialogue between John and Jesus.[88] John baptised Jesus in the Jordan and a new era was about to begin. Though the ministry of John is unique and the baptism of Jesus without parallel, still the narrative is rich in biblical allusions, setting the event within the wider scope of Salvation History.

---

88. Short pithy dialogues between Jesus and someone with whom he is engaging are common in Matthew.

B. The Baptism of Jesus Mt 3:16-17

As Jesus came up out of the water the definitive salvific work of God began with the rending of the heavens, the descent of the Spirit like a dove and the voice from heaven, marking a completely new initiative of God in the economy of salvation. The rending or tearing open of the heavens described in the immediate aftermath of the baptism of Jesus is an eschatological sign, announcing the inauguration of the final definitive action of God. It recalls the sentiment of Trito-Isaiah: 'O that you would tear open the heavens and come down ... to make your name known to your adversaries, so that the nations might tremble at your presence! When you did awesome deeds that we did not expect ...' (Isa 64:1-3; cf Isa 24:17-20; Rev 19:11). Here at the scene of the baptism of Jesus the rending of the heavens and the heavenly voice represent the divine presence, transcendent and immanent, joining earth and heaven, somewhat like the (Jacob's) ladder image in John's gospel (Jn 1:51). J. Marcus explains the significance exceptionally well: 'God has ripped the heavens apart irrevocably at Jesus' baptism, never to shut them again. Through this gracious gash in the universe, he has poured forth his Spirit into the earthly realm.'[89]

The descent of the Spirit signifies the anointing of the Messiah and is interpreted by the witnessing voice from heaven (Isa 42:1; Ps 2:7).[90] It signifies also the return of the quenched Spirit in a spirit anointed Messiah (Isa 11:2; 42:1; 61:1) and the eschatological event heralded by the rending of the heavens (Isa 64:1). It signifies, too, the new creation symbolised by the dove hovering above the water like the Spirit of God hovering over the waters at creation (Gen 1:2), just as a bird hovers above the nest inciting the young to fly, and the bird in question was interpreted by the rabbis as a dove brooding above the nestlings.[91] It is reminiscent also of a new definitive recon-

---

89. J. Marcus, *Mark 1-8*, 165.

90. The voice is not just the return of prophecy. The *bath qol* that took the place of the direct inspiration of the prophets is now superseded by the voice of the Father and the definitive return of the Spirit in a new creation initiative. See Dunn, *op. cit.*, 27.

91. G. R. Beasley Murray, *Baptism in the New Testament*, Grand Rapids: Eerdmans, 1963, 61, sees the dove as having eschatological significance. The Rabbis saw the hovering of the dove as an image of the Spirit breathing over chaos at creation. cf G. T. Montague, *The Holy Spirit: Growth of a Biblical Tradition*, New York/Toronto: Paulist Press, 1976, 240; C. K. Barrett, *The Holy Spirit and the Gospel Tradition*, London, SPCK, 1947, 39.

ciliation, reminiscent of the dove sent out by Noah heralding the ending of the flood, the completion of the punishment and the new covenant about to be made. Furthermore, the river has salvific significance in the biblical tradition where it can be seen to symbolise life (Ezek 47:1-12), forgiveness (LXX Ezek 47:3) and healing (2 Kings 5:14). For the readers in the Hellenistic world, comparing the Spirit to a dove highlighted the divinity of the Spirit since the dove was regarded as a divine bird in the Hellenistic world.[92] The descent of the Spirit points to the divine origin and power of the one about to be declared Beloved Son by the voice from heaven.

After the end of the prophetic times when the Spirit no longer spoke through the prophets the rabbis spoke of the *bath qôl*, 'daughter of the voice', the faint echo of the divine voice uttered in heaven. This 'voice from heaven' at the baptism, accompanied by the return of the quenched Spirit is no faint echo, but the sound of the voice (*phônê*) of the Father, transcendent and immanent at this moment, proclaiming: 'This is my Beloved Son in whom I am well pleased' (Ps 2:7). There is a density of meaning here. First of all it recalls Psalm 2 which probably reflects an enthronement ceremony, where the metaphor of adoption as God's son (Ps 2:7) assures the royal prince of God's protection at his enthronement as Davidic King. However, Jesus' sonship transcends the general sonship of the anointed king, the righteous priest, prophet or prince and the suffering righteous one, or the collective sonship of the people. The term *agapêtos*, 'beloved', reflects the Hebrew *yahid*, 'unique', as in 'only son' (as *monogenês* in Jn 1:18) and therefore especially beloved, as in the case of Isaac (Gen 22:2,12,16). It also reflects the Hebrew *bakîr*, 'chosen', as in the appointment of the chosen servant of God, in whom God is well pleased and in whom he puts his spirit. This recalls the suffering servant, obedient to God to the end in spite of persecution, and suffering vicariously on behalf of others, taking their faults on himself and praying all the time for sinners (Isa 42:1-2; 52:13 – 53:12). The divine voice in the baptism scene speaks in the third person, addressing anyone who listens or reads: 'This is my Beloved Son …' and later in the ministry at the Transfiguration the voice will specifically address the disciples, saying of Jesus: 'This is

92. R. H. Gundry, *Mark. A Commentary on his Apology for the Cross*, 4.

my Beloved Son ...'(Mt 17:5).[93] Jesus is thus declared a messianic prince-king, a prophetic style servant, but above all the Beloved Son in a unique way.[94]

The 'installation' of Jesus in his role resembles (though in a much less dramatic way) that of Ezekiel who was also installed at the bank of a river as winged creatures (Ezek 1:1ff) appeared in the sky, and was then transported to another place by the spirit. The difference here is that Jesus does not become son at this point but his sonship is revealed, as it will be revealed to the three chosen disciples at the Transfiguration (Mt 17:1-13). He is not sent on a mission, told what to say or do like the prophets of old, as in the case of Ezekiel eating the scroll or Jeremiah accepting that God would 'put my words in to your mouth' as he was sent 'to tear up and knock down, to build and to plant'(Jer 1:9f). Jesus' authority and mission spring from who he is, the Beloved Son, which has been declared at his baptism and from the power of the Spirit, an integral constituent of his role as Messiah. His testing in the desert will show that the Spirit has not just paid him a fleeting visit, but in the words of John's gospel, the Spirit remains/dwells (*menein*) with him (Jn 1:32).

Contrary to the image given by many works of Christian art, the Spirit was not conferred on Jesus by the ministrations of the Baptist but marks a completely new initiative of God in the economy of salvation. Matthew and Mark state that John the Baptist baptised Jesus, but make it quite clear that he had already been baptised and had come up out of the water when the Spirit descended upon him (Mt 3:16; Mk1:10). Luke says that he had been baptised and was at prayer when the Spirit descended on him (Lk 3:21). The gospel of John emphasises the divine initiative rather that human action by omitting any reference to the actual baptism and referring only to the descent of the Spirit on Jesus, an event witnessed by John who is significantly not styled 'the Baptist' in the Fourth Gospel, but is presented as the key witness to Jesus, in this case the witness to the descent of the Spirit upon him showing him to be the Son/the Chosen One of God (Jn 1:32).

---

93. In Mk 1:11 the divine voice addresses the son, Jesus, directly in the second person.
94. Towards the end of his ministry in Jerusalem Jesus challenges the general understanding that the Messiah is (merely) son of David and goes on to point out that David himself calls him 'Lord', elevating him to the divine plain (Mt 22:41-46).

C. The Testing in the Desert Mt 4:1-11//Lk 4:1-13; cf Mk 1:12-13)

Testing his Sonship

The imagery and associations of the desert and Jordan locations are continued. All three synoptics mention 'forty days in the desert' but Matthew adds 'and forty nights' thereby including a further layer of allusions. The number forty conjures up the memory of Israel's wandering in the desert on escaping from Egypt, experiencing the presence of God in their midst and the role of Moses leading them through the wilderness for forty years. Forty days (or years) became a canonised symbolic term for a period of testing in the desert. It conjures up also the memory of their struggle in the desert between accepting the unfolding if yet unclear plan of God and the desire to return to Egypt. When God called his son (Israel) out of Egypt (Hos 11:1), that son failed time and again during the testing period in the desert. Here again Jesus' experience is tied in to the paradigmatic experience of the people of Israel. The temptations to turn the stones into bread, to enter the Holy City and throw himself from the pinnacle of the temple and to worship the devil in return for power over the kingdoms of the world parallel the failures of the people in the desert when they complained about hunger, put the Lord God to the test and worshipped a false god (the golden calf) in the desert. However, unlike the son called out of Egypt (Hos 11:1) this son, the Beloved, will not complain about hunger and produce miraculous food, put the Lord God to the test or worship a false god as the people did in the desert. He will be tried and found to be the genuine Beloved Son of God. The temptations stand at the outset of Jesus' ministry as a benchmark like the Book of Deuteronomy stands as a benchmark providing the criteria for the Deuteronomic History (Joshua through 2 Kings) in which the Israelites' tenure of the Promised Land came to be assessed.

Matthew expands the 'forty days' formula into ' forty days and forty nights.' The sojourn of Jesus in the desert therefore recalls for Matthew not only the general picture of the forty years in the desert, but also the forty days and forty nights of Moses' fast on Mount Sinai (Exod 34:28; Deut 9:9,18) prior to the making of the covenant and the revelation of the Law. It recalls also the experience of Elijah's journey of forty days and forty nights to Horeb (Sinai) when he was in mortal danger and was assisted in his exhausted and hungry state by the angel (1 Kings 19:1-8).

The imagery of the crossing of the Jordan is continued with the citations from Deuteronomy that recall the sermon of Moses as the people prepared to cross the Jordan into the Promised Land. He spelled out for them the significance and obligations of the covenant. The call to obedience and wholehearted worship of God, together with the reminder of their failure and their putting God to the test, are the subject of chapters six to eight of Deuteronomy. It is from these chapters that the citations of Jesus in response to the tempter are taken.

Jesus has already been introduced to the reader as Son of God. He is now about to set out on his mission in which he is obliged to carry out the will of the Father, 'to fulfill all righteousness'. The 'tempter', the devil, the source and personification of the forces of opposition throughout the story about to unfold, is now introduced to the reader as he tempts Jesus in order to see 'if' he is really the Son of God. The battle lines are being drawn for Jesus' ministry. The longer account of the temptations, which appears both in Matthew and Luke, is a very clever piece of religious storytelling reflecting the experience of Jesus' life and illustrated by apt quotations from the Book of Deuteronomy. It is a reflection on the main factors which operated against his proper task as Son of God sent to do the will of his Father and to fulfil all righteousness in establishing the kingdom rather than responding to human, even diabolical, promptings, insights and considerations.

The temptations are best understood by looking at the response of Jesus, in each case a citation from the Book of Deuteronomy. The temptation to turn the stones into bread is countered by 'Not by bread alone does man live, but by every word that comes from the mouth of God' (Deut 8:3). The temptation to throw himself from the pinnacle of the temple receives the response: 'You must not put the Lord your God to the test' (Deut 6:16), and the temptation to worship the devil and thus receive power over the kingdoms of the world receives the reply: 'The Lord your God you must adore and him only will you serve' (Deut 6:13). These citations by way of response to the tempter point out respectively that the kingdom is not just about physical well being but about the whole person's need of God, neither is it a means whereby God proves himself to human satisfaction through miraculous displays of power and thereby receives his due honour and service, nor is it a power-based society established by an acceptance of the worldly standards of human politics, power and influence, the acceptance of which would entail accepting and worshipping the god of the world, Satan. Reading through the gospel stories, one can see these forces at work – pressure to respond to physical hunger and need at the expense of providing spiritual nourishment; pressure to replace genuine religious response of repentance and faith with a quasi-superstitious religion of miraculous displays of power which gratify 'religious' curiosity but leave heart and mind unchanged, unrepentant and ultimately unbelieving; and pressure to establish the kingdom by acknowledging the spirit of earthly power, influence, status, social upheaval and political rebellion. Faith on human terms and conditions is really no faith.

The Spirit has already been mentioned in the account of Jesus' birth, in John's description of Jesus' coming 'baptism in Holy Spirit', in the description of the descent of the Spirit on Jesus immediately after his baptism and in the action of the Spirit in leading Jesus into the desert to be tested by the devil. The Spirit is constitutive of the role of the Messiah/Christ, the Anointed One. The devil represents the spiritual power and embodiment of the forces that will operate against the Spirit. During the ministry, when Jesus' role and the power behind it are challenged and he is accused of casting out demons by the power of the prince of devils, Jesus describes it as blasphemy against the Holy Spirit, and designates it 'an eternal sin' (Mt 12:24-32//Mk 3:22, 29-31).

Though the Matthean and Lukan accounts of the temptations are virtually identical and both begin with the temptation to turn the stones into bread, the order of the second and third temptations differs between Matthew and Luke. Both seem to order the temptations according to the overall structure of their gospels. Luke ends each major section of his gospel with a scene in Jerusalem. His Infancy Narrative ends with the finding of the child Jesus in the Jerusalem temple (Lk 2:41-52), the temptations end with the temptation to throw himself from the pinnacle of the temple in Jerusalem (Lk 4:9-12) and the gospel ends with the disciples returning from the Mount of the Ascension to pray in the temple in Jerusalem (Lk 24:52-53). Matthew, on the other hand, has the temptation in the temple in Jerusalem second and the temptation on the high mountain third. This is in keeping with the emphasis on the mountain as a highly symbolic location in the gospel. Jesus will deliver his major teaching on the Torah in the Sermon on the Mount (Mt 5-7). He will be transfigured on a high mountain (Mt 17:1-8) and deliver his eschatological discourse on the Mount of Olives (Mt 24-25). In the final scene in the gospel the Risen Jesus brings his disciples to a high mountain in Galilee and sends them into the whole world to make disciples of all nations (Mt 28:16:20). The final temptation in Matthew, where the devil takes Jesus up to a high mountain and shows him the kingdoms of the world and their glory, is reflected in this final scene of the gospel where Jesus commissions his disciples to bring the nations under the authority of God, making them disciples and baptising them in the name of the Father, the Son and the Holy Spirit, a direct reversal of the temptation to worship the devil in the world as he inhabited and controlled it (Mt 28:16-20).

Here the battle lines are drawn between the devil, Satan, the strong man, and Jesus the stronger man in the gospel.[95] The Beloved Son, empowered by the Spirit, has been tested and not found wanting. The tempter began his adversarial activity in Matthew and Luke by saying, 'If you are the son of God ...'. Jesus' response to the temptations in Matthew and Luke removes the 'if'. The attitude of Jesus displayed during the temptations is seen throughout the ministry. He will first of all teach the multitudes and because they stay with him he will feed them, not however as a display of power or for personal gratification, but as the compassionate shepherd in keeping with his role as Messiah, shepherd king, and Son of God (Mt 14:13-21; 15:32-39). He will enter Jerusalem humbly amidst the royal acclaim (Mt 21:1-11) and, far from performing a mighty miracle in the Holy City and its temple, he will move resolutely through his passion, accepting the will of the Father in spite of the taunt 'If you are the Son of God come down from the cross' (Mt 27:40, 42).

---

95. For Mark the desert was the place of testing, of temptation, of fiery serpents. In popular imagination it was the place of dangerous wild beasts, the home of demons and forces of destruction. It was the opposite of the Garden of Eden where harmony existed between God, humanity, the animals and the earth. Jesus was led there by the Spirit to be tested by Satan. He is like a new Adam, in harmony with God and at home with the wild beasts, a reminder of the prophetic promise that in messianic times the harmony of man and beast would be restored when 'the lion lies down with the lamb, the cow and the bear make friends and the infant plays over the cobra's hole' (Isa 11: 6-9). The Markan narrator leaves the reader wondering about the exact nature of the testing/temptation but the gospel story itself unpacks much of the enigma.

Matthew and Mark close their account of the tempting/testing of the Son with the assertion that the angels ministered to him (Mt 4:11; Mk 1:13). One could see the assertion in the Markan tradition that 'he was with the wild beasts' as a summary statement symbolising the evil powers that tempt and threaten Jesus and his mission. But tradition, as seen in Psalm 91, also associates the protective care of the angels with the one present among the wild beasts. The Psalmist reflected: 'He will give his angels charge over you, to keep you in all your ways ... on the lion and the viper you will tread and trample the young lion and the dragon ...' (Ps 91:11-13).[96] Daniel emerged from the lions' den with the affirmation, 'My God sent his angel who sealed the lions' jaws so they did me no harm since in his sight I am blameless ...' (Dan 6:21-23). Similarly, the men tested in the fiery furnace were protected by the angel of the Lord (Dan 3:49). In his desert sojourn the angel came to the aid of Elijah in his hunger and weakness (1 Kings 19:1-8). St Luke speaks of the angel comforting Jesus in Gethsemane (Lk 22:43). These are examples of the biblical experience behind the statement that the angels ministered to him (Mt 4:11).

Practical considerations

These temptations of Jesus, placed here at the beginning of the gospel, represent the tests that will come his way during the ministry. The gospel of John, for example, does not have a temptation narrative at the beginning of the ministry but the sixth chapter dealing with the Bread of Life has a remarkably parallel series of 'real life' temptations. The crowd on the first day want to make him king, the crowd on the second day come looking for ordinary bread without any concern or realisation of the meaning of the Bread of Life, the Bread from Heaven, and the crowd also demand signs of a religious nature to convince them of his authority (Jn 6:15, 26-27, 30).

Throughout the ministry, everyone will want his healing touch but not everyone will want his challenging message. Many will think of him as a revolutionary Messiah who should overthrow the Romans, establish an earthly kingdom and bring about a social revolution, but reject his role as a suffering, serving Messiah who sees the greatest in the kingdom as the one who serves or as the child full

---

96. This psalm is actually quoted in the temptation accounts in Mt 4:6 and Lk 4:10.

of innocence but without power and influence. Many will want miraculous signs to replace the challenge of genuine repentance, faith, hope and love. They will call on him to come down from the cross so that they will believe, but he dies in obedience to the Father's will.

The temptations have provided spiritual writers, preachers and moralists, with much food for thought and speculation. Novelists like Dostoevsky in his portrayal of the Grand Inquisitor in the *Brothers Karamazov* or the portrayal of Jesus in the film *Jesus of Montreal* have dealt with the subject in very practical ways. From a practical pastoral point of view, these tests that Jesus experienced are also the tests that confront his followers in all ages. The church as institution, in its community life and in the lives of individual believers, is always in danger of absorbing the values of the society in which it lives. There is always the temptation to put the immediate pressing needs of the day ahead of the longterm spiritual goal, to yoke the success of the church to the establishment with its influence, power and money in the hope of achieving the desired goals of the church but at the expense of allowing the one who pays the piper to call the tune. There is also the ever present danger of responding to genuine spiritual hunger with less than wholesome 'spiritual' food, be that a hiding behind empty rituals and platitudes, or cultivating an unhealthy dependence on half-superstitious practices and suspect signs or visions.

The preparation of the way of the Lord is complete. The recognition, empowering and testing of the protagonist have taken place and the scene is about to change. 'After John had been arrested Jesus withdrew into Galilee.' The story of John's arrest and murder will be by way of reminiscence after his death (Mt 14:1-12//Mk 6:14-29). In contrast to the Johannine tradition, which has a chronological overlap between the ministries of John and Jesus, the synoptics put a clear division between the two eras by having Jesus' ministry begin after John's arrest. A new era has already begun, and it is accompanied by a change of time and place as Jesus returns to Galilee whence he had come for the baptism of John and all that accompanied it. The activity at the Jordan and in the desert comes to a close. A new mission in a new area is about to begin.

The reader has now been led to see that God is the prime mover behind the coming of Jesus Christ, Son of God, the Lord for whom the precursor was sent to prepare the way. Jesus from Nazareth in

Galilee is the Christ, the Son of God, the one on whom the Spirit descended at baptism and whom the Spirit subsequently led out into
the desert. He is the one proclaimed as 'my Son the Beloved on
whom my favour rests' by the Father through the heavenly voice.
The devil, the tempter, Satan, represents the forces to be confronted
and the protecting forces of God are represented by the presence of
the angels. The reader is now equipped to read the story from a privileged position shared with the 'omniscient' narrator (though the
narrator has a lot more to reveal). From the prologue one has ac-
quired the necessary key to interpreting the gospel.

D. Jesus returns to Galilee (Mt 4:12-16)

A new beginning is taking place. It is an important temporal and
geographical marker in the narrative. The summary events marking
the beginning of the ministry (Mt 4:17-25) can be seen as the second
'kernel' or hinge in the text, emerging from what precedes and
opening on to the following block of 'satellite' material, the major
discourse (Mt 5-7) and the miracle cycle (Mt 8-9) showing Jesus' authority in word and deed, and the transfer of his authority to his
apostles in the missionary discourse (Mt 10).

When Jesus heard that John had been handed over, he withdrew
into Galilee. The era of John is completed. Jesus enters the public
arena. 'Handed over' (*paredothê*) stands out at the beginning of
Jesus' ministry as the fate of the precursor, the one who initiated the
proclaiming of the imminence of the kingdom by calling on Israel to
repent and to prepare the way of the Lord. It prefigures exactly the
fate of Jesus who is now beginning his public ministry. He too will
be *handed over*[97] and will warn his disciples and followers that the
same fate may lie in store for them also (Mt 10:17).

For the second time in his life Jesus arrives in Galilee, at
Nazareth, because of the danger posed in the area of Judea.
However, this time he moves on from Nazareth to Capernaum. This
gives Matthew the opportunity to highlight again the meaning of
what is unfolding by way of geographic references with Old
Testament significance. His move from Nazareth to Galilee is seen
in terms of obedience to a divine plan already laid down in scrip-

---

97. 'He will be handed over into the hands of men ...' (Mt 17:22); 'He
will be handed over to the chief priests and the scribes' (Mt 20:18); ' one
of you will hand me over' (Mt 26:21).

ture. The fulfilment citation from Isaiah 9:1, which does not correspond exactly to the wording of either the Hebrew or the Greek text
of the Old Testament, is carefully crafted to bring out the significance of Jesus' change of location (Mt 4:15). The context in Isaiah is
the celebration of the ending of the Assyrian war and the Syro-
Ephraimite threat. It celebrates the dawning of the light and the end
of the terrible period when the prophet Isaiah had said that the
child to be born of the maiden would be called Emmanuel, signifying the presence of God with his people, 'God with us'. The 'people
who walked in darkness' were the northern tribes who lost out in
the war and were taken in exile after the disastrous events of
722/721BC. Zebulon and Naphtali stand here for the deported
tribes, lost to Israel. Now the light not only dawns, but shines out in
their area. New beginnings are in store and they are emanating
from Galilee of the Gentiles where the chosen people lived among
the pagan nations. That very area now becomes the springboard of
the mission to Israel and to the nations. 'The way of the sea', in its
original setting in Isaiah, referred to the Via Maris along the
Mediterranean. Now the term is applied to the way along the Sea of
Galilee where the ministry of Jesus will unfold to Jew and Gentile in
Galilee of the Gentiles. Though Jesus' initial call is to the people of
Israel, it is a call that will not stop at the borders of Israel.

The Inauguration of The Kingdom of Heaven
The Authority of Jesus
Mt 4:17 – 11:1

Introduction

From Mt 4:17 to 11:1 there is a relatively clear-cut arrangement of material into narrative and discourse sections, as can be seen from the following general outline:

1. *Narrative*: Jesus Begins his Mission (Mt 4:17-25)
2. *Discourse*: The Sermon on the Mount (Mt 5:1–7:2)
3. *Narrative*: Miracles and Challenges (Mt 8:1–9:34)
4. *Discourse*: Commissioning of the Twelve Apostles (Mt 9:35–11:1)

The return of Jesus to Galilee functions as a hinge or bridge bringing the prologue to a close with a significant citation from Isaiah (Isa 8:23-91) which sets the tone for the in-breaking of the kingdom with the mission of Jesus to Israel, beginning in Galilee. This next major portion of the gospel (Mt 4:17-11:1) contains two sections of narrative and two of the major discourses of the gospel. It begins with the statement: 'From that moment Jesus began his preaching with the message, "Repent for the kingdom of heaven is close at hand".' (Mt 4:17) The consistent theme running through this whole section is the authority of Jesus and its impact. It begins with the immediate response of the disciples to his authoritative call to discipleship (Mt 4:18-22) and is followed by the summary of his preaching and mighty works and their impact on the people (Mt 4:23-25). His authority in word is then seen in the Sermon on the Mount (Mt 5-7) and his authority in deed is seen in his mighty deeds in the miracle section (Mt 8:1-9:34). It is further emphasised in his conferring of a share in his authority on his chosen Twelve Apostles and in the instruction he gives them in the Missionary Discourse (Mt 10:1-11:1). His authority is so much in evidence that his opponents cannot deny it and ascribe it to the power of the prince of devils (Mt 9:34).

From Mt 11:1 on the spotlight will move from Jesus' authority to the questioning, criticism and hostility that will gather momentum until the final denouement in the Passion Narrative.

1. JESUS BEGINS HIS MISSION MT 4:17-25

Outline of the section:
- a. Call for Repentance. Imminence of the Kingdom (Mt 4:17)
- b. Calling of the First Disciples (Mt 4:18-22)
- c. Summary of Jesus' Mission (Mt 4:23)
- d. Response of the People (Mt 4:24-25)

A. CALL FOR REPENTANCE. IMMINENCE OF THE KINGDOM (MT 4:17)
Now Jesus begins his own (and the reader's) adventure through his ministry as he comes into Galilee proclaiming the imminence of the kingdom and calling on all and sundry to repent, repeating verbatim the proclamation of the Baptist. Calling for repentance Jesus, just as John had done before him, is seen to be solidly within the tradition of the prophets who time and again called on the people of Israel to turn from their evil ways and return to the God of the covenant. The evangelists make it clear that Jesus sees the inauguration of the kingdom in his own person and ministry. The following comment on Mark is equally true of Matthew:

> Jesus shared the belief of his Jewish contemporaries that the fullness of God's kingdom is future, and yet, according to Mark and the other evangelists, Jesus saw in his own person and ministry the beginning or inauguration of God's reign: 'Now is the time of fulfilment; and the kingdom of God is at hand' (Mk 1:15a). Whatever Jesus said or did was in the service of God's kingdom.[1]

---

1. J. R. Donahue and D. J. Harrington, *The Gospel of Mark*, Sacra Pagina, 72.

B. CALLING OF THE FIRST DISCIPLES MT 4:18-22//MK 1:16-20 CF LK 5:1-11

Discipleship

The announcement of Jesus' arrival in Galilee is followed by the calling of the first disciples and their immediate unconditional response. These disciples, the whole group, the Twelve or the inner group of Peter, James and John, will be 'with him' throughout his ministry until they abandon him in Gethsemane and take flight. Matthew, like Mark, presents the call of the disciples as stark and sudden, prior to any miraculous action on Jesus' part, like the calling of a prophet in the Old Testament, without forewarning. It is a reversal of the usual rabbinic procedure where the disciple seeks out the rabbi. It resembles the calling of the prophets (Isa 6:1-13; Jer 1:14-19; Ezek 1:1-3), where the parentage and profession of those called are often given together with their response. The details of leaving family and livelihood, though far less dramatic, are reminiscent of Elijah's call of Elisha, son of Shaphat, who left his family and his servants and sacrificed his oxen using the wood of the plough for the fire (1 Kings 19:19-21). Matthew's account, like Mark's, is in sharp contrast to the account in John's gospel which portrays a previous knowledge of the disciples on Jesus' part during the ministry of the Baptist, or Luke's account of the call after they have already experienced Jesus' works, especially the miraculous catch of fish (Jn 1:35-51; Lk 5:1-11). Unlike Luke or John, Matthew and Mark give no hint of any preparation or previous experience of Jesus' mighty deeds, just a stark call as in the case of the prophets.[2] Furthermore, Jesus' call is not a result of seeing some particular gift or aptitude in those called, but a free act of graciousness on his part.

---

2. This resembles also the calling of some famous philosophers in the Greco-Roman world, such as the calling of Xenophon by Socrates who said to him: 'Follow, then, and learn.' Diogenes Laertius, *Lives of Eminent Philosophers*, 2:48.

The Brothers

The two call narratives are in similar form. The first one, the calling of Simon called Peter, and his brother Andrew, describes Jesus moving, (*peripatôn*)[3] along the shore and seeing the prospective disciples and their work. It describes their relationship as brothers, recounts Jesus' call to them to 'come after me (*deute opisô mou*) and I will make you fishers of men (people)',[4] and their immediate response: 'They immediately (*eutheôs*) left their nets and followed (*êkolouthêsan*) him.' Matthew describes Simon as 'Simon called Peter', which is significant in the light of his future designation as the rock on which Christ builds his church (Mt 16:18). In the calling of the second pair of brothers Jesus is again described as moving: 'having moved on from there' (*probas ekeithen*), he saw two other brothers, James son of Zebedee and his brother John. The narrator tells their names and the fact they were brothers, and names their father and describes their activity, mending the nets in the boat. He called them and 'immediately (*eutheôs*) leaving the boat and their father they followed him (*êkolouthêsan autô*).' In both cases the initiative is entirely with Jesus. He called whom he willed. The two descriptions, 'they followed him' (*êkolouthêsan autô*) outline the response in discipleship which will be very important throughout the story of the ministry.

The reader immediately sees a distinction between the second and the former pair whose father is not named. The former pair are probably older, their father deceased, the second pair younger, their father still alive. The first pair left their nets, symbols of their occupation and security; the second left the boat and their father (Mark adds also the hired men, indicating a successful business), pointing to leaving behind the security of family and occupation. The peer group's criteria of success in life are abandoned: family and tools of trade (nets and boats). They had

---

3. Mark has *paragôn*.
4. See J. Murphy-O'Connor, 'Fishers of Fish, Fishers of Men', *BR* 15/3 (1999) and G. Fischer and M. Hasitschka, *The Call of the Disciple. The Bible on Following Christ*, NY: Paulist, 1999.

left the security of family and livelihood. It is interesting that the mother of the second pair will be inquiring of Jesus later on about positions of prominence in the kingdom (Mt 20:20-23). The call narrative in both cases could be illustrated as follows, with Jesus' act of calling at the centre.

    a. Jesus passes along
        b. He sees them. Family ties/livelihood described
            c. He calls them
        b. They leave family/livelihood
    a. They follow him

The call of Matthew will follow a similar pattern, but in his case it will be a calling of a controversial kind because he is a tax collector, a very unpopular profession putting him on the wrong side of the boundary of acceptability in Israel (Mt 9:9//Mk 2:14). By way of contrast, later on in the ministry, Jesus' calling of the rich young man, whose name is not given or whose parents are not mentioned, but whose personal dispositions and circumstances are described, will fail to elicit a positive response because of his attachment to his many possessions which he fails to leave and follow Jesus (Mt 19:16-22//Mk 10:17-22).

C. SUMMARY OF JESUS' MISSION MT 4:23

Jesus went throughout Galilee teaching in their synagogues and proclaiming the good news of the kingdom, and curing every disease and every sickness among the people. (Mt 4:23)

This summary statement functions, together with the summary in Mt 9:35, as an inclusion or bracket around the Sermon on the Mount (Mt 5-7) and the series of healings (Mt 8-9) which illustrate the actual teaching and healing activity of Jesus, showing him to be mighty in word and deed. His words and deeds form a continuum. What he says is authenticated by the power manifest in his deeds and his deeds are themselves a teaching through action about the nature of the kingdom. They show him to be the shepherd moved to compassion for the sheep (Mt 9:36). He then prepares his disciples/apostles to carry on his mission (Mt 10).

Jesus' healings and exorcisms not only show his power over the forces of sickness and the evil spirits but they restore the ill or possessed person to full active participation in the people of God. Healing a sick or possessed person points beyond the physical healing to a healing of the destructive and alienating effects of sin and highlights the gift of forgiveness. Healing the deaf and the blind are in themselves a call to listen to the word and to see the activity of the kingdom in the person and ministry of Jesus.

D. RESPONSE OF THE PEOPLE   MT 4:24-25

His reputation spread throughout all Syria. Syria was the wider Roman Province and so his reputation is spreading already among the Gentiles, as will be obvious in the next verse from the reference to the crowds coming not only from Galilee (of the Gentiles) but from the (pagan) Decapolis, the ten Greek cities, as well as from (the pagan territory) Transjordan – in addition to the crowds coming from the Jewish area of Jerusalem and Judea. They brought to him all those suffering with every kind of sickness and ailment, together with the possessed, the mentally disturbed and paralytics, and he healed them.

2. THE SERMON ON THE MOUNT: MT 5:1-7:29
Jesus: Mighty in Word

INTRODUCTION TO THE SERMON

i. *Classifying the Sermon*

The Sermon on the Mount is one of the most well known sections of the entire New Testament. It stands out prominently in the gospel of Matthew, and indeed in the New Testament as a whole, somewhat like the Farewell Discourse in John (Jn 14-17). It is nearly four times the length of the somewhat similar 'Sermon on the Plain' in Lk 6:20-24. In its setting in Matthew it outlines a fitting lived response to the proclamation of the kingdom and to the first manifestations of its arrival in the ministry of Jesus. As Jesus' sojourn and testing in the desert recalls the paradigmatic history of the Israelites' testing in the desert, so also this inaugural sermon of Jesus at the approach of the kingdom recalls the great sermon of Moses on the threshold of the Promised Land.

The Sermon has been variously classified as the charter of the kingdom, the law of discipleship,[5] an authoritative interpretation of the Torah for Christians,[6] and a compendium or epitome of the essential teaching of Jesus for Jews. It serves to show Jewish Christians how Jesus' teaching relates to their Jewish background.[7] In showing how the sermon relates to their traditions and fulfils their hopes, it aims to show that far from destroying or rendering obsolete the Law and the Prophets Jesus has come to fulfil them. The sermon, therefore, challenges Israel to find in Jesus' teaching the authentic interpretation of God's will as it is revealed in the Torah. At the same time the sermon interprets the Torah for non-Jewish Christians as they become

---

5. J. P. Meier, *Matthew*, 38.
6. D. J. Harrington, *The Gospel of Matthew*, Sacra Pagina, 76.
7. Luke tends to relate his Sermon on the Plain to converts of a more Hellenised, Gentile or Diaspora background. See H. D. Betz, *The Sermon on the Mount*, Hermeneia, Minneapolis: Fortress, 1975, 70-88.

disciples of Jesus in consequence of his command to 'make disciples of all nations' (Mt 28:19).

ii. Setting in the gospel

The sermon is set in the context of Jesus' teaching the crowds and the disciples (Mt 4:23; 7:29). It is followed immediately and complemented by the section of the gospel that deals with his healing activity (Mt 8:1–9:35). Both sections go together (Mt 5:1–9:35) to illustrate in striking fashion the authority of Jesus in word and deed, the sermon evoking the response of the crowd: 'He taught them with authority and not like their own scribes' (Mt 7:29), and the healings evoking the response: 'Nothing like this has been seen in Israel' (Mt 9:34).[8]

The sermon is set against the background of Jesus' touring of Galilee, teaching in the synagogues, proclaiming the good news of the kingdom and curing all kinds of diseases and sicknesses among the people. As his reputation spread beyond Galilee into Judea and throughout the Roman province of Syria, the crowds came to him from Galilee, the Decapolis,[9] Jerusalem, Judea and Transjordania (Mt 4:23-51). The sermon is his response to seeing these crowds, and though the disciples have a prominent place among the listeners, the crowds are also an essential part of the audience. This is evident from the narrator's comment that when he had finished saying these things his teaching made a deep impression on the crowds (Mt 7:28-29). The crowds here are like the people of Israel assembled at Sinai waiting for Moses to come from the Mountain of Sinai with the Law (Exod 19:17; 34:32) or the people assembled to listen to the Sermon of Moses at the threshold of the Promised Land (Deut 1:1), two pivotal moments in the history of the people of Israel.

---

8. The Sermon on the Mount balances the discourse in Mt 24-25 in the overall structure of the gospel.
9. The term *Decapolis*, literally meaning 'ten cities', refers to the federation of ten Hellenised, Greek-speaking pagan cities across the Jordan. Pliny the Elder gives their names as Damascus, Philadelphia, Raphana, Scythopolis, Gadara, Hippos, Dion, Pella, Gerasa, and Canatha.

'On seeing the crowd he ascended the mountain.' This is an unspecified mountain in Galilee and from the setting one would presume it to be along the western shore of the lake.[10] Reference to the mountain is familiar to readers of the synoptics[11] and reminiscent of Sinai/Horeb with its connotations of the presence and glory of God, the gift of the Law to Moses (Exod 19-20) and the gentle breeze heralding the word of the Lord to Elijah (1 Kings 19). However, the New Testament does not specify the exact location, as to do so would take from the deeper symbolic meaning of the mountain, with its connotations of the divine presence and memories of the encounters on Sinai/ Horeb. Even outside the experience of Israel, in the Ancient Near East and in Greek mythology the mountain was seen as a home of the gods, a place of divine presence, action and revelation.

'He sat down.' The solemnity of the occasion is highlighted by referring to his taking up the official position of the teacher, 'in the chair of Moses', sitting on a seat or bench as the pupils or disciples sat at his feet on the floor. It was the ancient practice of teachers to sit during their teaching, highlighting their dignity and authority.[12] Jesus is regularly described as 'sitting' to teach. He is so described here in the Sermon on the Mount, in the boat (Mt 13:2) and on the Mount of Olives (Mt 24:3). Jesus uses the imagery of 'the chair of Moses' to highlight the importance of the official teachers (Mt 23:2). The solemnity of the occasion is further borne out here in the introduction to the Sermon on the Mount by the liturgical, oracular, prophetic, hieratic formula 'he opened his mouth'.

---

10. Traditionally the Mount of Beatitudes is identified with the area between the Sea of Galilee and the Horns of Hattin, and the Mount of Transfiguration has been identified as Mt Tabor, but it is really the symbolism of ' the (high) mountain' that is important rather than the identity of the locations.

11. The Sermon on the Mount (Mt 5-7), the Transfiguration (Mt 17:1-8) and the final appearance of the Risen Lord (Mt 28: 16-20) are on a (high) mountain in Galilee.

12. J. P. Meier, *Matthew*, 38.

The scene is reminiscent of the scene at Sinai, but with a significant difference. Jesus, though at first glance appearing to wear the mantle of Moses, is not a new Moses receiving a new Law. He stands in the role of the supreme Lawmaker, God, who gave the Law to Moses, and it is the disciples who now fill the role of Moses as they come to receive the 'new', 'fulfilling' interpretation of the Law from Jesus. This role of Jesus is highlighted especially in the antitheses as he repeats 'it was said (that is, 'God said'), but I say to you' and goes on to internalise, deepen, abrogate or extend the precepts of the Law (Mt 5:20-48). This 'authoritative' attitude to the Law and the established customs will be carried through in a practical way in his ministry of word and deed as evidenced in his actions of challenging the current understanding of the Sabbath and the prescriptions for its observance (Mt 12:1-14), in his forgiveness of sins (Mt 9:1-8), in his touching the leper (Mt 8:2-4), in his eating with tax-collectors and sinners (Mt 9:10-13) and in his dramatic and challenging action in the Temple (Mt 21:12-22).

iii. Sources

Three main sources are evident in the sermon as in the gospel as a whole: Mark (or an earlier source edited by Mark and Matthew), Q and M (and both Q and M seem to be composites).[13] Scholarly discussion centres on whether Matthew composed the sermon directly from his sources, whether he inherited a fairly substantial sermon already formed, and whether or how much of the sermon can be traced back to Jesus himself. Even if the sermon originated as an independent collection of Jesus' instructions, an epitome of his essential teaching put together from these various sources, as it now stands it is integrated into the gospel of Matthew. It reflects the main themes of the gospel and fits into the immediate context and into the overall structure of the work. It is this final redaction of the sermon within the gospel that interests us here.

13. For an extensive exposition on the theories about the sources of the Sermon on the Mount, see W. Carter: *What are they saying About Matthew's Sermon on the Mount?* 9-34.

iv. Overarching themes

Fulfilment (*plêroun*) and righteousness (justice) (*dikaiosunê*) are the overarching themes used by Matthew to describe the arrival of the kingdom and the required response to its arrival. The Infancy Narrative and the narratives of Jesus' baptism, temptations and inauguration of his mission in Galilee so far have been replete with references to the fulfilment of scripture, and by implication, the fulfilment of the salvific plan of God. Furthermore, Jesus has come, not to destroy the Law and the Prophets, but to fulfil them (Mt 5:17).

A very important key to Matthew's presentation here and throughout the gospel is his emphasis on the theme of *dikaiosunê*, righteousness (justice). It is used seven times throughout the gospel. Jesus submits to the baptism of John in order to fulfil all righteousness (Mt 3:15). He declares blessed those who hunger and thirst for righteousness and those persecuted for the sake of righteousness (Mt 5:6,10). One is exhorted not to fret and worry about material things but rather to 'seek first the kingdom and its righteousness and all these other things will be given you as well' (Mt 6:33). In relation to obeying the Law (and the Prophets) Jesus appeals for a greater righteousness than that of the scribes and Pharisees (Mt 5:20) and introducing the pious works he warns that righteousness should not be practised in the sight of people to win their admiration (Mt 6:1).[14]

What is this righteousness (justice)? It refers first to God's salvific plan and activity (Mt 5:6, 6:33) and the covenant relationship it sets up between God and the people, resulting in or demanding a spiritual and ethical response to God that responds to and carries out the will of the Father in heaven (Mt 5:10, 20;

---

14. Whereas Luke emphasises love as the overarching category, Matthew emphasises justice/righteousness. Some commentators draw attention to the fact that the great teacher in the Qumran community was known as 'The Teacher of Righteousness'. There is however a significant difference. He taught a community a way of life as they awaited and prepared for the arrival of the messianic figure. Jesus *is* the awaited figure and has inaugurated the kingdom so his teaching on righteousness is a response to its arrival.

6:1).[15] The disorder of sin has broken that saving order, and now the Messiah promises the restoration of covenant righteousness (justice).

The preaching and baptism of John call for repentance, acknowledging that sin has undermined the covenant relationship, which the 'one following him' comes to renew. Jesus' initial statement in the gospel when he approaches John for baptism highlights the fact that his ministry is 'to fulfil all righteousness' (Mt 3:15), that is, to carry out in obedience the saving will/plan of the Father in restoring that relationship. This is almost identical to the sentiments of Jesus in John's gospel: 'I do not seek my own will but the will of him who sent me' and 'We must carry out the work of the one who sent me' (Jn 5:30; 9:4). Righteousness is a fundamental category for all spirituality and moral action, as is evident from Jesus' generalisation: 'Unless your righteousness exceeds that of the scribes and the Pharisees you shall not enter the kingdom of heaven' (Mt 5:20). In the apocalyptic/eschatological context the righteousness of the just will be their vindication at the last judgement.[16]

'Righteousness (justice)' is inextricably related to the theme of fulfilment. It signifies both God's saving activity (Mt 5:6; 6:33) and man's response to it by way of acting in accordance with God's will. Joseph the righteous/just man (*dikaios*) changed his own plans to facilitate the fulfilment of God's plan, so that the scripture was fulfilled (Mt 1:19, 22-23; Isa 7:14). Jesus submitted to John's baptism 'in order *to fulfil all righteousness*' (Mt 3:15). Acting to fulfil God's plan, to carry out God's will in obedience, is the core meaning of righteousness and it constitutes the main challenge of discipleship.

The sermon focuses on fundamental and overarching principles and attitudes that guide both the individual disciple and

---

15. Luke on the other hand, emphasises love and social justice.
16. The devotees at Qumran followed 'the teacher of righteousness' but there is a significant, radical difference to the Teacher of Righteousness at Qumran. Jesus is Son of God, Son of Man, Emmanuel, and Saviour and assumes the authoritative role of lawgiver as he interprets the Law in his teaching and carries it out in his activity.

the community of disciples in the way of righteousness. This is different to the *halakic* or legalistic approach to ethics with its numerous prescriptions, or to impossible counsels of perfection for idealists, such as those in monastic communities. It is far different also to the sermonising of fiery preachers harping on the human weakness of people who fall short of impossible standards. Neither is it a 'putting down' of the Law and the Prophets with a 'superior' teaching but a bringing of them to a new level in the light of Jesus' inauguration of the kingdom.[17] In this sense one can speak of the sermon as 'an ethics of discipleship' and it is a challenge for everyone who allows Jesus to call him/her to God. E. Schweizer states:

> Undoubtedly the Sermon on the Mount is an ethics of discipleship. Sayings concerning discipleship are introduced immediately after the Beatitudes, and the disciple is required to exhibit a righteousness superior to that of the Pharisee. Nevertheless, anyone who allows Jesus to call him to God is a disciple, and so the Sermon on the Mount is addressed to the whole crowd.[18]

D. Senior points out in his commentary on Matthew[19] that a reference to the Law and the Prophets forms a bracket around the body of the sermon, highlighting a fundamental theme of the sermon as a whole. 'Think not that I have come to destroy the Law and the Prophets. I have not come to destroy but to fulfil them' (Mt 5:17) and 'Always treat others as you would like them to treat you. That is the meaning of the Law and the Prophets' (Mt 7:12). The scribes and Pharisees have been the great exponents and teachers of the Law and the Prophets and their teaching should be respected. 'They occupy the chair of Moses.' However, their way of life was not in keeping with their teaching and preaching. 'They do not practise what they preach'

---

17. D. J. Harrington, *The Gospel of Matthew*, 76, points out that the history of the Sermon's interpretation is a miniature history of Christianity.
18. E. Schweizer, *The Good News according to Matthew*, 78f.
19. D. Senior, *Matthew*, Abingdon New Testament Commentaries, Nashville, 1998, 68.

(Mt 23:3) and so the righteousness required of Jesus' disciples is contrasted with that of the scribes and Pharisees. The Sermon on the Mount spells out the implications of the challenge of discipleship in terms of *the greater righteousness*, that is, righteousness greater than that of the scribes and Pharisees (Mt 5:20).

The sermon also has a strong eschatological dimension. It looks ahead to the coming of the Kingdom in its fullness. It is seen in the beatitudes (Mt 5:3-12), in the prayer for the coming of the Kingdom (Mt 6:10) and in the final warnings of the sermon (Mt 7:21-27). The righteous (just) will be vindicated on the Day of Judgement. At the same time the sermon provides an interim ethic, prescribing principles and attitudes for the real situations in which the disciples live in the concrete circumstances of their world in the here and now. This ethic is both individual and communal, avoiding the extremes of an individualistic ethic of perfection or a communal ethic of an unachievable utopia.

It is worthy of special notice that the moral demands follow, rather than precede, both the proclamation of the imminence of the kingdom and the beatitudes which proclaim the blessedness of those for whom it can be said that 'theirs is the kingdom of heaven' (Mt 4:17, 23; 5:3-12).[20] As D. J. Harrington puts it, 'The beatitudes are not entrance requirements but delineation of the characteristics and actions that will receive their full and appropriate eschatological reward.'[21]

v. The Outline of the Sermon

Many suggestions have been made about the outline or main divisions of the sermon but no one suggestion has won the approval of all scholars. A particular difficulty arises when the somewhat obvious structure of the early part of the sermon breaks down into a series of apparently unrelated sayings in the section of the sermon running from Mt 6:19 to 7:12 (from the Lord's Prayer to the warnings about judgement). W. Carter reviews some of the main contributions to the debate in his book,

20. J. P. Meier, *Matthew*, 39.
21. D. J. Harrington, *Matthew*, 83.

What are they saying about the Sermon on the Mount.[22] He draws attention to the fact that the Beatitudes, the greater righteousness and the Lord's Prayer have been taken as the organising principle by different commentators. M. Goulder, for example, sees the first eight beatitudes as the basis of the sermon, functioning as a summary or heading in the rabbinic style of the *kelal*, like the covenant blessings in Deut 27-28, announcing the blessings of the new Law, and then expounding them in reverse order with triple illustrations, again in rabbinic style.[23] D. Patte[24] sees the sermon structured as a chiasm or ring structure, with the greater righteousness, as illustrated by the six antitheses, at the centre of the chiasm (Mt 5:21-47). U. Luz[25] regards the Lord's Prayer as central to the sermon and sees it surrounded and highlighted by a series of ring-like structures. E.Schweizer,[26] H.Hendrickx[27] and W. Grundmann[28] also see the Lord's Prayer as providing the centre for the sermon. G. Bornkamm[29] sees Mt 6:19 to 7:12 as an elaboration of the Lord's Prayer, giving a coherence to the diverse contents of that section which poses a special problem for scholars seeking a neat structural outline.

D. Allison points to the rabbinic use of triads.[30] Triads are very obvious in the sermon. There are three examples of pious living (almsgiving, fasting and prayer) (Mt 6:1-18) and three warnings about judgement that round off the sermon (enter by

---

22. W. Carter, *What are they saying about the Sermon on the Mount*? 35-55.

23. M. Goulder, *Midrash and Lection in Matthew*, London: SPCK 1974.

24. D. Patte, *The Gospel According to Matthew: A Structural Commentary on Matthew's Faith,* Philadelphia, Fortress, 1987.

25. U. Luz, *Matthew 1-7*, Minneapolis: Augsburg, 1989.

26. E. Schweizer, *The Good News According to Matthew*, Atlanta: John Knox, 1975

27. H. Hendrickx, *The Sermon on the Mount*, London: Geoffrey Chapman, 1984.

28. W. Grundmann, *Das Evangelium nach Matthaus*, THKNT 1; 3rd ed.; Evangelische Verlaganstalt, 1972, 204-206.

29. G. Bormkamm, 'Der Aufbau der Bergpredigt,' *NTS* 24 (1977-78), 419-32.

30. D. Allison, 'The Structure of the Sermon on the Mount', *JBL* 106 (1987), 423-45.

the narrow gate, watch out for false prophets and build on rock rather than sand) (Mt 7:13-27).

There are, however, some clear indicators of a general nature that facilitate a general commentary on the sermon. Two pronouncements of Jesus on the Law and the Prophets frame the body of the sermon between the introductory section (the beatitudes and metaphors) and the final warnings: 'Think not that I have come to destroy the law and the Prophets. I have not come to destroy but to fulfil' (Mt: 17) and 'So always treat others as you would like them to treat you; that is the meaning of the law and the Prophets' (Mt 7:12). Seeing these references to the Law and the Prophets as a frame around the body of the sermon leads to the following general outline of the sermon, which I shall basically follow in this commentary.

A. Beatitudes and Metaphors (Mt 5:1-16)
B. The Greater Righteousness (Mt 5:17-7:12)
    a. The Law: The Antitheses (Mt 5:17-48)
    b. Acts of Piety (Mt 6:1-18)
    c. Wisdom Teachings (Mt 6:19-7:12)
C. Warnings about Judgement (Mt 7:13-29)

A. BEATITUDES AND METAPHORS (MT 5:1-16)

a. The Beatitudes: 'Blessed/Happy are they ...'

The Greek word *makarioi*, equivalent of the Hebrew *asharê*, 'blessed', describes a deep, enduring state of happiness or blessedness essentially bound to one's standing before God, a standing that endures through changing and challenging situations and emotions. Such a state is a gift of God, like the 'peace' Jesus promises when he said in the Last Supper discourse in St John's gospel 'Peace I leave with you, a peace the world cannot give I give you' (Jn 14:27). It is often translated as 'happy' which is somewhat inadequate as a translation because it is a word usually used to describe a passing emotional state of happiness or contentment of a purely human kind. The *Catechism of the Catholic Church* puts it very well:

The Beatitudes respond to the natural desire for happiness. This desire is of divine origin: God has placed it in the human heart in order to draw man to the One who alone can fulfil it.[31]

The people declared blessed because of their state, actions or virtues in the beatitudes are said to be the people who constitute, or in whom is found, the kingdom of heaven. The assertion that 'theirs is the kingdom of heaven,' occurring in the first and eighth beatitude, frames the main body of the beatitudes. The state, actions or virtues of those declared blessed are already well rooted in and reflect various Old Testament values and traditions and are reminiscent of a wide variety of scriptural texts. Understanding the biblical background to their state, actions or virtues helps significantly in interpreting and understanding the sermon as a whole. The poor in spirit and mourners, for example, recall Isa 61:1-3, the meek who inherit the earth recall Ps 37:11 and those who hunger and thirst for justice recall Ps 107:5, 8-9. However, the gospel settings bring a critical new dimension to the Old Testament background.

Eight of Matthew's beatitudes in the sermon are in the third person; the ninth is in the second person. The beatitudes in the Wisdom Literature tend to be universal, valid for all people at all times, and so they are stated in the third person. They point to the 'blessedness' or 'happy' state 'in the here and now' of those who live according to the insights, advice and rules of Wisdom (Sirach 25:7-10; cf Ps 1:1). The beatitudes in the prophetic writings, as in Luke, on the other hand, and the blessings and curses in Deuteronomy tend to be addressed to the audience physically present to, or in the mind of, the speaker/writer, and so they are in the second person. In the processional psalms the pilgrims are greeted on their arrival at the temple with a proclamation about their blessed state in the here and now as pilgrims (Ps 84:5-6, 12; 128:1). Often the beatitude comes in a double expression of blessedness (Ps 84:5-6; Sirach 25:7-10).

---

31. *Catechism of the Catholic Church*, English Translation, Dublin: Veritas, 1994, 386.

The opposite of the beatitude is either the 'woe' or the 'curse'. In the Old Testament they both figure widely (Isa 5:8-23; Amos 6:1) but not often together[32] as opposites except in the sermons in Deuteronomy where Moses puts before the people a blessing and a curse (Deut 27:1-28:46).

For Matthew 'blessedness' is inherent in the kingdom, which is already here but not yet fully, so there is both a 'here and now' and an eschatological dimension to the beatitudes. The passive voice and future tense used in the beatitudes (e.g. 'they shall be comforted') emphasise God's future activity while respecting the Jewish reverence for the name of God by not pronouncing it or predicating direct action to God. The main difference in the beatitudes in Matthew, as in the New Testament generally, therefore, is the setting of the promised 'state of blessedness' in the context of the kingdom of heaven. There is a strongly eschatological dimension, though a present dimension is also in evidence through the happiness that accompanies the anticipation of the final possession of the kingdom. The wisdom and eschatological/apocalyptic aspects function together. 'Theirs *is* the kingdom of heaven' and 'They *shall* be comforted.' The timing of the reward is therefore different to that in the Old Testament. The future verbs evoke the final eschatological judgement. So also do the eschatological paradox and reversal of values – the ones the world regards as miserable, Jesus proclaims blessed in anticipation of the final outcome.[33] The promises of comfort, inheriting the earth, experiencing satisfaction, receiving mercy, seeing God, being called children of God all refer primarily to the final judgement and state of blessedness, though they are also enjoyed in the here and now by way of anticipation.

Luke's four beatitudes and four corresponding woes are couched in the second person plural (Lk 6:20-24). They represent Jesus' forthright address, in the manner of the prophets, to the literally poor and hungry. They are usually regarded as older

---

32. Greek Eccles 10:16-17 has a blessing and a curse: 'woe to you, city whose king… blessing to you land, whose king …'
33. J. P. Meier, *Matthew*, 39.

than Matthew's beatitudes and come from the traditional material which scholars call Q. Matthew, on the other hand, spiritualises and universalises eight beatitudes for everyone by using the third person plural which is in fact the more common form of the beatitudes in the Wisdom Literature and related traditions.

Matthew's ninth beatitude is, however, in the second person plural and addressed directly to those suffering persecution.[34] The second person plural is then continued from the ninth beatitude into the metaphors of salt and light in statements which are addressed to the immediate audience (Mt 5:13-16).[35] The beatitudes in Mt 13:16 ('Blessed are your eyes because they see the things you see') and Mt 16:17 ('Blessed are you, Simon bar Jonah, because it was not flesh and blood but my Father in heaven who revealed this to you') are also addressed to the immediate audience. The woes against the scribes and Pharisees are also in the second person and directed at specific targets (Mt 23:13-32).

Matthew has nine beatitudes at the beginning of this sermon. The first eight are stated in the third person and they are expressed in similar form – a promise or assertion of blessedness, and a reason given for the promise: 'Blessed are X for Y.' The first and the eighth close with the declaration/promise 'Theirs is the kingdom of heaven', so they open and close on the same note. The group of eight are divided into two groups of four beatitudes. The final beatitude in each of the two groups of four, numbers four and eight, emphasise 'righteousness/justice'. These eight beatitudes have all the appearances of a tightly knit group to which the ninth was added. The ninth differs in form, in being much longer and in being stated in the second person. The first eight are general, appealing to all persons at all times, but the ninth is directed to the immediate audience/readership,

---

34. The beatitudes in Mt 13:16 and 16:17, 'Blessed are your eyes that see.' and 'Blessed are you, Simon bar Jonah …' are also in the second person, whereas 'Blessed is anyone who takes no offence at me' is in ther third person (Mt 11:6).
35. Matthew reserves his woes for his major confrontation in Mt 23. The woes are loosely parallel to, and in reverse order to the beatitudes.

who appear to be actually experiencing or in danger of experiencing persecution.[36]

i. *Blessed are the poor in spirit, theirs is the kingdom of heaven* (Mt 5:3)

The biblical background to 'the poor in spirit' is the spirituality of the *anawim/annouim*, the poor people of God. Who were they? A look at the spirituality that grew from the awareness of God's care for the poor and suffering in the Old Testament throws light on the question.[37]

God's care for the poor, the humble, the meek, the mourning, the marginalised, the outcast, the exile and the contrite of spirit is a theme running through the Old Testament in the legal, prophetic, and wisdom traditions. Already written into their foundation charter as the Hebrews became the covenant people of God (Exod 22:25-27; 23:11; Lev 19:9-10; Deut 15:7-11), God's care for them became a major theme in the preaching of the prophets. The Books of Isaiah and Hosea contain, for example, some of the most striking passages about God's love and compassion (Isa 57:15; 61:1-3; 66:2; Hos 11:1-9). Furthermore, Amos and Isaiah excoriated the social injustice which militated against God's care for the people (Amos 2:6-16; 8:4-8; Isa 1:16-17; Micah 6:8) assuring those discriminated against that God was on their side and exhorting them to keep God at the centre of their lives.

Nowhere is the spirit of the *anawim* more obvious than in the utterances of the psalmists. Ps 22:25 states: 'When the poor cried the Lord heard/He has never despised the cry of the poor' and Ps 34:18 is in similar vein: 'The Lord is near to the broken hearted and saves the crushed in spirit.' The poor turned to God in

---

36. In the opinion of scholars the beatitudes concerning the poor, the mourners, the hungry, and the longer beatitude on persecution seem to come from Q, and those dealing with the meek, the merciful, the pure of heart and the shorter beatitude about persecution come from M.

37. The Psalms of Solomon (10:6; 15:1) and *The War Scroll* of Qumran (14:7) show that the contemporary community spoke of itself in similar terms as 'poor' and 'poor in spirit'.

their poverty, seeing in God their protector and vindicator, sentiments powerfully reflected in the Ps 23:1: 'The Lord is my shepherd, there is nothing I shall want' and in Ps 16:5-6: 'The Lord is my chosen portion and cup, you hold my lot.' Having God at the centre of their lives enabled them to see the wealth of the unjust as a shifting and deceptive sand. 'Such is the lot of the foolhardy; the end of those who are pleased with their lot ... death shall be their shepherd. Mortals cannot abide in their pomp; they are like the animals that perish' (Ps 49:13, 14, 21). They contrasted that insecurity of the unjust rich with the sure footing of the just person who has little material wealth but has God at the centre of life. The psalms highlight the contrast very well, saying of the unjust and uncaring: 'You set them in slippery places. You make them fall to ruin ... they are destroyed in a moment; slippery are the paths on which you set them' (Ps 73:18), and pointing out that 'The just man's few possessions are better than the wicked man's wealth; for the power of the wicked shall be broken and the Lord will support the just' (Ps 37:16-17).

This 'spirituality' of the 'poor people of God', the *anawim*, evolved and developed over the centuries and righteous Jews who were no longer materially poor adopted it as a way of life and outlook on the world and its riches. They realised their own dependence on God and their utter spiritual poverty without God. God was their only support, other supports were but an illusion, and so they bowed humbly before God in complete trust and were willing to await everything at God's hands.[38] They received everything from God as gift and recognised God's kingdom as a gift that cannot be forced.[39] E. Schweizer states that the title 'poor (in spirit)' became, in the Judaism of Jesus' time, a title of honour for the righteous, and 'poor' and 'righteous' became largely parallel concepts. He makes a very incisive and apt comment:

---

38. J. P. Meier, *Matthew*, 40.
39. D. J. Harrington, *The Gospel of Matthew*, 78.

As early as Isaiah 61:1 the terms 'poor' and 'broken-hearted' or 'broken in spirit' are juxtaposed (cf Prov 16:19; 29:23; Ps 33 (34): 19). In the Judaism of Jesus' time 'poor' had also become a kind of title of honour for the righteous (Ps Sol 5:2, 11; 10:7; 15:1; 18:2- first century BC), because it was an important mark of righteousness and devotion to accept in faith the difficult way of God and not to resist. At the time of Deutero-Isaiah, 'poor' was still a term applied to all Israel, deprived of its own land and living among aliens; in the centuries that followed, the social class of the poor began to apply this term to themselves as distinct from the upper classes. Thus 'poor' and 'righteous' became largely parallel concepts (Sirach 13:17-18; 4QpPs 37 ii.8-11; CD xix.9). Finally, at Qumran we find a formula most closely resembling the one in Matthew: 'poor (or humble) of spirit' (1QM xiv. 6-7); these are people who 'have knowledge of God' and he 'gives firm stance to those whose knees are weak and upright posture to those whose backs are broken' so that they may 'walk perfectly' (cf Mt 5:48).[40]

Whereas Luke's term 'poor' addresses a materially deprived audience, calling them *ptôchoi*, the term usually used for persons reduced to begging, Matthew's 'poor in spirit' casts a much wider net and draws on a broader spirituality which can be enjoyed by all people irrespective of position or social class. The beatitude pronounces them blessed because 'of such is the kingdom of heaven.' It is among these people that the kingdom is accepted, takes root and bears fruit.

ii. *Blessed are those who mourn they shall be comforted*
(Mt 5:4)
The many psalms of individual and communal lamentation show the poor in spirit and the broken hearted turning to God in their distress. They call out in their trouble and sorrow expressing their confidence in the God who listens to their prayers, sees

40. E. Schweizer, *op. cit.*, 86.

their distress and comes to their aid with comforting words and actions. Looking at their history, the people of Israel could say of their ancestors in Egypt or Exile: 'To you they cried and were saved, in you they trusted and were not put to shame' (Ps 22:6). Their covenant-based faith was rooted in the God who heard their cry, saw their toil, their oppression and their misery in Egypt and led them out 'with mighty hand and outstretched arm' and brought them to the land where milk and honey flow (Deut 26:5-9). They felt confident therefore to assert that 'He looked down from his holy height; from heaven the Lord looked at the earth that he might hear the groans of the prisoners and free those condemned to die' (Ps 102:18, 20-21). As a people in crisis they could pray with confidence, knowing that God hears their cry. 'Awake, O Lord, why do you sleep? Arise, do not reject us forever! Why do you hide your face? Why do you forget our affliction and oppression?' (Ps 44:24-25).

During the trauma of the Exile they mourned the loss of freedom and feared the loss of identity when they had lost the land, the temple and the civil and religious institutions that gave expression to their identity as a people and their covenant relationship with God. That terrible experience was the occasion for God's consolation of the mourners of Zion, as had been the case when they cried out to God in Egypt (Sirach 48:24; Deut 26:5-9). God sent the prophets to comfort the mourners and the distressed during the Exile. The prophet, who is usually referred to as Deutero-Isaiah, was commanded to speak comforting words to the people: 'Comfort my people, comfort them, says your God' (Isa 40:1). That 'comforting' activity is again spelled out in Trito-Isaiah as the servant-prophet proclaims the message of comfort to the poor and the mourners. He proclaimed:

> The spirit of the Lord God is upon me, because the Lord has anointed me; he has sent me to bring good news to the oppressed, to bind up the broken-hearted, to proclaim liberty to the captives, and release to the prisoners; to proclaim the year of the Lord's favour, and the day of vengeance of our God; to comfort all who mourn; to provide for those who

mourn in Zion – to give them a garland instead of ashes, the oil of gladness instead of mourning, the mantle of praise instead of a faint spirit (Isa 61:1-3).

Their historical experience as a people enabled the Israelites both as a people and as individuals to pray: 'In you our ancestors put their trust; they trusted and you set them free; to you they cried and were saved; in you they trusted, and were not put to shame' (Ps 22:5-6). Underpinning the prayer in distress was the understanding that, 'The Lord is close to the broken-hearted, those whose spirit is crushed he will save' (Ps 34:19). One can pray with confidence, 'For he did not despise or abhor the affliction of the afflicted (the poverty of the poor). From him he has not hidden his face, but he heard the poor man when he cried' (Ps 22:24). The comforting action of God touched also the sense of guilt and alienation and offered forgiveness of sins. 'Relieve the troubles of my heart and bring me out of my distress. Consider my affliction and my trouble and forgive all my sins' (Ps 25:17-18).

As already seen, the terms 'poor' and 'broken-hearted' or 'broken in spirit' are thus juxtaposed as early as the text of Isaiah 61:1 and that order is followed in the beatitudes. Following the beatitude dealing with *the poor in spirit* the beatitude referring to *those who mourn* assures them that they will be comforted, that is, God will comfort them. The comforting speech and activity of the prophets is re-echoed by Jesus. His ministry is now the moment of comforting for those who are open to seeing the comforting action of God in the here and now of Jesus' ministry and in the promise of the definitive arrival of the kingdom. This will be spelled out, for example, in Jesus' reply to the messengers of the Baptist when Jesus interprets his ministry in these prophetic terms: 'Go and tell John what you have seen and heard. The blind see, the lame walk, the lepers are cleansed, the deaf hear, the dead are raised and the poor have the good news preached to them' (Mt 11:4-5). Similarly, in his programmatic sermon in Nazareth in Luke's gospel, Jesus explains his ministry in similar terms (Lk 4:18-19). Simeon was waiting for the comforting of

Israel (Lk 2:25) and in the Farewell Discourse in John's gospel Jesus promises to send the Paraclete as comforter (Jn 14:16-17; 26; 16:7-11).[41]

All kinds of mourning are covered in the reference to those who mourn. People mourn their own and others' oppression, poverty, dislocation, and every kind of physical and mental suffering. They mourn the loss of innocence and the presence of sin in the world. They mourn their own mortality and the mortality of those around them. As Jesus inaugurates the kingdom the mourners encounter the comforting action of God in the here and now, in anticipation of the eschatological establishment of the kingdom when in a final and irreversible way 'they shall be comforted,' that is, God will comfort them

iii. Blessed are the meek they shall inherit the earth (Mt 5:5)

The third beatitude recalls the words of Psalm 37:11 which states that 'the meek/humble (anawim/praeis) shall possess (inherit) the earth.' In many ways the 'meek' resemble the 'poor in spirit'. In our world today the terms 'meek' and 'humble' have connotations of being a weak or soft person, a 'wimp'. This is definitely not the meaning of the LXX and New Testament word praeis, which translates the Hebrew anawim, the same word as that in general use for the poor of YHWH. Perhaps the best way to describe the meek is to say that they are the opposite to the proud, the self assured and the overconfident, who are described in the psalms as 'wearing their pride like a necklace' and 'having their mouths in the heavens and dictating to the earth' (Ps 73:6, 9). The meek are those aware of their true position as creatures before God the creator, subject to God's law, in need of God's grace and forgiveness, docile and willing to learn, considerate, unassuming and well disposed to God and other people. God is on their side and they will survive when the wicked and proud are defeated (Ps 37:10, 17). The wisdom tradition points out that it is 'better to be humble among the lowly than to share

41. The paraklêtos brings paraklesis, that is, comforting words and/or action.

the booty with the proud' (Prov 16:19), and that 'a man's pride brings him humiliation but he who humbles himself will win honour' (Prov 29:23). Jesus is the supreme example of the meek/humble person. J. P. Meier puts it very well:

> The truly meek are, in the Bible, the considerate, the unassuming, the peaceable towards God and man. They do not push their own plans to the detriment of God's saving plan. Jesus, the Wisdom of God, is the model of the meek man who gives rest to others (11:29), the meek King who brings salvation through his own sufferings (21:5), the Son who through meekness gains all authority (28:18).[42]

'Inheriting the earth' is a promise reflecting the biblical promise to Abraham that he would inherit the land of Canaan (Gen 17:8), the promise to the Israelites that they would inherit the land of Canaan, flowing with milk and honey (Deut 1:7-8) and the promise in Ps 37:11 that the poor/meek would inherit the land. Jesus was promised the kingdoms of the world if he worshipped Satan (Mt 4:11). At the end of the gospel he will reverse that process and send his own representatives into the whole world to make disciples of all nations and to baptise them in the name of the Father, the Son and the Holy Spirit (Mt 28:16-20). The promise of 'inheriting the earth' is the promise to share in the kingdom of heaven established by the one who is 'meek and humble of heart' (Mt 11:29) as the world responds to his messengers.[43] This universal mission is in keeping also with the apocalyptic tradition, which sees the promise to inherit the earth in terms of the righteous inheriting the whole world (1 Enoch 5:7). The *Catechism of the Catholic Church* states the matter very clearly:

> The Beatitudes are at the heart of Jesus' preaching. They take up the promises made to the chosen people since Abraham. The Beatitudes fulfil the promises by ordering them no

---

42. J. P. Meier, *Matthew*, 40.
43. Ibid.

longer merely to the possession of a territory, but to the kingdom of heaven.[44]

iv. *Blessed are those who hunger and thirst for righteousness
(justice) for they shall be satisfied* (Mt 5:6)

In the Old Testament the poor and lowly are promised that
their hunger will be satisfied (1 Sam 2:5: Pss 107: 5, 8, 9, 36-41;
146:7). The hungry will be fed in days of famine (Ps 37:19). The
beatitude on hunger in Luke's Sermon on the Plain, in its direct
address to 'you who are hungry now', reflects very closely this
attitude of confidence in God while actually experiencing
hunger (Lk 6:21).

Matthew, on the other hand, spiritualises and universalises
the beatitude by expanding the hunger into 'hunger and thirst'
and describing the object of the hunger and thirst as 'righteousness'. He thus fits the beatitude into his overall programme of
righteousness. Already in the Old Testament, hungering and
thirsting were regular metaphors for seeking God's word,
mercy and presence (Amos 8:11; Isa 55:1-2, 7; Ps 42:3). According
to Baruch 2:18, only the 'soul that hungers' can extol God's glory
and righteousness. The imagery of Psalm 42 is striking: 'As a
deer thirsts for flowing streams so my soul thirsts for you, my
God. My soul thirsts for God, the living God, when shall I come
and behold the face of God?' (Ps 42:2-3). Furthermore, hungering
for righteousness also means a longing for the anointed one, the
spirit-filled servant or Davidic king who will bring justice to
those suffering from poverty, social injustice, exclusion or violence among the people (Ps 146:7-10) and the one who will bring
true justice and peace to the nations (Isa 9:7; 42:1-4; 49:6). This
longing looks forward to the coming kingdom and the righteousness of God that will be realised in it.

The gift of the land flowing with milk and honey, the fertility
of the land and the animals, the richness of harvest and vintage
and the signs of plenty were seen as a blessing from God.
Conversely, want and hunger were seen in Old Testament times

---

44. *Catechism of the Catholic Church*, 385.

and in the Judaism of Jesus' period as God's beneficent chastisement.[45] Hunger caused people to turn to God in repentance, remembering his beneficent actions in the past and seeking his provident action in the present and future. As in the case of 'the poor in spirit', the repentant attitude and spirituality of the people surviving in times of famine lived on beyond the point of crisis and a 'spiritualised hunger and thirst' replaced the actual hunger and thirst. The life force and survival instinct driving one in the case of hunger or thirst provide a most powerful image for the total focus on the will of God driving one to seek *righteousness/justice*

Though Jesus inaugurates the kingdom, righteousness will only come fully at the eschatological time laid out in God's plan since righteousness means God's saving activity and the covenant relationship which that activity sets up between God and man.[46] The disorder of sin has broken that saving order, and Jesus at the last supper will promise the restoration of covenant righteousness/justice under the image of the sacrificial meal in which the bread and wine become his body given and his blood poured out for sin. This covenant in his death looks forward to satisfying all hunger and thirst at the table of the eschatological banquet where the covenant is made anew (Mt 26:26-29).[47]

In an apocalyptic context, righteousness refers to the vindication of the just at the last judgement. The satisfaction promised is ultimately eschatological.[48] Jesus looks forward to this time when righteousness will be finally established fully and promises that 'many will come from the east and the west and will take their places with Abraham and Isaac and Jacob at the banquet in the kingdom of heaven (Mt 8:11; cf Mt 22:1-14 / / Lk 14-16-24; cf Lk 22:30). The real fulfilment will be God's eschatological act, emphasised by the use of the future tense. Those who hunger

---

45. For example, *Psalms of Solomon and Testaments of the Twelve Patriarchs*.
46. J. P. Meier, *Matthew*, 41.
47. J. P. Meier, Ibid.
48. D. J. Harrington, *Matthew*, 79.

and thirst for righteousness are blessed because at the eschatological banquet they will be satisfied.

v. *Blessed are the merciful for they will obtain mercy* (Mt 5:7)

A more 'active' dimension in the beatitudes now becomes
obvious. Showing mercy, making peace and pursuing righteousness to the point of being persecuted are clearly 'active'
roles (*eleêmones, eirênopoioi, dediôgmenoi heneken dikaiosunês*).

Mercy is an attribute of God and is seen above all in his forgiveness. God forgives and expects those who receive or expect
to receive his forgiveness to forgive others in return. This is
spelled out in the Lord's Prayer (Mt 6:12) and in the admonition
about forgiveness that follows it (Mt 6:14-15). It is strikingly illustrated in the parable of the debtor who begged for and received remission of a huge debt and then refused to show mercy
and remit a far smaller debt, a parable which is rich in the language of mercy and equally stark in the description of the lack of
mercy and the punishment it incurred: 'Showing compassion,
he forgave him the debt ... You should have shown mercy as I
showed mercy to you.' When the fellow servants appealed to
the master (*kyrios*) in the face of such a lack of mercy on the part
of the one who had been shown mercy the master rescinded his
own remission of the debt and imposed a severe punishment
(Mt 18:23-25). Jesus' own compassionate ministry illustrates
great mercy (Mt 9:13; 12:7) but his teaching makes it clear that
anyone who does not show mercy cannot count on God's mercy,
especially when those refused mercy appeal to God (Mt 6:15;
18:35).

Mercy also finds expression in kindness to the poor. The wisdom tradition in Proverbs pronounces a blessing on those who
show such kindness (Prov 14:21 and 17:5) (LXX). Showing
mercy is the mark of the 'just man' (Ps 37:21). In his condemnation of the Pharisees Jesus rejects a legalistic piety that neglects
mercy, a quality which he describes as 'one of the weightier matters of the Law' (Mt 23:23). The Pharisees are condemned because they put great emphasis on some aspects of the Law but

they neglected 'the weightier matters such as justice, mercy and good faith' (Mt 23:23). Jesus also states that mercy is more important than rituals and sacrifices. He twice quotes Hosea's remark that God requires mercy, not sacrifice (Hos 6:6; Mt 9:13; 12:7). The scene of final judgement in Mt 25:31-46 makes it clear that mercy/compassion for the poor and the marginalised will be the acid test for inheriting the kingdom.

The beatitude states that the merciful are blessed because they will obtain mercy. A similar view is expressed in the Letter of James that states that human mercy triumphs over God's judgement (James 2:13).

vi. *Blessed are the pure of heart for they shall see God* (Mt 5:8)

Placing this beatitude about the 'pure of heart' between the beatitudes about mercy and peacemaking alerts one to its active character. Though it appears to be a passive state or condition, 'pure of heart' sits comfortably between these beatitudes and is in keeping with the broader biblical background/context where righteous actions and speech are seen to proceed from a pure heart.

In biblical thought the heart is not only the seat of the emotions but a person's innermost being which shapes one's entire life, often unconsciously.[49] From early on in their history the people of Israel were reminded that purity of heart was more important than pious acts and ritual sacrifice (1 Sam 15:22; Isa 1:10-17). One must be clean in one's inmost being, in the heart, where one thinks and makes decisions (cf Ps 24:3-5). The call for circumcision of the heart in contrast to purely ritual circumcision of the flesh is heard on several occasions (Deut 10:16; 30:6; Jer 4:4; Jer 9:24-26; Ezek 11:19). The prophets regularly criticised the people for their purely external religion not matched by internal dispositions. Isaiah uttered the well known harsh words that are re-echoed in the gospels: 'This people honours me with their lips but their heart is far from me' (Isa 29:13; cf Mt 15:8; Mk 7:6). Jeremiah delivered a scathing attack on the temple personnel,

---

49. E. Schweizer, *Matthew*, 93.

the cult, the people, and the religious and political leaders (Jer 7-9). He issued a threat of punishment for all who were 'circumcised only in the flesh' together with other nations and groups who are 'uncircumcised in heart' (Jer 9:24-26). He spoke of a new covenant with a new law written on their hearts (Jer 31:33) and in this he was followed by Ezekiel who spoke of a new covenant in which God would take out the heart of stone from the people and give them a heart of flesh (Ezek 36:26).

This concern with the disposition of the heart is a central theme in many of the Psalms. There is an acute awareness of God as the observer of one's inner disposition. The psalmist feels free to address God in the words: 'You who test the minds and hearts, O righteous God' (Ps 7:10) or to say: 'O Lord, you have searched me and known me ... you discern my thoughts from far away ... even before a word is on my tongue, O Lord, you know it completely' (Ps 139:1-4). The righteous can say to God: 'Examine me Lord, and try me; test my heart and my mind' (Ps 26:2), and 'If you try my heart, if you visit me by night, if you test me, you find no wickedness in me; my mouth does not transgress' (Ps 17:3).

This disposition of the heart is not just a passive attitude or disposition. It manifests itself in right conduct and wise speech before God and neighbour. Again this is obvious in the Psalms. 'Who shall ascend the mountain of the Lord? Who shall stand in his holy place? Those who have clean hands and pure hearts.' (Ps 24:3-4; cf Ps 15:1-2). The psalmist prays: 'Let the words of my mouth and the meditation of my heart be acceptable to you, O Lord' (Ps 19:14). Repentance is also a mark of the pure heart. David's prayer of repentance makes an appeal to God in the words: 'in the secret of my heart teach me wisdom' (Ps 51:4, 12). Thus the sinner prays for inner cleansing, a simple directness of intention and attitude, and a pure or uncontaminated motivation in the things relating to God. The righteous one prays: 'I will study the way that is blameless ... I will walk with integrity of heart ... perverseness of heart shall be far from me' (Ps 101:2.4).

In line with this Old Testament insight, the New Testament

focuses on the importance of proper inner dispositions. Jesus warns the Pharisees about their fixation on external cleanliness by pointing out that real decisions involving clean and unclean take place in the heart. It is not the things that go in through the mouth but the things that come out through the mouth from within a man, from his heart, that make him unclean (Mt 15:16-18). 'A man's words flow out from what fills his heart '(Mt 12:34). Matthew's account of Jesus' severe criticism of the Pharisees points to the difference between their external piety and their internal dispositions. Inside they are full of extortion and wickedness/intemperance (Mt 23:26). Jesus warns against judging by external appearances. One's outward performance may be very different from one's inner disposition, as in the case of the false prophets who come 'disguised as sheep, but underneath are ravenous wolves' (Mt 7:15).

Contemporaneously with the New Testament the community at Qumran practised ritual baptism as an external manifestation of inner cleanliness and the Manual of Discipline, emphasising the importance of inner dispositions, warned that mere washing could not make a person clean. It is God himself who will finally 'purge all the acts of man and refine him by destroying every spirit of perversity in his flesh, cleansing him by a holy spirit and sprinkling upon him the spirit of truth like waters of purification to cleanse him' (IQS 3:7-9; 4:21; 5:4; 1QH 16:12; cf Ezek 36:25-27).

On the broader New Testament canvas Paul tells the Romans that 'the real circumcision is in the heart' (Rom 2:29). Elsewhere he speaks of innocence and purity (2 Cor 1:12; Phil 1:10; 2:15). The letters to Timothy advise the young church official that 'there should be love, coming out of a pure heart, a clear conscience and a sincere faith' (1 Tim 1:5) and exhort him to 'fasten your attention on holiness, faith, love and peace, in union with all those who call on the Lord with pure minds' (2 Tim 2:22). D. J. Harrington puts it well:

... 'pure in heart' characterises people of integrity whose

moral uprightness extends to their inmost being and whose actions and intentions correspond.[50]

'Pure of heart' indicates sincere, unfeigned devotion to God, resulting also in one's attitude and activity towards one's neighbour. Being pure in heart implies that one is not harming or plotting harm against anyone. Such a disposition is characteristic of those 'who seek the face of the God of Jacob.' Only such undivided hearts can see God (Ps 51:4,12; Isa 6:5). They will be vindicated (Pss 24:3-6; 51:10; 73:1). This overarching insight of the scriptures is crystallised in the beatitude: 'Blessed are the pure of heart for they shall see God.'

The promised vindication or reward for the pure of heart is that they shall see God. In the Old Testament the vision of God was deemed impossible for man. No one can see God and live (cf Isa 6:5). Jesus speaks of such a vision as a prerogative of the angels (Mt 18:10). The Old Testament emphasis on interior attitude and purity of heart was linked to ritual cleanliness and guaranteed access to the temple and to the experience of God in worship. When the psalmist prayed: 'When can I enter and see the face of God? '(Ps 42:2-3), the desire was to see the vision of God in the Temple. In New Testament times the emphasis shifted to an eschatological experience of God's presence. The apocalyptic and rabbinic understanding saw the vision of God as reserved for the just in paradise. No longer does the hope of seeing God refer to visiting the Jerusalem temple but to the last judgement. However, it also has a relevance to the here and now approach to God in prayer and worship, as is obvious from the repeated statements about forgiveness of one's fellows and the command to leave one's gift at the altar, to go and be reconciled to the estranged brother, and then to enter the presence of God to offer one's gift (Mt 5:23-24). Matthew twice highlights Jesus' statement in which he contrasts mercy with the merely outward performance of cultic acts, quoting the words of Hosea: 'What I want is mercy not sacrifice' (Mt 9:13: 12:7; cf Hos 6:6). The beati-

---

50. D. J. Harrington, *op. cit.*, 79.

tude of the pure of heart follows naturally on the beatitude of the merciful and is in turn followed by the related beatitude referring to the peacemakers.

vii. *Blessed are the peacemakers for they shall be called sons (children) of God* (Mt 5:9)

This beatitude refers not simply to 'lovers of peace' or 'peaceful people', but to those who actively cooperate in bringing about peace, the peacemakers, *eirênopoioi*. This beatitude blends with Matthew's strong emphasis on forgiveness, mercy and reconciliation. The Hebrew word for peace, *shalôm*, basically means fullness and as a greeting refers to the fullness of God's gifts. It can be seen also as 'wholeness' in the sense of 'a perfect state of wellbeing and integration in the individual and society on every level.'[51] The peacemakers will be called, that is, they will be, and will be seen to be, children of God because they act in accordance with God's own forgiveness, mercy and reconciling love. They thus prove themselves to be children of God who causes his sun to rise on good and bad alike and his rain to fall on the just and the unjust alike (Mt 5:45). A similar emphasis on peacemaking was to be found in rabbinic circles in the wake of the destruction of Jerusalem and the temple. Those who made peace were promised the salvation that could formerly have been obtained only by a sacrifice at the altar.[52]

In the Old Testament the term 'son of God' was used for the angels, the people of Israel, the prophets, the just ones and the anointed king. It signified various kinds of special relationship with God. In the New Testament Jesus brings this relationship with the Father to a new level, but distinguishes between his own relationship with the Father and that of his disciples, as for example by his use of 'my Father' and 'your Father' (cf Jn 20:17). However, J. P. Meier points out that there was no close association of peacemaking and being a son of God in the Old Testament except perhaps in the case of Solomon, who was a

---

51. J. P. Meier, *Matthew*, 42.
52. E. Schweizer, *Matthew*, 94.

peaceful man (whose name signifies peace) and, as anointed king, he was an adopted son of God.[53] Peace is God's gift and perfect peace will come only with the kingdom. However, the following of Jesus in the here and now demands the active pursuit of peace. The required attitude and work of the peacemakers will be spelled out in practical detail in the exhortations to reconciliation and love of enemies further on in the sermon (Mt 5:21-26, 43-48) and in other sections of the gospel (Mt 18). The peacemakers 'will be called sons (children) of God' especially when they are so declared by God at the judgement.

viii. *Blessed are those who have been persecuted for the sake of righteousness, for theirs is the kingdom of heaven* (Mt 5:10)

As seen already, righteousness signifies both God's saving activity (Mt 5:6; 6:33) and man's response to it by way of acting in accordance with God's will. It refers first to God's justice and then to human response to God and neighbour. The beatitude declares blessed those who are persecuted in the cause of righteousness and states that theirs is the kingdom of heaven. These are the people who respond to the will of God in their lives and pursue justice, mercy, and peacemaking. In this they manifest the presence of the kingdom. They may provoke a reaction and incur the wrath of people whose lifestyle, interests and values are threatened or challenged by their pursuit of righteousness / justice.

'Those who have been persecuted in the cause of righteousness' (*dediôgmenoi heneken dikaiosunês*) refers to all those who have been persecuted and still suffer as a result. The perfect tense has the connotation of a past action or experience that has consequences in the present. The prophets and the Baptist had preached repentance, justice, mercy and peacemaking and had suffered as a result, and by the time of Matthew's gospel Jesus himself and many of his followers had followed in their footsteps. The fiercely savage persecution of Nero had already taken

---

53. J. P. Meier, *Matthew*, 42.

place in Rome and was obviously known to the broader Christian community. Suspicion on the part of secular authority and society as a whole, and hostility on the part of other Jews in the divisions that emerged after the tragic events of 70AD, were already a reality for many of Matthew's intended readers. The kingdom of heaven is taking root and manifesting itself in the lives of the people who pursue righteousness, the carrying out of the will of God in the face of such hostility and persecution.

This beatitude forms an inclusion with the first beatitude so the collection of eight beatitudes opens and closes with the declaration that those whose beatitude is being declared are those to whom the kingdom belongs, 'for theirs is the kingdom of heaven' (Mt 5: 3, 10). This eighth beatitude also parallels the fourth with its emphasis on righteousness (Mt 5:6, 10). This emphasis on righteousness will again emerge in the sermon in the criticism of the shallow righteousness of the scribes and Pharisees (Mt 5:10). The theme of persecution forms a link with the following beatitude, the ninth, which changes style and addresses a specific audience, applying the universal statement of beatitude to a particular group.

ix. *Blessed are you when men revile you and persecute you*
and utter all kinds of evil against you falsely on my account.
Rejoice and be glad, for your reward is great in heaven, for so
men persecuted the prophets who were before you. (Mt 5:11-12)

The previous 'general' beatitude expressed in the third person is now expanded and addressed to a particular audience in the second person. The persecution in the eighth beatitude is 'for the sake of righteousness' and here in the ninth it is described in terms of 'for my sake', that is 'for Jesus' sake'. It parallels the direct address of Luke's beatitude on persecution (Lk 6:22). This beatitude can be taken along with the following statements on salt and light as an address to the disciples (and all followers) about their life and role in the world. The beatitude, however, speaks more of suspicion, calumny and false accusations as though the active persecution is past and the ripples continue in

society. A warning about persecution from Jew and Gentile will
be spelled out in both the mission and eschatological discourses
(Mt 10:16-31; 24:9; cf 23:24).

Luke, on the other hand, is very forthright and addresses the
community right in the midst of active persecution as he speaks
of 'hatred, exclusion, reviling and casting out' (Lk 6:22). Luke
makes no explicit mention of the false accusations (Lk 6:20).
'False accusations' (*pseudomenoi*) reflect the comment on persecution in 1 Pet 2:19-20.[54]

The reference to 'your reward' is in line with the biblical tradition that God rewards the just ones who are persecuted.
Matthew's addressees stand in the succession of the martyred
prophets, of the Baptist and of Jesus himself. In his series of
woes Jesus will place the scribes and Pharisees in the line of succession to those who killed the prophets whose tombs/monu-
ments they are now building (Mt 23:29-30).

Summing up in relation to the call to rejoice in their sufferings, J. P. Meier states:

> Christians must constantly exult with the eschatological joy
> of the saved, who have learned to see in their suffering the
> sign of their election.[55]

b. Metaphors of Salt and Light: The Nature of Discipleship

The second person address of the ninth beatitude provides a
transition to the assurance now given to the disciples (and all
followers) with an accompanying exhortation, that they are the
salt of the earth and the light of the world. The contrast with
what has preceded is as striking as it is ironic since the two beatitudes about persecution are followed by two metaphors pointing to the important role these same persecuted, despised disciples can have in society. The persecuted disciples might be
despised, slandered or pitied by the world, but they are pointers

---

54. The participle *pseudomenoi* (falsely) is omitted in western texts. See
M. W. Holmes, 'The Text of Mt 5:11', *NTS* 32, (1986), 283-6.
55. J. P. Meier, *Matthew*, 43.

to the presence of the kingdom and play their part in its establishment. They serve to define the identity of the faithful followers of Jesus. Those who see their good works will give glory to the Father in heaven. Though their identity is firmly rooted in Israel's identity as God's people, their significance now reaches beyond Israel. There is a universal ring to 'salt of the earth', 'light of the world' and 'in the sight of men.' The final commission to make disciples of all nations is foreshadowed here (Mt 28:16-20).

Striking sayings and metaphors, like those about salt and light, were transmitted independently in the various New Testament traditions and are applied and edited into their texts by the various evangelists and writers. Some of them are to be found also in the apocryphal writings. The parable of the light is to be found in the Gospel of Thomas and the image of the city is found both in the Gospel of Thomas (32) and in the Oxyrhynchus papyri. Matthew's version of the sayings about salt (cf Mk 9:49-50//Lk 14:34-35) and light (cf Mk 4:21//Lk 8:16) are found widely in the New Testament

Salt

Salt is needed for the proper functioning of the body and its vital presence in the body is witnessed in blood, sweat and tears. It purifies and disinfects. It destroys impurities and it preserves life and health. In New Testament times long before the invention of the refrigerator it was vital for preserving food and for keeping it wholesome. Salt also seasons food and makes it palatable and pleasant to eat. It was used to prevent wounds from festering. It could be a catalyst in making fire. It was used in making covenants and in sacrifices (Lev 2:13; Ezek 43:24). The rabbis spoke of the Torah as salt. It was so important that soldiers were paid in part with a ration of salt, hence the saying 'worth one's salt' and the modern term 'salary'. The imagery points to the followers of Christ as persons who are penetrated with the life, vision and message of Christ. Such persons' presence and witness, expressing itself in teaching and example is an

agent of health and preservation in society, and it seasons living
with the good deeds of the kingdom initiated in Jesus' ministry.
Such a presence and influence are aptly described as 'salt of the
earth', the earth symbolising the whole of humanity. Salt does
not lose its flavour but can be adulterated with other chemicals
(as in the Dead Sea) or diluted through contact with water and
so lose its effectiveness. So, too, there must be nothing insipid in
discipleship, for if it is watered down, if the witness ceases or is
not in evidence, it loses its effectiveness, and may be rejected.
Like the insipid salt it is cast aside, overlooked and regarded as
having no value. It is thrown out and trodden on by the people.

Light

Jesus now applies the imagery of light to the disciples and
followers. 'You are the light of the world' highlights the obligation to witness to the world by 'good deeds/works' which will
result in the world's giving of glory to the Father in heaven. 'Let
your light so shine before men so that seeing your good works
they will give glory to your Father in heaven' (Mt 5:16).

Matthew introduced Jesus' mission in Galilee with the imagery of light, drawn from Isaiah: 'The people that walked in
darkness have seen a great light'(Mt 4:12-17; Isa 9:1). The Old
Testament spoke in terms of the light of God's dwelling, presence and influence. It was the vocation of God's people Israel to
be a light to the nations (Isa 42:6; 49:6). John's gospel places huge
emphasis on light and walking in the light. For John, Jesus is the
light of the world (Jn 8:12; 9:5) and the disciples are exhorted to
walk in that light (Jn 3:21; 11:9-10; 9:4). People who are afraid to
come into the light are those who are aware that their evil deeds
will be exposed (Jn 3:20). The New Testament has several texts
that deal with Christians as 'children of light' (Rom 2:19; 13:11-
14; 1Pt 2:12; 2:9; 5:8; Col 1:13; Eph 5:8-14; Heb 6:4).[56]

Here in the Sermon on the Mount, Jesus tells the disciples
(and through them all followers) that they are the agents of the
light. 'You are the light of the world.' They are like the city on

56. Cf M Mullins, *Called to be Saints*, Veritas, Dublin, 1991, 181, 308-310.

the hill that is seen by all. It is so prominent that it cannot be hidden. Similarly their light is to shine for all in the house. It is lit in order to be placed on a lamp-stand, not to be hidden under a tub (measuring bowl). In the small windowless one-roomed house the rush lamp would be quenched by placing a measuring bowl on it to contain the smoke, the unpleasant smell of fumes and any possible sparks. In other words one does not light a lamp in order to hide or extinguish it. The disciples and followers are told that they must be witnesses to others. They must not be afraid, shy or turned in on self, but witness openly to the light that has come in Christ.

They are called to witness through what they are (salt and light) and what they do (their good deeds). The good deeds are not specified here. The rest of the Sermon on the Mount and the other discourses and example of Jesus will supply the details of such deeds.

The ultimate goal is the glory of the Father in heaven. 'Father in heaven' is a designation characteristic of Matthew. The emphasis on the glory of the Father is very close to the theme of glory in John's gospel.

B. THE GREATER RIGHTEOUSNESS (MT 5:17-7:12)

a. The Law/Torah: The Antitheses (Mt 5:17-48)

Statement of Principle (Mt 5:17-20)

Matthew presents Jesus' programmatic statement of his attitude to the Law and of the absolute observance, 'the greater righteousness', which he requires of his disciples and followers in Mt 5:17-20.[57] These verses serve as an introduction or transition to the six antitheses that follow where six examples of 'the greater righteousness' are spelled out. They give an assurance of continuity in the face of what may be perceived as a radical reassessment of the six precepts examined. They serve to underline the organic relationship or continuity between Jesus' teaching and the Torah, and consequently between Judaism and

---

57. D. Senior, *Matthew*, 73.

Christianity, especially as lived in Matthew's community. They show the relationship as one of fulfilment, a far cry from any idea of abolishing or destroying the Torah. Jesus affirms and establishes the Law rather than downgrading or nullifying it.[58]

In stating, 'I have come' Jesus is pointing to the fulfilment of the messianic expectation of the 'one who is to come', 'the one coming into the world'. He combines the Law and the Prophets as together they signify the forward movement of the Old Testament scriptures towards their fulfilment at the coming of the Messiah and the inauguration of the kingdom. This understanding will be highlighted in Jesus' statement that 'all the Prophets and the Law prophesied until John' (Mt 11:13).[59] There is, however, a fundamental shift in emphasis. Traditionally the Law stood at the centre of the religious universe of the Jews, but now for Matthew, it is Jesus, and not the Law who stands as the decisive centre of his religious universe.[60] The question is now: 'How do Jesus and his teaching relate to the Law? What does he mean by saying he has come to fulfil the Law and the Prophets?'

'Amen I say to you' introduces Jesus' solemn statement about the enduring quality of the Law, somewhat parallel to the statement in Deutero-Isaiah and the First Letter of Peter about the word of the Lord enduring forever (Isa 40:6-8; 1 Pet 1:24-25). To illustrate his point Jesus uses the imagery of two aspects of the alphabet. 'No *iota* and no *hook* will pass from the Law.' The *iota* was the smallest letter in the Greek alphabet and is probably meant to represent the *yodh*, the smallest letter of the Hebrew alphabet. The *hook*, sometimes called *tittle*, may be the small stroke at the angular base of the letter *beth* (b) to distinguish it from the curved base of the letter *kaph* (k). The point being made, however, is quite clear. The Law will endure in all its integrity until 'heaven and earth pass away' and 'until all things are fulfilled' (Mt 5:18).

---

58. D. J. Harrington, *Matthew*, 83.
59. Luke does not mention 'prophesied' in the // statement in Lk 16:16. He just states 'the Law and the prophets until John'.
60. J. P. Meier, *Matthew*, 46.

The *iota* and the *hook* are now interpreted in terms of the least commandment. Some rabbis distinguished between grave and light commandments. For example, the command to honour one's parents (Deut 5:16) was seen as a grave commandment, the commandment not to capture a mother bird sitting on a nest of eggs was seen as a light commandment (Deut 22:6-7). Some rabbis like Rabbi Judah was wary of this distinction and recommended that one should pay heed to the light precept as to the grave one.[61] So too Matthew rejects the distinction and regards the whole Law as important. The scribe's question later in the gospel about the first or most important commandment reflects this debate (Mt 22:34-40; Mk 12:28-34).

Teachers who are not faithful to the Law, even to its least commandments, are condemned to the last place in the kingdom. Those who are faithful in its interpretation and in carrying it out in their lives will be the great ones in the kingdom. Teaching must be accompanied by action, by 'doing' what one teaches and practising what one preaches. Later in the gospel, as Jesus excoriates the scribes and Pharisees (a collective characterisation in Matthew for official Judaism opposed to Jesus), he accuses them of not practising what they preach. He says to do what they say, but not what they do (Mt 23:1-3). In the final instruction to the disciples when he gives them their universal mission he tells them to 'teach (all nations) to observe all that I have commanded you' (Mt 28:20). Observing/doing all the precepts is of absolute importance, not just knowing, extolling and preaching them. It is of supreme importance also not to be selective in one's observance.

The Antitheses Mt 5:21-48

There are six antitheses, contrasting Jesus' teaching with what the audience had heard before. 'The righteousness greater than that of the scribes and the Pharisees' required of the followers of Jesus is now spelled out in terms of six antitheses, so called

---

61. *m. Aboth* 2:1. See D. J. Harrington, *Matthew*, 81.

by scholars because there is a tension or opposition between what Jesus is teaching and what they have been taught before.

'It was said' is Matthew's respectful way of saying 'God said' in the Torah revealed to Moses. 'But I say to you' highlights an enormous claim to divine lawmaking on Jesus' part. He is no new Moses receiving the Law. He is issuing interpretations with the authority of the Divine Lawgiver. 'You have heard' refers to the reading of the scriptures in the synagogue and the accompanying teaching on the texts. Jesus' interpretations differ from these older teachings in different ways, deepening, spiritualising, radicalising or changing them. The words of the Torah are subjected to the scrutiny of Jesus and give way to his words. The impact of this claim to authority on the part of Jesus in first century Palestine may be lost on a present day Christian reader who believes in the divine nature and authority of Jesus. The full impact of Jesus' claim to authority in his 'but I say to you' approach to the Torah and how it sounded then, and still can sound to a Jewish audience, is captured in a comment by A. Ginzberg:

> Israel cannot accept with religious enthusiasm, as the Word of God, the utterances of a man who speaks in his own name – not 'thus saith the Lord' but 'I say to you'. This 'I' is in itself sufficient to drive Judaism away from the gospels forever.[62]

Five of the antitheses begin with 'You have heard that it was said … but I say to you.' The third antithesis has a slightly different form: 'It was said, but I say to you.' The change in form may point to its having been added to five original antitheses which are here under scrutiny, symbolically reflecting the five books of the Torah, the number five being reflected also in the five great discourses in the gospel. The 'odd one out' is imported from the treatment of divorce in Mt 19:1-12 and inserted here because of

---

62. A. Ginzberg, *Ten Essays on Zionism and Judaism*, London, 1922, 232, quoted by D. R. Catchpole in 'The Problem of the Historicity of the Sanhedrin Trial' in E. Bammel (ed), *The Trial of Jesus*, London: SCM Press, 1970, 50.

similarity of theme, as a further illustration of the point being
made and in the context it serves the purpose perfectly as a contrast with former teaching on the subject.

i. Murder (Mt 5:21-26)

*'You have heard that it was said to our ancestors: Thou shall not
kill but whoever kills will be liable to judgement.'*

Responding to this commandment Jesus looks behind the act
of killing to the roots of such a violent action. Three possible motives are given. They are failure to control one's anger, branding
someone a renegade (to religion or nation) or regarding someone as foolish or inferior. Each example is condemned to a hearing in court and the authority of the court in question is in ascending order from the local court to the Sanhedrin and to hell
itself. J. P. Meier sees in the ascending order of crime and punishment a mocking parody on casuistry, since in the radical, eschatological judgement of Jesus, insulting one's brother by calling him a fool betrays the same murderous heart as that which
homicide displays.[63]

The response to offence and division must be reconciliation.
The merciful have already been declared blessed in a beatitude
(Mt 5:7). The biblical insight into the God who demands mercy,
not sacrifice (Hos 6:6) underpins the admonition not to approach God in worship while un-reconciled to the brother.
Being un-reconciled to the brother one is also un-reconciled to
God, not only in the temple service, but also in the eschatological judgement. One should therefore leave one's gift before the
altar, go and be reconciled to the brother and then come to offer
the gift. The sermon later states in the context of Jesus' teaching
the disciples to pray that they should say: 'Forgive us our tres-
passes as we forgive those who trespass against us' and goes on
to emphasise the point with a further *logion* about God's forgiveness being dependent on one's human forgiveness (Mt 6:12, 14,
15), a point emphasised later in the gospel in Jesus' answer to

---

63. J. P. Meier, *Matthew*, 51.

Peter's question about forgiveness (Mt 18:21-22) and in the parable of the unforgiving servant (Mt 18:23-35).

The reasons which may cause one to be angry, to brand someone as a renegade or traitor or regard someone as a fool may arise from one's own faulty judgement or prejudice. One should not be too confident of one's own judgement in regard to other people and of being in the right in a contested issue. If tested in court the judge may well find otherwise. One is never a judge in one's own case. For the person too confident in his/her own judgement a triple level of judgement/punishment may be in store – the sentence of the judge, the arrest by the guard and the confinement of the prison. A solemn 'Amen I say to you' introduces the salutary warning about not getting out of prison till the last penny is paid. The Jews did not imprison debtors, but the Romans did and so the reference reflects a Roman practice, as the reference to pressgang service does in the antithesis about hating enemies. Paying the last *kodrans* is also a Roman expression, since the *kodrans* is the Roman *quadrans*, the smallest Roman coin, usually translated into English as a penny.

ii. Adultery (Mt 5:27-30)

You have heard that it was said 'you shall not commit adultery ...'

As in the case of murder, Jesus here looks behind the actual sinful act of adultery to see its roots in one's attitude and behaviour prior to the sinful act. Adultery is first committed in the heart in lustful gaze and resulting desire (another example of the importance of being pure in heart). The woman is already violated, her marriage threatened and her husband sinned against by the lustful gaze of the would-be adulterer. The sin has already been committed in the impure heart.

By adding Mt 5:29-30 about mutilating the offending organ Matthew gives to the right eye and hand a sexual reference. The rabbis also warned against adultery of heart, hand, and eye.[64] The statement about tearing out and throwing away the right eye or right hand that causes one to sin is not simply hyperbole

---

64. J. P. Meier, *Matthew*, 52.

but actually reflects the punishments often meted out for crimes, including those of a sexual nature. Some biblical scholars and moral theologians see in these references a connection with rabbinic teaching as seen in the Babylonian Talmud, *b. Niddah* 13b, about sexual sins of child abuse (the little ones), masturbation (the hand), adultery (the foot), lustful glances (the eye).[65] Similar punishments were known also among other nations. Loss of hand or foot was a punishment for theft, and of eyes for adultery.[66]

Mentioning the right eye and right hand (the more dominant of each pair for the much larger percentage of the population and so representing both eyes and hands), both essential to life in the world, Jesus points out in two similar statements that if any one of them is a cause for leading one into sin it would be better for that person to be at the loss of it and living in the kingdom than able-bodied and excluded from it. There is a similar use of hand, foot and eye in Mk 9:43-47 in the context of scandalising 'the little ones'. Hand, foot and eye together seem to have been regarded as the basic essentials for healthy living. Job, for example, sees the moral and physical health of the person in terms of purity of eyes, feet and hands (Job 31:1-7). Loss of any or all of them is therefore a serious loss of life in the world, but it is preferable to loss of life in the kingdom.

iii Divorce (Mt 5:31-32)

It was also said: 'Whoever divorces his wife let him give her a writ of divorce.'

Jesus is quoting the Mosaic rule about giving one's wife a certificate when divorcing her (Deut 24:1) but goes on in his antithetical statement to say: 'But I say to you that everyone who di-

---

65. See R. F. Collins, *Sexual Ethics and the New Testament: Behaviour and Belief,* New York: Crossroads, 2000, 62-72 and W. Deming, 'Mark 9:42-10:12, Matthew 5:27-32 and *B.Nid* 13b: A First-Century Discussion of Male Sexuality,' *NTS* 36 (1990), 130-41.

66. See D. Derrett, *Studies in the New Testament,* I, 4-31. See also the discussion in J. R. Donohue and D. J. Harrington, *The Gospel of Mark,* 290.

vorces his wife except for *porneia* makes her an adulteress; and
whoever marries a divorced woman commits adultery.'[67]

The writ of divorce was a legal document showing the proof
that the marriage had ended and the husband had no further
legal rights. The former wife had protection from further claims
on his part (as for example, concerning financial matters like a
dowry). The writ also showed a prospective new husband that
the woman was free to marry again and protected him also from
any claims by the first husband.

Whoever divorces his wife, except for porneia, commits adultery,
and whoever marries a divorced woman commits adultery. All
records of Jesus' statements are strongly opposed to divorce[68]
(Mt 5:31-32; 19:1-12; Lk 16:18; Mk 10: 2-9,11-12; 1 Cor 7:10).
Matthew, however, has an 'exceptive clause' in both places
where he deals with the issue. Here in Mt 5:31-32 he has the
clause *parektos logou porneias,* 'except in the case of *porneia*' and in
Mt 19:3-9 he has *mê epi porneia,* 'except for *porneia*'. What is
meant by *porneia* and why does Matthew alone have the 'exceptive' clauses? Since Mark, Luke and Paul do not have such exceptions when dealing with Jesus' teaching on divorce it is obvious that the question of *porneia* arose in the Matthean community,
and is not part of the original statement of Jesus. There are differing interpretations of its meaning, and they will be dealt with
in the commentary on Mt 19:3-9 in which the question of divorce, the grounds for divorce, the writ of divorce and the exceptive clauses will be treated at greater length. Suffice it to say
at this point that Jesus is challenging an understanding that sees

---

67. For studies on the question of marriage and divorce in the New
Testament see B. Vawter, 'Divorce and the New Testament,' *CBQ* 39
(1977) 528-42; J. A. Fitzmyer, 'The Matthean Divorce Texts and Some
New Palestinian Evidence,' *TS* (1976) 197-226.
68. Matthew does not have Mark's prohibition forbidding the wife to
divorce her husband. It appears to be a spelling out of the implications
of Jesus' teaching in the changed circumstances of the Roman world
where the role and status of women had changed since the early days
of the empire and women were in a position to initiate divorce proceedings.

Moses' prescription about a writ of divorce as an acceptance of divorce as a normal, quite acceptable practice. Jesus, however, is re-establishing a more fundamental norm or ideal of marriage. The compromise should not be taken as the ideal.

iv. Oaths and Vows (Mt 5:33-37)

Again you have heard that it was said to the ancients, 'You shall not swear falsely; but you shall carry out your oaths to the Lord.'

'Swearing' in the sense of taking oaths was a well-established practice, and there was clear legislation governing it in the Torah. The commandment in the Decalogue states: 'You shall not bear false witness against your neighbour' (Exod 20:16; Deut 5:20) and an injunction appears in Lev 19:12: 'You shall not swear by my name falsely.' However, far from replacing solemn oaths with a milder form of oaths, Jesus does away with the practice altogether when he says: 'Do not swear at all', an admonition found also in the Letter of James (James 5:12). Jesus uses a triple formula, showing the ubiquity of God – in heaven, God's dwelling place, on the earth, God's footstool, a world completely under his control (Isa 66:1) and in Jerusalem, the city of the Great King (God), where God has chosen to dwell (Ps 48:3). None of these places should be used in an oath since they are special to God's presence, majesty and authority, and ultimately are beyond man's authority and power.

One should not swear by one's own head either. One is not ultimately master of one's own life. It too, belongs to God. The reference to hair colour may contain a note of irony or even humour since colouring one's greying hair was known in antiquity. The ageing process is beyond one's control. The years are there in spite of cosmetics and the hair is still grey beneath the artificial colour.

In the Lord's Prayer Jesus will state: 'May your name be held holy' as the first 'wish/petition' following the address to 'Our Father in Heaven', the 'in heaven' also emphasising the transcendence and holiness of the Father. Keeping the Lord's name holy must involve preserving it from being used (and abused)

for human convenience in the matter of taking oaths. Calling
God to witness in human affairs is treating God like a servant at
man's beck and call. Simply say 'yes' if you mean 'yes' and 'no'
if you mean 'no'. Jesus then adds that anything else comes from
evil/the evil one. What does this imply? Oaths taken in haste,
anger, passion, hatred or self-interest are given to extravagant
expression and proceed from the evil that touches our lives and
circumstances. Two such oaths are in evidence in the gospel, the
hasty and extravagant oath of Herod (Mt 14:7) and the terror
driven oaths of Peter (26:72-74). The first resulted in the murder
of the Prophet, the second in the denial of the Master.

v. Retaliation (*Lex Talionis*) (Mt 5:38-42)
*You have heard that it was said, an eye for an eye and a tooth for a
tooth ...*
The 'law of retaliation' is found in the Bible in Exod 21:23-25,
Lev 24:18-20 and Deut 19:21. In origin the 'eye for an eye and
tooth for a tooth' was a significant step ahead in civilisation. The
law code of Hammurabi who reigned in Babylon from 2285 to
2242BC had framed a similar law. It demanded controlled response and exact retribution for injury caused to another. It took
the right of vengeance away from the individual and placed it in
the objective competence of a judge. It stands out as a major departure from blood feuds and excessive acts of revenge like the
retribution seen in the case of the rape of Dinah, for example,
when the whole male population of an area paid with their lives
for the crime of one man (Gen 34). One eye for one eye and one
tooth for one tooth meant that the offender could not be blinded
by the removal of both eyes or lose a whole mouthful of teeth. It
was an extremely careful measurement of retribution/punish-
ment. It had, however, become something quite different with
the passage of time, a formula and justification for vengeance,
and could be seen, in the oft-quoted words of Mahatma Gandhi,
as a formula for a world of blind and toothless people. Wilfrid J.
Harrington gives a very apt quotation from G. B. Caird's comment on Rev 13:10:

When one man wrongs another, the other may retaliate, bear a grudge, or take his injury out on a third person. Whichever he does, there are now two evils where before there was one; and a chain reaction is started, like the spreading of a contagion. Only if the victim absorbs the wrong and so puts it out of currency, can it be prevented from going any further. And this is why the great ordeal is also the great victory.[69]

Jesus goes straight to the heart of the matter, behind the letter of the Law, and builds on its essential humanising and moderating concerns. He looks beyond court proceedings for obtaining retribution and compensation, beyond civil law and judicial principles and seeks the eschatological justice/righteousness of the kingdom. In doing so, he looks beyond the injury and the right of retaliation to the person who has caused the injury. 'Do not resist the evil one' seems to refer to the offending party in the suit (rather than to Satan, the author of evil who has to be resisted).

Jesus gives a number of practical examples of what he means by offering no resistance. He speaks of 'turning the other cheek' (or turning one's back and walking away)[70] when struck on the right cheek. A stroke on the right cheek is more likely to be an insult rather and an act of physical violence, since it would mean a slap with the back of the hand, in the majority of cases when most people are in fact right-handed, a slap on the cheek would be on the left cheek. Does Jesus mean that one should just walk away and pretend the injury did not happen? By no means. The following antithesis about love of enemies offers a very definite, but very different, response to the evildoer.

The Law prescribed that if someone sued an opponent and got his shirt/garment, he should restore it at night for it was the only covering the person had (Exod 22:26-27). Jesus implies that one should forego this right and let the opponent take the cloak

---

69. W. J. Harrington, *Matthew: Sage Theologian*, 45, quoting G. B. Caird, *The Revelation of St John the Divine*, London: A& C Black, 1966, 170.
70. D. J. Harrington, *Matthew*, 88, suggests that there may be a mistaken translation between the similar words for 'other' and 'back' in the Aramaic '*uhrâ/ahorâ*. The point is still the same. Do not retaliate.

as well. The Roman law allowed soldiers to press people into service, often carrying baggage from place to place or doing other physical tasks, like Simon of Cyrene carrying the cross for Jesus (Mt 27:32). The 'victim' forced into going a mile is here exhorted to go an extra mile rather than put up resistance.

The Law prescribed generosity in the giving of alms and a loan (Deut 15:7-11). Jesus here goes beyond the 'regulated' examples of alms to deserving cases and loans to reliable debtors and says to give alms or a loan 'to anyone who asks' (i.e. even if they are hostile or unreliable persons). No restrictions are placed on the alms and no conditions are put on the loan.

These examples of non retaliation and non assertion of one's rights and claims show how the offended or injured party should take positive action, turn the difficult situation into an opportunity for strengthening character, building a relationship and bringing about a change for the better in the offending party. They lead on to the final antithesis that deals with love of enemies.

vi. Love of Enemies (Mt 5:43-48)

You have heard that it was said, 'You shall love your neighbour and hate your enemy,' but I say to you, love your enemy and pray for those who persecute you ...'

The command to love one's neighbour is found in Lev 19:18 but the prescription to hate one's enemies does not appear in the Torah. However, some Old Testament texts do show such hostility (e.g. Ps 139:19-22) and the Manual of Discipline in Qumran commands 'hatred of the sons of darkness', that is, of the enemies of the community, some of whom may even be Jews.

Jesus' response, 'but I say to you, love your enemy and pray for those who persecute you' is backed up by way of reference to God's own treatment of good and bad alike as he makes his sun to shine on evil and good and his rain to fall on righteous and unrighteous alike. Those who love their enemy and pray for their persecutor will be sons (children) of their Father in heaven. In the beatitudes those who show mercy are told that they will be called sons/children of God. In similar vein those who love their enemies and pray for their persecutors will be sons/children of their Father in heaven. The Father in heaven is associated with forgiveness as will be seen in the Lord's Prayer. Being children of God, they must be like God who shares his creation with the good and bad alike, and sends his sun to shine on them and his rain to fall on them, sun and rain being two of the most essential supports of life in the world. This understanding of God's beneficence in creation was commented on also in Greco-Roman literature. Seneca states: 'If you are imitating the gods then bestow benefits also upon the ungrateful; for the sun rises also upon the wicked and the sea lies open also to pirates'.[71] The sun and rain are metaphors for God's gracious beneficence, his 'indiscriminate and radically gracious love that envelops even the enemy'.[72] Jesus rejects limitations put on love. The Father loves all, good and bad alike.

Reciprocity, whereby people love those who love them, is normal human behaviour practised even among the tax collectors and Gentiles. The tax collectors, regularly coupled in the New Testament with sinners and prostitutes, were suspected and despised because they were bullies who leaned on the weak, collected more than their due, pocketed much of it and gave the rest to the Romans, the foreigners with whom they were collaborating. The Gentiles were seen as pagan and ritually unclean. However, even these tax collectors and Gentiles respond to those who treat them well. The followers of Jesus are to have a much more radical code of behaviour in responding well to those who treat them badly.

Summary: *Be Perfect as your heavenly Father is perfect*

The final exhortation in the section, 'Be perfect as your heavenly Father is perfect' (Mt 5:48) has its nearest Old Testament equivalent in the exhortation 'Be holy as your God is holy' (Lev 19:2; cf. 20:26; 21:8). Luke translates the corresponding sentence

---

71. *De Ben*, 4.26.1.
72. D. Senior, *Matthew*, 80.

as 'be merciful as your heavenly Father is merciful' (Lk 6:36) and this would come close to Matthew's idea of completeness or perfection, a sincere, single-hearted devotion to God and neighbour. Holiness, in so far as it is an attribute of God in himself, his being totally other, is a quality of God alone. However, God's holiness touches his people through his presence and work of salvation. Man is made holy through God's gift and work. God's covenant relation with his people makes them a holy people. They reflect God's holiness when they live according to the covenant. The Greek term *teleios*, reflects the Hebrew words *tamim* and *shalom*, both meaning 'perfect' in the sense of complete. It is related to the noun *telos*, which means end or goal, so it signifies that which is complete since it achieves its goal. Man's goal and God's goal coincide in the perfection of man, when man achieves his fullness through God's plan for him. In this sense man becomes holy in the language of Lev 19:2, perfect in the language of Mt 5:48, and merciful in the language of Lk 6:36. To achieve this he models his life, attitudes and actions on those of God for the people, on the prescriptions of the Torah and now on the radical challenge of Jesus at the onset of the kingdom, especially in following his example and his teaching on love and forgiveness. Later in the gospel Matthew gives a practical example as he relates the story of Jesus' invitation to the rich young man that if he wishes to be perfect he should sell all he has and give the money to the poor, and thereby have treasure in heaven, and 'come follow me' (Mt 19:21).

b. Acts of Piety Mt 6:1-18

Statement of Principle (Mt 6:1)

As the six antitheses in legal teaching were introduced with a statement of principle in Mt 5:17-20, so now a series of 'antitheses' in attitudes to three central pious practices are introduced with the statement of principle: 'Beware of practising your piety/righteousness before men in order to be seen by them; for then you will have no reward from your Father who is in heaven' (Mt 6:1). The person practising these pious exercises should do so for the glory of God, not for the praise of people. The point running through the section is clear. Do God's will and avoid ostentation. God will see and give due reward.

Jesus in the sermon now turns his attention to the attitudes motivating the three central acts of piety that were seen to be constitutive of righteousness (*dikaiosunē/sedaqâ*). Here the major theme of righteousness is translated into terms of the acts of piety and the inner disposition, purity of heart, is emphasised. The acts of piety are almsgiving, prayer and fasting. They are interconnected since fasting and almsgiving often accompanied prayer. All three are a response to the awareness of the immanence, transcendence and mercy of the Father in heaven. Jesus affirms the value of almsgiving, prayer and fasting but issues a stern caution about the motivation underpinning these acts of piety.

The basic formula in each of the three cases is similar, containing four elements. There is a description of hypocritical, ostentatious action, a solemn 'amen' pronouncement that the 'reward' is already exhausted in the human praise, a prescription for private performance of the exercise known only to God and a promise of God's reward. In dealing with prayer, the basic formula is expanded to deal with babbling prayers after the fashion of the Gentiles, instruction on prayer in the form of the Lord's Prayer, and a precondition for the sinner's prayer to be effective, that is, the sinner's own forgiveness of others.

In all three cases the essential dichotomy between mere ostentation on the part of the 'hypocrites' and a sincere internal disposition (another example of purity of heart) is highlighted. It reflects the prophetic warnings about 'honouring me with their lips while their hearts are far from me' (Isa 29:13) and Hosea's remark that God requires mercy, not sacrifice (Hos 6:6; Mt 9:13; 12:7).

i. Almsgiving Mt 6:2-4
The comment on giving alms refers to the practice of collecting alms in the synagogue or giving alms in a public place. In the

synagogue one could make a display of giving and thereby receive admiring glances and comments. In the street or in the
market place one could easily make a public display of giving
alms when approached and appealed to by beggars or even by
throwing or dropping coins into the begging receptacles on onto
the street. Those who do that are labelled 'hypocrites', *hypokritai*,
which literally means 'actors'. They create their own stage and
attract an admiring audience. Their performance is ironically
described as being announced by a trumpet call (like the opening of a stage performance) and the solemn pronouncement
'amen I say to you' states that they have received their 'wages'
(*misthon*), usually translated as 'reward', a translation which
may easily miss the satirical irony of the actor being paid for the
performance. It is a far cry from the motivation of compassion or
mercy that should inform the almsgiving. Interestingly the
Greek word for alms *eleêmosunê* and the word for 'merciful' *eleêmones*, already used in the beatitude, are similar, both coming
from a common root in Greek. They reflect the essential motive
for almsgiving.

Jesus prescribes the antithesis to this 'performance' beginning with: 'When you give alms ...' The one giving alms must do
so with no thought of receiving praise from people, even one's
own self must be removed from any sense of self congratulation,
a point emphasised by not letting the left hand know what the
right hand is doing. But God knows what is done in secret and
will respond not with mere 'wages' (*misthon*) or reward of a material or passing kind but with 'Your Father's' 'reward' (*apodôsei*,
'he will give in return') which will be of another order entirely in
the kingdom which is now partly present and manifest in such
actions, and will be fully manifest at the end of the age when
hidden things are made known and roles and status are reversed (cf Mt 20:16).

ii. Prayer Mt 6:5-15

The temple and synagogue services and the pilgrimage
feasts provided a form and timetable for the people's prayer life.

The liturgical horarium of temple, synagogue and religious movement set a pattern of prayer that could be 'exploited' by the 'actors' who liked 'to perform' in the worshipping assembly or in public at the official hours for prayer, assuring themselves of an admiring audience. Since the standing position was the norm for prayer it afforded an advantage for those who wished to be seen.

Jesus never criticised formal worship and liturgical assembly as such and later in the ministry he assured those who gather in his name that he will be present in their midst (Mt 18:19-20). In these cases the focus is on the worship of God and the abiding presence of the Risen Christ, not on the individual seeking attention and admiration. For personal, private prayer, however, one should seek out a quiet, secret place away from the gaze of others. A storeroom or outhouse would give such privacy. Your Father sees in secret and will respond. J. P. Meier gives two striking examples from the Old Testament of such private seclusion for prayer.[73] 'Go into your rooms my people; shut your doors behind you. Hide yourselves a little while until the wrath has passed' (Isa 26:20), and '(Elisha) went in and shut the door on the two of them and prayed to *YHWH*' (2 Kings 4:33).

Matthew expands this simple antithetical formula to include three key aspects of Jesus' teaching on prayer. First there is an antithesis to the Gentile practice of repetition of prayers. This may well point to the fact that some of Matthew's intended audience/readership came from pagan religious background and had been brought up in their traditions of prayer. This is followed by the instruction to pray in the words of the 'Our Father'/'The Lord's prayer'. Thirdly there follows the pre-condition for prayer that the person praying is disposed to the neighbour as he/she hopes God is disposed to himself/herself. This focuses on the acid test of forgiveness.

(i) Praying like the Gentiles (Mt 6:7-8)
Formulas and incantations were repeated over and over and

73. J. P. Meier, *Matthew*, 59.

the names of every deity and spirit may have been called on to ensure the petition would be heard and the appropriate divinity addressed.[74] Paul in Athens noticed and commented on the altar to 'the unknown god', a provision against overlooking and offending any player in the divine protection organisation (Acts17: 23). The impression given is that the gods are like the fruit machines or the lottery numbers that give a reward if the right combinations of deities and incantations come up after several attempts. The follower of Jesus has two advantages. There is no element of chance involved or lack of identity of the God to whom they pray. They pray to the God whom Jesus tells them is their 'Father in heaven'. Furthermore they have no need to formulate lengthy petitions, excuses, descriptions and explanations of their needs because 'Your Father knows what you need before you ask him.'

This assurance leads on to his teaching them the prayer usually described as the 'Our Father' or 'the Lord's Prayer' though in fact it would be more accurately described as 'the Disciples' Prayer' which was taught to them by the Lord![75]

(ii) The Lord's Prayer (The Disciples' Prayer) (Mt 6:7-13)

Matthew's version of the 'Lord's Prayer' is longer than Luke's (Lk 11:1-4) and reflects both Matthew's overall outlook and the liturgical formulation of the prayer in his community. The address, 'Our Father in heaven' rather than Luke's straightforward 'Father' (which reflects more closely Jesus' own *abba* and 'my Father' forms of address), is a case in point. 'Our Father' reflects the address of the assembly of disciples to the Father, the address of the community at prayer. Whereas Jesus speaks of

---

74. The word 'adore' may well have its origin in this context. It refers to the practice of putting the hand over the mouth (*ad-orare*) in order to ensure the wrong incantation or the incorrect name of a divinity would not be uttered.

75. The term 'The Lord's Prayer' would more accurately describe Jesus' own prayers such as the thanksgiving prayer of Jesus (Mt 11:25-26), his prayer of resignation in Gethsemane (Mt 26:39,42 and / /s) or his prayer *par excellence* in Jn 17.

'my Father', the followers speak of 'our Father', maintaining the distinction between the relationships. In John's gospel this distinction is made very clear when the risen Jesus commissions Mary Magdalene to tell the brethren: 'I am ascending to my Father and your Father, to my God and your God' (Jn 20:17). The qualifying 'in heaven' in Matthew's version emphasises the transcendence and majesty of God, adding a formal, solemn, worship-based dimension to the familiar 'Father' relationship and address.

The structure of the prayer is simple. After the opening address, there are three wishes or petitions regarding the Father, touching on his name, his kingdom and his will. There follow three petitions relating to the needs of those offering the prayer, touching on the provision of food (spiritual and physical), the forgiveness of sins and the preservation from evil.

The first three 'wishes' are in the passive voice, 'may your name be held holy', 'may your kingdom come', 'may your will be done'. The passive voice here as elsewhere is a way of avoiding predicating direct action of the Holy One. It means 'may you bring it about that your name be held holy, your kingdom come, your will be done'. God is the agent who will bring about the desired effect. The aorist tense signifies a single action and emphasises the once-for-all action of God in bringing about the final time.

Having opened the prayer with the address 'Our Father in heaven', the three petitions are rounded off with the description of the desired effect, that it be 'on earth as in heaven' which relates to all three petitions. This is reminiscent of the prayer for the 'tearing open of the heavens' to bring about the apocalyptic, eschatological time when the name of God is known and the kingdom is established on earth: 'O that you would tear open the heavens and come down … to make your name known to your adversaries, so that the nations might tremble at your presence '(Isa 64:1-3; cf Isa 24:17-20; Rev 19:11). It reflects the promise of God in the Old Testament that he will display his holiness before the nations: 'But I had concern for my holy name … I will sanctify my great name which has been profaned among the nations ... and the nations will know that I am the Lord ... when through you I display my holiness before their eyes' (Ezek 36:21-23). The prayer 'may your name be held holy, your kingdom come, your will be done' is a prayer for this eschatological realisation of the end-time and the arrival of the kingdom, when the will of God will be done on earth, among the Jews and the Gentiles. This end time is being inaugurated in the life, death and resurrection of Jesus. A parallel can be found with the final words of Jesus' 'priestly' prayer in St John's gospel which sum up his ministry in the words: 'I have made your name known and will make it known' (Jn 17:26). In Matthew's gospel Jesus' final prayer will be 'your will be done' just before the signal for the final battle, temptation or trial, the *peirasmos*, is given by Judas (Mt 26:42).

The second group of petitions relates to human need and appeals to God's providence. It is God who gives, forgives and does not subject one to the test (*peirasmos*) but delivers from evil. The verbs here are also in the aorist imperative signifying a final once-for-all mighty action of God.

The appeal to our Father in heaven to give food/bread (*ton arton hêmôn epiousion*) has been understood both as an appeal for the daily bread needed to sustain physical life and also as an appeal for the final eschatological food, the banquet of the kingdom. It may be a reflection also of the food referred to in the first temptation where Jesus is confronted with physical hunger but in replying to the tempter reminds him of the fact that the word of God is another and even more necessary form of food (Mt 4:4; Deut 8:3). 'The word from the mouth of God' sustains the petitioner with its promise of the eschatological food.

For Matthew, the liturgical setting of the prayer may be the Eucharist, seen as the first instalment on that eschatological meal. The term *epiousion* in Greek seems to come from the verb *epienai*, 'to come'. Whereas Matthew has given it an eschatological dimension, Luke has interpreted it as the food that is necessary for sustaining physical life, and qualified his interpretation accordingly with the addition of the phrase *kath' hêmeron*, 'day by day', showing an awareness of the ongoing history of the church and its continuing needs, rather than an immediate appeal for the eschatological food as in Matthew's presentation of the petition as a prayer for the 'daily' bread with the appeal for it to be given right now, today (*sêmeron*).

Forgiveness of 'debts' is predicated on the petitioner's own forgiving attitude to debtors. This is further borne out in the *logion* or saying on forgiveness that follows immediately on the prayer, and later in the gospel it will be illustrated very graphically in the parable of the unforgiving debtor (Mt 18:23-35).

The final petition is like a Semitic parallelism, a double statement about saving us from the great test (*peirasmos*), the final onslaught of the powers of evil before the final triumph of the kingdom. Do not put us to the test, do not lead us to, or allow us to be put to the test, but rather save us from *ponêros*, evil or the evil one (either translation is possible). In Gethsemane Jesus will exhort the disciples to watch and pray lest they be led into temptation, put to the test unexpectedly and unprepared: 'Watch and pray lest you enter into temptation' (Mt 26:41). Even if the final great eschatological test is the main focus of the petition, the prayer also encompasses the many 'testings' along the way, as in the case of Jesus' own testing in the desert and the great test facing Jesus and the disciples in Gethsemane.

(iii) Precondition for Forgiveness (Mt 6-14-15)

The *logion* in Mt 6:14-15 is a parallelism. If you forgive, your Father in heaven will forgive you, if you do not neither will your Father forgive you your sins. This carries on the final petition of the prayer and also fits in with the beatitude about the merciful and the parable of the unforgiving servant/debtor (Mt 5:7; 18:23-35). In the prayer itself 'debtors' (*opheiletai*) and 'debts' (*opheilêmata*) are used, whereas in the following *logion*, the term *paraptômata*, failings/sins, is used. 'Debt' (*hôbâ*) was a metaphor for sin in Aramaic. Luke uses the straightforward *hamartias* 'sins' together with 'debtor' possibly for his Gentile audience on whom the Semitic metaphor would probably be lost (Lk 11:4).

Readers familiar with the bibles, prayers and liturgy used in Reformed and Eastern traditions will be aware of their use of the doxology added to the Lord's Prayer: 'For thine is the kingdom, the power and the glory, forever and ever.' This is a typical biblical doxology, reflecting closely 1 Chron 29:11. It is added in the *Didachê* and from early on has been added in some manuscripts of Matthew. Since the liturgical reforms of Vatican II the Roman Missal has included it as a response to the prayer for deliverance from evil that follows the Lord's Prayer in the Mass.

iii. Fasting (Mt 6:16-17)

Proceeding to fasting, the third work of piety, one finds again the underlying formula, 'When you fast, do not … but rather …'

Fasting regularly accompanied private and public prayers of petition, repentance and devotion. The Day of Atonement, *Yom Kippur*, was a day of public fast. Other days of public fast could be proclaimed for particular reasons such as mourning, supplication in time of pestilence, famine or war, and repentance.[76] Waiting for the promised one to come and repentance by way of preparation for his coming, or for the coming of the kingdom, would have been the order of the day among some religious groups such as the Essenes, the Baptist and his followers, and other pious groups and individuals. The Pharisee in the temple in Jesus' parable in Luke's gospel, who prides himself on his virtuous life in contrast to the sinful tax-collector, and boasts about fasting twice a week, provides an insight into the practice of fasting (Lk 18:9-14). Jesus himself was challenged about fasting when it was pointed out that the disciples of John and the Pharisees were fasting and his disciples were not (Mt 9:14-17; Mk 2:18-22; Lk 5:33-39). On that occasion he pointed out that it would be inappropriate to fast while the bridegroom was with them but the day would come when the bridegroom would be taken away and on that day they would fast. Some manuscripts of Mark's gospel add 'and fasting' to Jesus' statement that some

---

76. 2 Sam 12:23; 2 Chron 20:30; Joel 1:14; 2:12-15; Ezra 8:21; Jer 36:9; Pss 35 (34):13; 69 (68):10; Neh 9:1; Zech 8:19.

demons are only driven out by prayer, when he explained to the disciples why they failed to heal the demonic/epileptic boy (Mk 9:29), a further pointer to the link between prayer and fasting.

The person fasting is not to be like the 'dismal', 'sad-looking' hypocrites. They make strange, funny, disfigured, faces in order that their fasting would be seen by people. Making faces, funny looks, painting faces: all are associated with the actors putting on their performance. The actors do so for the applause of the crowd. So too those disfiguring themselves (by putting ashes on their head, not washing or shaving, deliberately looking emaciated and so on) receive the reward of the actors, the admiration and applause of the crowd. That was their goal, their payment (*misthon*) for their performance, and they received it there and then from the onlookers rather than from the Father in the final reckoning.

On the other hand, the person who is really fasting for genuine religious, spiritual and self-disciplinary motives will not be interested in the praise of people but in the religious significance of the activity. That person will appear well groomed, 'puffed, powdered and shaved', looking happy and no one will know of the fasting, except, of course, the Father who sees all things done in secret, and the Father will 'see in secret' and give the reward in the eschatological time.

c. Wisdom Teachings: (Mt 6:19-7:12)[77]

The Wisdom Tradition

Throughout the Ancient Near East the teachers of wisdom had built up a store of proverbs, parables, riddles and stories that conveyed the accumulated experience of the generations. The underlying insight of the wisdom teachers was simple. It asserted that no one is born wise. Only experience brings wisdom. No one individual's experience is broad enough or long enough to bring sufficient wisdom for life. Therefore learning the wis-

---

77. G. Bornkamm in 'Der Aufbau der Bergpredigt,' NTS 24 (1977-78), 419-32, sees Mt 6:19–7:11 as an elaboration of the Lord's Prayer, giving a coherence to the diverse contents of the section.

dom of the ancients handed on by the teachers was of supreme importance. From the wisdom schools of Egypt through the Books of Proverbs, Sirach, Wisdom of Solomon and a host of others, the wisdom of the generations was learned. How to be a good ruler, secretary, teacher, gardener, husband or wife, all were subjects dealt with in the wisdom traditions. How to be happy, prosperous and free of undue anxiety were also important themes. Of importance too were wisdom in speech, knowing when to speak or to be silent, sobriety in food and drink and prudence in choosing friends and confidants. Learning wisdom was a sure way of living in peace and tranquillity. Jesus here at this point in the Sermon on the Mount fits into this category of wisdom teacher. His approach, however, differs in that he sets the wisdom teaching in the context of the kingdom. Though his sayings here are more in the nature of a collection of separate sayings or proverbs and images, there is a definite line running through them. It could be summed up as finding true security and happiness in God and the kingdom rather than in earthly things that are illusory, ephemeral and promise but do not deliver happiness.

i. God or Mammon Mt 6:19-32

'Do not store up treasure on earth' is the first of a series of strong prohibitions and commands in this section of the sermon. It will be followed by equally strong prohibitions on worrying, judging and inappropriate sharing of sacred things. A dominant theme running through Mt 6:19-32 is the need to choose between two masters, whether to serve God and worship the Father in heaven or the false god mammon.

(i) The heart's treasure (Mt 6:19-21)

The word treasure, in its verbal and noun forms (*thêsaurizete, thêsauros*) occurs five times in this saying. The repetition emphasises the attachment of the person to the thing treasured for 'where your treasure is there will your heart be also'. Again the spirituality of 'poor in spirit' comes into view with the emphasis on real treasure and the true source of happiness. It resonates also with the beatitude of 'the pure in heart'. One must be single-minded in one's attachment to God. Otherwise one can spend a lifetime minding the treasure, hoarding possessions, hiding money, stashing away food or other necessaries in a society where poverty was never far from the door. All these 'treasured' things are subject to decay, attack or thievery and so may prove to be a very false security. Also they demand our attention, cause us worry and attachment to them can determine our value system and behaviour. In short, they demand our allegiance. Such allegiance to possessions runs counter to the allegiance due to God and God's kingdom. Finding one's treasure in heaven was an established theme as seen especially in a comment like that in 4 Ezra 7:77: 'For you have a treasure of works laid up with the Most High; but it will not be shown to you until the last times.' The Psalmists can say: 'In his riches man lacks wisdom, he is like the beasts that are destined for slaughter' (Ps 49:12-13) and 'The Lord is my chosen portion and my cup' (Mt 16:5). Elsewhere Jesus uses the image of buried treasure when he compares the kingdom of heaven to a treasure hidden in a field which someone finds, hides again and goes away full of joy and sells everything in order to buy it (Mt 13:44). The teaching of 'the scribe trained for the kingdom' is like the householder drawing from his store 'treasure new and old' (Mt 13:52). The rich young man was so attached to his earthly possessions that he refused to sell them, give the money to the poor and so have treasure in heaven (Mt 19:16-22; Mk 10:17-22; Lk 18:18-23), a refusal which caused Jesus to remark that it is easier for a camel to pass through the eye of a needle than for a rich man to enter the Kingdom (Mt 19:24).

(ii) The lamp of the body (Mt 6:22-23)

Taken on its own and out of context this saying could point to the greedy eye of avarice, the green eye of envy, the evil eye of ill will, the blind eye of hardheartedness and so forth (cf Deut 15:9). Taken in the overall context of the sermon the lamp of the

body is probably the eye that sees the light of Christ as it illumin-
ates the realities of living with one's eye focused on the kingdom
of heaven and its treasures. Not to see in this way is to see only
the illusory, ephemeral, decaying things of the earth, an attitude
decried in the preceding *logion* about one's treasure. The unhealthy eye is a metaphor for possessiveness, greed and avarice
as distinct from the healthy eye which is a metaphor for openness to others in seeing their need and responding in generosity
and expansiveness.

(iii) Serving two Masters (Mt 6:24)

This admonition flows naturally from the warning about
one's treasure and one's heart being where one's treasure is. As
noted above, riches or possessions demand our attention, cause
us worry and attachment to them can determine/distort our
value system and behaviour. In short, they demand our allegiance. Such allegiance to possessions runs counter to the allegiance due to God and God's kingdom. Similar to the saying
about the heart being where the treasure is, this saying shows
that service and worship cannot be given to two gods/two masters. One must serve either the Father in heaven or mammon, a
term used for property, money and wealth. One has to make the
choice. Both options are not available.

(iv) Human anxiety and God's Providence (Mt 6:25-34)

This 'little sermon' on providence flows from the admonition
not to be anxious about life, about food, drink, clothing and so
forth. Storing up treasure in heaven by seeing things in the light
of the kingdom and serving one master only is possible for those
who open their eyes and look around at the providence of 'your
heavenly Father' as seen in his care of the natural world around
us. The beauty of the birds and their plumage outstrips the
splendid robes of Solomon, and the birds received their beautiful plumage without labour and spinning (unlike the huge
labour force working for Solomon to keep him in his splendour).
Appreciation of this providence is the opposite to, and drives

out, unnecessary anxiety about the necessities of today and the uncertainties of to-morrow. Such anxiety is a mark of the Gentiles. The admonition does not decry or forbid ordinary prudent provision for everyday living, but sees it in the overall context of God's providence. Removing such anxiety with its accompanying attitudes and conduct keeps the way clear for the pursuit of the kingdom and its righteousness. The theme of the 'little sermon' is summed up in the admonition: 'Seek first the kingdom and its righteousness and all these things will be added on for you' (Mt 6:33). Again the divine passive signifies: 'God will add it on for you.'

ii. Dispositions for Prayer (Mt 7:1-12)

In turning to God in prayer one must have the dispositions required, a forgiving, non-judgemental attitude to others, a sense of the holy (ultimately all holiness comes from God and glorifies his name) and an attitude of complete trust in the Father's providence

(i) Not Judging others (Mt 7:1-5)

Another clear admonition follows. 'Do not judge.' This instruction about not judging others is really a corollary to the sayings about 'forgiving us as we ourselves forgive' (Mt 6:12, 14-15). The provocative juxtaposition of the splinter and the log in the eye highlights our self-justifying attitudes and our judgemental attitudes to others. Again the condemnatory word 'hypocrite' is used of those who condemn others for a little fault (a splinter) and fail to see the enormity of their own faults (a beam/tree). A modern expression conveying the same meaning states that if you point a finger accusingly at someone you still have three fingers pointing back at yourself! No one is a judge in his/her own case and so no one should be too self-assured because when his/her own judgement is put to the test the independent judge may find differently and one could end up in prison (Mt 5:25-26). Only when we remove the beam, that is, repent of our own sins, can we see clearly enough to know another's sins. Lev 19:17 legislates for fraternal correction and provision for fraternal correction will be made in Mt 18:18:15-17. Anyone engaged in such correction must do so in full awareness of one's own, possibly greater faults. Otherwise one is but a 'hypocrite', motivated by prejudice or acting out a part for selfish reasons.

Commentators have pointed out that Jesus, though coming from a town background, raised in a carpenter/building environment, usually draws his images from farming and fishing, but the one image he uses from carpentry is a painful one, that of a splinter in the eye!

(ii) Preserving the Holy: Dogs and Swine (Mt 7:6)

Dogs were unclean animals to the Jews who did not keep them as family pets. 'Dog' was even used as a pejorative term for describing the 'unclean Gentiles'. Swine were particularly unclean to the Jews and eating swine flesh was a mark of the unclean Gentiles. Not giving to dogs what is holy strikes the reader as an adaptation of a proverb about not giving to dogs the meat made holy through sacrificial rites in the temple. But what about casting pearls before swine? The saying may well be a known proverb as it reflects the form of a typical synthetic Semitic parallelism, two lines saying essentially the same thing.

> Give not that which is holy unto dogs;
> Lest they trample them underfoot;
> Neither cast your pearls before swine
> Lest they turn and tear you. .

There may be a pun involved or a play on a popular saying or proverb. C. H. Dodd makes an interesting suggestion. He points out that the word 'holy' in Hebrew, written without vowels is *kdsh* and the Aramaic for an earring, also written without vowels is *kdsh*. This may point to an original parallelism which could be translated:

> Give not an ear-ring to the dogs;

78. C. H. Dodd, *The Gospel of Matthew*, The Daily Study Bible, St Andrew Press, Edinburgh, 1975, Vol 1, 267f.

Neither cast ye your pearls before swine.[78]

He draws attention to a phrase in the Talmud 'an ear-ring in a swine's snout' as a metaphor for something incongruous and out of place. Jesus' saying may be a word play on such a proverb.

In forbidding the giving of that which is holy to dogs and the casting of pearls before swine, what exactly is in mind? The kingdom is represented as a pearl of great price in a parable related by Matthew (Mt 13:45-46). By implication membership of the kingdom or the teaching of the kingdom should not be given to swine. The saying has all the marks of a protective measure that denies access to membership, teaching and Eucharist to persons who are fundamentally hostile and use their 'insider' knowledge to the detriment of the community in mockery, misrepresentation, calumny and even persecution. The ninth beatitude makes strong reference to such ill treatment by way of calumny. Is this a practical injunction in the light of such treatment? The advice that 'they will trample underfoot that which is holy' and 'turn and tear you' on being given the pearls, seems to point clearly in that direction.

One such group of hostile people may be, as J. P. Meier suggests, apostates or persons expelled from the community who still want to be part of the community, hear the word or share the Eucharist, but do not really belong because of their way of life or lack of real belief. He points to the use of the saying in the *Didachê* for keeping the unbaptised and the unrepentant from the Eucharist.[79] D. J. Harrington points to the rabbinic parallels that prescribe keeping the Law from non-Jews.[80]

(iii) Prayer (Mt 7:7-11)

Three forms of request, ask, seek and knock, are used to describe a prayer of petition. The granting of the request in each case is emphasised by the repetition of the promise that the Father will respond. As is typical of Matthew, the action of God

---

78. J. P. Meier, *Matthew*, 69f.
80. D. J. Harrington, *The Gospel of Matthew*, 103, n. 6.

is expressed in the passive voice or indirectly as 'it will be given', 'you will find' and 'it will be opened'. Verse 8 essentially repeats verse 7 but with a universal emphasis, 'for everyone (*pas*) who asks receives, who seeks finds and to the one who knocks it (the door) is opened.'

Jesus poses a rhetorical question: 'Is there a man among you who if his son asks for bread will give him a stone, or if he asks for a fish will give him a snake?' The very idea of doing such a despicable thing shocks the listeners into the realisation of the instinctive concern of parents for their children. Jesus now builds on the reaction and makes the *a fortiori* argument that if 'you who are sinful know how to give good things to your children, how much more will your Father who is in heaven give good things to those who ask him?' The examples of the stone instead of bread and the snake instead of a fish play on the similarity in appearance of a loaf to a stone and of a fish to a small snake. Even a sinful father will not give his son a counterfeit, even dangerous, substitute in response to his request for his 'daily bread'. How much more generously will the infinitely good, all provident and foreseeing Father in heaven respond to the request of his children. This is like a commentary on the petition for daily bread in the Lord's Prayer.

iii. The Golden Rule (Mt 7:12)
The 'golden rule' rounds off the central 'preaching' of the sermon before the final exhortations to take the sermon seriously, to live accordingly and to keep in mind the final judgement.

The Golden Rule, though something of an isolated statement here in this sermon, fits into a broader teaching context. Sometimes a teacher/rabbi would be asked a question such as, 'Could the entire body of law be summed up in a sentence, or recited while standing on one foot?' A famous example is that of Hillel, quoted in the Babylonian Talmud.[81] Shammai and Hillel were two of the most well known rabbis who were more or less contemporaries of Jesus. The former was regarded as more

---

81. *b. Shabbat* 31a.

strict, the latter as more liberal in their interpretations of the Law. A Gentile approached Shammai promising to become a proselyte if he could teach him the whole Torah while he stood on one foot. Shammai chased him away with a stick. He came to Hillel who responded to the same request with what has been called the 'silver rule' of Hillel, 'What you yourself hate, do not do to anyone; this is the whole law, the rest is commentary; go and learn it.' This reflects very closely a maxim stated in Tobit: 'Do to no one what you would not want done to yourself' (Tob 4:15).

Whereas the 'silver rule' was stated in negative terms, saying what should not be done, Jesus' 'golden rule' is like a corollary stated in positive terms, stating what should be done. The 'golden rule' of Jesus in Matthew's gospel is spoken in the context of an underlying principle running through the teaching of the Law and the Prophets: 'So always treat others as you would like them to treat you, that is the meaning of the Law and the Prophets' (Mt 7:12). In Luke the 'golden rule' is included as one of a series of maxims in the sermon on the plain (Lk 6:31). St Paul quoted it in his letter to the Galatians: 'The whole Law is summarised in a single command: "Love your neighbour as yourself"'(Gal 5:14) and in his Letter to the Romans: 'The one who loves his neighbour has fulfilled the law ... All the commandments ... are summed up in this single command: "You must love your neighbour as yourself." Love is the one thing that cannot hurt your neighbour; that is why it is the answer to every one of the commandments' (Rom 13:8-10).

Matthew's comment on the Golden Rule, 'For this is the Law and the Prophets' relates back to, illustrates and forms an inclusion with, Jesus' statement about his coming to fulfil the Law and the Prophets (Mt 5:17). These two references form an inclusion or bracket around the central body of the sermon.

C. WARNINGS ABOUT JUDGEMENT. THE ESCHATOLOGICAL CHOICE (MT 7:13-29)

Just as Moses put before the people a blessing and a curse to illustrate the outcome of their keeping or not keeping the prescriptions of the Torah when they crossed into the Promised Land (Deut 11:26ff), so too Jesus here puts forward two options and their consequences, following or not following the prescriptions of the sermon. In so doing, he uses well established biblical imagery in a series of antithetical parallel statements pointing to 'the two ways', the way to destruction and the way to life, the way of the kingdom and the way of judgement/condemnation. The choice of opposites is highlighted by the use of contrasting images – the narrow gate and difficult way are contrasted with the wide gate and easy way, the good tree that bears good fruit is contrasted with the bad tree that bears bad fruit and the wise man who builds his house on rock is contrasted with the foolish man who builds on sand.

There is an emphasis throughout on 'doing'. Entering by the narrow gate, being wary of false prophets, doing the will of the Father rather than saying 'Lord, Lord', and building one's house on rock rather than on sand are the final exhortations of the sermon. This is in keeping with Matthew's emphasis throughout the gospel on praxis and his aversion to words that are not followed through with actions.

i. The Narrow Gate/The Broad Way (Mt 7:13-14)

The saying about entering the door and following the way to salvation in Matthew is followed by a warning about false prophets who come in sheep's clothing but inwardly are ravening wolves. This is very close in sentiment and vocabulary both to the description in John's gospel of the evil shepherds who climb over the wall and to the hireling who runs away and abandons the sheep when he sees the wolf coming (Mt 7:15; Jn 10:12f.). The synoptic and Johannine traditions seem to draw from the same general store of imagery. The vocabulary is strikingly similar in the synoptic and Johannine sayings.[82] Following

---

82. The same words are used: entering, door/gate, being saved; *eiser-*

the 'parable' of the ideal/model shepherd in St John's gospel, Jesus uses a solemn 'Amen, Amen' declaration in which he proclaims himself to be the door or gate (*thura*) of the sheepfold (Jn 10:7-9). In the synoptic tradition Jesus speaks of the 'narrow gate' (*thura/pulê*) and the 'hard road' (*hodos*) that lead to life (salvation) (Mt 7:13f; Lk 13:24), and in the Johannine tradition he says, 'I am the door (gate)' and 'I am the way, the truth and the life' (Jn 10:7,9; 14:6).[83]

The opening and closing of the door is an image that figures quite prominently in Jesus' teaching, especially in the parables of the kingdom. Entering through the door symbolises entering the kingdom and the role of the doorkeeper in opening or closing the door is therefore very important. Peter is given the keys of the kingdom (Mt 16:19). The foolish virgins knock on the locked door only to be told: 'I do not know you' (Mt 25:11-13). The wicked people who claim that Jesus ate and drank with them and preached in their town appeal to their former friendship with the master of the house who has just locked the door. He responds saying, 'I do not know where you come from' and they find themselves locked out (Mt 25:10-12//Lk 13:25-27). The servant who watches the door for his master's return is praised (Lk 12:36). The unwilling master of the house when the friend called at night does not want to open the door (Lk 11:5-8). In his teaching on prayer Jesus says the door will be opened for the one who knocks (Mt 7:7-11//Lk 11:9f). The door thus figures very large in the language of entry into or exclusion from the kingdom.

'The Two Ways' was a long established image in religious and ethical teaching both in Israel and further afield in the Ancient Near Eastern and Greco-Roman worlds.[84] The Two Ways figure in the Old and New Testaments and in early Christian writings. It was part of the general ethos of the east to see things in 'dual' fashion. The wisdom tradition saw life and

chomai, thura/pulê, sôzomenoi/sôthêsetai.
83. Luke, like John, uses *thura* and Mt uses *pulê* for gate, but the imagery is the same.
84. M. Mullins, *Called to be Saints*, Dublin: Veritas, 188-190.

behaviour in dualistic terms and spoke of the influence of (Lady) Wisdom and (Dame) Folly. The prayer life of the Israelite as reflected in Psalm 1 highlights the two ways and their outcome: 'The Lord guards the way of the just but the way of the wicked leads to doom' (Ps 1:6). Alexandrian Judaism spelled this out in the Wisdom of Solomon where the destinies of the righteous and the unrighteous are contrasted (Wis 3:1-12). The Old Testament and later Jewish writings regularly reflect this 'dualism', (e.g. Deut 30:15f; Jer 21:8; Prov 2:12f; 4:18; 19:4; Ps 1:6; 1 Enoch 94:1-4; 2 Enoch 30:15; *Pirke Aboth* 2:1). In the *Testaments of the Twelve Patriarchs* Asher speaks of the basic duality of the universe, of life and death, of two inclinations, two kinds of activity, two dispositions and two outcomes (Asher 1:3-5; 5:1-3), Levi speaks of 'light and darkness, the law of the Lord and the works of beliar' (Levi 19:1) and Judah describes two spirits (Judah 20:1-5). Overall the *Testaments of the Twelve Patriarchs* is a very comprehensive statement of dualism and reflects an ethos permeated by it. The rabbis spoke of the 'two inclinations', *yetzer ha-tov* and *yetzer ha-ra'* and the choice between them was seen by the rabbis as a choice between 'the way to Eden' and 'the way to Gehinnom'.[85] The Qumran Community Rule spoke of the Two Ways and of the war between the powers of light and darkness (IQS 3:13–4:26). The Sermon on the Mount therefore fits into this tradition as it comes to a climactic conclusion putting the stark choice before its listeners.

ii. False Prophets (Mt 7:15-23)

False prophets had always posed a problem for the people of God whether they were court prophets telling the king what he wanted to hear, apostate prophets leading the people into idolatrous worship or political prophets leading them into dangerous liaisons with pagan peoples or into violent action against the Romans. False prophets could lead rulers and people to their spiritual, social and political ruination. Laws concerning false

---

85. See J. I. H. McDonald, *Kerygma and Didache*, SNTS, Cambridge University Press, 1980, 77.

prophets, guidelines for discerning the true from the false prophets and punishments for the latter like those laid down in Deut 18:9-22 were therefore very necessary. The emerging Christian community was equally exposed to false prophets. The imagery of the sheep's clothing conjures up the apparently harmless, smooth, innocent, and sincere but utterly false and dangerous nature of these people posing as leaders. In the gospels of Matthew and John Jesus uses the image of the wolf to describe their cunning, rapacious and dangerous inner dispositions (Mt 715; Jn10: 12). Similarly, in his farewell speech in Miletus to the leaders of the Church of Ephesus Paul warned them about 'fierce wolves that will invade you and have no mercy on the flock' (Acts 20:29).

The acid test is their fruit. You will know them by their fruit. The nature/species of the plant or tree determines the nature/species of its fruit, and the quality of the plant or tree determines the quality of that fruit. Grapes do not grow on thorns or figs on thistles even if there is some external similarity in their shape or form that may cause one to misidentify them.

The sombre note of judgement is sounded here, re-echoing the sombre tone of the Baptist: 'Every tree that does not bear good fruit is cut down and thrown into the fire' (Mt 3:10).

False prophets can appear to be very 'religious'. Paul had a great difficulty with the people in Corinth who placed charismatic experiences above love and unity in the church (1 Cor 12-13). They set themselves up above others, enjoying privileged status as 'holier' and more charismatically endowed than everyone else. This caused serious division in the community. Something of a similar experience seems to be the target of this remark: 'Not everyone who says "Lord, Lord'", or who says "Did we not prophesy in your name, and cast out demons in your name, and do many mighty works in your name?" shall enter the kingdom of heaven.' Whereas Paul combats empty or divisive enthusiasm by calling attention to the centrality of love, Matthew's Jesus combats deceptive pious words with 'doing the will of my Father who is in heaven', that is, doing the 'righteousness' already emphasised in the gospel narrative, and in the sermon. 'On that day', the biblical term for the Day of the Lord, the day of judgement, they will be shown up to be 'evildoers' and no true disciples of the one they called 'Lord, Lord'. He will say to them: 'I never knew you, away from me you evil men ' (Mt 7:21-23).

iii. Building one's house on rock or sand (Mt 7:24-27)

The final challenge of the sermon is to take Jesus' words seriously and it uses the contrasting imagery of a wise and foolish builder, the wise one building on a firm foundation of rock, the foolish one building on the insecure, shifting ground of sand. This imagery of a solid foundation carries a dire warning for the one who does not build a life of commitment on the solid rock of Jesus' teaching, on 'these words of mine'. The wise man sees ahead to the oncoming judgement, the wind and floods that will wash away a life not built on the word spoken in the sermon. The foolish man, on the other hand, built his house on sand, without a solid foundation, and so it was swept away in the wind and the floods. The wise man built on a solid rock foundation and his house withstood the onslaught of wind and floods.

Matthew's emphasis on 'doing' is again in evidence. It is not sufficient to *hear* the word; one must *do* it, put it into practice in one's life. The foolish man hears, probably thinks it a wonderful sermon, even praises it highly, builds a false security around the ideas, but does not put it into practice and so is heading for collapse when the wind and rain of judgement sweep away his 'castle in the air', to use a contemporary expression. Saying and doing were earlier emphasised, now hearing and doing are put forward as the necessary requirements to avoid the fate of the foolish one who does not do and whose ruin will therefore be complete.

Conclusion and Transition Mt 7:28-29

'It came to pass when Jesus had finished saying these things ...' This concluding formula is similar to the formula used at the conclusion of all five major discourses. The reference to the crowds points back to the introduction to the sermon, to the scene of the crowds gathering in Galilee (Mt 4:23-25). The reader is told: 'They were astonished at his teaching because he taught them as one who had authority, not like the scribes' (Mt 28:29). Not the content only, but the authority manifest in his teaching, made an impression on them. This reference to the crowd serves as a transition from the lengthy sermon showing Jesus' authority in word to the section showing his authority in deed. The crowd had gathered around Jesus bringing their sick, those afflicted with various diseases and pains, demoniacs, epileptics and paralytics. The narrator will now focus on Jesus' response to their suffering. His authority in word will be matched by his authority in deed in the series of miraculous actions that follow (Mt 8-9).

3. MIRACLES AND CHALLENGES MT 8:1 – 9:34.
Jesus: Mighty in Deed

Plot and Outline

As Jesus comes down from the mountain (Mt 8:1) great crowds follow him. The same comment, 'great crowds followed him' (* êkolouthêsan autô ochloi polloi*) also set the scene for the Sermon on the Mount (Mt 4:25). It is now repeated at the end of the sermon, forming an inclusion with the former description of the crowd and it leads into the miracle section of the gospel. The general narrative, interrupted by the sermon, now continues.

As the crowd following him grew (Mt 4:23-25) Jesus at first responded with powerful words (Mt 5-7). He now follows through with powerful (and challenging) deeds (Mt 8-9). Having demonstrated his authority and power in word and deed he will give authority to the Twelve whom he appoints to carry on his work and he will instruct them for their mission (Mt 10:1-.42). Chapter eleven will then open with reference to 'the deeds of the Christ', that is the works of Jesus and of his disciples, commissioned to work on his behalf.

The word *exousia*, 'authority/power' and related terms are now emerging as a dominant motif and will appear repeatedly in this major section of the gospel. His miracles for those individuals who emerge from the crowd and approach him in faith are followed by the miracles that show his power over the elements, over the demons and even over sin, and then over fatal illness and death. The leper will open his plea to Jesus with, 'If you have the power', the centurion will marvel at his authority and the disciples will be awestruck at his power over the elements. Most spectacularly he will demonstrate power and authority to forgive sin. Before they are chosen and sent out to act in his name the disciples are thus exposed to his authority and power.

They are also warned about the cost or dangers of discipleship. The danger from the elements during the storm at sea

when they 'follow' Jesus into the boat, the aggression of the demoniacs on their arrival at the other side of the lake and the
withering effects of criticism are all brought into the open before
Jesus shares his authority with them and commissions them to
act in his name.

This major section of the gospel (Mt 8-9) ends with a summary
of Jesus' activity and a reference to his seeing the crowd as sheep
without a shepherd (Mt 9:35-38). This forms an inclusion with
the earlier references to the crowd and at the same time sums up
and rounds off this major section which shows Jesus as 'mighty
in word and deed' (Mt 5:7; 8:3, 9). Following on this observation
about the sheep without a shepherd Jesus will instruct the disciples to 'pray to the Lord of the harvest to send labourers into his
harvest' (Mt 9:38). This in turn will set the scene for the appointment and giving of authority to the Twelve and the accompanying commissioning or missionary sermon.

Mt 8:1– 9:34 contains a series of miracle stories interspersed
with explanatory summaries, Old Testament allusions/citations
and reflections on the meaning and demands of discipleship.
Some scholars have seen a pattern of ten miracles reflecting the
ten plagues of Egypt. However, the story of the healing of
Peter's mother-in-law and the healings at sundown are best
taken together as a unit, since there is no introductory indication
of change of place as in the other stories. It seems that the best
way to understand the section is to see it as a series of three sections each made up of three miracle stories, separated from each
other by the explanatory summaries, allusions and reflections.

Outline
A. The First Triad: (Authority and Boundaries) Mt 8:1-17
    a. The Leper: 'If you can?' Jesus' authority/power
    b. The Centurion. His comment on Jesus' authority
    c. Peter's Mother-in-law and the Crowd at Evening
    d. *Summary and Citation from Isaiah (Isa 53:4)*

B. The Second Triad: (Authority and Danger) Mt 8:18 – 9:17

Introduction/Commentary
a. Rebuking the Wind and the Waves
b. Exorcising the Demons
c. Forgiving Sins and Healing
d. Call of Matthew; Dining with outcasts. Fasting

C. The Third Triad: (Danger of Calumny) Mt 9:18-34
a. The Two Daughters[1]
b. Two blind men cured
c. The dumb demoniac cured
d. Response: Awe and Accusation/Calumny
e. Summary and focus on the distress of the crowd

It is worth noting that many pericopes in Matthew's narrative are shorter, starker and without the detail and secondary characters which one meets in Mark's rendering of their common tradition. In the case of personal healings, Matthew concentrates on the meeting of the petitioner and the healer. The word or action of faith on the part of the petitioner is met by the word or action of healing on the part of Jesus. Secondary characters and explanatory or descriptive details tend to be either omitted or kept at a minimum. It has become a widely accepted view, especially in the light of the work of G. Bornkamm,[2] that Matthew severely edited Mark's narrative in this regard. However, it is also quite possible that both Matthew and Mark were working on an older tradition (oral or written?) which both redacted differently. This second possibility would account for both the similarities and differences in the order, approach and emphasis in the various pericopes and also account for how both evangelists

---

1. The official's daughter and the woman with the haemorrhage whom Jesus addresses as 'daughter'.
2. G. Bornkamm, 'The Stilling of the Storm in Matthew' in G. Bornkamm, G. Barth, and H. J. Held, *Tradition and Interpretation in Matthew*, Philadelphia: Westminster/London, SCM, 1963; see M. Mullins, *Mark*, Columba, 2005, 468-9; S. O'Connell 'Towards the First Gospel. Redactional Development in the Gospel of Mark', *PIBA*, 26 (2003), 66-88, 73.

have a consistent and coherent narrative in spite of the differences.

Each of the three stories begins with a verb (participle) of motion, signifying Jesus' arrival at the place of his activity, *katabantos, eiselthontos, elthôn,* 'descending, entering, approaching'. All three deal with a crossing of boundaries to heal. First of all, Jesus touched a leper. Among the Jewish people a leper was regarded as unclean and therefore treated as a social and religious outcast and a danger to society. Any physical contact with a leper made one unclean. Secondly, Jesus crossed a significant boundary when he signalled his willingness to enter the house of a pagan centurion who represented an occupying foreign power to heal his servant. Thirdly, in Matthew's account Jesus is alone in the house with a sick woman, Peter's mother-in-law, whom he touches in the process of healing. All three actions of healing would have raised eyebrows and made him ritually unclean in the eyes of strict observants.

The double story of the sick-mother-in law and the crowd of ill people who were brought at sunset probably came to Matthew as an already formed single unit as they are together also in Mk 1:29-34 and Lk 4:38-41. The healings at sunset supply a good summary of his activity and a context for the fulfilment citation from Isaiah (Isa 53:4.).

a. The Leper Mt 8:1-4//Mk 1:40-45//Lk 5:12-16

Matthew begins his miracle stories with the healing of the leper when Jesus came down from the mountain.[3] A participial verb of motion (*katabantos*) opens the pericope with a reference to Jesus' movement to the place of his healing activity.

Matthew's stylistic phraseology 'and behold, a leper coming,

---

3. In Mark the healing of the leper comes after the healing/exorcism in the synagogue, the healing of Peter's mother-in-law and the healings at evening, and it is followed by a cycle of controversies (Mk 1:40-3:6).

pays homage to him saying', introduces a significant shift in the storyline as something unexpected and socially unacceptable happens. The message of Jesus is now put to the test as the mould of centuries is about to be broken and the breaking of this mould will stand as a significant rubric in the entire narrative of the gospel. The approach of the leper signifies that someone has taken Jesus' message really seriously, that entrance into the kingdom is open to everyone. A significant boundary is about to be crossed in both directions. Leprosy was just one of the factors which placed people in the category of the unclean, the unholy or polluted and separated them from the clean, the holy and the pure. The separation was strictly observed and violation of it was seen as an undermining of the appropriate social order. 'The purity system' made it very clear who belonged to normal civil and religious society and who did not, who were the 'insiders' and the 'outsiders', the 'clean' and the 'unclean'. Unfortunately this sense of belonging or not belonging reached beyond social and liturgical belonging and was regarded by some strict observants as a pointer to acceptance and non-acceptance in the salvific plan of God. The rule of Qumran, for example, was very specific about who was excluded from their messianic community in waiting. Jesus' touching of the leper, his association and eating with tax collectors and sinners, and his entering the house of a Gentile are prophetic actions which challenge these regulations and assumptions and in doing so proclaim that everyone is welcome in the kingdom.

The leper crosses the boundary of convention as he comes to Jesus, pays him homage and says to him: 'Lord, if you wish you have it in your power to make me clean.' Breaking the purity rules, going against social custom, exploding the taboo, the leper approaches Jesus.[4] He addresses him as 'Lord', *Kyrie*, an expres-

---

4. There is an extensive section of legislation in Lev 13-14 dealing with leprosy. In the biblical context leprosy may not be exactly the same as the disease covered by the technical definition of leprosy in the modern world (Hansen's Disease). In Greek the verb *leptein* means 'to peel off' and so the term *lepros,* could cover a variety of conditions. The Hebrew term *sara'at* refers to the kind of fungus growth like that which one sees

sion used in contradistinction to 'rabbi' to show that the petitioner has a deeper faith in Jesus than in a simple teacher or
rabbi. Jesus responds in kind, reaching out to touch the untouch-
able. The legislation in Lev 13-14, which follows a detailed description of symptoms of the disease and regulations for the examination of them by the priest, prescribed that the leper wear
torn clothes, keep dishevelled hair, live 'outside the camp' and
cry out 'unclean, unclean'. This warned off the unsuspecting on-
comer. Should someone, even unwittingly, touch a leper that
person incurred both the unclean state and its penalties. Leprosy
meant isolation from social and religious gatherings, death of
human relationships, and its pallor resembled that of a corpse,
so it was regarded as a sort of death and curing it was seen as
restoring life to one effectively dead (Num 12:10-12; 2 Kings 5:7).
Leprosy was often seen as a punishment for sin.[5] Its effects in
bodily destruction leading to death and a life of isolation from
community paralleled the effects of sin and so the rabbis used
leprosy as a metaphor for sin with its destructive effects on the
person and on his/her relations with the social and religious life
of the community.

The combination of *thelês* (if you wish) and *dunasai* (you have
in your power) in the leper's plea highlights the leper's perception of Jesus' power to heal. In response, Jesus stretches out his
hand and touches him, saying: 'I (so) wish, be cleansed.' The result is immediate. 'And immediately (*kai eutheôs*) his leprosy
was cleansed.' Matthew, unlike Mark, concentrates on the healing action of Jesus without mentioning Jesus' being moved to
compassion at his plight (or anger at his treatment by society
and the establishment).[6]

Jesus' action in reaching out to touch the leper is a radical

---

on clothes or associated with dry rot in houses (cf. Lev 13:47-58; 14:13-
45).

5. Num 12:10-15; cf Deut 28:27, 35; 2 Kings 5:25-27; 2 Chron 26:16-21.

6. Most mss of Mark (Mk 1:41) say Jesus' action was motivated by compassion. 'Being moved to compassion (*splagchnistheis*), he stretched out
his hand and touched him.' Some mss, however, have 'being moved to
anger (*orgistheis*), he stretched out his hand and touched him.'

step in proclaiming in action and attitude the inclusive nature of the kingdom. Touch is a bridge, an embrace across the divide, and in the embrace Jesus healed the leper. The story is reminiscent of, and yet very different from, the healing of Naaman when he came to Elisha for healing of his leprosy. Naaman was an 'outsider', an 'unclean Gentile' and he approached the prophet in Israel, in faith that showed itself in his coming a journey and in his persistent manner. Elisha, however, did not touch him but sent him to the river Jordan to bathe and be healed by *YHWH* (2 Kings 5:8-14).

Jesus instructed the leper to tell no one. He sent him to show himself to the priest who would witness his cure and authorise his return to the community and instructed him to offer the gift laid down by Moses. Witnessing to the healing was an elaborate process. It shows that the term leprosy was used for a variety of apparently similar conditions, which at that time were usually regarded as incurable. The witnessing, according to Lev 13-14, was an elaborate process of sacrifices, washings, shaving of head and eyebrows, and a second and final examination confirming the healing after seven days. Jesus again shows how he has not come to destroy the Law and the Prophets as he explicitly instructs the healed leper to offer the gift required by the Law of Moses

Jesus instructed the leper to tell no one. This command to silence is a particularly striking feature of Mark's gospel and was the key to Wrede's[7] insight that Mark produced a highly theological work rather than a clumsy but close to eye-witness account of Jesus' life. Matthew mentions but does not put the same emphasis in his gospel on the command to silence.[8]

---

7. Wrede, W., *The Messianic Secret*, London: Clarke, 1971 (E. T. by J. C. G. Grieg of *Das Messiasgeheimnis in den Evangelien*, Göttingen 1901).
8. In so far as 'the messianic secret' (the term scholars have given to the injunction to silence) represents a fact of the historical Jesus' life it can be accounted for by a concern about false messianic hopes of a political and social nature. In so far as it was a matter of importance to the early Christian community it may well reflect a certain anxiety about the fact that Jesus whom they now widely refer to as Christ/Messiah did not

b. The Centurion Mt 8:5-13//Lk 7:1-10 cf Jn 4:46-53

The account again begins with a reference to Jesus' coming to the place of his activity 'coming to Capernaum', again a Greek genitive participial phrase (*eiselthontos*).

Jesus' descent from the mountain is now followed by his approaching Capernaum. A centurion approached him beseeching (*parakalôn*) him and like the leper addresses him as Lord, *Kyrie*. The condition of the *pais* is emphasised by two expressions *beblêtai paralytikos*, 'lying paralysed' and *deinôs basanizomenos*, 'terribly tormented'. Jesus responds immediately with the offer to go and heal him, a journey to a Gentile house that would incur ritual uncleanness in the eyes of the strict observants.

The centurion replies, again addressing Jesus as *Kyrie*, and stating his sense of unworthiness that Jesus should enter under his roof. In an extraordinary statement of faith he says to Jesus: ' Say but a word and my servant shall be healed.'[9] He further elaborates on what he means by explaining that he has seen extraordinary authority/power in Jesus. Being a military person he has been subject to higher commanding officers and has in turn exercised authority over soldiers in his own command. 'I say to this one, "Come" and he comes, and to my servant, "Do this", and he does it.' He recognises authority because he has doubly experienced it.

Jesus' amazement takes expression in his solemn 'amen' pronouncement to those following (note the word 'following', signifying those who are becoming his disciples). He says of the Gentile's faith, 'Nowhere have I found such faith in Israel.' This sets the tone for further negative comment on Israel's faith in the gospel and prepares for a future rejection by Israel and a mission to the accepting Gentiles.

He foreshadows the future incorporation of the Gentiles in the kingdom when he continues: 'Many will come from the east and the west and sit down with Abraham and Isaac and Jacob in

himself make explicitly messianic claims during his ministry. Mark is far more emphatic on the injunction to silence than Matthew or Luke.
9. Literally, 'Only speak with a word and my servant shall be healed.'

the kingdom of heaven.' Foreshadowing the rejection by Israel he proclaims 'the sons (children) of the kingdom will be cast out into exterior darkness where there will be weeping and gnashing of teeth.'

Dismissing the centurion Jesus says: 'Go, may it be done to you according to your faith.' Jesus' word was, as the centurion stated, sufficient. The boy was healed at that same hour. The 'divine' or theological passive 'was healed' is a circumlocution for 'God healed him' which avoids using the divine name and predicating action of God. This use of the passive is particularly obvious in Matthew and throughout the New Testament in the healings carried out at a distance.

This story is not told by Mark but it appears in Luke's gospel (Lk 7:1-10) and so it seems to come from the traditional material which Matthew and Luke have in common, conventionally referred to as Q. John has a somewhat similar story (Jn 4:43-54) which may reflect an original common account that has been handed on with different details and emphasis. The synoptic and Johannine traditions are both set in Galilee and both seem to be dealing with a person of pagan birth. In both traditions the petitioner shows strong determination and faith and in both cases the healing takes place at a distance. Whereas the synoptic tradition speaks of a servant or slave, and the Johannine account speaks of a son, the close bond of a household slave to the family members, particularly if born in the master's household, could easily account for his being treated by the master and spoken of as a son of the family. Furthermore, the Greek word *pais* used by Matthew (Mt 8:6,13) can mean boy/ child, whether a servant, slave or son. Luke uses both *doulos*, a slave or servant (Lk 7:2,3,10) and *pais* (Lk 7:7). John uses *huios*, son (Jn 4:46,47,50,53) and also uses *pais* in Jn 4:51 and *paidion*, a diminutive of *pais*, in Jn 4:49.

c. Peter's Mother-in-Law Mt 8:14-15//Mk 1:29-32//Lk 4:38-39

Again a participial verb of motion (*elthôn*) opens the pericope with a reference to Jesus' movement to the place of his healing activity. Entering the house of Peter[10] he found Peter's mother-in-law lying down and feverish. The language of 'healing touch' (*êpsato*) and the resurrection language of 'raising up' (*egeirein*) are used in the account of the restoration of the woman to health. He touched her hand and she rose up. Whereas Matthew speaks of 'touching her hand' in the corresponding story Mark uses the expression 'taking a powerful grip of her hand', *kratêsas tês cheiros* (Mk 1:29f).

Touch was a well-established dimension of healing in biblical and extra biblical experience and literature. The language of 'raising up' recurs in the gospel. It has connotations of restoring to health and wholeness and also of restoring the dead to life. Before the writing of the gospels it was a long established term in the proclamation of the resurrection of Jesus whom 'God raised from the dead.' The immediacy and completeness of the cure is evidenced by the statement that she 'ministered to him', *diêkonei autô*, an activity requiring a level of energy not associated with someone who has just been in a fever (Mt 8:15).

'She ministered to him', *diêkonei autô*.[11] Here in this case the verb *diêkonei* does not have connotations of a 'servile' service but rather ties into the whole biblical idea of a ministry of hospitality within home and community, particularly to the ministers of the gospel (Mt 10:11f; Mk 6:10f; Lk 9:6; 10:5ff). It is also the verb used for describing the task for which the seven were appointed in Acts 6:1-6. Like Martha in St John's gospel (Jn 12:2) the mother-in-law of Peter is said to 'serve/minister to' (*diakonein*) her guest. In the mind of the evangelists and those for whom they were originally writing it was not a relegating of her to a 'menial' kitchen sink role but an elevation of her to what was seen by

10. The parallel accounts in Mark and Luke call him Simon at this point. 1 Cor 9:5 may imply that Peter/Cephas brought his wife with him on his missionary journeys. Paul writes: 'Do we not have the right to be accompanied by a believing wife as do the other apostles and the brothers of the Lord and Cephas ?'

11. F. J. Moloney, *op. cit.*, 55, points out that in Jesus' time it may have been a departure from custom, in fact a breaking of a taboo, to have a rabbi or religious leader 'served' by a woman. However, by the time of the writing of the New Testament that attitude had radically changed.

them as an established, highly prized and important role in the hospitality ministry of the community. Hospitality was seen as the mark of the God-believing and God-fearing person in the Old Testament (cf Gen 18:1-15). Hospitality was very important in early Christian communities. It was to be the acid test for the apostles in discerning the good, receptive person when they entered a town or village (Mt 10:11-16). The house churches grew up around the hospitality of those who received the missionaries. It should be kept in mind that very early on there was a debate in the Jerusalem church about the neglect of hospitality in overlooking the Hellenist widows. In response to the criticism the seven were chosen for this service of hospitality. The apostles prayed over them and laid hands on them (Acts 6:1-6). Furthermore, the criteria for enrolment as a widow in the First Letter to Timothy emphasise such hospitality: 'She must be well attested as one who has brought up her children, shown hospitality, washed the saints' feet, helped the afflicted and devoted herself to doing good in every way' (1 Tim 5:10). Some communities had an established order of 'deacon' already in New Testament times (Phil 1:1; 1 Tim 3:8, 12, 13;Rom 16:1).

There is no mention in Matthew's account of anyone else being present with Jesus in the house of Peter's mother-in-law, drawing his attention to her illness or being 'ministered to' by her after her healing. The story focuses on her and Jesus alone. Being thus alone in the house with a woman who was not a relation and touching a woman, which a rabbi or religious leader would not have done, have strong connotations of Jesus' breaking a taboo, as in the case of touching the leper.

d. Summary and Citation from Isaiah Mt 8:16-17//Mk 1:32-34//Lk 4:40-41; Isa 53:4

As evening drew on they brought to him many possessed people and he drove out the spirits with a word (again the power of his healing word is in evidence) and he healed all who were ill. There is no reference to a change of place and this is a reason for seeing the two accounts as a unit. Why did they wait till evening? A reader who had read only Matthew's gospel would be inclined to think that maybe the cool of the evening facilitated the carrying of stretchers, or the end of the day's work made it possible for people to be free to come together and co-operate in bringing the sick to Jesus. Having read Mark's gospel where the evening comes at the end of a Sabbath, one immediately thinks of the end of the Sabbath and the lifting of its restrictions on work, movement and transportation. Mark's account probably influences readers to consider the same reason for the crowd waiting till evening in this gospel. Matthew emphasises the universal impact of Jesus' actions by saying that they brought many possessed people and he cured all those who were sick.[12]

Matthew rounds off this first triad of miracle stories by pointing to the fulfilment of scripture: 'So that the saying of Isaiah the prophet would be fulfilled' (Isa 53:4). The citation comes from the Fourth Song of the Suffering Servant (Isa 52:13-53:12). The main thrust of that song is that the servant took on himself our weaknesses and suffered vicariously on our behalf (Isa 53:4). As the citation is presented here to further Matthew's point of view it does not follow exactly either the Hebrew Masoretic Text or the Greek Septuagint text (as was also the case in the citations earlier in the gospel). The emphasis in the first half of the citation (*tas astheneias elaben*) emphasises his taking away, in the sense of doing away with, our sicknesses but the second half (*tas nosous ebastasen*) follows the sense of the overall hymn with its emphasis on his vicarious suffering on our behalf, taking our sufferings on himself, 'he carried them' on our behalf.

---

12. Mark brings out the same emphasis by the hyperbolic use of 'all the sick', 'the whole city', 'many kinds of sicknesses' and 'he healed many sick and expelled many demons.' The Greek word for 'many' (*polloi*), used here by Matthew, has much stronger connotations in the New Testament than its English translation, especially when reflecting a Semitic word such as *rabh* which has the connotation of 'a very large number.'

B. THE SECOND TRIAD: JESUS' AUTHORITY AND THE DANGERS OF DISCI-
PLESHIP MT 8:18- 9:8

The term 'following' has been used in a particular way of the
disciples and in a general way of the crowds. Now it will begin
to be emphasised in terms of the cost and the danger to the individual who has already become, or wishes to become a disciple
or follower.

Just as Capernaum figures as the central location in the first
triad of stories, now the Sea of Galilee figures as a central location in the second triad. Crossing the sea to the other side has
strong overtones of entering Gentile territory and foreshadows
the future missions to the Gentiles which will be more strongly
foreshadowed in the latter part of the gospel and commanded in
the final scene (Mt 28:16-20).

In this second triad of miracle stories the awesome figure of
Jesus is now emerging more strongly and the christology of the
gospel is developing in and through the narrative, as Jesus exercises divine control over the natural elements, casts out demons
and pronounces the forgiveness of sins.

*a. Rebuking the Wind and the Waves: Mt 8:18-27//Lk 8:22-25 //Mk
4:35-41*

On seeing the crowds around him Jesus gave orders to go to the
other side (of the lake). The reason for wanting to leave the
crowd is not explained, but one can assume that Jesus needed
rest, quietness and a place apart to pray and be with his disciples.

At this point in the narrative Matthew introduces two characters whose approach to Jesus give him the opportunity of issuing
a serious warning about the cost and the dangers of discipleship.
These two initial encounters enable and lead into the particularly
Matthean redaction of the story of the storm on the lake.[13]

---

13. Matthew's redaction of the story is the subject of a very influential
treatment by G. Bornkamm, 'The Stilling of the Storm in Matthew' in G.
Bornkamm, G. Barth, and H. J. Held, *Tradition and Interpretation in
Matthew*, Philadelphia; Westminster/London, SCM, 1963.

The first to approach Jesus is a scribe who is not yet a disciple (follower). He addresses him as 'teacher', the usual address of those who are not disciples or followers, showing an inadequate understanding and faith in Jesus. He says: 'I will follow you (be your disciple) wherever you go.' It was customary for potential disciples to seek out a famous rabbi and apprentice themselves to him wherever he was domiciled. This seems to be his intention as he approaches Jesus and addresses him as 'teacher'. The opposite is true of Jesus and his disciples. It was Jesus who picked his disciples. In response to the scribe Jesus points out in clear imagery drawn from nature, that foxes have holes, the birds of the air have nests but the Son of Man has nowhere to lay his head. Far from being apprenticed to an established teacher with a fixed abode and a body of knowledge and wisdom to impart, Jesus is of no fixed abode and being apprenticed to him means sharing his lifestyle with its challenges and outcome. In referring to himself, Jesus uses the term Son of Man and in so doing a whole new christological dimension is being introduced into the narrative.

This first reference to the Son of Man is an example of a *prolepsis*, a gap in information leaving the reader to await further revelation before discovering who this Son of Man is. Though the term 'Son of Man' can mean simply 'a human being' just as in English one may say 'any mother's son', it has taken on a series of theological meanings in the Bible and is particularly in evidence in the New Testament where it is applied to Jesus.[14] It is often used as a corrective by Jesus against titles that convey false messianic expectations. In this regard it is used to convey the notion of the humble servant of God carrying on the ministry to establish the kingdom and in a particular way it is applied to his role as the suffering servant who will be rejected,

---

14. Matthew uses the term ' Son of Man' twenty nine times, Mark uses it fourteen times, John thirteen times and Luke twenty seven times. Outside of the gospels the term occurs in the New Testament only in Acts 7:56 where Stephen alludes to Dan 7:13, and in Rev 1:13, 14:14.

cast out and put to death.[15] Here the lifestyle of the Son of Man
has now been described and his fate has been hinted at in Jesus'
response to the potential disciple and there is a definite implication that his followers will share both in his lifestyle and his fate.

The second person to approach Jesus is already 'one of the
disciples'. He addresses Jesus as disciples and believers do with
the title Lord, *Kyrie*, and makes a request to Jesus about letting
him go to bury his father. The reader is reminded of the call of
Elisha when he asked Elijah for permission 'to kiss his father
and mother' before leaving them (1 Kings 19:20). Is this disciple
of Jesus asking simply to go to attend to the funeral arrangements of an already dead father or is he speaking of a return to
look after him until he dies or is he homesick for his father's
house? Even more pertinent is the question: 'Is he returning because his father objects to his following Jesus?' Jesus' answer is
sharp and to the point. It is in keeping with his remarks elsewhere that 'anyone who loves father or mother more than me is
not worthy of me; anyone who loves son or daughter more than
me is not worthy of me' (Mt 10:37-38). One draws the conclusion
from Jesus' response that there is more than just a temporary absence for a funeral or a longer absence for a genuine filial obligation involved. It seems to reflect a situation where the father
objects to the son's following of Jesus and so he wishes to put his
discipleship on the long finger until after the death of his father.
Jesus' further remark seems to bear this out as he comments on
the 'dead' state of the father: 'Let the dead bury their own dead.'
This exchange probably resonates with the experience of famil-
ial tensions about Christ and his followers on the part of members of Matthew's community.

Having thus commented on the cost of 'following him' in
'discipleship' Jesus entered the boat and his disciples followed

15. It is also used to give expression to the glorious return of the Son of
Man, when he will come to exercise the functions ascribed to 'the One
like to a Son of Man' in Daniel (Dan 7:13), specifically the power to
judge and to give life. As a foreshadowing of this glorious, authoritative role he forgives sins (Mt 8:6) and declares himself master of the
Sabbath (Mt 12:8).

him. Here Matthew's emphasis is very obvious when the opening of the story is compared with Mark's statement that the disciples 'took Jesus just as he was into the boat' (Mk 4:36). In
Matthew's account the disciples follow Jesus into the boat. In so
doing they have followed him into very dangerous waters!
Following Jesus on land, in the open spaces, into a house or synagogue is very different to following him (a carpenter's son with
no experience of seafaring) into the boat at night when the little
boat, open to the elements, will be battered by earthquake, wind
and sea. Against all odds it does not break up and sink when a
'great earthquake' (*seismos megas*) struck and the boat was en-
gulfed by the waves. The power of God protected it in spite of
the superior forces ranged against it. Commentators see in the
boat with its endangered, troubled passengers and sleeping, but
protecting Jesus, an image of the church in a troubled, and persecuting world.

The lake was notorious for sudden storms as the land cooled
after the heat of the day and tornado style whirlwinds resulted
from the difference in air temperatures over the lake and the surrounding land. Mark describes such a 'great storm', but
Matthew increases the effect of the upheaval and the resulting
terror engendered by referring to it as a 'great earthquake' (*seismos megas*), whereas Mark and Luke speak of a (violent) storm
(*lailaps megalê*) (Mk 4:37; Lk 8:23).[16] The waves breaking over the
boat, as in a tsunami caused by an underwater earthquake, create the sense of chaos emerging from the disturbed sea, often
seen in biblical times as the home of the primeval monster and
the forces of chaos. The vivid description sets the scene for the
terror of the disciples and Jesus' powerful word of command to
the wind and the sea.

The terror of the disciples stands out in great contrast to the
untroubled sleep of Jesus – manifesting his lordship over life,
death and chaos and his awareness of the power and protection

16. Mark speaks of a violent storm of wind (*lailaps megalê anemou*) (Mk
4:37 breaking upon them and Luke speaks of a storm of wind (*lailaps
anemou*) (Lk 8:23).

of God, expressed so clearly in the psalms of confidence: 'I will lie down in peace, and sleep comes at once, for you, Lord, make me rest in safety', and 'Now I can lie down and go to sleep, and then awake, for *YHWH* has hold of me' (Pss 4:8; 3:5 *inter al*). The description of Jesus asleep in the boat is reminiscent of the account of Jonah sleeping in the ship during a violent storm when the other passengers were terrified and calling on their gods until the boatswain woke Jonah up in a less than gentle manner and commanded him to call on his god: 'What do you mean by sleeping? Get up. Call on your god! Perhaps he will spare us a thought and not leave us to die' (Jonah 1:4-6).[17] Both Jewish and Gentile readers of the gospel would be aware of the power of the sea, and Jewish and pagan literature has many stories of travellers calling on the god of the sea.

Whereas Mark says 'they woke him' Matthew says 'they approached him', that is like the leper and the centurion who also approached him and appealed for his powerful help. Approaching and waking Jesus, the disciples address him with the title 'Lord', appropriate for disciples who are beginning to understand that he is more than just a teacher. They simply cry out to him: 'Save (us), Lord, we are perishing!'[18] This is in stark contrast to Mark's account where they address him at this point simply as 'Teacher' and rebuke him with the words 'Do you not care if we perish?' A further contrast with Mark's account is seen in Jesus' response to their appeal. In Mark's account Jesus first calms the storm and then rebukes them for their little faith. Here in Matthew's account Jesus first addresses them in the midst of the seismic upheaval with the words 'Why are you afraid (*deiloi* / cowardly / timid), men of little faith?'[19] Addressing these words

17. By way of contrast, Jonah was on his way west to avoid his God-given mission to the Gentile Ninivites. Jesus is on his way east to the Gentiles' side of the lake to carry on his mission in Gadarene territory, when they encountered the storms.

18. Peter will also cry out 'Save, Lord' *Sôson, Kyrie*, when he begins to sink in the waves (Mt 14:30).

19. Mark emphasises their fear: 'They feared a great fear', *ephobêthêsan phobon megan*. Matthew does not give it so much emphasis and does not have Jesus 'rebuking' them for it but rather he seems to be teaching and preparing them for such adversity.

to them right in the midst of the crisis highlights the point made earlier about the insecurity involved in following him. In the vocabulary of both Matthew and Mark the opposite of faith is fear. It is because of their little faith they are so very frightened in the crisis. Having made his point in such traumatic circumstances, Jesus then displays his power in action.

'Rising up' (*egertheis*) conveys the powerful picture of Jesus rising up in the boat where he had been sleeping, to confront the life threatening forces of the winds and the sea. Seeing them in personalised terms as forces to be controlled, he rebuked them. 'He rebuked (*epitimêsen*)' is the verb regularly used in the New Testament for rebuking the demons and silencing them. Here Jesus rebukes and silences the wind and the sea, so often seen as the abode of monsters and demons of chaos. At his word the great seismic upheaval (*seismos megas*) becomes a great calm (*galênê megalê*).

Exercising this power over wind and wave casts Jesus in the role of one having extraordinary possession of the divine powers evident in control over creation. God's creative power is seen at its most spectacular in the control of the sea. The control and separation of the waters at creation and the leading of the people through the waters of the sea as they fled from the Egyptian army at the Exodus stand at the foundation of biblical understanding of God's role in creation and in their own history as a people.[20] This biblical awareness of the divine presence in, and power over, creation, especially as manifested in the case of the angry sea is found all through the Bible. Job affirmed: 'He alone stretched out the heavens and trampled the waves of the sea' (Job 9:8), and Deutero-Isaiah proclaimed: '... the redeemed pass over the depths of the sea ... *I am, I am*, the one comforting you, how then can you be afraid ...' (Isa 51:10,12).[21] The psalms have many references to God's control over the sea and to his protec-

---

20. Cf Gen 1:6-8; Exod 14; 15; Deut 7:2-7; Job 38:16; Pss 29:3; 65:7; 77:19; 89:9; 93:4; Isa 43:1-5; 51:10.
21. '*I am, I am*, the one consoling/comforting you.' LXX *ego eimi, ego eimi ho parakalôn se* (Isa 51:10,12).

tion of those threatened by its power: 'Your way was through
the sea, your path through the mighty waters yet your footprints
were unseen' (Ps 77:19). 'Some went down to the sea in ships ...
they cried to the Lord in their trouble and he saved them from
their distress. He made the storm still and the waves of the sea
were hushed. They rejoiced because of the calm and he brought
them to the desired haven' (Ps 107:23-30). 'You rule the raging of
the sea, when its waves rise you still them' (Ps 89:9). 'When the
waters saw you, O God, they were afraid and the very deep
trembled' (Ps 77:16). This understanding of God's power over
the sea permeated the thinking and prayer life of the people of
Israel. Here, to the amazement of the disciples, Jesus shows that
same divine power emanating from his rebuke to the winds and
the sea. The 'men' (mere human beings) were awestruck at his
power over the elements and how they obeyed him.

In the story of Jonah, after the people in the boat experience
the calming of the storm by *YHWH*, the God of Jonah, 'they were
seized with dread of *YHWH*; they offered a sacrifice to *YHWH*
and made vows' (Jonah 1:16). The people of the Greco-Roman
world would have been familiar with prayers to the gods of the
sea, sky and earth for protection. The disciples in the boat with
Jesus have an even more awe-inspiring experience as they see
that power of *YHWH* exercised by their master in the boat. Their
awesome terror prompts them to ask the central question of the
gospel 'What kind of man (*potapos*) is this for the wind and sea
obey him?' 'Obey' (*hypakouein*) is a reinforced form of '*akouein*',
to listen/hear. The whole story thus comes to a climax in the
christological question which points to the identity of Jesus and
the nature of the kingdom he proclaims.[22] The use of the term
anthrôpoi, 'men' in the sense of 'mere human beings' in describing the amazement of the disciples, rather than referring to them

22. Even though the story was important for the first Christians as a
consolation in the midst of persecution, pointing to the fact that an apparently sleeping Jesus was still very much with them in their suffering,
and in control, still as it is told here in the gospel the point of the story is
also seriously christological and directed at the disciples to warn them
of the cost and dangers of discipleship.

as the 'disciples' at this point highlights both the human power-lessness before the forces that Jesus had controlled and their human amazement at his power/authority as they exclaim 'What kind of man is this that the winds and sea obey him?'

The demons, speaking through the possessed men whom Jesus and his company encounter immediately on landing in pagan territory, will have no such problem knowing Jesus' true identity! They address him as 'Son of God' and are seized with fear that the final judgement has already begun with his appearing.

b. Exorcising the Demons Mt 8:28-34//Mk 5:1-20//Lk 8:26-39

Jesus and his disciples have reached the other side of the Lake of Galilee. The goal of Jesus' journey has been achieved, facilitated by his saving action on the water. They have arrived safely in pagan territory. The troublesome distance between Jewish and pagan territory has been well experienced in the dangers of the seismic upheaval on the sea, and will be further highlighted in Jesus' reception on the other side where they encounter the frightening scene of the demoniacs and the danger they posed to anyone who came near them.

The story of the Gadarene demoniacs is shorter and some-what less dramatic than the parallel account in Mark. The focus is firmly on Jesus and his power, and the two demoniacs fade immediately from the picture as soon as the demons are driven from them. The story manifests Matthew's liking for pairs of examples or witnesses to Jesus' power. This interest in pairs may well be related to the fact that a pair of witnesses was a legal requirement for accepting a testimony.

In the handing on of the story of the Gadarene (or Gerasene) demoniacs confusion about the exact location has crept into the accounts.[23] However, the purpose of the story and its place in the overall narrative of the gospel are the important points and

23. Matthew and some Markan manuscripts speak of the territory of the Gadarenes. Most manuscripts of Mark speak of 'the territory of the Gerasenes' but some, following a conjecture of Origen, have 'Gergesenes'.

the exact location is of purely academic interest, except in so far
as it points to a location in Gentile territory, in the general area of
the Decapolis. Locating a mighty work of Jesus in Gentile territory foreshadows, and could be used subsequently by the
Christian community to legitimate missionary work among the
Gentiles.

On his disembarking from the boat, two demoniacs, coming
out from the tombs, accosted Jesus. Their condition is referred to
as 'demon possessed' *daimonizomenoi*. They were so fierce that
no one could pass along that way.[24]

They call out: 'What is between us and you, Son of God', a
clear acknowledgement of Jesus' extraordinary identity and a
recognition of the irreconcilable difference between him and
them and the respective powers they represent. They ask fear-
fully if he has come to torture them before the time, that is, before the eschatological judgement, when Satan and the demons
will be judged and finally overcome and eternally punished.
The verb *basanizein*, to torture/punish is also used in Mt 18:34 of
eschatological judgement and in Lk 16:23, 28 of the damnation
of the heartless rich man.

The demons beg of him, as of a superior power, that if they
are cast out (of the possessed men) that he send them into the
herd of swine that were feeding some distance away. In this way
they will not be sent away out of the territory (a request made

---

Luke speaks of 'the territory of the Gerasenes which is opposite Galilee'.
Gadara is five miles from the sea and has no steep cliffs. Gerasa (modern Jerash) is thirty-seven miles from the sea. Both sites are therefore
problematical. Maybe 'territory of the Gadarenes' (or Gerasenes) refers
to territory where they shepherded their flocks in summer months
away from their homes, as was customary with nomadic people. The
presence of the herd of swine seems to support this view.

24. Other examples of pairs of healings are those of the two blind men
in Galilee (Mt 9:27-31) and two blind men in Jericho (Mt 20:29-34), corresponding to the story of the one blind man (Bartimaeus) in both Mark
and Luke (Mt 20:29-34 cf Mk 10:46-52; Lk18: 35-43). Also he puts together
as a pair the stories of the cure of the blind men and the deaf mute in
Galilee (Mt 9:27-34). This interest in pairs may well be because a pair of
witnesses was a legal requirement for accepting a testimony.

explicit in the Markan account) that reflects the ancient belief that demons were territorial. Remaining in the district would facilitate other possessions there.[25] The superior status and power of Jesus are seen in his allowing the transfer. Appropriately the demons enter what to the Jews were the most unclean of the unclean, a herd of pigs. Not alone were Jews forbidden to eat pig meat, they were forbidden to keep pigs and swine herding was seen like tax collecting and prostitution as an unacceptable occupation for a Jew. Minding the pigs for a Gentile was the ultimate degradation for the Prodigal Son (Lk 15:15f).

The demons get their new abode but they are 'sold a dummy'. Some say that the folkloric motif of the 'duped demon' may be present here in the story.[26] Their presence causes even the unclean animals to go into such a frenzy that they rush down the hill into the very waves from which Jesus has so recently saved his disciples. He has consigned the demons to a place in the deep with the forces of chaos. Of significance also is the fact that demons were reputed to be afraid of the sea.[27]

So far the story has followed the usual form of an exorcism story – a meeting with Jesus, the demons cry out in fear as they identify and address Jesus as Son of God, thereby trying to control him. Jesus controls and expels the demons, and by implication (though it is actually described at greater length in Mark) the possessed persons are restored to health and society. Instead of a command to silence and the usual brief statement about the effect of the miracle on the people who observed it, the reactions to the extraordinary happening are told by the herdsmen who 'fled' and 'announced/publicised' in the city everything that

---

25. See the article by D. H. Juel, 'Plundering Satan's Household: Demons and Discipleship' in D. H. Juel, *A Master of Surprise. Mark Interpreted*, 65-75.

26. J. R. Donohue and D. J. Harrington, *op. cit*, 166.

27. R. H. Gundry, *op. cit.*, 9., in his commentary on Mark, detects a note of humour in Mark's telling of the story as the demoniacs, having been reduced to 'grovelling supplication' are described as 'drowning' (*epnigonto*), the imperfect of the verb functioning as a humorous 'slow-motion playback.' Matthew simply says, 'They died in the waves'.

had happened, and all about the demoniacs. Matthew's univer-
salising emphasis is again in evidence as he reports that 'the
whole city came out to meet Jesus'. Mark simply says 'the people came to see what had happened'. The colourful description
of the healed man sitting clothed and in his right mind does not
appear in Matthew. The stark statement of the people's reaction
to, or rather against, Jesus as they begged him to leave their territory comes as a surprise, or rather as a shock, to the reader.
Jesus embarks and returns to his own side of the lake to his own
city/town (Mt 9:1).

Why did the people ask Jesus to leave? Some have speculated
that the loss of the pigs was an economic blow that they did not
want repeated – the price of the men's healing was the loss of the
pigs! It is much more likely that the fear/awe with which they
were struck in the presence of this Jew who had come over the
lake was too much for pagan people to handle at the time. They
may have feared Jesus, thinking that an ever greater and more
evil power than the demons in the possessed men was at work
in him. Even among his own people the Pharisees will believe,
or at least they will spread the malicious rumour in order to
make others so believe, that he was driving out demons through
the power of the prince of demons (Mt 12:24)! Had some such
rumour preceded him over the lake or were the people genuinely
afraid of such a superior demon working through him? It is also
quite possible that Matthew tells the story knowing that this
kind of experience is being repeated in the case of some of the
first Christian missionaries among the pagans.

Though there is a foreshadowing of the mission to the
Gentiles in the story and the possibility of a rejection of the disciples' powerful work in their midst, still the subject is not further
developed and, unlike the story in Mark, there is no mention of
the healed demoniacs wanting to stay with Jesus or being sent
by him to bear witness among their own Gentile people (cf Mk
5:19f).

The reader of the gospel has been assured of Jesus' power
over the evil spirits. In this triumph over the frightful demons

that terrorised the people passing along the road the final eschatological victory has been foreshadowed and in fact has already begun in the ministry of Jesus.

Jesus embarks and returns to his own side of the lake to his own city/town (Mt 9:1).

c. Forgiving Sins and Healing Mt 9:1-8//Mk 2:1-12//Lk 5:17-26

As Jesus embarks and returns to his own side of the lake to his own city/town (Mt 9:1) the change of location again sets the scene for another initiative. This third miracle in the triad, describing Jesus' healing of the paralytic after pronouncing the forgiveness of his sins, is an example of a story common to Matthew, Mark and Luke.[28] As Jesus is accused (though silently) of blasphemy, the danger of criticism, misrepresentation, calumny and false accusation are becoming evident and will gather momentum as the gospel narrative progresses.

'And behold they brought to him a paralytic lying on a stretcher/bed.' This typical Matthean introduction to the story ('and behold') replaces the colourful scene of the stretcher-bearers climbing onto the roof in Mark and Luke (Mk 2:1-12//Lk 5:17-26). Jesus' reaction on seeing the faith of the stretcher bearers is to address a word of encouragement to the sick man: The exhortation to 'Take courage' just like 'Do not be afraid' is associated very much with theophanies and angelic appearances throughout the Bible. The biblical reader should therefore expect some divine initiative or healing action to follow. There follows the astounding proclamation: 'Your sins are forgiven.'[29] With these words Jesus strikes at the perceived root of all suffer-

---

28. The reader wonders why the narrator, if he were following the story in Mark, would have omitted the vivid and colourful detail of the crowd blocking the entrance to the house and the carriers of the stretcher climbing onto the roof, stripping off the roofing materials and letting the stretcher down in front of Jesus, even taking into account Matthew's usual economy of words, images and characters. It may point to Matthew's working on an earlier narrative subsequently edited differently by Mark and Matthew.

29. 'Faith', *pistis*, has connotations of their faith in Jesus and their fidelity to the sick person.

ing. In saying this, he is assuming an authority that belongs to God alone, a fact spelled out explicitly in the account in Mark in the thought rising in the hearts of the scribes: 'Who can forgive sins but God alone?'(Mk 2:7)

What has had all the appearances of a typical healing/miracle story up to this point now becomes a typical controversy story. The authority he assumes in his remark on the forgiveness of sins gives offence to the scribes who say to themselves: 'This man is blaspheming.' This first recorded criticism of Jesus in the gospel foreshadows the final, fatal criticism, the charge of blasphemy at his Jewish trial, which will signal his definitive rejection and condemnation by the Jewish authorities, resulting in his being handed over to the Romans and put to death.

Even the term 'this man' (houtos) has overtones of disapproval. Jesus immediately knew that they thus thought to themselves and asked them: 'Why do you have these wicked thoughts in your hearts?' Then he poses a question and places them in a no-win situation. He asks: 'Which is easier to say to the paralytic, "Your sins are forgiven" or to say "Rise up take up your pallet and walk"?'[30]

Words are usually easy to say and they can equally easily deceive. Deeds are not. They are transparent. But in this case words are not easy as the only words possible would have been either: 'It is easier to say: "Your sins are forgiven"' or 'It is easier to say: "Rise up take up your bed and walk."' The first option was impossible because, if they said: 'It is easier to say: "Your sins are forgiven"' it would implicate the critics in the very blasphemy that provoked their criticism. Their other option, to say: 'It is easier to say: "Rise up, take up your pallet and walk"' would have exposed them to huge embarrassment and ridicule when, unlike the one they were criticising, they proved unable to match their words with deeds.

Then, having thus reduced his opposition to a shamed silence, Jesus showed the deeper meaning of his ministry and the words

---

30. See Hunter, Faith and Geoffrey, 'Which is Easier? (Mk 2:9)', *Exp Times* 105 (1993) 12f.

and deeds in which it found expression, deeper than just winning an argument. He said: ' To prove to you that the Son of Man
has power on earth to forgive sins (he addressed the paralytic),
"I say to you, rise, take up you pallet and go to your home".'
And rising up he departed to his own home. The verb 'rise up',
so often associated with Jesus' life-giving power, appears three
times in this healing. Seeing it the crowds were filled with awe
and gave glory to God 'for giving such power to men'. This resembles the awe of the disciples in the boat when they said:
'What kind of man is this? The wind and waves obey him.' In
Mark the enthusiasm of the crowd is expressed in the words 'We
have never seen anything like this' and Luke has a similar expression. Matthew's version, however, 'They praised God for
giving such power to men' seems to carry an apologetic note
against ongoing scepticism about forgiveness of sins in the
(Matthean) community, or on the part of their former Jewish co-
religionists.

This enthusiasm of the crowd as they acknowledge the miracle
as an act of God overshadows for the moment the criticism in
the hearts of the scribes. But that criticism will smoulder and
gradually assert itself openly. In the honour-shame consciousness of society Jesus has scored a major victory and put his critics to shame.

The fact that there were scribes present, as if in formal teaching position, seems strange in a crowded house, if Mark's location is taken into account, though Matthew does not state
where the incident occurred. The description is reminiscent of
an occasion in the synagogue.

This second reference to the Son of Man, now stating that he
has power on earth to forgive sins is another example of a *prolepsis*, a gap leaving the reader to await further revelation before discovering who this Son of Man is and why he has power on earth
to forgive sins, a prerogative of God alone. The original audience
and the implied or original readers, may have had some knowledge of the Son of Man passages in Daniel and Ezekiel but such
knowledge would have served to whet the appetite rather than to
explain the term and its function at this point in the narrative.

The faith of the infirm man's friends figures in the story of the paralytic giving them the role of a communal character manifesting a very positive attitude towards Jesus. They also represent, very likely, people in the Christian community who bring their sick for healing. Interestingly, the man himself does not figure as a character at all. There is no mention of his appeal to Jesus, his faith or lack of it, his response to his healing or to the forgiveness of his sins. He merely fulfils a function. Perhaps his story was (and still is) important also for Christians who bring their sick, maybe unbelieving or sceptical family members or friends, for healing.

The critics of Jesus in this episode were the scribes. They were not a religious organisation or movement like the Pharisees, Sadducees or Essenes. The term is a professional one covering a broad array of people such as biblical scholars, legal experts and official secretaries of various kinds. They probably belonged to different religious and philosophical associations, as is evident from Mark's reference to the scribes who belonged to the Pharisee party (Mk 2:16). However, their knowledge of scripture and Law probably predisposed a large number of them to become members of the Pharisee movement, but in the Jerusalem area many would have allied themselves with the very influential Sadducees and priestly class.[31]

d. Controversy: Call of Matthew; Dining with Tax Collectors and Sinners; Fasting Mt 9:9-17

This section functions as a sequel to the second triad of miracle stories and as a lead into the third and final triad. Jesus has just pronounced the forgiveness of sins (*hamartias*) and cured a physical ailment as a pointer towards and authentication of his authority and power to forgive sins. The natural sequel to such an event is to show how he relates to sinners. He calls sinners (*hamartôloi*) and the religiously and socially excluded to discipleship in the kingdom and gathers them around him in his circle

---

31. For a study of the Scribes see C. Schams, *Jewish Scribes in the Second-Temple Period*, Sheffield: Academic Press 1998.

of disciples and in his social circle. In so doing he displays and defends an attitude that will draw on him the criticism of the Pharisees. Matthew now traces a series of words and deeds of Jesus dealing with his attitudes towards the marginalised and the excluded. This marks a new beginning in the story of salvation following the proclamation of the kingdom. His attitudes and actions are a source of controversy. For this Matthew uses the material used in the Galilee controversies in Mark and Luke (Mt 9:9-17//Mk 2:13-22//Lk 5:27-39), all three making the same points but with differences of detail.

i. The call of Matthew Mt 9:9; cf Mk 2:13-14; Lk 5:27-28

Jesus proceeds on his way, whence or whither is not clearly defined, but the description of his movement is an integral part of the synoptic call narratives as seen already in the call of the two pairs of brothers (Mt 3:18-22). Jesus was passing, he saw the potential disciple, noted his profession, called him to follow him and he followed. The person called to discipleship here is named Matthew but the person called in the parallel story in Mark and Luke is called Levi, son of Alphaeus (Mk 2:13f; Lk 5:27f). Why are there two different names for what appears on the surface to be the same person? Some scholars maintain that this disciple had two names. It is always possible that someone gets a nickname or a pet name in life from family or associates, sometimes a term of endearment in a family circle or a name that fits the person's appearance, character, habits or influence in a circle of friends so well that it almost replaces one's official name. One thinks of Jesus' designation of Simon as Kephas/Peter, the brothers James and John as 'sons of thunder' (Mk 3:17), Nathanael as 'a true Israelite without deceit' (Jn 1:47) and Saul's change of name to Paul. In the case of a founder or significant figure in a community (as Matthew appears to have been) it is possible that a title of honour may have been intended. Levi may be a descriptive title used as a nickname because of Levitical background, somewhat like Macantsagairt or Taggart in Irish and Scots Gaelic. Or it may be that in Hebrew the corre-

sponding name *Mattatiyah* means 'gift of God' and its Greek
form *Mattaios* sounds somewhat like *mathêtês*, a disciple and a
loose play on both words would serve well as a title of honour.
However one explains either name it is more likely that a nickname or title of honour is being used than an intrusion of
Matthew (because of his later importance) into the story of the
call of Levi and into the lists of the Twelve in place of Levi (as is
sometimes suggested). In the lists of the Twelve which appear in
all three synoptic gospels and in the Acts of the Apostles, it is
significant that Matthew, and not Levi, is mentioned, and the list
in Matthew adds 'the tax collector' after his name (Mt 10:1-4; Mk
3:13-19; Lk 6:12-16; Acts 1:13).

Here we again encounter the call of Jesus, in a form akin to
the calling of the Old Testament prophets. The name of the addressee, his livelihood, and the location of the call are given,
similar to the case of the two pairs of brothers already called.
Like them Matthew left his means of livelihood, rose and followed Jesus. However, calling Matthew is a very radical step
and a provocative gesture on Jesus' part since the collectors of
tolls or taxes were seen as operating a system for a foreign government, often in the interests of their own pockets and regularly
carried out through putting pressure on the more vulnerable
members of society. Needless to say the tax and toll collectors
were held in disfavour, or more accurately, they were greatly
despised, by the people generally.

Though Julius Caesar had discontinued the system of farming out the tax collecting to rich and often dishonest grasping
people, in Galilee under Herod the Great and his son Antipas
the tolls or taxes continued to be collected by royal officials, who
in turn sub-contracted minor officials to carry out the task. Tax
collectors get a bad press from Roman, Greek and Jewish writers
alike. Cicero and Dio Chrysostom link them with beggars,
thieves and robbers.[32] The *Mishnah* associates them with robbers, murderers and sinners.[33] In the New Testament they are

---

32. Cicero, *De Officiis*, 15-21; Dio Chrysostom, *Orations*, 14.14.
33. *m.Tohar* 7.6; *m. Baba Qamma* 10.2; *m. Nedarim* 3:4.

regularly associated with sinners in the phrase 'tax collectors and sinners' (*telônôi kai hamartoloi*) (Mt 9:10; 11:19; Mk 2:15; Lk 7:34; 15:1) and sometimes they are associated with 'immoral persons' (*pornai*), which signifies sinners in the area of sexual immorality, such as prostitutes (Mt 21:31; Lk 18:11). Matthew also associates them in a negative way with unbelieving and unclean Gentiles (Mt 5:46; 18:17). The term 'sinners' did not apply primarily to people who committed occasional transgressions, but rather those who lived outside the Law in a constant and fundamental way.[34] The toll or tax collectors, prostitutes, idolators and the non-circumcised were considered sinners in this way (e.g. 'Gentile sinners' in Gal 2:15). Furthermore the toll/tax collectors were not only regarded as sinners but were despised as a class, and considered outsiders in the community of Israel.

Jesus now takes the initiative and calls Matthew, a toll/tax collector to follow him. Jesus sees him working at the *telônion*, very likely a sheltered counting desk or booth placed strategically near the route out of the area of Galilee where the fishermen would transport their catch and along which caravans would pass *en route* from Egypt and Palestine to Syria and the East. Jesus called this man of unacceptable status and he got up and followed him. Implied in the following of Jesus is the leaving of his desk, symbol of his profession and root of his sinfulness.

ii. Dining with Tax Collectors and Sinners Mt 9:10-13//Mk 2:15-17; Lk 5:29-32.

Not only the unacceptable individual himself but also the company he kept, the circle of associates in which he moved, are now brought into the ambit of Jesus' acceptance as he dines with them.[35] Beginning again with the 'biblically sounding' expression *kai egeneto*, 'and it came to pass', Jesus is described as 're-

---

34 J. R. Donahue and D. J. Harrington, *op. cit.,102.*
35. Mark says 'in his house', leaving readers to question whether Jesus dined in Levi/Matthew's house or whether they dined in Jesus' house. Matthew's comment ' in the house' is so general that the reader may not be prompted to ask the question.

clining' (*anakeimenou*) in the house and many tax collectors are reclining (*synanekeinto*) with Jesus and his disciples.

The criticism of Jesus this time is actually spoken and addressed to his disciples. The term *mathêthês* for 'disciple' (lit. 'pupil', from the word *manthanein*, to learn) and the description *didaskalos* (teacher) reflect the usual understanding that a disciple became the pupil of a rabbi in order to learn his wisdom and knowledge. Jesus understands discipleship in a much more radical way. The criticism of Jesus for his actions does not remain unspoken in the hearts of his critics, identified on this occasion as the Pharisees (Mk 2:16 speaks of them as the scribes of the Pharisee party) but it is spoken openly and challengingly to his disciples: 'Why does your master eat with tax collectors and sinners?' In the criticism the present tense of the verb 'eats' (*esthiei*) implies a habitual eating with such people. Placing 'with tax collectors and sinners' before the verb 'eats' emphasises the objectionable nature of the company and association with them. The sentence could be translated: ' Why is it that it is with tax collectors and sinners that your teacher eats?' It could refer to meals given for Matthew and his associates by Jesus or, more likely, to meals given by them in Jesus' honour, since it was a common practice for wealthy people to give banquets for important teachers, philosophers and religious leaders.

These meals also display aspects of a Greco-Roman banquet at which the guest of honour, a philosopher, teacher or religious figure, would lead a symposium after the meal proper. Following a transition in which a libation was poured to a god, a hymn or prayer recited, the women withdrew to pursue their own company and interests and the men drank and discussed. In New Testament times many Jews had adopted and adapted this kind of meal for special occasions. Luke's account of Jesus' meal with Simon the Pharisee where he 'reclined' at table and a woman 'invaded' the male space, only to be defended by Jesus' pointing to her love and Simon's failure in hospitality and etiquette, is a case in point (Lk 7:36-50). Aspects of Greco-Roman practice, such as reclining for the meal, are mentioned twice in the pericope (*anakeimenou* is used of Jesus himself and *synanekeinto* of those dining with him). In such a setting Jesus would be expected to speak as a Jewish Wisdom Teacher, and his audience would function very much like the interlocutors in a symposium. In Greco-Roman society the symposium was the opportunity for establishing reputation and showing off social status. In this context, however, Jesus' presence and activity are countersigns to the 'status' game and the occasion for a very significant statement about the nature of his mission and of the kingdom he proclaims.

The canonised wisdom, as stated so clearly in Psalm 1 about not associating with sinners or sitting in the company of scorners, is seen to be violated by Jesus. The traditional wisdom warned the just not to associate with the unjust for fear of contamination and becoming like them. The 'just' and the 'unjust' are regularly contrasted in moral discourse in the scriptures. Their paths and their destinies are contrasted. Psalm 1 contrasts the way of the just, like a tree planted by the waterside giving its fruit in due season, with the way of the wicked which leads to doom. Psalm 37 is a treatise on the fate of the just and the unjust and Wisdom of Solomon states that 'the souls of the just are in the hands of God ... but the godless will be duly punished for their reasoning' (Wis 3:1-12). Jesus reverses the maxim about the righteous not associating with the unrighteous by pointing out that in fact it is precisely those unrighteous people who need a physician. The wisdom of Psalm 1 is reversed. The influence is going in the other direction, from the righteous one to the unrighteous. Jesus bridges this age old gap and reverses the process of influence, bringing the unrighteous into the sphere of influence of the kingdom. It is the sick who need the physician.

The physician's place was with the sick and the philosopher was often seen as a physician to those morally sick.[36] Jesus' comment here in the gospel: 'It is not the healthy who need the physician, but those who are sick', would have been well re-

---

36. cf Dio Chrysostom, *Orations*, 3.2.14-30; Epictetus, *Discourses* 3.23,30; Plutarch, *Moralia*, 230f.

ceived both in the Jewish and Greco-Roman worlds. The long tradition of prophetic criticism of religion and rituals without the inner dispositions of justice, mercy and knowledge, love of God and neighbour are here brought to the fore and summed up in the words of Hosea: 'I desire mercy and not sacrifice' (Hos 6:6). He adds: 'I have not come (a technical phrase for the coming of the Messiah, the expected one) to call the righteous, but sinners.' 'The one to come' whom they expected 'has come' but in spite of the righteous legality of the scribes, the piety of the Pharisees and the ascetic, threatening warnings of the Baptist and his followers, he has come to call sinners, the very ones they excluded from Israel, from the messianic community-in-waiting at Qumran and for whom, in their estimation, the kingdom would have no place.

In the manner of a Jewish wisdom teacher or Greco-Roman philosopher Jesus replied in a vein that would have been as natural to Sirach as to Epictetus or Dio Chrysostom when he said: 'It is not the healthy who are in need of a physician but those who are sick.' Sirach, commenting on medicine and illness, wrote:

Honour the physician with the honour that is his due, in return for his services; for he too has been created by the Lord. Healing itself comes from the Most High, like a gift from a king ... The Lord has brought medicines into existence from the earth, and the sensible man will not despise them. Did not a piece of wood once sweeten the water, thus giving proof of its virtue? (Sir 38:1-5. cf Exod 15:23-25)

iii. Fasting. Bridegroom/Wedding Guests Mt 9:14-15//Mk 2:18-20//Lk 5:33-35.

The next criticism, concerning his disciples, is directed to Jesus himself by the followers of John.[37] He is challenged about his attitude to fasting when it is pointed out that the disciples of

---

37. Mark and Luke have the criticism spoken by an unidentified group who quote the practice of fasting on the part of the Baptist's followers

John and the Pharisees were fasting and his disciples were not. As already stated in the comments relating to Jesus' teaching about fasting in secret (Mt 6:16-18), fasting was practised as a private and public exercise. It regularly accompanied private prayers of petition, repentance and devotion. In addition to the Day of Atonement, *Yom Kippur*, which was a day of public fast, other days of public fast could be proclaimed for particular reasons such as mourning, supplication in time of pestilence, famine or war, and repentance.[38]

The criticism about Jesus' disciples' failure to fast is the cue for Jesus to reply in terms of his being the bridegroom of Israel. The imagery of the bridegroom is so well established in the Old and New Testaments that just a mention is needed in the gospel. As *YHWH* was the bridegroom of Israel in prophetic imagery, now in the New Testament the imagery shifts onto Jesus as bridegroom of Israel. This is an extremely significant claim about the nature of his presence and ministry. He is filling the role ascribed to *YHWH* in the Old Testament. However, Jesus here adds another radically new and ominous dimension: He begins with a statement that cannot be denied: 'Surely the bridegroom's attendants would never think of mourning (Mk 2:19 says fasting) while the bridegroom is still with them?'[39] He asso-

---

and the followers of the Pharisees (Mk 2:18; Lk 5:33). The disciples of the Pharisees were obviously people who followed, or were learning to follow, the devotional life of the Pharisees. The disciples of John are mentioned here in all three synoptics and will be mentioned again by Matthew and Luke when they are sent by John to inquire of Jesus: 'Are you he who is to come or shall we look for another?'(Mt 11:2ff; Lk 7:18ff). Matthew and Mark record how they came to bury his body after he has been beheaded (Mt 14:12; Mk 6:29). In John's gospel they are mentioned prominently, and some of them become the first disciples of Jesus (Jn 1:35-39).

38. 2 Sam 12:23; 2 Chron 20:30; Joel 1:14; 2:12-15; Ezra 8:21; Jer 36:9; Pss 35:13; 69:10; Neh 9:1; Zech 8:19.

39. The significance of this pithy statement in the synoptics is brought out clearly in John's gospel where John the Baptist uses the imagery of the bride and bridegroom for Jesus and his following, an imagery long established for the covenant relationship of God and Israel. 'The one who has the bride is the bridegroom, the friend (the best man) stands by

ciates the fasting with mourning. Then he goes on to focus on a future violent event of eschatological significance. Using the established biblical phrase for a significant eschatological event, 'days are coming' (*eleusontai hêmerai*), Jesus points to the eschatological significance of his own death. 'Days are coming when the bridegroom will be taken away from them, and then on that day they will fast.' It will be a time of mourning. Again the reader is left wondering and waiting for further clarification as the story unfolds.

Days will come when the bridegroom is taken away. The word 'taken away' (*aparthê*) signifies more than a simple departure. It warns of a forced or violent removal. Here Jesus' teaching pinpoints a future critical event that will usher in a new era and a new regime of fasting, an era known to the readers of the gospels. The theme of his being taken away by force will be developed in the predictions of the Passion in terms of his being rejected, handed over to the Gentiles and put to death (Mt 16:21-23; 17:22-23; 20:17-19; 26:2). It will be realised in the Passion Narrative. Mourning (*penthein*) and repentance for the death of Jesus will call for fasting. The early Christian experience of fasting following the death of Jesus was a new departure unrelated to traditional Jewish practices. That the early Christians fasted on Wednesdays and Fridays is recorded in the *Didachê*.[40] Matthew here sets the precedent for their fasting in the saying of Jesus, 'When the bridegroom is taken away, then they will fast.'

Now, however, it is a time for rejoicing as the groom claims his bride and the wedding feast is being prepared. The covenant was graphically described as a marriage bond between God and the people.[41] The restoration of the divine authority in the messianic time and the attendant blessings are encapsulated in the imagery of the kingdom. Jesus in his parables uses the wedding

and rejoices at the voice of the bridegroom'(Jn 3:29f). John's joy is to see the stage set for that accomplishment as the bridegroom of Israel receives his bride, and John's task is accomplished.
40. *Didachê* 8:1.
41. Hos 2:19f; Isa 25:6-8; 62:5; Jer 2:2; 3:14.

banquet as a metaphor for the kingdom, with all it entails by way of reconciliation, restoration and abundance.[42] Speaking of himself rather than God as the bridegroom is a whole new departure in Judaism, and having his disciples not fast while he is present not only says something very special about himself and his mission but sets his disciples apart from other Jews and their traditions of fasting.

iv. New Garment, New Wine Mt 9:16-17//Mk 2:21-22//Lk 5:36-39

Jesus uses two metaphors, or to use the word loosely, two 'parables' to focus on the radical newness of what is taking place in his ministry. What he is accomplishing cannot be fit neatly into, or contained within, the categories of the old dispensation, no more than a patch of unshrunken cloth can be sewn onto an old garment or new wine put into old skins. The inherent dynamism of the shrinking new cloth and the expansion of the fermenting wine are too powerful for the already shrunken garment and stretched wineskin and will cause damage, destroying the garment, spilling the wine and ruining the skins.[43] Israel's traditions have done their task as garment and wineskin, but something radically new is happening and cannot be contained or imprisoned in the old. To attempt to do so will destroy both the old and the new.

---

42. The Book of Revelation, for example, looks forward to the final establishment of the Reign of God in terms of the eschatological banquet, the Wedding Feast of the Lamb (cf Mt 8:11). The parables of the wedding feast appear in Mt 22:1-14, Lk 14:15-24.

43. The garment may conjure up the images of creation and community. A new creation is unfolding and the untorn garment signifies a unified community. The new wine conjures up the image of the kingdom, the messianic time when the hills will flow with new wine (Amos 9:13). The new reality being brought about should not to be hampered by hankering after the old.

C. THE THIRD TRIAD MT 9:18-37

a. The Two Daughters Mt 9:18-26//Mk 5:21-43//Lk 8:40-56.

Intercalation: Intermingling of the Two Stories

The stories of the official's daughter who has died and the woman suffering from the terminal haemorrhage whom Jesus addressed as 'daughter'[44] are placed together as an intercalation or 'sandwich' highlighting each other. They come at the climax of a series of miracle stories where Jesus overcomes various powers. Both recount the healing of a woman. Both, very significantly, recount very great faith on the part of two people, apparently at the extreme opposite ends of the social scale. The man is a 'ruler/leader/official' and so a person of standing in the community. The woman is unnamed in all three synoptics. She is alone, chronically and probably fatally ill, frightened, and excluded from the synagogue and the society of the chosen people because her constant bleeding made her ritually impure and socially excluded. Both come to Jesus displaying great faith. The official abandoned the dignified stance of his status and office and humbled himself by showing him great respect. The verb *prosekunei* signifies bowing low or performing some such gesture. Mark says he 'fell at his feet'. The woman braved serious disapproval by touching with her ritually impure hands the garment of an important religious figure surrounded by his disciples and followers. Jesus puts his saving, life giving power ahead of any considerations of ritual impurity or taboo. Contact with the haemorrhaging woman or touching the dead body of the girl would be seen as incurring ritual impurity in the eyes of the strict observers and the purity enforcers.

Matthew's double story is shorter than the parallel accounts in Mark and Luke; in fact it is only about a third of the length of the longer Markan account (Mk 5:21-43; Lk 8:40-56). These two

---

44. The significance seems to be 'daughter of Abraham', (honorary title for a Jewess, a member of the chosen people) as is spelled out in the healing of the crippled woman in Lk 13:16. As daughter of Abraham she had every right to seek the healing power of God's anointed agent to the people.

'intercalated' stories are reduced to their bare bones with the faith of the petitioners eliciting the healing power of Jesus over fatal illness and death itself emerging as the dominant theme. Matthew, as is his custom, focuses on the word/action of faith on the part of the petitioners, in these two cases the faith of the official and of the woman with the haemorrhage, and the word/action of healing and restoration to normal life on the part of Jesus. The reader familiar with the accounts in Mark and Luke will notice the obvious omission of the name of the official and the bringing of the three special disciples, Peter, James and John to the room where the dead girl was lying. The reference to the crowd pressing all around him as he followed the official, the tension engendered by the report that the girl was on the point of death followed by the arrival of the servants to announce the death are also missing. Matthew's story begins with the statement that she had just died. Matthew omits also Jesus' use of the Aramaic expression *talitha koum*, 'little lamb arise.' In the case of the woman with the haemorrhage, her wasting her fortune on doctors (Mark) and their inability to cure her (Mark and Luke), the questioning of Jesus about who touched him and the obtuse remark of the disciples are all omitted.

The Official's Daughter (Part 1) Mt 9:18-19

After a typical genitive participial phrase 'as Jesus was saying these things to them' (*tauta aotou lalountos autois*), as distinct in this case from the more usual reference to where he was going or coming from, this story also begins with the typical Matthean 'behold' (*idou*) followed by the description of the petitioner 'approaching' and paying homage to Jesus. The petitioner whose name is not given is described in very general terms as a certain *archôn*, an official (leader/ruler) as distinct from the more specific description 'official of the synagogue' in Mk 5:22 and Lk 8:41 where his name is given as Jairus. He says to Jesus that his daughter is already dead and asks him to come and lay his hand on her and she will live. Mark at this point says she was on the point of death and Luke says she was dying.

He begs Jesus to come to his daughter who has already died. This is an even more striking request than the request in Luke or in Mark where Jairus begs Jesus to come to his 'little daughter' or 'dear daughter'[45] who was 'dying' or 'on the point of death', (*eschatôs echei/in extremis est*), and lay his hands on her so that she may be saved, that is, saved from the power of death, and live.

In response to his petition Jesus 'rises up' as he did in the boat when he 'rose up' and rebuked the winds and the sea. In this case Jesus rises up and goes together with his disciples towards the house of the petitioner. His progress, however, is interrupted by a second petitioner, the woman with the haemorrhage. As Jesus accompanies the distraught father to his house the seriously (probably fatally) ill woman approaches him, interrupting the father's crisis with her own.

Both stories highlight each other in the telling. The process of intercalation in this case heightens the dramatic tension as the urgent movement towards the house of the ill child is delayed, and also heightens the contrast of the little girl growing into life for twelve years as the older woman gradually loses her life force in the issue of blood during those same twelve years.

The woman with the Haemorrhage Mt 9:20-22

Matthew introduces the story of the woman with the haemorrhage with the typical, 'behold!' Again the petitioner is said 'to approach' the healer, this time from behind, emphasising her exclusion and need to stay hidden due to her 'unclean' condition and the 'inappropriate' nature of a woman, not to mention a 'ritually unclean' woman approaching a male religious leader in public. Having heard about Jesus she is the first woman to approach him in public and her example of forthrightness stands out as an example for all followers.[46] Coming from behind in the crowd, she touched the hem of his garment, for she was saying,

---

45. 'Dear daughter' would be the translation if the diminutive *thugatrion* from *thugatêr* is seen as endearment rather than referring to her young age.
46. See the study by Marla J. Selvidge, *Woman, Cult and Miracle Recital. A Redactional Critical Investgation on Mark 5:24-34*, Lewisburg, NJ: Bucknell University Press,1990.

'If I can but touch his garment I shall be saved (healed).' Healers were considered to be possessed of spiritual power that was channelled to the person being healed, and the laying on of hands or touching the sick person was the means of channelling that power. Here the woman in her desperation and determination 'short circuits' the process by touching the healer herself. Matthew does not elaborate further on the condition of the woman or the reaction of Jesus in seeking out who had touched him, nor on the disciples' reaction, but focuses on the direct contact of the faith-driven action of the woman, the fact of the healing and the comment of Jesus, in typical Matthean style, exhorting her to have courage and commenting on her faith: 'Have courage, daughter; your faith has saved you.' The effect of the cure is emphasised. The woman was 'saved' from that hour.

Jesus addressed her as 'daughter'. Like the 'daughter' of the official this woman too is a daughter. It is a familiar address in the midst of an awe-inspiring experience. It is reminiscent of his remark to his critics in Luke's gospel when they criticised him for healing a long-suffering woman on the Sabbath. He spoke of her as a daughter of Abraham (Lk 13:16). 'Saved' has connotations beyond those of the physical healing. She was restored to the religious life of Israel, to society, family and friends. Furthermore her cure, like that of the invalid on the stretcher, was symptomatic also of her rescue from the global effects of sin and its power at the approach of the kingdom.

The Official's Daughter (Part 2) Mt 9:23-26

The story of the official and his daughter now continues. The narrative is shorter than that in Mark. The death of the girl has already been stated in Matthew, whereas at this point Mark describes messengers coming with news of her death. Jesus enters the house; there is no mention of his bringing Peter, James and John with him. On seeing the flute players and the crowd making a tumult, he dismisses them with the statement that the girl is not dead but sleeping. They scoffed at him. The scene reflects the elaborate mourning rituals common both to Jewish and

Greco-Roman society. Lamentations, funeral dirges, keening women, flute players, fasting, rending of garments, scattering ashes and so forth were all part of the process. Into such a scene Jesus enters and clears out the whole company. They ridicule his remark about sleeping. Though sleeping was a common euphemism for death it also carried the nuance that no one is dead to God. For many Jews in the New Testament period death is seen as the sleep from which the believer will waken. This is most likely the meaning of Jesus' remark. He will make the point strongly in the debate with the Sadducees (Mt 22:23-33).

When the crowd had been put out he entered and 'took her powerfully' by the hand. As in the case of touching the leper, Jesus breaks a very serious taboo incurring ritual impurity for touching a corpse. The verb *ekratêsen* has strong connotations of power, so it may be translated, 'He took her hand in power', 'he took her powerfully/he manifested his power in the taking'.[47] The little girl (*to korasion*) rose up, *êgerthê*, which means not only 'rose up as from a lying down position' but as already seen the verb is very much associated with raising/resurrection from the dead.[48]

The scoffing of the mourners may reflect some experience of

---

47. Some scholars point out that the girl was not really dead and that Jesus' remark is pointing out that fact to the mourners. If that were the case would the story have been significant enough to command such attention in the gospel, in fact in all three synoptics (Mt 9:18-26; Lk 8:40-56)? Were the messengers, the mourners and the family all mistaken? In the case of Lazarus in John's gospel Jesus says he is sleeping and then has to correct the mistaken view of the disciples who think that he is simply asleep (Jn 11:11f). 'Sleeping', *koimesis*, becomes a common Christian word for death and the related word 'cemetery' is used for the place of such sleeping (1 Thess 4:13-18). Would the healing of a seriously ill child have caused the Markan Jesus, for example, to issue such a very strict order about keeping the matter secret (Mk 5:43)?

48. Matthew does not include the Aramaic expression used by Jesus in Mark, *talitha koum*, 'little lamb, arise', which Mark translated into Greek as *korasion*, 'young lady or young woman', the diminutive of *korê*, maiden, the term used here also by Matthew. For such a Jewish gospel it is a little surprising that Matthew does not have the Aramaic expression. Perhaps he was considering his Diaspora and Greek readers.

the early Christians of scoffing reaction to their belief in resurrection. Scoffing and mockery of the believer are a common motif in biblical literature and Hellenistic miracle stories.

Raising the dead would not have seemed as incredible to people in Jesus' time as it would in our day. The biblical stories of Elijah and Elisha raising the dead would have been known and believed (1 Kings 17:17-24; 2 Kings 4:18-37). Matthew, Mark and Luke tell the story of the daughter of the official (Jairus) (Mt 9:18-26; Lk 8:40-56). Luke tells the story of the raising of the widow's son at Naim (Lk 7:11-17) and John tells the story of the raising of Lazarus (Jn 11:1-44). Jesus' response to the messengers of the Baptist includes 'the dead are raised' (Mt 11:2-6; Lk 7:18-23) and Jesus' programmatic statement in his sermon in Nazareth refers to the story of Elijah and the widow at Zarephath (Lk 4:26; 1 Kings 17:8-24) which comes across as an indirect reference to raising the dead during his own ministry.

For readers familiar with the Bible there are echoes of the raising of the son of the Shunammite woman by Elisha (2 Kings 4:25-37) in the account of the raising of the official's daughter. The pleading and faith of the parent, the going privately into the room where the child lay and the restoration of the child are points in common to both stories.

Whereas Mark at this juncture has Jesus issuing one of his sternest injunctions to silence, to maintain what scholars have called the messianic secret, Matthew simply points out how the news of what happened, spread throughout the whole countryside. This reference to the effect on the crowd and their reporting of what happened is a typical conclusion to a miracle story.

b. The Two Blind Men Mt 9:27-31 (cf Mt 20:29-34)

Again this healing story is introduced with a statement of Jesus' moving on to another place. As he does so, two blind men followed him, saying: 'Have pity on us, Son of David.' Calling him 'Son of David' recalls the royal descent emphasised in the genealogy and in the account of the birth and infancy, which not only placed Jesus in the royal line, but also designated him as the Davidic shepherd king. As such he is present to and shows mercy on the flock of Israel, forgiving their sins, hearing the cry of the poor and ministering the comforting action of God on their behalf (cf Ps 72:12-13; Ezek 34, *inter al*). Furthermore, as J. P. Meier points out, compassion and healing are an apt context for such a confession since the title was applied to Solomon who was seen as a healer in first century writings.[49] Furthermore, the expectation of a messianic Son of David is reflected in the Psalms of Solomon 17, contemporary with the New Testament, especially in the prayer: 'See, Lord, and raise up for them their king, the Son of David, to rule over your servant Israel in the time known to you, O Lord.'

Jesus apparently kept the two blind men in suspense and they followed (is there more than just a physical following implied?) as far as the house. On his entering the house they approach him. As in the case of other petitioners *they approached* Jesus. He says to them, testing their faith: 'Do you believe that I can do this?' Faith in Jesus' power to heal is obviously the vital factor. Again there is emphasis on Jesus' authority / power. They say to him: 'Yes, Lord.' Their faith that caused them to call out for pity, to address him as 'Son of David' and to follow him to the house and make an approach to him, is now brought out clearly in their answer to his question, both in their affirmative 'Yes' and in their use of the believers' address 'Lord'. Responding to their faith, Jesus applies his healing touch to their eyes saying: 'According to your faith let it be done to you!' Their eyes were opened and Jesus sternly warned them (*enebrimêthê autois*): 'See that nobody knows.' The verb *enebrimêthê* has strong overtones of severity. Probably false expectations were growing around his healing activity and the gathering and activity of the crowds he was drawing. This would have caused a certain alarm to both Jewish and Roman authorities since crowds could be manipulated or used as a cover for revolutionary activity. But again, in spite of the warning, the healed people went out and

---

49. J. P. Meier, *A Marginal Jew*, 2:689f; Josephus, *Ant.*, 8:46-49; *Test. Sol.* 20:1; cf F. J. Moloney, *op. cit.*, 209.

spread the news in the whole countryside. For Matthew, the good news cannot be suppressed.

Matthew's focus on two blind persons is most likely evidence of his interest in having 'two witnesses' (the legal requirement in Deut 17:6; 19:15; Num 35:30; 2 Cor 13:1) to the miraculous power of Jesus. He will again speak of two blind men in the healing in Jericho (Mt 20:29-34). Mark also recounts two healing stories involving a blind man, one in Bethsaida (in Galilee) and the other in Jericho but in both there is only one blind man mentioned (Mk 8:22-26; 10:46-52). Was there an older tradition of a healing of two blind men in Galilee (Bethsaida) and Jericho, which both evangelists used for their own redactional purposes? Matthew is here building up a picture of the works of the Messiah, with the required two witnesses, which will be used in the response to the messengers of the Baptist by way of an allusion to or composite quotation from Isaiah's prophecy of the healing works of the Messiah (Mt 11:2-6). Mark, on the other hand, uses the Bethsaida healing as a literary pivot in the middle of his gospel which functions as a symbolic summary of the first section and a preview of the second half of the gospel. For this purpose he needs to refer to just one person (Mk 8:22-26).[50] In both Matthew and Mark the Jericho healing is used as a springboard for the acclaim accompanying Jesus on his final approach to Jerusalem. Mark may have focused on Bartimaeus, because his name and possibly his subsequent role as a 'follower on the way' were known. One can only speculate but such speculation helps to show the tradition, history and editorial work that has gone into the final version of the stories involved.

The two healings in Matthew, in Galilee and subsequently in Jericho, describe the blind men addressing Jesus as Lord, Son of David. Mark has the address 'Lord, Son of David' on the lips of the blind man in Jericho (Bartimaeus).[51] The stories in both

50. Similarly John needs just one person in the healing in Jn 9 which serves the purpose of illustrating belief and unbelief by way of reference to sight and blindness.

51. Matthew also recounts the healing of a blind man, who is also dumb, to which the people responded with the question, 'Could this be the Son of David (Mt 12:22-23)?'

gospels contain a very public recognition of Jesus through the use of faith-based titles. 'Son of David' was already well established as a messianic title in the narrative of Matthew's gospel, and 'Lord' was established as the address used by believers and disciples when addressing Jesus.

c. The Dumb Demoniac Mt 9:32-34//Lk 11:14-15

As they (the healed blind men) departed, they (unspecified subject) brought to him a deaf and dumb (kôphôs) demoniac. When the demon was driven out, the deaf mute spoke. The crowds were amazed, saying 'Nothing like this appeared in Israel.' The verb 'appeared', ephanê, has overtones of epiphany, christophany and divine visitation. Typical of miracle stories the reaction of the people highlights the power and effect of the miracle. But in this case it also provides the contrast with the negative reaction of the Pharisees.

The conclusion of the miracle stories with the account of the healing of the blind, the deaf and the dumb recalls for the reader the prophecy of Isaiah: 'Then shall the eyes of the blind be opened and the ears of the deaf unstopped' (Isa 34:6). These two healing stories, one a healing of two blind men and then a healing of a deaf/mute, are told in summary form, and in a polished Greek[52] that suggests they may have already been in the tradition as summaries of stories later told at greater length by the three synoptic writers. They are used here by Matthew to fill out his messianic portrait so that Jesus will be able to reply to the questioning of the Baptist by quoting Isaiah's prophecies about the messianic work of healing, giving sight to the blind, speech to the dumb, hearing to the deaf, cleansing to the lepers, a mission that can be summarised as 'good news for the poor' (Mt 11:2-5; Isa 26:19; 29:18f; 34:6; 35:5f; 61:1). Jesus has himself ac-

---

52. Note the dative participial phrase 'paragonti ekeithen ...' instead of the more regular genitive participial phrase and the stylish accurate genitive absolute autôn de exerchomenôn, 'as they departed', introducing respectively the healing stories of the blind and the deaf. Note also the stylish genitive absolute ekblêthentos tou daimoniou, 'the demon having been driven out'.

complished this messianic work of healing and now will send his disciples / apostles out to continue this work on his behalf.

d. Response: Awe and Accusation Mt 9:34//Mk 3:22

By the Power of the Prince of Devils

The crowds marvelled, but the Pharisees, unable to deny the marvels that had taken place, seek to discredit them by ascribing them to the power of the prince of devils. Already the scribes have accused him of blasphemy and now the Pharisees ascribe his healing powers to the prince of devils. The coming rejection of his mission and his trial for blasphemy are already casting their shadows. The charge that he casts out devils by (the power of) the prince of devils will be dealt with at greater length when the charge is made again and on that occasion Jesus will respond / react to the charge (Mt 12:24-32). The apostles are warned in the missionary discourse that they too will be subjected to similar, possibly even greater, calumny (Mt 10:25).

Summary Mt 9:34

The narrative of the gospel has been through its initial stages of introducing the protagonist and his main support and opposition. The reader has been securely brought on side. Now the plot of the narrative is becoming complicated and will continue to manifest the complication of reactions and threats to the protagonist until the resolution at the end of the narrative.

D. COMMISSIONING OF THE TWELVE APOSTLES MT 9:35 –11:1

Outline:
a. Jesus' Compassion on the Crowd Mt 9:35-37
b. Jesus' Appointment of the Twelve Mt 10:1-5
c. Mission/Apostolic Discourse Mt 10:6-42

a. Jesus' Compassion on the Crowd Mt 9:35-37

The summary in Mt 9:35 states that Jesus toured the towns and villages, teaching in their synagogues, proclaiming the good news of the kingdom and healing every disease and every infirmity. The next two verses (Mt 9:36-37) spell out the motivation of Jesus. He is moved to compassion through his concern for the crowd because they are like sheep without a shepherd. These verses serve a number of functions in the narrative. First of all they form an inclusion with the emphasis on the crowd in Mt 4:23-25 and so bracket together the Sermon on the Mount and the Miracle Stories, illustrating the authority/power of Jesus in both word and deed. The crowd have responded to his word with the comment: 'He taught them with authority and not like their own scribes' (Mt 7:29), and the healings evoked the response: 'Nothing like this appeared in Israel' (Mt 9:34). He has shown his messianic authority in word in Mt 5-7 and in deed in Mt 8-9. Secondly some of the miracle stories and accompanying comments (Mt 8:19-27 and 9:14-17) have prepared the reader for the transfer of Jesus' authority to the Twelve, those sent to represent him and do his work, hence the term Apostles. Thirdly, the comments of the crowd have struck a note of criticism of the teachers and healers in Israel. Their criticism has not gone unnoticed by those unfavourably compared to this new religious figure and they feel it necessary to undermine his influence with the crowd. They have already criticised him on several aspects of his behaviour and have even accused him of casting out devils by the power of the prince of devils.

The reference to Jesus' compassion on the crowd and the reference to the harvest leads into the next section of the gospel, the

Mission Discourse, where Jesus calls the Twelve and shares his own authority and power with them. The reference to the sheep without a shepherd sets the context for their being sent to the lost sheep of the House of Israel (cf Num 27:17; 1 Kings 22:17; Zech 10:2; Ezek 34; Jer 23:4). Jesus' compassion for the flock casts him in the role of shepherd, reminiscent of the caring activity of God, the Shepherd of Israel, for the people in the desert. It is reminiscent of the role and leadership of Moses as he fed the people in the desert and provided them with the Torah, and of the role of the Davidic shepherd king.

As Jesus is moved to compassion on seeing the crowds because they were harassed and dejected like sheep without a shepherd, he proceeds to appoint twelve of his followers / disciples to assist him in his work. The Bible reader will remember Moses' distress as he realised the enormity of the task of looking after all the people, and how he chose the seventy to help him in the task (Num 11:16-17; cf Exod 18:13-27). Jesus is moved to say to his disciples that the harvest is great but the labourers are few. He asks them to pray to the Lord of the harvest to send labourers into the harvest. The harvest is a common way of referring to the eschatological gathering of the elect into the kingdom. Here the reference to the harvest is like a foreshadowing or first instalment on that final eschatological harvest.

The sentiment of Moses' prayer in the desert is recalled when Jesus had compassion on the crowd who followed him out in the countryside, because they were harassed and dejected like sheep without a shepherd (Mt 9:36//Mk 6:34; cf Lk 12:32).[53] Moses prayed: 'Let the Lord ... appoint someone over the congregation who shall go out before them and come in before them, who shall lead them out and bring them in, so that the congregation of the Lord may not be like sheep without a shepherd' (Num 27:16f). Micaiah son of Imlah, contradicting the lying spirit of the false prophets, proclaimed to the kings of Israel and Judah: 'I saw all Israel scattered on the mountains like sheep that have no

53. cf Lk 12:32. Luke portrays Jesus' comforting words: 'There is no need to be afraid, little flock, for it has pleased your Father to give you the kingdom', a saying that evokes the image of a shepherd-king.

shepherd' (1 Kings 22:17). Both Jeremiah and Ezekiel severely
condemn the shepherds of the people and echo each other in the
promise of God to raise up good shepherds for them. Ezekiel
proclaimed that for want of a shepherd the people were scattered and had become the prey to any wild animal (Ezek 34:5)
and promised a new David who would be a true shepherd to the
sheep. 'I will set up over them one shepherd, my servant David,
and he shall feed them and be their shepherd ... I, the Lord, will
be their God, and my servant David shall be prince among them'
(Ezek 34:23-4; cf Ps Sol 17:40-41). A similar sentiment is expressed in Jeremiah, where God promises to raise up shepherds
for the sheep who have been abandoned by bad shepherds and
left to wander uncared for and become dispersed (Jer 23:1-4).

The role of the shepherd is to protect, care for, feed and gather
together the flock, to seek the lost and not lose any of the flock.
The imagery of the shepherd, shepherding and shepherd-king
was widely applied to religious and secular leadership in the ancient world.

b. Jesus' Appointment of the Twelve Mt 10:1-4//Mk 3:13-19//Lk 6:12-16

The account of the calling and commissioning of the Twelve is
reminiscent of and builds upon the calling of the first disciples:
'Follow me and I will make you fishers of people' and it foreshadows the universal mission: 'Going, therefore, make disciples of all nations' (Mt 4:19; 28:18).[54]

The call narrative emphasises both the initiative and the free
choice of Jesus. The deliberate intention of this action of Jesus is
emphasised by the use of the 'fortified' verb to call *proskale-
samenos* (in the Greek middle voice showing a certain reflexive
meaning, 'call to himself', strengthened by the prefix *'pros'*).
Whereas the indicative, simple, unfortified active verbs *legei autois* ('he says to them') and *ekalesen autous* ('he called them') were
used in the call of the two pairs of brothers (Mt 4:19, 21), the very

---

54. The discourse that follows the calling of the Twelve balances the
'community / ecclesiastical' discourse in Mt 18 in the overall structure of
the gospel.

deliberate nature of the action here makes the same point as the very explicit statements in the Farewell Discourse in John's gospel: 'You have not chosen me, I have chosen you and commissioned you to go out and bear fruit' (Jn 15:16), and similarly in the crisis following the discussion on the bread of life when he says: 'Have I not chosen you Twelve, and yet one of you is a devil' and the Johannine narrator goes on to explain that he was referring to Judas Iscariot, one of the Twelve, who was going to betray him (Jn 6:70-71). Both synoptic and Johannine traditions emphasise the same point of Jesus' initiative and very deliberate choice, even of the one who will betray him.

'He called his twelve disciples and he gave them power/authority over unclean spirits to cast them out and to heal every disease and every infirmity.' The authority/power of Jesus, so much in evidence heretofore in the gospel, is now shared with the Twelve. The 'power over unclean spirits to cast them out' is in direct continuity with Jesus' own activity (Mt 8:28-34; 9:32-34) and the reference to healing 'every disease and every infirmity' further emphasises the continuity with Jesus' work by repeating the description of his healings in Mt 9:35.[55]

The names of the twelve apostles[56] appear in all three synoptic gospels and in the Acts of the Apostles, but there are some minor variations in the lists (Mt 10:1-4; Mk 3:13-19; Lk 6:12-16; Acts 1:13). Every list begins with the two pairs of brothers, Simon (Peter) and Andrew, James and John.[57] In all lists (Simon) Peter is mentioned first. Matthew and Luke mention Andrew after Peter and before James and John but Mark mentions him after James and John. Matthew significantly further highlights

---

55. Mark refers only to the power over unclean spirits at this point (Mk 6:7). Luke speaks of power over evil spirits, power to heal and a commission to proclaim the kingdom of God (Lk 9:1-2).

56. Matthew uses the term, *apostoloi*, 'apostles', 'the ones sent' in this section of the gospel which deals with their commissioning as his representatives, but he prefers the terms *mathêthai*, disciples, and *hoi dôdeka*, the Twelve, throughout the rest of the gospel.

57. Matthew does not state that he gave a special name, *Boangeres*, 'sons of thunder', to James and John, the sons of Zebedee. This is in keeping with Matthew's avoidance of Hebrew and Greek expressions.

the pre-eminence of Peter by explicitly referring to him as the 'first'. He begins his list: *prôtos Simon ho legomenos Petros*. Since *prôtos* is an adjective this is best translated as 'Simon called Peter was the first', that means the first in rank or leadership, since the second, third fourth and so on are not mentioned and so mentioning the first makes sense only in terms of rank, since if it were purely numerative the numbering would have been continued throughout the list. This giving of rank to Peter is very much in keeping with Matthew's emphasis on Peter. 'First' foreshadows the prominence given to Peter in the gospel story that has yet to unfold. John mentions 'the Twelve' but does not supply a list of their names or a narrative of their call or appointment as a group of twelve (Jn 6:67, 70, 71; 20:24). Paul mentions the Twelve but names only Cephas (Peter) in his list of appearances of the Risen Lord (1 Cor 15:5). Every list ends with Judas Iscariot. In Matthew's gospel at the point where Mark and Luke describe the call of Levi at the custom house (toll booth), Matthew calls the toll (tax) collector in question Matthew. Matthew and Mark speak of Simon the Cananaean where Luke and Acts speak of Simon the Zealot. (Coming from Cana in Galilee he was probably seen as a Zealot, since Galilean and Zealot were nearly interchangeable in many people's minds). In Luke's list Thaddeus is omitted and Judas, son of James, is inserted. Nathaniel figures in the initial calling of disciples in John's gospel and tradition later identified him with Bartholomew.

The name *Iscariot* has been variously interpreted. The most straightforward meaning is *'ish Keriot,* man of Keriot, identifying him by his place of origin. Some see it as a condemnatory adjective describing his act of betrayal and derived from the Hebrew *skr,* which means to 'deliver', 'hand over' or 'betray'. Others speculate on a Semitic version of the Latin *Sicarii,* 'men of the dagger', a name for revolutionaries working to overthrow the Romans and their Jewish collaborators and so described from the short daggers they carried. Others think it may be derived from the Hebrew verb *saqar,* to act falsely. The New Testament writers generally heap opprobrium on Judas. His mind and motives have been a subject of discussion throughout history. Luke and John see the Prince of Evil at the root of Judas' actions. Both say that Satan entered into Judas (Lk 22:3; Jn: 13:27) and John also says that Judas was a devil (Jn 6:70). This 'religious' interpretation is accompanied by terms relating to what is often seen as the root of all evil, love of money. Mark and Luke show the chief priests tempting Judas with the offer of money. Matthew shows him demanding the money. John further develops this money loving weakness in terms of stealing from the common fund in his charge (Mk 14:11; Lk 22:5; Mt 26:15; Jn 12:4-6). Mark, probably very wisely, simply draws attention to the fact of the betrayal and avoids speculation on the motives. Since New Testament times historians, priests, poets, playwrights, novelists and many others have continued to speculate on his motives.

Several of those mentioned do not figure in any prominent way in the gospels or in the Acts of the Apostles. However, Matthew and Luke portray them as the eschatological judges presiding over the twelve tribes (Mt 19:28//Lk 22:28-30)[58] and the pressing desire to fill the vacancy left by Judas, signifying a vacancy 'on a bench' or 'college' of twelve is striking (Acts 1:15-26), as is the subsequent emergence of a volume of apocryphal literature that emerged in the early church in their names.

The number twelve is symbolic. It is inspired by the number of the sons of Jacob after whom the tribes of Israel take their names and represents the fullness of Israel in the eschatological people of God. Here Jesus is embarking on a mission to renew Israel, not to establish 'a new Israel' but the renewal will have far-reaching effects beyond the traditional boundaries of the people of Israel. Giving the names of the Twelve is another example of telling the story of Jesus against the background of the Old Testament. The Book of Numbers describes Moses appointment of twelve helpers, representing each of the twelve tribes, and gives their names: 'These are the names ...' (Num 1:5).

---

58. Mt 19:28//Lk 22:28-30 represents material the majority of scholars designate as coming from the Q source, the material common to Matthew and Luke which Mark does not share.

Similarly in the account of the sons of Jacob/Israel going down to Egypt the expression 'these are the names ...' is used (Gen 46:8). Only Matthew uses the phrase 'These are the names', which points to his rooting the story of Jesus in the great narrative of Israel's history.

These twelve apostles of Jesus are sent out to proclaim, that is to be his heralds or representatives, and to have power to cast out demons and to heal every disease and infirmity, the very things Jesus himself was doing. The phrase, *apesteilen autous*, 'he sent them' makes them *apostoloi*, 'apostles' of Jesus, as well as disciples.

c. Mission Discourse. Part 1. In the Jewish World Mt 10:6-11:1

Sent to the lost sheep of Israel Mt 10:6-15

Having chosen the Twelve, Jesus proceeds to instruct them (Mt 10: 5). 'Jesus sent out these twelve having instructed them saying ...'

The first thing to note about Matthew's version of the instruction which forms the basis of the second major discourse in the gospel is the clear direction to the Twelve not to go on the way of the Gentiles nor to enter any town of the Samaritans.[59] Their initial mission is to Israel, and specifically 'to the lost sheep of the House of Israel'. Setting out they are to proclaim that the kingdom of heaven is near at hand. This is a re-echoing of one half of the proclamation to Israel by the Baptist and Jesus. The other half, the call for repentance is not included. Why? It is not included probably because it is now replaced by the call for faith in the powerful preaching and works of Jesus that are inaugurating the kingdom.

The Twelve are told to do the works that Jesus has been doing, to heal the sick, raise the dead, cleanse the lepers, the messianic activities prophesied by Isaiah. In addition they are to drive out demons, an activity marking the arrival of the king-

---

59. Note the elegance of the Greek sentence: *eis hodon ethnôn mê apelthête kai eis polin Samaritôn mê eiselthête*, 'Unto the way of the Gentiles do not go and into the city of the Samaritans do not enter.'

dom and its attack on the kingdom of Satan. It is significant that at this point they are not told to teach. They still have to receive the instruction in the remaining major discourses, and to experience the power of God in the death, resurrection and glorification of Jesus. After that they will be commissioned to teach all nations (Mt 28:18-20).

Their attitude is of supreme importance. Generosity and trust in providence must be the hallmarks of their mission. They have received freely as a gift and they must give freely as a gift. They must not take gold, silver or coppers in their belts. Matthew seems to have a different social stratum in mind to that of Mark since he mentions gold, silver and coppers. Mark mentions only coppers. They are not to take a bag for the journey, nor two tunics, nor footwear (slaves, servants went barefoot) nor a staff (for defence?). They are to rely on the generosity of those to whom they bring the news/work of the kingdom.[60] Those to whom they minister will give them the just reward of their labour because 'the labourer is worthy of his wages.' The wages in this case are in recognition of what the labourers do, what they stand for and whom they represent.[61]

---

60. The nature of their mission is described in an article on the parallel passage in Mark by J. A. Draper, 'Wandering radicalism or purposeful activity? Jesus and the sending of messengers in Mark 6:6-56', *Neotestamentica* 29 (1995) 183-202.

61. In Mark they are sent out in twos. In addition to any consideration of prudence concerning their safety and well being, there was a long tradition of seeing two persons as necessary for juridical witness (Deut 17:6; 19:15; Num 35:30; 2 Cor 13:1). Representing Jesus, acting in his name and with his authority is a bearing of witness to him and to his mission to establish the kingdom. This concept of 'witnessing' is brought out clearly in Jesus' farewell and commissioning at the beginning of Acts when he tells the disciples: 'You will be my witnesses not only in Jerusalem but throughout Judaea and Samaria and to the ends of the earth' (Acts 1:8). The sending of the seventy-two in Luke also emphasises their going in pairs (Lk 10:1). This was also very likely the practice of the early church. Barnabas and Paul went together, and when they fell out, Paul brought Silas on his missionary journey and Barnabas brought John Mark (Acts 15:39f). Peter and John went together to Samaria (Acts 8:14-17).

The missionary must be detached, relying on the providence of God who sent Jesus whose representatives they now are, and on the hospitality of those to whom they minister. They therefore are to bring no bag (*pêra*) for the journey, no money in their belt, no sandals, no staff and no spare tunic. The *pêra* mentioned is very likely a 'begging bag' like that used by wandering Cynics or philosophers, or begging priests and officials of pagan deities and their shrines. The latter were described in antiquity as 'pious robbers with their booty growing from village to village.'[62] Jesus' ambassadors must behave very differently and avoid any such reputation and image.

Emphasising this point of dependence on providence and hospitality, Matthew emphasises that they are to bring no staff and no sandals (Mt 10:10). Luke states that they are to bring no staff (Lk 9:3). Matthew has already made the point when he recounted Jesus' saying: 'the Son of Man has nowhere to lay his head' (Mt 8:20). E. Schweizer puts it succinctly:

> Messengers who wish to provide for every emergency do not have faith. Messengers are not to be believed if they rely on their own resources (material or spiritual) rather than on the One whom they proclaim.[63]

M. D. Hooker points to a passage in the *Mishnah* which forbids entry to the Temple Mount with staff, sandal or wallet, or with dust on one's feet. Jesus' instruction to the apostles resembles this instruction about respecting the sacred nature of the Temple Mount and T. W. Manson suggests that Jesus' instruction similarly reflects the sacred nature of their mission.[64]

The witness across all three synoptics points very clearly to dependence on God's providence and the generosity of the recipients of the gospel in the sacred task of representing Jesus and

---

62. Quoted by W. Barclay, *The Gospel of Mark*, 143.
63. E. Schweizer, *The Good News According to Mark*, 130.
64. M. D. Hooker, *op. cit.*, 156, quoting *m. Berakoth* 9.5 and T. W. Manson, *The Sayings of Jesus*, London, 1949, 181.Though the *Mishnah* was codified later than the New Testament, it must reflect traditions formed over a long period of time.

the kingdom he proclaims. However, though all three emphasise the same overall understanding of the nature of the mission
task, Mark differs from Matthew and Luke on the instruction
about not bringing a staff or wearing sandals. According to
Mark Jesus tells them to bring a staff and to wear sandals (Mk
6:8-9). One asks, 'Why the difference?' Is it a practical suggestion
for those who may have taken the original command too literally
at a cost to their health and safety? That may be partly the case,
but there is probably a more theological reason, one that highlights the nature of the mission without in any way compromis-
ing their dependence on providence and generosity as already
outlined.

The restless movement of Jesus throughout his ministry in
Galilee and his fateful journey to Jerusalem paint a picture of a
wandering prophet and teacher, a charismatic wanderer. F. J.
Moloney points out that the staff and sandals symbolise very
well such a wandering lifestyle. Mark is obviously conscious of
the fact that almost every pericope dealing with Jesus' ministry
begins with a verb of motion. The staff and sandals are the symbols of the missionary lifestyle into which the Twelve are now
being commissioned.[65] For these reasons Mark may be placing
an emphasis on staff and sandals.

But there is another aspect that may be very relevant to
Matthew at this point in the gospel. The shepherd's staff was a
symbol of the shepherd's role and care, and was widely used
even by political rulers in the secular cultures of the east. It is
very prominent in stories of God's envoys among the Gentiles.
The staff of God's envoy symbolised the authority and power
conferred for the mission or office. Moses and Aaron used the
staff to demonstrate their God-given power (Exod 4:20; 7:9-20;
8:16f; 14:16). Gehazi, the servant of Elisha was told to place the
staff of Elisha on the face of the Shunammite woman's son prior
to the healing (2 Kings 4:29-37). Here in Matthew's gospel Jesus
is commissioning the apostles to carry out a 'local' mission to the
'lost sheep of the house of Israel.' It does not call for a display of

---

65. F. J. Moloney, *op. cit.*, 122.

the power of the God of Israel among the Gentiles. Mark (Mk 6:7-13) and Luke (commissioning the seventy two)(Lk 10:1-16) are sending them out on a far broader, universal mission. For Mark the staff and sandals are not only necessary, but the staff of God's representative will continue its significant historical role in their encounters with the Gentiles.

Similarities have been pointed out between Jesus' mission charge to his apostles and the 'mission' of the Cynics. Their setting out without food, clothing and other accessories is similar but their purpose and behaviour are quite different. The Cynics shunned company and hospitality, rejected tradition and authority and addressed people in an aggressive manner, decrying the system and society wherever they saw the need to challenge the smug and the arrogant. The work and attitude of the Twelve was to be very different in spite of superficial similarities.

The Twelve are told to inquire who is worthy in any town or village that they enter. 'If the house is worthy let your peace/greeting come upon it. If it is not worthy let your greeting return to you.' This is a Semitic antithetic parallel statement making a point by highlighting opposites. If they find a welcome then let them bring the blessing of their presence and work to that house. If not, let them take themselves and their blessing elsewhere. On entering a house (i.e. when they take up lodgings in a house because they receive a welcome there) they should stay there until they depart from the district. And in the case of not being welcomed Jesus tells them: 'If anyone does not welcome you or listen to what you say, as you leave that house or town shake the dust from your feet.'

In biblical tradition hospitality is a mark of the God-fearing person and the hospitable household is a sacred congregation in itself into which one did not take staff, begging bag or money belt, just as one left them outside the temple.[66] Inhospitality is

---

66. Mark amplifies the command to 'stay there in the house until you leave' by adding 'do not move from house to house.' Stability within an area is necessary for good communication. But there is a deeper reason. Hospitality once offered should not be rejected, especially in the interests of better accommodation or more interesting company. To do so would

the mark of a non God-fearing people. Where the apostles meet inhospitality they are instructed to treat that area symbolically as 'a pagan place', shaking the contaminated pagan dust from their feet, the gesture they used on returning from Gentile territory into the Holy Land.

The final judgement is again brought to the fore in the solemn 'amen' pronouncement about the condemnation of that town on the Day of Judgement, a condemnation worse than that which befell Sodom and Gomorrah.

Mission Discourse. Part II. In the Wider World Mt 10:16-11:1

Persecution Mt 10:17-25

The reader clearly senses in the strict instruction about not going on the way of the Gentiles or entering a Samaritan town but going to the lost sheep of the House of Israel an emphatic apologetic directed at the Jews or the Jewish Christians who may have felt that they were somewhat overshadowed or overlooked in favour of the mission to the Gentiles which had taken place so quickly, even so spectacularly, after the life of Jesus. Matthew therefore emphasised the priority of the mission to Israel at the outset of the discourse. Now at this point he opens the discourse onto a much broader consideration of the missionaries in the wider world. From here on the discourse is close to the 'apocalyptic' discourses in the synoptics (Mt 24; Mk 13; Lk 21) and to the Farewell Discourse in John (Jn 14-16). No longer does it appear to be directed just to the original Twelve, but to all disciples, followers and missionaries. The reference to the Gentiles and the kings, princes and their courts envisages a universal rather than a local mission, a bearing witness to the nations.

The 'missionaries'/apostles are given a piece of very solid advice, worthy of a wisdom teacher and a prophet: 'Behold I am sending you as sheep in the midst of wolves; so be wise as serpents and guiltless as doves.' The imagery is then unpacked.

---

reject and demean the goodness of those who first showed hospitality and such an action would put material and social concerns ahead of the missionary way of life. Their lifestyle should reflect their preaching.

'Beware of men for they will hand you over to sanhedrins and
scourge you in their synagogues, and you will be dragged before governors and kings for my sake to bear witness to them
and to the nations ...' The verb 'hand over' (*paradidômi*) is a
'loaded' term in Matthew and in the New Testament generally.
It is used again immediately in the exhortation to them not to
worry about what to say when they are handed over. It rever-
berates with the fate of the Baptist who was handed over to
Herod Antipas (Mt 4:12) and with Jesus' predictions of being
handed over himself to his fate. It appears in the second passion
prediction (Mt 17:22), twice in the third (Mt 20:18,19) and in the
fourth (Mt 26:2), several times in the passion narrative, and Paul
uses it in Rom 4:25 and 8:12. The readers are aware that Judas
handed Jesus over to the Jewish authorities (Mt 10:4; 26:15-16)
who handed him over to Pilate (Mt 27:2) and Pilate handed him
over to be crucified (Mt 27:26). The disciples are destined to follow Christ in being handed over themselves, and in fact the
readers of Matthew had directly or indirectly experienced the
fulfilment of Jesus' prophetic warning. The first readers of
Matthew were aware that the prophetic warning of Jesus about
persecution had become a stark reality before the gospel was
written.

First of all Jesus warned his disciples that they would be
brought before the *synedria*, the local Jewish courts in each town
with powers of discipline to scourge them, a punishment carried
out in the synagogue.[67] In this regard, Peter and his companions
were flogged in Jerusalem (Acts 5:40). Paul states that he was
given the 'forty lashes less one' five times and beaten three times
with rods on their authority, the punishment laid down in
Deuteronomy (Deut 25:1-3; 2 Cor 11:24).

According to Jesus' warning they would also be brought before pagan courts, before governors and kings 'to bear testimony
to them and to the nations.' The reader thinks of Paul bearing
testimony before Felix, Festus and Agrippa (Acts 23:24; 24:27)
and being sent under guard to Rome where he was held under

---

67. *Sanhedrin* 1:6.

house arrest. Tradition places the martyrdoms of Peter and Paul in Rome, together with the 'huge number' who died in the Neronian persecution and who are referred to by Clement of Rome and Tacitus.[68] Matthew's readers may well be aware of these terrible events. All these had taken place before the writing of Matthew's gospel.

They are encouraged not to worry when they are *handed over* about how to speak or what to say because 'it will be given to you in that hour what you will say', that is, God will give you what to say. This is reminiscent of God's promise to the anxious prophet: 'I am putting my words into your mouth' (Jer 1:9-10). Witnessing to the nations was also the task of Jeremiah into whose mouth God placed the words to enable him to 'tear up and to knock down, to destroy and to overthrow, to build and to plant' (Jer 1:9-10). Facing the court would have been a very terrifying experience particularly for so many early Christians who would not have been well educated or well off people able to afford an advocate or call on influential friends. Jesus promises that it will be given (i.e. God will give) to them what to say. 'You will not be speaking but the Spirit of your Father will be speaking in you.' John's gospel speaks of the role of the Spirit as Paraclete/Advocate and further develops and spells it out in terms of a divine comforter and advocate who will defend them in the face of an unbelieving and hostile world, lead them into understanding, and cause them to recall all that Jesus had said and done (Jn 14:16, 26; 15:26; 16:7). This promise of divine presence, protection and inspiration so obvious in John's gospel appears here in Matthew in a less elaborate but equally clear form.

The warning about hostility from the authorities and from society in general is followed by a warning about hostility within the family circle. 'Brother will hand over brother to death and the father (his) child, and children will rise up against parents and put them to death'. Warnings about family division figured

---

68. *I Clement* 5 written in Greek and Tacitus, *Annals*, xiv, xliv written in Latin both speak of 'a huge number' (*poly plêthos*/*multidudo ingens*) having been put to death in Nero's persecution of the Christians.

in prophetic condemnations of the corruption of the people and also in Jewish apocalyptic imagery.[69] Jesus' prediction that 'brother will hand over brother to death and the father his child, and children will rise up against parents and have them put to death' is reminiscent of the description in Micah: 'For the son treats the father with contempt, the daughter rises up against her mother, the daughter-in-law against her mother-in-law; your enemies are members of your own household' (Mic 7:6).[70] This citation appears also in *m. Sotah* 9:15b as part of a passage on 'the footprints of the Messiah' after the statement 'children will shame elders, and elders will stand up before children.' Matthew's first readers may well have been aware of a fulfilment of Jesus' prediction in the betrayal and handing over of family members during the Neronian persecution. Tacitus describes how some of those arrested betrayed their fellow Christians and Clement of Rome reflects on the disastrous results of fanatical zeal.[71]

Predictions about general hostility and family divisions are followed by a very strong prediction of universal hatred. 'You will be hated by all on account of my name.' The Farewell Discourse in St John's gospel conveys a similar message. Jesus says to the disciples: 'If the world hates you remember that it hated me before you ... because you do not belong to the world ... therefore the world hates you' (Jn 15:18f). He also says: 'If they persecuted me, they will persecute you too' and '... the hour is coming when anyone who kills you will think he is doing a holy duty for God' (Jn 15:20; 16:2). The evangelists had good reason for emphasising the reality of persecution, hostility and hatred. Tacitus, for example, reflects the hostile opinion of society in his description of the Neronian persecution. He described the victims as 'the notoriously depraved Christians' and described the Christian movement as 'a deadly superstition'.[72]

---

69. Mic 7:6; Jub 23:19; 4 Ezra 5:9; 6:24; 2 Bar 70:3.
70. Matthew and Luke have an adaptation of this quotation from Micah (Mt 10:35; Lk 12:53).
71. Tacitus, *Annals*, XV, xliv; *I Clement* 6:1.
72. Tacitus, *Annals*, XV, xliv.

In Jewish and Christian tradition patience (*hypomenê*) is seen as a necessary virtue which accompanied one's waiting 'to the end', *eis telos*, that is 'to the full unfolding', 'to (the) end or completion', of the divine plan (Dan12:12; 4 Ezra 6:25; 7:27; Rom 5:4f). Perseverance is vital. The one who thus endures with patience (*hypomeinas*) to the end will be saved, not just saved from persecution and suffering, but saved in the sense of spiritual and eschatological salvation. 'If they persecute you in one town flee to the next.[73] 'Amen I say to you, you will not have exhausted the towns of Israel before the Son of Man comes.' With these words the reader is brought back to the commissioning of the original Twelve. Jesus tells them that the Son of Man will come before they have exhausted all the towns of Israel. The Son of Man is again mentioned. This time there is a different context. He is mentioned in connection with the final, eschatological judgement when the false judgements and prejudiced attitudes towards the disciples will be reversed and their persecution ended.

The disciple is called to share the same fate and undergo the same ill treatment as his master. 'A disciple is not above his teacher, nor a servant above his master; it is enough for the disciple to be like his teacher and the servant like his master.' This is very close to the teaching in the farewell discourse in John when Jesus says: 'If the world hates you, remember it hated me before you ... A servant is not greater than his master. If they persecuted me they will persecute you too. If they persecute you remember they persecuted me before you' (Jn 15:18, 20). Matthew recalls the slur that Jesus casts out demons by the power of the prince of demons (Mt 9:34) when he warns them: 'If they branded the master of the house Beelzebul, how much more will they (brand) the members of his household. Jesus will later respond to the charge of casting out demons through the power of Beelzebul (Mt 12:22-37)

---

73. Some mss add: 'and if they persecute you there flee to another'.

Triple exhortation to fearlessness Mt 10:26-33

'Do not fear them'. Exhortations to fearlessness were a long established element in the accounts of the call and commissioning of prophets. Usually the exhortation not to fear is first of all an exhortation not to be overcome with reverential fear or awe in the presence of the Divine or the divine messenger. Secondly the exhortation was often accompanied by an assurance of divine presence, inspiration and protection as a counterbalance to the causes of fear. 'I will be with you to protect you' (Jer 1:8; Exod 3:12) and 'I am putting my words into your mouth' (Jer 1:9-10).

As Jesus says to his apostles, 'Do not fear them', the reader asks: 'Who is not to be feared?' Obviously those who are not to be feared are the opponents and persecutors already mentioned in the discourse. They will try to suppress the proclamation of the kingdom and silence its witnesses. However, the revelation of Jesus, during his ministry so far and throughout the rest of the gospel, and the witness borne to him by his present and future followers, cannot be suppressed. Revelation will out in spite of calumny, silencing and persecution. 'What I say to you in the dark say it in the light and what is whispered in your ear proclaim from the housetops.' The persecution of Jesus or of his witnesses and the attempted suppression of their message will fail. Already in the gospel, even the efforts of Jesus himself to have some of his healings kept secret have failed and the news of them has been widely proclaimed.

'*And do not fear* those who kill the body and cannot kill the soul; fear rather the one who can destroy both body and soul in hell.' Human beings can kill the body but there is a greater power that can destroy the body and soul in hell. This 'body and soul' language is somewhat Hellenistic though it is set in the eschatological context of final judgement. A somewhat similar saying about finding and losing one's life 'for my sake' is found a few verses further on in the discourse (Mt 10:39).[74] The Greek word for 'life' (*psychê*) in this context should not be taken in the

---

74. There is a parallel passage in Mark where Jesus, following his first passion prediction, is instructing his disciples and the crowd about

philosophical Platonic sense of soul as distinct from body. Neither should it be taken in the straightforward sense of life just as we know it in this world, the biological life between birth and death. It is more the Hebrew concept of the essential person, the *nephes*, with the connotation of the survival of that which is essential to the person after death. What one should fear is not the one who can destroy only one's physical life and wellbeing but the one who can destroy the essential person by frustrating one's ultimate goal and destiny as laid out in God's plan. Instead of being afraid of those who can kill the body one should be afraid of believing or trusting in the false promises of those who can destroy body and soul in hell, that is, those who can frustrate the ultimate purpose of one's life.

Instead of *being afraid*, and fear comes across in the gospels as the opposite to faith, one should trust in God's providence, so evident in his care for even the smallest and, from the point of view of the market place, the cheapest of his creatures. 'Are not two sparrows sold for a penny, and yet not one of them falls to the ground without (the knowledge and will of) your Father.' The *a fortiori* argument follows: 'And all the hairs of your head are numbered, *therefore do not be afraid*.[75] You are of more value than many sparrows'.

Acknowledging Jesus Mt 10:32-33

Acknowledging Jesus before people in this world will result in acknowledgment by him before his Father in heaven. Conversely, denying him in this world will lead to denial by him before his Father in heaven.[76] Jesus here speaks of 'my Father in

---

'saving and losing one's life'. 'Anyone who loses his life for my sake and the sake of the gospel will save it. What gain is it for someone to gain the whole world and lose his life?'(Mk 8:35-36)

75. Italics added.

76. Mark uses stronger language for the same saying: 'If anyone is ashamed of me and my words in this adulterous and sinful generation, the Son of Man will be ashamed of him/her when he comes in the glory of his Father with the holy angels' (Mk 8:38). Instead of having Jesus refer to himself as 'I' he has him refer to himself as 'the Son of Man', coming in the glory of his Father with the holy angels.

heaven' rather than 'your Father in heaven' (a change from Mt 10:29) emphasising the fact that 'your Father' ultimately depends on the relationship with Jesus who can speak of God as 'my Father.' At the eschatological tribunal Jesus will be both judge in his own right, identifying his brothers and sisters, and advocate before the Father. J. P. Meier puts it in a nutshell:

> But failure to witness before the earthly tribunal will mean disgrace before the heavenly tribunal, where Jesus will disown the weak disciple as not being truly his brother and therefore not truly a son of the Father.[77]

The Sword of Division (Mt 10:34-39)

In the Sermon on the Mount Jesus challenged a false perception of his relation to the Law and the Prophets with the statement: 'Think not that I have come to destroy the Law and the Prophets. I have not come to destroy but to fulfil'(Mt 5:7). In a similar statement he here challenges a false perception that the messianic era will mean peace and harmony. It will in fact be a time when people will opt for or against the Messiah and serious divisions will emerge, most keenly felt in one's own household. The line up of members seems to point to a generation gap, where the younger members oppose the older, the man[78] against his father, the daughter against her mother and the daughter-in-law against the mother-in-law. Though not explicitly stated it seems the younger ones are opting to follow the call of the Messiah and the older ones opposing it. As pointed out already in the discourse in relation to the statement about being universally hated, and brother handing over brother to death and the father his child (Mt 10:21), 'a man's enemies will be those of his own household'. Micah's prediction again comes to mind (Micah 7:6).

No human relationship must be allowed to come between

---

77. J.P.Meier, *Matthew*, 112.
78. The word *anthrôpos* means human being, man or woman, but in the overall balance of the sentence it seems man is meant since the other examples are of the younger opposing the older of the same gender.

the follower and the Christ, not even the parent-child relationship, the love of son and daughter or father and mother. Luke uses the more Semitic expression, 'hating father and mother' rather than 'not loving more' (Lk 14:26). The personal decision for or against Christ made by the people in Jesus' time and in the time of his followers resulted in division in families. One therefore had to decide between love of parent, brother or sister, and the love/following of Christ. It is quite possible that the community for which Matthew wrote had experienced such family divisions and that some followers had even been turned out of their families, and out of their synagogues. In Mark's gospel the same point is made. A man's enemies will be those of his own household (Mk 13:12, cf Mic 7:6). Already in Matthew's gospel Jesus has told the disciple who wished to go and bury his father to let the dead bury their own dead (Mt 8:21f).

The statement about loving/hating parents is followed by the necessity of taking up one's cross and following Jesus (as in Lk 14:27). The follower must share the fate of Jesus, even to the unspeakably awful and disgraceful death by crucifixion. Speaking of taking up the cross reminds the reader of Jesus' own carrying of his cross. However, the reference need not necessarily have its origin in the post Good Friday recollection of Jesus' own carrying of the cross because crucifixion was a common experience, as was the sight of the victims carrying the crossbeam to the place of execution. This fact is borne out by Plutarch's remark in his work on punishment and providence that every criminal who is executed carries his own cross.[79]

The saying about finding and losing and losing and saving one's life: 'Whoever finds his/her life will lose it and whoever loses his/her life for my sake will save it' is a typical Semitic antithetical parallel. As seen already the word 'life' (*psychê*) in this context should not be taken in the philosophic Platonic sense of soul as distinct from body. Neither should it be taken in the straightforward sense of life just as we know it in this world, the biological life between birth and death. It is more the Hebrew

---

79. Plutarch, *De sera numinis vindicata*, 9.554b.

concept of the essential person, the *nephes*, with the connotation
of the survival of that which is essential to the person after
death. 'Finding' (or 'saving') one's life and then losing it implies
directing all one's energies to preserving, securing and enriching one's own life for this world only, and missing out on something far more fundamental at the eschatological judgement.
Losing one's life implies an acceptance of suffering, rejection,
death, loss and failure 'for my sake' and being prepared to appear foolish to people for living such a way of life.[80] Such an apparent loss of life results in 'saving one's life', that is, it brings triumph to the 'essential person' at the final judgement.

Accepting the Missionaries of Christ Mt 10:40-2

After the warnings about rejection, persecution and division
the discourse ends on a positive note, with three statements or
logia about acceptance of the 'apostles', the missionaries of
Christ.

It is a basic tenet of political, social, synagogue and church
practice that the one sent, the emissary, ambassador or apostle is
treated with the respect due to the one who sends him/her and
to deny such respect and acceptance is to deny respect to the one
who sent the emissary.[81] The first and most fundamental of the
statements states that the person who welcomes those sent by
Christ (the apostles) welcomes Christ, and in turn the one who
welcomes Christ welcomes the One who sent him. This fundamental truth turns up with only slight variations in all gospels
(Mk 9:37, Lk 9:48; 10:16, Jn 12:44-45; 13:20).

The second statement is a corollary of the first. The prophet
and righteous[82] man are also representatives of God. Accepting
them gives one a share in their role and righteousness with its

80. Matthew and Luke have 'for the sake of me'. Mark has 'for the sake
of me and of the good news'.
81. This is a central theme of St John's gospel where it is strongly emphasised that rejection of the one-sent results from not knowing, not
hearing and not obeying the Father who sent him.
82. Note again Matthew's emphasis on *dikaios* 'righteous' as the mark of
the follower of Christ.

due reward. Here this pair is representative of the Christian followers (a somewhat similar pairing, 'prophets and saints' appears in Rev 11:17-18).

The third statement, introduced solemnly with 'amen I say to you' is a promise that generosity to the apostles / representatives of Christ, even a cup of cold water given to the little ones (the ordinary disciples that could easily be overlooked or forgotten) will not go without its reward (/ / Mk 9:41).

Conclusion Mt 11:1

The discourse ends with the usual formula: 'And it came to pass when Jesus had finished ...' followed by a reference to a change of location and new activity (Mt 11:1). The narrative now resumes after the discourse.

The Challenge of the Kingdom
Mt 11:2 – 13:58
Questions, Controversies and Parables

The Plot

As is customary in Matthew, the statement that Jesus had finished his discourse leads on to a new section of the gospel, which begins with a change of place and a summary of Jesus' activity (Mt 11:1). 'When he had finished instructing his twelve disciples he went on to teach and preach in their towns/cities.' This summary functions as a bridge binding the discourse and the following narrative. Already obvious in the gospel, the hostility and intransigence of the leaders now becomes more and more obvious and from now on the performance of miracles is less frequent in the antagonistic, non-believing atmosphere. Chapters 11 and 12 trace the rejection of Jesus through a series of incidents involving several characters and events and include some material from Mark's Galilean controversy cycle. The narrative prepares the ground and the reader for the parabolic discourse in Mt 13:1-52 and then this section of the gospel reaches its climax in the dramatic and poignant rejection of Jesus in his hometown and among his own people (Mt 13:53-58).[1]

The inauguration of the kingdom in the person, words and deeds of Jesus poses a challenge, even a serious problem, for those who had very different expectations of the Christ and the kingdom. The reactions portrayed in chapters 11 and 12 range from the genuine questioning of the Baptist through the calumny of the Pharisees who say he casts out devils through Beelzebul, prince of devils, and the hostile demanding of a sign by the scribes and Pharisees, right through to the outright rejection ex-

---

1. From the rejection in Nazareth (Mt 13:53-58) onwards the narrative of the gospel will be a very close parallel to Mark, including almost all the material from Mark 6:1 onwards. The neat arrangement of materials seen in the Infancy Narrative, the Sermon on the Mount and the collection of miracle stories gives way to a less obvious arrangement.

perienced in his native place by his own people. The parables in chapter 13 are Jesus' response to this questioning and negativity, a counter challenge to friend and foe alike to think in a whole new way about the nature of the kingdom, the challenge it poses and the response it demands.

Outline of Mt 11:2-13:58
1. Jesus and John Mt 11:2-19
2. Jesus' Response to Unbelief Mt 11:20-30
3. Controversies Mt 12:1-50
4. Parabolic Discourse 13:1-52
5. Jesus Rejected in his Native Place Mt 13:53-58

1. JESUS AND JOHN MT 11:2-19
Chapter 11 has three units dealing with John the Baptist and Jesus. It begins with John's question about Jesus, continues with Jesus' question about John and concludes with a reflection on the negative reactions to both Jesus and John. This leads to Jesus' condemnation of the unbelieving generation in prophetic style and his invitation to come to him, delivered in the style of the Wisdom literature.

a. John's Question about Jesus Mt 11:2-6
It was when John heard the works of the Christ that he asked, through his messengers, if he (Jesus) was the one who was to come or should they look for another. The reader is surely surprised to hear the Baptist asking if he is 'the one who is to come', a well-established designation of the Messiah. After all, he had proclaimed the superior nature of Jesus' person and mission and contrasted his own baptism with Jesus' baptism in spirit when Jesus came to him at the Jordan. He had performed the baptism and witnessed the accompanying events, the voice from heaven and the descent of the Spirit. He was the key witness to the events authenticating and empowering the ministry of Jesus and played a central role at its launch (Mt 3:11-17). Now he is asking a question, as though he is confused or has lost confidence in his previous perceptions and declarations.

Why did such a question arise at this juncture? One may ask whether the question was really posed for his own sake or the sake of his disciples but, in either case, the basic question remains the same. Looking again at the preaching of the Baptist before his arrest, one can see from the accounts of both Matthew and Luke (the Q tradition), that his preaching envisioned an apocalyptic style judgement which would herald the arrival of the kingdom, destroying at its arrival the sinners and their sin. The axe laid to the root of the tree and the burning of the chaff were powerful images of such an apocalyptic event (Mt 3:10-12 / / Lk 3:9, 17).

But the ministry of Jesus (and of his newly appointed apostles) turned out to be very different from what the Baptist, and like-minded people, expected. Far from destroying sin and the sinner, Jesus proclaimed the forgiveness of sin and he ate and drank in the company of sinners. He crossed the boundaries of taboo in matters of ritual purity. He touched the leper, the sick and the corpse. He preached that the kingdom belongs to the 'poor in spirit' and to those persecuted for the sake of righteousness. He announced that the merciful would receive mercy. Far from promoting self-righteous zeal in the face of wrongdoing he emphasised an attitude of forgiveness of others as a precondition for one's own forgiveness from God. All of these aspects of his ministry must have raised self-righteous and even genuinely perplexed eyebrows.

In response to the question of the Baptist, Jesus sends his disciples back to him with the simple instruction to tell him what they have heard and seen: 'The blind see, the lame walk, the lepers are cleansed, the deaf hear, the dead are raised, and the poor have the good news preached to them.' This answer to the Baptist, far from being argumentative, apologetic or theological, is just a simple statement of what the observers of Jesus' ministry 'have heard and seen'. Typical of Matthew, he is pointing to the fulfilment of the prophesies of Isaiah (even though there is no introductory formula of fulfilment). Jesus' words and deeds are authenticated, in Matthew's understanding, by their fulfilment of scripture (Isa 25:8; 29:18-19; 35:5-6; 61:1).[2] The summary and climax of the recital of deeds is the preaching of the good news to the poor (in word and deed).

The response concludes with the beatitude, 'Blessed is the one who is not scandalised in me.' The one who does not find in Jesus' way of carrying out his ministry a stumbling block to faith, such a one is blessed. Matthew may well be keeping his own audience in mind as there may have been lingering worries in the minds of his Jewish Christians about the obvious difference between widely expected hopes and visions of the Messiah and his role and the actual nature of Jesus' ministry. For Matthew's Jewish and Gentile audience this difficulty would have been compounded by the official rejection of Jesus and his ministry and by the terrible nature of his death. His death after all was, in the words of Paul, 'to the Jews a stumbling block and to the Gentiles foolishness' because 'the Jews looked for signs and the Greeks looked for wisdom' (1 Cor 1:22).

For Matthew's Jewish Christians also the figure of the Baptist, a widely respected prophet among the people, giving voice to a problem about Jesus and his ministry would legitimate both their own questions and create the space for the authoritative answer of Jesus to them.

b. Jesus' question about John Mt 11:7-15

Jesus then questions the crowd about why they followed the Baptist into the wilderness. Who did they think he was and what was the nature of his mission? Was he 'a reed blowing in the wind', a popular demagogue keeping his ear to the ground, picking up every wind of change and telling the people what they wanted to hear? Was he 'someone dressed in fine garments' like a well-dressed official agent or spy giving the people the official line and propaganda? If so would he not be in the palace as a well dressed, well housed official rather than a prisoner in the palace dungeon?

---

2. This is entirely contrary to the oft repeated, but erroneous, notion that the evangelists had to include a miracle tradition to keep Jesus on a par with the wonder workers of their day.

John was obviously a prophet. He lived an ascetic life
dressed in a garment of camel hair, wearing a leather belt and
feeding on locusts and wild honey. Like the prophets before him
he called sin and incest for what they really were and in doing so
he offended the powerful people who had him imprisoned (Mt
4:12) and would bring about his death (Mt 14:1-12). But here
Jesus proclaims that he was a prophet but still more than a
prophet. He was the precursor, the one sent to prepare the way
(of the Lord/the Messiah).

To illustrate his point Matthew quotes the scriptures, without naming the source. The citation is adapted from the prophet
Malachi about the sending of the one 'to prepare a way before
me'. The adapted citation introduces the main protagonist, God,
into the narrative, as God addresses Jesus through the scriptural
citation: 'Behold, I am sending my messenger before you, he will
prepare your way, before you' (Mal 3:1). The adaptation to a
triple emphasis on 'you/your' is striking.[3]

Matthew continues the comments of Jesus beginning with
the statement that 'of all the children born of women a greater
than John the Baptist has never been seen'. After this assertion of
the unsurpassed greatness of the Baptist in the old dispensation,
Jesus contrasts the new dispensation in the kingdom with the
old dispensation of which the Baptist was the final exemplar.
Even the least in the kingdom is greater than the greatest in the
old dispensation. All the prophets and the Law were leading up
to John.[4] All the prophetic activity and the Law would lead, according to the final prophecy of Malachi 3:23, to the return of
Elijah to usher in the messianic era. Jesus adds: 'and if you will
believe me, he (the Baptist) is the Elijah who was to return'.
Following this declaration is the well established biblical call to
listen: 'If anyone has ears to hear, let him listen', a New
Testament equivalent of the prophetic statements closing or in-

---

3. Mark (1:2-3) expands on the idea of 'your way' with a quotation from
Isaiah and ascribes the whole quotation, an amalgam of Mal 3:1, Exod
23:20 and Isa 40:3, to Isaiah.
4. 'The Prophets and the Law' is a reversal of the usual order of importance. This may be to highlight the important role of John as prophet.

troducing and emphasising a speech: 'Thus speaks the Lord' or 'These are the words of the Lord.'

c. Hostile Reaction to John and Jesus Mt 11:16-19

Jesus speaks of 'this generation', a pejorative term used frequently in the gospel for the unbelievers he encounters in Israel. Taken on its own the verse describing the children in the marketplace playing dance music and dirges and expecting their playmates to dance to their tune could be a reference to the leaders who want to manipulate the people according to their wishes. However, taken in context with the succeeding verse describing the difference between the ministries of John and Jesus the focus passes from the players of the music to the children who cannot be satisfied by either kind of music. The ascetic lifestyle and 'apocalyptic' style preaching of the Baptist provoked the reaction and criticism that he had a demon (a criticism that is also leveled at Jesus). The ministry of Jesus[5] in which he shared the table, eating and drinking with outcasts and sinners, and declaring the forgiveness of sin, did not suit the critics either (Mt 9:6, 10-13). They called him a glutton, a drunkard and a friend of tax collectors and sinners.

The statement that since the coming of the Baptist, up to the present time, the kingdom of heaven has been subjected to violence and the violent are taking it by storm can be understood in different ways. Some ancient mss speak of the kingdom coming violently, but the more likely reference is to the fact that John the precursor has already suffered through his arrest and imprisonment and Jesus has already warned against the likelihood of a similar violence against himself and his followers (Mt 10:16-31).[6] The Pharisees are already showing hostility and will soon be plotting how to destroy him (Mt 12:14).

Jesus responded to the Baptist's question by way of drawing

---

5. He describes himself here as 'the Son of Man' probably because of his forgiveness of sin/sinners.

6. Immediately following the transfiguration Jesus will again address the question of John the Baptist as the returned Elijah who has been badly treated (Mt 17:10-13).

the messengers' attention to, 'what you have heard and seen,' and describing a series of deeds that recalled the prophecies of Isaiah. Now he sets his actions, and by implication his words, in the context of another great biblical tradition, the tradition of Wisdom. The power and wisdom of God were manifested through his work in creation, his guidance of history and his revelation of a way of life to the chosen people. Wisdom was personified as Lady Wisdom in several Old Testament texts (Prov 8:1-9:6; Wis 7:22-8:8 *inter alia*). Now Jesus is seen as the embodiment of Wisdom. He is the revealer of God and the establisher of God's kingdom through his words and actions. These words and actions are the fruit of Wisdom. Just as the goodness of the tree is proved by its production of good fruit, so Jesus and his messianic deeds will be proved to be 'just/righteous' by their fruit. In the face of rejection the mighty (words and) deeds of Jesus (and his followers) will prove who was 'righteous', by their success in working according to the will and plan of God for the establishment of the kingdom. 'Wisdom is justified by her deeds.'

2. JESUS' RESPONSE TO UNBELIEF MT 11:20-30

a. Woes on the cities of Galilee Mt 11:20-24

Continuing the note of rejection and returning to the language of the prophets, Jesus pronounces woes on those who have refused to repent and believe. The woes are the opposite of the beatitudes. Whereas the beatitudes point to a gift and reward from God, the woes warn of God's displeasure and threat of punishment. Traditionally the prophets pronounced woes on the cities, the rulers, the priests and the people who transgressed the covenant.

The Galilean cities, where Jesus' ministry, including his call to repentance, his preaching and his mighty deeds had taken place, should be in the forefront of his following. But they had not heeded his call to repentance. Chorazin and Bethsaida that refused to repent are therefore described as worse than pagan cities. They are unfavourably compared to the cities of Tyre and

Sidon that would have repented in sackcloth and ashes (like Nineveh long ago) (Jonah 3:5) if the mighty deeds done in Corazin and Bethsaida had been done in their midst.[7] The refusal of Capernaum to repent was worst of all because (again by implication) it was at the centre of his ministry and was most favoured. It would suffer the greatest judgement instead of experiencing the reward of its privileged position. 'And you Capernaum, will you be exalted to heaven? No, you will be brought down to Hades. For if the deeds of power done in you had been done in Sodom it would have remained until this day. But I tell you that on the day of judgement it will be more tolerable for the land of Sodom than for you' (Mt 11:23f). Again the clearly eschatological note of judgement emerges.

These 'woes' present an interesting scenario since Matthew has given no account so far of any mighty deeds done either in Chorazin or Bethsaida, and his picture so far of Capernaum has been quite positive in relation to the general response of the people. The woes therefore represent an independent piece of early tradition introduced into the narrative at this point to emphasise the growing rejection of Jesus. Furthermore, they represent an early tradition of miracles, which, combined with some of the summaries in the New Testament point to the existence from the very beginning of a 'miracle stratum' in the gospels.[8]

b. Thanksgiving Prayer for Revelation Mt 11:25-27

The connecting phrase, 'At that time', highlights the contrast between the aforementioned rejection by the 'establishment' of the lake towns and the acceptance by the 'unimportant' people of the area, the 'mere children.' The following sublime utterances of Jesus about the Father's revelation to the mere children and Jesus' relationship with the Father stand out against the dark background of rejection and hostility already described. The Wisdom theme introduced in Mt 11:19 with a reference to Wisdom being justified by her deeds is followed through here in

7. Tyre was quite hostile to the Jews in New Testament times.
8. This is a pointer against those who regard the miracles as a later addition to put Jesus on a par with the miracle workers of the day.

two essential aspects of the Wisdom tradition which are fulfilled in Jesus' ministry. Jesus is revealer and host.

The Father-Son relationship revealed here will underpin all subsequent christology, expressed in the Son of God and Son of Man titles in the gospel. These verses are almost like a digest of the Father-Son theology in the gospel of John. They are spoken at a time when the religious leaders, those who know the laws and traditions, are rejecting him, and the poor; the outcasts and the sinners are coming to him and finding 'rest for their souls'. The question of the Baptist about 'the one to come' finds its most sublime solution in these verses.

Two verses (Mt 11:25-26) praise the Father, 'Lord of heaven and earth', for his revelation, not to the wise and the clever, the religious leaders and teachers (could they be classified in modern idiom as 'the know-alls'?) but to the 'little ones', the ordinary people who may be overlooked and even looked down upon by 'the wise and the clever'. But they are the Father's 'little ones', 'his children'. They are the ones who can pray the words 'Our Father.' In so revealing himself to them God has shown his 'graciousness'.

The next verse focuses on the mutual knowledge of Father and Son. This relationship is known to people only through the revelation by the Son. In the language of John's gospel they know the Father and so they know the Son, the one the Father has sent. The 'wise and the clever' do not know the Father, the love of the Father is not in them, and so they do not know the Son, the one he has sent (Jn 8:19, 55). No one has ever seen God / the Father (Jn 1:18; 6:46). It is God the only Son, ever in the bosom of the Father, who has made him known (Jn 1:18). Those who know the Son come to know the Father in a whole new way. 'I know my own and my own know me, just as the Father knows me and I know the Father' (Jn 10:15). No one comes to the Son unless the Father draws him (Jn 6:44) as Jesus says in John's gospel: 'To hear the teaching of the Father and to learn from it is to come to me' (Jn 6:45). Those who have heard the Father now hear the invitation of the Son.

c. Wisdom-Style Invitation. Jesus as Host. Mt 11: 27-30

Like Wisdom, Jesus is a gracious host inviting devotees to his banquet and to a place of rest, refreshment and well being (Prov 9:1-6). Three verses (Mt 11:28-30) spell out that invitation of the Son to come to him to find rest from the burdens of life, for his way of life is life giving and dispels unnecessary worry and anxiety. His yoke is easy and his burden light, unlike the yoke and burden of self righteous rigorists who bind up heavy burdens for others to carry and do not lift a finger themselves to help them (Mt 23:4). His rest is ultimately the eschatological rest, a sharing in his life and relationship with the Father. The gospel of John sums up this as being with Jesus where he is, as he prayed at the Last Supper: 'I want those you have given me to be with me where I am' (Jn 17:24).

3. CONTROVERSIES. (GALILEAN DISPUTE CYCLE) MT 12:1-50

a. The Sabbath Disputes: Mt 12:1-14

The phrase 'at that time' not only acts as a connecting phrase with what has gone before but also keeps the reader's attention focused on the emerging atmosphere of opposition and criticism. Matthew now recounts two disputes about Sabbath observance that form part of the Galilean dispute cycle in Mark 2:23-3:6.

(i) The Charge: Plucking grain on the Sabbath Mt 12:1-8

Jesus is passing through a cornfield on the Sabbath. His disciples are hungry and they pluck ears of corn and eat them. Plucking corn and eating it as one passed through someone else's field was permitted, but putting a sickle into another person's corn was strictly forbidden (Deut 23:25). The difficulty arose because they were plucking the corn on the Sabbath and in the eyes of legal rigorists it was seen as harvesting work that was forbidden on the Sabbath.[9] The Pharisees saw them and

9. Exod 34:21; cf *m. Shabbat* 7:2; Philo, *De Mosis.*, 2:22; CD 10:14-11:18. There may be a concern also about not having prepared their food prior to the Sabbath. cf *CD10*: 22.

challenged Jesus about the actions of his disciples whom they accused of breaking the Sabbath.

Jesus' response

Jesus responded with two lessons from scripture both of which he introduced with the devastating and challenging remark to persons setting themselves up as experts in scripture and enforcers of the Law: 'Have you never read?'

The first *halakic* or legal interpretation is crystal clear even though the story Jesus quotes differs in a number of ways from the known texts of the Old Testament. The story of David to which Jesus refers is found in 1 Sam 21:1-6 (LXX 21:2-7).[10] No companions of David are mentioned in the Old Testament story, neither is there reference to their being hungry and eating the bread of the presence, the twelve loaves baked specially to be set before the tabernacle every Sabbath and which were to be eaten only by the priests. This consecrated bread is often referred to as 'the bread of the presence' or 'shewbread'. The story as told here may reflect a lost tradition of the Old Testament or a lost Targumic reflection on it. It may also reflect a New Testament tradition earlier than Matthew's (or Mark's) written gospel. The narrator adds the explanatory note about the bread: 'which it is not permitted for anyone except the priests to eat.'[11] Jesus tells the story to highlight the fact that compassionate response to human need, such as hunger, is of greater importance than scrupulous observance of laws governing Sabbath observance or temple ceremonial.

The second *halakic* example is also quite clear. The temple duties of the priests, which involve work in preparing the sacrifices, do not break the Sabbath. The temple ceremonial outranks the

---

10. Mark further complicates the historical details of the story by referring to Abiathar as High Priest at the time. In both the Hebrew and Greek texts of the Old Testament which have survived, Ahimelek, the father of Abiathar and not Abiathar himself was the priest in question. Furthermore, he was the priest, not the High Priest.

11. J. P. Meier, *Matthew*, 129, points out that in David's time there was not a prohibition against eating the shewbread.

Sabbath observance. There is clearly an ascending order of importance in matters religious. Jesus builds on this ascending order when he goes on to say: 'I tell you something greater than the temple is here.' This was a very important claim on Jesus' own lips for the early community at a time when the temple and its rituals had been destroyed. The gospel reader already knows that Jesus fulfils the role of Emmanuel, signifying the Divine Presence and that his divinely given name, 'Jesus' points to the fact that he is the one who saves his people from their sins, the two main functions of the temple (Mt 1:2-22).

Jesus then issues another broadside at his critics with the remark: 'If you had known what it is (means): "I demand mercy not sacrifice" you would not have condemned the innocent.' Quoting the saying of Hos 6:6 Jesus again emphasises the theme of mercy, a prominent theme so far in Matthew (Mt 5:7; 9:13). Then he goes on to say ' The Son of Man is master of the Sabbath.'[12] The Son of Man, whose power to forgive sins was already demonstrated, is mentioned again and this time his status and authority are shown to outrank the sacred institutions of Sabbath and Temple.

(ii) The Charge: Healing on the Sabbath Mt 12:9-14

Jesus is again on the move and enters their synagogue. Matthew's use of 'their synagogue' highlights the distancing that is or has been taking place in his time and sees in it a continuation of the tensions evident in Jesus' own ministry. Mark and Luke in the parallel passages simply say 'the synagogue' (Mk 3:1; Lk 6:6). As in Mark this incident follows the incident in the cornfield (Mk 2:23 – 3:6). Here in the synagogue is a man with a withered hand. The withered hand was most likely not life threatening and so, in the eyes of the strict observants, it did not qualify as an emergency that could be treated on the Sabbath. The description xêra (withered) seems to suggest a long-term condition, possibly from birth.

---

12. Mark's *logion* in this context is: 'The Sabbath was made for man, not man for the Sabbath' (Mk 2:27). It does not appear in Matthew or Luke.

The atmosphere is charged with tension as 'they' (identified at the end of the account as the Pharisees) put the question to Jesus: 'Is it lawful to heal on the Sabbath?' They question him thus in order to find some accusation against him. The reader senses that the unfortunate person with the withered hand is either deliberately 'planted' or conveniently used in the synagogue as a bait to trap Jesus into an act of healing on the Sabbath. In their 'religious' zeal and controlling legalism they both degraded the person and demeaned the Sabbath with their cunning approach.

Jesus' response

Jesus realised the situation and threw down the gauntlet with a penetrating argument against his critics, beginning with: 'Which of you will have one sheep that falls into a pit on the Sabbath and you will not pull it out?' 'Which of you' makes the reply almost into an *ad hominem* argument and the specification of 'one sheep' may be a further 'put down'. The overall meaning could be stated as: 'Which of you would have difficulty in finding yourselves excused from the Sabbath observance in order to rescue just one sheep?' They cannot in honesty disagree with his rhetorical question. Thus using the example of saving one sheep that had fallen into a pit on the Sabbath he makes the *a fortiori* argument for healing a person who is of much more value than one sheep. Concluding his argument he states categorically that it is (therefore) lawful to do good (in this case to heal) on the Sabbath.

Jesus said to the man with the withered hand: 'Stretch out your hand.' It was cured and restored to the same condition as his good hand. No law or custom was transgressed in simply stretching out one's hand. Jesus thereby scored a multiple victory. He proved his superior insight into his opponents; cured with a word, transgressed no law or custom in doing so, and his manifestation of power underpinned his rhetorical question and manifested his authority. In an honour-shame context he won the argument and shamed his opponents. But they were not content to learn, admit their mistake or credit his power. The Pharisees withdrew into council to discuss how to destroy him.[13] The end of the gospel is here foreshadowed. Jesus had already warned that the bridegroom would be taken away and now the likelihood of its happening is beginning to emerge as the Pharisees scheme about doing away with him. The dramatic effect is palpable as the reader/audience senses that the outcome of the gospel has been foreshadowed in this story. It remains to see it unfold.

b. Jesus' Withdraws from the District. Mt 12:15-21. The Servant of YHWH cf Isa 42:1-4

The next pericope is also introduced with a statement of Jesus' change of location. 'He withdrew from there' because he was aware of the hostility and plotting of his opponents. Just as he withdrew into Galilee after the arrest of the Baptist, so now he again withdraws from a fraught situation. However, many people followed him, and he cured them all, a typical statement of Matthew concerning Jesus' universal healing power. However, he instructed them not to make him known. Whereas Mark developed this 'tell nobody' motif into a significant theological construct that scholars have called 'the messianic secret', Matthew sees it partly as a prudential move to keep him out of trouble and to prevent the wrong kind of publicity leading to further controversy. But even more so, in this present context, it is in keeping with the character of Jesus who has described himself as 'meek and humble of heart' and invited people to take up his yoke for it is easy and his burden light (Mt 11:28-30). This is in contrast to the rigorous legalism to which they were often subjected. In this case it was a legalism resulting in a threat of violence against Jesus himself.

13. At this point Mark says the Pharisees conspired with the Herodians about how to destroy him (Mk 3:6). Mark's association of two mutually hostile and extreme opposites on the political, social and religious scene highlighted the extent to which Jesus' opponents were prepared to go to destroy him. Luke shows Jesus leaving his critics to draw their own conclusion in their confused embarrassment (Lk 14: 6).

This aspect of Jesus' character and ministry, which caused him to withdraw from where the controversies and plotting took place, will be further borne out in the fulfilment citation from the prophet (Deutero-) Isaiah which follows and which shows Jesus' withdrawal to be in keeping with the divine plan in the scriptures. To illustrate this, Matthew introduces the longest Old Testament citation of his gospel in order to portray Jesus in the role of the humble, obedient, beloved and spirit endowed servant of God, described and foretold in the (Suffering) Servant hymns of Isaiah. The citation does not match exactly the MT or the LXX so it is either from another tradition of the Old Testament or, more likely, Matthew has, as in the case of the other citations, tailored it to fit his point of view. In this case he tailors it to fit the context of opposition to Jesus and his humble reaction, marked by his compassion. He introduces the citation with a fulfilment formula: 'This was to fulfill what was spoken by the prophet Isaiah.'

The citation (Mt 12:18-21) is from the First Song of the (Suffering) Servant (Isa 42:1-4). The opening verse of the citation, 'This is my servant, whom I uphold, my chosen in whom my soul delights. I have put my spirit upon him; he will bring forth justice to the nations', recalls the baptismal scene with the voice from heaven and the descent of the Spirit. The heavenly declaration will be repeated in the account of the Transfiguration (Mt 17:5). The Greek term *pais* can mean servant or son and the connotation 'son' is picked up by Matthew and he uses *huios*, son, in the divine declaration in the Baptismal and Transfiguration scenes (Mt 3:17; 17:5). Here in Mt 12: 18 the term 'servant', *pais,* is retained. The Spirit will be upon him and he will proclaim justice, that is God's plan of salvation to the pagan nations, the Gentiles. It will not be a justice or salvation built on prejudice, propaganda and self-importance. The term *krisis* is the LXX translation of the Hebrew *mishpat* meaning judgement 'which signifies the divine statute that governs the relationship of God with man, in so far as it is known through revelation and the true religion that is founded on it.'[14] The mission to the Gentiles is foreshadowed here and reinforced at the end of the citation with the emphasis on the victory of justice, a victory that will cause the Gentiles to hope.

The second verse of the citation, 'He does not shout aloud or have his voice heard in the street' points to the fact that he does not get embroiled in loud and controversial disputes or wrangle and engage in loud hostilities in public. He does not make great displays of power and destroy his opponents or those branded as sinners. He has in fact just withdrawn from the scene of possible turmoil.

The third verse in the citation (Mt 12:20), 'He will not break the bruised reed or quench the smouldering wick until he has brought justice to victory', has been clearly demonstrated in Jesus' ministry to date in his compassion for the weak and needy, a far cry from the apocalyptic destruction of the axe laid to the root of the tree or the burning of the chaff, the very difference that probably prompted the Baptist's question: 'Are you he who is to come or shall we look for another?' Bringing justice to victory signifies the victory of God's justice. E. Schweizer explains it very well:

> It is the justice of one who does not spout propaganda or destroy what is weak. In the face of all messianic expectations, the text emphasises what Jesus does not do ... Despite its totally different language and theology, this passage is remarkably reminiscent of Paul's proclamation of the righteousness of God which seeks to establish itself on earth among all the nations ... it is not a shattering judgement but a supportive justice, under which victory goes to the one whose purpose is not to carry the day for his own cause but to intervene on behalf of the weak.[15]

The final verse of the citation (Mt 12:21) states that in his name the nations will put their hope. 'In his name' sums up his

14. Footnote to Mt 12:18 in the Jerusalem Bible (1966 ed).
15. E. Schweizer, *op. cit.*, 282.

identity, authority, salvific purpose and the nature of his mission. These have just been summarised in the citation and will be the source of hope for the nations. The goal of the gospel and the universal mission are foreshadowed.

c. Healing by the power of Beelzebul Mt 12:22-24

Already in his ministry Jesus healed two blind men who called him 'Son of David' as they appealed to his compassion (Mt 9:27-31) and, following on their healing, he healed a dumb demoniac (Mt 9:32-33). In response the people said: 'Nothing like this was ever seen in Israel' and the Pharisees said: 'It is through the prince of devils that he casts out devils' (Mt 9:34). These reactions now come to the fore again. In a 'double' healing he cures a blind man who is also dumb (and by implication probably deaf as well). Recounting the miracle affords Matthew the opportunity again to recall two reactions. The first is the positive reaction of the crowd who wonder if this sign points to the fact that Jesus is the Son of David, a confession heard earlier on the lips of the two blind men. The messianic significance of the title was examined in the commentary at that point (Mt 9:27-31). The second reaction is negative, as in the case of the earlier healings when the Pharisees accused him of casting out devils by the power of the prince of devils (Mt 9:34). This time they name the prince of devils Beelzebul.[16]

The name Beelzebul for a demon is not found in the LXX. It occurs in the synoptics both in the triple tradition (Mt 12:24 // Mk 3:22//Lk 11:15) and in the double tradition, the material usually designated as Q (Mt 12:27//Lk 11:18f). There are some variations in the name such as Beelzebul, Beelzeboul, Beelzebub. Looking for a possible origin of the name, scholars point to the likelihood that Beelzebul and Beelzeboul are variations on the name of an old Canaanite god meaning 'Baal the Prince' or 'Baal

---

16. The parallel account in Mk 3:22ff states that the comment was made by the scribes from Jerusalem. They were among Jesus' most formidable opponents and many of them would very likely have been Pharisees.

the exalted abode'.[17] The name Baalzebub ('Lord of the Flies') appears in the Second Book of Kings as a satirical version of the name of the Canaanite god of Ekron and in the Testament of Solomon Beelzeboul is a fallen angel who is called 'prince of demons' and 'ruler of demons'.[18] Obviously popular usage kept alive the name and its demonic associations with the usual variations and approximations typical of folk tradition.

Responding to the charge, Jesus calls 'the prince of demons' Satan. In the Book of Job 'Satan' means 'adversary,' much as we would speak of 'devil's advocate' in a discussion (Job 1:6-12). In this pericope in Matthew Satan is identified with Beelzebul, the prince of demons. Satan is the tempter in the desert (Mt 4:10; Mk 1:13) and Luke says the devil departed from there to return at 'the appointed time', at 'his opportune moment' (*achri kairou*) (Lk 4:13), generally seen as the moment when Satan entered into Judas and motivated the betrayal (Lk 22:3; Jn 13:27). He is seen in the New Testament generally as the adversary of Jesus. In a more general way any person operating against Jesus or inspired by thoughts and plans contrary to his could be regarded as a 'Satan' figure, as Peter was when Jesus said: 'Get behind me Satan, you are a hindrance to me; for you think not the things of God but of men' (Mt 16:23//Mk 8:33).

Whatever the exact derivation of the names the accusation is quite clear. Jesus is accused of having, in the sense of being possessed by, a leading spirit of a pagan pantheon who wields authority over other evil spirits, all of whom, by very definition, operate against God and God's rule in creation and among his people. They are the forces opposed to the kingdom of God and Jesus is accused of being their instrument. He warned his apostles that they will be subjected to a similar slander (Mt 10:25).

---

17. J. R. Donahue and D. J. Harrington, *op. cit.*, 129, n.22.
18. Ibid. cf 2 Kings 1:3,6. *Test. Sol.* 3:1-6.

Jesus' Response

i. Divided Kingdom; Divided City; Divided House Mt 12:25-29

'Knowing their thoughts' Jesus responds to their accusation using the images of a divided kingdom and how it is so easily laid waste, and of a divided city and a divided house, and how they cannot stand. 'If Satan casts out Satan he is divided against himself. How can his kingdom stand?' These examples are gnomic, proverbial, and applicable to all situations at all times, not depending on any particular set of circumstances for their validation. However, Jesus' audience would have seen how they reflected their own experience and Matthew's audience would have plenty of contemporary examples to illustrate the maxims. The experience of having five emperors in the years 68-69AD,[19] four following in quick succession after the suicide of Nero was demanded by the military and the Senate, with the empire-wide upheaval caused by military and dynastic rivalry for the throne was an example to everyone in the empire of the consequences of a kingdom divided against itself. So too the destruction of the house of Herod Antipas, after he divorced the daughter of the Nabatean king Aretas in order to marry Herodias, would have been well known. Well known also was the enmity in the Herod family which led to the deposition and banishment of Antipas by Caligula at the instigation of Herodias' brother, his own nephew, Agrippa, (c. 38-39AD). The powerful family that hounded the Baptist had been destroyed from within, divided against itself, by the time the gospels were written.

Following the universally applicable examples of the consequences of internal division, Jesus launches an *ad hominem* broadside at his own critics, asking them by whom their own sons cast out demons. Does he mean that they are by implication condemning the good people in their own families who do healing work? If so, those good people will be their judges and condemn them for their condemnation of another exorcist/healer. Or is he pointing to the charlatans in their midst who go unchecked by them, and whose toleration by them will be a

19. Nero, Galba, Otho, Vitellius and Vespasian.

source of judgement on them? Either or both meanings are possible.

Jesus clinches the argument with the challenge to his critics that if it is by the Spirit of God that he casts out demons, then the kingdom of God has come upon them. This has very serious implications for the strong man (Satan) whose house is being broken into and despoiled (by the agents of the kingdom of God). By implication, therefore, his critics ought to be very careful about rushing to negative statements and judgements. Instead of his usual expression 'kingdom of heaven' Matthew here uses 'kingdom of God' in this response of Jesus, either because it was a well established response in the tradition at this point, or even more likely because it highlights the opposition between God and Satan and their kingdoms, and the attack being launched on the kingdom of Satan by the kingdom of God.

To despoil the strong man's house one must first bind and render powerless the strong man. By implication this is what Jesus is doing to Beelzebul, Satan, the prince of demons, as he plunders his house and establishes the kingdom of heaven (of God). Raiding the house of the strong man, the oppressor, is an established pattern in biblical thought. The Israelites 'despoiled' the Egyptians as they left in the Exodus (Exod 3:21f; 11:2f; 12:35f; cf Ps 105:37). Isaiah celebrates the fact that God despoils the mighty of his captives and the tyrant of his prey and the servant of God divides the spoils with the mighty/strong (Isa 49:24f; 53:12).

ii. No Sitting on the Fence Mt 12:30

The next saying is another broadside, this time against those who like to 'sit on the fence', determined not to commit themselves, to avoid any difficult decision and its consequences, and wait to see the outcome before, hopefully, joining with the eventual victors. 'Those who are not with me' says Jesus of these people, 'are against me.' Those not siding with him lend credence and silent support to those who reject him. There is no neutral position. 'Those who do not gather with me, scatter.' The opposite of activity on behalf of the kingdom is not neutral inactivity, it is in effect activity against the kingdom.

iii. The Sin against the Holy Spirit Mt 12:31-32

Having delivered his response in images to the substance of the allegations made against him, Jesus now delivers a judgement on the nature of the offence involved in making such allegations. In response to the serious criticism and allegation of the Pharisees that he casts out devils by Beelzebul, the prince of devils, Jesus responds: 'Therefore I say to you that people will be forgiven all sins and blasphemies, but the one who blasphemes against the Spirit will never be forgiven in this age or the age to come.'

To blaspheme is to offer insult. Jesus' response begins with a reaffirmation of a belief in God's universal forgiveness current among many of the people at the time. This belief has been fortified and extended by the radical nature of Jesus' ministry in his embracing of people branded as sinners and in his inclusion of the marginalised and outcast.[20] Jesus describes the universal nature of God's forgiveness for all sins committed and blasphemies uttered, even those against the Son of Man (whose true identity may be hidden from their eyes). The distinction between blasphemy against the Son of Man and blasphemy against the Holy Spirit seems to point to the distinction between a reaction to the Son of Man, seeing him as a human being, though he is acting in the name of God and representing humanity before God, and a reaction against the Spirit of God that empowers him and his ministry. Jesus highlights the heinous nature of the accusation made against the Spirit of God manifest in him and in his ministry by stating that there is a sin that can never be forgiven, in this age or the age to come.

The work of the Spirit is manifest for all to see and not hidden like the identity of the Son of Man. As already seen in the gospel, Jesus' ministry is one of Spirit-empowered healing and forgiveness. He is the one on whom the Spirit descended at his

20. 1QS 11:11-14; cf also *The Prayer of Manasseh*.

baptism, the one driven into the desert by the Spirit and empow-
ered by the Spirit as he 'baptises in Holy Spirit'. This ministry of
Jesus, aptly named a baptism in Holy Spirit by John, has been
branded by Jesus' accusers as the work of the Prince of Devils.
They have not only refused the gift, they have seen it as evil.
Where else can they find forgiveness? They have refused it at
source. They have branded it as the work of the prince of devils.
This is no 'ordinary' blasphemy like uttering the Divine Name.
It is a blasphemy that has eternal consequences.

The incident is rounded off by a reminder that the blasphemous dispute started because they were saying: 'He has an unclean spirit', which could be paraphrased as 'the spirit he has,
which the reader knows is the Holy Spirit of God, is unclean'.
There is nowhere else to seek forgiveness, no other power to forgive. There can be no forgiveness where forgiveness itself is refused and condemned. The consequences are eternal.

iv. Words issue from the heart Mt 12:33-37

Jesus now turns to the inner dispositions that find expression
in one's words and deeds. He begins with the image of the good
and bad tree that produces good or bad fruit. 'Either make a tree
sound and its fruit will be sound or make a tree rotten and its
fruit will be rotten. By its fruit will the tree be known.' Jesus
poses a rhetorical and damning question: 'How can your speech
be good when you are evil, for from the abundance of the heart
the mouth speaks?' He looks to the spoken words as the fruit
produced by the inner life and disposition of the person. 'The
good man puts forth good things from his good treasury (i.e.
from his inner treasury of good things), the evil man puts forth
evil things from his evil treasury.' The reader here recalls the
beatitude about the pure in heart (Mt 5:8).

The wisdom literature of Israel, and the literature of the
Ancient Near East with which it shared common cultural roots
put great emphasis on speech and how speech reveals one's true
inner disposition. Addressing his adversaries in the words formerly used by John, Jesus uses the term 'brood of vipers' as he

points to their evil dispositions that come out into the open in their speech. They will account in the judgment for every foolish or idle word. The foolish or idle word is not just a harmless or neutral word spoken without any great deal of thought. It reflects a recurring theme of the wisdom tradition dealing with the words of the fool. The fool is the one who scorns wisdom and discipline, neglects duty to God and due care for self and others. The thoughts of his heart find expression in words spoken or unspoken. A good example is found in Ps 14:1-4: 'The fool says in his heart, "There is no God above"; such are his thoughts. His deeds are corrupt.' The fool is the opposite of the sage who is lauded in the wisdom tradition and the opposite to 'the pure of heart' lauded in the beatitude (Mt 5:8). One's words will eventually be the evidence for or against one in the eschatological reckoning on the Day of Judgement. One's words will stand as testimony to the state of one's heart.

d. Seeking a Sign Mt 12:38-42

The Challenge

Then some of the scribes and Pharisees responded to Jesus saying: 'Teacher, (didaskale) we wish to see a sign from you' (Mt12:38). The scribes and Pharisees are two of the strongest groups opposed to Jesus. The address 'teacher/master' in Matthew's gospel usually indicates insincerity or lack of genuine or adequate belief in Jesus. In seeking a sign, sêmeion, the scribes and Pharisees are looking for a significant proof of the divine authority behind Jesus' teaching and actions.[21] Their request, however, comes across in this context more like an aggressive challenge rather than a genuine seeking of authentication for his mission.

The deuteronomic prescription concerning true and false prophets presumes that prophets demonstrate their authenticity by predicting some happening (Deut 18:20-22). In the Old Testa-

---

21. In the Markan and Lukan traditions the sign is described as 'a sign from heaven', that is a sign from God rather than a sign 'in the heavens' (Mk 8:11-12; Lk 11:16).

ment demanding a sign or the prediction of a future event was a way of establishing a prophet's credentials. In addition, a specific prophetic message was often confirmed by a divine sign as when Isaiah predicted the receding shadow of the sun as a confirmation of his message to Hezekiah (2Kings 20:8-11) and the birth of the Emmanuel child was a sign and a prediction of God's protection from the Assyrian hordes and the threats of the Syro-Ephraimite coalition (Isa 7:11-14).[22]

All the gospels record such a demand for a sign being made of Jesus. It is in line with the tradition of Old Testament prophets and their authenticating signs. However, in the New Testament the seeking of signs is regarded as a negative or hostile attitude to Jesus in all gospel traditions. Paul reflects critically on the Jews' penchant for signs: 'The Jews look for signs and the Greeks look for wisdom ...' (1 Cor 1:22). In the Johannine tradition Jesus did not trust himself to the enthusiastic crowd who were impressed with him in Jerusalem on his first visit because of the 'signs' he performed (Jn 2:23-25). Back in Galilee he responded to the request of the royal official with the saying: 'Unless you see signs and wonders you refuse to believe' (Jn 4:48) and later in the ministry he refused to go to the Feast of Tabernacles with his brothers because they were urging him to perform signs in Jerusalem (Jn 7:2-8). The overall New Testament witness is consistent in its negative attitude to the seeking of signs. The temptation accounts in Matthew and Luke also focused on the question of signs when Jesus was tempted to throw himself from the pinnacle of the temple. He answered in the words of Deuteronomy: 'You shall not put the Lord your God to the test' (Mt 4:5-7; Lk 4:9-12; Deut 6:16).

Jesus' Response

i. An evil generation seeks a sign / The sign of Jonah

Returning to the text of Matthew one reads: 'An evil and adulterous generation seeks a sign.' They are an evil generation because of their unbelieving reaction to his mighty words and

22. cf also Isa 55:13; Ezek 12:11; 24:27, *inter alia*.

works which have manifested the kingdom taking root in their midst. These critics, and the generation like them, had not been open to what was taking place. In fact they saw his mighty deeds and said they were done through the power of Beelzebul. They have seen but not accepted the signs God has given in Jesus' mighty works. As noted already, Tyre and Sidon would have repented in sackcloth and ashes had these works been done in their midst (Mt 11:21). In this they have broken the covenant, the marriage bond between God and the people (Hos 2:2-13; Jer 3:6-10). They are therefore, in the language and imagery of the prophets, guilty of adultery for this lack of faithfulness to the marriage bond, and so he calls them an adulterous generation. Jesus is not now going to jump to their command and perform to their requirements.

Jesus responds to 'the evil and adulterous generation' saying that no sign shall be given 'except the sign of Jonah'. His statement that no sign will be given is a 'divine passive' meaning, 'God will give no sign', except the sign of Jonah the prophet. He develops this further into a lesson on reading the signs of the times and a comparison between Jonah's time in the belly of the sea creature and the time the Son of Man would spend in the belly of the earth (Mt 12:38-42; 16:1-4). Matthew, like Luke, has Jesus replying again at a later stage to a second request for a sign with the same response 'no sign will be given except the sign of Jonah (Mt 16:14; Lk 11:16; 11:29).[23]

What is the sign of Jonah the prophet? Jonah preached with outstanding success to the Ninivites, though earlier he had resolutely resisted the command to do so because of his prejudice against those sinful Gentile people, as he would have considered them. Eventually he obeyed the divine commission and his

---

23. In the gospel of Mark Jesus simply replies to the Pharisees' request for a sign with the response that no sign shall be given (Mk 8:11-12) and in Luke he responds to the first request for a sign with the statement that a house divided against itself shall fall (Lk 11:16), and a second request some time later draws a response contrasting the response of the Ninevites to the preaching of Jonah with the reaction of 'this evil and adulterous generation' to the Son of Man (Lk 11:29-32).

preaching of repentance was greeted with an overwhelming response. The Gentiles recognised and responded to the prophet of God. Jonah's surviving the shipwreck and swallowing by the sea monster points to the action of God on behalf of his reluctant agent and emphasises the importance of his mission (Jonah 3).

Jesus draws attention to the parallel between Jonah who was three days and three nights in the belly of the sea creature and the Son of Man who will be three days and three nights in the heart of the earth.'[24] Jesus' predicted survival of death and burial manifested in his Resurrection points to the supreme action of God, the central role and identity of the Son of Man, and the importance of his mission. Comparing the two experiences, or saving acts of God, and the two agents and their missions, Jesus is 'a greater than Jonah'. The unclean, sinful Gentile Ninevites acknowledged the identity and role of Jonah and responded to his preaching. The people of the covenant have not acknowledged the identity and role of 'the one greater than Jonah' or responded to his call to repentance. The people of Nineveh will therefore be their judges on the Day of Judgement. They will be the benchmark for judgement.

ii. One greater than Jonah; One greater than Solomon

Not only the pagan Ninevites but the Queen of the South (the Queen of Sheba) will stand against them in the Day of Judgement because when she heard of the wisdom of Solomon, she came 'from the ends of the earth' to verify for herself the truth of his reputation, and to recognise the man of God and the God who gave him such a gift of wisdom and such power, splendour and prosperity. This example is particularly apt here in the gospel following so closely on the treatment of the wisdom themes of speech and the inner condition of the heart that finds its expression in spoken and unspoken words. These examples show up

---

24. There is a slight generalisation or poetic/prophetic licence here, since the Son of Man was two nights in the heart of the earth between the crucifixion and the first day of the week, the third day, the day the Resurrection was proclamed to the women and the disciples.

the slowness and hesitancy of God's own people in responding to the one who is greater than Jonah, the prophet of repentance and greater than Solomon, the teacher of wisdom.

As the rejection of Jesus by his own people becomes more obvious, the signs of a future mission to the Gentiles come more and more into view. The stories of Jonah and the Queen of the South (of Sheba) foreshadow that mission and its success. On Judgement Day the example of the Ninevites and of the Queen of the South will be a benchmark for judging and condemning 'this evil generation'. In this sense they will rise up in judgement against them.

iii. Return of Unclean Spirit Mt 12:43-45

Spirits or demons were believed to be territorial and to be always in search of a dwelling. The casting out of the demons from the men who emerged from the tombs in Gadara is a good example. The demons asked not to be expelled from the territory and to be allowed to enter into the pigs (Mt 8:31). The warning here about the return of the evil spirit is a pointer to the fact that if one does not allow the Spirit of God into one's life after the expulsion of the evil spirit(s), there is a serious danger of falling into a far worse situation. One is ready for reoccupation by the former spirit, and possibly other even more malevolent spirits as well. The last state of that person will be worse than the first. There is no 'neutral' position. Jesus then concludes his line of argument with the warning: 'So will it be with this evil generation'. If they do not accept the 'baptism in Spirit' that Jesus brings after the repentance preached by the Baptist and the attack on Satan's kingdom and the expulsion of the demons initiated by Jesus, they will be ripe for the taking by any evil spirits that need some place to lodge.

iv. Jesus' 'New Family' of Disciples Mt 12:46-50

'While he was still speaking to the crowds, behold, his mother and brothers stood outside seeking to speak to him.'[25] This account is less critical of Jesus' family than the parallel story in Mark where his family come to take him by force because they are convinced that he is out of his mind (Mk 3:31-35).

It is noteworthy that Jesus' family stand outside and send a messenger to him with the message that they wished to speak to him. A distinction between 'insiders' and 'outsiders' is obvious and his family are among the outsiders.

When the message is brought to him that his mother and brothers are 'outside' wishing to speak to him, he responds to the messenger saying: 'Who is my mother and who are my brothers?' Then stretching out his hand towards his disciples[26] he uses the metaphor of family relationships and says: 'Behold my mother and my brothers.' Then he explains his meaning. 'Whoever does the will of my Father in heaven, he is my brother, and sister and mother.' Matthew's emphasis on doing the will of the Father, which constitutes the better righteousness, is once again highlighted in the gospel.

Commentators have noticed the absence of 'father' in the reply. Some have speculated on the fact that this is because Joseph was already dead and so the parallel with his human family did not include the father.[27] It is much more likely, though not explicitly stated, that the absence of a reference to 'father' reflects the understanding that his new family of disciples are the family of his Father in heaven, those who carry out

---

25. The genitive participial phrase connecting this pericope to what went before is followed by 'behold', which alerts the reader to an important turn of events.

26. At this point Mark has Jesus refer not just to the disciples, but also to the larger group of followers: 'Looking around at those sitting in a circle around him he said ...'

27. Similarly in Mk 10:30 fathers are not mentioned in the restoration after persecution when the persecuted will be 'repaid a hundred times over with houses, brothers, sisters, mothers, children and land'. In the parallel accounts Matthew and Luke simply refer to their being paid a hundred times over and inheriting eternal life (Mt 19:27-30; Lk 18:28-30).

his will. Furthermore, this understanding will form the basis of the teaching that 'you must call no one on earth your father, since you have only one Father, and he is in heaven. Nor must you allow yourselves to be called teachers, for you have only one teacher, the Christ' (Mt 23:10).

Relationship in the kingdom has replaced biological relationship. A related point was made in the comment of the Baptist that God could raise children to Abraham from these very stones, when he suspected that the Pharisees and Sadducees were claiming special privileges for being descended from Abraham (Mt 3:9). Earthly family ties have been replaced with the ties of the kingdom. This reminds one of the blessing of Elizabeth in Luke's gospel when she proclaimed that the mother of Jesus was blessed, not because she was his biological mother, but because she believed. 'Blessed is she who believed that the word spoken to her would be fulfilled' (Lk1: 45).

4. THE PARABOLIC DISCOURSE MT 13:1-52

Introduction Mt 13:1-2

'On that day' serves as a connection with what precedes the discourse and a change of location signals a new departure or initiative. Jesus withdrew from the house to the shore of the sea (of Galilee). As the hostility shown to him becomes more obvious he concentrates on his 'new family', the disciples chosen 'to be with him' and the broader circle of the friendly crowd of followers who are disciples in the general sense. In this tranquil oasis of calm, peace and harmony, he teaches the friendly crowd from the boat. The whole crowd stands along the shore. The emphasis on 'sitting' highlights the teaching position (as 'in the chair of Moses'). Here Jesus uses the boat as a 'chair of teaching' or pulpit. Getting into the boat kept him from being crushed and having his voice absorbed by the immediate section of the crowd in too close proximity. Furthermore, sound travels well over the water.

Jesus teaches seven parables, explains why he speaks in parables, gives allegorical explanations of the Parable of the Sower and the Parable of the Darnel and concludes with the assessment of the scribe trained for the kingdom as one who, like a householder, brings from his treasury things new and old.

a. 'He told them many things in Parables'

The use of parables is one of the aspects of Jesus' teaching with which most readers are familiar. The Greek word for parable, *parabolê*, is made up of two words: *ballein*,' to throw', and *para*, 'alongside', in the sense of throwing, or placing, two things alongside each other as a means of comparison or contrast. In the gospels the term 'parable' is sometimes used of a 'parable story' such as the very well known examples in Luke of the Good Samaritan or the Prodigal Son (Lk 10:29-37; 15:11-32) but it is more often used in the New Testament in a broader and relatively loose sense and can refer to short metaphorical sayings, similitudes, allegories, riddles and lessons for illustration. For example, in the gospels *parabolê* is used for short metaphorical sayings (Mt 12:26,29//s), allegories (Mt: 13:18-23; 24:42-44//s); riddles (Mt 13:10-15; 15:10-20//s), lessons or illustrations (Mt 24:32-36//s) and longer narratives, (Mt 13:4-9; Mt 21:33-46//s).

This broader use of the term *parabolê* reflects the Hebrew *mashal* (Aramaic *matla*) which captures the more enigmatic element of *mashal/matla* and covers various forms of speech and figurative discourse such as parabolic narrative (Judges 14:10-18; Prov 1:1-7; 1 Sam 10:12), riddles, proverbial sayings or aphorisms (Judges 14:10-18; Prov 1:1-7; 1 Sam 10:12), allegories (Isa 5:1-7; Ezek 17: 3-24.), satires and taunt songs (Mic 2:4; Hab 2:6), apocalyptic revelatory texts (Dan 7:1-28; 8:1-27; 1 Enoch 37-71) and so forth. All these function in the Old Testament as figures of speech which can at the same time both conceal the truth from the spiritually obtuse and reveal it to the spiritually open who are on the way to fuller understanding.

Since parables function as figures of speech which can at the same time both conceal the truth from the spiritually obtuse and reveal it to the spiritually open on the way to fuller understanding, they are far more than stories with a straightforward moral or religious message, which is how they are often inadequately described. Such a description is more suitable to Aesop's fables each of which has a moral message, than to Jesus' parables. Parables are unsettling confrontations with the realities of life. Sometimes they are immediately obvious like the warning about the divided kingdom (Mt 12:25-26). At times they can be like a shot across the bows as in the case of the parable of the wicked tenants (Mt 21:33-46). At other times they are like a hard sweet to chew on for a time as in the case of the parable of the labourers entering the vineyard at different hours (Mt 20:1-16). Sometimes they provoke an immediate response as in the case of the parable of the wicked tenants where the immediate reaction on the part of the people is a spontaneous judgement on the evildoers and on the part of the authorities the reaction is a desire to arrest Jesus (Mt 21:33-46; Lk 20:9-19). At other times they only yield their meaning later when the listeners have had time to go away and think about them. In his book *The Parables of the Kingdom*, C. H. Dodd described the parable as 'a metaphor or simile drawn from nature or common life, arresting the hearer by its vividness or strangeness and leaving the mind in sufficient doubt about its precise application to tease it into active thought.'[28] F.Kermode in his book *The Genesis of Secrecy* puts it very well: 'The parable isn't over until a satisfactory answer or explanation is given, the interpretation completes it.'[29] The process of understanding can take time, and may produce different levels of understanding on the part of the original audience and the intended and actual readership.

Jesus often resorted to the use of parables when he was under pressure by way of criticism or outright attack, or when he wanted to go on the offensive against his critics. He also used parables to shock, provoke and stimulate his listeners into thinking through the implications of his words and deeds. A parable can be like a weapon in the hand of a speaker. It can function as a

---

28. C. H. Dodd, *The Parables of the Kingdom*, 5.
29. F. Kermode, *The Genesis of Secrecy*, 24.

shield to divert criticism and turn the tables on an adversary or it can sink a thought-provoking shot into the mind and heart of the audience causing a change of outlook and attitude, confronting the listeners with a decision that needs to be made.

i. The Parable of the Sower Mt 13:3-9

The first of the parables told by Jesus on this occasion is usually called 'the parable of the sower', and is so called in Mt 13:18. It is not introduced at the beginning as a parable but is referred to as such in Mt 13:18. It is a parable story that contrasts frustrated growth, or failed harvest, with abundant harvest. Perhaps it would be more in keeping with the dynamic of the parable to call it the parable of the seed, the parable of the ground, the parable of failed growth or the parable of the abundant harvest. However, the setting of the parable in the overall gospel story and the allegorical explanation which follows (Mt 13:18-23) point to the preacher of the word who is compared to the sower. This accounts for the use of the term 'parable of the sower'. Jesus, like the sower, 'went out to sow' the word and the intended readers obviously include Christian preachers. Calling it the parable of the sower makes it their story.

Matthew has set the 'parable of the sower' in his own redactional framework to reflect the fact that in spite of the growing rejection and apparent failure of Jesus' mission, it will be followed by an abundant harvest. He underscores this understanding of the parable by following it immediately with Jesus' explanation of why he speaks in parables. The allegorical explanation of the parable further bears this out as it focuses on the obstacles to growth and is in turn followed by the parable of the weeds/darnel in the wheat which also addresses the question of obstacles to growth (Mt 13:18-23; 24-30).

When the parable is taken together with the parable of the seed growing secretly and the parable of the mustard seed, all three are seen to focus on a growth beyond expectation. However, this parable describes the spectacular growth against the background of a triple failure in growth and the emphasis seems to fall on the impediments to growth. The triple abundance, however, more than compensates for the triple failure. The audience and reader are here left to ponder on what exactly is meant by the parable. The very nature of a parable story is to get the listeners to tease out the meaning for themselves. This is obvious from the fact that the disciples must have been left to tease out the meaning as Jesus has to explain it to them later. Listening, however, is not just hearing and understanding intellectually. It is hearing and taking to heart what is heard in such a way that it becomes effective in one's life. Serious pondering is called for in Jesus' concluding remark: 'Let the one who has ears, listen!' In the actual telling of the parable Jesus does not spell out in detail the possible applications to life of the various types of ground and the images used. The listener / reader has to think it through.

What can the listener / reader say at this point about the parable? It is meant to present a comparison or contrast. The sower is the agent of the sowing but does not figure in any level of the comparisons. The manner of sowing, whether on ground subsequently ploughed or scattered widely on already ploughed ground, is not really relevant to the point of the story. It is not a critique of agricultural or horticultural methods. The comparisons or contrasts come really in the nature of the ground and of the harvest produced. Of the four sowings there are three failures – instant failure on the path due to the birds, failure after an initial growth on rocky ground due to the sun and poor roots, and failure after more promising growth due to the choking activity of the thorns. The contrast comes with the fourth sowing that produces a huge harvest from the good ground. The triple failure is contrasted with the triple abundance. The one point is clear. Seed on three kinds of bad soil fails, seed on good soil produces abundantly, some a hundredfold, some sixty and some thirty.

While the reader is figuring out the parable, Jesus addresses the broader question of why he speaks in parables.

b. 'Why do you speak to them in Parables?' Mt 13:10-17

These verses are inserted between the 'parable of the sower' and its allegorical explanation. In keeping with the rabbinic practice of subsequently explaining to disciples a public statement or teaching,[30] Jesus regularly explains later to his disciples what he had been teaching in public. In this case the disciples have a particular question for him. They approach him and say: 'Why do you speak to them in parables?' In his response Jesus makes a clear distinction between 'you' (the disciples) and 'them'. 'To you (*hymin*) it has been given to know the mysteries of the kingdom of heaven but to them (*ekeinois*) it has not been given.' The distinction between the disciples and 'them', the non-believers, is much more clear-cut here in Matthew than in Mark. Here there is something of a shift from the benign, even praiseworthy portrayal of the friendly crowds, to a portrayal of an obtuse, even hostile group.

Again there follows a *logion* that emphasises the impossibility of 'sitting on the fence'. 'The one who has to him will be given more in abundance.' It signifies the growth of understanding and participation in the life of the kingdom on the part of the follower/believer. On the other hand, 'The one who has not, even what he has will be taken away.' Those who do not accept, believe and understand will find that even the belief that they have will be taken away. The little faith they have will wither and die. Again Israel is being warned as it becomes apparent that many are rejecting Jesus' message. Rejecting the new dispensation they will lose out on the blessings of the old in which they are trying to take refuge. It is 'a warning against resting on one's spiritual privileges.'[31] The sight of the miracles, and the message of Jesus' preaching, both of which they have experienced, have fallen on blind eyes and deaf ears and so they do not understand what is taking place. Though seeing they do not see and hearing they do not hear or understand. Jesus therefore has to resort to parables. 'For this reason I speak to them in parables because

---

30. D. Daube, *The New Testament and Rabbinic Judaism*, 141-50.
31. D. J. Harrington, *The Gospel of Matthew*, 195, n. 12.

seeing they do not see and hearing they do not hear or understand' (Mt 13:13). For Matthew, in the words of J. P. Meier, 'the
problem of the parables has become the problem of Israel's unbelief.'[32]

Jesus sets the negative reaction in the broader context of the
history of Israel's response to God's messengers. He sees in it a
fulfilment of the prophecy of Isaiah: 'With them indeed is fulfilled the prophecy of Isaiah which says ...' This same passage
from Isaiah (Isa 6:9-10) is quoted or paraphrased not only in the
parallel synoptic passages (Mk 4:12; Lk 8:9) but in two later
Christian documents explaining the rejection of Jesus' claims (Jn
12:40) or of his followers' claims on his behalf (Acts 28:26f).

Matthew quotes Isa 6:9-10 (LXX) in full and unusually for
him, he follows the Greek text exactly.[33] The citation begins with
a prediction: 'You will listen and listen and not understand and
see and not perceive.' The prediction is followed by a description of the reason for their neither understanding nor perceiv-
ing. 'For the heart of this people has grown hard, their ears have
grown dull of hearing and their eyes blind of seeing.' Mark
omits these explicit references to hardening of hearts, stopped
ears and blind eyes from the citation. Matthew includes them
and points them specifically at unbelieving Israel, seeing in this
hardening of heart the reason for their not seeing with their
eyes, hearing with their ears or understanding with their hearts.
For Matthew seeing, hearing and understanding with one's
heart are the marks of the disciple. Hardness of heart is the block
on the road to discipleship. There is however a note of hope in
the citation pointing to the possibility of making a choice, a

---

32. J. P. Meier, *Matthew*, 144.
33. These verses of Isaiah are more loosely quoted or alluded to in Mk
4:12 and are among the most difficult verses in Mark's gospel. Much of
the sting is removed from the original text of Isa 6:9, 10 by Mark's omission of references to hardening of the heart, stopping of the ears and
closing of the eyes. Mark sees the hardening as an act of God resulting
in the lack of understanding and perception. Matthew sees the lack of
understanding and perception as the result of their hardness of heart,
implying their own culpability rather than an act of God.

'turning round': 'Unless they see with their eyes, hear with their ears and turn round (be converted) and I will heal them.'

The purpose of revealing the secret of the kingdom is the putting before the hearers of the choice that demands acceptance or rejection. Just as in the case of Moses and the prophets, now in the case of Jesus, God's intervention provokes a reaction of acceptance or rejection. In the language of the Johannine tradition, the acceptance or rejection of the Word is itself the judgement, and results from one's knowing or not knowing God and having or not having the proper dispositions towards the Father and the Son whom he sent. One's dispositions enable one to be drawn to the Father and the Son, summed up in the Johannine statement: 'No one can come to me unless the Father who sent me draws him' (Jn 6:44). The Word came into the world so that the blind would see and those who see would turn blind (Jn 9:39). The purpose of the coming was to separate them, but which side of the separation one found oneself on was not determined by God but by the dispositions of the hearers. Those with the right dispositions were drawn to God and consequently to God's envoy (and vice versa). Paul deals with the same problem of rejection in terms of 'the hardening of Israel' (Rom 11:25). The New Testament writers face up to the fact that whereas many within Israel and in the larger world accepted God's intervention in Jesus, very significant numbers of the people of Israel and of the larger world did not. In the words of Simeon in Luke's Infancy Narrative the child was to be 'a sign to be contradicted' (Lk 2:34).

It is, however, the disposition of the listeners that does not allow them to understand the parables and that divides them into those who see only riddles and those who question and seek further insight and clarification. This differs essentially from divine predestination or the revelation of a long-hidden secret to privileged witnesses while others remain in ignorance, a scenario reminiscent of the apocalyptic tradition in which select privileged persons or groups are given privileged knowledge.

Matthew's very positive attitude to the disciples is evident in his use of the beatitude pointing to their being blessed above the great figures of the past, the prophets and righteous ones[34] who longed to see and hear what they have seen and heard. As in the case of the Baptist, the greatest of those born of woman, who is less than the least in the kingdom, so too the great people in the old dispensation are less than these 'ordinary folk', the disciples in the new dispensation. They are 'blessed' for they have received the gift of God: 'To you it has been given to know the secrets of the kingdom of heaven.' They see, hear and understand, unlike the outsiders and their predecessors castigated by Isaiah, who see but do not see, and hear but do not hear or understand. Matthew's positive picture of the disciples at this juncture stands out in stark contrast to the very negative picture of them painted by Mark in which Jesus' rebuke about their lack of understanding is emphasised: 'You do not know/understand this parable. How can you know/understand all the parables (Mk 4:13)?

Jesus began his ministry by proclaiming the imminent arrival of the kingdom of heaven and calling for repentance. Following his initial proclamation, his mighty words and deeds manifested the power of God working through him as he expelled and silenced the demonic powers, overcame the power of sickness and displayed power to forgive sin, all manifestations of the presence of the kingdom (reign) of heaven in the world. There is a 'givenness' about Jesus and his ministry to date, but it is a pointer to the greater reality of the as yet to be revealed 'mysteries of the kingdom of heaven.' It is a gift, as yet unwrapped.

The 'mysteries' are described here in Matthew in terms of 'the mysteries of the kingdom of heaven.'[35] What are those mysteries? The term 'mystery', *mystêrion* (from *myein*, to be silent) is a Greek word which is used in the New Testament with a very different set of meanings to its general usage in the Greek language of the time. Outside the New Testament it was used (often

---

34. Lk 10:23-24 has 'prophets and kings' at this point.
35. For an overall treatment of the question see J. Marcus, *The Mystery of the Kingdom of God*, S.B.L. Dissertation, Atlanta, 1986.

pejoratively) of the 'mystery' religions, like those of Mithras, Isis and Osiris, Cybele and Attis and others. It conveyed the sense of the secret rites and initiations into enlightenment that the devotees conducted away from the gaze of outsiders. In the Bible, however, the term *mystêrion* is used to convey a very different and thoroughly biblical meaning. Daniel, for example, had used the Hebrew equivalent, the term *raz*, 'mystery', for the hidden purposes of God (Dan 2:18f; 27-29; 30, 47). In the Pauline writings, the term *mystêrion* is used twenty one times and with different shades of meaning. It refers to the hidden salvific plan of God made manifest in the Christ event (1 Cor 2:7; 4:1; Rom 16:25f; Eph 3:9). The formerly hidden plan of God for salvation is being made manifest in the mighty words and works of Jesus. 'Mystery' appears as a summary term in the Christian proclamation (Col 2:2; 4:3; Eph 3:4; 6:19; 1 Tim 3:9, 16) and Paul also uses the term *mystêrion* to describe the incomprehensible rejection of Jesus by his own people which must in some way fit into the divine scheme of things (Rom 11:25). He also describes the Christian preachers as 'stewards of the mysteries of God'(1 Cor 4:1).

'Given to know' signifies a revelation and the 'divine' passive voice points to a gift of God. Whereas Mark just says 'given', Matthew, in line with his emphasis on revelation and understanding, goes further and says 'given to know the mysteries/secrets.' The fact that the mysteries of the kingdom are revealed is noted, but their exact nature is still to be revealed. J. Jeremias put it succinctly:

> ... the secret of the kingdom of God which constitutes God's gift must not be understood as implying information about the kingdom of God, but ... a particular piece of information, the recognition of its dawn in the present.[36]

---

36. J. Jeremias, *The Parables of Jesus*, (revised edition), SCM Press, London, 1972, 16.

i. Interpretation of the Parable of the Sower Mt 13:18-23

Jesus now returns to the parable of the sower. He says: 'You therefore will hear the parable of the sower', that can mean both that you will be told the meaning of the parable and you will hear it in the sense of understanding it. This is in keeping with the former statement 'to you it is given to know ...' The allegorical interpretation most likely does not have its origins with Jesus, but Jesus' preaching is being interpreted for a subsequent audience/readership of the gospel. M. D. Hooker makes the point very clearly:

> Parables spoken by a wandering teacher in Galilee sounded very differently when recited as words of the Master whom the community acknowledged as risen Lord. Inevitably parables took on a new meaning in a new situation, and inevitably, in the process, their relevance sometimes seemed obscure.[37]

This is very likely the reason why a preacher or teacher explains them in allegorical fashion. In the case of a parable it is the hearer who reflects on it and applies it to life. In the case of an allegory, on the other hand, it is the teacher rather than the hearer who makes all the practical connections between the story and its application to life. The parable is a conversation between the speaker, the parable and the hearer. It challenges the hearer to think, respond or react. The allegory does the interpreting by giving significance to the various details of the story rather than leaving it speak for itself as the hearer teases out the meaning from the simple thrust of the comparison or contrast which often builds up to a punch line at the end.

As 'the parable of the sower' is redacted by Matthew it refers to listening, hearing, accepting and persevering in the word first sown by Jesus during his ministry and subsequently sown by the Christian preachers in the community, and among the implied readership.

---

37. M. D. Hooker, *op. cit.*, 120.

As noted already, Matthew speaks of 'the parable of the sower',[38] but the sower does not really figure in the contrasts and allegorical interpretation of the details. By implication the sower is the preacher, and the sower 'goes out to sow' as Jesus 'went out' on his journeys to preach and as Christian preachers continued to do following the example of Jesus and those whom he sent. Like Jesus, they too encountered many bad receptions but also some extraordinary responses.

The fate of the seed represents the response to the word. The seed is healthy but the ground can be unhealthy because of its composition (rocky) or circumstances (overgrown with thorns or trampled into a path and exposed to the birds). Three failures in sowing are followed by three outstanding successes. The birds that eat the seed on the path are interpreted as Satan taking the word from the heart of the listener. Interestingly, demons were portrayed as birds in apocalyptic tradition. In 1 Enoch 90:8-13 and in Jubilees Prince Mastema, a Satan-like figure sets the crows to eat the seed that is being sown. The seed on the rocky ground, *petrida*,[39] does better initially but there is no root and it dies under the heat of the sun, like those who after several initial displays of enthusiasm, fell away or were scandalised, under the threat of persecutions and trials on account of the word. The seed among thorns is interpreted as those who have heard the word and have an initial positive response, but the worries of the world and the lure of riches choke the word. Interestingly, thorns were seen as a metaphor for the irrational passions by Philo in his comments on the thorns in Gen 3:18.[40] All categories

38. There is a significant history of using the imagery of 'sowing' in the Bible. Already in the New Testament Paul used sowing as a metaphor for preaching in 1 Cor 3:5-9. In the Old Testament it is used as a metaphor for planting the Law among the people (4 Ezra 9:30-37). It is used for moral living, for sowing righteousness and reaping love (Hos 10:12), and sowing virtue and reaping a solid reward (Prov 11:18). It is also used for negative actions and their consequences, for sowing the seeds of grief and reaping the results (Job 4:8).
39. Some commentators say *petrida* may also contain a pun on Peter and his falling away under pressure.
40. Philo, *Legum Allegoria*, 3.248.

heard the word initially and made an initial positive response but, depending on their inner disposition or external circumstances, they responded with different degrees of commitment. The triple failure is more than compensated for by the seed that fell on good ground. This represents the people who heard the word, accepted it, and produced an abundant harvest, a hundredfold, sixty and thirty.

In its original form the parable of the sower would most likely have been a single-point discourse on the huge harvest that comes unexpectedly from successfully sown seed in spite of the failure of the other seed. Like the parables of the seed growing secretly, the insignificant mustard seed becoming a great plant and the small amount of yeast leavening a huge batch of flour, the emphasis was probably on the outstandingly successful result in spite of insignificant or difficult beginnings.

ii. The Parable of the Weeds/Darnel Mt 13:24-30

Jesus now tells three other parables dealing with growth. It may be more accurate to call them similitudes since all three begin with a formula of comparison: 'The kingdom of heaven may be compared to' or 'The kingdom of heaven is like'. The first of the three, the parable of the weeds in the wheat, is found only in Matthew.[41] The comparison in each case is with the entire range of actions and process that take place in the story.

The weeds/darnel (*zizania*) sown by the enemy while the people were asleep grow, look like and intertwine their roots with the wheat. The desire to root them out is a natural reaction on the part of the servants but the master counsels against it. For Matthew's community the master's reaction gives a headline for how to react to the influence of those who did not accept and even violently opposed the Messiah and his work for the king-

---

41. It bears a resemblance to the parable of the seed growing by itself in Mk 4:26-29. Maybe there was an early seminal parable about growth that was differently adapted. Matthew adapts it here for his specific purpose of explaining the continued presence of sinners and hostile elements in synagogue and church in spite of the inception of the kingdom.

dom and why God allows them to continue to exist and exert influence.[42] It could also be applied to the question of hostile or heretical elements in the church. All elements must exist together until the day of the harvest, the Day of Judgement, when the *zizania* will be gathered and burned and the wheat will be gathered into the barn. Again this teaching manifests a strong eschatological motif.

iii. Parable of the Mustard Seed Mt 13:31-32

The parable of the mustard seed and the parable of the yeast (leaven) that follows it are very similar and go together as a pair of parables emphasising extraordinary growth from insignificant (and suspect?) beginnings.

The parable of the mustard seed emphasises first of all the tiny size of the seed from which (with literary exaggeration) the largest of the plants grows and becomes a tree.[43] The mustard plant in fact grows to a height of two to six feet and was common along the shore of the Lake of Galilee. It was noted for spreading in an invasive way and quickly taking over a garden.[44] The image of a great tree was often used as the symbol of a nation and its power or the beauty of its terrain. The cedars of Lebanon are proverbial as symbols of power and beauty. Daniel describes the power and personal status of Nebuchadnezzar in terms of the great tree 'under which lived the beasts

---

42. The reaction of the servants who wish to root it out reflects the apocalyptic preaching of the Baptist about the axe being laid to the root of the tree and the chaff being burned in the fire. It reflects the withdrawal of the Essenes from Jewish, Jerusalem and Temple society, and against the attitudes of the Zealots who would have driven the Romans and their collaborators from Israel and set up the pure state. It reflects also the exclusivist attitude of the strict Pharisees (whose attitudes are particularly targeted by Matthew due to the post 70 tensions with the Pharisaic Judaism and its programme of reconstruction).
43. In Mt 17:20 the tiny size of the mustard seed and its potential are used to show that even the tiniest amount of genuine faith can achieve great miracles.
44. Pliny, *Natural History*, 19:170-171.

of the fields, and in its branches dwelt the birds of the sky' (Dan 4:19-21). Even closer to the imagery in Matthew is the statement in Ezekiel that God will take a sprig of a great cedar and plant it to produce fruit and become a noble cedar under which 'every kind of bird will live; in the shade of its branches every kind of winged creature' (Ezek 17:22f). Jesus thus portrays the kingdom where every creature will find refuge. But in the irony of the gospel, the great tree develops from an intrusive bush grown from the tiniest of seeds. Furthermore, great results have been achieved in spite of the fact that the mustard seed was often seen as a nuisance plant growing and spreading rapidly in an otherwise very controlled and cultivated garden. From insignificant beginnings the greatest of kingdoms, the kingdom of heaven, will emerge, because the gift of God's life-giving power is in its beginnings and in its process of growth. J. Marcus puts it succinctly: 'For the dominion of God is like the word: paltry in appearance, but hiding a tremendous divine potency behind its apparent insignificance.'[45]

iv. Parable of the Leaven Mt 13:33

Leaven/yeast is an essential ingredient in making bread, but in fact it is in itself a corrupting agent in the fermentation process. It causes the bread to rise and expand. It does so, however, by a decaying process during the fermentation which eventually causes the bread to become stale and mouldy and thereby unhealthy and unpalatable if not eaten soon after baking. Jesus will warn the disciples about the leaven of the Pharisees and Sadducees (Mt 16:6, 12; cf Mk 8:15; Lk 12:1). St Paul used leaven as a metaphor for a morally corrupting influence or agent (1 Cor 5:6-8; Gal 5:9) and in so doing was in line with Greco-Roman writers like Plutarch and Perseus.[46]

Here in this parable the emphasis is on the life-giving power and growth potential of such a small amount of leaven. Though it is small enough to be hidden in the flour it can be used to leaven

45. J. Marcus, *Mark 1-8*, The Anchor Bible 27, 323.
46. Plutarch, *Quaestiones Romanae*, 109 and Perseus, *Satires* 1.24.

three measures (*sata*), a huge amount of dough/flour. *Sata* is plural of *saton*, a dry measure of 21.6 pints and three measures would be 64.8 pints, about fifty pounds. That would be enough to provide a meal for a hundred people.[47] From such unpretentious beginnings the yeast when mixed with the flour produces an enormous amount of bread. Here too great results are achieved from tiny beginnings in spite of secrecy and apparent corruption in the process. This parable or similitude possibly responds also to a negative image and hostile comment on the community.

c. He spoke to the crowds only in parables Mt 13:34-35 cf Mk 4:33-34
'He said (*elalêsen*) all these things in parables to the crowds and without a parable he said (*elalei*) nothing to them.' Matthew does not have Mark's comment 'in so far as they could understand'. The verb *elalei* is the imperfect tense of the verb *lalein*, signifying continual or repeated speaking. It is a change from the more familiar *elegen*. *Lalein* has overtones of prophetic speech and the prophetic quality is highlighted by the statement that his speaking in parables was to fulfill the word spoken through the prophet. Matthew has a flexible approach to the idea of prophecy as is seen from the fact that the citation is not from a prophet but from Ps 78:2 (LXX, 77:2). Here again the overall influence of prophecy is seen as in Mt 11:13 which spoke of 'all the prophecies of the prophets and the Law'. The first half of the citation follows the Greek LXX, but the rest is a loose translation in which Matthew highlights the 'secret' aspect. The heretofore 'hidden quality' of the mystery/secrecy, and its impending revelation are emphasised: 'I shall open my mouth in parables, I shall declare things hidden from the foundation (of the world).'

Jesus continues the discourse in the house with the disciples. In Mark the comment on speaking in parables signals the end of the discourse (Mk 4:33-34).

---

47. J. Jeremias, *The Parables of Jesus*, 147.

i. Interpretation of the Parable of the Weeds/Darnel Mt 13:36-43

A change of audience takes place. Many see this as a turning point in the gospel where Jesus begins to devote more and more time to the disciples as he withdraws from hostile opponents and ambivalent crowds. Jesus leaves the crowds and goes to the house and his disciples approach him saying: 'Explain to us the parable of the darnel in the field.' The disciples of a rabbi often asked him subsequently to explain his public teaching. Jesus again responds with an explanation that is in fact an allegory. The fact that they ask him for an explanation does not take from the fact that they are regarded as 'seeing, hearing and understanding'. Asking for an explanation in this context emphasises their eagerness to learn and shows how they are teasing out the parables.

In the explanation Jesus points out that the sower of the good seed is the Son of Man. The field is the world. The good seed is the sons/children of the kingdom. The darnel/weeds are the sons/children of the evil one. The enemy who sowed them is the devil. The harvest is the end of the world, the reapers are the angels. Just as the darnel is gathered up and burned by fire so will it be at the end of time. The Son of Man will send his angels and they will gather from his kingdom all the scandals and those who do evil (lawlessness) and he will cast them into the furnace of fire where there shall be weeping and gnashing of teeth. Then the just will shine like the sun in the kingdom of their Father.

Matthew's eschatological emphasis again strikes a dominant note as the point-by-point allegory builds up to the description of the final judgement at the end of the age (*synteleia tou aiônos*), a Matthean designation for the end of the world. The terrible fate of those who cause scandal or do evil is contrasted with the glorious reward of the *dikaioi*, 'the righteous/just ones' (another favourite description of Matthew). The Son of Man appears again. This time he is cast in the role of the eschatological judge.

The warning, 'Let the one who has ears, hear/listen!' serves a function similar to the Old Testament prophetic formulae: 'These are the words of the Lord' and 'Thus speaks the Lord' which opened, punctuated or closed many prophetic speeches.

ii. Three Parables/Similitudes of the Kingdom:
Treasure, Pearl, Dragnet Mt 13:44-50

Another three parables, or similitudes, associated together
by the introductory formula: 'The kingdom of heaven is like ...'
follow the explanation of the parable of the darnel. The first two
are quite different from the third. They are about finding, recognising, and committing oneself to owning the kingdom with resulting rejoicing. The third is similar to the parable of the darnel
in that it is about patience and tolerant endurance for the present, and severe punishment at the judgement accompanied by
'weeping and gnashing of teeth'.

The Treasure Mt 13:44

The kingdom of heaven is like a treasure hidden in the field,
a person finds it, hides it, and with great joy goes and sells
everything he has and buys that field. The unexpected nature of
the find, the astuteness of the finder who realises its value and
hides it again in the field without removing or stealing it, the
commitment involved in selling everything to buy the field and
the rejoicing at the find, all are illustrations of the process of
finding the kingdom, becoming a disciple even at great personal
cost and then experiencing the joy of the kingdom.

The Pearl Mt 13:45-46

The kingdom of heaven is like the merchant in search of fine
pearls. Unlike the worker in the field he does not come unexpectedly upon a hidden treasure. He is a person searching for
fine pearls. He too recognises the value of the pearl, sells everything he has and buys the pearl. This activity also illustrates the
process of finding the kingdom, recognising and valuing it, becoming a disciple even at great personal cost and then experiencing the joy of the kingdom.

The Dragnet Mt 13:47-50

The kingdom of heaven is like a dragnet. The dragnet does
not discriminate between the fish it catches. Whatever lies in its

path is snatched up into the net. However, when the net is full
the fishermen separate the good from the bad fish, placing the
good in the basket and discarding the bad. It will be like that at
the end of time (again Matthew's phrase, *synteleia tou aiônos* is
used). The angels will appear, separate the wicked from the
midst of the just (again a favourite designation of Matthew) and
throw them into the furnace of fire where there will be weeping
and gnashing of teeth, as in the case of the burning of the darnel.

iii. The Scribe Trained for the Kingdom Mt 13:51-52

Jesus asks the disciples: 'Have you understood all this?' They
answer 'Yes'. 'Understanding' is one of Matthew's main criteria
for a good disciple. His positive portrait of the understanding
disciples here stands in stark contrast to the rejection that will
follow in his home town and among the people of Israel
throughout the rest of the gospel. It stands in stark contrast also
to Mark's negative portrait of the disciples to whom Jesus can
say in frustration or desperation: 'Are you still without understanding (Mk 8:21)?'

Jesus now gives the formula for a wise scribe. 'Every scribe
who has been trained for the kingdom is like a householder who
brings from his treasury things new and old.' Looking back to
the Sermon on the Mount Jesus had proclaimed that he had not
come to destroy the Law and the Prophets but to fulfil them (Mt
5:17). He then went on to present the six antitheses in which a
new understanding of the old was proclaimed, underpinning
the Law and at the same time introducing a whole new set of
challenging insights. The wise scribe trained for the kingdom
must do the same as he realises the value of all that has gone before and is open to embrace every new initiative of God.

Again this discourse finishes on the familiar note that Jesus
'had finished (*etelesen*)' these parables and moved away to a new
location.

5. Jesus Rejected in His Native Place

Mt 13:54-58//Mk 6:1-6//Lk 4:16-24

Having finished his parabolic discourse, Jesus left that district and came to his hometown and taught in the synagogue.[48] The mighty words and works of Jesus during his ministry in Galilee have drawn great admiring crowds from far and near but at the same time he has been subjected to sharp criticism and hostility from official circles. Now he comes to his own town, in many ways the acid test of the response to his ministry. His home town is not named, probably because it stands representatively for all Israel and for his own people who reject him, as the gospel of John states it: 'He came unto his own domain and his own people did not accept him' (Jn 1:11).

Matthew's account typically focuses on Jesus and the reaction to him.[49] It was the prerogative of any layman to teach in the synagogue if invited to do so by the synagogue officials. At first the people in the synagogue were astonished (*ekplêssesthai / ekplessein*) at his preaching, a response of amazement that immediately turns sour.

They ask: 'Where did this fellow get this wisdom and these mighty works?' The ensuing questions about his background and origins are cynical. 'Is not this fellow the son of the carpenter (manual worker, artisan, craftsman)? Is not his mother called Mary and his brothers James and Joseph and Simon and Judas? And are not all his sisters with us?' The biting cynicism of their question is difficult to render directly into English. It could be rendered as: 'Where did the likes of this fellow get the likes of all that?' seeing 'this fellow' (*houtos/toutô*) as a cynical comment on someone who had risen above his station. It is probably meant as a slur implying that he has no distinguished background and therefore no education or training other than using his hands for his trade in the family business. It is a typical statement of jeal-

---

48. *Patris* could be translated as 'home country' or 'home town'. The context appears to favour 'home town'.

49. Some details found in Mark's account such as the reference to the Sabbath and to the presence of the disciples are omitted.

ous small mindedness that could be summed up as: 'Indeed we
know all his people and all about them, so how can he teach us!'

The reference here to Jesus' family members also serves the
purpose of showing how ordinary he was in the eyes of the people among whom he grew up and who now think he has risen
above his station. There is no mention of his father's name. Is it
because Joseph was long dead or known not to be his biological
father? Or is it a theological point on the part of Matthew who
has portrayed him throughout the infancy and baptism narratives as Son of God, and introduced him as Son of David, Son of
Abraham (Mt 1:1)? Elsewhere Matthew has recorded Jesus' saying: 'Call no man on earth your father' (Mt 23:9).

The brothers and sisters of Jesus are mentioned, and the
brothers are identified by name as James, Joseph, Simon and
Judas. The 'ever-virgin' status of Mary is a matter of long standing tradition, not a dogma of faith and is independent of the
question of the virginal conception of Jesus. Some ancient and
modern scholars see them as the children of Mary and Joseph
but the dominant Catholic tradition, shared by many other
Christians, has been that Mary was 'ever virgin' and so in that
tradition these brothers and sisters of Jesus are seen not as children of Mary and Joseph but children of an earlier marriage of
Joseph, or cousins, members of the extended family, possibly
children of Mary's sister.[50]

The outcome of their speculations about Jesus' background
and family is 'scandal', a stumbling block to belief that anyone
so like themselves, one of their own, about whom they thought

---

50. In the ancient church Hegesippus (2nd cent), Tertullian (2nd-3rd
cent) and Helvidius (4th cent) held that they were the biological children of Mary and Joseph, an opinion held by many 'non-Roman
Catholic' scholars and by some recent Catholic commentators, such as J.
P. Meier, *A Marginal Jew*, 1:327-32 and Rudolf Pesch, *Markusevangelium*,
1:322-24). See also J. P. Meier, 'The Brothers and Sisters of Jesus in
Ecumenical Perspective', *CBQ* 54 (1992), 1-28 and R. Bauckham, 'The
Brothers and Sisters of Jesus: An Epiphanian Response', *CBQ* (1994),
686-700.

they knew everything, with nothing in background or education to recommend him, should be so possessed of power to preach and to work wonders. This poses for them a 'scandal', 'a stone causing them to stumble'. They reject him. He responds: 'A prophet is only without honour (*atimos*) in his native place and in his own house.'

Whereas Mark says 'he was unable to do' many mighty works (*dynameis*) there because of their lack of faith (Mk 6:5), Matthew simply says 'he did not do' many mighty works there. His not doing many mighty works in the face of a lack of faith is a pointer to the fact that Jesus was not a wonder worker performing mighty deeds in order to convert people to his cause. Belief usually precedes a healing on Jesus' part and he is careful to ascertain the belief and the motive of the petitioner, often in a short dialogue (Mt 8:2-4, 5-13; 9:20-22; 27-31; 15:21-28) before responding with a healing. There is no compelling of people into belief.[51]

Jesus is now in the tradition of the rejected prophet,[52] the servant of God without honour,[53] the wisdom teacher not listened to.[54] This sentiment is reflected across the gospels. Mark reports the saying in the same words as Matthew, 'A prophet is only without honour (*atimos*) in his native place and in his own house' but with the addition of 'and among his relations' (Mk

---

51. This is very obvious in the temptation narratives in Matthew and Luke which highlight the main factors that will bedevil his ministry – the pressure to respond to physical need such as hunger for food instead of seeing the deeper needs of people for the word of God, the temptation to grasp at political power and influence to further his cause or to promote it by performing compelling religious signs (Mt 4:1-11; Lk 4:1-13.) These would satisfy people and win them to his cause but they would not open them to the word of God, and the call to conversion, repentance and belief. This truth is clearly seen here in Mt 13:58 (//Mk 6:5f) where healings are seen to follow faith, not the other way round.

52. 2 Chron 24:19; 36:16; Neh 9:26, 30; Jer 35:15; Ezek 2:5; Hos 9:7; Dan 9:6,10.

53. Isa 53:3 (LXX), the suffering servant is *atimos*, without honour.

54. Significantly Matthew uses the term *sophia* for Jesus' teaching here in the gospel, in the context of the rejection of his teaching.

6:4). Luke reports the saying as: 'No prophet is accepted in his native place' (Lk 4:24) and John has: 'A prophet does not have honour in his own native place' (Jn 4:44). The Gospel of Thomas reflects a combination of New Testament and other sayings: 'A prophet is not acceptable in his home town, a doctor does not heal those who know him.'[55] Similar experiences and sayings are found among philosophers and healers in the wider world. Among those in Hellenistic literature is the comment in Philostratus' *Life of Apollonius of Tyana*, that it is the universal opinion of philosophers that life is difficult in their native land.[56]

Rejection by his own people now leaves Jesus in the position of gathering a new people, a new family, around himself, not bound by bonds of blood or sharing of a homeland but a family of disciples bound together by their response to his call to embrace the kingdom, 'to do the will of my Father in heaven'.

---

55. *Gospel of Thomas*, 31.
56. Letter 44, quoted by J. R. Donahue and D. J. Harrington, *op. cit.*, 185.

Rejection: New Beginnings: New Authority
The Petrine Section/Building on Rock
Mt 14:1-19:2

Plot and Outline

Rejection: New Beginnings: New Authority
Jesus is rejected by the authorities and by his own people in his own place. A very significant milestone has been reached. From now on there is an ever-widening gap between him and official Israel, a gap that will eventually bring about his downfall, trial and execution.

The narrative in Mt 14:1-17:27 traces the ongoing rejection of Jesus and the new beginnings as he gathers his followers around him and provides them with a new authority and leadership. The discourse that follows the narrative (Mt 18:1-19:1) provides a blueprint for the exercise of authority and interpersonal relationships in the new community or *ekklêsia*, the church, which is forming around Jesus.

At the centre of this major narrative. there is a pivotal section at Mt 16:5-20, around which the overall plot of the gospel turns. It follows on Jesus' refusal to perform a sign for the Pharisees and Sadducees. On that occasion 'he left them and walked away', a definitive action highlighting his symbolic leaving of the teaching authorities in Israel (Mt 16:4). A little further on another definitive moment is signalled by the narrator at Mt 16:21 as a new direction and a new dimension of the gospel are introduced with the statement, 'From that time onwards Jesus Christ began to point out to his disciples that he must depart for Jerusalem and suffer many things at the hands of the elders and the chief priests and the scribes and be put to death and be raised on the third day' (Mt 16:21). The movement of the gospel from then on is towards Jerusalem and Jesus' teaching is punctuated by the predictions of the Passion (Mt 16:21-23; 17:22-23; 20:17-19; 26:1-2).

Between these two definitive moments Matthew has placed the pivotal section of the narrative (Mt 16:5-20). It has two parts. The first highlights symbolically what Jesus has rejected in Israel, namely, 'the leaven of the Pharisees and Sadducees' (Mt 16:5-12) and the second focuses on Peter's confession of faith and Jesus' triple response to him, pronouncing a beatitude, conferring a title on him and granting him authority in the community of followers, the *ekklêsia* (Mt 13-20).

The narrative (Mt 14:1 – 17:27) contains within itself a number of indicators of structural outline, some older than Matthew's redaction. As said already, it contains the pivot of the gospel in Mt 16:5-20 between Jesus' symbolic leaving of the authorities (Mt 16:4) and his definitive turning his attention towards Jerusalem (Mt 16:21). The narrative contains also the two more or less parallel ' bread sequences' which are found also in Mark (Mt 14:13-15:28 and 15:29-12//Mk 6:30-7:37; 8:1-26). Each consists of a multiplication of loaves (and fishes), a sea crossing, a dispute with the Pharisees, teaching about bread, food or eating, and healings. The second 'bread' sequence in both gospels is followed by the pivotal section of the gospel. In Matthew it contains in its final pericope Jesus' warning about 'the leaven of the Pharisees, which forms part of the pivotal section.'[1]

Important also for the overall structure of Mt 14:1-17:27 are the stories about Peter with which he punctuates the narrative. Peter figures very prominently throughout the entire section. Already in the gospel he was the first disciple called (Mt 4:18) and was given prominence when he was ranked ' first' (*prôtos*) in the list of apostles. In this section he is given a very high profile. He responds to Jesus' invitation to join him on the storm tossed sea and calls out to Jesus to save him when he begins to sink (Mt 14:22-33). He emerges as spokesperson asking for an

---

1. In the pivotal section Mark illustrates the turning point at Peter's confession by way of placing the double healing of the blind man immediately before Peter's confession of faith (Mk 8:22-30) and Matthew illustrates the turning point at Peter's confession of faith by way of contrast with the leaven of the Pharisees and the Sadducees.

explanation of the parable/metaphor about what goes into the mouth (Mt 15:15) and it is he who responds to Jesus' question to the disciples: 'Who do you say that I am?'(Mt 16:13).[2] He professes his faith in Jesus as the Christ, the Son of the living God and Jesus responds to him with a beatitude, confers on him a title and grants him authority in his newly forming *ekklêsia* (Mt 16:17-19). He reacts to Jesus' prediction of the Passion and earns Jesus' rebuke (Mt 16:22-23). He speaks out on the Mountain of Transfiguration (Mt 17:4) and the narrative section ends with Peter speaking and acting on Jesus' behalf with regard to paying the temple tax (Mt 17:24-27).[3] Furthermore, in the discourse, which follows the narrative, it is Peter's question about forgiveness that elicits Jesus' response by way of a *logion* and a parable on forgiveness (Mt 18:21-22, 23-35).

Some of these stories about Peter are found only in Matthew or have a uniquely Matthean flavour. Only Matthew describes how Peter left the boat, came over the water to Jesus and cried out to him as he sank (Mt 14:28-31). The style of Peter's confession is unique to Matthew (Mt 16:16) and only Matthew has Jesus' triple response to Peter's confession (Mt 16:17-19). Only Matthew has the story of Peter and the temple tax (Mt 17:24-27). Peter's question about forgiveness is found only in Matthew (Mt 18:21-22).[4] The distinctively Matthean stories about Peter divide Mt 14:1-17:27 into three sections, each building up to a story about Peter, and the following discourse (Mt 18) culminates in Peter's question about forgiveness and Jesus' response.[5]

2. After his incident on the waves he emerges as spokesperson for the disciples, asking for an explanation of the parable (Mt 15:15). In other places in the common tradition Peter is portrayed as spokesperson. In Mt 16:16//Mk 8:29//Lk 9:20 he utters the confession of faith in Jesus' Messiahship and in Mt 17:4//Mk 9:5//Lk 9:33 he comments during the Transfiguration. In John's gospel he speaks on behalf of the Twelve proclaiming faith in, and continuing loyalty to Jesus when others were falling away (Jn 6:67-69).
3. There is no parallel to this pericope in the other gospels.
4. A similar teaching about forgiveness is found in Lk 17:4 but there is no mention of Peter.
5. See, for example, P. Ellis, *Matthew: His Mind and his Message*, Collegeville, 1974, 63-67.

Outline of Mt 14:1–18:35
1. Mt 14:1-14:33 culminates in the account of Peter on the storm tossed sea calling on Jesus to save him.
2. Mt 14:34-16:20 culminates in Peter's profession of faith and Jesus' triple response.
3. Mt 16:21-17:27 culminates in Peter's paying the temple tax for Jesus and himself.
4. Mt 18:1-35. The discourse on life in the community culminates in Peter's asking the crucial question about forgiveness in the community and Jesus responding with a *logion* and a parable.

PART 1. MT 14:1-33
a. John and Herod Mt 14-1-12//Mk 6:14-29//Lk 3:19-20; 9:7-9
The lot of the rejected prophet is now brought home to the reader by way of completing the story of the Baptist. It may appear at first glance that this is a story in the gospel that does not directly relate to or directly concern Jesus and his ministry. That, however, would be an understanding that seriously misses the point. John is the precursor. He began the process of announcing the imminence of the kingdom and preaching repentance as preparation for its arrival. He presented Jesus as the one who would baptise in the Holy Spirit. When John was arrested Jesus stepped into the breach and carried on the mission of preaching and now his representatives are going about Galilee preaching. John, the first of the preachers now meets the fate which will await Jesus and threaten the others. In his death, therefore, he is also the precursor, preparing the way. Jesus will soon begin speaking about a similar fate awaiting himself, and possibly also awaiting his representatives. The precursor is again preparing the way on which Jesus will follow.

The story of the arrest and execution of John the Baptist stands at this point as a prefiguring of the ultimate fate of Jesus. As John was precursor to his ministry so will he be the precursor to his death (Mt 14:3-12). Herod (Antipas) arrested and executed the precursor and now he is turning his attention to Jesus.

Jesus had escaped the wrath of Herod the Great, father of Herod Antipas, at his birth. The Baptist now falls victim to his son, and that same son is being given information about Jesus. He has heard of Jesus' reputation[6] and remarks to his servants/ members of his court that this is John the Baptist, that he has risen from the dead and this is why these miraculous powers (*dunameis*) are at work in him (though in fact there are no accounts of miraculous powers exercised by the Baptist).

Herod Antipas was very disturbed by John's rebuke for taking his brother's wife, Herodias. 'It is not lawful for you to have her,' he had said. According to Matthew he wanted to kill the Baptist but was afraid of the people who regarded him as a prophet. Mark has a more complicated picture. He says that Herod feared him but liked to listen to him and the murderous intentions were on the part of Herodias, his wife (Mk 6:14-29). Both Mark and Matthew are mistaken in saying Herodias had been the wife of his brother Philip. In fact she was wife of another brother, Herod. The story of the beheading of John is based on some essential historical facts relating to the preaching, arrest and beheading of John. The reasons for the arrest given by Matthew and Mark are religious and moral, relating to his preaching against Herod Antipas' incestuous marriage. The reasons given by the historian Josephus are political, relating to the fears surrounding a very popular figure who draws crowds that may encourage or give cover to revolutionaries.[7]

Herod Antipas was a son of Herod the Great and succeeded his father as tetrarch (not king) of Galilee and Perea. Matthew and Luke give him his proper title, but Mark calls him a king. Some scholars see this as a straightforward mistake or the result of editorial fatigue on Mark's part. It is more likely that it reflects popular usage. It may be deliberately used as a literary associ-

---

6. According to Luke, Herod's curiosity was aroused by the discussion among the people and their speculation that John the Baptist had risen from the dead, or that Elijah or some other ancient prophet had appeared. He was anxious to see Jesus, and pleased when Pilate sent him to him, hoping to see a miracle performed by Jesus (Lk 9:7-9; 23:8-12).
7. Josephus, *Ant*, xviii. 5, 2.

ation with the stories of king Ahab and queen Jezebel (1 Kings 19 & 21) and the king in the Esther story (Esther 5), both of which have strong echoes in the Baptist's story. Furthermore, it must have been well known that Antipas' downfall some years later resulted from his ambition to be king, so there is a great irony in calling him 'king'. His own, and particularly his wife's, ambition that he be made king, caused him to be dismissed and sent into exile by the emperor Caligula shortly after his accession to the imperial throne circa 38-39AD. His downfall was brought about in large measure at the jealous instigation of Herodias' brother, Herod Antipas' nephew, Agrippa, who laid charges against him. Matthew gives Herod Antipas his proper title 'tetrarch' in the introduction to the story, but reverts to the title 'king' later in the account when describing his regret for making a rash promise on oath (Mt 14:9).

As Elijah condemned Jezebel for her patronage of the cult of Ba'al and subsequently for the murder of Naboth and the impounding of his vineyard, so John criticised the incestuous marriage of Herodias and Herod Antipas. As Jezebel was wont to force her will upon her weaker and vacillating husband King Ahab, though Elijah luckily escaped her murderous designs, so too Herodias watches her opportunity and traps Herod Antipas into serving up the head of the Baptist on a dish at his birthday party (cf 1 Kings 19 & 21). According to Matthew and Mark, the dancing girl is prompted by her mother to ask for the head of John the Baptist on a dish.

Matthew's account of the dancing girl is much shorter and less polished than Mark's. The dancer (whose name is given by Josephus as Salome) 'pleased' Herod and his fellow diners. The verb êresen/areskein, 'pleased', has the meaning of 'entertained' in a non-erotic sense, though popular representations of the scene usually take it in the erotic sense. The promise to give her whatever she would ask is a less colourful promise than Mark's version of a promise of half his kingdom, a promise with its antecedent in the Esther story (Esther 5).[8] The solemn oath to make

8. This was a highly ironic statement on the part of Mark because Herod

a generous gift was very serious. In Jewish culture it invoked the Holy One with all the solemnity that such a gesture entailed. In Hellenistic culture a royal oath was the pinnacle of binding one-self in honour and to Christian ears it was similar to the Jewish religious obligation. The 'king' realised how badly he had been trapped and he was *lupêtheis*, distressed, regretful. Mark has the stronger expression *perilypos*, very distressed, the same verb being used only one other time in Mark's gospel, for Jesus' distress in Gethsemane (Mk 14:14).

Beheading brings dishonour to the victim and to the victim's followers and family, a very serious concern in a culture with an honour-shame consciousness and value system.[9] The beheading of John was a blow struck against his person but also against his following and it could pose a threat also to the reputation and standing of Jesus, the one for whom he prepared the way and for whom he bore solemn witness in public. His disciples, however, remained faithful to him. They came, took the body and placed it in a tomb and went and told Jesus (Mt 14:12).

The reference to the disciples of John is but a small window on the phenomenon of John's following. His influence seems to have been far greater and more widespread than appears at first glance. Josephus has a significant comment on the influence of the Baptist,[10] the Acts of the Apostles speaks of people as far away as Ephesus having received the baptism of John (Acts 19:1-7) and Apollos knew of the baptism of John when he came from Alexandria to Ephesus (Acts 18:25). The New Testament seems to be in a constant state of unease with the fact that many people still believed that John was the Messiah. All the accounts of John in the New Testament insist on John's own admission of the superiority of Jesus' baptism, person and mission over his own.

---

was a client ruler under Rome and did not have power to do any such thing and furthermore, as seen above, he was not a king and did not have a kingdom to divide!

9. Josephus points out that Anthony beheaded Antigonus to dishonour him and diminish his fame among the Jews (*Ant* 15:9f). He points out also that beheading is similar in that intent to crucifixion (*War* 2.241).

10. Josephus, *Ant* xviii. 5,2.

This banquet of royal guests opens what can be called the 'bread/food' section of the gospels of Matthew and Mark. It stands in great contrast to the open-air banquets for the ordinary people, which follow where the little food available feeds the masses at the command of Jesus. The murderous banquet of the elite that comes to a climax at the command of the host, the ruler of the people, with a dish bearing the head of the prophet, is followed by the banquets for Jew and Gentile at the command of the shepherd-king who had compassion on the people, healed their sick and fed them in the desert.

b. Feeding the Five Thousand Mt 14:13-21//Mk 6:32-44//Lk 9:10-17

As the reader pictures the disciples of John gathering to give a fitting burial to their murdered leader and bringing the news to Jesus, the spotlight turns to Jesus. On hearing the news, he withdrew alone by boat to a desert place. A change of location again introduces a new initiative.

Jesus withdrew 'to a desert place' (*eis erêmon topon*) alone. The nature of the place is stressed again further on in the remark, *erêmos estin ho topos*, 'the place is a desert'. However, when he arrives there the desert place he sought for solitude will be peopled with an enthusiastic crowd. As the people guessed his destination they set out on foot from the towns and reached the place before him, so on emerging from the boat (or from his secret location?) he saw the crowds and had compassion on them and healed their sick. Earlier when he made the tour of the cities and villages teaching in their synagogues, preaching the gospel of the kingdom and healing every disease and infirmity, the crowds came to him and he had compassion on them because they were harassed and helpless, like sheep without a shepherd (Mt 9:35-36). Here in Mt 14:12-14 Jesus' compassion on the crowds is again emphasised as he sets about healing their sick and then feeding them in the desert.[11]

---

11. Mark makes a similar remark at the beginning of his account of the first multiplication. In Mark Jesus' reaction on seeing the crowd was to teach.

The multiplication of the loaves and fishes is one of the few miracles recounted in all four gospels (Mt 14:13-21; 15:32-39; Mk 6:35-44; 8:1-10; Lk 9:12-17). In fact there are two accounts in Mark and Matthew who have two parallel blocks of material at this point.[12] The 'Bread Section', as it is sometimes called, is composed of two parallel blocks of material, each beginning with a feeding of the multitude, followed by a sea crossing,[13] a dispute with the Pharisees and a teaching on the theme of bread (Mt 14:13–15:20 and Mt 15:21–16:12). Whether or not they inherited from the tradition a cycle of miracle stories containing two catenae[14] or lists with doublets, they have integrated the two 'bread' cycles with great skill into their overall narratives.

As evening came on, the disciples approached Jesus and pointed out that it was evening and they were in a desert place and the time had slipped by. They remark on the loneliness of the place and lateness of the day and advise Jesus to send the people away to buy food for themselves in the surrounding villages. Jesus responded in a solemn, more or less oracular tone: 'There is no need for them to go away.' Then he says that they should give them something to eat themselves.[15] Quite taken aback, they reply that they have only five loaves and two fish.

As Jesus issues the instruction to the Twelve to feed the crowds themselves he heightens their awareness of the problem and creates an appreciation of the gift which follows and its sign

---

12. See the studies by G. van Oyen, *The Interpretation of the Feeding Miracles in the Gospel of Mark*, Turnhout: Brepols, 1999 and A. Grassi, *Loaves and Fishes: The Gospel Feeding Narratives*, Collegeville: The Liturgical Press, 1991.

13. Luke's account stands alone among the six accounts in not having a sea crossing following the multiplication.

14. See P. J. Achtemeier, 'Toward the isolation of pre-Markan miracle catenae' in *JBL*, 89 (1970), 265-91.

15. Mark at this point describes their reaction in a manner reminiscent of Moses' reaction in the desert as he questions the Lord: 'Where am I to get meat to give to all these people?' and 'Are there enough flocks and herds to slaughter for them? Are there enough fish in the sea to gather (LXX *synagein*) for them?'(Num 11:1-3, 13, 22). This same theme is reflected in the psalm: 'They spoke against God saying: "Can God spread a table in the wilderness?" '(Ps 78:19).

value. The disciples' statement that they have only five loaves and two fish and Jesus' command to bring them to him is curt and to the point when compared to the account in Mark where there follows a discussion about the expense involved. Jesus then tells them to make the people sit down on the grass.[16] The shorter description in Matthew highlights the solemn 'Eucharistic' character of the account, taking the spotlight off the disciples and their anxious questioning and placing it on Jesus and his words and actions. (There is no mention of the little boy with the loaves and fish who appears only in John's account (Jn 6:9) but whose presence has become an established part of the popular telling of the story in harmonised versions and in works of art.)

Having solemnly commanded them to bring him the loaves and fishes and having instructed the crowds to sit on the grass, Jesus' subsequent words and actions reflect the words and actions by then established in the Eucharistic Liturgy. *Taking* the five *loaves*, and the two fish, *having looked up to heaven*, he *said the blessing, having broken* the loaves, *he gave them* to the disciples, and the disciples gave them to the crowds. All are actions and words familiar from the liturgy. The focus of attention is on the bread rather than the fish, because the allusion to the Eucharistic celebration is highlighted.[17] The fish will not even be mentioned in Mt 16:9-11//Mk 8:18-21 when Jesus later reminds the disci-

---

16. Matthew does not have Mark's allusion to the Exodus in the *symposia symposia*, usually translated as 'in groups.' This recalls the organisation of companies of hundreds and fifties during the wandering in the desert (Exod 18:21-25; Num 31:14; Deut 1:15). Neither is there a reference to green grass (Matthew just says grass), an allusion to Psalm 23 with its emphasis on green pasture, rest after a journey and safety under the caring eye of the shepherd as they ate and had not only their fill but had food left over.

17. Bread was not usually eaten on its own but would have some 'filling' as in a sandwich. In John *opsarion*, a double diminutive, was used to describe such a filling (Jn 6:9). It literally means 'a small, little fish'. Combined with bread such a 'filling' is referred to as 'food' or, in the more general sense of the term 'bread'. The 'fish' is not therefore left 'redundant' in the narrative.

ples of both multiplications.[18] As the account of the multiplication reflects the established practice of the Eucharistic Liturgy it points forward to the institution of the Eucharist at the Last Supper and to the eschatological banquet in the kingdom.

They ate and had their fill. The number who ate was about five thousand men, not counting the women and children. Emphasising the large numbers recalls the feeding of the people during the wandering in the desert. The gathering of the fragments (*klasmata*) recalls the gathering of the manna and with it the desert scenario of Moses and the Exodus-Wandering when the people gathered the manna each day, until they had what they needed (Exod 16:8, 12, 16, 18, 21). The account emphasises the compassionate response of God to the people's plea for food, the gift of God and the fact that whether a person gathered less or more manna, everyone had enough. The noun *klasmata* has overtones of the breaking into shared pieces of the Eucharistic bread and is so used to signify the Eucharistic fragments in the First Letter of Clement of Rome, in the *Didachê* and in the letter of Ignatius of Antioch to Polycarp.[19] The mention of twelve baskets, however, shifts the focus of attention from the food to the people, pointing to a number representative of the complete number of the tribes of Israel, thus referring to the completeness of God's people, a number used also in the choice of twelve apostles, like the twelve sons of Israel (Jacob), and now signifying the full number of believers in Jesus (Mt 14:20; Mk 6:43; Lk 9:17).

Jesus' compassion for the flock casts him in the role of shepherd, reminiscent of the caring activity of God, the Shepherd of Israel, for the people in the desert. It is reminiscent of the role and leadership of Moses as he fed the people in the desert. His compassion, manifesting itself in his healing and feeding activity makes Jesus a worthy leader, a true shepherd whose role is often

---

18. The account focuses on the bread and the Eucharistic language is very much in evidence. Keeping the fish in the story shows how its presence was well established in the more primitive accounts before the Eucharistic language was developed.

19. *I Clement* 34:7; *Didachê* 9:3,4; Ignatius, *Polycarp*, 4:2.

associated with the role of king, and particularly with David the divinely appointed shepherd king (Ezek 34; Ps 22/23). Jesus' compassionate feeding of the multitude in the desert stands out in severe contrast to what has taken place at the banquet in the palace of the earthly 'king' at which the prophet's head was served on a dish. Jesus challenges the Twelve to share in this shepherding work by telling them to feed the crowd themselves. One feels that there is a double meaning to feeding throughout. As well as the physical feeding the Twelve are commissioned to feed the people with the word.[20]

The multiplication of the loaves is both a christological and eucharistic miracle. Unfortunately its significance on both counts has been overlooked and its many rich seams of meaning have been diminished by rationalistic attempts to explain away the miraculous. J. R. Donahue and D. J. Harrington in their commentary on the feeding in Mark's gospel make a point, which is relevant to all six multiplication accounts in the New Testament:

> One way not to actualise the passage is to say that the people were so moved by the preaching of Jesus that they divided their food with others. This 'nice thought' interpretation goes back to the nineteenth century rationalistic attack on miracles but has now achieved a strong foothold in mainline Christian preaching. Rather, the narrative offers a picture of Jesus as compassionate towards the leaderless people and concerned about their physical hunger. A church that invokes the name of Jesus must be concerned about the spiritual and physical hungers of people today. The location in a desolate place evokes God's care of the Jewish people during the wilderness wanderings. Since Vatican II has chosen 'pilgrim people' as one of the central metaphors for the church, this aspect of the narrative can readily be actualised.[21]

---

20. This teaching dimension is picked up and greatly developed in the sixth chapter of St John's gospel in which the idea of the Bread of Life, both as Word and Eucharist, is developed at length.
21. J. R. Donahue and D. J. Harrington, *The Gospel of Mark*, 211.

c. Jesus and Peter on the Water Mt 14:22-33//Mk 6:45-52

Jesus on the Water

Following the multiplication of the loaves there is a scene on the sea where Jesus comes to the disciples in distress. The double action, the feeding of the multitude and his saving presence on the sea, re-echo the double action of Moses in feeding the people in the desert and leading them through the sea.

Matthew (like Mark) describes Jesus sending the disciples away in a boat to the other side of the lake while he himself dismisses the crowd and goes alone to the mountain to pray. Going to the mountain has significant resonances in the history of salvation. The mountain was the special place associated with the Divine Presence (Gen 22:14; Exod 3:1; Deut 11:29; Joshua 8:70) and with encounters with the Divine. Moses encountered *YHWH* on the mountain (Exod 19:3, 16, 24) and the word of the Lord came to Elijah on the mountain (1 Kings 19:9-18). Moses returned from the mountain bathed in light and his altered appearance terrified the people (Exod 34:29f). On this occasion Jesus will come from the mountain and the disciples will be terrified by his appearance as they see him coming over the water. He will later be transfigured on the mountain in the presence of Peter, James and John (Mt 17:1-13//Mk 9:2-13//Lk 9:28-36).

In Matthew (and Mark) Jesus is very swift and deliberate in his sending the disciples away from the scene of the multiplication. He immediately forces them to embark and go before him to the other side (of the lake), while he dismisses the crowd (*kai eutheôs ênagkasen ... embênai*). The implied reason may well be his desire to remove them from the misguided messianic enthusiasm of the crowd caused by the feeding of so many in the deserted place. John's account emphasises the enthusiastic reaction of the crowd from which Jesus himself escapes into the hills alone to avoid their taking him away to declare him king (Jn 6:15-17).

As Jesus goes to the mountain alone to pray the reader now picks up on the imagery of Moses going to the mountain alone to encounter the Lord, especially in the wake of the Mosaic-Exodus allusions in the story of the multiplication of the loaves.

The 'Mosaic' action of feeding the multitude is now followed by another great miracle reminiscent of the Passover and Exodus event, the safe passage through the sea, guaranteed by the divine name and presence. The focus, however, is not on the miracle of calming a storm or stilling a difficult head wind. It is on the terrified state and perplexity of the disciples at the sight of Jesus coming towards them over the water, an epiphany interpreted through the divine name, *I am*, with its accompanying reassurances, *have courage* and *do not be afraid*.

As evening fell Jesus was alone on the land. The boat was many *stadia* out from the land in a distressed state, being beaten by the waves since the wind was against them. Jesus came to them walking over the sea, during the fourth watch (between three and six o'clock in the morning).[22] As he approached them the disciples were terrified thinking he was a ghost. They cried out in fear. He immediately responded to their terrified state saying: *Tharseite, egô eimi, mê phobeisthe*, 'Have courage. I am / It is I. Do not be afraid.' Jesus thus fulfils the role of the comforting saviour, pronouncing the *egô eimi*, 'I am' and exhorting the disciples not to be afraid. Having repeated the miracle of Moses in feeding the people in the desert, a sign expected to herald the arrival of the messianic age (2 Baruch 29:8), he proceeds to repeat the other Mosaic miracle of leading his followers through the water. However, unlike Moses, Jesus himself pronounces the *ego*

---

22. Mark's account helps to throw light on the meaning of the event. Mark states that, 'He (Jesus) wished to pass by them', *êthelen parelthein autous*. It does not mean simply he was going to pass them by and go on his way. It is a phrase canonised in the tradition of the theophany / epiphany. It signifies 'passing by' in the sense of 'passing in front of, and in view of them'. It recalls Moses' plea to God: 'Show me your glory, I beg you' and the response: 'I will let all my splendour pass in front of you and I will pronounce before you the name *YHWH*' (Exod 33:19) and '*YHWH* descended in the form of a cloud, and Moses stood with him there. He called on the name of *YHWH*. *YHWH* passed before him and proclaimed, "*YHWH, YHWH*, a God of mercy and compassion, slow to anger, rich in loving kindness and faithfulness" '(Exod 34:5f). The theophany is marked by God 'passing by' or 'passing in front of' Moses and pronouncing the Divine Name.

eimi, 'I am' and issues the exhortations to have courage and not to be afraid.

The context, following the Mosaic-Exodus allusions, alerts the reader to the deeper significance of *ego eimi*, 'I am' which is significantly more than a simple self identification such as 'It is I' meaning, 'This is Jesus whom you left on the shore a few hours ago.' When God's name was revealed to Moses in the words usually translated as 'I am who I am', the revelation was followed by the command to go to the people and say: '*I am* sent me to you' (Exod 3:14f). Isaiah develops this *I am* designation for God in several passages, and the LXX use of *ego eimi* for the Divine Name springs immediately to mind,[23] as for example, '*I am, I am,* the one comforting you' (Is 51:12), and 'therefore my people will know my name on that day because *I am he*, the one (who is) speaking to you (Is 52:6).'[24] D. M. Ball, writing about the use of *ego eimi* in John's gospel, makes a point equally relevant to its use here in Matthew. He states the case clearly as he points out how the single phrase containing *egô eimi* may alert the implied reader to an entire thought world, which is shared with the implied author since they are within a shared cultural framework. The implied reader, therefore, would automatically understand the implications of the words *egô eimi*, which is clear from the fact that they are not explained. Furthermore when Jesus uses these words, it is not only the words themselves but also the thought world to which they point which helps to explain what he means.[25] Ball also points out that:

> The absolute use of *egô eimi*, 'I am', in the Old Testament is striking as the only conclusive parallel to the use in the New

23. Isa (LXX) 41:4; 43:10; 46:4; 48:12; 51:12.

24. cf Isa 51:12: *ego eimi ego eimi ho parakalôn se:* ' I am I am, the one (who is) consoling you.' Isa 52:6: *dia touto gnôsetai ho laos mou to onoma mou en tê hêmera ekeinê, hoti egô eimi autos ho lalôn soi:* 'Because of this my people will know my name on that day, because *I am* is the one speaking to you.' (*egô eimi autos*, in Hebrew, *ani hû*).

25. D. M. Ball, *'I Am' in John's Gospel: Literary Function, Background and Theological Implications,* Journal For the Study Of The New Testament, Supplement Series, 124 Sheffield Academic Press, 1996, 177.

Testament. However ... it is not only in the words *egô eimi* that John points back to Isaiah, but also in the way that those words are presented.'[26]

This is equally true of Matthew. The *egô eimi* is in the context of an epiphany and furthermore it is enclosed between the standard expressions used in an epiphany/theophany, 'have courage', and 'do not be afraid'. This epiphany reflects the biblical awareness of the divine presence in, and power over, creation, especially as manifested in the case of the angry sea, seen already in relation to the calming of the storm (Mt 8:23-27//Mk 4:35-41).[27] The saving power of God and the call to believe and not to fear run through these biblical passages.

The *egô eimi* statement of self identification and reassurance is inextricably linked to the words 'Have courage' and 'Do not be afraid'. This injunction not to be afraid is a recurring feature of Old Testament theophanies. *YHWH* spoke to Abram, saying: 'Do not be afraid, Abram, I am your shield' and went on to promise him the land from the Wadi of Egypt to the Great River (Gen 15:1,18). In the apparition to Isaac at Beersheba, *YHWH* said; 'I am the God of your father Abraham, do not be afraid for I am with you' (Gen 26:24). To Jacob *YHWH* said: 'I am God, the God of your fathers, do not be afraid of going down to Egypt, for I will make you a great nation there' (Gen 46:3). The injunction not to be afraid is found in Isaiah, 'I am holding you by the right hand; I tell you do not be afraid, I will help you', and 'Do not be afraid for I have redeemed you; I have called you by your name, you are mine. Should you pass through the sea I will be with you, or through rivers they will not swallow you up ... do not be afraid for I am with you' (Isa 41:13f; 43:1-5). Several times Jeremiah is assured that he has no need to fear his enemies, because *YHWH* will be with him (Jer 1:8, 17; 42:11; 46:28).[28]

---

26. Ibid.
27. Ps 106 (107): 9, 30. cf Exod 14:15; Deut 7:2-7; Job 38:16; Pss 29:3; 65:8; 77:20; 89:10; 93:3f; 51:9f; Isa 43:1-5; 51:9f.
28. In the annunciations to Zachary and Mary the angel tells them not to be afraid (Lk 1:13, 30). Before performing some of his healings Jesus

Peter on the Water

The call to have faith and not to fear is now put to the test in the case of Peter. Matthew alone among the gospel writers includes here the account of Peter coming to Jesus over the water. Peter responds to the saving implications of Jesus' *egô eimi* as he returns the statement, 'If you are, bid me come to you over the water.' True to his character elsewhere in the four gospels, he enthusiastically responds to Jesus' invitation to come to him over the water. Finding himself in the midst of the storm he is confronted with his own frailty as he feels the wind and begins to sink in the sea, and then calls out to the Lord.

The christology is significant. Peter called out to Jesus to save him, acknowledging his power to save and using the believer's title 'Lord', *Kyrie, sôson me*, 'Save me, Lord'. Jesus stretched out his hand and took him, and significantly Jesus' comment 'You of little faith, why did you doubt?' is directed in the singular to Peter, not to the group as in the earlier boat scene (Mt 8:26). When they enter the boat the wind ceases. The disciples in the boat react with an act of homage, bowing down and saying: 'You are the Son of God', again a higher christology than the parallel account in Mark, but typical of this gospel.[29]

His action is somewhat similar to his jumping into the sea on seeing the Lord on the shore after the Resurrection, in John's gospel (Jn 21:7). It also prefigures the initial response of Peter to Jesus' arrest, following him to the house of the high priest, but then collapsing into denial on finding himself in the midst of the crisis.

---

told the petitioner not to be afraid (Mk 4:40; 5:36; Lk 8:50) and in the Resurrection appearances the terrified or perplexed recipients of the appearances are told not to be afraid (Mk 16:6; Mt 28:5, 10; Lk 24:5).

29. Mark points out that they failed to recognise him precisely because they had not understood about the loaves (*epi tois artois*) because their heart was hardened.

Part 2. Mt 14:34-16:20

a. Healings at Gennesaret Mt 14:34-36//Mk 6:53-56
Having crossed over they came to land at Gennesaret, the fertile ground on the north west shore between Tiberias and Capernaum. The area, known as Gennesaret, was a thickly populated area. On recognising him the people of the area sent word around the whole district and they brought to him all who were ill and begged him that they might only touch the hem of his garment, and 'as many as' (whoever/everyone) touched him were healed.

The verb *parakalein* is used of their request to Jesus to heal the sick. Literally it means 'to call alongside', and is usually translated as 'to beg, to implore'. It is a pointer to Jesus' acknowledged power and status among the people. Like the woman with the issue of blood who believed that touching his garment would bring her healing (Mt 9:20-21), they too saw the holy man as a reservoir of power so they begged him to let them touch the hem of his garment.[30] All those who touched him were saved.

b. Dispute with the Pharisees and Scribes. Tradition and Purity Laws Mt 15:1-20
'Then' links the following passage with the preceding. There approached Jesus from Jerusalem Pharisees and scribes ...' The emphatic position in the sentence of the designation 'from Jerusalem' raises the spectre of the long hand of Jerusalem authority reaching into Galilee.[31] Furthermore, at the mention of the Pharisees and scribes approaching Jesus the reader immediately expects a confrontation because of their former appearances in the gospel. Some of the scribes had already accused

---

30. *Kraspedon*, fringe, tassel, can refer to the tassels prescribed to be worn by Num 15:38-39 and Deut 22:12.
31. The long arm of Jerusalem stretched into Galilee when there was unauthorised religious activity in the air. The questioning of the Baptist as seen in John's gospel is a good example (Jn 1:19-28) and Mark states that it was scribes from Jerusalem who accused Jesus of casting out devils by the power of the Prince of Devils (Mk 3:22).

Jesus of blasphemy when he told the paralytic his sins were forgiven (Mt 9:3). Pharisees had questioned his disciples about his reason for eating with tax collectors and sinners (Mt 9:11). Pharisees had scolded him about his disciples' breaking of the Sabbath in the cornfield (Mt 12:2). They questioned him about healing on the Sabbath and when he outwitted them they conspired about how to do away with him (Mt 12:14). They accused him of casting out demons by the power of Beelzebul (Mt 12:24). Now they confront him about his disciples' transgression of the tradition of the elders.

The Dispute

Their criticism is severe and to the point. 'Why do your disciples transgress the tradition of the elders, for they do not wash their hands when they eat bread?' Jesus immediately picks up on the references to 'transgression' and 'the tradition of the elders'. He responds with prophetic fury to the attack on his disciples. He points to their own far greater 'transgression' with the challenge: 'And why do you transgress the commandment of God because of your tradition?' His counter-accusation about transgressing the commandment of God far outweighs their accusation about transgressing the tradition of the elders. Instead of outlining Jewish customs of ritual washing at this point (as Mark does) Matthew goes on immediately to outline Jesus' counter argument. To illustrate his point Jesus takes the example of the commandment to honour parents and not to speak evil of them (speak in any way to their detriment), under pain of death (Exod 20:12; Deut 5:16; Exod 21:17; Lev 20:9). The prescriptions of the Torah were seen as the commandments of God, not simply the commandments of a pivotal figure like Moses. So when Jesus equivalently says: 'God said ... *but you say*' he really highlights their arrogance or blindness. He illustrates his point by highlighting a teaching of theirs and how it transgresses the law of God. 'Whoever may say to father or mother: "Whatever you should gain from me is a *gift*" shall not honour his father or mother.' In making such a vow one is speaking to the detriment of one's parents. The 'gift' is a reference to a practice specifically named by Mark as *Corban*. The exact meaning, extent and practice of *Corban* is unclear and the particular practice criticised here by Jesus is elsewhere unknown. *Corban* is an Aramaic word whose basic meaning is 'an offering made to God with an oath'.[32] What Jesus is here criticising therefore seems to be either the allowing or encouraging of a practice in the name of religion which denied due support to parents by dedicating to the temple with an oath what would have been necessary for their support, or refusing to permit someone who makes a hasty or ill-judged oath of dedication to *Corban* to annul it later in the interest of due concern for the parents. In fact the *Mishnah*, codified later than the New Testament but very likely reflecting practices of the New Testament period, allows for the setting aside of a vow that contravenes a biblical precept, especially in the case of a resulting neglect of parents.[33] It is at least a possibility that this *Mishnaic* excusation clause arose in response to something similar to what Jesus was here criticising. In thus neglecting parents in the interest of religion one is failing to obey the commandment to honour father and mother, and in doing so makes void the word of God. The statement about 'speaking evil of father or mother' can be seen as a reference to speaking the words of a vow or oath that will have the effect of doing evil by way of economic deprivation to the parents.

In speaking of 'the tradition of the elders' his opponents are probably referring to biblical texts like Num 18:8-13 and Lev 11:15 which deal with things consecrated to God and things 'clean and unclean' respectively, and to the traditions that had developed relating to their practical application. 'Unclean' is designated as *koinos*, which literally means 'common', that is 'in common secular use' and therefore ' tainted' by contact with the world, as distinct from *hagios*, blessed by, or dedicated to God

---

32. Josephus speaks of *Corban* as a gift offered to God, *Ant* 4.73; *Against Apion* 1:167.
33. *m. Nedarim* 9:1;11:11.

(*hagiazein/qaddes*).[34] The 'tradition' (*paradosis*) was an unbroken chain of teaching believed to stretch from Simeon ben Gamaliel in the late second century BC back to Moses.[35] Josephus points out that the Pharisees had included traditions of the fathers not found in the Book of Moses. The Sadducees rejected these additions.[36]

The challenge put to Jesus gives him the opportunity to play the role of the prophet who challenges stringent tradition that kills healthy religion and ignores basic obligations such as filial duty and compassion. Quoting the words of Isaiah as prophecy Jesus recalls the major prophetic theme of external rituals that do not reflect internal dispositions. Ritual without internal moral and spiritual dispositions is performance (*hypokritein*), so he calls them 'performers', persons who play a part, acting out a role. The Greek *hypocritês*, does not necessarily carry the connotations of deviousness and deception that 'hypocrite' carries in English. Its connotation in this context is more that of 'empty performance', 'going through the motions' and 'lip service', rather than 'deliberately deceiving.' Jesus points to it as an attitude well summed up by Isaiah:

> This people honours me with their lips, but their heart is far from me, the worship they offer me is worthless, teaching as doctrines the commandments of men' (Isa 29:13; cf Mk 7:6f).

The second part of the Isaian quotation moves the discussion from 'empty performance' to the relative values of divine command and human tradition. The quotation is closer to the Hebrew text than to the LXX Greek text, but even at that it adapts the original 'teaching human precepts and doctrines' to 'teaching as doctrines the precepts of men (human beings)'.

---

34. *Koinos* means 'common' and in classical Greek it signifies the opposite to *idios*, private, but it is used of unclean animals in 1 Macc 1:47, 62 and of unclean food in Acts 10:14, 28; 11:8; and Rev 21:27.
35. *m. Abot* 1:1-18;
36. Josephus, *Ant* 13.297 and 18.12.

Teaching the crowd and the Disciples Mt 15:10-20//Mk 7:14-23

A change of audience signals a further shift in the argument. 'Calling the crowd to him Jesus said to them: "Listen and understand".' The Pharisees and scribes from Jerusalem are no longer the sole audience. The original point of dispute was how they should eat. The argument now moves to what they should eat and Jesus clinches his argument with the *logion*: 'It is not what goes into the mouth that makes a man unclean, but what comes out of the mouth that makes a man unclean.'

The audience changes again as the disciples come to Jesus and ask him if he knows that the Pharisees were scandalised at what he said. Jesus replies in the severest tones. 'Every plant that my heavenly Father has not planted will be rooted out. Leave them alone (take no notice of them). They are blind guides of blind men and when a blind man leads a blind man both fall into a ditch.' This response is in line with the long established imagery of God's people as a vine or a vineyard planted by God from which he expected fruit in due season (Isa 5:1-7) and with the imagery of the fig tree (Mt 21:18-22) and the tree bearing no fruit (Mt 3:10). Either they are not sown by God or they have not produced fruit and will be rooted up.

In response, Peter asks him to explain the 'parable' (really a *logion* or *mashal/matla*). Jesus responds to their question by asking them: 'Are you also still lacking in understanding (*asynêtoi*)?' 'Do you not know that everything going in through the mouth passes through the stomach and is expelled into the drain, but the things coming out of the mouth come from the heart and those things make a man unclean.' Food from outside passes through the digestive system and then out into the sewer without making any negative moral or spiritual impact on the person. The things going in through the mouth only enter the stomach, but the things coming out of the mouth come from the heart. What is in the heart is manifest in what comes out of the heart, in what one does and says. Using a list of vices Jesus then spells out the bad things that come from the heart. The heart is mentioned twice in the pericope, signifying the centre of one's

life, the seat of one's emotions, convictions, motivation and actions, in short, one's character. Already in the gospel there has
been an emphasis on the condition of the heart. 'The pure of
heart' are declared blessed and promised that they will see God
(Mt 5:8) and Jesus also warns that a man's words flow from
what fills his heart (Mt 12:33-37).

The heart is often portrayed in the Bible as the arena or battle-
ground where good and evil forces confront one another. As
seen already in the comment on the 'pure of heart', there are
many positive and negative examples throughout the Bible,
summed up in terms such as learning wisdom in the secret of
the heart, giving praise from the heart, rending the heart and not
the garment, evil thoughts arising in the heart, plotting malice in
the heart, being hard of heart and so forth. Originally the saying
'what goes into a man' may not have been in the context of a dispute about clean and unclean food, but an independent *logion*
emphasising the contrast between external influences and the
true state of one's heart.

Jesus' response to the disciples' request for clarification spells
out the dispositions of the evil heart with a catalogue of vices.
Teaching morality by way of lists of virtues and vices, a method
referred to by scholars as *catalogical paraenesis*, was widespread,
both in biblical and secular literature.[37] Virtue lists are also used
in a variety of contexts and show a great variety in content.[38] In
the handing on of the tradition it is quite possible that Jesus'
original explanation has been transformed into this list which
would represent a familiar style of teaching where the teacher
makes the practical connections with life, while maintaining the
essential meaning.

Beginning with the emphatic phraseology 'for it is from out

---

37. The vice lists appear at Rom 1:24, 26; 29-31; 13:13; 1 Cor 5:10f; 6:9f; 2
Cor 12:20; Gal 5:19-21; Eph 4:31; 5:3-5; 1 Tim 9f; 6:4f; 2 Tim 3:2-5; Tit 3:3;
1 Pet 2:1; 4:3f; Jude 8:16; Rev 9:20f; 21:8; 22:15; Mt 15:19 / /Mk 7:21f. The
most common evils mentioned in the vice lists are fornication (8 times)
and idolatry (5 times).
38. The main virtue lists are found in Mt 5:3-11; 2 Cor 6:6f; Gal 5:22f;
Eph 6:14-17; Phil 4:8; 1 Tim 3:2f; 6:11; Tit 1:7f; Jas 3:17; I2 Pet 1:5-7.

of the heart that "evil machinations" (*dialogismoi*) come', Jesus goes on to spell out the significance and results of the 'evil machinations' or 'designs of the heart' in terms of a list of actions and dispositions – murder, adultery, fornication, theft, perjury, blasphemy/slander.[39] The point being made is abundantly clear. People are not made unclean by 'external' factors like eating certain foods. They are unclean because of their 'inner' state and motives, which result in external actions. Jesus repeats his point at the end of the list: 'These are what defile a man: but to eat with unwashed hands does not defile a man.'

c. The Canaanite Woman Mt 15:21-28//Mk 7:24-30

As usual a new initiative of Jesus is signalled by a change of location. Jesus departed from there and withdrew to the territory of Tyre and Sidon. The controversy with the Pharisees and scribes and the teaching to the crowd and to the disciples, which dealt with ritual purity, are now significantly followed by an account of Jesus' dealings with the 'unclean' Gentiles. 'And going out from there' Jesus went on to Gentile (and potentially hostile) territory, the region of Tyre and Sidon. He will encounter a Canaanite woman, hold a discussion with her about food and feeding Gentile children before healing her daughter.

Even though he was already rejected in his own town and by his own people he had subsequently carried on a mission and miraculously supplied food to the crowds in a desert area in Jewish territory. Since it was in Galilee of the Gentiles and crowds were probably coming from the surrounding Gentile areas, he may well have fed Gentiles together with the Jewish crowd. Now he leaves the land of Israel and travels into thoroughly Gentile country to the north as he heads for the region of

---

39. Mark gives a list of twelve evil actions and dispositions. Six of them are in the plural signifying 'acts of' fornication, theft, murder, adultery, avarice and malice and six are in the singular signifying dispositions or qualities of actions such as deceit, licentiousness, envy, slander, pride and folly. All except the general *dialogismoi*, machinations, and *ophthalmos ponêros*, 'the evil eye' signifying envy, are found in the Pauline lists of vices.

Tyre and Sidon. Tyre is not only Gentile territory but the inhabitants were particularly hostile to the Jews, a fact borne out by their imprisoning and killing many Jews at the outbreak of the Jewish war against the Romans in 66AD.[40]

Whether he was already in the pagan territory when the woman from that region 'came out' to him or whether she 'came out' of that region and met him in Galilee, the point is that she was a Canaanite. This is a more significant description of her than Mark's 'Syro-Phoenician' because it showed her to be one of a race traditionally seen as the pagan opponents of Israel.[41] Like the pagan slave girl in Philippi who later calls after Paul and his companions in the streets (Acts 16:16-18) this woman calls out to Jesus and calls after his disciples in public until his disciples ask him to send her away.

More striking still is her address, 'Lord, Son of David', as she called out to Jesus to have mercy / compassion, and begged him to cast the unclean spirit from her daughter: 'Lord' (*Kyrie*) is the address used by believers in approaching Jesus, and three times in the story the woman addresses Jesus as 'Lord'. 'Son of David' is a title central to the healing stories of the gospel, rooted in the genealogy and birth story of Jesus and heard on the lips of the various Jewish people coming to him for healing. Here it is on the lips of a Canaanite. She declares that her daughter 'is severely possessed', *kakôs daimonizetai*.

Though the story begins as a miracle story, a plea for help, a description of the possession suffered by the girl, it becomes a debate on the appropriateness of helping the Gentiles and thereby letting them into the arena of God's saving work.[42] Jesus at

40. Josephus, *Against Apion*, 1.13; *War* 2.478.
41. See J. Dewey, 'Jesus' Healings of Women: Conformity and Non-Conformity to Dominant Cultural Values and Clues for Historical Reconstruction', *BBT* 24 (1994), 122-31.
42. In Mark's account Jesus enters a house there, not wishing anyone to know, but he is unable to remain unnoticed. The text can be read on two levels. On one level Jesus crosses and is provoked into crossing, boundaries between Jew and Gentile and on another level there is the parallel experience of the Christian readers of the gospel. Boundary issues in Jesus' ministry foreshadow similar issues encountered by the first Christians.

first does not utter a word in response to her appeal and then the disciples ask him to 'dismiss her' because she is calling after them. What exactly is meant by 'dismiss her' (*apoluson autên*)? Does it mean 'send her away forthwith because she is a nuisance' or 'send her away with her request granted because she will continue to pester us till it is', or does it refer to the demon possessed daughter, meaning 'release her from the demon'? Jesus' response would imply that they expected him to grant her request and then she would go away, for he responded to their request saying: 'I have been sent only to the lost sheep of the House of Israel.' This refusal reflects Jesus' mission instruction to his apostles (Mt 10:6) and further emphasises his role as Messiah for the Jews.

The woman reacts immediately to his refusal in determined fashion with a pleading gesture of homage, *prosekunei*, manifesting the depth of her plea and her respect for and faith in the one she approached, saying: 'Lord, help me!' Jesus replied: 'It is not good to take the children's bread and throw it to the little dogs.' The term 'dogs' was often applied by the Jews to the non-believing, unclean Gentiles. The word used here is *kunaria*, a diminutive of *kuôn*, dog. It seems to mean 'pups', offspring of dogs, as distinct from the offspring of the householder. In the context of the story the children of the householder are the children of God, the Jews. 'Dog' was a pejorative term applied by some Jews to the Gentiles. In Jewish eyes dogs were unclean animals, and being touched by them was a contamination. In the Sermon on the Mount Jesus says 'Do not give to dogs what is holy '(Mt 7:6). Dogs had a very bad press and the term dog was very insulting when applied to persons with whom one disagreed. The 'dog language' here is symbolic of the deep chasm between Jew and Gentile. In the light of Jesus' recent controversy and discussion on 'clean and unclean' it is more than surprising to find him make such a remark. But the remark serves to reflect a general prejudice which will be successfully challenged in the reaction it provokes. There is no basis for trying to soften the remark by pointing to the fact that it is a diminutive term, 'little dogs', and possibly even an endearing term, as though someone would be less offended or feel less belittled by being considered 'a little dog' or 'a dear little dog' rather than a dog. Saying that Jesus said it with a smile or in a jocose or playful way, even if it is true, is not suggested by the text and there is no evidence for Jesus behaving in such a manner elsewhere in any of the gospels.

The narrator shocks the reader with this apparently racist, offensive remark on the lips of Jesus and thus prepares the reader for something dramatic or very significant to follow. What did Jesus mean by his remark about dogs? In her commentary on the parallel story in Mark's gospel, M. D. Hooker makes what seems to be the most apt comment: 'In its present context, the term is a challenge to the woman to justify her request.'[43]

Why would a Gentile come to a Jew for healing? Was it because she saw in him, for example, some magical power or exceptional natural healing power? Was it because of some level of religious faith in the God of Israel and in Jesus as God's prophet or envoy? Is it a recognition of the special role of the Jews in the history of God's dealings with humanity? If so, it is the exact point made by Jesus in John's gospel in his conversation with the Samaritan woman when he says: 'Salvation is from the Jews, but the hour is coming ... when the true worshippers will worship the Father in Spirit and in truth' (Jn 4:22f). Jesus is challenging the Canaanite woman to justify her request with some articulation of the faith that prompts her to come to a Jewish prophet-preacher and fall at his feet in a reverential gesture as she pleads with him to heal her daughter.

She responds with articulate confidence, again using the address 'Lord'. 'Yes, Lord. But the (little) dogs also feed on the crumbs that fall from their masters' table.' The direct address adds to the vividness of the story. Jesus' responds: 'O woman, great is your faith! Be it done for you as you desire', and her daughter was healed from that hour. She showed a level of appreciation for the gift of God that was absent in the critics of Jesus among his own people. This Gentile woman displays a

43. M. D. Hooker, *op. cit.*, 183.

level of faith akin to that on the part of the centurion when Jesus praised him saying: 'I have not found such great faith in Israel' (Mt 8:10). As in the case of the centurion's servant, the Canaanite woman's daughter is healed[44] at a distance.[45] In fact many of the miracles performed for Gentiles in the Bible are at a distance, symbolic of their coming 'from far away'. All these stories of Gentiles approaching Jesus helped subsequently to root the church's mission to the Gentiles in the ministry of Jesus.

Again the story is told with an eye to the Old Testament, specifically to the Elijah and Elisha cycle of stories. The story is reminiscent of the prophetic figures of Elijah or Elisha entering into dialogue and acceding to the request of the distraught and forthright mother. Elijah went to Zarephat, 'a Sidonian town' and miraculously fed the woman and her son. When the son died the woman challenged the prophet, and after performing the life-giving miracle he finally said 'your son lives' (1 Kings 17:8-24). Elisha raised the son of the Shunammite woman, a woman persistent like the Canaanite woman as she grasped the feet of the prophet to implore his help. This story also happens after a miraculous feeding by the prophet (2 Kings 4:18-37). These stories bring out the repeating pattern and consistency in God's plan of salvation for Jew and Gentile.

The form of the story is the usual miracle format with two differences. In the usual form a problem is presented, a request made, a response or reaction of Jesus is described, a healing or exorcism follows and then there is a reaction of amazement on the part of the onlookers. One difference here is the lack of response on the part of the onlookers. The other difference is Jesus' response, or perhaps more accurately, his reaction to the

---

44. The expression 'was healed' is a 'divine/theological' passive, a circumlocution for 'God healed her' in keeping with Jewish respect for the divine name.

45. Healing at a distance appears in both Jewish and Gentile traditions. The Talmud contains the story of the healing of the son of Rabban Gamaliel by Hanina ben Dosa (*b.Berakot* 34b) and Philostratus tells of a healing by Apollonius of Tyana in *Life of Apollonius* 3:38.

request and the exchange it provoked between himself and the woman.

The exchange between the woman and Jesus brings out the fact that although the Jews are the children (of God) the Gentiles also belong to the household of God, even if in a different capacity. She finds a role in the household for those regarded as outsiders and unclean, as the 'little dogs.' They can eat the crumbs from the masters' table.[46] They share one house. Together they constitute an overall domestic scene.[47]

The Canaanite, Gentile woman acknowledges who she is, who Jesus is and the priorities in the history of salvation with regard to Jews and Gentiles. Her story prepares for and reflects a debate about the relations of Jew and Gentile in the early church, very much in evidence in the letters of Paul and in the Acts of the Apostles.[48]

d. Healings along the Sea of Galilee Mt 15:29-31

Again the opening words of a pericope describing a change of location set the scene for a new initiative. Jesus goes from there to the Sea of Galilee and then up the mountain where he sat down. As already seen, the mountain is an example of symbolic geography in the gospels as it is throughout the whole Bible. On this occasion the mountain is the setting for the crowds coming for healing. They bring the lame, the crippled, the blind, the dumb and many others. They put them down at Jesus' feet and he healed them so that they were amazed to see the dumb speaking, the cripples healed, the lame walking and the blind seeing. They praised the God of Israel. 'Praising the God of

---

46. See the study by J-F Baudoz, *Les Miettes de la table. Étude synoptique et socio-religieuse de Mt 15:21-28 et Mc 7:24-30*, E.B.n.s. 27. Paris: Gabalda, 1995.

47. The rather domestic scene of throwing food to the little dogs under the table in the house stands out in contrast to the possible negative connotation of throwing food to dogs in the street.

48. Paul on his missionary journeys in Gentile territory explains his approach as 'to the Jew first, then to the Greek' though his mission to both was simultaneous (Acts 13:46). The priority was not chronological.

Israel' seems here to point to a Gentile presence among those giving praise. 'The crowd was amazed to see the dumb speaking, the cripples whole again, the lame walking and the blind seeing and they gave praise to the God of Israel.' This proclamation of Jesus' messianic potential in line with prophetic expectations comes on the lips of the Gentiles. It forms a striking contrast with the hostility he encountered on the part of the Jewish authorities and the disbelief of his family.

Matthew's cumulative picture of healings creates an overall effect and can be seen as a fulfilment of the prophecies of Isaiah (Isa 35:5-6; 29:18-19; 61:1-2). The reaction of the crowds mirrors the reaction of the crowds to the deeds of the Lord predicted by Isaiah: 'They will stand in awe of the God of Israel' (Isa 29:23). Jesus himself in the gospels of Matthew and Luke proclaims a similar sense of fulfilment. In replying to the Baptist's question, Jesus told his messengers: 'Go and tell John what you have heard and seen, the blind see again, the lame walk, the lepers are cleansed, the deaf hear, the dead are raised and the poor have the good news preached to them' (Mt 11:2-5/ / Lk 7:22).[49]

This final summary of the effects of the Galilean ministry reflects and brings to a climax and conclusion the summaries already contained in the narrative at Mt 4:23-25; 8:16-19; 9:35; 14:14. The crowd have been taught, fed and healed.

The first 'bread cycle' is now complete. It consisted of the multiplication of the loaves (which probably included Gentiles in the mainly Jewish multitude), the sea journey with the christophany and Peter's experience on the water. It contained the 'clean and unclean' dispute arising from the disciples eating with unwashed hands, the discussion with the Canaanite woman about the priority of the mission to the lost sheep of the House Israel and feeding the Gentile children, and concluded with the healings of Jews and Gentiles. The cycle has shown a definite movement of Jesus' ministry in the direction of the

---

49. Mt 11:2-5; Lk 7:22. The response of Jesus is a medley of allusions to Isaiah. Isa 26:19; 29:18f; 35:5f; 6:11; cf Lk 4:18-19 quoting Isa 61:1-2.

Gentiles, even though he emphasises the priority of his mission to the lost sheep of the house of Israel.

e. Feeding the Four Thousand Mt 15:32-39//Mk 8:1-9
The highly symbolic and significant action of Jesus in 'calling' his disciples to share his company, teaching and mission is again brought to mind as 'he calls his disciples to him' and tells them of his compassion for the crowds who have been with him now for three days and have nothing to eat, and how he is unwilling to send them away hungry lest they collapse on the way. He is calling them to share in his compassionate response to their plight.

The description of the crowd is a reminder of the crowd that gathered before the first miraculous feeding. On that occasion Jesus had compassion on the crowd because they were like sheep without a shepherd, and he healed their sick (Mt 14:13-14). However, on that occasion it was the disciples who drew Jesus' attention to the lateness of the hour and the need to let the crowd go to buy food. On that occasion also Jesus told the disciples to supply the food themselves (Mt 14:15-16). Here in the account of the second multiplication his compassion comes in his own words when he says: 'I have compassion on the crowd because they have been with me for three days and have nothing to eat. If I send them away hungry they will collapse on the way for many have come a great distance' (//Mk 8:1-3). The mention of three days is a pointer to the extent of his involvement in healing (and presumably teaching as well). The compassion of Jesus for this crowd is the dominant theme, a straightforward humanitarian concern. The question of the disciples: 'Where would anyone get enough bread in a deserted place for so great a crowd?' resonates with the desperation seen in the accounts of Moses' wondering how to feed the people in the wilderness. The reader remembers the desperation in Moses' questions to the Lord in the desert: 'Where am I to get meat to give all these people?' and 'If all the flocks and herds were slaughtered would that be enough for them? If all the fish in the sea were gathered (LXX *synagein*) would that be enough for them (Num 11:1-3, 13, 22)?' This same theme is reflected in the psalm: 'They even spoke against God. They said, "Is it possible for God to prepare a table in the desert?" '(Ps 78:19)

Jesus asks them: 'How many loaves have you?' They answer seven, and a few small fish. The numbers of loaves and of baskets of fragments are different from the first feeding and their use here highlights again the importance of symbolic numbers in biblical narratives. Seven, the number of loaves and of baskets of food left over, is a number very much associated with the Gentiles and the broader world. It is the number of commandments in the Noachic covenant with all humanity before the call of Abraham (Gen 9:4-7), the number of the pagan nations of Canaan (Deut 7:1; Acts 13:19), the number of Hellenists chosen as deacons (lit. 'to serve') (Acts 6:3) and the number of churches in Revelation (Rev 2-3). The number 4000 is probably a combination of the use of 'four' and 'thousands'. Since there was no word in the Hebrew vocabulary for 'infinity', 'thousands' tended to be used for huge numbers. The multiple four was probably intended to reflect the four points of the compass, the four winds, the four corners of the universe, from which the Gentiles were gathering, so 'four thousand' signifies a vast number of Gentiles from all directions. The mention of 'collapsing on the way' may well refer to the long distance they have come and shows the expansion of Jesus' reputation and ministry among the Gentiles. 'Coming from afar' is a recurring theme in the Old Testament used for the Gentiles who come to learn about, and worship, the God of Israel,[50] a theme that comes to the fore in the New Testament in the coming of the Magi (Mt 2:2,12), the coming of the Greeks (Jn 12:20f) and the gathering of all the peoples at Pentecost (Acts 2:39).

The words and deeds of the Eucharistic 'ritual' are reflected here as in the first feeding. *Taking the bread, breaking the bread* and *distributing it* are common to all multiplication accounts. There

---

50. Josh 9:6,9; Isa 2:1-4; 60:2-22; 40:4; Mic 4:1-3; Ps 72:10f; Mt 2:2; Jn 12:20f; cf also Acts 22:21; Eph 2:12,17.

are two traditions of the prayer over the bread (and fish). The first feeding in Matthew and Mark and the one feeding in Luke say 'having looked up to heaven he said the blessing' (Mt 14:19; Mk 6:41; Lk 9:16), reflecting the Hebrew *berekah*, as the prayer over the bread. This corresponds to the 'institution' of the Eucharist narratives at the Last Supper where *eulogêsas*, 'having said the blessing' is the description of the prayer in Matthew and Mark (Mt 26:26; Mk 14:22). In the second multiplication account the term *eucharistêsas*, 'having given thanks' is used for the prayer over the bread (Mt 15:36//Mk 8:6). Luke and Paul use *eucharistêsas* in their accounts of the institution of the Eucharist (Lk 22:19; 1 Cor 11:24). It was probably more in keeping with Greco-Roman or Hellenistic Jewish vocabulary.

They ate as much as they wanted ('they were satisfied'), as after the first feeding, but here there is a heightened awareness of their having been well fed because of the emphasis at the beginning of the account on their hunger and the danger of their collapsing on their way home without food. Now Jesus has fed both Jew and Gentile, a significant follow up to the challenge of the Canaanite woman's comment on the need to feed not only the children of the household but also the 'little dogs' under the table (also part of the household).

Jesus is the one who brings the Messianic/Eucharistic Banquet to Jew and Gentile alike, as he demonstrates and foreshadows in the feeding of both multitudes. This will be very important for Matthew's readers in the early church as they struggle with the questions that arise about sharing the table with Jew and Gentile, as seen both in Acts and the letters of Paul (Acts 10-11; 15; Gal 2:11-21).

The Sea Crossing Mt 15:39//Mk 8:10

After both multiplication accounts in Mark and Matthew, and the account in John, when the crowd are dismissed and disperse there follows a sea crossing. Here Jesus crosses to 'the region of Magadan'. Mark says he crossed to 'the region of Dalmanutha.' Both are references to unidentified placenames about which scholars have made various suggestions of a textual, translation, transliteration and geographical nature. Change of location is a standard literary device for ending an episode, and a sea crossing is a standard ending for a miraculous feeding story, so no further meaning need be attached to the crossing at this point.

f. The Pharisees and Sadducees seek a Sign Mt 16:1-12//Mk 8:11-13; cf Lk 11:16, 29; 12:1, 54-56

The Pharisees and Sadducees came and set about testing him, seeking from him a sign from heaven. The critical attitude of the Pharisees has already been in evidence many times in the gospel. Here the Pharisees are joined by another major section of official Israel, the Sadducees[51] with whom they have already been associated in this gospel in the context of the baptism of John, when he called them 'a brood of vipers' (Mt 3:7-8). They emerge at this point in the narrative for a brief encounter because Matthew is painting a clear, stark picture of the united forces of official Israel, which were negatively questioning and testing Jesus. The brief appearance at this point of such an unlikely alliance is Matthew's way of showing the broad spectrum of official opposition to Jesus and providing the setting for Jesus to 'leave them and depart', a definitive moment in his rejection of the leadership in Israel (Mt 16:4). It also provides a cue for Jesus' warning about the leaven of the Pharisees and the Sadducees.

Already some scribes and Pharisees had sought a sign from him and Jesus responded that 'an evil and adulterous generation was demanding a sign and no sign would be given except the sign of Jonah the prophet' (Mt 12:38-42). Again Jesus repeats his former response to a similar request for a sign with the remark that an evil and adulterous generation are seeking a sign but no sign will be given except the sign of Jonah. A number of early manuscripts do not contain verses 2-3 in which Jesus comments on their ability to predict the weather from the appear-

---

51. The Sadducees' focus of attention was on their power and position arising from their association with the religious, civil and economic powers.

ance of the sky in the evening or morning, but fail to read the signs of the times. These verses, which were possibly interpolated here into Matthew, reflect closely Jesus' criticism of the crowds in Lk 12:54-56.

In seeking a sign from heaven, *sêmeion ek tou ouranou*, the Pharisees and Sadducees may appear to be in line with the tradition of Old Testament prophets producing their authenticating signs but, as seen already in relation to the Pharisees' former request for a sign (Mt 12:38-42), the seeking of signs is indicative of a negative and unbelieving attitude in all gospel traditions. They have failed to read the signs of the very significant happenings taking place as the kingdom is being inaugurated. They have not been open to what is taking place. This point is very clearly brought out in the interpolated verses. In fact they saw his mighty deeds and said they were done through the power of Beelzebul.

Jesus is not now going to jump to their command and perform to their requirements. Very deliberately at this point he leaves his critical questioners standing there and walks away. This is a very significant turning point in the narrative. It is a climactic moment when Jesus 'leaves them', a definitive rejection and a further milestone in the narrative and in his ministry. Placing this encounter with the Pharisees and Sadducees at this point provides the cue for Jesus' warning to the disciples about the leaven of the Pharisees and Sadducees.

His outright criticism and turning from the 'official' teaching authority in Israel will now be followed by his laying down the foundations of a new authority for a renewed community, a faithful remnant.

g. The Pivot of the Gospel Mt 16:5-20

> i. The Leaven of the Pharisees and the Sadducees Mt 16:5-12
> / /Mk 8:14-21/ /Lk 12:1

The theme of bread continues. The narrator tells us that the disciples having crossed to the other shore had forgotten to take any loaves (*artous*) with them.[52] Jesus said to them: 'Watch out, beware of the leaven of the Pharisees and the Sadducees!' Matthew joins this warning to the disciples to beware of the leaven of the Pharisees and the Sadducees very closely to Jesus' distancing himself from official Israel.

The disciples discussed (his warning) among themselves saying: 'It is because we have brought no bread.' Jesus responded: 'You men of little faith, why do you discuss among yourselves the fact that you have no bread?' His address 'men of little faith' and his rhetorical question 'Do you not yet understand?' are followed by his reminding them of the multiplication of the loaves. 'Do you not remember the five loaves for the five thousand and how many basketfuls you took up and the seven loaves among the four thousand and how many basketfuls you took up?' Then he asked them how they failed to understand that he did not speak simply about bread (when he said to beware of the leaven of the Pharisees and the Sadducees). Jesus is here less severe in his criticism of the disciples' failure to understand than in Mark's account.[53]

Matthew is following the same narrative outline as Mark, but whereas Mark at this point tells the story in order to criticise the disciples very severely about their obtuseness and lack of understanding (Mk 8:14-21), Matthew, on the other hand, reports the

---

52. Mark changes this traditional story of their forgetting to take bread along into a story about taking only one loaf, and then he develops the one loaf theme giving it both a christological and eucharistic interpretation.

53. In Mark Jesus goes on to say: 'Do you not grasp or understand what has happened, is your heart still hardened? Having eyes do you not see, having ears do you not hear? Do you not remember? Do you still not understand?' The 'hardness of heart' was already used by Mark to describe their lack of understanding after the first multiplication in Mk 6:52.

criticism of the disciples in a much milder tone and uses the story primarily to launch a scathing attack on the 'leaven of the Pharisees and the Sadducees', repeating the term ' leaven of the Pharisees and Sadducees' three times in the story. As he repeats his warning about the leaven of the Pharisees and the Sadducees the disciples come to understand that Jesus was speaking not about actual leaven but metaphorically about the teaching of the Pharisees and Sadducees.

The metaphors of bread and banquets were regularly used in the bible for Torah, Wisdom and the Word of the Lord. The metaphor of leaven, the essential ingredient in making bread, is here applied metaphorically to the process of learning and teaching and used as a critique of the Pharisees and Sadducees. It carries a double meaning full of irony. As noted already, leaven is an essential ingredient in making bread, but in fact it is in itself a corrupting agent in the fermentation process. It causes the bread to rise and expand. It does so, however, by a decaying process during fermentation, which adulterates the pure flour and eventually causes the bread to become stale and mouldy and thereby unhealthy and unpalatable if not eaten soon after baking. St Paul used leaven as a metaphor for a morally corrupting influence or agent (1 Cor 5:6-8; Gal 5:9) and in so doing was in line with Greco-Roman writers like Plutarch and Perseus.[54]

What is the leaven in question?[55] Matthew makes it quite clear that the leaven of the Pharisees and Sadducees is their teaching. This is in keeping with his overriding concern about teaching and his portrayal of Jesus as the teacher *par excellence*. Matthew has Pharisees and Sadducees in this scene because both groups were involved in teaching, unlike Mark who has Pharisees and Herod in the scene. The emphasis throughout on listening to the teaching of Jesus and the clash between his teaching and that of his opponents leads the readers to under-

---

54. Plutarch, *Quaestiones Romanae,109* and Perseus, *Satires* ,1.24.
55. Mark mentions the leaven of the Pharisees and of Herod but Matthew focuses on the leaven of the Pharisees and of the Sadducees (Mt 16:12), since Herod was not involved in teaching.

stand the leaven of the Pharisees and Sadducees as the mindset
by which their teaching is processed, whereby good teaching is
allowed to grow stale, unpalatable and lacking in nourishment,
resulting in a feeling of threat from anything new and challenging. From this there springs their questioning attitude and outright hostility towards Jesus, their failure to understand him and
their demanding a sign from heaven when he has the nerve to
challenge their teaching. Their leaven does not produce good
bread that nourishes life and supports healthy action.

ii. Peter's Confession of Faith Mt 16:13-16//Mk 8:27-30//Lk 9:18-21; cf Jn 6:67-71

The setting of Peter's profession of faith is Caesarea Philippi,
the most northerly point in the Holy Land near the source of the
Jordan close to Mount Hermon. An ancient city Paneas (modern
Banyas) was replaced on the site by the Roman city, which was
called after its founder the tetrarch Philip, and dedicated to
Caesar, hence the name Caesarea Philippi. From this most distant point in the land, Jesus from now on will be making his way
to Jerusalem, a way punctuated by predictions of the rejection,
passion, death and resurrection awaiting him there. In the context of his passion, death and resurrection he will refer to himself in terms of the Son of Man (a term he will also use in the context of his second coming in glory at the judgement).

Jesus asked his disciples: 'Who do men/people say the Son
of Man is?'[56] In the corresponding passage in Mark Jesus uses 'I'
rather than 'the Son of Man'. There may be a word play in
Matthew's use of *anthrôpoi* (men) and *huios tou anthrôpou* (Son of
Man) as though to ask: 'What do ordinary men, mere mortals,
think of this extraordinary or enigmatic figure, the Son of Man?'
In using the title Son of Man Matthew is certainly adding a tone
of solemnity and focusing attention on this figure who has already been described as one who has nowhere to lay his head
(Mt 8:20), has power on earth to forgive sins (Mt 9:6), is greater

---

56. Mark and Luke say: 'Who do people say that I am and who do you
say that I am?'(Mk 8:27).

than the Sabbath (Mt 12:8), will come at the *parousia* (Mt 10:23), the sower of the good seed who will send his angels to collect out of his kingdom all causes of sin and all evildoers and to throw them into the furnace of fire, where there will be weeping and gnashing of teeth (Mt 13:37-43).

In asking the question about the Son of Man, Jesus is not only seeking 'feedback' on the reaction of the people to his ministry to date and to his sayings about the Son of Man, but he is also preparing the disciples, and the reader, for his forthcoming teaching about the Son of Man as the one who serves, offers his life as a ransom for many, endures the Passion and comes in glory with his kingdom.

Jesus' question and Peter's response will bring together the Son of Man and Son of God titles and associate them with the role and title of the Messiah (Christ). Jesus' response to Peter's christological confession will then illustrate how the christology of the gospel underpins its ecclesiology.

The response of the disciples throws light on the general discussion among the people about Jesus' identity and role. In doing so it reflects some of the messianic expectations current at the time.[57] 'Some say John the Baptist, some say Elijah and others say Jeremiah or one of the prophets' (Mt 16:14). The speculation that Jesus was John the Baptist risen from the dead was already reported in the worried deliberations of Herod Antipas who thought John may have risen and that was why miraculous powers were at work in him (Mt 14:1-2). This popular speculation was probably prompted by John's widespread appeal and by the popular revulsion at the violent cutting short of his fiery mission which resembled, even in his dress and appearance, that of the equally fiery Elijah whose return was expected to usher in the time of the Messiah, the Day of the Lord or the ap-

---

57. The synoptic accounts at this point are somewhat similar to the opinions articulated in St John's gospel by the messengers sent by the Jerusalem authorities to question John the Baptist: 'Are you the Christ … Elijah … the Prophet?' Though the exactness of the Johannine formula, especially in relation to 'the Prophet' is not seen here in Matthew, the multifaceted nature of the expectation is in evidence.

pearance of the apocalyptic lamb (Mal 3:1, 4, 5; 3:23f; Enoch 90:31; 89:52). He would turn the hearts of fathers towards their children and restore the tribes of Jacob (Sir 48:10f; cf Lk 1:17). The New Testament in fact presents the mission of John the Baptist in terms of the return of the spirit of Elijah (Mt 17:9-13; Lk 1:17; cf Mk 9:13; 1:4-8).

Only Matthew mentions Jeremiah in this context. He was the model of the rejected, suffering prophet, who himself fell foul of authority because of his criticism of the temple, its rituals and its administration. Matthew has a particular interest in Jeremiah and sees him as a model or prototype of Jesus. He actually names him in three texts, first in relation to the mourning of Rachel, then in the opinion of the crowd about the Son of Man and finally in a comment on the thirty pieces of silver (Mt 2:17; 16:14; 27:9). He alludes to the Book of Jeremiah several times, to his dealing with false prophets, with the prophet's appeal to the people and with the city that murders the prophets (Mt 7:15-23; 11:28-30; 23:37-39). A Jeremiah style tone is heard throughout the criticism of the temple and of the authorities. The condemnation of the commercialism of the temple is stated in a phrase from Jeremiah, 'the robbers' den' (Mt 21:13; Jer 7:11). The story of Jeremiah is largely reflected through Jesus' action in the temple and the criticism and lethal hostility it provokes. Finally, the people's reference to 'one of the prophets' may be a reflection of different expectations about prophetic figures such as Malachi, or it may be a loose understanding of the promised 'prophet like Moses' (Deut 18:15-18).

This unclear vision, manifest in the responses to Jesus' question: 'Who do people say that the Son of Man is?' shows positive, but inadequate and somewhat confused understandings of Jesus and his mission on the part of the people at large. Now Jesus directs the question to his disciples, those who have been closely associated with him in public and private, who have witnessed his works and heard his public and private teachings. 'But *you*, who do *you* say that I am?' Jesus' question could be paraphrased: 'In the light of what has gone on to date in the ministry, you who have been chosen to be with me and have been sent out to represent me, you who have heard my public and private teaching and seen my works, you who should be 'on the inside', who do you say that I am?' The reader or listener to the gospel knows that this is the central question directed to disciples of Jesus in all ages. Interestingly, in the first question about the opinion of the people Jesus refers to himself as 'the Son of Man' and in the question addressed to the disciples he refers to himself simply as 'I'. The wording of the questions thus identifies Jesus explicitly as the Son of Man already referred to in the gospel.

Simon Peter replies: 'You are the Christ, the Son of the living God' (Mt 16:16). As in the parallel passages in Mark and Luke, and in a similar situation in John, it is Peter who answers on behalf of the disciples, confessing belief in Jesus' special identity and role. In Mark Peter says: 'You are the Christ' (Mk 8:29). In Luke he says: 'You are the Christ of God' (Lk 9:20). In John, when the followers were leaving Jesus because of his 'hard saying' about his body and blood, Simon Peter said on behalf of the other disciples: 'Lord, to whom shall we go? You have the message of eternal life and we believe; we know that you are the Holy One of God' (Jn 6:68-69).

Matthew renders Peter's response in terms of the double profession acknowledging Jesus both as Christ/Messiah and Son of the living God (cf Jn 20:31; Mk 1:1).[58] The language is solemn, liturgical and in keeping with customary prayer formulae with reference to 'the living God', that is, the God who is life, gives and sustains life here and promises eternal life in the hereafter. The term 'the living God' will next be heard on the lips of the High Priest Caiaphas as he interrogates Jesus during his trial (Mt 26:63).

Jesus has already been implicitly designated 'Son of God' in the birth story (Mt 1:18-25) and explicitly so designated by the citation from Hosea relating to the sojourn and return from

---

58. In Mark Jesus is not acknowledged as Son of God by a human being until the confession of the centurion at the crucifixion when he saw how Jesus died (Mk 15:39).

Egypt (Mt 2:15) and by the voice from heaven at the Baptism (Mt 3:17). He was addressed as 'Son of God' by Satan during the temptations in the desert (Mt 4:3, 6), by the Gadarene demoniacs (Mt 8:29) and by the disciples in the boat after they experienced his coming to them over the water and his saving the sinking Peter (Mt 14:33). Peter's confession now gives the title a solemn, liturgical tone with the reference to 'the living God'. The title Christ/Messiah has already been used in the title/superscription of the gospel (Mt 1:1), in the Infancy Narrative at the end of the genealogy, in the summary of the generations and in the opening of the birth story (Mt 1:17, 18, 19). Peter now joins it to the Son of God title and does so in close association with Jesus' question about the Son of Man. The three main titles are thereby brought together here at the pivotal point in the gospel.

iii. Jesus' Triple Response Mt 16:17-20 cf Jn 21:15-18

Jesus makes a triple response to Simon Peter, each response being itself a triple statement. The first line of each response is followed by antithetical parallel statements, one negative and one positive or as a pair of opposites (binding and loosing), the second line bringing out the meaning of the first. The responses are respectively a beatitude, a conferring of a title and a granting of authority. There is a certain parallel to the Johannine post resurrection scene at the lakeside when Jesus tells Peter three times to feed his lambs and feed his sheep in response to Peter's triple protestation of his love (Jn 21:15-17).

a The Beatitude:
Blessed are you Simon, bar Jonah
because flesh and blood did not reveal this to you
but my Father in Heaven (has revealed it).

b. The Title
I say to you: 'You are Peter (*Kephas, Kephâ*)
on this rock I will build my church
the gates of Hades will not prevail against it

c. The Authority

I will give to yoú the keys of the kingdom of heaven
   whatever you bind on earth will be bound in heaven
   whatever you loose on earth will be loosed in heaven

The Beatitude

Jesus proclaims that Peter is blessed because 'flesh and blood' (a mere mortal) has not revealed the content of his confession of faith. He has not arrived at this faith by human perception, reasoning or argumentation, but by way of a gift of God, a revelation by 'my Father in heaven'.[59] This is a corollary to what was already on Jesus' lips: 'No one knows the Son but the Father and no one knows the Father but the Son and those to whom the Son chooses to reveal him'(Mt 11:27). Again the closeness to the Johannine theology is striking (cf Jn 1:18; 3:35-36; 10:15; 17:25-26).

The Title

Jesus follows through on the beatitude with the conferring of a title and a role on Peter. He tells Simon Peter, 'You are Rock.' Conferring a name can signify the recognition of personality, character or achievement and/or signify the giving of a new task, and purpose, resulting in a new relationship.[60]

Jesus addresses Peter as ' Simon bar Jonah', that is in Aramaic 'Simon, son of Jonah', a version of the name John which is the name actually used in John's gospel where he is called 'Simon, son of John' (Jn 1:42, 21:15). Matthew (like John) refers to Peter as 'Simon Peter' when Jesus calls him to discipleship (Mt 4:18; cf Jn 1:39-42), when he commissions him as an apostle (Mt 10:2) and when Peter professes his faith in Jesus as Messiah, Son of the living God (Mt 16:16). In the Johannine tradition he is called 'Simon Peter' when he professes his faith in Jesus as the Holy One of God (Jn 6:68-69). Though already called Peter in the gospel at his

---

59. Matthew's favourite way of referring to the Father.
60. Abram and Sarai became Abraham and Sarah when Abraham was told he would be father of many nations and that in his name all nations would be blessed (Gen 17:3-5,15-16).

call to discipleship (Mt 4:18) and at the appointment of the
Twelve (Mt 10:2), the formal conferring on Simon of the name
'Peter' (*Kephâ*/ Rock, cf Gal 2:7-8), a name not otherwise known
in Palestine at the time, is described here as Jesus responds to
Peter's confession with a reciprocal statement about Peter. This
conferring of the name is anticipated at an earlier stage in the
ministry in John's gospel when Andrew, Simon's brother, who
declares he has found the Christ (Messiah), brings him to Jesus
and Jesus looked hard at him and said: 'You are Simon, son of
John, you are to be called *Kephâ*, (*Kephas*) meaning Rock' (Jn 1:39-
42). There appears to be a common underlying Petrine source/
tradition deeply rooted in the Aramaic substratum of the gospels
of Matthew and John. J. P. Meier remarks:

> The M-material in vv. 17-19 is probably not a creation of Mt.
> Many of its phrases reflect an Aramaic background, and the
> play on Simon's new title is directly intelligible only in
> Aramaic.[61]

Calling him 'rock' and saying he will build his *ekklêsia* 'on
this rock' is very significant in the light of the use of the term in
the Old Testament. In the military history of Palestine the pre-
cipitous crags in the mountainous areas were extremely important for establishing a position against attack. The metaphors
'rock of Israel', 'rock of refuge', 'rock of deliverance' and other
similar titles were applied to *YHWH* (2 Sam 22:3; 23:3; Isa 17:10;
30:29; Deut 32:15, 37; Pss 18:3; 62:3, 7, 8; 89:27; 94:22; 95:1 *et al*).
YHWH is the rock who bore Israel (Deut 32:18). The metaphor
was also applied to Abraham and Sarah who are described as
the quarry and rock from which the people were hewn:
'Consider the rock from which you were hewn, the quarry from
which you were cut/Consider Abraham your father and Sarah
who gave you birth' (Isa 51:1-2). Related to the metaphor of the
rock are the metaphors of the cornerstone, the keystone and the
pillars (Eph 2:2:20; 1 Pet 2:4-5), the stone rejected by the builders
(Mt 21:42//Mk 12:10-11//Lk 20:17; cf Ps 118:22-23), the stone

---

61. J. P. Meier, *Matthew*, 179.

that crushes (Lk 20:18) and the rock on which the wise man builds a house which withstands the onslaught of rain, floods and gales (Mt 7:24-25). Here the rock imagery is applied to Simon Peter as he is conferred with the title/name 'Rock'. On this rock Jesus will build his church. Like a new Abraham he will be the new patriarch of Jesus' *ekklêsia*.

Now Simon Peter, Rock, will be the rock on which Jesus, the Christ, Son of the living God will build his church, his community, his *ekklêsia* (a term repeated in the community discourse at Mt 18:17). As he says 'On this rock I will build my church' (*ekklêsia*) the reader senses the note of distance from or opposition to the community with which he is in conflict. Together with the authority he bestows, Jesus guarantees protection against and victory over 'the gates of Hades' (the power of death/the underworld/hell).[62] The footnote in the Jerusalem Bible explains very well the meaning of such protection from the gates of Hades. Explaining that Hades is the Greek translation of the Hebrew *Sheol*, the dwelling place of the dead, the note goes on to say:

> Here its personified 'gates' suggest the powers of evil, which first lead man into that death which is sin and then imprison him once for all in eternal death. The church's task will be to rescue the elect from death's dominion, from the death of the body and above all from eternal death, so that it may lead them into the kingdom of heaven ... In this the church follows its Master who died, descended into the underworld ... and rose again.[63]

The authority

Jesus then presents 'the keys of the kingdom' to Peter. Having distanced himself from the authorities in Israel, he now

---

62. Some commentators point out that the expression 'gates of Hades' is non-Semitic and draw the conclusion that it points to a late origin of the entire saying. This overlooks the fact that Matthew may well be editing an earlier more Semitic expression for his Gentile and Diaspora Jewish members. Furthermore, the gospel of Matthew tends to omit or avoid Semitic terms.

63. Footnote to Mt 16:18 in the 1966 edition of the Jerusalem Bible.

confers authority on Peter.[64] He is given the keys of the kingdom and told that what he binds on earth will be bound in heaven and what he looses on earth will be loosed in heaven. The striking imagery replicates an incident in the Book of Isaiah where the oracle of the Lord is pronounced against the major-domo Shebna who was dismissed from his post in Hezekiah's palace and Eliakim son of Hilkiah put in his place. 'Thus says the Lord ... I will commit your authority to his hand ... and I will place the key of the house of David on his shoulder' (Isa 22:15, 21-22). To signify his supreme control over the palace he was told that he 'would open and no one would shut, and shut and no one would open' (Isa 22:22). He would hold his office and authority with security: 'I will drive him like a peg into a firm place' (Isa 22:23). This incident is the background providing the imagery for the parallel statement signifying complete authority. There is a similar parallel statement in John's gospel where the apostles are given the Holy Spirit and told, 'whose sins you shall forgive, they are forgiven; whose sins you shall retain, they are retained' (Jn 20:23). The terms binding and loosing are used in rabbinic literature to cover several functions, including the authority to determine membership, to impose or lift excommunication, to impose rules and sanctions, to grant exemptions, and even to confer the power of exorcism.[65] The same power 'to bind and loose' is given to the community itself for the purpose of accepting or excluding from membership of the community (Mt 18:18). The promise is that God ('in heaven') will ratify the decision made or the stand taken on earth. In the case of Peter it is a mandate relating to 'my church', the overall or universal community whereas in Mt 18:18 it refers to the ' local' community.

In the imagery of the keys Peter is given charge of the 'palace', as *major domo* or prime minister. The palace is the com-

---

64. Speaking of that authority as *magisterium* (literally, teaching authority) at this point anticipates the command to teach in Mt 28:20 and can be seen as a counter to the leaven (the teaching) of the Pharisees and Sadducees.

65. D. Senior, *Matthew*, 191-2. D. J. Harrington, *The Gospel of Matthew*, 248.

munity among whom the kingdom is taking root as they await the *parousia* and the final gathering of the elect. The opening and closing of doors is a widely used image in the New Testament. The wise virgins/bridesmaids enter the marriage feast (a metaphor used for the kingdom and the eschatological banquet in the kingdom), but the foolish ones find the door shut on them (Mt 25:10-11). The Sermon on the Mount issued the warning about entering the kingdom saying that it is not those who say 'Lord, Lord' will enter (Mt 7:21-23) and the 'woes' against the scribes and Pharisees condemns them because they shut (the door to) the kingdom in people's faces, neither going in themselves nor allowing others to go in (Mt 23:13). In a similar 'woe' Luke states that the lawyers have taken away the key of knowledge and block people from entering (Lk 11:52). Peter has the keys, and the responsibility of opening and closing that goes with them.

A Note on the Reception of the Petrine Texts (Wirkungsgeschichte)
Throughout the history of Christianity generations have looked to these Petrine texts through the lens of their own theology and experience.[66] They have become therefore very important for a study of Reception Criticism since they have been central to inter-Christian debate, both ecumenical and polemical.[67]

U. Luz gives a summary of four main lines of interpretation.[68] They are the Typical, the Eastern, the Augustinian and the Papal. All four capture an important dimension of the texts. In the Patristic writings Origen saw Peter as a type, the prototype of the pneumatic human being who 'comprehended the building of the church in himself, effected by the word, and thus gained strength' (*Contra Celsum* 6.77). He saw faith as the rock

---

66. For a study of the Petrine Office in the church see Hans Urs von Balthasar, *The Office of Peter in the Church*, San Francisco: Ignatius Press, 1989.
67. See for example, the study by J. A. Burgess, *A History of the Exegesis of Matthew 16: 17-19 from 1781 to 1965*, Ann Arbor: Edwards, 1976.
68. U. Luz, 'The Primacy Saying of Matthew 16:17-19 from the Perspective of Its Effective History', in U. Luz, *Studies in Matthew*, Grand Rapids: Eerdmans, 2005, 165-182, esp 168-172.

on which the spiritual person is founded. This arises from the fact that the rock saying follows from a beatitude in praise of Peter's faith. This is the 'typical' interpretation. Tertullian saw Peter as the guarantor of genuine and public apostolic tradition (*De praescriptione haereticorum*, 22.4f). This became the dominant understanding in the Greek and Syrian churches and so it is referred to as the Eastern interpretation. The Augustinian interpretation is christological in the sense that it sees Jesus as the rock and Peter standing on that rock (*In Johannem* 124.5; *Retractiones* 1.20.2).[69] The Papal interpretation focuses on the link between the primacy of Peter and the ongoing apostolic succession and juristic interpretation of Peter's primacy.

Already in the early church, as reflected in the Acts of the Apostles, there appears to have been an emerging understanding of apostolic tradition and continuity of apostolic office. The prominent role of Peter subsequent to the earthly life of Jesus (Acts 1:13, 15; 2:14-36, 37; 3:1, 3, 5, 11, 12-26; 4:1-12, 13, 19; 5:3, 9, 15; 8:15, 20; 9:32-35; 36-43; 10:3-48; 11:1-18; 12:1-19; 15:5-12) and the concern to fill the number of the 'college' of apostles after the departure of Judas (Acts 1:15-26) point to an understanding already present of a necessary continuation of the roles established during Jesus' life and ministry.

The interpretation of the Petrine texts has been particularly polarised since the 'Protestant' and 'Catholic' or 'Counter' Reformations in the sixteenth century. The 'Protestant' emphasis on *sola scriptura* (already in vogue since the middle ages in some religious movements) led to a denial of the papal claim to a hereditary role for Peter's successors since it was not explicitly stated in the text. The Reformers did not develop their own interpretation of Mt 16:18 but handed on the traditional Augustinian and Eastern readings, giving them an at times antipapal emphasis.[70] The Catholic position emphasised a primacy of honour and

---

69. For further discussion on the Patristic approach see Henri de Lubac, *The Motherhood of the Church*, San Francisco, Ignatius Press 1982, in particular Part II, 275-335.
70. U. Luz, *op. cit.*, 171.

leadership (in vogue since the early centuries of the church) and of jurisdiction in the universal church (already in vogue since the days of Hildebrand, Pope Gregory VII in the eleventh century). Since the Counter-Reformation the *papal* interpretation has been supported with reference to the keys in Mt 16:19. U. Luz quotes an example from Cornelius a Lapide: 'Keys are the attribute of kings and rulers, not of teachers or preachers.'[71] However, it must be said that Luke's reference to the key of knowledge (i.e. teaching) and the importance of the teachers who hold it (Lk 11:52) would argue against, or a least add a further important dimension to this comment of Cornelius a Lapide.

Catholic theology maintains that doctrine and practice develop within the tradition under the guidance of the Holy Spirit the Paraclete, as promised in St John's gospel (Jn 14:16-17, 25-26; 16:13-15) which teaches that the Spirit leads the church into further and deeper understanding of Jesus, his actions and his teaching. This understanding is stated clearly in the teaching of Vatican II: 'This tradition which comes from the apostles develops in the church with the help of the Holy Spirit.'[72] In this regard one sees the Petrine texts in Matthew as seminal and their implication has grown in the living experience and tradition of the church. They are an important dimension of a broader tradition of New Testament Petrine texts with which they should be studied when there is discussion on their implication for the life of the church.[73]

U. Luz points out how this Catholic understanding is in fact in keeping with the hermeneutical principles of Hans-Georg Gadamer who says that 'understanding is always a productive activity, never simply reproductive, and that if we understand at all we understand "in a different way".' For Gadamer the temporal gulf between text and interpreter is not a 'gulf to be

---

71. *Commentarius in quattuor Evangelia. Argumentum in S. Mattaeum,* Antwerp: Jacobus Meursius, 1670, p 319, quoted by Luz, ibid., 168.
72. *Dei Verbum,* II, 8. cf Vatican I, 'Dogmatic Constitution on the Catholic Faith, Chapter 4,'On Faith and Reason' (Denziger 1800).
73. See, for example, G. Claudel, *La confession de Pierre, trajectoire d'une péricope évangelique,* Paris: Gabalda, 1988.

bridged' but the productive factor, which makes different understanding and new understanding possible.[74] For Catholics that distance in time and culture is not a gulf but a living tradition under the influence of the Spirit who leads the church into deeper understanding (Jn 14:16-17, 25-26; 16:13-15). The understanding of the Petrine texts over the centuries is an example of such new and developing understanding.

Sadly, the Reformation resulted in a polarisation of interpretations and the post-reformation positions (and polemics) were rigidly adhered to until the second half of the twentieth century when a significant amount of ecumenical study was carried out on the texts and their interpretations, and a significant amount of consensus achieved.[75]

Command to Silence Mt 16:20

Following his response to Peter Jesus warns the disciples not to tell anyone that he is the Christ/Messiah (Mt 16:20). This injunction is recorded also in Mk 8:30 and Luke 9:21. The obvious reason is that there were all kinds of wrong understandings and expectations about the role of the Messiah as a political and apocalyptic figure and social activist. This was especially true of the very nationalistic element of the crowd (and possibly true also of some of the disciples, e.g. Simon Zealot whose name may indicate a political outlook and/or former affiliation). The Messiah is about to be shown in a very different light as the serving and suffering Son of Man. Furthermore encouragement of such wrong expectations could lead to political or social disturbances drawing down the wrath of Roman authority with disastrous consequences not only for Jesus' ministry but for the ordinary people who might be led into activity for which they would pay dearly.

---

74. Hans-Georg Gadamer, *Truth and Method*, New York: Seabury, 1975, 264f.

75. See the ecumenical discussion in R. Brown, K. P. Donfried and J. Reumann, *Peter in the New Testament*, Minneapolis, Augsburg, 1973 and O. Cullman, *Peter, Disciple, Apostle Martyr: A Historical Study*, English trs SCM, 1966; Joseph Ludwig, *Die Primatworte Mt 16:18,19 in der altkirchlichen Exegese*, NTA, 19.4, Münster: Aschendorff, 1952, 61-70.

a. First Prediction of the Passion Mt 16:21-23//Mk 8:31-33//Lk 9:22
'From that time', *apo tote*, is a telling expression. It could be paraphrased, 'From that important point onwards'. It signifies the
time when he 'left the official representatives of Israel and went
away' followed by the time when Peter, on behalf of the disciples, recognised Jesus' messianic role and special relation to God
as 'Son of the living God' and the time when he in turn conferred
a special title, role and authority on Peter.

J. D. Kingsbury draws attention to the fact that the phrase
'From that time Jesus began to ...' is used at two very important
pivotal moments in the gospel.[76] At Mt 4:17 it is used to mark the
beginning of Jesus' public ministry and at Mt 16:21 it is used
again to mark the beginning of the section of the gospel which
deals with his forthcoming death and resurrection. It introduces
the second half of the gospel.

A very significant series of events has taken place, and an important turning point has been reached. From now on Jesus begins to point out to his disciples that it is necessary for him to go
to Jerusalem and to suffer many things at the hands of the elders, the chief priests and the scribes, and to be put to death and
to be raised on the third day.[77] This first prediction of the passion, the reaction of Peter and the teaching of Jesus on the conditions of following him (Mt 16:24:28), mark a serious turning
point in the narrative. This is a 'hinge' or 'kernel' passage in the
narrative. It brings what has preceded to a climax and opens
onto the succeeding narrative block of 'satellite' stories.

Matthew is following the same narrative line as Mark, very
closely at this point, but Matthew, always very influenced by
Old Testament biblical texts, sharpens Mark's expression 'after

---

76. J. D. Kingsbury, *Matthew: Structure, Christology, Kingdom*, Philadelphia: Fortress, 1975, 8.
77. Matthew is closer to the kerygmatic formula 'God raised him up' (1
Cor 15:3-5; Acts 2:23; 3:15; 4:10) than to the Markan 'he will rise' or the
Johannine 'laying down his life and taking it up again' (Jn 10:18).

three days he will rise' to read 'on the third day he will be raised'. 'The third day' was an established biblical expression pointing to the restoration of the one who had been struck down: '... after a day or two he will bring us back to life; *on the third day* he shall raise us up and we shall live in his presence' (Hos 6:2-3). It also alludes to the manifestation of the glory of God in the story of Moses and his preparation of the people in the desert for the revelation of the glory of God *on the third day* (Exod 19:9-25).[78] 'Go to the people and consecrate them today and tomorrow ... and prepare for the third day, because *on the third day* the Lord will come down upon Mount Sinai in the sight of all the people' (Exod 19:10f). The third day subsequently became a 'canonised' term for the day of God's presence in glory when he gave the people the gift of the Law.

The expression 'From that time Jesus began to point out to his disciples' (*êrxato deiknuein*) points to the beginning of a habitual or repeated teaching. This first prediction of the passion and resurrection is presented in indirect speech in the third person, and it is presented as a summary of ongoing or repeated instruction. (Mark adds that he was saying this openly/boldly, *parrêsia ton logon elalei*). Underlining this understanding of his identity, role and destiny, so very different from the expectations of the people and the disciples, Jesus does not use the title Messiah of himself, but in the context where one would expect him to do so he uses 'Son of Man' as he speaks of his destiny in Jerusalem.[79] Jesus' use of the Son of Man title as a term to indicate his messianic role as one who suffers sets the Danielic Son of Man imagery (Dan 7:13f) in an ironic position of one who, instead of receiving all authority over men, suffers at the hands of men before being glorified at the resurrection and 'given all authority in heaven and on earth' (Mt 28:18).

Though Jesus is Messiah and Son of the living God, his

---

78. Exod 19:9-25. The term 'the third day' occurs four times in the passage.

79. See H. F. Bayer, *Jesus' Predictions of Vindication and Resurrection*, Tübingen: J. C. Mohr (Paul Siebeck), 1986.

Messiahship and role as Son are very different from popular expectations. Whatever ideas the disciples and the people had of the expected Messianic figure, however unclear, all had one thing in common. For them the Messiah, the anointed one, would be chosen and empowered by God. For them this God-given power would confound the forces of moral, political or social evil experienced by the people, even if assessed differently by different individuals or groups. However, Jesus' understanding of his role runs counter to all three – moral, political and social forces will appear to overpower him – his fate will be one of ignominy, defeat and suffering. Peter voices the shock which all the disciples surely felt.

The Reaction of Peter Mt 16:22 / /Mk 8:32-33

The expression 'it is necessary', *dei* (he *must* go to Jerusalem and suffer many things) reflects a theme in apocalyptic literature that certain future events were part of the firmly decreed will of God. For Matthew also the carrying out of the plan of God is a major dimension of righteousness. Asking him to shrink from such a divinely decreed event is therefore asking him to disobey the will of God, not to 'fulfill all righteousness' as he had done in coming to the Baptist for baptism. This explains Jesus' response to Peter: 'Get behind me Satan', followed by the comment that his attitude is that of human beings and not of God. It reflects the human desire for the Messiah to carry out his work and win people by spectacular means not involving suffering or a change of heart through repentance and faith. This reflects closely the point of the temptation narratives where Jesus is tempted by Satan in the wilderness (Mt 4:1-11 / /Lk 4:1-13; cf Mk 1:13).

Peter's reaction is not just a failure to understand intellectually but rather an indication of not wanting to see Jesus fail, and to find that he himself and the other disciples are followers of a failure, 'a loser'. These are naturally very human thoughts, 'the thoughts of men and not of God', to quote the response of Jesus. Peter has already spoken in the name of the disciples. When Jesus tells Peter, who has taken Jesus aside to advise him as

though he were the master, to 'go behind me', (*hypage opisô mou*),
he is in fact telling him to resume his position as a disciple, one
of those 'following', 'coming after Jesus', as designated in the
original call to 'come after (follow) me' (*deute opisô mou*) (Mt 4:19).
Addressing him as 'Satan' recalls the various ploys of Satan in
the temptation narratives where Jesus is presented with, and rejects, 'plausible' human shortcuts to the establishment of the
kingdom. Such thinking, like Peter's, is an obstacle (*skandalon*) to
Jesus.

A Historical Note on the Predictions

The passion predictions in the synoptics are like neat, tightly
expressed summaries of what actually came to pass. These 'formulae' are obviously the result of repeated telling and are most
likely influenced by the actual historical outcome. However,
there is a real experience of threat behind the formula. Already
the Pharisees have conspired about how to destroy him (Mt
12:14//Mk 3:6). After the parable of the wicked husbandmen
the Jerusalem authorities will have similarly lethal intentions in
his regard (Mt 21:45-46//Mk 12:12//Lk 20:19) and finally the
chief priests and elders of the people will plot against him and
accept the help of Judas in handing him over (Mt 26:3-5; Mk 14:1,
2, 10, 11; Lk 22:1-2). The passion predictions serve a similar function to the references to 'the hour' (*hôra*) and 'the time' (*kairos*) of
Jesus in John's gospel where his hour and his time signify his
glorification when he will be lifted up from the earth and draw
all to himself (Jn 12:32). Though John's gospel is very different in
many ways to the synoptics there is a striking parallel to the
sense of foreboding and future vindication contained in the synoptic predictions. Time and again there are attempts to arrest,
stone or kill him but they are unsuccessful because his hour has
not yet come.[80] After the raising of Lazarus, Caiaphas announced to the Sanhedrin that it was better for one man to die
for the people than that the whole nation should be destroyed

---

80. Jn 5:16-18; 7:20, 25f, 30, 32, 44, 46; 8:20, 59; 10:30-33, 39; 11:8, 49, 57.

(Jn 11:50). Jesus' pronouncements about 'being lifted up' are somewhat equivalent to the synoptic passion predictions but they are set in thoroughly Johannine theology: 'When you have lifted up the Son of Man then will you know that I am' (Jn 8:28) and 'When I have been lifted up from the earth I shall draw all to myself' (Jn12: 32). In the parable of the good/model shepherd Jesus speaks of laying down his life for his sheep and laying it down and taking it up of his own accord (Jn 10:11, 15, 18). These references in John and the predictions in the synoptics toll like a bell throughout the gospels signalling the oncoming salvific event.[81]

Looking at this very varied material from different gospel traditions it is obvious that there is a solid historical basis for Jesus' expectation of a violent death and his faith in a divine vindication. It is quite possible that Jesus, like the prophets, had a clear prophetic insight into the outcome of his ministry. But even from the point of view of a shrewd human being he must have had an awareness of the forces lining up against him, together with his faith that God would ultimately have the last word. M. D. Hooker sums up the case very well in her commentary on Mark:

> ... it seems incredible that Jesus should not have foreseen at least the likelihood (if not the inevitability) of his death. The conviction that suffering was likely may well have arisen from the hostility of the authorities and would have been confirmed from his reading of scripture, where obedience to God frequently involves suffering. The pattern of suffering of the righteous and prosperity for the wicked is especially prominent in the psalms ... Although the details of the passion predictions may be *vaticinia ex eventu*, there seems no reason to deny that he spoke of his rejection in general terms.[82]

---

81. J.Ernst, *Markus*, 59 writes: *Die drei Leidenankundigungen Jesu sind wie das Wetterleuchten vor dem Drama der Passion. Der Weg nach Jerusalem hat durch die Todessignale eine klare Orientierung erhalten.*
82. M. D. Hooker, *op. cit.*, 204-205.

b. Teaching on Discipleship Mt 16:24-28 //Mk 8:34-9:1

Jesus' rebuke to Peter marks the beginning of the intense instruction of the disciples on the way of discipleship. The shocked disciples (and readers) are embarking on a steep learning curve. Three important 'moments' of instruction follow. First of all Jesus teaches the disciples about discipleship. Secondly he brings the inner group, Peter, James and John, to the mountain where they experience the Transfiguration (Mt 17:1-8). Thirdly he gives further instruction following the disciples' failure to heal the ill/possessed boy (Mt 17:19-20).

Teaching the Disciples

Following Peter's expression of horror at the idea that Jesus would be ill-treated and put to death at the hands of the authorities, Jesus spoke to the disciples about the conditions for following him. The disciple must follow the master who renounced messianic glory to follow the path of the rejected and suffering Son of Man, by renouncing self, taking up one's cross and following Jesus, even losing one's life for his sake.

Whoever wishes …

The invitation to discipleship is both individual, emphasised by the use of the singular *tis*, 'if any person wishes' (*ei tis thelei*) and universal, emphasised by the use of the more indefinite 'whoever may wish' (*hos gar ean thelê*).

The nature and personal cost of discipleship are spelled out in a collection of sayings that may have existed as individual sayings or *logia* prior to their being collected and edited by the evangelists or someone before them during the process of transmission prior to the writing of the gospel. The collection builds up to the promise of eschatological reward by the vindicated, glorious Son of Man when he comes in the glory of his Father accompanied by his angels, to reward everyone according to their behaviour. All people are afraid of pain and suffering and ashamed of failure, and of appearing foolish before others. The challenge of discipleship is to follow Jesus through these 'negative' experiences to a sharing of his final glorious vindication.

Taking up one's cross

The first saying (Mt 16:24) is about renouncing self, taking up one's cross and following Jesus. It arises directly from Peter's rejection of suffering. 'If anyone wishes to come after me (i.e. to follow me, to be my disciple), let him deny himself and let him take up his cross and follow me (i.e. persist in following me in spite of the cross).'[83] Denying oneself means taking oneself out of the centre of the picture and selflessly placing oneself at the service of Jesus and the kingdom. Speaking of taking up the cross reminds the reader of Jesus' own carrying of his cross. However, the reference does not necessarily have to have its origin in the post Good Friday recollection of Jesus' own carrying of the cross because crucifixion was a common experience, as was the sight of the victims carrying the crossbeam to the place of execution. This fact is borne out by Plutarch's remark, in his work on punishment and providence, that every criminal who is executed carries his own cross.[84] Carrying one's cross and following Jesus is a very apt description of discipleship at this point in the narrative as Jesus sets out on the fateful way to Jerusalem together with his disciples, a way that will end in his carrying of his cross to Calvary, and the enlisting of a stranger to assist him after the disciples have left him and fled.

Saving and losing one's life

The second saying (Mt 16:25) is a paradoxical teaching about saving and losing one's life. 'Whoever wishes[85] to save his/her life will lose it and whoever loses his/her life for my sake will

---

83. This is an example of a sentence where the impact and clear focus of the original masculine form, intended inclusively, is slightly dulled in translation by the need to translate inclusively, especially when the translator uses the plural. An attempted inclusive translation would be: 'If anyone wishes to come after me, let that person deny self, and let that person take up his/her cross and follow me.'

84. Plutarch, *De sera numinis vindicata*, 9.554b.

85. *hos gar ean thelê*, lit.,'If anyone would wish', 'whoever might wish'.

save it.'[86] The word 'life' (*psychê*) in this context has posed problems for translators. The Greek word should not be taken in the philosophic Platonic sense of soul as distinct from body. Neither should it be taken in the straightforward sense of life just as we know it in this world, the biological life between birth and death. It is more the Hebrew concept of the essential person, the *nephes*, with the connotation of the survival of that which is essential to the person after death. Saving one's life and then losing it implies directing all one's energies to preserving, securing and enriching one's own life for this world only, and missing out on something far more fundamental, the final sharing in the glory of the vindicated Son of Man. Losing one's life implies an acceptance of suffering, rejection, death, loss and failure 'for my sake' and being prepared to appear foolish to people for living such a way of life. Such an apparent loss of life results in 'saving one's life', that is, it brings the 'essential person' to the glory of the vindicated Son of Man.

What price for one's life?

The third saying (Mt 16:26) is couched in the commercial language of the world: profit, loss, gain, exchange. 'What will it profit a human being to gain the whole world and suffer the loss of one's life (*psychê*) or what can one give in exchange for one's life?' Jesus poses the question as a challenge to make them think about what possible profit it is to someone to gain the whole world and lose one's life (that which is most essential to their person, and which will survive this present biological phase of life), or what can one give in exchange for (as a price for) one's life.

c. The Son of Man coming in Glory Mt 16:27-28

The Son of Man who could forgive sins on earth (Mt 9:6) and

---

86. Matthew (16:25) and Luke (9:24) both have 'for the sake of me.' Mark has 'for the sake of me and of the good news' (Mk 8:35), though some mss of Mark have 'for the sake of the good news' rather than 'for the sake of me and of the good news'.

who was declared master of the Sabbath (Mt 12:8) and who will be rejected, suffer many things, be put to death and raised on the third day (Mt 16:21), is now presented as one who will come in the glory of the Father, accompanied by his angels. Jesus will again refer to his coming as the Son of Man in glory in his eschatological-apocalyptic discourse (Mt 24:30,44) and in his statement at his Jewish trial (Mt 26:64). At his coming he will repay everyone according to their conduct (*praxis*). The emphasis on 'doing' is typical of Matthew, evident already in the final section of the Sermon on the Mount (Mt 7:15-27), and it will be the dominant criterion in the account of the last judgement (Mt 25:31-46). Jesus' final word in his commissioning the disciples to make disciples of all nations will be to 'teach them to *observe* all the commands I gave you' (Mt 28:20).

The prophetic oracle or promise, 'Amen I say to you there are some people standing here who will not taste death until they see the Son of Man coming in his kingdom', functions as a bridge, being both a climax to the teaching on following Christ and an interpretative opening to the account of the Transfiguration.

The reader has now been alerted not only to the final coming of the Son of Man and the accompanying judgement but also to another, more immediate, dimension to the coming of the Son of Man. At the end of the apostolic discourse Jesus had solemnly promised the newly commissioned apostles that they would not have gone round the towns of Israel before the Son of Man comes (Mt 10:23). Now he declares that some of them standing there will not taste death before they see the Son of Man coming in his kingdom (Mt 16:28). What is to be understood by this more immediate coming? The vindication of the Son of Man when God raises him from the dead, and the experience of him as risen and glorified Lord on the mountain where he had arranged to meet them, is an obvious example (Mt 28:16-20). But an even more immediate example is the experience of the inner group of disciples, Peter, James and John when they perceive him glorified on the mountain of transfiguration in a scene that follows immediately on the prediction in the gospel narrative.

The reader is not left to ponder on this prediction since the account follows immediately and so the reader wonders if the chapter division between Mt 16:28 and 17:1 is not only artificial but also misleading since instead of binding the event to the prediction with the connecting 'and after six days', it seems to distance it and make it a new departure.

d. The Transfiguration/Transformation of Jesus Mt 17:1-13// Mk 9:2-10//Lk 9:28-36

The Transfiguration scene which follows can be seen as a first instalment on the glory of the Son of Man, whether one sees the glory in terms of the Resurrection or the Second Coming (*parousia*). Both are aspects of the future vindication of the Son of Man over the imminent rejection, suffering and death, which he has foretold.

A fulsome confession in Jesus as the Messiah/Christ and Son of the living God, followed by a command to silence, dashed hopes, a menacing future for Jesus and probably also for the disciples in the short term, Jesus' rebuke and the promise of a final coming of the Son of Man in glory, set the scene for the Transfiguration. The scene itself is unique to the gospels and the lack of other examples for the purpose of comparative study makes it difficult to interpret. It is set between the promise that some here present with Jesus will see the Son of Man coming in his kingdom and the prediction about Jesus' resurrection from the dead. These utterances help to interpret aspects of the Transfiguration. The scene confirms Peter's profession of faith that Jesus is the Son of the living God to whom they should listen even though as Son of Man he will suffer but afterwards be glorified.[87]

'After six days ...' is somewhat unusual as a measure of time between events.[88] It is significant in that it binds the event about

---

87. See J. P. Heil, *The Transfiguration of Jesus: Narrative Meaning and Function of Mark 9:2-8, Matt 17:1-8 and Luke 9:28-36*, Rome, Biblical Institute Press, 2000.

88. Matthew (17:1) and Mark (9:2) mention 'six days later' but Luke (9:28) speaks of 'eight days later'.

to take place to the preceding material. Taken at face value it may refer back to one or all of the preceding conversations – Jesus' dispute with the Pharisees and Sadducees and his walking away from them, his discussion with the disciples and Peter about the identity of the Son of Man, the conferring of the 'keys' on Peter and the subsequent teaching on discipleship. However, the mention of 'six days' most likely has a deeper symbolic significance.

In the original form of the story some period of preparation may have been implied or described.[89] 'Six days' traditionally represented the time for preparation and self-purification before an encounter with the divine (cf Exod 24:15-17). The gospel narrative so far has been rich in allusions to Moses and the foundation events in the formation of Israel at Sinai and during the sojourn of the people in the desert. Symbolically this story too contains echoes of Moses' ascent of Mt Sinai when he and his servant Joshua spent six days on the mountain, when the Glory of the Lord settled on Mount Sinai and the cloud covered it for six days, before God called to Moses from out of the cloud on the seventh day (Exod 24:12-18). It recalls also the story of Moses and his preparation of the people in the desert for the revelation of the glory of God on the third day (Exod 19:9-25).[90] 'Go to the people and consecrate them today and tomorrow ... and prepare for the third day, because on the third day the Lord will come down upon Mount Sinai in the sight of all the people' (Exod 19:10f). *The third day* subsequently became a 'canonised' term for the day of God's presence in glory when he gave the people the gift of the Law. The memory of the event at Sinai came to be celebrated at Pentecost on the third day of a three-day preparation as described in the Exodus narrative. Later still these three days of immediate preparation were preceded by four days of remote preparation, creating a six-day period of preparation for the

---

89. D. E. Nineham, *op. cit.*, 234.
90. Exod 19:9-25. The term 'the third day' occurs four times in the passage.

manifestation of the glory on the seventh day.[91] Echoes of such a
six day preparation with a manifestation of the divine on the
seventh may very well be present in the reference: 'after six
days', *meth' hêmeras hex*.

The reference to the 'high mountain' is very symbolic. Jesus
brings Peter, James and his brother John, by themselves, up a
high mountain, an unspecified mountain in Galilee familiar to
readers of the synoptics and John[92] and reminiscent of Sinai/
Horeb with its connotations of the presence and glory of God,
the gift of the Law to Moses and the gentle breeze heralding the
word of the Lord to Elijah (Exod 19-20; 1 Kings 19). The mountain
has been variously identified as Mt Hermon, Mt Carmel and Mt
Tabor. Since the fourth century Mt Tabor (modern *Jebel et Tor*)
has been the most frequently accepted venue, probably due to
its location, and nowadays it is to the church at its summit that
pilgrims are taken to commemorate the event. However, the
New Testament does not specify the location as to do so would
take from the symbolic meaning of the mountain with its
connotations of the divine presence and the encounters on
Sinai/Horeb.

Jesus was transformed, transfigured, *metemorphôtê*. 'He had a
change of form.' Commentators point out that this probably
refers to a manifestation of the glorious form he would assume
after death, resurrection and exaltation in glory to the right hand
of the Father. It is a foretaste, a glimpse beforehand of Jesus in
the final state of lordship and glory to which he would finally be

---

91. In St John's gospel a four day period comes to a climax with Jesus'
promise to the disciples that they will see greater things with the rending of the heavens and the vision of the angels of God ascending and
descending on the Son of Man (Jn 1:51). Then the climax of the inauguration narrative comes at Cana 'on the third day' when Jesus manifests
his glory and his disciples believe in him; that is, after a six day period
of preparation (Jn 2:1). See J. Potin, *La Fête juive de la Pentecôte*, 314-317.
92. The Sermon on the Mount (Mt 5-7), The appointment of the Twelve
(Mk 3:13-19//Lk 6:12-16), the healing of the crowd (Mt 12:29), the
Transfiguration (Mt 17:1-8//Mk 9:2-8 //Lk 9:28-36) and the final appearance of the Risen Lord (Mt 28) are all on a mountain in Galilee, and
so too is the multiplication of the loaves in Jn 6:1-15.

exalted. It is 'conceived as actual ethereal substance ... the sort of body generally supposed to belong to heavenly beings and indeed to be the vesture of God himself.'[93]

Matthew (Mt 17:2) and Luke (9:29) mention that Jesus' countenance shone like the sun.[94] The reader recalls the brightness shining in Moses' face when it shone so brightly with the reflected glory of his encounter with God on Sinai (Exod 34:29). Jesus' garments became shining white like light. The concept of garments reflecting glory was common, as seen from the comment in 1 Enoch: 'The elect will be clothed with garments of glory from the Lord of spirits, and their glory shall never fade away (1 Enoch 62:15f).' It is found also in 2 Enoch: 'Take Enoch from his earthly garments and clothe him in garments of glory (2 Enoch 22:8).'[95] In the vision of the heavenly court in Daniel the heavenly being is described in terms of brightness and having a robe white as snow (Dan 7:9-10). In the Book of Revelation the martyred saints are described as those clothed in robes washed white in the blood of the lamb (Rev 6:11; 7:13-14).

There are, however, other factors to be taken into account such as the appearance of Moses and Elijah.[96] The mention of Moses and Elijah sets Jesus in the context of salvation history. Both figures are associated with divine encounters on the mountain of Sinai/Horeb (Exod 19:16-25; 24:12-18; 34; 1-28; 1 Kings 19:11-18). Their presence bears testimony to Jesus in the face of those who accuse him of being a law-breaker or false prophet. The Law and the Prophets are represented by these two central characters who are in conversation with Jesus.[97] Moses repre-

---

93. D. E. Nineham *op. cit.*, 234, quoting G. H. Boobyer, *St Mark and the Transfiguration Story*, 23.

94. Mark does not refer to his countenance.

95. cf Rev 4:4; 7:9; 3:5 *inter alia*.

96. Mark mentions Elijah before Moses, unlike Matthew and Luke who mention Moses first. If putting the more significant figure second after *syn* (with) as in 'Elijah with Moses' is Mark's purpose, then the intention of all three synoptics is to see Moses as the more important figure. See J. P. Heil,'A Note on '"Elijah with Moses" in Mark 9:4', *Bib* 80 (1999), 115,

97. Luke specifies that they were speaking about his 'exodus', i.e. his Passion, Death, Resurrection and Ascension.

sents the Law but was also seen as the prophet *par excellence*. Elijah is the father figure of classical prophecy. They bear witness by their presence to the authentic nature of Jesus's mission as the one whose coming is heralded by Elijah and fulfils the promise that a prophet like Moses will appear. Their presence also highlights the fact that he has come not to abolish the Law and the Prophets but to fulfil them (Mt 5:17-18).

There was a belief in Jesus' time that prominent figures from the Old Testament would appear in the end time and play a part in the kingdom.[98] Particularly from the time of Malachi onwards Elijah's name is most frequently used, as in the words of the prophecy: 'Know that I am going to send you Elijah the prophet before my day comes, that great and terrible day' (Mal 4:5-6).

Both Moses and Elijah are also associated with ascensions into heaven.[99] Elijah ascended in a fiery chariot (2 Kings 3:9-12), an incident that received much consideration in subsequent biblical and extra-biblical writing.[100] Moses' death is recorded but his burial place is unknown (Deut 34:5-8) and later tradition associated his death with ascension into heaven as reported in the apocryphal *Ascension of Moses* (11:5-8), in Josephus, (*Ant* 4:8.48) and in Philo, *Moses* (2.288, 291-2). Their presence therefore is also symbolic of Jesus' future ascension to the glory of the Father with the angels after his rejection, suffering, death and resurrection, mentioned in Jesus' recent remark to the disciples (Mt 16:27).

The reaction of the disciples is again articulated by Peter. 'Lord, it is good that we are here.'[101] His address to Jesus 'Lord' reflects the full faith of the believer in the Risen Lord, again a foretaste of the forthcoming resurrection. He goes on to say: 'If

---

98. Mt 8:11 and Lk 13:28f speak of the role of Abraham, Isaac and Jacob in the kingdom.
99. Some scholars see a connection with the two eschatological witnesses sent by God in Rev 11:3-13.
100. Further reflection on this takes place in Sir 48:9; 1 Macc 2:38; 1 Enoch 89:52; 93:8; Josephus, *Ant.*, 9:28.
101. Literally: 'It is good that we are here.'

you wish I will build three tents (*skênai*), one for you, one for Moses and one for Elijah.'

What exactly had Peter in mind by offering to build tents (booths)? He is suggesting the building of a permanent dwelling place or shrine for the transfigured Jesus and his heavenly companions, to preserve the moment forever.[102] It ignores the fact that they will have to come down from the mountain, leaving the extraordinary experience behind and face into the rigours of daily life as disciples and the fateful journey to Jerusalem and what it holds in store, in short, all that Jesus has said about his having to suffer rejection, ignominy and death.

The reference to the cloud that enveloped them recalls the intervention of God in the life of the people of Israel, the cloud by day in the desert, the cloud on Sinai, the cloud on the Tent of Meeting and the cloud covering the Temple at its dedication, associated also with the 'glory' of the Lord's presence.[103] The cloud became a circumlocution for God's presence, the *shekinah*, (from *shakan*, 'to dwell'). 'The cloud covered them,' appears to mean it covered Jesus, Moses and Elijah, as the disciples experienced the voice coming from out of the cloud.

The divine command: 'Listen to him!'

The voice comes out from the cloud just as on Sinai Moses heard the voice from out of the cloud (Exod 24:16) and Ezekiel heard the voice speaking in the vision in which the light of the glory of the Lord was like the bow in the clouds on a rainy day (Ezek 1:28). The voice of God identifies Jesus: 'This is my Son the Beloved in whom I am well pleased.' Then God commands them to listen to the Beloved Son, just as Israel's foundation creed begins with the command to: 'Listen, O Israel' (*shema' Israel*) and when the people were promised a prophet like Moses they were told: '*YHWH* your God will raise up for you a prophet like myself, from among yourselves, from your own brothers; to him

102 St John's Gospel speaks of the Word becoming flesh in terms of ' pitching tent among us', *eskênôsen en hêmin* (Jn 1:14).
103. Exod 13:21f; 24:16; 33:7-11; 34:5; 40:34f; 1 Kings 8:10f; Ezek 1:28; 11:23.

you must listen' (Deut 18:15). Jesus himself has many times called on them to listen. Now the voice of the Father identifies Jesus as 'my Son the Beloved' and instructs them to *listen to him*.

The truth of Jesus' Messianic role and status as Son of God is confirmed by the voice from out of the cloud saying: 'This is my Beloved Son', a repetition of the words spoken at the baptism but this time spoken to the disciples in the context of a manifest-ation of his glory (the reader already overheard the voice from heaven at the baptism). The heavenly voice raises Jesus above the prophets and shows him to be more than the 'prophet like Moses' (Deut 18:15, 18-19) or the returned Elijah (Mal 4:5-6), but far above both in that he is God's own Beloved Son to whom they are commanded to listen. This is very significant given the fact that soon the authoritative voices claiming to speak with the authority of the Law (Moses) and of the prophets (Elijah) will ac-cuse him of being a blasphemer at his trial precisely when he af-firms that he is Christ, the Son of God and the Son of Man who will return in glory (Mt 26:64-66). In doing so they will imply that he is a lawbreaker and a false prophet. They will reject him and his claims. However, their religious authority and judge-ment are rendered void in anticipation by the authority of the Father's voice from the cloud. This voice from heaven also, and very significantly, commands the disciples, the very people who such a short time previously found Jesus' teaching about the nature of his messianic role and the suffering it will entail so challenging, to 'listen to him.' It will be important also, not only for the characters in the story, but also for the readers of the gospel to listen to the voice of Jesus amid the contending voices and claims in their own time.

On hearing the voice the disciples fell on their faces and great fear/awe came upon them. This is the standard biblical reaction of mere mortals to a divine encounter or apocalyptic vision (Dan 8:17; 10:9-11; Rev 1:17).

Jesus came and touched them and said: 'Rise up and do not be afraid.' This kind of reassuring gesture, reported only by Matthew, is also reminiscent of apocalyptic visions, and is yet another example of the healing and raising touch of Jesus and his calming word, seen already in the gospel (Mt 8:3, 15; 9:25, 29).

The disciples then raise their eyes and find themselves alone with Jesus in his usual state/form. The moment has passed. The injunction, as they came down the mountain, to tell no one about the vision until the Son of Man is risen from the dead links the experience with the future vindication of Jesus over his rejection, suffering and death.

A Revelation during the Ministry

The scene involves the inner group of disciples, Peter, James and his brother John, a representative group of disciples who will be with Jesus again in Gethsemane.[104] The whole event seems to be directed at them, and here lies the key to its interpretation. The whole experience is for the benefit of the central group of disciples at this critical juncture in the ministry and for this reason it must be seen as an experience during the ministry rather than a relocation of a post-resurrection experience as is sometimes suggested.[105] Peter has already professed Jesus to be 'Christ the Son of the Living God', a fact already made known to the reader in the narratives of the infancy, baptism and temptation of Jesus. Here that information is confirmed in a dramatic way for these chosen disciples. R. H. Lightfoot, commenting on the Transfiguration in Mark, makes a point equally valid in the case of Matthew:

> ... the whole event, from first to last takes place solely for the sake of the three disciples. 'He was transfigured *before them*';

104. They figure much more prominently in Mark where Jesus gave them special names, Simon whom he called Peter, James and his brother John, whom he called Boangeres, 'sons of thunder'. In Mark's account they accompanied Jesus to the house of Jairus, the synagogue official and the same three (together with Andrew) were the recipients of the eschatological-apocalyptic discourse on the Mount of Olives. Finally they were associated closely with him in the garden of Gethsemane (Mk 3:16f; 5:37; 14:33f; cf Lk 8:51).

105. See M. Mullins, *The Gospel of Mark*, Dublin: Columba Press, 2005, 242-245 for an outline of various approaches to the interpretation of the Transfiguration.

'there appeared *unto them* Elijah and Moses'; 'there came a cloud overshadowing *them*'; 'this is my only Son; hear *ye* him'.[106]

This corporate experience may in large measure be explained as a mystical experience of a group associated with Jesus and caught up in his intimate prayer with the Father in which the reality of his nature and identity shines through his changed appearance. It confirms his status and authority and lays the ground for their acceptance of his assertion of the necessity of his suffering, death and resurrection.

The narrative of the Transfiguration is, however, very symbolic, and the Old Testament imagery and typology is striking, even if not always clearly spelled out and therefore difficult to interpret exactly. Its overall purpose and impact is nonetheless clear. In the words of M. D. Hooker:

> ... the story spells out the truth about Jesus and confirms their belief in him as God's beloved son. For a brief moment, the three disciples are said to have a shared vision of the understanding of Jesus which belongs to the post-resurrection situation.[107]

This is borne out by the fact that Jesus commands the disciples to tell no one about the vision until the Son of Man is raised from the dead, when presumably the experience could be put into the context of his vindication by the Father as subsequently it was proclaimed by all believers.

M. D. Hooker, also commenting on Mark, but equally relevant to Matthew, points out that the best explanation for this experience of the disciples, subsequently presented in the traditional language and categories canonised in the Old Testament is:

> ... an historical ' happening' of some kind has been interpreted with the aid of Old Testament allusions to produce the narra-

---

106. R. H. Lightfoot, *The Gospel Message of St Mark*, Oxford: Clarendon Press, 1950, 44.
107. M. D. Hooker, *op. cit.*, 214.

tive as we have it, but the two have been so fused together that it is impossible for us now to separate the two ... The true nature of Jesus is a hidden mystery which breaks out from time to time, and for Mark these revelations do not require explanations.[108]

Neither do they require explanations for Matthew.

e. Elijah and John the Baptist Mt 17:9-13//Mk 9:11-13

In an apparently abrupt change of theme the disciples ask Jesus why the scribes say that Elijah must first come. The reference is very likely to the scribes' teaching about Malachi's prophecy which states: 'Remember the teaching of my servant Moses, the statutes and ordinances that I commanded him at Horeb for all Israel. Lo, I will send my prophet Elijah before the great and terrible day of the Lord comes' (Mal 3:23-24). The evangelists, or an older tradition or source, may well have had this passage in mind and wanted to show both the presence of Moses and Elijah together bearing witness to Jesus, and at the same time to present this fleeting glimpse of Elijah as his promised reappearance. Maybe there was a need for the Christians to answer a question posed by Jews, about how they could regard Jesus as Messiah when Elijah had not yet come in accordance with the prophecy. Jesus responds to the question, obviously prompted by the fleeting vision of Elijah, with the confirmation of the scripture and its fulfilment: 'Elijah does come and he is to restore all things.' Having alluded to the scripture he goes on, using the authoritative formula used in the antithesis, 'but I say to you that Elijah has already come and they did not know him, but treated him how they pleased.' Then he adds: 'So too the Son of Man is going to suffer at their hands.' The disciples then realised that he was speaking about John the Baptist.

Elijah was expected to carry on a mission of repentance and reform expressed in terms of coming in the spirit and power of Elijah to turn the hearts of fathers to their children, a text applied

---

108. Ibid.

specifically to John by Luke (Lk 1:17; Mal 3:23-24). John carried
out such a mission of repentance, which drew all Jerusalem and
Judea to him confessing their sins. People also came from
Galilee as one can see from the presence of Jesus. In addition
Elijah had to suffer, as seen in the treatment and attempt on his
life in 1 Kings 19:1-3, and John the Baptist suffered imprisonment and execution. Both Elijah and John prefigure the suffering
about to fall on the Son of Man. They are forerunners, precursors
in suffering just as in glory. John had even dressed in the manner traditionally associated with the prophets, especially Elijah.
Elijah in fact had returned in the person of the Baptist.

f. The Disciples' Failure to Heal Mt 17:14-20//Mk 9:14-29//Lk 9:37-43
Matthew tells the story of the man with the epileptic/possessed
boy in about half the length of Mark's account, as he has done
with the earlier miracle stories in chapters eight and nine. He
does not recount the dispute between the disciples and the
scribes. Neither does he describe the amazement/enthusiasm of
the crowd on seeing Jesus.

When Jesus and the three disciples came from the mountain
and approached the crowd, a nameless man in the crowd ran
forward and in a gesture of faith and acknowledgement of Jesus'
status knelt before him and addressed him as 'Lord'. He begged
him to have mercy on his son who was a ' lunatic' (*selêniazetai*)[109]
suffering severely and his condition put him into mortal danger
when he fell into fire or water. He drew Jesus' attention to the
failure of his disciples to heal him.

In a reaction that parallels Jesus' reaction to the Canaanite
woman (Mt 15:21-28) or to the royal official in John's gospel (Jn
4:48), Jesus responds with an apparently harsh reply which in

---

109. The Greek *selêniazetai* reveals how the ancients believed that the
moon and its phases affected the mental state of certain people. J. P.
Meier, *Matthew*, 194, points out that this is the only place where the verb
selênizomai is used in the New Testament, and possibly it is its first appearance in Greek literature. (The Greek *selênikos* and the Latin *lunaticus*,
from *selênê* and *luna* would be accurately translated by 'moonstruck'.)

turn elicits a strong statement of faith from the petitioner. Jesus exclaims: 'You faithless and perverse generation, how much longer must I be with you (*meth' hymôn*)? How long am I to bear with you (*hymôn*)?' However, 'you', *hymôn* is in the plural. Jesus' reaction of criticism targets a broader audience than the father or the disciples, as in the case of the royal official in Jn 4:48. He targets the whole unbelieving generation in Israel, whose criticism and rejection of Jesus has been recounted already in the narrative. Just as Jesus himself did not perform any healings in his native place because of their lack of faith (Mt 13:58) maybe the disciples had encountered such lack of faith, and suffered from lack of faith themselves, and they also could not or did not perform healings for this reason. As Jesus condemns 'this faithless generation' for their failure to believe, the reader recalls the Song of Moses in which he laments over the faithless people (Deut 32:20).[110]

The boy is brought to Jesus. He 'rebukes' the demon. It leaves him and the boy is cured instantly. The story has the marks of a conflation of two original accounts. The boy's condition is first described as 'madness' and in terms very similar to an epileptic seizure in which he falls into fire or water but the healing is described as driving out a demon. The story therefore may be a conflation of more than one story, and they are conflated, shortened and fashioned into a teaching on faith. The basic outline of the story is that of a miracle, a healing or exorcism story where a problem is presented, Jesus first reacts and then responds. Jesus heals and/or exorcises the demon. However, in this case the story of the disciples' inability and Jesus' instruction are woven into the story of the healing/exorcism. This means that the focus is not so much on the power of Jesus as on the lack of power on the part of the disciples and their little faith. This furnishes Jesus with the opportunity of giving them an instruction on faith as the source of power.

---

110. At this point Mt 17:17 and Lk 9:41 use the term 'perverse' which is the actual term used in Deut 32:20.

Jesus' Teaching

The disciples approached Jesus in private and asked him why they were unable to cast out the demon. Jesus told them that it was because of their lack of faith.[111] He then made a solemn 'Amen I say to you' pronouncement using the example of a grain of mustard seed which he had already used as a simile for the kingdom. 'If you had faith like a grain of mustard seed, you would say to this mountain, "Move from here to there" and it would move. Nothing would be impossible for you.' Moving mountains was a common metaphor used by rabbis for doing things of great difficulty, and a rabbi who could explain particularly difficult passages of scripture was regarded as a 'mountain-remover'.[112]

At this point v 21 is added in some mss. It reads: 'As for this kind (of devil) it is cast out only by prayer and fasting.' This is obviously an interpolation from the tradition shared with Mark (Mk 9:29) which has two mss traditions, some saying 'by prayer' others 'by prayer and fasting'. Fasting was often seen as an accompaniment to prayer, creating a disposition for prayer rather than an activity in its own right.

g. The Second Prediction of the Passion Mt 17:22-23//Mk 9:30-32//Lk 9:43-45

Unlike Mark who describes a secret journey through Galilee during which Jesus instructs his disciples in private (cf Mk 9:30), Matthew introduces the second, and shortest, prediction of the passion with the simple phrase, 'as they were together in Galilee.' In this second prediction of his passion, death and resurrection Jesus states, 'The Son of Man is to be delivered into the hands of men, they will put him to death and he will be raised on the third day.'

---

111. Mark has Jesus replying that it is because of their lack of prayer, and some mss of Mark add 'and fasting' which was a regular accompaniment of prayer (Mk 9:29).

112. D. E. Nineham, *op. cit.*, 305. See also the article by C. W. Hedrick, 'On Moving Mountains. Mark 11:22b-23/Matt 21:21 and Parallels', *Forum* 6 (1990), 219-37.

Unlike the second prediction in Mark (Mk 9:31) the 'persecutors' are not specified as 'the elders, the chief priests and the scribes,' but simply as 'men' (human beings). Similarly the verb *paradidosthai* 'handed over' is used in a general sense here, not yet in its specific sense of 'betrayal' by Judas. The general nature of the prediction and the (divine?) passive 'handed over' seems to refer to God's divine plan rather than to any specific human agency. Some scholars speculate that this may be the most primitive form of the prediction which has been expanded in the other predictions, while others think that they are three independent primitive sayings.

Whereas Mark, true to form, stresses the failure of the disciples, their inability to understand, their confusion and fear, and the fact that 'they were afraid to ask' (Mt 17:23//Mk 9:32), Matthew simply states that the prediction caused the disciples to be greatly distressed.

h. Peter and the Temple Tax Mt 17:24-27

As Jesus is about to leave Galilee and head for Jerusalem the setting in Capernaum recalls and forms an inclusion with Mt 4:13 when Jesus took up residence in Capernaum at the beginning of his Galilean ministry. Probably because of its location there were many tax collectors there (Mt 8:5,14; 9:1,9-13). This scene is recorded only in Matthew. It brings this narrative section of the gospel (Mt 13:53 to 17:27) to a close on a significant Petrine note.

There are two conversations about the tax, one between the tax collectors and Peter in which Peter speaks on behalf of Jesus (Mt 17:24-25) and one between Jesus and Peter in which Jesus accepts Peter's statement on his behalf and lays down two fundamental principles (Mt 25-27). As with so many stories in the gospels, this story has three levels of significance. It roots Jesus firmly in the traditions of Israel as he fulfils the prescription of the Law and the Prophets. It highlights Jesus' special status as Son of God and it provides an example for the life of the church.

Historical note on the tax

First of all, within the context of Palestine in Jesus' time paying the temple tax was a long-standing religious duty. The Book of Exodus laid down that:

> Every man of twenty years and over should pay half a shekel ... the rich man is not to give more nor the poor man less ... to the service of the Tent of Meeting ... It will remind *YHWH* of the sons of Israel and will be the ransom for your lives (Exod 30:11-16).

Nehemiah speaks of the obligation:

> We also lay upon ourselves the obligation to charge ourselves yearly with the third part of the shekel for the service of the house of our God' (Neh 10:32).

Paying the tax, according to Philo, was seen as a means of bringing all kinds of blessings such as freedom from slavery, healing of diseases, enjoyment of liberty and preservation from danger.[113]

Beyond Palestine in Jesus' time the Jews of the Diaspora were permitted to collect the tax throughout the empire. It was one of the concessions they had won following their taking the right side in two Roman civil wars, the war between Julius Caesar and Pompey and the war between the conspirators who murdered Caesar, (Brutus and Cassius), and Caesar's supporters Octavian (later emperor Augustus) and Anthony. The Jews had won the status of *religio licita*. They were allowed therefore to organise themselves into synagogues and to carry out religious and social duties associated with the synagogue. They were exempt from taking part in the public religious rituals of the state and from military service. They were allowed to gather the temple tax throughout the empire. Josephus states that in Babylonia the Jews organised a system for collecting the temple tax.[114] Apart from its religious value, therefore, the tax, like the observation of

---

113. Philo, *Special Laws*, 1:77
114. Josephus, *Ant* 18:312.

the Sabbath, was one of the marks of Jewish identity throughout the Diaspora.

Throughout the empire after the Jewish War, which resulted in the fall of Jerusalem and the temple, the Romans collected the tax, now known as the *fiscus Judaicus*, formerly the temple tax, for the temple of Jupiter Capitolinus in Rome.[115] This would raise issues for Jews and Jewish Christians, as it was collected for a pagan temple, but its refusal could be a sign of disloyalty to the state.

(i) The tax collectors conversation with Peter Mt 17:24-25a

The question put to Peter: 'Does your master not pay the *didrachma* (tax)?' could be paraphrased 'Surely your teacher will pay the *didrachma*?' The Greek coinage mentioned, *didrachma*, (a two *drachma* coin) is the equivalent of the Jewish half shekel. Obviously expecting an affirmative answer, they recognised in Jesus someone who would not play on his role as teacher to avoid the tax, though apparently some priests and teachers claimed exemption.[116] Peter spontaneously answers in the affirmative. This would be in keeping with Jesus' own teaching that he had not come to destroy, but to fulfil the Law and the Prophets (Mt 5:17), in this case to fulfil a pious Jew's obligation towards the temple and its services.

(ii) Jesus' conversation with Peter Mt 17:25b-27

On his return to the house Jesus takes the initiative and puts a searching question to him. It touches on Jesus' own relationship to God and God's house, and by extension to that of Jesus' followers.

As in the introduction to a parable, *mashal* or proverb, Jesus asks Peter to consider the question he is about to ask: 'What do you think?' Then he asks about the king and his imposition of taxes. Peter must respond that kings collect taxes from their subjects, not from the children of the royal family. The glaring con-

---

115. Josephus, *War*, 7:218.
116. J. P. Meier, *Matthew*, 196.

clusion to be drawn is that Jesus is not only the royal son of David, but more so, he is the Son of the living God and the temple is his Father's house. He is free. He needs no divine or royal ransom like that implied in Exod 30:11-16. Neither do his followers. Like him, they are free.

Jesus then states a second principle. Though he need not pay the tax, he is conscious of the possible misunderstanding that could arise from his not paying, 'lest we scandalise them'. J. P. Meier explains it well:

> If the sons are free from tax, they are not free from the claims of love, even love of enemies ... In their freedom they are obliged to avoid unnecessary scandal ... From this vantage point of practical love, Jesus confirms Peter's 'yes', but for a totally different reason.[117]

The story of paying the tax is therefore important as a precedent for behaviour in the primitive church. Paul gave a similar instruction to the Corinthians on the matter of food offered to idols. Some of the more educated and self-assured people were contending that idols and food offered to them are of no significance, but other people were worried about the apparent involvement in idol worship through eating the meat consecrated to idols. Paul responded that the demands of love meant they should not cause scandal or offence. He wrote: 'knowledge gives self importance – it is love that makes the building grow' (1 Cor 8:1-13).

(iii) Jesus tells Peter to pay for both of them Mt 17:24- 27

Jesus tells Peter to cast a hook into the lake and he will find a *statêr*, a coin equal to four drachmas, the equivalent of a shekel, in the mouth of the fish. The shekel will pay the tax for Jesus and Peter.[118]

Paying the tax allows Peter to be a both a Jew and a follower

---

117. Ibid, 197.
118. There is a similar rabbinic story about a pearl found in a fish (*b. Sabbat* 119a).

of Jesus. As such there is an example *par excellence* for those in Matthew's church who wanted to maintain their Jewish identity, while at the same time remaining followers of Christ. Peter's example and Jesus' confirmation of his activity provide precedent and authority for their position.

The Coin in the Fish's Mouth

For many general readers and preachers questions about the quasi-miraculous account of finding the coin in the mouth of the first fish caught overshadows the various levels at which this story is operating.

It is interesting to note that there is no actual account of Peter's catching a fish with a coin in its mouth. The saying about the coin may be a proverb or local saying[119] among a fishing community which Jesus uses or adapts and which has been absorbed into the narrative. There was a rabbinic story of a pearl found in the mouth of a fish and similar incidents may have given rise to a local saying. It may well be another way of saying to those who were instructed to carry no gold, no silver, not even a few coppers in their purses, to trust in God who provides in unexpected ways (Mt 10:9).

The point at issue is Jesus' acceptance of Peter's answering on his behalf and his commissioning of Peter to act on his behalf. This may even account for some envy on the part of the other disciples who ask: 'Who is the greatest in the kingdom of heaven?' (Mt 18:1).

---

119. Is Jesus simply adapting a proverb about divine providence as he tells Peter to go fishing to earn the money?

This is the fourth of the five major discourses in the gospel. It deals with matters of concern within the community. It falls into two clear sections, the first deals with how to show proper concern for the 'little ones', the weaker and more vulnerable members (Mt 1:1-14), and the second deals with how to respond to errant and offending members (Mt 18:15-35). The advice is given by Jesus to the disciples in the gospel story. For Matthew's church (and the church today) it is directed at those who are strong, upright and authoritative members of the community.

Scholars have made various suggestions about the divisions in the discourse. It seems best to divide it along the lines of the two concerns just mentioned (Mt 18:1-14 and 15-35). Not only do the two concerns suggest such a two-fold division, but there is also a literary parallel between the two sections thus marked off. The first section has the teaching about 'the little ones', followed by a parable and ending with a reference to the will of 'your Father in heaven'. The second section has the teaching on errant and offending members, followed by a parable and ending with a reference to what 'my heavenly Father' will do.

a. The ' Little Ones' Mt 18:1-14

i. Becoming as a little Child Mt 18:1-4

'At that hour'[1] the disciples came to Jesus and said: 'Who is the greatest in the kingdom of heaven?' There may be something of an envious reaction to the apparent preferment of Peter who 'received the keys of the kingdom' and spoke and acted on behalf of Jesus in the payment of the tax, but it is not explicitly stated. In Matthew, however, the disciples are more positively portrayed at this point than in the parallel scene in Mark where Jesus intervenes in an argument about personal status in the kingdom (Mk 9:34-35).[2]

---

1. The connecting temporal phrase *en ekeinê tê hôra* ('at that hour') differs from the more usual *en ekeinô tô kairô* ('at that time').
2. At this point in the narrative Mark, true to form, again has a very negative portrait of the disciples. He portrays Jesus intervening in an argu-

Jesus responds to their question about the greatest in the kingdom with a parable in action followed by a solemn, apocalyptic style 'amen' pronouncement. He called a little child placed him in their midst and said: 'Amen I say to you, unless you turn/change and become like little children you will not enter the kingdom of heaven.' The term *paidion* is a diminutive of *pais* (child) and signifies a little child. The disciples are told to 'turn', that means to change radically their outlook and values concerning status and adopt those of the little child or they will not enter the kingdom of heaven. The verb *straphein* 'turn' is very like a Greek translation of the biblical *subh*, to 'return' as in returning to the Lord in repentance. Becoming like little children means taking on the status of the child in society at the time. The child had no influence, power, control or standing in society. It related only to the parents and family on which it was totally dependent. So, too, the disciples must not seek power, position or influence on the model of secular society. The followers of Jesus must focus their attention on the kingdom of heaven, and by implication, on the relations within the kingdom, all of which are the concern of 'your Father in heaven'. J. P. Meier states it well:

> Jesus is recommending … a child-like trust in a loving Father, a trust that awaits everything and grabs at nothing.[3]

Jesus goes on to say: 'Whoever, therefore humbles himself like this little child is the greatest in the kingdom of heaven.'

ii. Behaviour towards the little ones Mt 18:5-14
Accepting the little child 'in my name'

The kingdom consists of those who have humbled themselves like this little child. The focus of the teaching now shifts from the dispositions of the child to the attitude of others to the child and to those who have humbled themselves and become

---

ment and when he asks the source of their disagreement he is met with a sullen silence. He knows the source of the disagreement was internal rivalry for positions of preferment and so he delivers his teaching accordingly (Mk 9:34-35).

3. J. P. Meier, *Matthew*, 201.

like the child. One's attitude to those who have so humbled themselves is central to one's own membership of the kingdom / community. Accepting 'the little one' in Jesus' name (that means for Jesus' sake, because Jesus said so) means accepting the authentic humble member. In respecting the choice he / she has made and the 'turn' he / she has taken, one accepts Jesus himself. 'Whoever accepts one such little child in my name accepts me.'

Scandal

The image of the member of the community as a little child leads on to the realisation that some are 'little ones' in an even more literal sense. They are young in the faith, impressionable and vulnerable. One can therefore be the cause of scandal to one of these little ones who believe in Jesus. Being a scandal means being an obstacle to their belief or a cause of their stumbling into unbelief or falling into sin. To behave in such a manner towards a new or weak member of the community is a heinous crime and in typical Semitic hyperbole Jesus describes it as worse than execution by drowning in the depths of the sea with a donkey's millstone round one's neck.[4] 'Whoever scandalises one of these little ones who believe in me, it were better for him that a millstone were put about his neck and he were drowned in the depths of the sea.' Drowning, in fact, was a form of capital punishment practised by the Romans, and not unknown in Galilee.

Solemnly and apocalyptically Jesus now pronounces a 'woe' on the world from which scandals must come and a 'woe' on the person through whom they come. Following the statement about capital punishment by drowning, Jesus mentions other forms of punishment such as deprivation of hand, foot and eye and says they are preferable to 'stumbling'.[5] 'If your hand or foot cause you to stumble, cut it off and cast it from you, for it is

---

4. *Mulos onikos*, a donkey's millstone, i.e. a large millstone turned by a donkey.
5. Josephus speaks of cutting off the hands for forgery and sedition, *Life* 34f; *War* II, 21:10. D. Derrett, *Studies in the New Testament*, I, 4 -31, points out that these punishments were known in other nations. Loss of hand or foot was a punishment for theft, and loss of eyes for adultery.

better to enter life crippled or lame than having two hands and feet to be cast into eternal fire.' Similarly in the case of an eye that causes one to stumble Jesus says it is better to enter life with one eye than having two eyes to be cast into the Gehenna (hell) of fire.

In a comment similar to that made in the antithesis on adultery (Mt 5:27-30) Jesus mentions the hand, the foot and the eye, all three essential to life in the world, and points out in three similar statements that if any one of them is a cause of leading one into sin it would be better for that person to be at the loss of it and enter into (eternal) life than to be able-bodied and excluded from eternal life. Hand, foot and eye together seem to have been regarded as the basic essentials for healthy living. Job, for example, sees the health of the person in terms of purity of eyes, foot and hands (Job 31:1, 5, 7). Loss of any or all of them is therefore a serious loss of life, but it is preferable to loss of life in the kingdom, or as Jesus puts it more solemnly and apocalyptically, such loss is better than being thrown into 'the *Gehenna* of fire'.[6]

It is possible that Matthew, or others before him in the handing on of the tradition, also meant the sayings to have a communal application in relation to removing certain members from the community. Commentators point to the widespread use of the body and its parts as a metaphor for the functioning of a social unit or organisation. The Roman general Agrippa used it to restore harmony in the army during the threat of a mutiny. St Paul used it in his discussions on the community as the body of Christ, and in his appeals for the community to work in harmony as the parts of the human body (1 Cor 12:12-26; Rom 12:3-8). Paul also advocated the expulsion of certain elements from the

---

6. Matthew was particularly fond of the term *gehenna*, cf Mt 5:22, 29, 30; 10:28; 23:15, 33). *Gehenna* or the Valley of Hinnom was a deep wadi to the south of Jerusalem, adjoining the village of Silwan/Siloam where rubbish was burned and there was a continual fire, a stench and a worm or beetle that seemed immortal because it emerged from the fire. The scene came to be used as a symbol of hell fire. Mark adds 'where the worm will not die nor the fire go out' as a further description (Mk 9:47).

body, the community, lest they corrupt the whole (cf 1 Cor 5:1-5).

'See to it that you do not despise one of these little ones.' 'Do not despise' is a way of saying 'accept', 'receive', 'value', 'do not overlook' or regard them as inferior or as of no importance. There was a strong belief in guardian angels in Jewish circles in the first century, especially among the Pharisees and the community of Qumran. D. Senior points to the fact that Jesus' words imply a symmetry between life on earth and life in the heavenly realm, as seen from the 'on earth as in heaven' setting of the petitions in the Lord's Prayer (Mt 6:10). Therefore the 'little ones' on earth should be regarded with the reverence due to those angels in heaven who are privileged to see the face of 'my Father in heaven'.[7]

Engaging the listeners' active participation in the discussion Jesus asks: 'What do you think?' He then presents the well-known parable of the Good Shepherd in the form of a rhetorical question. He asks: 'If a man has a hundred sheep and one strays will he not leave the ninety nine on the mountainside and go in search of the stray?' Whereas Luke uses the parable to focus on the goodness and concern of the shepherd, referring to the ministry of Jesus to the lost sheep of Israel when he was criticised for eating with tax collectors and sinners (Lk 15:1-7), Matthew, on the other hand, applies it to the leadership in the community and their duty to show the concern of the good shepherd for the stray or erring sheep in the community.

The efforts of the shepherd to find the one who has strayed or been led astray may or may not be successful, a fact borne out by the practical proviso, 'if he should find' (*ean genêtai heurein*). It is possible, however, that his search will not be successful. Matthew's church may have needed to hear that proviso. Luke has simply 'until he finds'. When and if he does find the stray it brings great joy, greater than the joy associated with the ninety-nine that have not gone astray.[8] The parable in Matthew has ap-

---

7. D. Senior, *op. cit.*, 208.
8. *Planâo* has the connotation of leading or being led astray, in the sense of being deceived.

pended to it a saying or *logion* that sums up the salvific intention of 'my Father in heaven' towards the little ones in the words: 'Thus, it is not the will of your Father in heaven that one of the little ones be lost.' Here again we find a parallel with Johannine thought (cf Jn 17:12).

b. The Sinning/Offending Member Mt 18:15-20

Mutual Correction

'If your brother sins (against you) ...' The words 'against you' are missing in many important manuscripts and so, as well as seeing the sin as a specific sin against a specific person, one can also see it as sin in a general sense. Three steps, each reflecting scriptural or established practice are recommended. The first step is to 'Go, reason with him alone.' This is in line with Lev 19:17 which recommends reasoned dialogue instead of harbouring a grudge or hatred and so sinning against one's neighbour. The text in Lev 19:17 reads: 'You shall not hate your brother in your heart, but you shall reason with your neighbour, lest you bear sin because of him.' Jesus continues: 'If he listens to you then you have won your brother.'

If he fails to listen, the second recommended step is to bring along one or two others, 'so that every word be confirmed by the mouth of two or three witnesses.' This step is also in keeping with scripture. Deut 19:15 lays down that 'only on the evidence of two witnesses, or of three witnesses, shall a charge be sustained.'

If he refuses to listen to them, tell the *ekklêsia*, the *qahal*, the (local) church community. This second use of the term *ekklêsia* in Matthew is probably in contradistinction to the local Jewish community, the synagogue. Telling the whole community, probably through its representatives or elders (presbyters), was an established custom in at least some Jewish congregations, as seen from the practice in Qumran where the assembly dealt with the expulsion of an errant member (1QS v 24 – vi1). If the sinner refuses to listen to the voice of the entire community then that member should be treated like a Gentile and tax collector, that is, like a pagan foreigner and a Jew who has taken on an acceptable way of life. Two valid conclusions can be drawn. Treating the erring member as Gentile or tax collector is a way of saying he / she is excluded from the community, no longer belonging to it as a member. It must, however, be kept in mind that Jesus' mission embraced the Gentile and publican, so the community does not turn its back completely on the one it excommunicates, but must see that former member as one to be called again to repentance, faith and true membership. Paul gives a similar instruction in 1 Cor 5:1-13.

The authority for such excommunication and admission to membership of the community is conveyed in the same terms as Peter was invested with authority 'to bind and loose', and again the symmetry of heaven and earth are in evidence in the solemn 'amen' formula: 'Amen I say to you, whatever you bind on earth shall be bound in heaven and what you loose on earth shall be loosed in heaven.' The passive voice is typical of Matthew's Jewish reverence for the name of God and his avoidance of predicating direct action to God.

Further continuing the symmetry between heaven and earth and continuing the juridical context of the assembly meeting to issue judgement and sentence, Jesus says 'Again I say to you if two of you agree about any case (*pragma*) on earth that they might ask (pray about), it will be done for them by my Father in heaven.'[9]

This promise is further underpinned by Jesus' affirmation that: 'Where two or three are gathered in my name, there am I in the midst of them.' This promise of divine presence and protection was foreshadowed in the name Emmanuel, God-with-us, given to the child at his birth, and foreshadows the final promise of the Risen Christ to his disciples on the mountain where they meet for the last time, when he commissions them to make disciples of all nations: 'Behold I am with you all days to the end of the age' (Mt 28:20). D. J. Harrington points out that it reflects also the rabbinic understanding that where two or three are

---

9. Some mss have the solemn 'Amen I say to you'.

gathered in the study of the Torah God is present with them: 'If two sit together and words of the Law pass between them, the divine presence abides between them' (*m. 'Abot* 3:2). He further points out that: 'The ideas of agreement, common prayer, and Christ's presence are here in the service of exercising the power to bind and loose in the case of the brother who sins.'[10]

c. Peter's Question Mt 18:21-22

i. No limits to Forgiveness

Peter, again the spokesman, addressing Jesus as 'Lord' asks the question, and probably thinks he is being very generous in his sevenfold suggestion. 'Lord, how often shall my brother sin against me and I forgive him? As often as seven times?' Jesus replied: 'I do not say to you seven times but seventy seven (or seventy times seven) times.'[11] Whichever translation one chooses, the meaning is the same. It signifies an unlimited number of times. There are no limits to forgiveness.[12]

ii. The Unforgiving Servant/Appeal to the Master Mt 18:23-35

Jesus goes on to tell them a parable (recounted only in Matthew) to illustrate his point. 'The kingdom of God may be compared to …' is a classical introduction to a 'parable of the kingdom'. The comparison is not with the king but with the whole narrative event. The king (referred to hereafter in the parable as the master, *ho kyrios*) settling accounts has a man brought before him who owes him ten thousand talents. One *denarius* was a day's wages. Several thousand *denarii* (scholars estimate between six and ten thousand) made up one talent. Consider then the absolutely astronomical value of ten thousand talents when reckoned in terms of *denarii* or day's wages. It

---

10. D. J. Harrington, *The Gospel of Matthew*, Sacra Pagina 1, 269, nn 19, 20.
11. The Greek *hebdomēkontakis hepta* can be translated either as seventy seven times or seventy times seven times (i.e. four hundred and ninety times).
12. D. J. Harrington, *The Gospel of Matthew*, 269, n 22, sees an allusion here to Gen 4:24 which states: 'If Cain is avenged sevenfold, truly Lamech (is avenged) seventy-sevenfold.'

would amount to ten thousand times many thousands of working day's wages. The debtor could never have paid it back. He faced the possibility of being sold into slavery, together with his wife and children, and having all his possession taken and sold, and so he begged for mercy and time to repay his debt. In fact he could never have repaid such a huge sum. Not only did the master not exact the penalty, or give him an extension of time to pay and so prolong the agony until another day of reckoning, he pardoned the debt. Consider the master's compassion and the loss to him of such a sum. The huge sum mentioned highlights the generosity of the master and the impossible burden removed from the debtor.

Typical of many parables, a comparison or contrast highlights the point at issue. The servant, having been the beneficiary of such great mercy on the part of the master, met a fellow servant who owed him a hundred *denarii*, a very meagre sum when compared to the ten thousand talents. Unlike his benefactor, he showed no mercy. The fellow servants were greatly distressed on seeing what happened and they went to their master and reported all that had taken place. The master on hearing of his behaviour responded to the distress of the fellow servants. He reverted to the strictures of the law and demanded restitution of the ten thousand talents. 'Wicked servant, I forgave you all that debt, when you begged me. Should you also not have had mercy on your fellow servant as I had mercy on you?' His lack of mercy not only cancels the mercy shown to him but in addition brings upon him the severest punishment. The master handed him over to the torturers till he would pay his debt in full.

The parable comes to a climax with Jesus' announcement: 'So also my heavenly Father will do to every one of you, if you do not forgive your brother from your heart.' God forgives our sins, enormous though they be. But God also has care for the people with whom we deal harshly and we are warned that if we do not show mercy we will not have mercy shown to us (Mt 5:7) and our prayer for forgiveness will not be effective (Mt 6:12, 14-15).

The Way to Jerusalem
Matthew 19-20

The first two verses of chapter nineteen function as a conclusion to the discourse, indicating that Jesus had finished what he wanted to say, and at the same time they function as a resumption of the narrative indicating a change of place and renewed activity. 'And it came to pass when Jesus had finished these words he departed from Galilee and came to the region of Judea across the Jordan. Large crowds followed him and he healed them there' (Mt 19:1-2). The summary of Jesus' activity is typical: 'And many crowds followed him and he healed them there.' Matthew 19-20 forms part of the larger section Mt 19-25.

Outline of Matthew 19-25:

1. *Narrative*	A. The Way to Jerusalem (Mt 19:1–20:34)
	B. Challenges in Jerusalem (Mt 21:1–23:39)
2. *Discourse*	The Eschatological Discourse (Mt 24:1–25:46)

1. THE WAY TO JERUSALEM MT 19:1-20:34

Jesus sets out on his final journey as he leaves Galilee for the region of Judea beyond the Jordan *en route* to Jerusalem. This was the traditional route from Galilee to Jerusalem for those, especially pilgrims, who wished to avoid travelling through Samaria.[13]

The incidents in Chapters 19 and 20 take place in the context of his journey to Jerusalem. D. Senior, quoting Warren Carter, sums up succinctly the nature of the material covered in these chapters:

> (They) have a certain 'domestic' hue, as Jesus takes up issues of divorce and remarriage (19:1-12), children (19:13-15), a young man's quest for eternal life (19:16-22), possessions (19:23-30), and a mother's ambitions on behalf of her sons

---

13. Luke tells a story of the hostile and inhospitable attitude of the Samaritans to Jews travelling to Jerusalem through their territory (Lk 9:51-56).

(20:20-28). Warren Carter suggests that Matthew may be interacting in these two chapters with elements of the patriarchal household, offering an alternate vision concerning husband-wife relations, the role of children, the dominant role of wealth in determining human worth, and uplifting Jesus' own model of service (Carter 1994).[14]

a. The Pharisees' Question about Divorce Mt 19:3-9//Mk 10:1-12 cf Mt 5:31f//Lk 16:18

The Pharisees again approach Jesus in order to test him. They do not come to him genuinely seeking informed legal opinion or knowledge. In the corresponding story in Mark they ask his opinion on the legality of divorce as such. Matthew, however, sets their question in the contemporary legal controversy between the rabbinic schools about the grounds for divorce, assuming that it is at least sometimes permitted.[15]

Already in the Sermon on the Mount Jesus has commented on the question of divorce in one of the antitheses. Quoting from the prescription of Moses Jesus says: 'It has also been said: "If a man divorces his wife let him give her a writ of dismissal" (Deut 24:1), but I say to you that everyone who divorces his wife, except in the case of *porneia* (*parektos logou porneias*) makes her an adulteress; and whoever marries a divorced woman commits adultery' (Mt 5:31-32). Since therefore his attitude to divorce was already made clear in the gospel, it is reasonable to assume that they came to contend with him because they knew his anti-divorce position. They came armed with a citation from scripture, the very citation that Jesus had already countered in the third antithesis.

They probably hoped to create for him the dilemma of either losing face through appearing to hold an anti-divorce position

---

14. D. Senior, *Matthew,* 213; See W. Carter, *Households and Discipleship: A Study of Matthew 19-20,* JSNT Sup 103. Sheffield: JSOT.

15. For studies on the question of marriage and divorce in the New Testament see B.Vawter, 'Divorce and the New Testament,' *CBQ* 39 (1977) 528-42; J. A. Fitzmyer, 'The Matthean Divorce Texts and Some New Palestinian Evidence,' *TS* (1976) 197-226.

which contradicted what was stated or a least implied by Moses in the Torah, or else show himself to be inconsistent and unreliable if he took sides in the current debate about the grounds for divorce and thus undermined his own earlier anti-divorce position. Their deviousness is obvious from the promptness with which they were able to respond to his anti-divorce citations from Genesis with their counter argument showing exact scriptural knowledge of Moses' regulation in Deut 24:1-2 which prescribed as follows:

> Suppose a man enters into marriage with a woman but she does not please him because he has found 'erwat dabar (something shameful) of which to accuse her; so he writes her a certificate of divorce, puts it in her hand, and sends her out of his house; she then leaves his house and goes off to become another man's wife. Then suppose the second man dislikes her, writes her a bill of divorce, puts it in her hand and sends her out of his house (or the second man who marries her dies), her first husband who sent her away is not permitted to take her again to be his wife after she has been defiled (Deut 24:1-2).

The writ of divorce was a legal document showing proof that the marriage had ended and the husband had no further legal rights. The former wife had protection from further claims on his part (as for example, concerning financial matters like a dowry, or taking her back if it suited him when she was subsequently divorced or widowed). The writ showed a prospective new husband that the woman was free to marry again and protected him also from any claims on the part of the first husband. However, Moses is not actually giving an instruction on the rights and wrongs of divorce itself when he speaks of the writ. He is in fact forbidding the first husband from remarrying his former wife if she has contracted another marriage in the meantime and has been subsequently divorced or widowed. The writ is really a legal prescription ensuring justice for the partners and preventing future disputes in a society where divorce was actually practised 'because of the hardness of their hearts (*sklêrokardia*).'

The Current Debate: *'erwat dabar*

They set the trap for Jesus by including in their question the hotly debated phrase 'for any cause whatever' (*kata pasan aitian*). They thus allude to the phrase *'erwat dabar* in Moses' prescription about the writ of divorce in Deut 24:1 the precise interpretation of which was disputed among revered rabbis and their learned followers at the time.[16]

The schools of Shammai and Hillel debated the interpretation of *'erwat dabar*, 'something shameful/displeasing' as a ground for divorce. Shammai held a strict position, that something serious like marital infidelity was intended. Hillel had the more liberal view that any matter causing the husband displeasure, such as spoiling a meal, was sufficient, and in the case of Rabbi Aqiba even finding a more attractive woman constituted a ground for divorce. These more liberal rabbis interpreted the two words *'erwat dabar* as alternatives, 'a shame' (*'erwat*) or 'some thing' (*dabar*) thus giving rise to 'some thing' as a basis for divorce, and this has found itself on the lips of the opposition to Jesus as they question Jesus about the grounds for divorce 'for any reason whatever', *kata pasan aitian*. This debate provided the Pharisees with the ammunition for putting Jesus to the test (*peirazontes auton*). They asked: 'Is it lawful to divorce one's wife for any cause whatever, *kata pasan aitian*?', 'for something displeasing' which motivates the husband to divorce his wife (Deut 24:1).

Jesus did not fall into their trap. He avoided the disputed phrase and so avoided being drawn into the debate. He also avoided the charge of opposing the teaching of the Torah and the authority of Moses. This he did by not only quoting the

---

16. In the corresponding account in Mark the question deals with the legality of divorce as such. Mark does not quote the phrase 'for any cause whatever (*kata pasan aitian*)' (Mk 10:2).

teaching of the Torah in Genesis (Gen 1:27 and 2:24) that was part of the Book of Moses but by using it to appeal to the authority of God the Creator. Having first cited the texts from Genesis he then restated his opposition to divorce. He frustrates the wily plan of his opponents because not alone is he not attacking either the scriptures or Moses but he is quoting the creation accounts which were also part of the Book of Moses, the Torah, and quoting an even higher authority than Moses, the Creator himself and his manifest intention enshrined for all to see in creation.

Basing his argument on the Torah, he rooted it not in texts about law or custom but about the creation itself. He put the questioners on a shaky footing when he asked: 'Have you not read?' and then introduced a far greater authority than that of Moses when he appealed to the Creator, 'He who created them from the beginning', thus drawing on the authority of God and pointing to the manifest will and purpose of God in creating them male and female. Combining Gen 1:27 and 2:24 he then said: 'He made them male and female. For this reason a man will leave father and mother and cling to his wife and the two will be one flesh; so the two are no longer two but one flesh. What God has joined together man must not divide.' The authority of God manifest in the creation shows that God has joined man and woman together in marriage and no man (no mere human being), a reference not only to a third party engaged in legal proceedings, faulty teaching or compromised moral standards but also referring to the husband himself, has authority to break that bond which is rooted by divine purpose in creation. He goes on to say that whoever divorces his wife 'except for *porneia*' (*mê epi porneia*) commits adultery against her.

Seeing the prescription of Moses as a compromise made necessary in a situation where divorce takes place because of their 'hardness of heart' (*sklêrokardia*), Jesus appeals to the scriptures that deal with creation where the ideal of marriage is laid down. The compromise had become the ideal and Jesus is in fact re-establishing the ideal of marriage and re-anchoring its definition in the theology of creation, removing its fundamental definition from the categories of law and custom.

Hardness of Heart: *sklêrokardia*

When his questioners ask why then did Moses command one to give a certificate of divorce when putting away one's wife, (Deut 24:1), Jesus countered their argument by pointing to the fact that Moses 'allowed' or catered for the *de facto* situation of divorce in a society where, because of their hardness of heart (*sklêrokardia*), it was necessary to ensure that the divorced partner be treated with justice. It does not say that a man should divorce his wife in any circumstance, but if a man divorces his wife then certain conditions apply. The prescription in Deut 24:1-2 is not about divorce as such but about the treatment of a woman who has been divorced. She must not be made the victim. A situation where she may be the victim of casual divorce and possible prearranged exchanges between husbands should not be countenanced.

'Hardness of heart' is mentioned here and also in the parallel passage in Mk 10:5. The term captures the idea frequently used in the Old Testament for resistance to God's word or plan as in the case of Pharaoh who refused to let the people go from Egypt or in the case of the Israelites in the desert when they hardened their hearts at Meriba, as recalled in Psalm 95, a prayer in which the people are asked not to harden their hearts. Jesus speaks of the hardness of heart in the former times, but now in the kingdom a new dispensation and set of attitudes are required. The opposite to hardness of heart is righteousness, the condition of the heart lauded in the beatitude of the one who co-operates with the will and plan of God even to the point of provoking persecution (Mt 5:10). The condition of the heart has been a repeating theme already in the gospel, summed up in the beatitude of the pure of heart (Mt 5:8).

The 'exceptive' *porneia* clauses Mt 5:31-32; Mt 19:9

In the third antithesis in the Sermon on the Mount Jesus said: 'The man who divorces his wife, except in the case of *porneia* (*parektos logou porneias*) and marries another, commits adultery (Mt 5:31-32).[17] He now says that whoever divorces his wife except for *porneia* (*mê epi porneia*) and marries another commits adultery against her. Jesus' anti-divorce stance is clear but what does he mean by the two uses of *porneia*?

Matthew alone has the exceptive clauses. Are they part of Jesus' original teaching or are they the product of Matthew's redaction? Since all other records of Jesus' attitude show him strongly opposed to divorce with no exceptions mentioned (Mt 5:31-32; 19:1-12; Lk 16:18; Mk 10: 2-9, 11-12; 1 Cor 7:10) it is very reasonable to say that they are most likely not part of Jesus' original statement. If, however, they are meant to reflect an original statement of Jesus which has come down to Matthew alone (which seems most unlikely) it is possible that he was saying 'leaving aside the matter of *porneia*,' in the sense of not getting involved in the *'erwat dabar* debate, a way of saying 'leaving aside the issue of *porneia*' or 'no comment on *porneia*'.

If, however, he actually took sides in the debate he would seem to be siding with the stricter side championed by the

---

17. Mark makes an equal case for men and women, implying that women can initiate divorce. This is because of the audience for whom Mark is writing and interpreting Jesus' message. In the Palestine of Jesus' day women did not initiate divorce. They were the vulnerable partner. Mark includes the prohibition on women divorcing their husbands because of the very different situation in Rome and the Roman cities under Italian law which gave them the same system as the mother city and the cities in Italy. There huge changes in the role, status and legal rights of women had taken place since the inception of the empire, and powerful Roman matrons regularly divorced their husbands. The implication in both cases is that a more powerful or influential partner, whether man or woman, does the other an injustice, and the person marrying the person who has been put away compounds that injustice. The adding of the prohibition against the woman initiating divorce has all the marks of an adjustment or 'spelling out' of the implications of Jesus' teaching on divorce for a (Greco-) Roman society with a legal system and customs very different to those among the Jews in Palestine. cf M. Mullins, *Called to be Saints*, 17ff.

school of Shammai. The exceptive clauses most likely, however, come from Matthew and not from Jesus. Since it is far more likely and far more widely accepted among scholars that Matthew is in fact referring to some matter of concern within the community, what did he mean or to what was he alluding in saying *parektos logou porneias* (Mt 5:32) and *mê epi porneia* (Mt 19:9)?

D. J. Harrington regards Matthew as having allied Jesus with the school of Shammai on the stricter side of the contemporary debate allowing divorce for marital infidelity (adultery) even though Jesus' position was in fact opposed to all divorce. He argues:

> By adding 'for any cause' in 19:3 and reserving the possibility of an exception in 19:9 ('except for sexual irregularity') Matthew has made Jesus a party in the first-century Jewish debate about the proper grounds for divorce … The two exceptive clauses in Mt 5:32 (*logos porneias*) and 19:19 (*epi porneia*) seem to take a stand with the School of Shammai against the more liberal views of the School of Hillel (even if the wife spoils a dish for him) and Rabbi Aqiba (even if he found another more beautiful than she is). Jesus' own teaching on divorce seems to have been even stricter (no divorce at all), perhaps in agreement with the Qumran Essenes (see CD 4:19-5:2; 11 Q Temple, though the interpretation of these texts remain controverted).[18]

J. P. Meier holds a different view, reflecting more closely the traditional Catholic understanding, in his commentary on Matthew. He points out that if *porneia* is taken to mean 'marital infidelity' in a sexual sense, then Jesus was making an exception in that case and was allying himself closely to the position of the Shammai school of thought. However, in so doing he would be undermining his own anti-divorce position. He holds that Matthew understood Jesus' prohibition to be absolute and without exception and that this is clear from his description of the disciples' horror at his stance and from Jesus' response to their

18. D. J. Harrington, *The Gospel of Matthew*, 274-5.

reaction (Mt 19:10-11). Had he just championed the position of Shammai over Hillel he would hardly have caused such a shocked exclamation that the unmarried state is preferable nor would he have followed that reaction with the statement that not everyone could accept what he had said except those to whom it had been granted. Meier goes on to say:

> *Porneia* in 5:32 refers rather to incestuous unions, i.e. marriages within prohibited degrees of consanguinity and affinity. All too common in the eastern Mediterranean, such marriages were forbidden by Lev 18:6-18. Some rabbis allowed a Gentile to maintain the incestuous union when he entered Judaism, and similar problems about these unions arose when Gentiles became Christians. The problem is mentioned in Acts 15:20, 29, 21:25 and 1 Cor 5:1. In all these texts *porneia* is used to describe the incestuous marriage. The 'exceptive clause' is thus the exact opposite of a relaxation of Jesus' radical morality.[19]

Summing up his comments on Mt 19:9 Meier says:

> Mt's point is that one cannot appeal to the Lord's prohibition of divorce to justify the maintenance of such unions. Thus, the 'exceptive clause' does not really weaken Jesus' absolute prohibition of divorce.[20]

Furthermore, on both historical and philological grounds 'adultery' is a doubtful interpretation because *porneia* has a broader range of meaning than 'adultery' as is obvious from Mt 15:19 where (in the list of evils that come from the heart) the plural forms *moicheiai* and *porneiai* are used for two different forms of 'unchastity', the former referring to 'adultery' the latter to 'fornication'. In fact in ten of the thirty-nine instances of its use in the LXX *porneia* is a translation of *zenuth* (fornication, association with prostitutes) and it seems to have the same meaning in Acts 15:28. In 1 Cor 5:1 it refers to a man living with his stepmother, a form of fornication that smacks of incest.

19. J. P. Meier, *Matthew*, 52-53.
20. Ibid, 216.

Another position, represented by Paul in 1 Cor 7:11, which may correspond in some measure to the situation which Matthew has in mind, allowed 'divorce' in the sense of separation without remarriage. It was not really divorce and the 'bond' was seen to endure. 'To the married I give this command – not I but the Lord – that the wife should not separate from her husband (but if she does separate, let her remain unmarried or else be reconciled to her husband), and that the husband should not divorce his wife.' One obvious reason for such a wish on the part of the wife to separate from her husband would be marital infidelity on the part of the husband. This was a practice of the early church in the early second century (*Hermas* 4, 1, 5-8).

The disciples' reaction Mt 19:10-11

The shocked reaction of the disciples and their outburst that 'if such is the case of a man with his wife, it were better for a man not to marry' highlights the radical and unexpected nature of Jesus' teaching on marriage and divorce. Had he allowed an exception, their shock would not be so great. Jesus goes on to say that not everyone could accept his teaching, only those to whom it is granted (by God).

Celibacy for the Kingdom Mt 19:12

The disciples' outburst is the cue for introducing Jesus' teaching on celibacy. These verses probably existed independently in the oral tradition and referred in a general way to celibacy 'for the kingdom'. Here they have taken on a certain affinity with the position of the rejected partner in the marriage and the prescription not to remarry (cf 1 Cor 7:10-11), but the basic meaning is that of celibacy for the kingdom.

Fidelity in marriage and celibacy for the kingdom, awaiting the kingdom, living as a sign of the kingdom or as a response to the arrival of the kingdom are ways of life which are given, that is, as a gift from God, which some people receive, and only those who receive the gift can accept and understand it. It is very different in nature from those born or determined in some other way to be unmarried, such as 'eunuchs from their mother's womb, eunuch's made so by men and eunuchs made so by themselves.'

Jesus' teaching on celibacy seems difficult to the disciples and he finishes it with an invitation to those who are able to accept celibacy for the kingdom.

b. Jesus and the Children Mt 19:13-15//Mk 10:13-16//Lk 18:15-17

Having dealt with Jesus' attitude to husbands and wives in the marriage and divorce discussion, it is a natural step to follow on with his attitude to the children. The people were bringing children to him so that he might 'lay his hands on them and pray.' Laying on of hands was a sign of blessing and healing, since blessing and healing could be obtained by contact with the holy person through an action like the laying on of hands or through the invocation by the holy one of a blessing from God.[21]

The action of the disciples in trying to prevent the people from bringing the children to Jesus is expressed in strong terms, 'they rebuked them', *epetimêsan autois*. Their attitude is unexplained here in Matthew, but Mark highlights Jesus' anger at their obvious misunderstanding which fits into Mark's ongoing portrait of their obtuseness (Mk 10:13-16).

Jesus said: 'Let the little children alone and do not prevent them coming to me; for of such as these is the kingdom of heaven.' Jesus has already spoken of the necessity of adopting the attitude of a child when he was asked (probably from selfish, ambitious motives) about the greatest in the kingdom of heaven (Mt 18:1-4). He also spoke of the importance of welcoming the child 'in my name' (Mt 18:5). Now he teaches, again accompanied by a parable in action in his laying hands on them, that 'of such is the kingdom of heaven'. The little children now join the company of 'the poor in spirit' and 'those who are persecuted

---

21. This story of Jesus and the children has been consistently used as an argument in favour of infant baptism. See J. Jeremias, *Infant Baptism in the First Four Centuries*, Philadelphia: Westminster, 1962; F.Beisser in his article, 'Markus 10:13-16 (parr) – doch ein Text für die Kindertaufe,' *Kerygma und Dogma* 41 (1995), 244-51, argues against such an interpretation.

for the sake of righteousness' of whom Jesus also said that 'theirs is the kingdom of heaven' (Mt 5:3,10).

The use of the diminutive *paidia*, 'little children' and the description of their 'being brought' to Jesus, highlight the point Jesus is making. The child's attitude to parents, family, society and the world is one of dependence and vulnerability. The child receives everything as gift, earns nothing and so depends on others for food, clothes, protection and all the other necessities of life. The child makes no display of self-sufficiency, much less of arrogance. The child's whole life is one series of receptive activities, seeing, hearing and touching as it embraces the world. The child is in a perpetual state of dependence and it expresses its needs in continually looking to the parents, an attitude the adult should have towards 'Our Father in Heaven' as Jesus has shown in his teaching on prayer. In the face of the kingdom we are all like children because we are all receivers and should display attitudes of receptivity, dependence and humility, rather than self-sufficiency, righteousness and arrogance.[22] These are the same dispositions displayed by the dependence of 'the poor in spirit' and the vulnerability of 'those persecuted for the sake of righteousness', of whom Jesus also says, 'Theirs is the kingdom of heaven.'

Jesus proceeded with the activity the disciples had tried to prevent. He laid his hands on the children. Then he went on his way from there (*eporeuthê ekeithen*).

c. Riches and Poverty Mt 19:16-30//Mk 10:17-31//Lk 18:18-30

This is one of the longest single treatments of an ethical issue in the gospels. It was probably put together from elements that were separate before being edited together in all three synoptics. It illustrates some important aspects of wealth, poverty and status. First of all the story of the rich man shows how a good, pious, law abiding Jew finds the attraction of wealth too strong

---

22. This attitude is summed up in the first beatitude in Matthew's Sermon on the Mount: 'Blessed are the poor in spirit, theirs is the kingdom of heaven' (Mt 5:3).

to give it away and become a benefactor of the poor and a disciple of Jesus. Secondly Jesus instructs his disciples on how difficult it is for the rich to enter the kingdom of heaven. Thirdly Jesus promises the disciples a hundredfold reward for following him and forsaking the things of the world. Fourthly there is the *logion* about being first and last and how these positions will be reversed.

i. The Rich Young Man Mt 19:16-22//Mk 10:17-22//Lk 18:18-23

'A certain man' (*eis*) approached him and said: 'Master (teacher) what good (deed/work) shall I do to obtain eternal life?' Unlike Mark and Luke Matthew does not tell us at the outset that he was a rich young man. He addresses Jesus as 'master/teacher', a title usually used by Matthew as an indicator that the questioner does not really have an adequate faith in Jesus.[23] He asks about doing good, maybe wishing to undertake some stricter way of life as a pious Jew, and so ensuring himself of eternal salvation.[24] Jesus' responded: 'Why do you ask me about the good? There is (only) One who is good (cf Deut 6:4). If you wish to enter into life keep the commandments.' The man said to him: 'Which ones?' His question may reflect the practice among the rabbis of discussing the relative weight of different commandments, as seen in the question: 'What is the greatest commandment of the Law?' (Mt 22:36 and//s).

Jesus first draws the attention away from himself to 'the One who is good', the One acknowledged in the *Shema*, the daily prayer of the Jews: 'Listen, O Israel, the Lord our God is One' (Deut 6:4). From this drawing of attention to 'the One', almost as a summary of the commandments about one's obligation to God, Jesus now reiterates the rest of the commandments, the second half of the Decalogue, those dealing with the neighbour. 'You shall not kill, you shall not commit adultery, you shall not steal, you shall not bear false witness, honour (your) father and

23. Some mss have 'good master' as the address, as it appears in Mark and Luke.

24. J. P. Meier, *Matthew*, 219, points out the Johannine terms used, such as *eternal life, entering into life, being perfect, entering the kingdom* and *being saved*.

mother.' Having begun with a summary recognition of the One, Jesus now sums up the other commandments with the challenge to 'love your neighbour as yourself' (cf Lev 19:18; Mt 22:39//Mk 12:31//Lk 10:27).

The questioner, now described as 'the young man' (*neaniskos*), answered that he had kept all these commandments and asked what else was lacking.[25]

Jesus poses the great challenge. 'If you wish to be perfect (*teleios*) go and sell your possessions and give to the poor and you will have treasure in heaven, and come follow me.' The meaning of the word 'perfect' (*teleios*) here has been seen by many scholars as a call to a higher state of perfection than that of the ordinary pious Jew fulfilling the requirements of the commandments with regard to God and neighbour, or as a call to the Christian to follow some kind of higher calling to a life of perfection in some religious life and vows. This is to miss the point. The call is not to a state of static perfection but to a state or situation in life which allows one the freedom to leave all things and become a disciple.

The word *teleios* is from *telos*, which means goal, purpose, completion. What Jesus is saying to the young man is that if he wishes to reach his ultimate purpose or goal, to fulfil his full potential, what he must do is to shake off all the shackles of wealth and be a free man to follow Jesus' call to discipleship. This call is not a call to asceticism as such, or to a hostile attitude to the things of the world, but rather a call to the itinerant lifestyle of an apostle, as pointed out by J. R. Donahue and D. J. Harrington in their commentary on the parallel passage in Mark's gospel:

> Being with Jesus and sharing in his mission of teaching and healing demand the adoption of the simplest possible way of life ('one staff, no bread, no bag, no money') and subordinating one's personal comfort to the mission. The kind of poverty envisioned in Mark's gospel is apostolic or mission-oriented rather than ascetic in the sense that self-denial becomes an

---

25. Matthew, unlike Mark, does not mention Jesus' emotional reaction and affection for the young man on hearing his response (Mk 10:31).

end in itself. The man's rejection of Jesus' invitation arises from his unwillingness to adopt the simple and itinerant lifestyle suited to Jesus' ministry and the conditions of first-century Palestine.[26]

It is a call to discipleship like that issued at the beginning of the gospel to the two pairs of brothers and subsequently to Matthew. They left everything and followed Jesus. This young man failed to rise to the challenge and leave everything to become a disciple because of his great wealth. His possessions possessed him. Instead of experiencing the joy of the kingdom he went away sad. He did not find the joy of the man who found the treasure in the field or the merchant who found the pearl of great price and sold everything to posses it with great joy (Mt 13:44-46).

ii. Jesus' Teaching on Riches Mt 19:23-26//Mk 10:23-27//Lk 18:24-27

Then Jesus pronounced solemnly to his disciples: 'Amen I say to you, with difficulty will a rich man enter the kingdom of heaven. Again I say to you, it is easier for a camel to pass through the eye of a needle than for a rich man to enter the kingdom of God.'

The image of the camel passing through the eye of a needle is as striking as it is hyperbolic. In spite of the hyperbole it makes a very clear point. Riches can be a diriment impediment to entry into the kingdom. Suggestions that the eye of the needle was a gate in the walls of Jerusalem through which large animals like the camel passed with great difficulty, or seeing the word *kamêlon* (camel) as a mistake and 'correcting' it to read *kamilon*, (rope), as in some manuscripts, serve only to rob the hyperbole of its powerful effect.

Possessions and the pressures put on people by wealth which needs protection, care, planning and general expenditure of time and energy, distract from more important aspects of life and living. Furthermore wealth has an addictive character mak-

---

26. J. R. Donahue and D. J. Harrington, *op. cit.*, 307

ing one seek more and more. Paul used the term, avarice, the need for more that is never satisfied, which he describes as idolatry, *eidôlolatria* (Col 3:5; cf Mk 7:22).[27] Being a form of idolatry it turned people's minds away from the true God to serve the false god of wealth (cf Prov 15:16; 30:8-9). Wealth is a stumbling block and a cause of iniquity (Ezek 7:19; Sir 31:5-7). The biblical 'remedy' for wealth was to use it for good purposes, such as the relief of poverty. In biblical thought the good person prospers and becomes a benefactor, making friends with 'the mammon of iniquity', ensuring a welcome in the kingdom from the recipients of one's generosity (Job 1:1-5; 29:1-25; Lk 16:9). The failure to show concern for the poor, an attitude born of the addiction to wealth and the luxurious lifestyle it spawns, is the recurring target of the Law, the Prophets and the Wisdom Books (Amos 6:1-7; 8:4-6). There follows from this the understanding that 'the poor' are privileged in so far as they, unlike the rich, are not enslaved to wealth and worldliness and so Luke can write, 'Blessed are you poor' and 'Woe to you who are rich ...'(Lk 6:20,24). The receptivity of the poor to the gift of God is seen in the *Magnificat*. 'He puts down the mighty from their thrones and raises the lowly / He fills the starving with good things, and sends the rich away empty' (Lk 1:52f). The 'poor in spirit', the *annouim*, the subject of the first beatitude, were those who lived a spirituality focused on God and unattached to the lure of wealth and worldly attractions (Mt 5:3). The Essenes at Qumran also put an emphasis on detachment from wealth (1 QS 1:11-13; 6:19, 22; 9:8-9, 22).

Unlike the call to poverty in Luke-Acts where there is an emphasis on ideal communities sharing all goods in common (Acts 2:44-45; 4:32), the call to poverty in Matthew and Mark is geared in a very practical way towards an itinerant missionary life. It is very well described by J. R. Donahue and D. J. Harrington in their commentary on the corresponding text in Mark:

The kind of poverty promoted by Mark and other NT writers is not simply monastic community of goods or a primitive

27. Mark includes avarice in the list of evils that come out of a person (Mk 7:22).

form of communism as envisioned in the Qumran Rule of the Community. Rather it is first and foremost poverty undertaken voluntarily in the service of proclaiming and witnessing to the kingdom of God. It is intended to contribute to an appreciation of the centrality of God's kingdom by minimising the distractions involved in becoming and staying rich, and it promises rewards not only in the world to come but also in the present. Mark's addition of 'with persecutions' in 10:30, however, is a sobering reminder of the reality of the world in which Mark's community lived and worked ...[28]

The disciples again react with an almost despairing attitude towards Jesus' teaching and they ask: 'Who then can be saved?' Jesus responds with the profound reflection that 'for men (human beings) this is impossible', an affirmation of their own feelings of inadequacy in the face of the challenge put before them. Then he adds, in almost Pauline theology and phraseology, 'For God all things are possible.' The saving work of God overcomes human inadequacy and weakness, or to use Paul's expression: 'I can do all things in him who gives me strength, for when I am weak then I am strong' (Phil 4:11-13). A later theological language would say: 'God's grace overcomes human weakness.'

d. The Reward of Discipleship Mt 19:27-30//Mk 10:28-31//Lk 18:28-30
Peter, again acting as spokesman for the disciples, responds to Jesus: 'Look, we have left everything and followed you. What then will we have?' Peter's question 'What will we have?' is particularly pointed. In Mark and Luke Peter simply says; 'We have left everything/our possessions and followed you' (Mk 10:28; Lk 18:28) without adding the explicit request: 'What will we have?' The contrast with the man who refused to give up his possessions is highlighted by this remark about all that the disciples have left behind. Responding with the solemn formula, 'Amen I say to you', Jesus promises them an eschatological reward when all things are made new (*en tê palingenesia*). Unlike

28. J. R. Donahue and D. J. Harrington, *op. cit.*, 308.

Mark and Luke, Matthew does not mention a reward in the present life and a subsequent reward in the life to come, nor does he mention the accompanying persecution. Matthew focuses on the promise of reward 'when all things are made new'. The Twelve will share in his reign. 'When the Son of Man sits on the throne of his glory' they will be duly rewarded. They will 'sit on twelve thrones judging the twelve tribes of Israel.' In the days before the monarchy the twelve tribes of Israel were ruled by judges. Their function was to rule, guide, protect, lead and judge the people. The Twelve are here promised a leadership role in the eschatological people of God.

In addition, they are promised that their leaving of houses, brothers, sisters, father, mother, children or land (fields) 'for the sake of my name' would be rewarded a hundredfold (some mss have 'manifold') and they will also inherit eternal life.

The eschatological reversal of roles and status, when the rich and powerful, the 'high and mighty' of the present world are cast down and the rejected and persecuted Christ and his followers share in the glory of the kingdom, is well expressed in the *logion* or saying of Jesus: 'Many who are first will be last and the last first' (Mt 19:30).

This *logion* forms both a conclusion to the promise of reward and a link to the parable of the labourers in the vineyard, for which it provides a frame, being quoted at the beginning and end of the parable. It appears in the parallel passage in Mk 10:31 and in Luke at the conclusion of the parables on final salvation (Lk 13:30). It is obviously a well-remembered *logion* or saying of Jesus that has outlived its original context and has been used in different contexts. It may even be the case that Jesus used it himself in different contexts for that very purpose. It emphasises the reversal of values, status, roles and destinies in the final arrangement of the kingdom, when all things are made new.

i. The Labourers in the Vineyard Mt 20:1-16

The *logion* is ringing in the reader's ears as Jesus introduces a parable with the familiar introduction: 'The kingdom of heaven is like'. The simile refers to the whole parable and not just to the 'landowner'.

The householder (not his steward!) went out early in the morning (about 6 am) to hire labourers for his vineyard. He agreed with them that they would be paid a *denarius* a day. A *denarius* a day seems to have been the regular wage for a day's work at the time. At about the third hour (9 am) he found men standing idle in the market place and sent them into the vineyard saying he would pay them 'whatever was just'. They entered the vineyard. At the sixth and ninth hours (12 noon and 3 pm) he did the same. About the eleventh hour he went out and found others standing there and he asked them: 'Why have you been standing here idle all day?' They answered: 'Because nobody hired us.' He sent them also into the vineyard. There is no talk of payment at this point.

What has really taken place so far in this parable? The first hiring in the early morning was standard practice, a contract between men available for work and an employer. The reader wonders about the second, third and fourth hiring. Was there extra work because of an abundant harvest or was the householder concerned about the breadwinners not being employed, with serious consequences for themselves and their families? The reader is wondering about this when at the eleventh hour the householder goes out and asks the men why they were idle all day. Their answer provides the key to the householder's conduct. Not being employed all day and still standing there in the hope of work, evidenced by their going to the vineyard without even a discussion about pay, shows the character of the labourers and of the householder. He could have shown his concern for them by giving them an alms. That, however, would have injured their pride and self- esteem, turning working people, who were prepared to wait all day for employment, into beggars. He gave them the dignity of employment and preserved their pride as he also provided for their needs and those of their families.

When evening came and time to call the labourers to receive their wages the reader is confronted with the surprising fact that

the householder instructed his steward to call the labourers and
to begin by paying the last people hired and work back to the
first. Already there is a first-last reversal of order. But there is
something more striking to come. Those hired at the eleventh
hour, without any agreement on pay are given a full day's
wages. They would have worked for it if they had the chance.
The householder knew their predicament. He gave them a gift,
and instead of an alms for the poor, which would have demeaned them, they received a very generous wage for their
labours. When he came to the first he gave them the just wage on
which they had agreed. They had the advantage of being employed in the early morning. They needed no charity, no benev-
olent patron. They earned their wages and the employer gave
them their due. But they complained.

The reader is challenged at this point to judge both their complaint and the householder's defence of his action. They complained about bearing the heat of the day and only receiving the
same pay as those who came to work at the eleventh hour. The
householder defended his action by stating that he is free to do
with his own (money) as he pleases and challenges his critics on
the grounds that they resent his generosity.

The parable is rounded off with the *logion* about the reversal
of status with which it began. ' Thus shall the last be first and the
first last.'

The parable is left to the reader to ponder over. It is like the
story of the resentful brother in the parable of the Prodigal Son
and his forgiving father in Lk 15:11-32 where the compassion of
the father for the wayward son and his joy at his return is resented
by the older son who cannot see beyond his own selfish interests, thereby overlooking the goodness of the father and the desperate need of the brother.

e. The Third Prediction of the Passion Mt 20:17-19//Mk 10:32- 34//Lk 18:31-33

Jerusalem is now explicitly mentioned as the goal of the southward journey. 'And going up to Jerusalem,[29] Jesus took the Twelve aside by themselves, and on the way said to them: 'Behold, we are going up to Jerusalem and the Son of Man will be given over to the chief priests and scribes, and they will condemn him to death, and they will hand him over to the Gentiles to be mocked and scourged and crucified; and on the third day he will be raised' (cf Mt 16:21; 17:23).

Jesus makes this prediction of his forthcoming fate as he starts the final stage of his journey to Jerusalem. He takes the Twelve aside to instruct them privately. Matthew is more sparing of their feelings than Mark who emphasises their confusion and fear at this juncture (Mk 10:32). Matthew uses the more precise kerygmatic language of ' being raised, *egerthêsetai*, on the third day' rather than Mark's 'after three days *anastêsetai*, he will rise again'. In this the great reversal is again proclaimed. The rejected, tortured one, the 'last' in rank, status and earthly success, will be 'first' when vindicated by God on the third day.

Jerusalem has been the real centre of hostility to him throughout the ministry and he is now deliberately setting his face to go up to the city. He has already made two predictions of his rejection by the Jewish authorities in Jerusalem (Mt 16:21; 17:23), but he now mentions for the first time that they will hand him over to the Gentiles by whom he will be mocked and scourged and that the death awaiting him will be by crucifixion.[30] He again refers to himself in this third prediction as Son of Man. The third prediction reads like a programme for the dramatic events of Jesus' last day alive – being handed over to the chief priests and scribes; condemned to death; handed over to the Gentiles; being mocked and scourged and crucified

---

29. Some mss read: 'As he was about to go up to Jerusalem, *mellôn de anabainein.*'

30. Mark says 'kill' rather than crucify in this third prediction.

and then raised on the third day.[31] The detailed nature of this third passion prediction, making the description more detailed as Jesus came closer to his fate, may well reflect a tradition from the liturgy or from a catechism on which the evangelist drew.[32] E. Schweizer points out that the emphasis on 'being handed over to the Gentiles' (this is the first mention of the Gentile involvement in his predicted death) and the details of how they treat him may well point to a Jewish-Christian tradition, possibly in Palestine.[33]

i. The Mother of the Sons of Zebedee Mt 20:23

As in the case of the two earlier predictions, the disciples react with a mixture of misunderstanding, incomprehension and apprehension when they realise that this prediction may have implications for their own lives as well (Mt 16:21; 17:22-23//Mk 8:32f; 9:33ff). In the case of each prediction there follows a focus on the disciples' failure to understand. Peter's failure to understand resulted in his telling Jesus, 'This must never happen to you,' after the first prediction (Mt 16:22). After the second prediction 'a great sadness came over them' (Mt 17:22-23). This third prediction seems to fall on deaf ears because the request of the mother of the sons of Zebedee, which follows immediately, shows how they have not understood anything of what Jesus has been saying about the fate awaiting him in Jerusalem but keep thinking in terms of earthly status and importance.

The failure of the disciples and their families and associates to really 'take in' what Jesus is predicting is highlighted by the mother of the sons of Zebedee who came to Jesus with her sons, bowing low and saying she wanted to make a request of him. When Jesus asked her what she wished him to do for her she asked that her sons be given the places at his right and left side

---

31. Concerning the third prediction in Mark's gospel, D. E. Nineham, *op. cit.*, 278, makes a comment that is equally true of Matthew's account. He says that it reads 'like a printed programme of a Passion Play.'
32. E. Schweizer, *op. cit*, 217.
33. Ibid., 216.

in his kingdom. The request provides Jesus with the opportunity of furthering the discussion of his forthcoming fate and pointing out that they too may have to share in it: 'Can you drink the cup that I am going to drink?'

What exactly were they expecting from Jesus and why were the ten indignant with them? They were nearing Jerusalem and the end was in sight. They may have expected the great revolution and the establishment of the kingdom along the lines of the kingdom of David. The request on behalf of James and John then would have been to share the thrones of political power with the newly proclaimed messianic-warrior king. Or it may have been a reflection of the same thinking that manifested itself in the Qumran community where there was a detailed approach to where everyone would sit at the messianic banquet. Whichever it was, the other ten protested, probably not out of high moral principle, but because their own ambitions were being cut across as the brothers got their applications in ahead of them![34]

Places in the Kingdom

Jesus' immediate response to the request on behalf the sons of Zebedee was to say, 'You do not know what you are asking.' Sharing with Jesus meant sharing in his rejection, suffering and death. Those who were eventually on his right and left side were in fact those crucified with him!

Jesus asks them if they can drink the cup that he has to drink. 'Drinking the cup' is a well-established image in the Bible. It can signify something good as in 'my cup is overflowing' (Ps 23:5), but it usually refers to suffering.[35] In the second century AD the apocryphal Martyrdom of Isaiah speaks of the cup in terms of martyrdom: 'For me God has mingled the cup of martyrdom.'[36] Jesus replies that they will drink his cup, but 'to sit at my right or

---

34. C. Focant, *op. cit.*, 398, puts it succinctly: *'Le lecteur ne peut pas deviner si leur indignation est intéressée ou verteuse.'*

35. Isa 51:17,22; Lam 4:21; Ps 75:8, Jn 18:11 and Mk 14:36//Mt 26:42// Lk 22:42.

36. Martyrdom of Isaiah, 5:13. Mark adds a parallel metaphor of undergoing a baptism.

left hand is not mine to give, but it belongs to those for whom it is prepared by my Father'. The readers of the gospels then, and now, are reminded that sharing with Jesus means sharing in persecution and martyrdom.

Ironically James was to die at the command of Herod (Acts 12:2). There are various accounts of John's martyrdom but also a contrary tradition of his living to old age in Ephesus. If he lived to old age in Ephesus, he certainly knew of the persecution by Nero in Rome and would live to see the persecution by Domitian in Asia Minor, the area in which he was living. Furthermore, the evangelists and their intended readers may have been aware of tensions about status and privilege in the church/community and so in recounting this story they indirectly address the issue.

The disciples had already questioned Jesus about rank and status in the kingdom (Mt 18:1). Now he calls them to him and talks to them about the nature of worldly power.[37] The terms used for exercising power *katakurieuousin* and *katexousiazousin* are rare and point to an oppressive exercise of power that weighs heavily on people.[38] He tells the disciples: 'It is not to be so with you.'

ii. Son of Man/As one who serves/Ransom for many

The reversal of status theme comes up again as Jesus elaborates on the paradoxical nature of leadership and greatness in the kingdom. It has already been touched on after the first passion prediction when Jesus spoke about denying oneself, taking up one's cross and following him, and losing one's life for his sake (Mt 16:24-2). Now after the third prediction of his passion he states that the one who wants to be great (*megas*) among you must be your servant (*diakonos*) and whoever wishes to be first (*prôtos*) among you must be your slave (*doulos*) (Mt 20:26-27).

---

37. Mark has a stinging note of irony at this point as he speaks of 'the appearance' of worldly power, since he refers to *hoi dokountes archein*, 'the ones who appear to rule'.
38. C. Focant, *op. cit.*, 398.

Jesus does not teach this in the abstract or from a safe distance. He himself leads the way. He speaks of his forthcoming death as the death of the Son of Man. Here he now speaks of the Son of Man as one who serves.[39] This is a far cry from the picture of the glorious Son of Man in Daniel coming in splendour to subject the nations to his rule (Dan 7:14, 27), a role which would elicit thoughts of one who came to be served and to save others from death rather than one who comes to serve others and to submit himself to death.

The Danielic picture of a glorious saviour of the nation, a conquering hero on their behalf, comes from a period of persecution, represented also in the stories of the Maccabees and the great persecution the nation suffered at the hands of Antiochus IV (Epiphanes). Now, however, Jesus' climactic statement, or *logion*, in this collection of sayings allies the Son of Man with the persecuted rather than with the saviour-warrior. He sums up the teaching on discipleship in terms of service to the point of giving one's life. 'For the Son of Man himself did not come to be served but to serve, and to give his life as a ransom for many' (Mt 20:28//Mk 10:45).

In a corresponding collection of sayings a similar instruction to the one given here is given by Jesus at the Last Supper in Luke's gospel following a dispute among the disciples about who was the greatest (Lk 22:24-27). The teaching about 'greatness' in Lk 22:27 represents Jesus as stating simply: 'Here am I among you as one who serves.' Some scholars see the Lukan version as the older one going back to Jesus himself and they see the Matthean and Markan version as introducing a whole new theological dimension into the teaching, as he goes on to explain

---

39. God's power is the real power and it often works in a way completely opposite to human expectations and practices. Jesus himself submits to the will of the Father as he accepts the fact that 'it is necessary' for the Son of Man to suffer. He does not seek earthly power and status but accepts the role of one who serves and suffers. As he accepts the will of the Father, not determining his own status and glory, so must his followers accept the will of Father and the positions in the kingdom that are determined not by the one sent, but by the One who sent him.

the significance of his death as 'a ransom for many'. In John's gospel the washing of the disciples' feet is a parable in action showing how the disciples must accept the role of Jesus as servant, and as the one whose service implies his death on their behalf and how they too must imitate his service, even to the point of laying down their life for others (Jn 13:2-17; 15:13).

Matthew and Mark render this service of the Son of Man as *lytron anti pollôn*, usually translated as 'a ransom for many'. In the words of V. Taylor, 'This saying is one of the most important in the gospels.'[40] But what exactly does it mean? It is somewhat out of harmony in context and without parallel elsewhere in Matthew and Mark.[41] Each of the three words has provoked scholarly discussion. It represents a very sudden and radical departure in terminology since elsewhere during their accounts of the ministry Jesus does not speak of his death in terms of ransom (*lytron/lytroô*), as in paying the price for the release of a captive or the emancipation of a slave (Lev 25:47-55), or in ritual terms like the sacrifice offered in place of the first-born (Exod 13:13-16). Furthermore, the LXX never associates *'asham* (an offering for sin) and *lytrôn* (ransom).

The preposition *anti*, 'for', can be translated as 'in favour of', 'for the benefit of' or 'instead of'. Its meaning in this context depends on one's interpretation of *lytron*. 'Many' in the Greek usage of the gospel is a translation of the underlying Hebrew or Aramaic 'many' which serves for 'the multitude', 'a limitless number', 'all the people', an expression used in the Dead Sea Scrolls for ' the people of God / the community'.[42] In the Pauline tradition a parallel statement is translated as 'all' in the phrase *antilytron hyper pantôn*, 'ransom on behalf of all' (1 Tim 2:6).

This concept of 'ransom for many' picks up on the 'saving the

---

40. V. Taylor, *The Gospel of Mark*, 444.
41. See also A. Y. Collins, 'The Signification of Mark 10:45 among Gentile Christians', *HTR* 90 (1997) 371-82 and B. Lindars, 'Salvation Proclaimed. VII. Mark 10:45: A Ransom for Many,' *Exp Tim* 93 (1981-82), 292-95.
42. 1 QS 6:1,7-25; CD 13:7; 14:7.

people' motif of the Son of Man in so far as it speaks of the salvation of the people, and it may reflect also the understanding of the deaths of martyrs as compensation for the sins of the people (1 Macc 2:50; 6:44; 2 Macc 7:17ff; 4 Macc 6:29; 17:21f). But it seems closest to the Christian community's reflection on the death of Jesus and its significance for salvation, as seen first in the Pauline letters and also in the emerging Johannine tradition of service and laying down one's life for flock or friend, though not necessarily dependent on these traditions. In the Pauline tradition a parallel statement is found in the phrase *antilytron hyper pantôn*, 'ransom on behalf of all' (1 Tim 2:6). The correspondence between them is obvious also in the verbal similarities in *antilytron* and *lytron anti*. A corresponding idea is found in various New Testament documents using the related term *apolytrôsis* (Rom 3:24; 8:23; 1 Cor 1:30; Eph 1:7, 14; Heb 4:30; 9:15; 11:35).

In John the washing of the disciples' feet casts Jesus in the role of one who serves and in interpreting the gesture Jesus points to the necessity of accepting his servant model of salvation and he instructs the disciples to follow his example, since 'I who am Lord and Master have washed your feet, you should wash each other's feet … no servant is greater than his master' … 'greater love no one has than to lay down one's life for one's friends' (Jn 13:3-16; 15:13). Earlier in John Jesus had spoken of the ideal shepherd as one who 'lays down his life for his sheep' (Jn 10:11, 15, 17, 18). It appears that the connection between service and giving one's life was well established as the traditions of Jesus' teaching developed in the light of his saving death and resurrection. John also records the words of the High Priest 'prophesying' that Jesus would die for the nation (Jn 11:50, 51). Underlying the synoptic, Johannine and Pauline developments of the theme, is the basic concept of a service given by one who is prepared to render that service even if it is given at the cost of one's life.

The vicarious suffering of the Suffering Servant in Isa 52-53 as a background to 'ransom for many' has been both affirmed and denied by scholars. Some point to the fact that the LXX does

not use *diakonos/diakonein* for 'servant/serve' but renders the
Hebrew *ebed* (servant) as *pais*, sometimes as *doulos*. On the other
hand the 'ransom for many' does at least resonate with the vicarious suffering ' for many' and 'praying all the time for sinners' of
Isa 53:4, 5, 10-12. One must remember, however, that ideas and
images can persist and influence each other even if different vocabulary is used, especially when an idea is remembered in an
oral context without immediate access to a written text, and
above all when it is translated into another language. In this way
a *logion* or an idea can be established in popular tradition.

What is not in dispute is the call to service of others, in imit-
ation of the Son of Man who rendered that service to the point of
paying for it with his life. Whatever the earlier history of the *logion*, it is set in the Matthean and Markan context of the rejected,
suffering, Son of Man who goes to his death in accordance with
the plan or will of the Father looking forward in faith to a vindication by God for himself and those who follow him. R. H.
Gundry sums up very well:

> Jesus interprets his approaching death as supremely self-sac-
> rificial for the saving of many other's lives ... The Cross will
> not bring shame to its victim, but salvation to his followers.[43]

f. Two Blind Men in Jericho Mt 20:29-34//Lk 18:35-43 cf Mk 10:46-52
The location of the story, as Jesus leaves Jericho and a large (undefined) crowd follow him, emphasises the fact that Jesus is now
only fifteen miles or so from Jerusalem and from here on 'going
up to Jerusalem' is literally a journey from the lowest point on
the earth's surface up the steep incline to Jerusalem, built on the
central ridge of the highlands.

The healing of the two blind men, which takes place as Jesus
leaves Jericho, corresponds to the story of the healing of the
blind Bartimaeus in Mark's gospel. Matthew has a fondness for
pairs as is obvious from his having two Gadarene demoniacs
(Mt 8:28-34), two blind men healed as he went on his way after

---

43. R. H. Gundry, *Mark. A Commentary on his Apology for the Cross*,
Grand Rapids: Eerdmans, 1993, 2000, 581.

the restoration to life of the official's daughter (Mt 9:27-31) and the two blind men here at Jericho (Mt 20:29-34). Typical of Matthew, the story is told more briefly than in Mark, thus focusing on the encounter between the faith-driven petitioners and the mercy-driven healer. Unlike Mark who gives the personal name of Bartimaeus and explains it as 'Son of Timaeus' and describes him as a beggar and gives the detail of how he abandoned his cloak (probably used by him as a receptacle on the ground for collecting alms) as he followed Jesus 'on the way', Matthew does not give the personal names, or the fact that were beggars, or mention the cloak or 'the way'. Neither does he elaborate on the make up of the crowd.

This is the last of the healing stories and it fulfils an important function in the gospel. It rounds off the major section of the gospel dealing with the journey to Jerusalem, which was punctuated with the three passion predictions, the reactions to those predictions on the part of the disciples and others, and the instructions for the disciples about the way of discipleship. The two blind men stand out at the end of this major section of the gospel dealing with discipleship as a paradoxical example of two men 'without sight' who see what many sighted people failed to see. They manifest faith, understanding and courage, and become disciples, following Jesus. The story reminds the reader of the healing of the blind man in John's gospel and the comments of Jesus about blindness and sight (Jn 9:1-41).

They respond to the presence of Jesus with a faith-filled address: 'Lord, Son of David, have pity on us'. Like the Canaanite woman and the man with the dumb (epileptic)/possessed son, they call out to Jesus for mercy, calling out from the margins, bringing nothing to their call but faith. Their 'calling out' to Jesus increases after the crowd rebuke and try to silence them. They call out louder: 'Lord, Son of David, have pity on us.' In the context of his healings Jesus responds with compassion to the title Son of David (cf Mt 9:27; 15:22).

Jesus responds immediately to their cry for mercy. Three

times they use the address 'Lord' associated with faith in Jesus,[44] and they use the messianic term 'Son of David' twice, as they appeal to Jesus for mercy. J. P. Meier makes an interesting comment on their appeal. 'Considering the pleas to Jesus for mercy here and in 9:27; 15:22; 17:15, one wonders whether *Kyrie eleison* ('Lord, have mercy') was not already a liturgical cry in Mt's church.'[45] Jesus will subsequently challenge the Pharisees about their limited understanding of the Christ as Son of David, saying to them that David himself called him 'Lord', the title the blind men have just given him together with the title Son of David (Mt 22:41-46).

Again the roles are reversed as Jesus stands and calls these people who were nobodies in the eyes of the onlookers and an embarrassment on a public occasion with an important person present. They now take centre stage as Jesus called them and asked: 'What do you want me to do for you?' and they replied, 'Lord, that our eyes might open.' Hearing their request Jesus takes pity on them and renders them the great service of his healing touch, and as he touched their eyes they immediately received their sight and they followed him, that is, they became his disciples.

Their confession also sets the tone for what follows in the triumphal approach to Jerusalem as the crowds hail Jesus in terms of a royal son of David, and prepares the reader for what follows by way of Jesus' authoritative action in the temple, his disputes with religious leaders and his debates with teaching authorities, coming to a climax with his statement that the Christ is not only Son of David but also the one whom David addressed as Lord (Mt 22:41-46).

44. Some mss do not have 'Lord' in the first address.
45. J. P. Meier, *Matthew*, 230.

Royal Visit and Prophetic Visitation
Mt 21-25

Plot and Outline of Chapters 21-25

The final phase of Jesus' life and ministry consists of two major sections, his activity in the city and environs in chapters 21 to 25 and the Passion and Easter Narratives in chapters 26 to 28. The five chapters (Mt 21-25), though composed from previously independent materials, form a single overall unit covering the ministry of Jesus in Jerusalem. Chapters 21-23 are basically narrative interspersed with dialogue and controversy and chapters 24 and 25 consist of the final major discourse of the gospel.

The entire section has the character of a denouement. The royal, messianic visitation of the city heralds a radical change, an ending of temple worship (Mt 21:12-22) and of teaching authority (Mt 21:23–23:39). The visitation is carried out by one who not only manifests an authority greater than the temple and greater than the teaching authorities, but one who prophesies also the destruction of the temple (Mt 24:1-2), the universal mission of the gospel (Mt 24:14), the end of the world as we know it, and the coming of the Son of Man in glory to gather the elect (Mt 24:31).

There are indications that his final visit may have been of longer duration than may appear from the synoptic and Johannine accounts. That Jesus died during the Passover celebrations is clear from all four gospels but there are some indications in the text that his 'triumphal' entry may have taken place either during the autumn Feast of Tabernacles or the winter Feast of Dedication/Hanukkah. The waving of branches and palms was a prescribed ritual in these festivals. These branches were usually gathered outside the city (as is specifically stated in Mt 21:8//Mk 11:8). The palm, mentioned only by John (Jn 12:13), was brought for the Feasts of Tabernacles and Hanukkah from the area around Jericho, pointing to its not being a spontaneous gathering of palm branches on the occasion but a using of those branches already collected for these feasts. This may indicate a longer final visit to Jerusalem or a 'triumphal' entry on an earlier visit. D. E. Nineham suggests that possibly the early church was already celebrating a Holy Week and therefore the various elements were fit into the framework of one final week.[1]

Jesus acts and teaches with an authority that manifests his superiority over the religious administration and teaching authority. A significant turning point in the section occurs when Jesus asks the Pharisees: 'What is your opinion about the Christ? Whose son is he?' They answered 'David's.' Jesus then points to an authority greater than the traditional understanding of the Messiah as Son of David. It is the authority of one whom David, moved by the Spirit, addresses as Lord (Mt 22:41-44). From this point to the end of the section Jesus is building up to his prophecy of the coming of the Son of Man in glory to gather the elect. He adopts the mantle of eschatological-apocalyptic prophet and predicts the end of the temple and of the world, and the coming in glory of the Son of Man to gather the elect when the universal mission to preach the good news to all nations is complete.

This final phase of Jesus' life and ministry opens with his triumphal entry into Jerusalem.[2] The reader has two contending impressions as Jesus approaches the city. On the one hand, there is the sense of foreboding created by Jesus' own predictions of what lies ahead and, on the other hand, there is the enthusiasm of the crowd surrounding his approach and entry into to the city from his leaving Jericho to his arrival at the temple in Jerusalem.

---

1. D. E. Nineham, *op. cit.*, 289.
2. The synoptic gospels do not recount any visit of Jesus to the Holy City during his ministry prior to his final, fateful visit. In the synoptics therefore all the traditions dealing with his Jerusalem ministry are contained in this one visit. In St John's gospel, on the other hand, Jesus goes to Jerusalem on a number of occasions to attend and carry on his ministry at the pilgrimage feasts so the traditions dealing with Jerusalem are spread over a number of visits.

1. CHALLENGES IN JERUSALEM MT 21:1–23:39

a. Royal Visit Mt 21:1-11

i. Preparing to enter the City Mt 21:1-5//Mk 11:1-6//Lk 19:28-34

A royal visitor and significant prophetic figure is now coming to the city on the occasion of the festival. Both the geographical direction and the carefully prepared manner of his approach are laden with biblical significance. He approaches the city from the Mount of Olives and comes seated on a donkey.

Jewish expectations of a royal or prophetic Messiah fired the minds of the Jews at the pilgrimage feasts, especially at Passover. The authorities, Jewish and Roman, had to be very alert to the presence of any messianic figure and the prospect of revolutionary activity when crowds assembled for the pilgrimage feasts, especially for Passover with its historical connotations of liberation from slavery and the defeat of the apparently indestructible army of the oppressor.

The Mount of Olives

The association of the Mount of Olives with the coming of the Messiah was deeply rooted in the biblical tradition and the historian Josephus mentions it in the *Jewish War* and the *Antiquities*.[3] A ceremonial approach by a messianic figure from the Mount of Olives would conjure up the imagery of the Day of the Lord, the Day of Judgement and of the eschatological battle. Zechariah described the coming of *YHWH* for the eschatological judgement of Jerusalem and the nations: 'A day is coming for *YHWH* ... On that day his feet will rest on the Mount of Olives, which faces Jerusalem from the east' (Zech 14:1,4). Malachi also prophesied about the Day of *YHWH* when there would be a divine judgement on the temple (Mal 3:1, 2). This echo of judgement will run not only through the immediate approach of Jesus to the city and temple but right throughout the ministry in Jerusalem.[4]

---

3. Josephus, *War* 11,13,5; *Ant*, 20,8,6.
4. J. Radermakers, *La Bonne Nouvelle de Jésus selon saint Marc*, 304.

As Jesus approaches the city mention of the Mount of Olives is therefore more than a simple pointer to another milestone on the road from Jericho to Jerusalem. A formal or ceremonial entry into the city from the Mount of Olives is an action laden with promise and foreboding.

Riding on a Donkey

Zechariah prophesied concerning the entrance to the city of the royal Messiah: 'Say to the daughter of Zion: Look, your king comes to you, humble and riding on a donkey, on a colt, the foal of a donkey' (Zech 9:9).

The donkey was long since closely associated with the ruler that would arise from the tribe of Judah, and so it had associations with the house of David. Concerning the ruler from the House of Judah the blessing of Jacob had proclaimed: 'Binding his foal to the vine and his donkey's colt to the choice vine, he washes his garments in wine and his robe in the blood of grapes' (Gen 49:10f). In the mythology of the Ancient Near East the donkey (or mule) was at times associated with representations of the gods, very likely because it was the domestic animal *par excellence*, the one sharing the human burden of work. It was the opposite to the horse used since the time of Solomon as a mount for the warrior heading for war and seen as a symbol of power and prestige. Approaching the city on a beast of burden is a declaration that the king is coming with peaceful intent and humble bearing.

A significant historical incident involving a royal entry to the city by a son of David on a donkey also needs to be kept in mind as a background to this deliberate action on the part of Jesus. Towards the end of David's troubled reign the disputed succession to the throne was decided finally, after the intervention of Bathsheba, in favour of Solomon when David sent for the priest Zadok, the prophet Nathan, and Benaiah son of Jehoiada and commanded them: 'Take with you the servants of your lord and have my son Solomon ride on my own mule, and bring him down to Gihon. There let the priest Zadok and the prophet

Nathan anoint him king over Israel' (1 Kings 1:32-34). Then Solomon and his entourage went up to the city as the people accompanied them with loud rejoicing and the usurper Adonijah and his entourage broke up and fled as they heard that Solomon was made to sit on the king's mule, anointed king and entered the city to tumultuous rejoicing to sit on the throne of David (1 Kings 1:44).

Jesus was introduced at his birth as the king of the Jews (Mt 2:1), introduced in the opening verse of the gospel and addressed throughout the gospel as son of David and is now acclaimed as such in royal fashion by the enthusiastic crowd as he enters the city on a beast of burden.

The Prophetic Sign

As Bethphage on the Mount of Olives comes into view the goal of pilgrimage, the city of destiny, draws near. In anticipation of the messianic expectations of the crowd and of his disciples, Jesus takes the initiative and prepares to make his own statement by the direction and manner of his approach.

Pilgrims entered the holy city on foot, and Jesus himself walked everywhere. Now, however, he sends two of his disciples to the village opposite to requisition a tethered donkey together with a colt. This very deliberate action, involving the commissioning of two disciples to bring the donkey and colt points to his making a very definite statement by the manner of his approaching the city.

His careful preparation results in an approach to the city that is like a prophetic *ôt*, a sign worked out in mime.[5] The prophets regularly made use of symbolic gestures that were really parables in action to highlight their message and to set people thinking. Often a symbolic gesture (*ôt*) or mime was bizarre or designed to shock. Isaiah walked barefoot and naked through Jerusalem to highlight the forthcoming defeat of Egypt and

---

5. Jesus prepares carefully for approaching the city just as he subsequently prepares for the celebration of the Passover meal, in a parallel passage (Mt 26:17-19).

Cush by the Assyrians (Isa 20:1-6). For Jeremiah the spoiling of the loincloth, the breaking of the yoke on his neck and the buying of the field, all had significant political messages (Jer 13:1-11; 28:1-17; 31:1-15). For Ezekiel the eating of the scroll and his dumbness signified his prophetic role. His portrayal of the city under siege in illustration on a brick and the shaving of his hair foretold what lay ahead in the horrors of the siege (Ezek 2:1-33; 4:1-4; 5:1-4). Jesus realises and acknowledges the significance of his entry into the city and engages in a dramatic prophetic style action to proclaim and illustrate the nature of his kingship.

As he sends the two disciples to acquire the colt the reader may ask whether his knowledge of where they will find the colt is the result of divine foreknowledge, prophetic insight, prior arrangement or good guesswork, but in the context the nature of his knowledge is really secondary to his intention. Like the passion predictions and the preparation of the Passover Meal, which follows later, the gospels set Jesus' 'foreknowledge' in the context of his obedience to the unfolding divine plan.

The message sent by Jesus to those who might inquire about his disciples' reason for taking the donkey and colt can be understood in two ways: 'Their master (*ho kyrios autôn*) is in need, and he (the owner of the animals) will send them immediately' or 'The master has need of them (*autôn chreian echei*) and he will send them immediately.'[6] Does it mean it is needed for the plan of God (understanding *kyrios* as referring to God)? Or is it a declaration that Jesus is *ho kyrios autôn*, 'their master/owner', referring to the animals and implying a divine ownership, or a royal right since Jesus as king has the right to lay claim to them? Is it a setting down of a marker for his forthcoming statement in Jerusalem that the Messiah is not just Son of David but Lord, *Kyrios* (Mt 22:41-46)?

As Jesus now prepares to enter the city seated on a donkey he acknowledges his royal status but with a gesture that interprets

---

6. Mark understands 'he will send it immediately' as meaning the Master will send it back straight away to its owner. Matthew's meaning is that the owner will immediately send it to the Lord.

it in line with biblical expectations different to those uppermost in the mind of the enthusiastic crowd and disciples, and the possibly jaundiced eye of the authorities who may witness or come to hear of the event. Jesus, described and addressed throughout the gospel as Son of David, is now being hailed by the crowd in royal fashion as he enters the city on a donkey. He comes in peace and humility, a significant gesture on the part of the one who had declared himself 'meek and humble of heart' (Mt 11:29).

In royal fashion he approaches the city seated on a beast of burden, symbol of the king coming in peace. Jesus' action illustrates not only the 'humble' dimension as prophesied by Zechariah (and emphasised by Matthew's omission of 'victorious and triumphant' from the citation), but the whole symbolism of coming on a beast of burden is a demonstration of the peaceful nature both of his coming and of his kingship/kingdom. The warrior king would come on a war-horse! The gesture is a parable in action emphasising the peaceful nature of the coming of the king/prophet. Jesus thus acknowledges but significantly reinterprets the popular view of his kingship.[7] This is a far cry from the national liberator in the tradition of the Maccabees, and the revolutionary leader or warrior expected by many of Jesus' contemporaries, against whom the Jerusalem authorities and the Roman occupiers were constantly on guard, especially on the occasion of Passover and the other major pilgrimage feasts. It manifests what Jesus said of himself and his mission when he said: 'Come to me all you who labour and are heavily laden … I am meek and humble in heart'(Mt 11: 28-30).

The action recalls not only Solomon, the Son of David, entering the city to sit on the throne, but also recalls the prophecies of Zechariah and Zephaniah who speak of the victorious warrior-king humbly approaching the city proclaiming a message of peace. Matthew states that this took place to fulfil what was spoken by the prophet, saying:

---

7. As he does in his trial before Pilate in John's gospel when he says: 'My kingdom is not of this world' (Jn 18:36f).

Tell the daughter of Zion
See now your king comes to you
humble and riding on a donkey,
and on a colt, the foal of a beast of burden.[8]

The introductory phrase, 'Tell the daughter of Zion', is a classical Isaian phrase announcing the coming of salvation (MT) or of the saviour (LXX) (Isa 62:11): '*YHWH* proclaims to the ends of the earth: "Say to the daughter of Zion, 'Look, your saviour[9] comes, the prize of his victory is with him …' ".' The enthusiastic crowds do exactly that, and fulfil the divine command, throughout the entire scene. The rest of the prophecy is from Zech 9:9.[10]

ii. Royal Entry Mt 21:7-11//Mk 11:7b-10//Lk 19:35-40 Jn 12:12-19

The Royal Visitor

At the beginning of Jesus' final ascent to the Holy City, the blind men in Jericho proclaimed him Son of David, a title full of royal messianic significance and repeated throughout the gospel. What they said in faith is re-echoed in the messianic enthusiasm of the disciples and the crowd. The disciples decorated the donkey and colt with garments, decorating them as a throne and the crowds placed garments and 'a carpet of greenery' on the roadway. Placing garments on the roadway is a gesture of homage to a royal person, as seen in the case of the proclamation of Jehu as king. 'They all took their cloaks and spread them for him on the bare steps; and they blew the trumpet and proclaimed, "Jehu is king"' (2 Kings 9:13). John alone specifies that palm branches were used. Carrying such branches that they gathered or cut

---

8. Matthew omits 'victorious and triumphant' from the citation and, anxious to show the exact fulfilment of the prophecy, overlooks or mistakes the Semitic parallelism and considers the prophecy as referring to two animals rather than a double reference to the same animal. He even has Jesus riding into Jerusalem on the two animals (*ep' autôn*).
9. Saviour (Hb); salvation (Gk).
10. John has a fusion of quotations from Zechariah and Zephaniah (Jn 12:12-19; Zech 9:9; Zeph 3:16f; cf Lk 19:28-40) and though Mark is more understated this symbolism is there to be seen.

outside the city, and palm which was brought from the area
around Jericho, was a custom at the Feasts of Tabernacles
(*Sukkot*/Booths) and Dedication (*Hanukkah*) (2 Macc 10:7).
Matthew speaks of 'those who went before and those following',
describing a scene that could be regarded as a description of
Jesus and his entourage coming on pilgrimage to the sanctuary
of the Lord, like the rejoicing crowd coming on pilgrimage, described in Ps 68:25: 'cantors marching in front, musicians behind'. However, there is a great irony in the account. The king is
about to enter his city but it will prove itself to be once again the
city that rejects its prophet.

Meeting a royal visitor, a king or emperor, outside the gates
and escorting him into the city was a custom in the Greco-
Roman world. The usual term used for a pilgrim's approach to
Jerusalem is 'going up' to Jerusalem but here Jesus is hailed as
'the one who comes' to the city (*ho erchomenos*). This emphasises
the royal and messianic nature of his visit, or more accurately
perhaps, of his visitation.[11]

The crowds proclaim the coming of the 'Son of David'.[12]
'Hosanna to the Son of David.' Originally the word 'Hosanna', the
Hebrew *Hoshianna*, meant 'Save us, we pray' but by New Testament
times it had become, through usage, a shout of joy or praise.

In the context of Jesus' entry into the city, 'Hosanna' is more
an exclamation of joy and homage, an affirmation of what is taking place, a prayer of petition or simply a calling down of a
blessing on the recipient. It was associated with the enthusiastic
waving of the palm fronds and sheaves of foliage at the festivals
and so the *lulab* or bunch of foliage was often called a 'hosanna'.[13]

---

11. For background to the 'triumphal approach of a warrior or king to
the city, see P. B. Duff, 'The March of the Divine Warrior and the
Advent of the Graeco-Roman King. Mark's account of Jesus' Entry into
Jerusalem', *JBL* 111 (1992), 55-71.

12. Mark here has an unusual way of referring to David as 'our father
David', since the term 'father' was used more or less exclusively of the
Patriarchs (Mk 11:10).

13. *Sukka* 37b. At Tabernacles as the Psalm 118 was chanted the males
present waved the *lulab*, the bunch of greenery, at the words 'Blessed is
he who comes in the name of the Lord' (Ps 118: 25, 26).

The citation, 'He who comes in the Lord's name' is from Psalm 118, one of the Hallel Psalms associated with the entry of the pilgrim into the temple at Passover and Tabernacles. The line from the psalm, 'Blessings on the one who comes in the name of the Lord' was probably used as a prayer or blessing by the priests as they greeted the pilgrims on arrival at the temple (Ps 118:26).[14] Here the blessing is given a messianic connotation and directed towards Jesus. It emphasises the messianic significance of 'the one who comes' bringing the fulfilment of the messianic promise 'in the name of (i.e., by the power of) the Lord.' (In Mark it is accompanied by the blessing on 'the coming kingdom of our father David.') The messianic expectation in New Testament times, in terms of a prince from the House of David, is clearly expressed in the Psalms of Solomon: 'See Lord, and raise up for them their king, the Son of David, to rule over your servant Israel in the time known to you, O Lord' (Pss Sol 17). 'Hosanna in the highest' is a paraphrase of Job 16:19 and Ps 148:1 which literally means, 'Save us, we pray, you who dwell in the highest', but here it is more in the nature of a joyous acclamation or greeting in the form of a shout of praise to God who dwells in the highest heaven.

The 'one who comes', 'the one who is to come' or the 'coming one' is an established term in the gospels for the awaited messianic figure. Jesus' approach to the city and temple recalls in action the prophecy of Malachi: 'The Lord you are seeking will suddenly enter his Temple; and the angel of the covenant whom you are longing for, yes, he is coming, says YHWH Sabaoth. Who will be able to resist the day of his coming? Who will remain standing when he appears?' (Mal 3:1, 2). Significantly Jesus' entry into the city is followed immediately by his judgemental prophetic action in the Temple.[15]

---

14. Ps 118:26. Throughout the scene the crowd act almost like the chorus in a Greek play voicing the background issues, providing a stimulus and an interpretation of the event.
15. The short interval between entering the city and the 'cleansing' of the Temple in Mark's gospel serves the purpose of making a distinction between both episodes, the royal approach to the city and the prophetic,

Matthew, Luke and John paint a large canvas of pilgrims and citizens greeting Jesus.[16] John knits into the crowd of pilgrims and citizens, those who saw Lazarus being raised and those who came to see the one who was raised (Jn 12:17-18). These crowds naturally draw the hostile attention of the authorities.[17]

The last two sentences in the sequence describe Jesus' entry into the city. 'And on his entering Jerusalem the whole city vibrated (lit 'shook as in an earthquake', *eseisthê*). This reaction recalls the reaction of 'all Jerusalem' being plunged into turmoil (*etarachthê*) when the magi came inquiring about the birth of the King of the Jews. Now at the arrival of 'the Son of David' the city shakes as in an earthquake and the people ask: 'Who is this?' The crowds answer: 'This is the prophet Jesus from Nazareth in Galilee.' So the Son of David, the royal Messiah, is also seen as the prophetic figure, possibly 'the prophet like Moses (Deut 18:15, 18) or in a more general sense a prophet like Elijah, Jeremiah or one of the prophets of old (cf Mt 16:14).

He enters the temple of God and his action in the Temple will provoke a questioning of the authority by which he does these things. This questioning in turn provides the context for Jesus' display of a greater teaching authority than those who challenge him. His action in the Temple and his disputes with the religious and legal experts all reflect a negative judgement on the central institution and leadership of Israel very much in line with the

---

judgemental action in the Temple. Mark and John are in agreement in making such a clear distinction.

16. There are a number of points of contact between the accounts as told in the three synoptics and John (Mt 21:1-11; Mk 11:1-11; Lk 19:28-40; Jn 12:12-19). All four gospels record the enthusiasm, the approach or entry on a beast of burden, the royal overtones, the citation of, and/or allusions to scripture. Matthew, Mark and John prefix 'Hosanna' to the citation from Psalm 118, 'Blessed is he who comes in the name of the Lord' and John adds the suffix 'even the King of Israel' (Ps118: 25f). This royal dimension is reflected in Matthew's reference to 'Son of David' (Mt 21:9) and in Mark's 'Blessed is the Kingdom of our father David that is coming' (Mk 11:10).

17. In Mark the approach is not quite so spectacular and the crowd has dispersed before the solitary entry of Jesus into the city (Mk 11:10-11).

prophecy of Malachi: 'Who will be able to resist the day of his coming? Who will remain standing when he appears?' (Mal 3:1, 2).

b. Prophetic Visitation Mt 21:12-22//Mk 11:12-19//Lk 19:45- 48/Jn 2:13-22

i. The Cleansing of the Temple

In the synoptic accounts Jesus' action in the Temple takes place at the end of his ministry and is presented as the final challenge to official authority, bringing into sharp focus the question of his own authority, and setting in motion the events leading to his trial and execution. By way of contrast the incident takes place at the beginning of the ministry in St John's gospel and serves as a programmatic statement and a throwing down of the gauntlet to the establishment from the outset of the ministry (Jn 2:13-22). What really matters, however, is not the timing but the meaning of the event. In the synoptics it comes across as a prophetic style action or demonstration. It provides the motive and generates the energy for pursuing Jesus and bringing him to trial. One of the accusations at his Jewish trial will focus on an alleged threat to the Temple (Mt 26:61; Mk 14:58) and similar accusations about Jesus and his followers will be made at the trial of Stephen (Acts 6:14).

Since there is but one journey of Jesus during his ministry to Jerusalem in the synoptic gospels the reader can see that the event had to be placed in the context of his final days. However, the fact that this action, according to all four gospels and the Acts of the Apostles, attracted such hostile attention from the authorities and resulted in their questions about Jesus' authority, makes it likely that if the event took place early in the ministry it would have proved an obstacle to continuing his ministry especially in Jerusalem and above all in the temple area. One therefore is inclined to think that the synoptic location of the event towards the end of the ministry is well placed historically. It may well be that historically Jesus had an ongoing attitude to the temple during a number of visits, and it boiled over or came to a head at the end of the ministry. It is clearly placed early in John's gospel for theological and literary reasons where it functions as a programmatic event setting the tone of the ministry and offering a challenge, a catalyst provoking a reaction by way of a decision for or against Jesus (Jn 2:13-22).[18]

Jesus was not alone in his own day in having a strongly critical attitude towards the Temple. The Hellenists were less than enthusiastic and the Samaritans were quite hostile in its regard. The Essenes had opted out of the whole temple-based religious life of Jerusalem and the Qumran community saw itself as the messianic community in waiting, seeing a renewed people of God as the true temple. In having a critical attitude Jesus would also have been in direct line of descent from the prophets. The four accounts of Jesus' 'cleansing' of the temple stand in continuity with this prophetic tradition. It was commonplace for the prophets to adopt a critical stance on the temple, its worship, its authority and its ongoing role in the life of the people. They issued stern reminders of the holiness of the temple. They pointed out that it should be a place free from all kinds of corruption and venality, a place of true inner worship and a place that God would visit at some future time.

A public judgemental action or statement of a high profile religious leader in relation to the temple and its functioning came therefore laden with historical precedent and allusion. All four gospels record the action of Jesus in the temple and the inevitable questioning of his authority that it provoked. Matthew speaks of casting out the buyers and sellers and upsetting the tables of the moneychangers and the stools of the pigeon sellers (Mt 21:12f) and Luke speaks of driving out those who were selling (Lk 19:45). Among the synoptic accounts Mark's is the longest. It speaks of Jesus casting out the buyers and sellers, upsetting the tables of the moneychangers and the stools of the pigeon sellers, and not allowing anyone to carry anything through the temple area. Carrying things through the temple and taking a short cut through its precincts were forbidden in the Mishnah, and the carrying of moneybags was specifically

18. John's gospel portrays the raising of Lazarus as 'the final straw' for the authorities. Here again theological concerns are uppermost.

forbidden.[19] Jesus' reaction to carrying things would have been a reaction to the general carrying of things related to commerce, and that would necessarily have involved carrying quite a deal of money. All three synoptics include the statement that the temple should be a house of prayer but they had made it 'a den of thieves' (Jer 7:11).

Coins with the emperor's or other rulers' heads and inscriptions which, as graven images, would have been offensive in a sacred place, were exchanged for Jewish or Tyrian coins by the money changers. These acceptable coins could be used for buying the birds, animals, grain, wine and oil for various sacrificial rites, and also for giving as offerings to the temple treasury and for paying temple tax and dues. Birds were on sale for purchase by the poor who could not afford more expensive animals for the sacrifices. Pigeons or turtledoves were offered as sacrifices by women after childbirth if they could not afford a lamb (Lev 12:6-8; cf Lk 2:22-24) and lepers were to offer one pigeon or turtledove as a sacrifice for sin, and another as a holocaust (Lev 14:22).

Jesus' statement about the 'den of thieves' quotes the condemnatory phrase of Jeremiah against this commercial activity (Jer 7:11). John's gospel hammers home this point by saying they were turning the temple into an *emporion*, a market (Jn 2:16). Not only is the commercialism condemned but there is also a very strong implication of dishonesty in the expression 'den of thieves.' In the light of Malachi's prophecy (Mal 3:5) of the future purification when the Lord enters his temple and brings an end to the oppression of the wage earner, the widow and the orphan, the reader wonders if there is not also an implication that these vulnerable people are being robbed of their hard earned money by the vendors and money changers and by the payment of taxes and offerings to the temple and its officials. If so, Jesus' action could be seen also as a criticism of extortion on the part of the temple authorities or priests in regard to fees for religious services or a very rigorous attitude on the part of the temple es-

---

19. *m. Berakot* 9. 5.

tablishment with regard to the purity of offering, the unblem-
ished character of animals, the nature of the coinage used and so
forth, perhaps putting a burden on the poorer people, and so
meriting the phrase used by Jeremiah against the temple, 'a den
of thieves'.[20] The account of the widow's mite (Mk 12:41-44; Lk
21:1-4) may have originated as an example of 'devouring the
property of widows' (Mk 12:40). She gave (and they took!) 'all
she had to live on.'

However, with regard to the 'cleansing of the temple' one
asks if the action was simply a 'cleansing' of the temple in line
with the historical criticisms of the prophets and the reforms
they inspired or did it have a deeper significance? Is it simply a
reaction to the commerce and possible extortion being carried
on in the outer court of the temple even if it was legitimate and
in the service of the various rituals?[21] At first glance, at least, the
reader is most likely to see Jesus' action as a prophetic protest
against this commercialisation and secularisation of the temple
complex through the carrying out of commercial activity. Such
activity should have been done outside the temple complex itself out of respect for the sacred character of the temple precincts
and the prayerful atmosphere that should have been preserved.[22] But has it a further and even more radical significance?

Isa 56:7 spoke of the temple as a house of prayer for all the
nations. Mark gives the full quotation indicating the universal
scope of a new order, but Matthew does not include 'for all nations', simply saying 'my house shall be a house of prayer'. He
was writing in the aftermath of the destruction of the temple and
probably did not see the temple as relevant to the future of the

---

20. See C. A. Evans, 'Jesus and the "Cave of Robbers": Toward a Jewish
Context for the Temple Action,' *Bulletin of Biblical Research* 3 (1993) 93-
110.
21. For a recent comment on the action of Jesus against the moneychangers see the article by J. Murphy-O'Connor, 'Jesus and the Money
Changers (Mark 11:15-17; John 2:13-17),' *RB* 107 (2000) 42-55.
22. J. R. Donahue and D. J. Harrington, *op. cit.*, 332. See also D. Seely,
'Jesus' Temple Act,' *CBQ* 55(1993), 263-83.

universal mission. Even in Jesus' time the universal dimension did not seem possible in the context of the temple. Jesus' discussion on the barren fig tree will be a prefiguring of the doom of the temple and he will predict such a doom in his eschatological discourse on the Mount of Olives (Mt 24:1-2).

A striking new beginning is already taking place with the presence of the blind and lame in the temple (Mt 21:14). A saying recorded in the Old Testament (2 Sam 5:6-8) banned the blind and the lame from the temple. The Qumran community had a similar outlook, as it excluded all deformed people from its messianic community in waiting.

The wonders he was working bring from the lips of the children the cry of praise for the messianic prophet 'Hosanna to the Son of David.' This enthusiasm brings the chief priests and scribes back on stage, for the first time since they schemed with Herod at the birth of Jesus (Mt 2:4-6), though they have figured prominently in Jesus' prediction of his passion. The reader therefore feels apprehension at their appearance and the ensuing conversation fuels the apprehension further. They challenge Jesus with the words, 'Do you hear what they are saying?' to which he replies in kind with: 'Yes. Did you never read ...?', implying an inadequate understanding on their part. He quotes Psalm 8, 'Out of the mouths of babes and sucklings you have elicited perfect praise.' This is reminiscent of Jesus' saying: 'I thank you/bless you Father, Lord of Heaven and earth for hiding these things from the learned and clever and revealing them to mere children' (Mt 11:25-26). Jesus had already said in reply to the question about who is the greatest in the kingdom of heaven that ' unless you turn and become like little children you will not enter the kingdom of heaven' (Mt 18:1-5) and when he blessed the children that the disciples had tried to restrain he said of them 'of such is the kingdom of heaven' (Mt 19:13-15). They are experiencing and appreciating what the officials have failed to see.

The final trial of strength has begun between Jesus and the Jerusalem powers. At this juncture Jesus leaves the temple and

city and retires to Bethany, his base of operations during this
visit, where he spent the night.[23]

The question about the deeper meaning of his action in the
temple will be answered clearly in the eschatological-apocalyptic discourse. All the synoptics record Jesus' saying that: 'not a
stone will be left upon another. All will be destroyed', in response to the disciples' comments on the magnificence of the
temple buildings (Mt 24:1-3; Mk 13:1-4; Lk 21:5-7). In the parable
of the wicked tenants he will speak of the stone rejected by the
builders becoming the corner stone (referring to the cornerstone
of the new temple) (Mt 21:42).

The incident in the temple leads eventually to Jesus' arrest.
This is not surprising given the central role of the temple in the
life of the people, especially the people of Jerusalem. Not alone
did the temple function as the central place for worship, the exclusive location for sacrifice and the goal of pilgrimage, it also
played a crucial role in the socio-economic life of Jerusalem and
its citizens and was central to the power, prestige and welfare of
the Jewish religious and civil authorities.[24] Jesus' attitude would
therefore have made a deep impression on the citizens and
badly stung the establishment. This will be obvious when
Matthew (like Mark) records Jesus' attitude to the temple as one
of the accusations made against him at his trial (Mt 26:61; Mk
14:58) and a source of mockery at his crucifixion (Mt 27:40; Mk
15:29).[25] The Acts of the Apostles records similar accusations
about Jesus at the trial of Stephen (Acts 6:14). Misquoted state-

---

23. The modern name for Bethany is Al Azariah, a name that associates
the place with the story of Lazarus (Jn 11).
24. This socio-economic dependence was typical of all 'shrines', e.g. the
centrality of the Temple of Artemis-Diana in Ephesus, as seen from the
riot of the silversmiths, Acts 19:23-41.
25. Matthew uses another *logion* in the context of the dispute about
breaking the Sabbath. Having pointed out that the temple priests are
blameless in 'breaking' the Sabbath by carrying on their ministry, Jesus
makes a profound christological statement in the *logion* 'something
greater than the temple is here', and then goes on in true prophetic style
to quote the text: 'What I want is mercy, not sacrifice', before making a
second christological statement in the *logion*, 'The Son of Man is master

ments about destroying and rebuilding the temple are heard on
the lips of false accusers and mocking enemies.[26]

ii. The Barren Fig Tree Mt 21:18-22//Mk 11:12-14, 20-24

The action in the Temple is followed by the account of the
barren fig tree. This is no mere coincidence. The barren tree and
its fate are a pointer to the state and the fate of the temple. The
connection is further highlighted by Mark who uses the technique of intercalation. He places the 'cleansing of the temple' in
the middle of the story of the fig tree (Mk 11:12-14; 20-25). Like
the fig tree the temple is doomed. It may well be that the fig tree,
as its decaying process had taken hold, put out a final unhealthy
but apparently lush growth. So too the feverish activity around
the sacred precincts was like the lush growth giving the impression of life and health while underneath the plant is doomed
and is no longer producing fruit.[27]

---

of the Sabbath' (Mt 12:7f). The synoptics thus portray Jesus breaking the
mould and transcending the institutions and practices of Israel's past.
In all the gospels his attitude to temple, Torah and Sabbath is of central
significance and displays his greatest claims to divine authority. The
many variations on the statement point to a widespread diffusion of the
theme, which therefore must have sprung from historical reminiscence
rather than from the creation of a midrashic style commentator.

26. In St John's gospel, however, the statements about destroying and
rebuilding the temple are not heard on the lips of opponents, but form
the basis for a high christological statement, or *logion*, on the lips of
Jesus himself, and they serve the purpose of raising the issue onto another plane.

27. Mark says it was not the season for figs. Why then would Jesus, a
native of a land where figs grow, look for figs at a time when figs were
not in season, and react so strongly when he found none? The reader's
first reaction is to regard it as a pointless exercise and a very unreasonable reaction on his part. Did he inspect the tree in early spring to see if
it had the early indications of a good harvest to come or did he enter the
city at the autumn Feast of Tabernacles or the winter feast of Dedication
when he may have sought some late fruit? Is the phrase 'was not the
season for figs', an explanatory comment added subsequently to the
story in the course of transmission? It may well be that the fig tree as its
decaying process had taken hold put out a final unhealthy but apparently lush growth, as often happens with decaying vegetation. This

The story of Jesus' cursing of the fig tree has raised many an eyebrow among those who see it as an action out of character for Jesus, and out of character with the canonical gospels generally, though quite in line with some of the stories in the apocryphal gospels. Some see it as an aetiology, a story composed to explain the phenomenon of a withered fig tree. Others wonder if it was a misunderstanding on the part of the disciples or if the story began as a parable like that of the unfruitful fig tree in Luke 13:6-9, and was later transformed in the course of transmission from a parable into an account of an action. Others see it as a parable in action or prophetic sign (*ôt*) like the actions of the prophets in the Old Testament described above in connection with the 'triumphal' approach to the city.

One can only speculate on the historical question. Its significance for Matthew has to be sought within the gospel itself. Whatever the origin of the story and the history of its transmission, the significance of the story here lies in its relation to the action in the temple. Matthew uses it in this specific context and invests it with definite meaning.

As with the approach to the city this story of Jesus and the fig tree is like a prophetic sign (*ôt*) and to understand its significance the reader needs to hear the Old Testament echoes that would have been heard by the original audience to the story, possibly before the writing of the gospel, and by the intended readership. In the Old Testament the fig tree and the vine (or vineyard) were used as metaphors for Israel (Isa 5; 1-7; Hos 9:10; Mic 7:1; Jer 8:15). When God sought grapes or figs and found none it was a prelude to divine condemnation. Isaiah speaks of the condemnation of the vine (yard): '(God) expected it to yield grapes but sour grapes were all it gave ... I will lay it waste, unpruned, undug, overgrown by the briar and the thorn' (Isa 5:1, 2, 6). Jeremiah articulates a similar condemnation: 'I would like to harvest there, says *YHWH*, but there are no grapes on the vine,

---

appearance of healthy growth may have led Jesus to seek fruit or to go through the motions of seeking fruit as a parable in action for the disciples.

no figs on the fig tree, even the leaves are withered' (Jer 8:13).
John uses this same imagery evocatively in his passage on the
vine and the branches: 'Every branch in me that bears no fruit he
(my Father) cuts away' (Jn 15:2). For John the fruit comes
through the life-giving power of Jesus, the vine. The parable of
the wicked tenants of the vineyard who refused to give the fruits
of the harvest to the owner, and maltreated his messengers is another case in point and in fact will shortly be told in the gospel,
and told in relation to the cleansing of the Temple and Jesus' authority for acting as he did (Mt 21:33-46//Mk 12:1-12// Lk 20:9-
19). The fig tree had special messianic significance. Israel should
welcome the Messiah with a harvest of figs. Its absence is an impediment to the reception of the Messiah and the arrival of the
messianic age, and results in condemnation. M. D. Hooker sums
it up succinctly:

> ... in the messianic age the fig tree will bear fruit. The fig tree
> is an emblem of peace and prosperity: hope for the future is
> expressed in terms of sitting in security under one's vine and
> one's fig tree (e.g. Mic 4:4 and Zech 3:10) and gathering fruit
> from them (Hag 2:19). William Telford (*The Barren Temple and
> the Withered Tree*) argues that the fig tree would have been
> understood as a symbol for Israel, which should have borne
> fruit in the messianic era: yet when Jesus comes to the city,
> the tree is without fruit, and judgement inevitably follows.[29]

Here in Matthew's gospel, therefore, the 'cursing' of the fig
tree is not just a reaction of pique on the part of a hungry and
tired Jesus when he finds no figs on the tree. It is not just a cursing of a tree but a prophetic symbolic condemnation of Israel for
not producing fruit and for not recognising ' the one who comes'.
The disciples are greatly surprised at the immediate fulfilment of Jesus' prophecy or curse that the fig tree would bear no
more fruit and they asked what had happened to it. Jesus' response points to faith (which finds expression in prayer) as the
source and locus of all divine power in human life and activity.

28. M. D. Hooker, *op.cit*, 262.

His statement about the power of faith is very significantly placed here in the gospel and expressed in typical Semitic hyperbole. If they had faith and did not doubt at all, they would not only do what he has done to the fig tree but they would move mountains. Moving mountains was a common metaphor used by rabbis for doing things of great difficulty, and a rabbi who could explain a particularly difficult passage of scripture was regarded as a 'mountain-remover'.[29] Confidence in prayer, born of faith, opens the way for God to act in our lives and world. His action in the temple, its symbolic representation in the fig tree and Jesus' pointing to the centrality of prayer and its power, point forward to the fact that in Jesus there is a new way to God, a new way of faith and prayer replacing the temple and its sacrifice and rituals. 'And all things that you ask for in prayer, if you have faith, you will receive.'

2. DISPUTE: RECOGNITION / RESPONSE TO AUTHORITY MT 21:22-22:46

In Jerusalem the religious authorities, administrative, priestly and scholarly, will now question publicly the nature and source of Jesus' authority for acting as he does. His dramatic entry into the city showed a possible potential for revolutionary activity and his action in the Temple implied a level of authority that challenged the establishment. His healing of the blind and the lame in the temple area added to the messianic aura surrounding his person, especially since it was unusual. First of all the authorities ask him by what authority he does these things and who gave him such authority.[30] Then they put his authority in teaching to the test, in the hope of discrediting him publicly before his followers. Jerusalem had already stretched its long hand of authority into Galilee during his ministry, scrutinising his ac-

29. D. E. Nineham, *op. cit.*, 305. See also the article by C. W. Hedrick, 'On Moving Mountains. Mark 11:22b-23 / / Matt 21:21 and Parallels', *Forum* 6 (1990) 219-37.
30. Jesus' authority has significant implications for social, political and religious life and organisation. See A. Dawson, *Freedom as Liberating Power. A socio-political reading of the exousia texts in the Gospel of Mark*, Fribourg: Universitätsverlag, 2000.

tivity and teaching. References to Pharisees and scribes who had
dogged his path may imply that they came from Jerusalem even
when it is not specifically stated, since both groups are more
closely associated with Jerusalem and the surrounding area than
with the rural areas of Galilee (and the fact that they came from
Jerusalem is explicitly stated in Mk 3:22). This is a clear pointer
to their keeping a close eye on anything they do not initiate and
control themselves. Matthew clearly assumes that this attitude
was known to Jesus' audience and would be known or deduced
by his intended readers

A series of 'controversies', containing challenges and responses, centred on the issues of forgiveness of sins, association
with sinners, fasting, plucking corn on the Sabbath and healing
on the Sabbath were set into the narrative of Jesus' ministry in
Galilee. Now two highly significant gestures, his royal approach
to the city and his prophetic action in the Temple, provoke the
officials to question him about his authority, and then the other
debates or 'controversies' follow suit as the leaders of the various religious, scholarly and political groups challenge and are in
turn silenced by him.[31] The central controversial issues concern
the authority of the Baptist, the payment of taxes to Caesar, the
resurrection of the dead, the greatest commandment and the
teaching about the Messiah as son of David. These were probably well established as a Jerusalem 'controversy' tradition prior
to the writing of the gospels. Matthew includes three parables in
the cycle of controversies, those of the two sons, of the wicked
tenants and of the wedding feast.

---

31. The entire section (Mt 21:23-23:12) has close parallels in the other
synoptics (Mk 11:27-12:44; Lk 20:1-47; 10:25-38; 11:37-52) and therefore
points to an already well established block of material which J. P. Meier
has called 'The Jerusalem Dispute Cycle.' cf J. P. Meier, *A Marginal Jew*,
3, 414f.

*a. The Authority of John and the Authority of Jesus Mt 21:23- 27//Mk
11:27-33//Lk 20:1-8*

In John's gospel the emissaries from Jerusalem interrogated
John the Baptist in severe fashion about his authority and his
baptism (Jn 1:19-28). This questioning is not recorded in the synoptic tradition but it can be deduced that their attitude to John
proved to be an ongoing embarrassment to them, and that Jesus
did not shrink from reminding them of their obtuseness in this
regard when they began to question his own authority. His public question to them about the source of John's authority left
them the stark choice of admitting their own failure or facing the
hostility of the people.

This group of chief priests and elders of the people, representing the priestly, scholarly, legal and administrative authority of the Sanhedrin, approach Jesus as he is teaching in the temple and challenge him to tell them: ' By what authority (*exousia*)
do you do these things and who gave you this authority?' It is a
challenge issued in public by the people with responsibility for
keeping order in Jerusalem and for the running of the temple
and its affairs. Jesus' royal approach to the city and his prophetic
action in the temple naturally provoked a reaction on their part.
Great tension is in the air and the reader will now remember
with a certain amount of alarm that these are some of the characters mentioned in the first Passion Prediction when Jesus said he
would be rejected by the elders, the chief priests and the scribes
and put to death (Mt 16:21; cf Mt 27:1-2). They are now trying to
trap him into publicly laying claim to divine authority. Their
challenge and the response it provoked from Jesus leave them
publicly exposed as not being able to identify divine authority
even when they encounter it, as in the case of John the Baptist,
even though the ordinary people whom they are supposed to
lead and teach had recognised it.

The question of Jesus' own authority is intimately linked to
that of the Baptist. It was John who 'prepared the way' (Mt 3:3)
and proclaimed the arrival of the one following him, the more
powerful one, whose sandals he was unworthy to carry, the one

who would baptise in Holy Spirit (Mt 3:11-12). Jesus' revelation as the Beloved Son on whom the Spirit descended and to whom the heavenly voice bore witness happened in the context of his baptism by John. A positive response to the question of John's authority would therefore have huge implications for the question of Jesus' own authority.

Jesus' counter-question to them presumes knowledge on the part of the listeners (and readers) of their attitude to John the Baptist. As he did in Capernaum when challenged about forgiving sin (Mt 9:1-8), Jesus responds in rabbinic style with a searching ('no win') question designed to embarrass and undermine his challengers. He tells them that if they answer his question (and whichever way they answer they will lose), he will answer theirs. Either a positive or negative response would have very serious consequences for themselves and their standing with the people. Asking them about the source or nature of the Baptist's authority was 'very close to the bone' and in doing so Jesus scores two points.

First of all they are put in the position of having to answer a 'no-win' question. If they say John's baptism was from heaven (i.e. from God) they will admit to their own obtuseness in this regard and their failure to see what the ordinary people saw clearly. If they say it was ' from man' they will deny what they have now come to realise, and also provoke a hostile reaction from the crowd who had enthusiastically followed John, as Matthew pointed out. 'Jerusalem and all Judea and whole Jordan district made their way to him; they were baptised by him in the river Jordan and confessed their sins' (Mt 3:5). Their very embarrassment reveals their belated belief in the divine origin of the Baptist's mission and their failure to accept it at the time. To save face they have to admit (or pretend?) that 'we do not know.' This was a huge admission and embarrassment on their part.

Secondly they are now shown up as behaving in the same way towards Jesus, not having learned from their mistake. Jesus leaves them to their devices by saying: 'Neither will I tell you by what authority I act like this.' Since they do not answer his question neither does he answer theirs.

Their ' authority' as institutional figures has now been challenged by the charismatic, prophetic roles of both John the
Baptist and Jesus as heralds of the kingdom. The classical challenge between prophecy and institution is in evidence. The classical reaction of institution is also in evidence. The gospel speaks
of Herod Antipas' arrest of John because of his attitude to his
marriage to Herodias, but Josephus reports that he had felt a
threat from the Baptist because of his popularity with the
crowds and had moved against him as a protection against civil
unrest.[32] Now the Jerusalem authorities similarly fear the
crowds and possible civil unrest if they allow Jesus to continue
his highly significant activity, and equally fear unrest if they try
to apprehend him (Mt 26:5). They tried to make him discredit or
undermine himself and failed when he turned the tables on
them with the question about the Baptist's authority.

b. Parables

Having turned the tables on the interrogators and reduced them
to a state of public embarrassment, Jesus goes on the offensive
and tells three parables. All three point a finger at his interrogators as privileged persons in the religious scheme of things who
should know and behave better. All three deal with refusal, refusal to work for the father, refusal to render the fruits of the
vineyard and refusal of the invitation to the royal banquet. A
father and son figure in all three.

i. The Two Sons Mt 21:28-32

Jesus begins by asking: 'What do you think?' He thus provokes them into answering his question about the two sons.
There is a certain confusion due to two different readings in the
manuscripts. The more common reading is as follows. The first
son is asked by the father to go into the vineyard to work and answers: 'I will not', but later repents and goes. The second son on
being asked says: 'Yes, sir!' but changes his mind and does not
go into the vineyard. Jesus asked: 'Which of them had done the

---

32. Josephus, *Ant*, 18.118.

father's will?' and they answered 'The first', that is, the one who had a change of heart (repented) after an initial refusal. The second son paid lip service at first, when he agreed to do his father's bidding. 'He did the talk but not the walk' to quote a contemporary idiom. In this interpretation there is a clear polemic against the leaders and lawyers who proclaim and extol the Law but do not live by it themselves, whereas the one who at first said no and changed his mind are like the tax collectors, sinners and prostitutes who repented and changed their ways and are entering the kingdom ahead of the so-called 'righteous' people.

The alternative reading of the manuscripts reverses the order of the sons and portrays the first son saying 'Yes' but later changing his mind and not going into the vineyard and the second son saying 'No' and then changing his mind and going in. This would be a very simple difference touching only on the reversal of order except for the fact that in this variant reading the leaders respond that the one who said 'Yes' but then changed his mind was the one who did the father's will. This is the opposite of the response in the first reading. This response aligns the respondents with the attitude Jesus was condemning in the leaders. They are confirming their own wrong attitude with their response as their words show how they think. For them the important thing is 'to talk the talk without walking the walk'.

The point is the same in both cases. It illustrates one of Matthew's favourite themes, the dichotomy between words only and words accompanied by deeds. The tax collectors, in spite of their unacceptable profession and its attendant temptations to extortion and co-operation with foreigners, and the prostitutes, in spite of their immoral way of life, are entering the kingdom before the leaders. Why? Because when John came 'in the way of righteousness'[33] it was the tax collectors and prostitutes (representing the broad canvas of the unrighteous) be-

---

33. There is a double sense to 'the way of righteousness'. It signifies John's 'fulfilling God's will in carrying out his role in the plan of salvation' and 'proclaiming a way of righteousness' as seen in the account of his preaching repentance and baptising.

lieved him in a life changing way, but the leaders did not believe him, and even when they saw the effect he had on the unrighteous they still did not 'change their attitude' (repent) and believe him.

The reference to the Baptist maintains the continuity between this exchange and the former questioning about the Baptist's authority. John the Baptist, the precursor who prepared the way, the Elijah figure foretold by Malachi, has been mentioned now for the last time in Matthew's gospel. After his arrest Jesus had taken up the baton and as his ministry began to make an impact the crowds and Herod himself thought John's spirit had come back in Jesus. The discussion of his authority brings his role to the fore again as the gospel approaches its denouement. His role as precursor foreshadows also the arrest and execution of Jesus, the one for whom he had prepared the way.[34]

The theme of refusal together with the references to the son and the vineyard link this parable to the parable immediately following.

ii. The Wicked Tenants Mt 21:33-46//Mk 12:1-12

Jesus calls on them to listen to another parable. He regularly tells a parable when challenged, criticised or disappointed. It is meant to provoke thought, either immediately or later as one reflected on it. Sometimes a parable is like a shot between the eyes that provokes an immediate response or exclamation. Such is the case with this parable of the wicked tenants. It provokes an immediate response from the crowd and a menacing reaction from the authorities. Having referred to the case of John the Baptist and the reception he received, Jesus now tells a parable that illustrates the long history of such rejection of God's messengers.[35] This parable is no riddle with a mysterious or secret message for the few, but a blatantly transparent allegory on the

34. For an overview of John the Baptist and his role, see W. Wink, *John the Baptist in the Gospel Tradition,* Cambridge: CUP, 1969.
35. For recent study of the parable see K. Snodgrass, 'Recent Research on the Parable of the Wicked Tenants: An Assessment,' *Bulletin of Biblical Research* 8 (1998) 187-215.

history of leadership in Israel and the rejection of the messengers sent by God.

The parable is using a familiar scene. Building the fence to keep out animals, digging the pit for pressing the grapes and building the tower as a shelter and lookout post, set the scene for a well run operation which the absentee landlord entrusts to his stewards. They in turn are expected to work the operation, make a living from it, and ensure the profit due to the owner at the proper time (*tô kairô*). The vineyard with its operation and care, together with its production of a good vintage, was a long established metaphor for Israel and its spiritual harvest (Isa 5:1-7).[36]

In this parable the people responsible for the vintage/harvest and its fruits have not only failed miserably but have illtreated the servants who were sent to collect the fruit of the harvest. The tenants beat one of the servants, killed another and stoned a third. They behaved similarly towards a second, larger group of servants who came to collect the fruit of the harvest. Finally the owner sent his son. The tenants conspired to kill him and seize his inheritance. The killing of the son in the hope of making the vineyard their own is the final failure, and outrage. As Jesus reaches the culmination of the story and asks the listeners what the lord of the harvest will do, the listeners exclaim spontaneously that the lord of the harvest will make an end of the tenants and give the vineyard to others. This is a spontaneous condemnation of the leaders on the lips of the listeners.

In Jesus' time the vineyard would have clearly represented the people of Israel and the *geôrgoi*, the 'land workers', represented the people charged with their spiritual welfare, answerable for their spiritual fruits to the God of Israel. The succession of messengers sent to remind them of the fruits that were due to the owner represent the prophets and other messengers who were so often badly treated.

The parable is like the Bible or the History of Salvation in miniature. Throughout their history God repeatedly sent mes-

---

36. See W. J. C. Weren, 'The Use of Isaiah 5:1-7 in the Parable of the Tenants (Mark 12:1-12; Matthew 21:33-46),' *Bib* 79 (1998) 1-26.

sengers to the people even in the face of repeated infidelity (Hos 2:2,14-20; Jer 3:11-14; Ezek 16:59-63). The parable reflects through the actions of the tenants the hardness of heart whereby the eyes do not see nor the ears hear (Isa 6:10). It reflects closely the complaint in 2 Chronicles where the heads of the priesthood are condemned for defiling the Temple:

> Furthermore, all the heads of the priesthood, and the people too, added infidelity to infidelity … defiling the temple that *YHWH* had consecrated for himself in Jerusalem. *YHWH*, the God of their ancestors tirelessly sent them messenger after messenger, since he wished to spare his people and his house. But they ridiculed the messengers of God, they despised his words, they laughed at his prophets, until at last the wrath of *YHWH* rose so high against his people that there was no further remedy (2 Chron 36:14-16).

The parable of the vineyard and those charged with working it shows a process of development or clarification in transmission. As Jesus himself told the parable he may well have focused on John the Baptist as the last of the prophets, maybe even seeing him as the son in the parable, particularly if the parable was originally told in connection with the question about the Baptist's authority. However, as the parable comes to the evangelists and is portrayed by them, Jesus is clearly the son who was killed and cast out.[37] This would fit the christology of the gospel with the heavenly declaration at the baptism and transfiguration where he is described as 'my Son, the Beloved' (Mt 3:17; 17:5).[38] They killed the son and threw him outside unburied, to get possession of the vineyard, and thereby maintain their own control, authority and interests. But Jesus asks the question: 'What will the owner of the vineyard do?' They respond: 'He will make an end of the tenants and give the vineyard to other tenants who will give him the fruits in the proper

---

37. Hb 13:12f speaks of Jesus as 'suffering outside the gate'.
38. There are echoes of Abraham's beloved son Isaac and of Jacob/ Israel's beloved son Joseph against whom his brothers conspired: 'Come let us kill him' Gen 22; 37:20.

times.' So they lost the inheritance they coveted by killing the son and suffered a similar fate to the one they had inflicted on him.[39] 'The 'other tenants' to whom he gives the vineyard fit into the developing narrative of Jesus' turning his back on the Jewish leaders, setting up a new leadership, and eventually establishing the universal, Gentile (and Jewish) mission.

Jesus then asks in rabbinic style and ironic tone as on previous occasions: 'Have you never read in the scriptures: "The stone which the builders rejected became the cornerstone" (*kephalê gônias*)?' This citation from Psalm 118:22-23 (LXX), illustrates how God's choice and God's marvellous work, 'a wonder in our eyes', are achieved in spite of human rejection.[40] Some scholars think that perhaps the similarity in sound between the Hebrew words *ben* (son) and *'eben* (stone) prompted the joining of the *logion* to the parable. It was placed here as a reflection on the parable. The experts in the dressing of vines and the dressing of stones are both shown up very badly. They failed to identify the identity, value and quality of the person they rejected but God's purpose was achieved in spite of them. The rejected Son, the rejected stone, survived to become the cornerstone of the new temple.[41]

The question concerning the Baptist and the parable of the wicked tenants reduce the chief priests and elders, the leaders of

---

39. For a discussion on the identity of the son and the other characters see A. Milavec, 'The Identity of the " Son" and "the Others": Mark's Parable of the Wicked Husbandmen Reconsidered,' *BTB* 20 (1990) 30-37.

40. *Kephalê gonias* has been variously interpreted as the cornerstone in the foundation and the capstone on top and the keystone in the arch. Whichever understanding is taken, the point is the same. It fulfils a vital function in the whole edifice. This may well be one of a number of *Testimonia* or proof texts assembled from the OT to illustrate particular points. Note how it is spoken of as *graphê*/writing/text, instead of the more usual *gegraptai*, 'it is written.' cf 4Q 175-177 as anthologies of proof texts from the OT about the Messiah, the future consolation of Israel and the last days.

41. Some mss have an insertion at Mt 21:44 corresponding to the Lukan parallel text: 'He who falls on this stone will be dashed to pieces and anyone on whom it falls will be crushed' (Lk 20:18).

the people, to silence before the people, largely due to the fact that the people show discernment. The unwarranted superior attitude of the authorities and their failed interrogation technique turn now to hostility and aggression. The chief priests and the scribes realise that they were the target of Jesus' parables. They would have liked to arrest him but they were afraid of the crowd. This same fear will cause them to seek a means of arresting him away from the festal crowd and Judas will come to their aid in facilitating the arrest (Mt 26:5).[42] The third parable of refusal follows. The status of the one offended is raised to the level of a king and the punishment of those who maltreat his messengers is of the severest kind.

iii. The Wedding Guests Mt 22:1-14 / / Lk 14:16-24

The narrative sequence is maintained by the remark that Jesus again speaks in parables. He introduces the parable (more accurately the parabolic simile), with the familiar formula: 'The kingdom of heaven is like ...' The comparison is not simply with the king but with the entire setting and action of the story. The theme of rejection by those first chosen and invited and the invitation to the 'undesirables', foreshadows the mission to the Gentiles. The affront, however, is to a king and the ill treatment of his servants warrants the severest punishment.

The parable as it appears here is similar to the parable in Luke 14:16-24 though it functions in a very different context and displays added features. Elements of other parables or narratives have been knit into it in the course of transmission or by Matthew himself. Judging by the more primitive form of the parable as it appears in Luke one can see how Matthew elevates a great banquet given by a man to a wedding feast given by a king for his son, how he adds a description of the ill treatment of the messengers and a very violent reaction on the part of the king to the rejection of the invitations and the ill treatment of the

---

42. John's gospel mentions several occasions in Jerusalem when they wished to arrest him (Jn 7:30, 45; 10:39; 11:57).

messengers. In this it resembles very closely the preceding parable of the wicked tenants. Matthew further adds the account of a guest being thrown into prison by the king for not being appropriately attired at the banquet.

In the simpler version of the parable as it appears in Luke, the guests first invited refuse the invitation on the grounds of purchasing land, tending to oxen and being newly wed. They are obviously the well-to-do people who are absorbed in the things of the world. The second group of invitees are people in the highways and bye-ways. They stand for the economically and spiritually poor, the outcasts, the tax collectors and prostitutes who flocked to Jesus and shared his table, after the so-called leaders and teachers had rejected him (Lk 14:16-24).

The fact that Matthew elevates the feast given by an ordinary man to a wedding banquet given by a king for a king's son accentuates the royal and messianic allusions and thereby heightens the christological and eschatological dimensions of the story. The wedding feast had long been established as a metaphor for the messianic and eschatological banquets in the kingdom.

For Matthew the first invitation is refused, and then the second is refused by some on the grounds of looking after farm or business and the messengers bearing the invitations are ill treated and killed by yet another group of invitees. The reader naturally asks why they ill-treated the messengers (already a theme in the former parable) and why the reaction of the king was so violent, sending troops to destroy the murderers and to burn their town. The former parable spoke of the wicked tenants coming to a sticky end. It may very well be that Matthew uses the memory of the destruction of Jerusalem as an example of such a sticky end coming upon the people who rejected the invitation to the kingdom and tortured the messengers and the Son.

The final round of invitations, to everyone at the crossroads in the town, good and bad alike were accepted so that the wedding hall was full. The crossroads in the town would have been a place where Jew and Gentile, good and bad alike would be encountered indiscriminately. For Matthew such an invitation represents the invitation to the kingdom, and to membership of his own community, to Jew and Gentile, good and bad alike without discrimination.

Adding the section about the wedding garment highlights the fact that just answering the invitation was not sufficient in itself (Mt 22:11-13). One must respond in a manner and state appropriate to the dignity of the call and the state and position to which it gave access. Garments had long been used as a metaphor for traits of character and patterns of behaviour (Isa 11:5; 59:17; 1 Thess 5:8; Eph 6:14-17). Like the new garments at baptism, symbolising a completely new beginning in life, or the military garments (armour) symbolising the virtues and courage needed for spiritual warfare, the wedding garment symbolised the dispositions required for those who had received and accepted the invitation to the king's banquet on entering his kingdom. The king came to inspect the guests, an allusion to the judgement. The guest not suitably attired on being confronted by his benefactor had no excuse, and remained silent. The judgement and punishment followed. The king said to his servants: 'Bind him hand and foot and cast him into exterior darkness where there will be weeping and gnashing of teeth.'

Seeing the story of the wedding garment as an example of unreasonable behaviour on the part of the king when he called all and sundry from the crossroads, irrespective of their social status or economic circumstances, is to miss the metaphorical nature of the parable. It may have been part of another parable appended to this one which in its original setting would not have appeared so 'strange'. This strangeness, however, may be a ploy of Matthew to shock and alert the intended audience, forcing them to think out their own response to the invitation.

Finally, as in the case of the wicked tenants, a *logion* is appended to the parable (Mt 22:14). 'Many are called (*klêtoi*), but few are chosen (*eklektoi*).' Two time frames are involved. Many are called in the present to enter the kingdom, but at the judgement how many will have proven themselves worthy of that call and be chosen for eternal reward? How many will be like the guest without the wedding garment?

3. CONTROVERSY / HOSTILE QUESTIONING MT 22:15-46

Having challenged the authority of the powerful leaders of the temple priestly and political-religious class Jesus is now drawn into a series of controversies that deal with questions of Law and Scripture. David Daube in his study of Rabbinic Judaism and its influence on the New Testament pointed out how the following 'debates' reflect the groupings of questions in rabbinic literature, even though they do not follow the same order.[43] Twelve questions were put to Rabbi Joshua ben Hananiah, as reported in the Babylonian Talmud.[44] Three of the questions were concerned with *Hokmah* (wisdom) in the interpretation of *Halakah* (legal questions arising from legal texts), three with *Haggadah* (non legal questions dealing with apparent contradictions in scripture), three with *Bôrut* (ridiculing the opponent's belief in the resurrection) and three concerned with *Derek 'Erets* (matters of moral conduct). Though both the Jerusalem and Babylonian Talmud are later than the New Testament they reflect an established pattern of debate and controversy. This division of questions is followed in the debates (controversies) here in Matthew (as in Mark), but significantly the *Haggadah* question dealing with apparently contradictory scriptural texts, here dealing with the Son of David, is kept until the end, as a climax in the arguments and a turning point or pivot in the overall section.

a. On Tribute to Caesar Mt 22:15-22//Mk 12:13-17//Lk 20-26

The Pharisees' disciples and the Herodians question Jesus

The chief priests and the elders of the people were beaten in their attempt to entrap Jesus and discredit him with the crowd when Jesus raised the embarrassing issue of the Baptist's authority. Now the Pharisees, having conspired how to trap him in his speech, sent their disciples together with the Herodians to question him. The Pharisees were the saints and scholars of Palestinian Judaism, careful about the Law, the traditions that

---

43. D. Daube, *The New Testament and Rabbinic Judaism*, 158-169. J.Radermakers, *La bonne nouvelle de Jesús selon Marc*, 2, 313-14.
44. B. *Niddah* 69b-71a. J. *Pesahim* 10:37d.

grew up around its interpretation and its strict observance in
every aspect of life. They were a foil for Jesus in his public ministry, and in the period after the destruction of the temple they
were the driving force in the reconstruction of the Jewish way of
life.[45] In their way of seeing things Jesus was not an observant
Jew in regard to the Sabbath observance. He also fell short in instructing his disciples in purity regulations. Furthermore, the
scribes who thought he uttered blasphemy in pronouncing the
forgiveness of sins may well have been of the Pharisee party. It
was in their interest to undermine the influence that such a person had on the common people. Though no friends of the House
of Herod and its Roman connections, they made common cause
with the Herodians in the face of this common, but probably differently viewed, threat or nuisance.

The Herodians, on the other hand, were supporters of the
house of Herod, in this case, the house of Herod Antipas. They
were not necessarily officials of the court of Herod Antipas,
tetrarch of Galilee, but politically minded Jews actively supporting his dynasty and enjoying his favour.[46] Josephus points out
how Antipas was worried about the influence that John the
Baptist had with the ordinary people in case it would boil up
into revolution against himself or the Romans.[47] This concern
may well have been transferred to Jesus and his following after
the elimination of John, and may in part account for Herod's desire to see Jesus during his visit to Jerusalem for Passover, when
he was sent to him by Pilate, as Luke reports (Lk 23:5-12). Herod
Antipas was particularly careful not to let anything happen in
his jurisdiction that would upset the Romans lest they depose
him as they had deposed another of the Herodian family,
Archelaus, and divided his jurisdiction. In fact the emperor
Caligula will eventually depose Antipas and send him into exile.
Anxiety about Jesus' influence with the people would have

---

45. The tensions that arose in that period influenced their negative portrayal in the gospels of Matthew and John, and particularly in Mt 23.
46. Jerusalem Bible (1966), footnote to Mk 3:6.
47. Josephus, *Ant*, 18:118.

made Antipas nervous of Rome, but an obvious move against Jesus could have brought about the very disturbance that he tried to avoid. Maybe enlisting the support of the Pharisees with their religious and nationalist reputation would soften the blow in the eyes of the people if they could undermine him. This may well account for the unlikely association. Conversely the Pharisees probably saw in the Herodians an influence, and an arm of the law that would control this unconventional preacher and his following. The Pharisees were not on good terms with the Sadducees who had their hands on the levers of Jerusalem temple authority, so the Herodians were a tactical option and they held sway also in Galilee where Jesus had started his mission and had a large following. In fact, in Mk 3:6 there is an account of an earlier conspiracy of Pharisees and Herodians when they consider how to destroy Jesus after a healing on the Sabbath in a synagogue in Galilee.

Whether this alliance is mentioned here to give an overall historical picture of the wide range of opposition experienced by Jesus, or a more literary highlighting of the coming together of even the most unlikely groups from opposite ends of the political, religious and social spectrum in the face of a perceived threat from Jesus, the combination is striking.

An honorific address, *didaskale*, 'teacher', and feigned praise about his honesty and reputation for giving straight answers in keeping with the way of God and not 'respecting' personages, was an attempt to 'set Jesus up', in order to trap him with feigned praise, a *captatio benevolentiae*. It failed to trap him and he unmasked their hypocrisy. Their real plan was to trap him through pretended praise of his sincerity and forthrightness into responding to their question, which was presented as a typical example of seeking *hokmah* (wisdom) in relation to a question that required a *halakah* (legal) response, about whether or not it was right to pay tribute (*kênsos*) to Caesar.[48] It was an attempt to make public his attitude.

---

48. The *kênsos* was a tax imposed on Samaria, Judea and Idumea in 6BC when they became Roman provinces.

On the one hand if Jesus had said it was lawful to pay tax to Caesar (*exestin* means it is lawful according to the Mosaic Law), he would very likely have been seen as a collaborator and alienated the Jews among his followers who resented the Roman intrusion into their country, their imposition of taxes, their division of the country into Judea, Samaria and Idumaea as areas of Roman administration and their importation of a pagan coinage with the emperor's head and 'divine' title, all of which contributed to the resentment from which the Zealot movement was born.[49]

On the other hand, if he said it was not lawful, then there would have been an obvious case against him for treason against the emperor and his appointed administration. Such a case against him would have been easily believed by the Romans because he came from Galilee, home of the Zealot movement. The words Galilean and Zealot were almost synonymous in many people's minds. In that case the Romans could move against him. Furthermore, the two parties asking the question were on opposite sides of the issue. If he said a straight 'yes' at least some of the Pharisees' disciples in the questioning group would have taken umbrage. If he said 'no' the Herodians in the same group, supporters of the house of Herod who were clients of Rome, would have seen it as treason. He could not please both elements in the questioning party. He would fall foul of one or other group whether he answered 'yes' or 'no'.

Even among the Pharisees themselves the question of paying tax to Caesar may have been a divisive question. Was this the reason why they sent their disciples rather than an established teacher? Throughout their history they resisted foreign and pagan influences of any kind. They 'built a hedge' of detailed prescriptions around the Law to protect it from infringement. Their instincts would have been anti-Roman, and particularly opposed to the portrayal of the emperor's head and the inscription on coins claiming divine or quasi-divine status for the present and past emperors (Exod 20:2-6; Deut 5:6-11). However, the

49. Josephus, *Ant*, XVIII.1.1, 6.

Pharisees may also have had some concerns about the obligation of paying for the services of administration and security provided by the Romans, services for which, according to the Pharisees, the Romans too would have to render account since all authority came from God.[50] They may also have preferred to keep the status quo rather than risk the consequences of an open rebellion.[51] Their question therefore put Jesus in a really difficult situation even with the Pharisees themselves. On all fronts it seemed to be a win-win situation for Jesus' opponents, and a lose-lose situation for himself.

Jesus did not fall into the trap. He refused to answer the question on the terms and in the context in which it was asked. Pointing out how he saw through their ploy, and addressing them as on former occasions as 'hypocrites' (actors or pretenders), he responded to the question about tax with a counter question: 'Why do you set this trap for me?' Then he asked them to show him the coin used in the tribute. (Jesus asked for a coin. Maybe it was because he was not carrying a coin with the image of a pagan ruler on it in the temple precincts, but obviously someone among the questioners was.) As they produced the coin used in the tribute, the *denarius* (*dênarion*),[52] he asked them a question that made them admit that the image and inscription on the coin that they were so happy to use, and many did not want to part with by way of taxation, were in fact Tiberius' head and inscription. It would have read: *Tiberius Caesar Divi Augusti Filius Augustus* (Tiberius Caesar, Augustus, Son of the Divine Augustus). They lived in Caesar's world and engaged in the commerce and life of his world. Caesar provided the adminis-

---

50. J.Radermakers, *op. cit*, 317-18. *Les pharisiens s'en accomodaient pratiquement, estimant que les gouvernements païens recevaient aussi de Dieu leur autorité de gardiens de l'ordre, dont ils auraient à lui rendre compte.* This is similar to the advice of Paul, a former Pharisee, in Rom 13:1-7.

51. M. D. Hooker, *op. cit.*, 280. See also 'Numismatik und Neues Testament,' *Bib* 81 (2000) 457-88 and C. H. Giblin, 'The "Things of God" in the Question Concerning Tribute to Caesar (Lk 20:25; Mk 12:17; Mt 22:21),' *CBQ* 33 (1971) 510 –27.

52. The *denarius* was regarded as the equivalent of a day's wages.

tration, the security and the economic and financial system. The coin and all it stood for was Caesar's. Therefore they should 'give back' to Caesar what was Caesar's, pay it back as a debt that was owed, as pay for the services provided by Caesar's system.[53] Jesus did not comment on the rights or wrongs of the political system whereby they belonged to Caesar's world, so he did not upset the people who resented Caesar's rule. Neither did he upset the Romans by opposing the payment of the tax. Instead of a 'win-win' the opponents had lost out on both counts. Small wonder they were taken completely by surprise.

Then Jesus added, like a sting in the tail, awakening the listeners to a very different level of reality, 'and give to God the things that are God's.' This was no pious afterthought. It was a brilliant stroke in a situation unwittingly provided by his opponents. It drew a clear line of distinction between the kingdoms of the world and the kingdom of God. The opponents were using a question about the coinage of the world and its kingdoms, under the guise of religious concern, to frustrate the one coming to announce the kingdom of God and its concerns. The first part of Jesus' reply focused on the kingdoms of the world and one's obligations towards political authority. They owed to Caesar a debt for organising, governing and protecting the world they lived in, even if they would prefer to organise and govern it themselves. 'Give to Caesar what belongs to Caesar.' Earthly government and its rights, duties and obligations are the proper concern of the rulers of this world. The second part of the reply draws a clear line between what was owed to Caesar and what was owed to God.

One is left to chew over the question of 'what belongs to God' in the context of Jesus' reply. In the light of what has been taking place in the immediate context of the gospel, true and fruitful worship, unlike the current commercialism and possible ex-

---

53. This is a similar attitude to that of Paul in Romans 13:1-7, (especially 13:6-7), and in 1 Peter 2:13-17. Subsequent persecution by Nero and Domitian brought about a very different attitude to the Romans, as evidenced in Revelation where Rome is described as the scarlet whore drunk on the blood of the martyrs and saints, Rev 17:1-7.

ploitation by the 'den of thieves', and acceptance and proper treatment of the people sent by God to gather the fruits of the vineyard (in this case the Baptist and Jesus himself), could be regarded as the fundamental issues involved in 'giving to God what belongs to God.'

The growing trend, however of regarding the emperor as, *divus*, 'divine' and *filius divi Julii* (son of the divine Julius) or *filius divi Augusti* (son of the divine Augustus), a trend that developed into full-blown emperor worship in the days of Caligula, Nero and Domitian, is a trespassing into the area of God's domain. The human agent should not trespass on the divine prerogatives or the exclusive right of God to receive divine worship. The Jewish and Christian difficulty with emperor worship may well be a sub-text in the transmission of this saying of Jesus.[54]

Jesus left his interrogators amazed, having exposed their hypocrisy and beaten them in their argument, and they left him and went away.

b. On Resurrection Mt 22:23-33//Mk 12:18-27//Lk 20:27-40

The Sadducees' Question

As the disciples of the Pharisees and the Herodians depart defeated from the fray, the Sadducees now on the same day try their hand at trapping Jesus. The Sadducees were members of the Jewish priestly aristocracy, people of high standing in the socio-religious order of their day. Taking their name most likely from the High Priest Zadok who lived in the time of David and Solomon (2 Sam 8:17; 15:24; 1 Kings 1:8), and enjoying also a happy similarity of name with the term *saddiqim*, the righteous ones, they were conservative and suspicious of change and innovation in belief and practice. They were theologically opposed to the Pharisees, especially on the questions of the resurrection of the dead and the existence of angels and spirits,[55] and

---

54. Emperor worship eventually became a matter of life and death for Christians, in the days of Domitian.
55. Paul stirred intense passion between them by raising the issue of Resurrection in Acts 23: 6-10.

they recognised the written Law of Moses only, unlike the Pharisees who followed not only the written Law but also the oral tradition that grew up around the Law and its interpretation. They regarded the Prophets and the Writings as having less authority than the Torah (Pentateuch), and in the opinion of some scholars they completely disregarded them. They liked to enter into debate with distinguished teachers about their teaching and their memory lived on in rabbinic literature where they function as foils for discussions with the Pharisees. Being quite removed from the ordinary people they were of limited influence with them.[56] Being prosperous and comfortable in this life they did not see the necessity of looking to an after-life existence.[57] Their children would perpetuate their name when their mortal life had ended, a belief strongly supported by the obligation of the levirate law about the brother of a childless dead man taking his widow as wife and raising offspring to carry on his brother's name (and probably ensuring also that land and wealth remained within the family!).[58]

It is interesting that during this exchange Jesus adopts the theological position of his more usual adversaries, the Pharisees. The Sadducees ask Jesus a question, not because they want or respect his opinion, but in order to undermine the belief in resurrection by making it look ridiculous. This is a typical *Bôrut*, a question introducing a discussion designed to mock the belief of the opponent. Quoting the levirate law and citing the authority of Moses that lay behind the law, they put forward an argument that seems to make belief in the resurrection of the dead look ridiculous. The levirate law (so called from the Latin word *levir* which means 'brother-in–law') lays down that:

---

56. Josephus, *Ant*, XIII, 10,6; XVIII, 1,4,16; *War* II, 8.14.
57. See the treatment by J. P. Meier, 'The Debate on the Resurrection of the Dead: An Incident from the Ministry of the Historical Jesus?' *JSNT* 77 (2000), 3-24. See also E. Main, '*Les Sadducéens et la resurrection des morts: comparaison entre Mc 12:18-27 et Luc 27-37,*' *RB* 103 (1996), 411-32.
58. Deut 25:5f. *Levir* is the Latin term for a brother-in-law, hence the term 'levirate law' for the regulation instructing the brother of a dead man to take his wife and raise issue to carry on his brother's name.

When brothers reside together, and one of them dies and has
no son, the wife of the deceased shall not be married outside
the family to a stranger. Her husband's brother shall go in to
her, taking her in marriage, and performing the duty of a
husband's brother to her, and the firstborn whom she bears
shall succeed to the name of the deceased brother, so that his
name may not be blotted out of Israel' (Deut 25:5-10).[59]

The Sadducees (identified in the text as people who say there
is no resurrection) come to Jesus, address him as 'teacher' and
they quote the levirate law, identifying Moses as its authoritative source. Then they put to Jesus a case that they said was
familiar to them (*par hêmin*) involving seven brothers.[60] All had
died childless and all had been married to the same wife in keeping with the prescription of the levirate law. They ask which will
be her husband 'at the resurrection'. The authority of Moses
stands solidly behind their interpretation of the levirate law and
the question arising from its scrupulous application seems to
highlight the ridiculous nature of belief in resurrection where
the woman would have seven contending former husbands.
Jesus' response elaborates critically on their interpretation of
scripture and their understanding or, more accurately, their not
understanding the power of God to raise the dead, and elaborates also on the nature of the resurrection.

Jesus' reply to the questioners opens with the statement that
they are wrong. The verb *planân* means 'to lead astray', and it is
here used in the passive meaning 'you are led astray, you are
wrong/mistaken'. They are wrong on two counts. They do not
understand the scriptures or the power of God (to raise the
dead). Jesus appeals to both authorities in his response to their

59. The story of Judah and Tamar in Gen 38 arises from Judah's failure
to respect this law and Tamar's reaction that ensures the continuation
of the line of the promises. The story of Ruth and Boaz similarly shows
the woman's action ensuring the continuation of the line through a relative (Ruth 2-4).
60. The reader wonders if the Sadducees contrived this case on the basis
of the story of Sarah, daughter of Raguel, whose seven husbands died
very prematurely (Tobit 3:7-8).

question and in his refutation of their underlying misunderstanding. He answers their questions in reverse order to the two
mistakes he points out.

He begins by talking about the power of God to raise the
dead and then deals with the authority and interpretation of
scripture. They have not understood the power of God. God has
power to raise the dead to a new way of life. This new life at the
resurrection is a communion of life with God. It is not just a
resuscitation of the present life, a continuation of the present
physical existence with marriage and giving in marriage.[61] It is a
whole new life in communion with God, and it is in God's
power to bestow this new life. It is a different mode of life, 'like
the angels in heaven' (an undermining of another theory of the
Sadducees, that there are no angels!).

Jesus is confirming a long tradition of belief in an afterlife
and presents it in terms of a sharing in the life of God. The
Psalms speak a lot about an 'afterlife' but it is an ill-defined,
shady, 'limbo-like' existence. Isaiah has a clearer statement,
'Your dead shall live, their corpses shall rise. O dwellers in the
dust, awake and sing for joy!' (Isa 26:19) and Daniel says, 'Many
of those who sleep in the dust of the earth shall awake, some to
everlasting life and some to shame and everlasting contempt
…'(Dan 12:2f). The Wisdom tradition speaks of the reward or
punishments of a good and bad life after death: 'But the souls of
the righteous are in the hand of God, and no torment will ever
touch them … but they are at peace … because grace and mercy
are upon his holy ones … But the ungodly will be punished
…'(Wis 3:1-12). There is a much clearer hope of eternal life in the
speech of the mother in 2 Macc 7:29: 'Accept death, so that in

61. The active and passive forms of the verb *gamein* were used of the
man and woman respectively in regard to contracting marriage. J.
Radermakers, *op. cit.*, 319-20, comments: '… *celui que forgent les sadducéens apparaît singulièrement théorique: il révèle, de plus, une conception de
l'au- delà calquée sur les réalités terrestres, où les joies de l'union conjugale ap-
paraîtraient comme la suprême bénédiction divine… .Les relations sexuelles
appartiennent à la condition charnelle de l'homme terrestre, il ne faut pas les
transposer imaginativement au monde de la résurrection. La loi du lévirat est
donc transitoire.'*

God's mercy I may get you back again along with your brothers …' and in the words of the youngest son: 'Our brothers have drunk of ever flowing life under God's covenant' (2 Macc 7:36). In New Testament times Martha declares to Jesus that she believes her brother Lazarus will rise on the Last Day, a reflection of the belief of the ordinary people, in line with the belief of the Pharisees (Jn 11:24). The Thanksgiving Hymns of the Dead Sea Scrolls, the *Hodayoth*, reflect the belief in an angelic style existence in the heavenly court, celebrating the heavenly liturgy, an image reflected in the Book of Revelation (Rev 14:3-5,13). Significantly, Jesus, though he speaks of his resurrection in the Passion Predictions, does not base his teaching in this discussion with the Sadducees on his own resurrection, a pointer possibly to the fact that the tradition of this discussion goes back to Jesus' ministry and has not been influenced by later teaching in the light of Jesus' own resurrection.[62] St Paul emphasises the fact that resurrection will lead to a life that is not just a continuation of the present life but a whole new existence, 'what is sown is perishable, what is raised is imperishable … It is sown a physical body, it is raised a spiritual body' (1 Cor 15:42-44). Paul, however, roots his teaching in the resurrection of Jesus and the believer's participation in it.

The other point on which the Sadducees are mistaken relates to their misunderstanding of scripture. Here Jesus engages in a rabbinic style argument from the scriptures. Again asking: 'Have you not read?' he chooses a well known pivotal text in the Old Testament, the passage about Moses and the burning bush in which God addressing Moses identifies himself as 'the God of Abraham, Isaac and Jacob', the Patriarchs who had died many centuries earlier (Exod 3:6, 15, 16; cf 4:5).[63] Jesus uses this central

---

62. For a treatment of Jewish belief in resurrection in the inter-testamental period as a background for understanding New Testament issues and innovations, see G. W. E. Nickelsburg, *Resurrection, Immortality, and Eternal Life in Intertestamental Judaism*, Cambridge, Mass: Harvard University Press, 1972.

63. A belief was current that the Patriarchs were still alive, as is seen from 4 Macc 7:19 and 16:25.

text to illustrate his point. God is not just the God of dead heroes of the past. M. D. Hooker explains the biblical argument:

> ... if God is the God of the Patriarchs (and of those who came after them), he does not cease to be their God at their death; experience of fellowship with God demands belief in some kind of continuing relationship with him.[64]

The encounter ends with a statement of the reaction of the onlookers. His teaching made a deep impression on them.

c. On The Greatest Commandment Mt 22:34-40 //Mk 12:28-34 //10:25-28
The Pharisees' Question

Jesus has now got the better of the chief priest and elders of the people, the disciples of the Pharisees and the Herodians, and the Sadducees. Now, when the Pharisees heard that Jesus has silenced the Sadducees they came together, and in order to put him to the test, one of them, a lawyer,[65] asked: 'Master, which is the great commandment of the Law?'

The question introduces a discussion that deals with the *Derek 'Eretz*, 'the way of righteousness', the fundamental principles of moral conduct. It is about 'the first of all the commandments' and it is not so much a question about the most important commandment among all the others, but a commandment that encapsulates some basic principle that underpins and runs through the vast array of commandments that were later organised by the rabbis into the 365 negative and 248 positive commandments, a total of 613 in all. Here two commandments are brought together to form one great commandment.

In giving a single, combined commandment Jesus is stating an underlying principle that runs through all the command-

---

64. M. D. Hooker, *op. cit.*, 285.
65. Some mss have simply 'one of them', others state that he was a lawyer (*nomikos*), as in the Lukan parallel (Lk 10:25). Mk 12:28 has 'one of the scribes' (*eis tôn grammateôn*). Unlike the negative approach of the questioner in Matthew and Luke, the scribe in Mark approaches Jesus in positive mood like a student approaching a well established master, because he was impressed with how well Jesus had responded to his questioners / critics.

ments. He is also at the same time issuing a challenge to the approach to law which lost sight of the central insights of the Law and considered it necessary to legislate for every possible circumstance in everyday living, leading at times to an overburdening of people with obligations (and consequently with guilt).

Being asked about one commandment, Jesus takes two commandments and knits them together as one great commandment or principle. First of all there is the commandment to love God, and then, following on that there is the commandment to love one's neighbour, typical of biblical religion where moral injunctions flow from religious worship and doctrine. The two commandments in effect sum up the two tables of the Decalogue, the first dealing with our relationship with God, the second with neighbour.

Jesus responds with the citation from Deuteronomy: 'You shall love the Lord your God with all your heart, with all your soul and with all your strength' (Deut 6:5). In the text of Matthew (and also in Mark) 'with all your mind (*dianoia*)' is added to 'with all your heart and soul', probably reflecting an attempt, under Hellenistic influence, to cover every aspect of the human person's personal response. Matthew does not include 'with all your strength'.[66]

The commandment to love one's neighbour is a citation from Leviticus 19:18. The standard measure for love of neighbour is love of self. 'It assumes that people naturally love themselves enough to care for themselves, protect themselves, and look after their own interests. The challenge is to show the same kind of love to others.'[67] In Leviticus 'neighbour' is seen in terms of family, kin and friend. Gradually a broader concept emerges and this is hammered home by Jesus in the parable of the Good

---

66. The commandment to love God is taken from Deuteronomy which begins with the command to 'listen/hear', the *Shema*, recited morning and evening by the Jews as their prayer and renewal of commitment: 'Listen, O Israel, the Lord our God is the one Lord' (Deut 6:4f, 9; cf 11:13-21; Num 15:37-41). Mark quotes the *Shema* in this context (Mk 12:29).

67. J. R. Donahue and D. J. Harrington, *op.cit.*, 355.

Samaritan in Luke's gospel where being a neighbour is defined in terms of response to anyone in need, of whatever race or background, even someone from a background hostile to one's own, a traditional and national enemy (Lk 10:29-37).

It was not uncommon for a master to be asked questions about the relative seriousness of various commandments. Some were regarded as 'light', others as 'heavy'. In the Sermon on the Mount Jesus speaks of 'the least' of the commandments (Mt 5:19).[68] Sometimes, too, a master would be asked a question such as, 'Could the entire body of law be summed up in a sentence, or recited while standing on one foot?' A famous example is that of Hillel, quoted in the Babylonian Talmud.[69] Shammai and Hillel were two of the most well known rabbis who were more or less contemporaries of Jesus. They were mentioned earlier in the commentary in connection with 'the golden rule' (Mt 7:12) and the debate on the grounds for divorce (Mt 19:1-9). As seen already, Hillel responded to the request of the prospective proselyte with what has been called 'the silver rule' of Hillel which stated, 'What you yourself hate, do not do to anyone; this is the whole law, the rest is commentary; go and learn it.' This reflects very closely a maxim stated in Tobit: 'Do to no one what you would not want done to yourself' (Tob 4:15).

Whereas the 'silver rule' was stated in negative terms, saying what should not be done, Jesus' 'golden rule' is stated in positive terms, stating what should be done. The 'golden rule' of Jesus in Matthew's gospel is spoken in the context of an underlying principle in the teaching of the Law and the Prophets: 'So always treat others as you would like them to treat you, that is the

---

68. I. Abrahams, in 'The Greatest Commandment' in *Studies in Pharisaism and the Gospels*, First Series, Cambridge: Cambridge University Press, 1917, 18ff, is of the opinion that the attempt to isolate the basic principle(s) underlying the Law caused fear among some rabbis that this could result in regarding some laws as less important, whereas they regarded all the Law as important. He suggests that the original intention of the question put to Jesus was to see where he stood on the issue. See, D. E. Nineham, *op. cit.*, 324-25.
69. *b. Shabbat* 31a.

meaning of the law and the Prophets' (Mt 7:12). In Luke the 'golden rule' is included as one of a series of maxims in the 'Sermon on the Plain'. St Paul quoted it in his letter to the Galatians: 'The whole Law is summarised in a single command: "Love your neighbour as yourself"(Gal 5:14)' and in his Letter to the Romans: 'The one who loves his neighbour has fulfilled the law ... All the commandments ... are summed up in this single command: "You must love your neighbour as yourself. Love is the one thing that cannot hurt your neighbour; that is why it is the answer to every one of the commandments"'(Rom 13:8-10).

Jesus sums up and drives home his point: 'On these two commandments hang the whole Law, and the Prophets also.' Again Jesus is seen 'not to destroy the law and the Prophets but to fulfil them'(Mt 5:17).

Although Mt 22:37-38 consists almost entirely of verbatim quotations from two Old Testament passages (Deut 6:4, 5 and Lev 19:18 – both fully emphasised and commented on by the rabbis and scholars), 'the combination of these two widely separated texts as taking us to the heart of religion is clearly an original and creative achievement of the highest order.'[70] Was Jesus the first to combine them? It is worth noting that whereas Mark and Matthew portray Jesus as combining them in his answer to the question put to him, Luke places the combination on the lips of the scribe and maybe in so doing reflects a tradition that was in vogue and is drawn on and highlighted by Jesus (Lk 10:25-28). Luke portrays the scribe as asking the question: 'What must I do to inherit eternal life?' Jesus responds: 'What is written in the Law? What do you read there?' to which the scribe responds with the double commandment of love of God and neighbour. Jesus responds that he has answered right and if he acts accordingly, 'life is yours'. In spite of the negative introductory note about his trying to disconcert Jesus, the scribe in Luke's account represents a tradition of 'good' scribes whose openness and perspicacity bring them close to the essential

---

70. D. E. Nineham, *op. cit.*, 324.

teaching of Jesus. The combination of the two commandments is also seen in a number of places in the *Testament of the Twelve Patriarchs*, a work generally regarded as having come under Christian influence.[71]

d. On the Son of David Mt 22:41-46//Mk 12:35-37//Lk 20:41-44

Jesus' Counter-Question

While the Pharisees were gathered together, Jesus put this question to them: 'What do you think of the Christ? Whose son is he?' They say to him: 'David's.' This question was probably very important for the early Christians as they debated among themselves and with the Jews how best to understand, articulate and argue the identity, role and status of Jesus. Being well established in the tradition, the debate finds its way into the three synoptic gospels with some differences of setting and audience. In the parallel passage in Mark's gospel Jesus raises the question as a criticism of the opinion of the scribes (many of whom were Pharisees) (Mk 12:35-37). In Luke's account Jesus appears to address the scribes (Lk 20:41-44).

The Messiah/Christ, 'the anointed one,' was 'the one who is to come', variously expected to be a prophet, priest or prince/king. Isaiah spoke of the messianic figure in terms of a descendant of David, 'a shoot from the stump/root of Jesse (David's father) (cf Isa 11:1, 10). Jeremiah spoke of God raising up 'a branch from the root of Jesse' (Jer 23:5). Ezekiel looked to the day when God would raise up a new David, a shepherd-king to look after the flock of God (Ezek 34:23). After the Exile the expectation developed in different ways. As the people struggled with the remnants of what had been, some looked to a complete apocalyptic destruction and a new beginning, others looked to an ideal future with the hope of restoring the kingdom of David and Solomon when God would raise up a judge, king or warrior to establish it. The Psalms of Solomon 17 from the century before

---

71. *Dan 5:3; Issachar 5:2; 7:6.*

Christ testify to the expectation. The devotees at Qumran expected two, possibly three, persons to fulfil the priestly, prophetic and princely roles of the expected Messiah.[72] In John's gospel the questioning of John the Baptist by the emissaries sent by the Jerusalem authorities shows a triple expectation of 'Christ, Elijah and the Prophet' though this neat formula may be influenced by subsequent Christian reflection (Jn 1:19-28). A messianic figure, a descendant of David, was expected, but the actual terms 'Son of David' and 'Messiah' do not seem to have been closely associated in common usage in the period prior to the New Testament.[73]

The very first verse of the gospel, its programmatic title, speaks of Jesus as 'son of David, son of Abraham' and on several occasions when persons came for healing they addressed him or spoke of him as 'Son of David' (Mt 9:27; 12:23; 20:30, 31). This general and possibly diverse and unfocused expectation of a Messiah hung heavily in the air at Passover, and attached itself to Jesus in a very definite way on the occasion of his triumphal approach to the city when he was hailed as Son of David by the blind men at Jericho (Mt 20:30, 31) and the crowd calling down blessings on 'the one who comes in the name of the Lord' and 'Hosanna to the Son of David' (Mt 21:9).

Now Jesus poses a question, or rather he issues a challenge, about the identity of such an anointed figure. He quotes the opening verse of Psalm 110 which guarantees the assistance of God to the king at his enthronement, as though he sits with God in the heavenly court: 'The Lord said to my Lord, "Sit at my

---

72. On the Qumran material see J. J. Collins, *The Sceptre and the Star: The Messiahs of the Dead Sea Scrolls and Other Ancient Literature*, ABRL; New York: Doubleday, 1995, and also his article 'The Nature of Messianism in the Light of the Dead Sea Scrolls' in *The Dead Sea Scrolls in their Historical Context*, (eds T. H. Kim, L. W. Hurtado, A. Graeme Auld and Alison Jack), Edinburgh: T&T Clark, 2000, 199-219. See also the essays in J. H. Charlesworth (ed): *The Messiah: Developments in Earliest Judaism and Christianity:* The First Princeton Symposium on Judaism and Christian Origins, Minneapolis: Fortress, 1992.
73. cf F. J. Moloney, *op. cit.*, 243, text and note 145.

right hand, and I will make your enemies a footstool under your feet".' Both Jesus and the listeners associate the psalm with David as author and accept its authority as inspired scripture. Both he and his audience are also accustomed to hearing verses of scripture quoted 'out of context', taken on their own and presented as oracles or proof texts. The verse is quoted here in Matthew (as in Mark) without reference to the footstool: 'I will put your enemies beneath your feet.'[74] Here however, as God is seen to inspire the oracle through divine inspiration of scripture, and David articulates it in the psalm, a third person, understood here to be the Messiah, is seen to be the addressee.

The argument made by Jesus is even more striking when seen against the background of the Greek text, *eipen ho kyrios tô kyriô mou*, 'The Lord said to my Lord'. The term 'Lord' had become a standard translation for *Adonai*, which was in turn a substitute for *YHWH* in the reading of the Hebrew scriptures where, out of reverence, the Divine Name was not pronounced. In the Greek of the Septuagint and of the New Testament, therefore, the same title is used for God and the one to whom the psalm is addressed, the Messiah. It could be paraphrased: 'God said to my Lord.' David, speaking of the Messiah, in this understanding of the psalm, describes him as 'my Lord', thus putting him on a different plain altogether to any son or descendant of his own. Sitting at God's right hand and having his enemies (a footstool) under his feet became for the Christians the great expression of Jesus' glorification and victory over sin and death (Mt 26:64; Mk 14:62; Lk 22:69; Col 3:1; Heb 1:3; 1 Cor 15:25).[75] The verse is actu-

74. In the ancient world, as is evidenced, for example, from some of the artefacts from the Egyptian tombs, it was customary for the victor to paint the image of his conquered enemy on his footstool. Putting his feet on the footstool then represented having his foot on the neck of his enemy, the sign of victory in combat. Mark and Matthew (Mt 22:41-46) drop the LXX reference to the footstool and simply state 'under your feet'. Luke maintains the reference to the footstool (Lk 20:41-44). The point being made is the same with or without the reference to the footstool. 'Underfoot' is understood in both renderings as signifying 'vanquished'.

75. Artists have often pictured the risen Jesus with his foot on the tomb as a sign of his victory over death.

ally quoted in Acts 2:34-35 and Heb 1:13. It is quoted in the context of Peter's speech at Pentecost in Acts, and followed by the remark: 'For this reason the whole house of Israel can be certain that God has made this Jesus whom you crucified both Lord and Christ.' In Hebrews 1:13 the author says: 'God has never said to any angel: "Sit at my right hand and I will make your enemies a footstool for you".'[76] As the Christians proclaimed Jesus Lord, they did so in a world, and often against a background of persecution, where the emperor was seen as Lord/*kyrios*/*Dominus*. By the time of Domitian they will be required to choose between Jesus as Lord and God (the great faith profession of John's gospel on the lips of Thomas in Jn 20:28) and the emperor Domitian as *Dominus et Deus, Kyrios kai Theos*, Lord and God. The gospels represent a step on the way towards this public clash of lordships.

All three synoptics have an account of this discussion about the Son of David. All three accept the importance of the Davidic descent of Jesus. The genealogies and infancy narratives in the gospels of Matthew and Luke (Mt 1:1-16, 20; Lk 1:27; 3:23-38) carefully emphasise the Davidic descent of Joseph who gave Jesus his legal paternity and all four gospels highlight the Davidic element in the enthusiastic (even if misunderstood) reception of Jesus at his triumphal entrance into Jerusalem. Matthew emphasises the Davidic confession at various healings, and both Matthew and Mark emphasise it at the healing in Jericho as Jesus begins the final ascent to Jerusalem. Apart from Jn 7:42 where the crowds are discussing the fact that Jesus came from Galilee whereas the Messiah must be descended from David and come from Bethlehem, there is no denial or serious questioning of Jesus' Davidic descent in the New Testament. The oldest references are those in Paul's letter to the Romans where he writes: 'This news is about the Son of God who, ac-

---

76. See W. R. G Loader, 'Christ at the Right Hand. Ps CX.1 in the New Testament', *NTS* 21 (1974-1975), 81-108 and D. M. Hay, *Glory at the Right Hand. Psalm 110 in Early Christianity*, SBLMS 18. Nashville: Abingdon, 1973.

cording to the human nature he took was a descendant of David: it is about Jesus Christ our Lord who, in the order of the Spirit, the Spirit of holiness that was in him, was proclaimed Son of God ...'(Rom 1:3) and in Rom 15:12 he applies Isaiah's designation 'the root of Jesse' (David's father) to Jesus. In 2 Tim 2:8 Jesus is described as 'sprung from the race of David.'

The discussion about the 'Sonship of David' is not an attempt to deny the Davidic descent on the human level, but rather an opportunity to emphasise that he is more than the son/descendant of David, modelled on him and his role. The citation from Psalm 110 is used to show how David himself acknowledged his superiority. He is far superior to David himself and to any of the expected political messianic figures of contemporary Jewish hopes. As the reader knows, Jesus is Messiah/Christ and Lord, Beloved Son of the Father, in him the Father is well pleased, and on him the Spirit descended at the Jordan. The triumphal approach to the city and the action in the Temple of one publicly celebrated by the rejoicing crowd as 'Son of David', in fulfilment of their political hopes, is but a faint prelude to the 'coming' in glory of 'the Son of Man' when city, temple and the world as we know it have passed away, as Jesus will go on to point out in the eschatological/apocalyptic discourse' (Mt 24:29-30//Mk 13:26f) and in his Jewish trial (Mt 26:64; Mk 14:62). To sum up in a phrase borrowed from Paul, Jesus 'according to the human nature he took was a descendant of David' (Rom 1:3). But he is something much more. He is Lord. The reaction to Jesus' statement is stunned silence. 'Nobody could answer him a word, and from then on nobody dared question him on anything' (Mt 22:46).

Having silenced them, Jesus will now seize the initiative and condemn his critics.

4. CONDEMNATION OF THE SCRIBES AND PHARISEES MT 23:1-39

The temple and its worship, the leaders of the people represented by the chief priests and elders, the religious movements represented by the Pharisees and Sadducees, the scribes, the experts in Law and Scripture and the political movement of the Herodians, have all been scrutinised and found wanting.

Jesus now has centre stage and in good prophetic tradition speaks to the crowds and his disciples. Matthew here includes a lengthy and very severe criticism of the scribes and Pharisees. Many of the scribes were members of the Pharisee movement. Luke has a corresponding polemic earlier in his gospel (Lk 11:37-54). Having acknowledged the importance of teachers and their teaching of the Law, Jesus severely condemns teachers who do not practise what they preach, though they impose heavy obligations on others.[77]

This lengthy criticism fits in with the preceding controversy cycle which took place mostly in the temple area, rather than with the succeeding eschatological discourse, the fifth of the major discourses in the gospel in Mt 24-25, after Jesus definitively leaves the temple area and moves to the Mount of Olives. The criticism in content and style recalls the fiery preaching of a prophet like Amos or Jeremiah.

a. They Occupy the Chair of Moses ... but ...' Mt 23:1-12

Words without deeds (Mt 23:2-4)

Jesus spoke to the people and his disciples. He pointed out to them that the scribes and Pharisees are the official teachers, 'occupying the chair of Moses'. As the official teachers people should do as they say and observe what they teach (this represents Matthew's concern for the Law, in keeping with Jesus' statements in Mt 5:17-19) but they should not conduct themselves like the scribes and Pharisees because they do not practise

---

77. At this point Mark presents Jesus' severe criticism of those scribes who use religion to acquire human esteem and, even more seriously, 'swallow the property of widows making pretence of long prayers' (Mk12: 38-40).

what they preach (a favourite criticism in Matthew, reflecting Jesus' criticism in Mt 5:20). They use their authority to bind up heavy burdens and place them on the shoulders of people but they do not lift a finger to help them and remain aloof from those burdens themselves, unlike Jesus whose 'yoke is easy and his burden light' (Mt 11:30).

Vanity and Self Importance (Mt 23:5-7)

Jesus continues his criticism pointing out how they do everything in order to be seen by people. They attract attention to themselves and feed their self-importance by broadening their *phylacteries*[78] and lengthening their *tassels*. *Phylacteries* were verses of scripture written on parchment and enclosed in leather boxes that were attached to the forehead or arms during morning prayer (Exod 13:1-16; Deut 6:4-9; 11:13-22). The statement here is probably an ironic comment on their putting more scriptural texts on the parchment and not following them in practice. They functioned then only as 'pious objects', charms or amulets. *Tassels* (fringes) were to be worn on the corners of their outer garments 'to remind them of all the commands of *YHWH*' (Num 15:38-39; Deut 22:12). They were therefore public declarations of their status as people of the covenant. The irony here is that they increased their 'reminders' but did not follow through in practice. The tassels/fringes also became a religious display rather than a reminder of their obligations.[79] They (the scribes and Pharisees) like the places of importance at banquets and the front seats in the synagogues (probably facing the people, in order to be admired) and being obsequiously greeted outdoors in the market places and being addressed as 'rabbi'.

---

78. *Phylacteries* were known also in rabbinic circles as *tefillin*.
79. The woman with the issue of blood and the sick brought into the streets for healing wanted to touch the fringe/tassels of Jesus' garments. This shows how the fringe was a tangible symbol of his religious standing, authority and power (Mt 9:20; 14:36).

b. Five Logia. Equality before God Mt 23:8-12

A collection of five *logia* or sayings point to a very different approach, which Jesus' followers must adopt. Rather than seeking status they are to live a communal life in equality before God. They are not to seek status and power. This is in stark contrast to the vanity, hypocrisy and arrogance of the religious leaders.

The first *logion* stresses that they should not be preening themselves on the title 'rabbi' since there is only one Teacher, the Christ (Mt 23:8) and they are all brothers (and sisters), all equally students of the one Rabbi. The second *logion* points to the fact that there is but one Father in heaven, so no one on earth should be called 'Father'. 'Father' not only denotes one's biological parent, the giver of life, protector and provider, but in Aramaic and Hebrew *ab* and its diminutive *abba* are also honorific titles given to an esteemed teacher, elder or patron, as *abûna* is in modern Arabic (Mt 23:9). The third *logion* resembles the first, almost like a variant version of the same. 'Do not be called 'instructors', (*kathêgêtai*), for your one instructor is Christ' (i.e. you are all in need of instruction). The fourth *logion*, 'The greatest among you must be your servant' (Mt 23:11) recalls Jesus' teaching on greatness in the kingdom (Mt 20:26-27; cf 18:1-4). The eschatological reversal of status is recalled in the fifth *logion*, 'Anyone who exalts himself will be humbled, and he who humbles himself will be exalted' (Mt 23:12).

c. Seven Woes. Judgement on the Scribes and Pharisees Mt 22:13-32

In this fiercely critical polemic Jesus is in the tradition of the prophets who, often to their own detriment, never drew back from criticising the authorities, civil or religious, drawing the fire of officialdom on themselves. The same is true here of Jesus. He is a Jew criticising the Jewish leadership for its failures in teaching and example. He is not criticising Israel, or the people of Israel as such, and as such he is not anti-Semitic or anti-Jewish in a racist sense. Commentators and preachers must be very careful, however, to keep that in mind and to put the criticisms in proper historical context. As Matthew records these criticisms he has in mind the tensions between Rabbinic Judaism and the Christian Movement in addition to the factors at work in Jesus' own time. Matthew is writing in the context of the tensions that arose between the followers of Rabbinic Judaism after Jamnia and his own mixed Jewish and Gentile Christian community – two sibling communities who had lost the parent community in the terrible events of the Jewish-Roman War which culminated in the destruction of Jerusalem and its temple and spelled the end of the pilgrimage feasts, sacrifices and atoning rituals associated with the temple. Both groups clash as they struggle to secure their identity and future in the new situation after 70AD.

The prophetic literature abounds with 'woes' against civil and religious leaders, against worship without genuine inner dispositions, against social injustice and on various occasions against a faithless people (Amos 5:18-20; 6:1-7; Mic 2:1-4; Isa 5:8-10, 11-14; 18-19, 20, 21, 22-24; 10:1-3; 28:1-4; 29:1-4; 30:1-3; 31:1-4; 45:9-10; Jer 13:27; 48:46; Ezek 16:23). The 'woe' is addressed to a person or group, their misdeeds are enumerated and a forthcoming judgement and its punishments are announced. The woes are pronounced to warn the evildoers, but also to warn off any followers or persons likely to imitate the doings of those being denounced.

The woes against the scribes and Pharisees in many respects reflect the opposite to the beatitudes in the Sermon on the Mount, for example, shutting up the kingdom rather than being 'of the kingdom'; becoming a child of hell rather than children of God; being blind guides rather than seeing God; neglecting mercy rather than showing mercy; cleaning the outside of the cup and plate rather than hungering and thirsting for righteousness; being like whitewashed tombs rather than showing purity of heart; inheriting the blood of the martyrs rather than inheriting the earth (Mt 5:3-12; 23:13-32).[80]

The seven 'woes' against the scribes and Pharisees in Mt 23:13-31 correspond roughly to the three 'woes' against the

80. See P. F. Ellis, *op. cit.*, 81.

Pharisees[81] and three 'woes' against the lawyers in Lk 11:39-52. Matthew and Luke seem to have drawn on a common tradition as in the material usually classed as Q. The 'woe' is the opposite to a beatitude or blessing which points to a positive virtue, deed or state in the persons addressed or spoken about and promises a reward. At times a series of beatitudes and woes go together. In Luke's Sermon on the Plain four beatitudes are followed by four corresponding woes. 'Blessed are you who are poor/Woe to you who are rich; Blessed are you who are hungry now/Woe to you who have your fill now, Blessed are you who weep now/Woe to you who laugh now, Blessed are you who when people hate you/Woe to you when the world speaks well of you' (Lk 6:20-26). Matthew has heavily edited and sharply pointed the material at his targets, the combined scribes and Pharisees. The Pharisees are criticised in Luke for cleaning the outside of cups and plates and not looking within, taking tithes on spices and herbs and neglecting justice and the love of God, seeking the best seats in synagogues, seeking obsequious greetings in public and being like whitewashed tombs. The lawyers are criticised for loading burdens and not helping to lift them, building tombs for the prophets their forefathers killed, and for taking away the key of knowledge, not entering themselves or allowing others to do so. These criticisms are present in Matthew, either in the general criticism immediately preceding the 'woes' or in the 'woes' themselves.

The main target of the criticism running through the woes in Matthew is hypocrisy. In six of the seven 'woes' Jesus addresses the scribes and Pharisees as 'hypocrites'. The Greek word *hyprokitês* means an actor. Since they are actors the applause of their audience is important to them and they gear their activity to that goal, so their vaunted piety is a performance, an external show. Hypocrisy signifies, therefore, an appearance not matched by reality, words not matched by actions and emphasis

---

81. In addition, some scholars count Lk 11:39 as a 'woe' though the term 'woe', *ouai*, is not used. It reads: 'Now you Pharisees , you clean the outside of the cup and the plate ...' cf D. J. Harrington, *op. cit.*, 326.

on externals to the neglect of the interior life. Jesus has used the term 'hypocrites' several times already in the gospel. Those who attract notice to their alms giving, praying and fasting are branded as hypocrites (Mt 6:2, 5, 16), as are those who judge others and do not see the plank in their own eye (Mt 7:5). The term is applied to the Pharisees when Jesus accused them of doing away with the commandment of God in favour of the commandment of men in the matter of avoiding their duty to father and mother by recourse to 'gift', 'something dedicated to God' (*Corban*) and when they set the trap for him with their question about paying taxes to Caesar (Mt 15:7; 22:18). Jesus criticises them also because they emphasise the little, even insignificant details to the neglect of the bigger things and engage in casuistry by which obligations undertaken can be subsequently avoided (Mt 23:16-22).

i. The first 'woe'. Not Entering the Kingdom (Mt 23:13)

The first woe is addressed to the scribes and Pharisees calling them hypocrites and pointing out how they who, by implication, are the spiritual leaders and have the authority and learning to open up the kingdom for people, instead are an obstacle to people who wish to enter. They shut up the kingdom of heaven. 'You yourselves do not enter the kingdom and hinder those who are entering.' This is the opposite to the beatitudes of the poor in spirit and those persecuted in the cause of righteousness 'for theirs is the kingdom of heaven'. Far from pleasing the audience like the hypocrites/actors, they tell them what they do not want to hear and in so challenging them draw their fire on themselves (Mt 5:3,10).

(Some manuscripts have an additional 'woe' interpolated here at Mt 23:14 from Mk 12:40 or Lk 20:47. 'Woe to you, scribes and Pharisees, hypocrites, for you devour widow's houses and for a pretence you make long prayers; therefore you will receive the greater condemnation.' The scribes functioned as lawyers and as such would have been involved in business and property dealings. Creating an aura of piety around themselves would have won them a clientele among whom there were vulnerable people like the widows who could be exploited. The legal, prophetic and wisdom literature of the Old Testament singled out the widow, the orphan and the stranger in one's midst as vulnerable people who should be helped and the exploitation of whom was seen as a crime calling out for God's punishment.)

ii. The second 'woe'. Making Proselytes (Mt 23:15)

The second woe also addresses the scribes and Pharisees as 'hypocrites'. This time attention is drawn to their widespread journeys over sea and land and feverish activity in making one proselyte, a convert to Judaism (the Greek word *prosêlytos* means 'one who has approached'). But what do they teach their neophyte only what they do themselves, and, given the usual eagerness and zeal of new converts, they make their new novice twice as bad as themselves, making him 'a child of hell (*Gehenna*)'. This has the opposite outcome to the beatitude of the peacemakers who 'will be called children of God' (Mt 5:9).

iii. The third woe. Swearing (Mt 23:16-22)

The third woe varies the pejorative address to 'blind guides' and twice during the woe the term 'blind' will be repeated, combined once with 'foolish/stupid'. Already, in the context of the discussion on ritual cleanliness Jesus has criticised the Pharisees as blind guides and warned that when one blind man leads another they both fall into a pit/ditch (Mt 15:14). He had already dealt with the subject of swearing in the antitheses in the Sermon on the Mount (Mt 5:34-35). Now this 'woe' is an extended criticism of the casuistry involved in making and then avoiding the obligation incurred in solemn oaths and promises. First of all they avoid using the divine name in making oaths and vows but then believe that in some way they can avoid the obligations incurred. They are even casuistic in their distinctions about the substitutes they use for the divine name. For this they are addressed as 'blind guides'. They imply that the gold of the temple is more important than the temple, which makes holy the gold, so swearing by the temple, one is not bound, but swearing by the gold of the temple one is bound. Similarly one who swears by the gift of gold on the altar is bound, but the one who swears by the altar is not bound, even though it is the altar that makes holy the gift, and whoever swears by the altar swears by the altar and everything upon it, so one cannot make that distinction. Similarly whoever swears by the temple swears by it and the One who dwells in it. Whoever swears by heaven swears by the throne of God and by him who sits on it. The problem here addressed seems to have been a cause of concern to the rabbis because, as D. J. Harrington points out, it is subsequently addressed in the *Mishnah*. 'All substitute words for vows are as the vows' (*m. Ned* 1: 1).[82] This woe is the reverse of the beatitude proclaiming 'blessed' the pure of heart, and promising that 'they shall see God'. Those avoiding their obligations through self-interest and far too clever argumentation are far from pure of heart and turn out to be blind. As Jesus stated earlier (Mt 15:14) they are blind guides, not alone not seeing God, but not even seeing the ditch into which they, and the people they lead, will fall!

iv. The fourth 'woe'. Tithes (Mt 23:23-24)

The fourth woe again calls the scribes and Pharisees 'hypocrites' because they are concerned about tithes on such small items of produce as herbs and spices, mint and dill and cumin, even though the scripture states only that tithes (one tenth of the produce) should be paid on larger produce such as grain, wine, oil and flocks (Deut 14:23). In spite of their meticulous and unnecessary rigour in this regard, they neglect the weightier matters of the Law – judgement and mercy and faith. Jesus agrees that they should have paid their tithes but not neglected the other matters. As an illustration of their blindness Jesus speaks of their scrupulous practice of straining the wine of libation to ensure its purity by ridding it of any tiny insect, but at the same time they swallow the very large, but more significantly, the very ritually unclean animal, the camel, declared unclean in Lev

---

82. D. J. Harrington, *op. cit.*, 325, n 22.

11:4 and Deut 14:7. They overlook the fundamental obligations of the Law, justice, mercy and faith/trust. This woe is the reverse of the beatitude 'blessed are the merciful' (Mt 5:7). Legal scruples have replaced the basic social obligations of justice, mercy and trust/good faith as they lay heavy burdens on people with their interpretations and practices.

v. The fifth 'woe'. Inner Cleanliness (Mt 23:25-26)

The fifth woe again addresses the scribes and Pharisees as 'hypocrites', and uses a second address 'blind Pharisee'. This time their hypocrisy, the external show, is graphically portrayed by reference to their practice of cleansing the outside of the cup and the plate while inside they are full of robbery and self indulgence. Their blindness prevents them from seeing that the inside must first be clean so that the outside can be clean as well. This is reminiscent of Jesus' discussion with the Pharisees and scribes from Jerusalem, and subsequently with the people and his disciples in Mt 15:1-20 in which he says that it is not what goes into a man that makes him unclean but he is made unclean by what comes out of his heart by way of evil intentions, murder, adultery, fornication, theft, perjury and slander (Mt 15:18-20). This woe is the opposite of the beatitude that extolled purity of heart, the internal disposition which is the opposite of the blindness of those who purify only the outside of the cups and plates: 'Blessed are the pure of heart for they shall see God' (Mt 5:8).

vi. The sixth 'woe'. Whitewashed Tombs (Mt 23:27-28)

The sixth woe again uses the address 'hypocrites'. They look like honest and upright men on the outside but inside they are full of hypocrisy and lawlessness. The outward show this time is portrayed graphically in terms of the 'whitewashed tombs' which look quite attractive on the outside but inside are full of decay and dead men's bones. Apparently there was a custom of whitewashing the outside of the tombs so that the unsuspecting passer-by would not unwittingly come in contact with the dead and so become ritually unclean. This woe also seems like the reverse of the beatitudes 'blessed are the pure of heart' (Mt 5:8) whose outward appearance is matched by inner purity and 'blessed are those who mourn' for they see the death and inner decay that needs to be mourned for rather than covering it over with outward show or whitewash (Mt 5:5).

vii. The seventh 'woe'. The Tombs of the Prophets (Mt 23:29-32)

The seventh woe again uses the address 'hypocrites'. Their activity of building the sepulchres of the prophets and decorating the tombs of the holy men their fathers killed identifies them as the sons of those who did the killing. They are chips off the old block. There seems to have been a considerable amount of monument building in Jesus' time. In saying they would not have done it had they been alive in their fathers' day they are at the same time acknowledging that they are 'sons of the murderers.' Jesus challenges them to finish off the work their fathers began. This woe is the reverse of the beatitudes about persecution. It targets the persecutors whereas the beatitudes focus on the persecuted (Mt 5:10-12). It is the opposite of the beatitude about the meek who will inherit the earth (Mt 5:4). The sons of the murderers will inherit the blood of the martyrs.

d. Persecuting the Messengers Mt 23:33-36

Matthew follows the seventh 'woe' dealing with the blood of the martyrs with Jesus' predictions about the future in store for his followers. He tells his opponents to fill up the measure of their fathers, that is, to complete the work their fathers had begun by persecuting Jesus' own prophets, wise men and scribes (paralleling the prophets, wisdom teachers and teachers of the Law in the history of Israel) and so to bring forward the end time and the judgement.

Addressing the scribes and Pharisees in a manner similar to that used by John the Baptist in addressing the Pharisees and Sadducees (Mt 3:7), Jesus asks them how they will be able to flee from the judgement. 'Serpents, brood of vipers, how will you

flee from the judgement of Gehenna?' that is, from condemnation to hell. This is another ironic statement since the Pharisees
were believers in afterlife, judgement, reward and punishment.
The Baptist had said to the Pharisees and Sadducees: 'Brood of
vipers, who warned you to fly from the retribution that is coming?' Now as the woes come to a climax with a pointed reference
to the historical killing of the prophets and holy ones, and the
predicted killing of Jesus' own 'prophets and sages and scribes',
the note of judgement and retribution has now been introduced,
as was traditional in the case of the prophets who followed their
'woe' statements of criticism with threat of the punishment that
lay in store for the offenders.

The imagery of killing and crucifixion places Christian suffering in line with that of Jesus himself. Just as the failure of the
leaders of Israel manifested itself in the rejection, even the
killing of the prophets and holy ones, so will they continue to
persecute the 'prophets and sages and scribes' of Jesus. 'Some of
them you will kill and crucify, and some of them you will
scourge in your synagogues and you will pursue from city to
city' (Mt 23:33-36). Matthew's community could see in some
high profile cases how these predictions had been fulfilled. Paul
and his companions, for example, were pursued from city to city
(Acts 14:19) and he wrote to the Corinthians about the five times
he had the thirty-nine lashes from the Jews (2 Cor 11:24). Paul
himself earlier had pursued the people of the way from city to
city, from Jerusalem to Damascus (Acts 8:3). There had been attempts on Paul's life by the Jews (Acts 21:31, 36; 22:22; 23:10, 16-
22). James, Son of Zebedee was beheaded by Herod Agrippa in
44AD (Acts 12:1-2) and James of Jerusalem was either stoned to
death in Jerusalem in 62AD (according to Josephus) or thrown
from the pinnacle of the temple and clubbed to death in 66AD
(according to Hegesippus).

Jesus states that all the blood of the righteous they had murdered would come upon this generation. He repeats with a
solemn 'amen' declaration, 'Amen, I say to you, all these will
come upon this generation.' This generation will pay the price.

They will undergo the judgement and punishment for all those murdered from Abel to Zechariah. Mentioning Abel and Zechariah is intended to describe a *terminus a quo* and a *terminus ad quem* that bracket the entire span of salvation history. Jesus now speaks again of 'this evil generation' as he has done so often already. He did so when he compared his critics to those who criticised John for his asceticism and himself for his gluttony (Mt 11:16-19); when the scribes and Pharisees were asking for a sign from him (Mt 12:38-42; 16:1-4) and when the disciples failed to heal the epileptic demoniac because of their little faith (Mt 17:14-20).

The mention of Abel (Gen 4:8) and Zechariah is quite clear in its purpose, but there is an element of historical confusion in regard to Zechariah. The prophet Zechariah was son of Barachiah, son of Iddo (Zech 1:1),[83] but it was another Zechariah, son of Jehoida the priest who was murdered in the temple because of his sermon in 2 Chron 24:20-22. After the Jewish War a further confusion may have occurred before or during Matthew's time with Zechariah son of Bareis, who was killed in the war (Josephus, *War*, 4:334-44). A confusion of the first two persons is the most likely scenario. The point at issue is unaffected by the historical 'confusion'.

e. 'Jerusalem that kills the prophets' Mt 23:37-39//Lk 13:34-35

Matthew and Luke quote almost verbatim the lamentation over Jerusalem. 'Jerusalem, Jerusalem that kills the prophets and stones those who are sent to you!' This lamentation sums up the parables of the wicked tenants and the wedding feast, and follows from the seventh 'woe', focusing them on Jerusalem. It sums up also the attitude to Jesus manifest at his birth, hinted at in his ministry and foretold to his disciples. In response Jesus uses an image long established in the psalms for the caring concern of God for the chosen people. The image of the mother hen gathering her brood under her wings is heard in the phrase 'the children of men take shelter under the shadow of your wings' (Ps 36:7) and in the prayers 'hide me in the shadow of your

83. Zechariah, son of Iddo according to Ezra 5:1; 6:14; (cf Neh 12:16).

wings from the onslaughts of the wicked (Ps 17:8; cf Ps 91:1-4) and 'Let me stay in your tent forever, taking shelter in the shadow of your wings' (Ps 61:4). The Book of Deuteronomy speaks of the supporting pinions of the eagle (Deut 32:11) and Boaz wishes the blessing of *YHWH* on Ruth who has come to find shelter beneath his wings (Ruth 2:12). Now Jesus embodies in himself and his ministry the care of God for the people and transfers the image to his own ministry. But, like so often before, the agent of God is rejected. '*How often* I longed to gather your children ...' may be a historical reference in the Q tradition to many journeys of Jesus to Jerusalem, as described in John's gospel.[84]

In Matthew's time the statement 'Your house is left to you desolate' would have appeared as a clear reference to the desolation following on the destruction of city and temple (both were often combined in the concept of the place where God dwelt among his people). It was the city where God had chosen to dwell. Now it is desolate. Prior to the destruction, the saying may have been understood in a more general sense, perhaps like that of the Old Testament prophets such as Jeremiah who warned that the Lord would destroy the temple, 'the den of thieves', as he destroyed the sanctuary at Shiloh (cf Jer 7:11; 26-6; Mic 3:12; Amos 9:1) or Ezekiel who threatened and described the glory of the Lord leaving the temple (Ezek 10:1-22; 11:22-25).

The traditional welcome and blessing on the pilgrim, the heartfelt greeting for the Messiah, already proclaimed by many at Jesus' entry into Jerusalem in the words of Ps 118:26, 'Blessed is he who comes in the name of the Lord', will be the acid test on the lips of Jerusalem, its people and leaders, when the Son of Man comes again in his glory to judge and to gather the elect.

The reference to his coming to Jerusalem and the blessing from Ps 118 form an inclusion with the entry into the city and wind up the narrative of his controversy laden ministry in Jerusalem. He will now make a definitive break with city and temple as he goes to the Mount of Olives and delivers the fifth

---

84. J. P. Meier, *Matthew*, 274

major discourse of the gospel, the eschatological-apocalyptic discourse.

The 'woes' can be seen to stand as an introduction to the eschatological discourse somewhat like the beatitudes do to the Sermon on the Mount, but they actually form part of the Jerusalem controversy narrative rather than a part of the major discourse, a fact emphasised further by the difference in place, time and audience. Furthermore the intervening passage on apocalyptic judgement brings the whole controversy narrative to a climax and a conclusion, and forms an inclusion with Jesus' entry into Jerusalem as the crowds proclaimed 'Blessed in the name of the Lord is he who comes'.

A Note on Anti-Semitism

Given the frightful reality of anti-Semitism, one must be very careful in using, interpreting, preaching and writing about passages such as the seven woes and the surrounding criticisms in the text. Taken out of context they give a distorted picture of Jews, Judaism and the Pharisaic movement. Unfortunately they have all too often been used in this way. D. J. Harrington sums up this extremely important point very succinctly:

> The criticisms are levelled against those with power and/or influence as in the prophetic denunciations, not against the whole people of Israel. The aberrations denounced by Jesus were also denounced by other Jewish teachers in the rabbinic tradition. The goal of the denunciations is to highlight the error, to preserve others from it, and perhaps to bring back those who err to the way of righteousness ... The Matthean Jesus speaks as a prophet sent to Israel, not as an opponent of Israel ... That is why it is so important to attend to the Matthean context – the limited group being addressed and criticised, the literary form used, and the goal of the prophetic denunciation. Matthew's target was the leadership of a specific group, not all Israel.[85]

---

85. D. J. Harrington, *The Gospel of Matthew*, 327.

5. THE ESCHATOLOGICAL / APOCALYPTIC DISCOURSE MT 24-25

Introduction to the Discourse
A very sombre mood has been set by the controversies with the leaders and teachers and the woes against the scribes and Pharisees. The mood becomes even more sombre, in fact, quite menacing, when Jesus pronounces the severe judgement on Jerusalem that brings to a close the Jerusalem controversy narrative. The controversies were set in the temple area which Jesus entered at Mt 21:23 and now leaves for the last time. *'Exelthôn ... apo tou hierou'* emphasises the point that he *came out of* and *went away from* the temple and *eporeueto* points to the fact that he 'went on his way'. No mitigating story intervenes like the story of the widow's mite in Mk 12:41-44 but his definitive departure is marked by the approach of the disciples wishing to point out to him the buildings of the temple.[1] Their approach provides the cue for his solemn prediction of its destruction: 'Amen I say to you, not a stone will be left upon a stone, everything will be destroyed.' This shocking prediction is recorded in all three synoptic gospels (Mk 13:2; Mt 24:2; Lk 21:6):[2] The double negative *ou mê* emphasises the point. This is no simple prediction of a future event. It is 'a judgement on the nation in whose midst the temple stands.'[3] The disciples' questioning reaction to this prediction leads into the eschatological / apocalyptic discourse.

This is the fifth major discourse in the gospel. Whereas in Mark's gospel Jesus addresses the four original disciples (Peter, Andrew, James and John), Matthew portrays Jesus' audience in more general terms as 'the disciples (who) came to him privately

---

1. Josephus, *Ant* XV.11.5, 6,11; *War* V.5, comments on the extent of the building project, the size of the stones, the marble and gold façade which reflected the rays of the sun. The work was begun in 20BC and believed to be still in progress in Jesus' time.
2. See L. Gaston, *No Stone on Another: Studies in the significance of the Fall of Jerusalem in the Synoptic Gospels, NovT Sup 23,* Leiden: 1970.
3. G. R. Beasley-Murray, *Jesus and the Last Days: The Interpretation of the Olivet Discourse,* Peabody: Hendrickson, 1993, 381.

saying: "Tell us when these things will happen and what will be the sign of your presence and of the end of the age".'[4]

Though a significant turning point is reached as Jesus left the temple precincts and moved to a new location, the temple theme and setting are carried on from the vantage point of the magnificent view of the temple and city across the Kidron valley from the Mount of Olives which runs parallel to the eastern side of the city.[5] In fact the view of the temple from the Mount of Olives would have given an overview of the whole complex and of the city not possible from within or in close proximity to the temple. The change of location also reflects the movement of the narrative, combining the dominant view of the temple with Jesus' leaving it for the last time and his predictions of its destruction.

The location, steeped in biblical tradition, facilitates the ongoing theme of denouement, this time predicting the end of the temple and of the world. The area was steeped in allusions to the Day of *YHWH*, the Day of Judgement and the final victory of God. As already seen in reference to Jesus' entry into the city, Zechariah had prophesied that God would set his feet on the Mount of Olives and the intervening valley would be the setting for the final victory of God over the enemies of Israel (Zech 14:4). The view from here was ideal for contemplating the promise of Malachi that the Lord would suddenly enter his temple on the Day of Judgement (Mal 3:1-5). Josephus highlights the ongoing awareness of these associations and of the continuing expectation that the Messiah would come from the Mount of Olives to liberate the people when he tells the story of an Egyptian prophet who persuaded the crowd to follow him to the Mount

---

4. Luke's audience is more general still, *tinôn legontôn peri tou hierou*, 'some people who were talking about the temple'.
5. He is overlooking the city from where he began his 'triumphal' entry into Jerusalem near to the traditional sites of the graves of some of the later prophets. Jesus in Luke's gospel (Lk 19:41-44) wept over the city that rejected its opportunity for the peace that God had offered, and predicted the forthcoming tragic events of the siege. The traditional spot where he is said to have wept is to day marked by the church of the *Dominus Flevit*, ('The Lord Wept'), constructed in the shape of a tear.

of Olives where he would issue a command and the walls of Jerusalem would tumble down.[6]

a. The Beginning of the Birth Pangs

Jesus is already in the sitting position of the teacher (and judge), when the disciples approach him privately and say: 'Tell us when these things will happen and what will be the sign of your coming/presence (*parousia*) and of the end of the age.'

The reader naturally expects Jesus to talk first about the destruction of the temple, the subject which prompted the question, and then to address the question of his coming/presence (*parousia*) and the end of the age. The destruction of the temple, however, is part of a broader complex of events and the reader has to wait until some general warnings about the *parousia* and the end of the age are first given before the specific question relating to the temple is answered.

i. Beware. False Messiahs/Prophets Mt 24:4-5//Mk 13:5-7

'Watch out'/'Beware', *blepete*, is a call for discernment, a scrutinising of what lies behind plausible words and deceptively impressive signs. Jesus issues a warning against the activity of false Messiahs, saying: 'They will lead many astray.' He warns that: 'Many will come in my name, saying: I am the Messiah.' 'Coming' had a messianic significance prior to Jesus' ministry relating to the expectation of 'the one coming into the world' and later for Christians 'coming' was related to the return of Jesus as the glorified Son of Man. Here Jesus is warning about pretenders 'who will come'. ' Coming in the name of Jesus' can signify usurping his position and dislodging him from his messianic status, or it can mean coming in the name of Jesus pretending to be his representative, or even coming with the claim to be Jesus risen from the dead. As Jesus warns the disciples, the warning is directed also to the readers of Matthew who are very probably aware of the many false messiahs who preceded Jesus

---

6. Josephus, *Ant*, XX.169-72; *War* II.262.

and of the many such figures that emerged in the crisis of the war against the Romans and the siege, capture and destruction of Jerusalem and the temple.[7] The Acts of the Apostles and Josephus give accounts of these persons.[8] They will be referred to again during the discourse (Mt 24:11, 23-26).

ii. Do not be alarmed! Wars and Rumours of Wars; Earthquakes and Famines. Persecution Mt 24:6-13//Mk 13:5-13

Another theme is introduced with Jesus' exhortation to the disciples to 'see to it that you are not alarmed' (*orâte, mê throeiste*) when they hear of wars and rumours of wars. In prophetic and apocalyptic literature they were seen as a necessary part of the upheaval that preceded the end time and necessitated divine intervention (Jer 4:16-17; Zech 14:2; 4 Ezra 8:63–9:3). Wars, earthquakes and famines were traditional elements in prophetic and apocalyptic representations of the end of the age, of the world as we know it, and of the approach of the end. They were seen as judgements and punishments experienced in connection with the Day of *YHWH*. The wars and rumours of wars, however, do not necessarily signify the imminent arrival of the end but they are part of God's overall plan as affirmed in the phrase *dei gar genesthai* ('for it must take place, it is necessary')[9] which is widely used in the New Testament to express the necessity of fulfilling God's will/plan.

Wars and such troubles were often seen in the Old Testament prophetic and apocalyptic traditions as punishment by God in the process of chastising the people (Jer 4:16f; Zech 14:2). Wars and revolutions were part and parcel of the prophetic and apocalyptic expectation (Isa 19:2; 4 Ezra 13:31).[10] Earthquakes too

7. Even as late as 132AD Bar Cochba, (a name meaning 'son of the star', a messianic designation) led a revolt against the Romans.

8. Acts 5:36-37; Josephus, *Ant*, 17.261-85; 20:167-72; *War* II.433-34, 444, 652; 613; 7.29-31.

9. Var. *dei gar panta genesthai*, 'for it is necessary that all things take place'.

10. 4 Ezra 13:31 states for example: 'They shall plan to make war against one another, city against city, place against place, people against people, and kingdom against kingdom.'

were to be expected (Isa 13:13; Jer 4:24; 1 Enoch 1:6-7) and famines (Isa 13:13; 14:30; Jer 4:24; Joel 1; 1 Enoch 1:6-7; 2 Baruch 27:6). Ezekiel describes four deadly acts of judgement of the Lord. They are sword, famine, wild beasts and pestilence (Ezek 14:21).

Jesus reminds the disciples that these troubles would contin- ue throughout history as nation rose against nation and king- dom against kingdom after the present troubles were over. These present troubles are only the beginning, the ' birth pangs'. The pangs of childbirth had been used as an image by the prophets for the sufferings accompanying a momentous act of God in history, a judgement on the sinfulness of the people, a looking to a new future and the coming of the messianic king- dom (Isa 13:8; 26:17-18; 66:7-9; Jer 6:24; 13:21; Hos 13:13; Mic 4:9- 10). The rabbis spoke of the sufferings that would precede the end as 'the birth pangs of the Messiah', a phrase that probably had gained a good deal of currency. In St John's gospel Jesus speaks of the sufferings the disciples will endure in terms of the woman in labour who forgets her pain when the new life is born into the world (Jn 16:21).

These wars and rumours of wars, earthquakes and famines, are not yet signaling the end. Life goes on after them and will be marked by nation rising against nation and kingdom against kingdom. Jesus tells the disciples: 'Do not be *alarmed!'(mê throeis- the*), and assures them that the end is not yet. The verb *throeisthai*, 'alarmed' is the same as that used to calm the fears of the Thessalonians (*mêde throeisthai*) when false rumours were abroad that the day of the Lord had already arrived (2 Thess 2:2). More will be heard about these wartime troubles in Mt 22:15-22/ /Mk 13:14-20.

Having already warned his disciples to 'beware', to 'watch out for' false Messiahs and not to be alarmed in the face of wars and rumours of war, earthquakes and famines, Jesus now warns them of future persecutions and the destructive effect they will have on his followers. 'Then they will hand you over to be tor- tured (*thlipsis*) and put to death; and you will be hated by all the nations (Jews and Gentiles) on account of my name.' This is like a summary of what he had already told them in the apostolic discourse when he warned them that they would be 'handed over' to sanhedrins and scourged in synagogues and stand before governors and kings 'for my sake' as a witness to them and to the Gentiles (Mt 10:17-18//Mk 13:9-10). They will be persecuted by Jews and Gentiles, by the people and the authorities. Jesus had also warned them about the possibility of having to lay down their lives (Mt 16:24-26; 20:22). The verb 'hand over' (*paradidômi*) in the sentence 'when they hand you over' is a 'loaded' term in the New Testament generally. It is used in the second passion prediction (Mt 17:22//Mk 9:31), it appears several times in the passion narratives, and Paul uses it in Rom 4:25 and 8:12.

However, all the ' handing over' will not be done by (non-Christian) Jews and Gentiles. The pressure of persecution will cause many to stumble and in turn to 'hand over' one another and hate one another. Such internal divisions in the community were also predicted by Jesus in his apostolic discourse. He spoke there of divisions in families with brother handing over brother, the father handing over his child and children rising up against their parents (Mt 10:21-22). These family divisions were seen in prophetic and apocalyptic circles as a sign of the end times (Mic 7:6; 4 Ezra 5:9; 2 Bar 70:3; Jub 23:19; 1 Enoch 100:1-2).

Again Jesus warns of religious imposters, this time, false prophets who will arise and deceive many. The increase in wickedness will cause the love of many (*agape tôn pollôn*), that virtue and quality of life that binds the community to one another and to God, to grow cold.

Patience (*hypomenê*) is seen in Jewish and Christian tradition as a necessary virtue which accompanied one's waiting 'to the end', *eis telos*, that is 'to the full unfolding', 'to the end or completion' of the Divine plan. (Dan 12:12; 4 Ezra 6:25; 7:27; Rom 5:4f). The one who thus endures with patience will be saved, not just saved from persecution and suffering, but saved in the sense of spiritual and eschatological salvation.

The first readers of the gospels were aware that the prophetic

warning of Jesus about persecution had become a reality before
the gospel was written.[11] Jesus warned that his disciples would
be brought before the *synedria*, the local Jewish courts in each
town with powers of discipline to beat them, carried out in the
synagogue.[12] In this regard, Peter and his companions were
flogged in Jerusalem (Acts 5:40). Paul states that he was given
the 'forty lashes less one' five times and beaten three times with
rods on their authority, the punishment laid down in Deuteronomy (Deut 25:1-3; 2 Cor 11:24). According to Jesus' warning
they would also be brought before pagan courts, before governors and kings 'to bear testimony to them.' The reader thinks of
Paul bearing testimony before Felix, Festus and Agrippa (Acts
23:24; 24:27) and being sent under guard to Rome where he was
held under house arrest. Matthew's community members were
probably also aware of the betrayal of Christian by Christian in
the Neronian persecution, referred to by Tacitus (*Annals* XV,
xliv) and the destructive results of fanatical zeal referred to by
Clement of Rome (*I Clement* 6:1). All these had taken place before the writing of Matthew's gospel.

iii. The Universal Mission Mt 24:14/ /Mk 13:9-10

The end will come when the good news of the kingdom has
been preached in the whole world as a witness to all nations.
This is very significant in the light of the fact that the final command of Jesus, the risen Lord, to his disciples on the mountain in
Galilee will be to preach to all nations (Mt 28:19-20).

b. The Great Tribulation Mt 24:15-31//Mk 13:14-20
Flee to the Mountains

The mood and pace of the discourse change. Instead of caution,
calm and waiting with patience, a note of urgency and alarm
sets the tone for the recommendation to flee with all haste.

---

11. Matthew has warnings similar to those in Mt 24: 9, 11, 12 in the instructions to the Twelve in Mt 10:17-21.
12. *Sanh* 1:6.

Read the Sign: The Abomination of Desolation

The disciples' question: 'When will these things take place?' is now partly answered with an ominous warning. 'When you see "the abomination of desolation" spoken of by Daniel the prophet standing in the holy place then let those in Judea flee to the mountains.' Unlike Mark, Matthew draws attention to the source of the reference to the 'abomination of desolation' as a saying of the prophet Daniel and specifies its location in the holy place (i.e. the temple), unlike Mark who uses the more vague expression, 'standing where it (he) should not be' (Dan 9:27; 11:31; 12:11; cf Mk 13:14).

The 'wars and rumours of wars' mentioned already are now spelled out at greater length. The implied or originally intended readers of Matthew are most likely aware of the persecution of Nero and the empire-wide upheavals that followed on his forced suicide as contending armies fought to establish their candidates on the imperial throne. They were aware also of the war that had culminated in the destruction of Jerusalem and the temple, and the flight of the people from the city and surrounding area.

The original readers would therefore be very alert to Jesus' words to the disciples, and the narrator ensures that they take note, by directly inserting the comment into the text: 'let the reader understand / take note.' They realise that when one event takes place the other follows. When they see the 'abomination of desolation' (*to bdelygma tês erêmôseôs*) then the flight of the people will follow.

The 'abomination of desolation' or 'the desolating sacrilege' originally referred to the altar to Ba'al Shamen, an oriental version of Olympian Zeus, set up on the altar of burnt offering by the Seleucid king Antiochus IV (Epiphanes) on the 25th day of Chislev 168, on which sacrifice was offered to Zeus (1 Macc 1:54-59).[13] It appears from Dan 9:27 that a statue of Zeus, made in the

---

13. 168 or 167BC. There is a one year discrepancy in scholarly determining of dates in the history of the Maccabees.

image of Antiochus was erected in the temple.[14] This was part of his programme of forced imposition of religious uniformity along Hellenistic lines throughout the Seleucid lands. He forbade the traditional temple sacrifices and rituals, forbade the people to follow the laws and customs of the ancestors and burned copies of the Law. Incense was offered at the doors of houses and in the streets and pagan altars were set up in the surrounding towns of Judah. This action resulted in the armed revolt of the Maccabees, the writing of the Book of Daniel and the increase in numbers of holy people leaving the city to live outside in the wilderness as Hasidim.

The term used in the Book of Daniel, 'abomination of desolation' (Dan 9:27; 11:31; 12:11 LXX), seems to be a play on the name of the aforementioned deity Ba'al Shamen (Lord Shamen). The term 'abomination of desolation', *shiqqus somem* or *mesomem* is made up from *shiqqus* which means 'an abomination' and *shomem* or *meshomem*, means 'desolation' (probably also a cynical word play on the Hebrew *shamayim*, which means 'heaven') (Dan 12:11). The sacrilege defiled the temple so no Jewish rituals could take place, thus rendering it desolate until its purification after the Maccabees' victory on the 25th *Chislev* 164 which ended its desolation. The Feast of Dedication or The Feast of Lights (in Hebrew, *Hanukkah* or in Greek, *Enkainia*) celebrates the rededication. Sometimes it is called 'The Feast of Tabernacles of the month of *Chislev*', because of similarities in the rituals of the feasts.

To what is the narrator drawing the reader's attention in so specific a manner in the parenthesis, 'Let the reader understand'? The reference has been interpreted by scholars in different ways. As it draws the reader's attention to the image of the 'abomination of desolation' drawn from the Book of Daniel, it could be seen as an imaginative way of illustrating in general the difficulties of living under pagan or anti-Jewish or anti-Christian rule and comparing it to the experience under the Seleucid per-

---

14. There are, however, some differences of opinion about the exact interpretation of the verse.

secution. It appears more likely, however, to be a reference to some specific event or person, as though to say: 'The reader knows quite well to what or to whom I am referring.'

Luke speaks at this point explicitly of the Roman siege and attack on Jerusalem, without using the expression *abomination of desolation*. 'When you see Jerusalem surrounded by armies realise that she will soon be laid desolate' (Lk 21:20). In Mark the reference to the *abomination of desolation* 'standing where it (or he?) should not' contains a grammatical feature which gives rise to a question about the exact nature of what is meant by Mark's use of the term 'abomination of desolation'. In Greek, 'abomination' is a neuter noun. However, the participle 'standing', which qualifies and should be in agreement with it, is masculine, in the accusative singular case (*hestêkota*). Unless Mark made a grammatical error, which is not in keeping with his general ability in writing Greek, one thinks of the abomination in terms of a person. Is the personal nature of the abomination determined by an original image of Olympian Zeus placed in the sanctuary?

The outrage of placing the image of Olympian Zeus in the sanctuary was very nearly repeated by the threat of placing the (standards and) statue of Caligula in the Temple in 39-40AD, an action that would possibly have sparked the war with the Romans a quarter of a century earlier than it happened.[15] Is it a reference to the standard and possibly the image or person of Titus in the Temple, where he received the homage of his troops? Or is it a fusion of memories, a generalisation of various Roman imperial outrages caused by the Roman presence, images and standards in the holy city and temple area? Could it be a similar generalised reference to an Antichrist figure, like the one referred to in 2 Thessalonians as 'the man of lawlessness ... who ... takes his seat in the temple of God, declaring himself to be God' (2 Thess 2:3f), signifying an emperor claiming divine status and honour? Whichever option the reader follows it is obvious that the reference to the 'abomination of desolation' points clearly to

---

15. Caligula was murdered on the Palatine Hill in Rome in 41AD, so there was no further trouble about the statue.

a happening in the temple known to the implied reader, which will result in the desolation and flight of the people.[16] The references to Daniel and the general mood of the passage reflect the prophetic warnings of Jeremiah and Ezekiel about the desecration and destruction of the temple, the fall of the city and the devastation and scattering of the people (Jer 26:1-19; Ezek 7-11).

This general apocalyptic and prophetic vision and language of destruction combine to give the discourse its vivid character. Jesus is issuing a dire warning about the destruction to come, and flight is the appropriate and urgent response.[17] 'Let those in Judea flee to the mountains.' So urgent is the flight that the one on the roof, (the flat roof where they often slept, ate, worked, prayed and relaxed in summer months), should not come down to take anything from the house and the one in the fields (where they worked) should not turn back (to the headland or to go indoors) to fetch their outer garment (left aside during their work). The reader remembers the instruction 'not to turn back' at the flight from Sodom (Gen 19:17). Such a flight will be particularly difficult for pregnant and nursing mothers. Pray that the flight be not in winter or on the Sabbath. If it occurs in winter it would be particularly difficult because of the rains producing mud, flooded wadis, rising water in the Jordan and flash floods typical of the region, with no fruit or crops to sustain them in their flight. These warnings to flee create a very definite mood and sense of urgency. Matthew adds 'nor on the Sabbath' to the trad-

---

16. G. R. Beasley Murray, *op. cit.*, 411.

17. An early tradition of a flight in 67AD in the depths of winter may well colour the gospel narrative which owes its inspiration to a tradition later historicised and appearing as a flight of the Christians to Pella and more generally to areas around Perea. The tradition appears differently in Eusebius' *Historia Ecclesiastica* 3.5.3, in Epiphanius' *Panarion* 29.7.7f and *De mensuris et ponderibus* 15. A flight in the later stages of the war would have meant leaving the city to go to surrounding areas already occupied by Roman military, and Jerusalem itself, being on the central ridge, it seems unlikely that 'fleeing to the mountains' would be an exact historical reference. The 'abomination of desolation' and 'the flight' are brought together here in what seems to be a simplification of a more complex series of frightening events.

ition, further pointing to his Jewish Christian community, and to his/their respect for the Law which severely restricted travel on the Sabbath.

As the discourse speaks of 'a great tribulation' (*thlipsis megalê*),[18] 'sufferings like none ever seen since the making of the world until now or will never be seen again' the reader recalls further references to the Book of Daniel. 'There shall be a time of anguish such as never occurred since nations first came into existence' (Dan12:1).[19] The reader also recalls the descriptions of the plagues of hail (Exod 9:18), of locusts (Exod 10:14) and of the weeping for the first-born of the Egyptians (Exod 11:6) that were described in similar terms.

However, though the time of testing and waiting for the coming of God's kingdom is a time of stress, God seems to have a worked-out schedule of events (Dan 12:7, 11, 12) and so another theme of the apocalyptic traditions is introduced as Daniel strikes a note of hope.[20] 'But at that time your people shall be delivered, everyone who is found written in the book' (Dan 12:1) and 'You shall rise for your reward at the end of the days (Dan 12:13). Similarly, Matthew, like Mark, points to an act of God's mercy in the cutting short of that difficult time as Jesus declares: 'On account of the chosen (elect) he shortened the days.' God is Lord of history and out of mercy for the chosen who would otherwise run the risk of falling away, of breaking under persecution and suffering, he has put a limit on the suffering. God thus ensures the survival of the chosen, as he ensured the survival of the faithful remnant of Israel. God will not allow his people to be exterminated. The repetition of shortening the days emphasises the point. The people of Israel in the Old Testament and the Christian community in the New Testament are regularly referred to as 'the chosen', one of a group of four epithets, *called*,

---

18. Matthew adds 'great', *megalê*, to the tradition in Mark (*thlipsis*), bringing it even more into line with Daniel.

19. Josephus, *War*, proem 4, uses a similar expression to describe the suffering of the people at the destruction of Jerusalem.

20. 1 Enoch 82:2; 83:1; Baruch 20:2.

chosen, loved and holy, which are frequently applied to the people of the covenant.[21] God chose the people because he loved them, not for any merit of their own. He called them to himself as a people. He dwelt among them to make them holy (cf Deut 7:6-11).

Do not be deceived: False Prophets/Messiahs (Mt 24:23-28 //Mk 13:21-23)

The discourse now returns to the issuing of further warnings about not believing the false messiahs and false prophets with their followers who will draw attention to them, thus gathering a following, saying: 'Behold, the Christ is here, or he is there'. As in the warning given already in the discourse, there is emphasis again on the need to cool overheated messianic and end time expectations. Josephus testifies to the fact that several false messiahs (*pseudochristoi*) had appeared and caused little harm to the Romans but brought great slaughter on the people.[22] The actual use of the term 'false Christs' (*pseudochristoi*) occurs only here and in the parallel passage in Mk 13:21-23, whereas the term 'false prophets' (*pseudoprophêtai*) occurs much more frequently, showing a more widespread concern about the latter. False prophets were an ongoing phenomenon in the history of God's people and had been legislated for in Deut 18:20, 22. The stock in trade trick in the bag of the false prophets in the Old Testament was a display of signs and wonders towards which one must have a discerning and skeptical attitude, and the New Testament has a similar aversion to their tricks. In fact Jesus, especially in John's gospel (Jn 4:48), has a particular aversion to a faith that depends on *sêmeia kai têrata*, signs and wonders, and the Second Letter to the Thessalonians issues very strong warnings against the Rebel and the false signs and wonders (2 Thess 2:1-12, esp 9f).

Jesus warns them that many false christs and false prophets will arise and give (perform, display) great signs and wonders

---

21. M. Mullins, *Called to be Saints*, 280-284.
22. Josephus, *Ant*, 17.285.

in order to deceive even, if possible, the chosen. The warning is emphasised with the words: 'Behold, I have told you beforehand'. 'If they should say to you: "Behold, he is in the desert", do not go out there. If they should say: "Behold he is in the inner rooms, do not believe them".' The coming of the Son of Man will not be a secret or hidden event for the few or an event for which people will have to go in search but rather it will be an event seen by everyone as the lightning that lights up the sky from east to west. As the body of the dead animal is visible to the eagles (classed by the ancients as a species of vulture) with their eagle eyes, from their high vantage point, causing them to swoop on the dead body, equally visible to all will be the Son of Man at his coming.

c. The Sign of the Son of Man (Mt 24:29-31//Mk 13:24-27//Lk 21:25-27)
In apocalyptic language the discourse goes on to address the question of the end of the world as we know it and the coming of the Son of Man on the clouds in power and glory to gather the elect from the four winds, from the ends of the earth to the ends of heaven.

Jesus has already warned of the tribulation they will experience in the world. There will be frightening portents of an earthly nature such as wars, rumours of wars, earthquakes and famines. 'Immediately after the tribulation (*thlipsis*) of those days' the portents preceding the end time will take place. These portents will be of a cosmic nature and are described in imagery taken from Isaiah (Isa 13:10; 34:4). They reflect widespread biblical and extra biblical apocalyptic and prophetic style language and imagery for the end of the world as we know it. 'The sun will be darkened, the moon will not give its light, the stars will fall from heaven and the powers of the heavens will be shaken.'[23] The imagery should not be taken literally as an exact physical description of the final dissolution, but as an imaginative representation of the end of all things as we know them.

23. cf Isa 13:2-10; Joel 2:10-3:4; 4:15-16; Amos 8:8-9; Rev 6:12-13; 4 Ezra 5:4, *inter alia*.

The description reflects also the great reaction of nature described in the context of an Old Testament theophany, where great natural and cosmic phenomena mark the Day of *YHWH*. The imagery is drawn from various Old Testament passages. The Book of Amos opens with the menacing words announcing the theophany: 'YHWH roars from Zion and makes his voice heard from Jerusalem. The shepherds' pastures mourn and the crown of Carmel withers' and its description of the Day of *YHWH* emphasises the cosmic dimensions: 'That day – it is the Lord who speaks – I will make the sun go down at noon, and darken the earth in broad daylight' (Amos 1:2; 8:9; cf Joel 4:15). The Psalms have cosmic imagery of God's activity, borrowed, probably from other ancient literature; for example, Ps 68:4 describes *YHWH* as the one who 'rides on the clouds.'[24] Joel speaks of the day of battle when the 'earth quakes, the skies tremble, sun and moon grow dark and the stars lose their brilliance' and of the Day of *YHWH* when 'the sun will be turned into darkness and the moon into blood ... and all who call on the name of the Lord will be saved' (Joel 2:10, 31). In his oracle against Babylon Isaiah says: 'See, the day of the Lord comes, cruel with wrath and fierce anger, to make the earth a desolation ... for the stars of the heavens and their constellations will not give their light; the sun will be dark at its rising and the moon will not shed its light' (Isa 13:10, cf 34:4). This imagery persists into the New Testament in passages like 2 Peter 3:10-12 which speaks of the Day of the Lord coming 'like a thief and then the heavens will pass away with a loud noise, and the elements will be dissolved with fire, and the earth and everything that is done on it will be disclosed.' The Book of Revelation speaks in similar language of the cosmic reaction to the breaking open of the sixth seal (Rev 6:12-14). The cloud is the great symbol of the presence of *YHWH*. Moses entered the cloud on Sinai, the pillar of cloud covered the tabernacle by day and a fire shone through it by night and the cloud covered the Temple when the Ark was placed there (Exod 24:16;

---

24. An image possibly borrowed from the Canaanite storm god, Ba'al, described as' cloud rider'.

33:9; 40:36-38; 1 Kings 8:10f). At the Transfiguration the cloud covered the mountain and the voice from heaven was heard from the midst of the cloud. The cloud both reveals and conceals the glory of *YHWH* (Mt 17:5 and//s).

This wealth of cosmic imagery is now transferred to the time of the coming of the Son of Man, emphasising its cosmic significance, and the end of the world as we know it. In the midst of this cosmic dissolution 'the sign (banner/standard)[25] of the Son of Man will appear in the heavens, and all the tribes of the earth shall mourn and they shall see the Son of Man coming on the clouds of heaven with much power and glory.' The cosmic imagery is that of the Day of *YHWH* (the Day of the Lord). The 'one like a Son of Man coming with the clouds of heaven' is modeled on the description in the Book of Daniel. Stating that the one coming is 'like a son of man/a human being' implies that in fact he is both like and at the same time very different from 'a son of man' in the sense of a human being. In Daniel he is the one sent with the power to give life and to judge, two divine prerogatives, as he comes to vindicate the holy ones of God (Dan 7:13-14). The mourning of the tribes of the earth is a transferring of the imagery of Zech 12:10 (cf Jn 19:37; Rev1: 7) from the mourning of the clans at the murder of the only son to the universal plane where the tribes of the earth mourn for the treatment of the Son of Man as they see him appearing in glory and anticipate his judgement.

Already in the gospel the Son of Man title or role was used by Jesus to justify his forgiveness of the infirm man's sins in Capernaum (Mt 9:1-8) and again when he replied to the charge of breaking the Sabbath with the statement that 'the Son of Man is master of the Sabbath' (Mt 12:8). The future coming of the Son of Man in glory was already mentioned just before the Transfiguration (Mt 16:27-28) and he will mention it again at his

---

25. 'He will raise a signal for the nations and will assemble the outcasts of Israel, and gather the dispersed of Judah from the four corners of the earth' (Isa 11:12).

trial before the High Priest as he predicts the future when the Son of Man will be 'seated at the right hand of the Power and coming with the clouds of heaven' (Mt 26:64). He commanded the disciples to be silent about the Transfiguration until the Son of Man was risen from the dead (Mt 17:9). However, the title is frequently associated with Jesus in his predictions of his passion, talking about his being betrayed, his giving his life as a ransom for many and in his call to suffering and service as the marks of real discipleship (Mt 17:22-23; 20:17-19, 28). Now Jesus declares that the coming of the Son of Man will be an event of great cosmic significance for he will come on the clouds of heaven with much power and glory.

His coming will be heralded by a great cosmic cataclysm as the sun is darkened, the moon does not give its light, the stars fall from heaven and the powers in the heavens are shaken. This reflects the Day of *YHWH* imagery and the cosmic Christ of Colossians who has subjected all powers under his feet and the Christ of Galatians who has freed the believers from the slavery to the *stoicheia tou kosmou*, 'the elemental spirits of the universe' who were believed to control the fate of people, often with capricious and malevolent intent.[26]

The long history of God's care for the chosen, especially those who had been scattered throughout the world, 'to the four winds' is a common theme in the Old Testament (Ezek 36:19, 27; Isa 11:11, 16; 27:12; Zech 2:6; Deut 30:3-5). The promise to gather them together from wherever they have been scattered and to bring them back to their own land to dwell in peace, plenty and security is a recurring theme, especially in the prophetic books.[27] Isaiah even speaks of God raising a signal/standard/banner on the occasion. 'He will hoist a signal for the nations and assemble the outcasts of Israel; he will bring back the scattered people of Judah from the four corners of the earth' (Isa 11:12). 'I will soon lift up my hand to the nations and raise my signal to the peoples;

---

26. Col 2:8, 20; Gal 4:3. 2 Pet 10, 12 speak of the elements melting in the heat when the world dissolves in flames.
27. Isa 11:11, 16; 27:12; 60:4; Ezek 36:24; 39:27; Deut 30:3-5

and they shall bring your sons in their bosom and your daughters shall be carried on their shoulders' (Isa 49:22). The language and imagery of the scattering and gathering back together of the 'chosen (elect)' is now transferred to the larger cosmic community of the elect of the Son of Man, who will be gathered from the whole of creation. He will send forth his angels with a loud trumpet and they will gather the chosen 'from the four winds, from one end of heaven to the other.'[28] It will not be simply a gathering of the people of Israel into their ancestral homeland but an eschatological gathering of all peoples, when his banner appears in the heavens, since by then the gospel will have been preached to all the nations.[29]

d. Be Alert

i. Observe the Fig Tree Mt 24:32-36 / / Mk 13:28-32 / / Lk 21:29-33

'From the fig tree learn the parable.' The term 'parable' is used here in a general sense. It is really a similitude, though it is not introduced with the standard phrase introducing a comparison, such as 'it is like ...' Here it refers to observing the annual cycle of the fig tree and observing the signs of the things that are happening or about to happen. In a land whose climate disposes it to the growth of many evergreen trees, the fig tree stands out as a tree that loses its leaves in winter and appears rigid and dead, and its becoming supple and putting out new leaves is a sign of the arrival of spring and the approach of summer and harvest. Like the leaves of the fig tree announcing the approach of summer 'these things happening' will announce the approach of the Son of Man. Already the withered fig tree was used as a pointer to the ending of the life and rituals of the Temple (Mt 21:18-22). To what does the expression 'these things' refer? Do they refer to the siege of Jerusalem and the destruction of the

---

28. Mk 13:27 uses the expression 'from the end of earth to the end of heaven' (cf Deut 13:7 and 30:4).

29. Earlier in the gospel Jesus said that the angels will gather those who are to be judged and separate the wicked from the just, consigning the wicked to the blazing furnace where there will be weeping and gnashing of teeth (Mt 13:49-50).

temple or the end of the world and the judgement? 'He is at the
gates' could signify a general leading the army to capture a city
(as at the siege of Jerusalem) or a royal visitor approaching in
procession as the Son of Man coming to the chosen. Perhaps
both events are seen together as through one lens.

Jesus then pronounces a solemn statement introduced with
the 'Amen I say to you' formula: 'Amen I say to you, this generation will not pass away until all these things take place.' Is the
reader to understand 'this generation' as referring to the generation of Jesus or the generation of the evangelist? Whichever is
meant, the message is clear. 'These things' would happen in the
near future. The reference is not so much a 'time reference', a
fact borne out by the following remark about nobody knowing
it, but rather an emphatic call for readiness, a notification that
there is no time for prevarication and postponing decisions.[30] D.
E. Nineham puts it well in his commentary on the parallel verse
in Mark:

> Did this (verse) originally ... form the conclusion of the dis-
> course proper? ... this generation is to be taken literally but
> just possibly the saying referred originally to some specific
> event, such as the destruction of Jerusalem. However, in
> view of Mk 9:1 and Mt 10:23, it more probably referred origi-
> nally, as it does in effect here, to the *parousia*. If so, it is an ex-
> ample of that 'foreshortening of the perspective' so frequent
> in the prophets. 'When the profound realities underlying a
> situation are depicted in the dramatic form of historical pre-
> diction, the certainty and inevitability of the spiritual process
> involved are expressed in terms of the immediate imminence
> of the event.'[31]

The word of the Lord throughout the Old Testament stands
unchanged in the changing circumstances of the people's history.
It remained as the sole foundation of their faith, identity and

30. F. J. Moloney, *op. cit*, 269.
31. D. E. Nineham, *op. cit.*, 359f, including the quotation from C. H.
Dodd, *Parables of the Kingdom*, 71.

hope for the future when all other institutional expressions of their identity as a people had collapsed in the Exile. The prophet, conventionally known as Deutero-Isaiah, proclaimed in the midst of the Exile that there would be a new Exodus and immediately followed his proclamation with the assurance: 'All flesh is grass and its beauty like that of the wild flower, the grass withers, the flower fades but the word of our God endures forever' (Isa 40:8). He also prophesied that: 'the heavens will vanish like smoke, the earth will wear out like a garment … but my salvation shall last forever and my justice have no end' (Isa 51:6). Jesus here uses similar imagery: 'Heaven and earth will pass away but my words will not pass away.'

'About that day or hour no one knows, neither the angels in heaven, nor the Son, but only the Father.' This seems to subordinate the Son to the Father as did Jesus' response to the sons of Zebedee when he said that the places at table in the kingdom were not his to give (Mt 20:23). Mentioning the 'Son' rather than the ' Son of Man' or ' Son of God' (or indeed any other title such as Messiah/Christ) and speaking of 'the day' and 'the hour' places the saying in a category of Son-Father sayings, the majority of which dominate the theology of St John's gospel where the 'hour' and the '*kairos*' (equivalent to the synoptic 'day and hour') are determined by the Father. The relationship of the sender and the one sent is spelled out for the disciples after the foot washing, when Jesus affirmed that: 'No servant is more important than his master; no messenger is more important than the one who sent him' (Jn 13:16 cf Mt 10:24; Lk 6:40). It is the Father who brings everything to fulfilment. This is functional and not ontological subordination of Son to Father. The later and more developed theology/christology of John helps to throw light on the developing tradition in the earlier synoptic texts. Seeing the synoptic statements in the light of the trajectory that finds such a fuller development in John's gospel, one can agree with the comment of J. R. Donahue and D. J. Harrington: 'These sayings are not the kind of material that early Christians would have created on their own, and so they may well represent the authentic voice of Jesus and provide an important perspective on the Incarnation.'[32] However, these texts (together with those in John) provided ammunition throughout the centuries for those who question Jesus' divinity and equality with the Father in the Trinity.[33]

ii. The Example of Noah Mt 24:37-41

The example of Noah is quoted precisely to show how he was aware and prepared for the flood whereas his contemporaries carried on their everyday lives regardless, and then were swept away. They were eating, drinking, taking wives, taking husbands right up to the day when Noah went into the ark and the flood/cataclysm came and swept them all away.

Jesus warns that it will be similar when the Son of Man comes. Two men will be doing the same work in the field, apparently living and working in exactly the same way, yet one is taken and the other left. So also two women will be grinding at the mill, also apparently living and working in similar fashion, but one will be taken and the other left. The purpose of the warning is to ensure vigilance and preparedness for the crisis that is coming when least expected. 'Be vigilant/watch out, for you do not know the day on which your Lord/Master is coming.'

iii. The Thief in the Night Mt 24:42-44

'Know this' is a warning expression introducing the example: 'If the householder knew in which watch the burglar would come, he would not have allowed his house to be broken into.' Anticipation and vigilance would have averted the crisis. The call for vigilance is repeated: 'Be ready, therefore, for the Son of Man is coming at an hour you do not expect.'

---

32. J. R. Donahue and D. J. Harrington, *op. cit.*, 376.
33. Ibid.

e. Be Prepared: Three parables Mt 24:45–25:30

i. The Conscientious Steward Mt 24:45-51 / / Lk12:41-48

In a rhetorical question Jesus outlines the virtues and reward of the 'faithful' and 'prudent' servant (*pistos doulos kai phronimos*) by asking 'Who is this faithful and prudent servant whom the master sets over his household to give them their food at the proper time?' Returning unexpectedly he finds the servant faithfully carrying out his duties. He will promote him to 'the top job', make him manager of all his affairs. In a solemn 'amen' statement Jesus pronounces him 'blessed'.

On the other hand there is the wicked servant (*doulos kakos*). As so often in the New Testament parables, the impact of the parable is made by way of a comparison or contrast. Here the master returns unexpectedly, and in great contrast to the faithful and wise servant, the wicked servant is seriously misbehaving. He 'had said in his heart' that his master was long in coming and so he had ill treated his 'fellow servants,' *syndouloi*, as though he were not a servant himself, but the master. He was eating and drinking with drunkards. The master of that wicked servant suddenly returning, on a day he did not expect and at an hour he did not know, reacts angrily and 'cuts him to pieces' and casts him among the 'hypocrites', in the place where there is weeping and gnashing of teeth, to use Matthew's favourite expression for that place of exclusion from the kingdom (Mt 8:12; 13:42, 50; 22:13; 25:30).

ii. The Wise and Foolish Maidens Mt 25:1-13

The parable begins with the formula: 'The kingdom of heaven may be compared to ...' As usual the comparison is with the whole story that follows, not just with the maidens. This parable continues the teaching on the necessity of remaining vigilant/ prepared, for 'You do not know the day or the hour when your lord comes.'

The ten *parthenoi*, maidens or virgins, are 'bridesmaids' only in an extended sense since they seem to be associated with the house of the groom rather than the bride. The custom was for the groom to go to the house of the bride's father to complete the financial and other arrangements and then bring the bride to his home. The couple were seen off in celebratory fashion from the home of the bride's family and received in celebratory fashion *en route* to the home of the groom by the procession of light-bearing ladies who met them and accompanied them to the home of the groom where the marriage feast was prepared. In this story the ten young ladies set out to meet the bridal party *en route*, but the latter were delayed. One can speculate on the reasons for the delay, but they are irrelevant to the point of the story.

The waiting procession of virgins fell asleep. This is not the point of the story either. The point is that five of them were *phronimoi*, wise in the sense of prudent, and they foresaw the possibility of such a delay and so they were prepared with extra oil for their lamps. The other five were *môrai*, foolish, or foolhardy in the sense of setting out on a journey without foreseeing the possibility of needing the extra oil. They were unprepared for the eventuality.

The fact that the 'wise ones' did not share their oil lest they too be left short is a further pointer to their prudence, but hardly a major aspect of the parable. The important fact is that the foolish ones had to go looking for oil or travel in the dark and, furthermore, at night it may have been difficult to find sellers of oil. As a result they arrived late, and when they knocked and called, 'Lord, Lord, open to us' the groom answered solemnly: 'Amen I say to you, I do not know you.' Their lack of preparedness meant that they were excluded from the wedding feast. The wedding feast is the long established metaphor for the banquet of the kingdom, and exclusion from it by the bridegroom of the banquet signifies the great final loss of the kingdom.

The parable ends with a *logion* that highlights the meaning of the parable and repeats the advice of the previous parable: 'Watch, therefore, because you do not know the day or the hour.'[34]

---

34. Some interpreters have interpreted this parable as an allegory, seeing in each of its features a reference to the church waiting for the parousia, seeing the rejection of the foolish maidens as the final judge-

iii. The Talents Mt 25:14-30//Lk 19:11-27

The usual introduction 'The kingdom of heaven is like ...' is shortened here to ' like/just as', *hôsper*, obviously picking up on the longer and more usual introduction at Mt 25:1 which serves both parables.

Like the parables of the two servants and the ten virgins this parable focuses on the importance of being prepared for the return of the master/lord when he comes. The master entrusted his property to three servants, and significantly 'to each according to his ability' and then went away on his journey. The servants who received the five and two talents conducted business and doubled their amounts. The one who received the one talent, however, went away and buried it in the ground. It was a custom to bury money or treasure in the ground for safe keeping, a practice which was regarded as taking due care for its security and removing liability, whereas wrapped in a cloth and hidden in the house was not regarded as a sufficiently secure method of concealing money or valuables and incurred liability.

Again the story of the delay in the return of the master figures in this parable, but at last he comes and calls his servants to account. The servants who got the five and two talents and doubled their capital through their efforts are praised as 'good and faithful servants', promised promotion in the management of their master's affairs because they were faithful in the little things, and invited to 'enter into the joy of your master', to share in their master's happiness. The man who had received the one talent handed it back to the master, telling him he had hidden it in the ground because he was afraid, knowing the master to be a hard man who reaped where he did not sow and gathered where he had not scattered. The master calls him a wicked and lazy servant. He tells him that if he was afraid (of not being successful in using the talent in business and risking the master's anger) he could have lodged it with the bankers and been sure of

---

ment, the foolish maidens as representing Israel and the wise ones the Gentiles. This kind of allegory is certainly not the intention of the parable in its setting in the gospel.

the return of the capital and the interest that accrued. He should have had the foresight to know that, in keeping with his own clearly articulated judgement, the master was an exacting master who would expect him to show results for the trust placed in him when he was given the talent and expected to work according to his capability, which the master had assessed beforehand.

The talent was taken and given to the one who had the ten talents because he would make most use of it. The *logion* or saying: 'For to everyone who has it will be given, and he will have an abundance. But the one who does not have – even what he has will be taken away from him' contains the divine passive 'God will give, God will take away.' This wisdom saying has a deeply spiritual significance, very well summed up by J. P. Meier:

> A disciple who 'gives himself' fully to the gift God has given him ... will receive greater grace still. The spiritual life is not unlike the stock market; nothing is gained without risk and effort. The person who is stingy in his expenditure of self will receive nothing further and will lose what he has. God's grace is like our physical limbs and intellectual talents: exercise brings greater strength; neglect brings atrophy. The 'atrophied' disciple, the useless Christian, will be punished exactly like the dissolute and the thoughtless – with damnation ... For the supposed Christian, laziness comes at a high price.[35]

The wicked and good-for-nothing servant was cast, like the wicked servant who beat his fellow servants, into the darkness 'where there will be weeping and gnashing of teeth', the very opposite to 'entering into the joy of your master'.

f. The Last Judgement Mt 25:31-46

Following the parables about being prepared for the coming of the master, Jesus gives an account of the coming in glory of the Son of Man and the judgement that takes place when he comes. 'When the Son of Man comes in his glory, and all the angels with

---

35. J. P. Meier, *Matthew*, 300.

him, then he will sit on his throne of glory' (Mt 25:31; cf Mt 16:27; 19:28; 24:29-31). All the nations are gathered before him. He will separate them into those who are blessed or cursed, those who enter the kingdom prepared for them since the foundation of the world or those who are excluded from it. He will pronounce the judgement. The scene, unique to Matthew, recalls the scene in the Book of Daniel describing the Son of Man receiving all authority from the Ancient of Days (Dan 7:13-14). Now he comes to judge and 'all the nations are gathered', i.e. God has gathered them or caused them to be gathered by the angels (Mt 13:41; 24:31).

The Son of Man imagery dominates the scene with an emphasis on glory and the throne of glory and draws to itself the images of judge, messianic shepherd-king and Lord. The scene recalls the *Day of YHWH*, a theme present in the prophetic and apocalyptic literature where judgement of the pagan nations, the Gentiles, was a major theme in itself, and the judgement of Israel accompanied it, but as a separate judgement. The nations are judged and condemned for their treatment of God's chosen people, but the chosen people, to their surprise, do not escape judgement themselves (Amos 1-2; Ezek 39; Joel 3; 1 Enoch 91:14; Pss Sol 17:29; 4 Ezra 13:33-49; 2 Baruch 72; *Test. Benjamin* 10:8-9). Already in this eschatological/apocalyptic discourse in Matthew the chosen people, in the person of their leaders, have been severely judged in the 'woe' condemnations and the people have been told that their house will be left to them desolate (Mt 23:38). The followers of Jesus have been warned about watching, acting in a faithful, prudent and industrious manner and being prepared for the coming of the Lord, the master, the Son of Man. Now all the nations, *panta ta ethnê*, are gathered at the coming of the Son of Man, as he comes in his glory, sitting on his throne of glory, accompanied by his angels.[36]

The main emphasis is on the criteria for judgement. The trad-

36. Who is referred to in the gathering of *all the nations*? Is it all the nations, including Israel and the Christians, or is it the Gentiles, the pagan nations who are neither Jewish nor Christian? Usually Matthew uses the term *ethnê* for the pagan nations, the Gentiles (Mt 4:15; 6:32; 10:5,18; 12:18, 21; 20:19, 25). In some cases he seems to use it in the sense

itional 'corporal works of mercy' are spelled out, giving food to
the hungry, drink to the thirsty, hospitality to the stranger,
clothes to the naked, visiting the sick, and visiting the imprisoned.

These works of mercy are performed for 'the least of my
brethren' and whoever performs them performs them 'for me'.
The act of compassion is done for the Son of Man who identifies
completely with the 'least of the brethren'. The judge lists the
criteria and both groups respond 'When did we see you hungry
...?' To this he replies, 'As long as you did it to one of the least of
my brethren you did it to me.' The blessed had acted according
to these criteria of mercy, the 'cursed' had not done anything
and are guilty by default.

The scene is composed of the opening description of the glorious Son of Man taking his seat as judge on his glorious throne.
He separates the 'sheep' and 'goats' and sends the sheep, the
blessed, into the kingdom prepared by his Father for them since
the foundation of the world. He sends the 'goats', the cursed,
into the eternal fire prepared for the devil and his angels. Like
the Israelites on the brink of the Promised Land when Moses offered them a blessing and a curse, here the nations are about to
come under a blessing or a curse.

The image of the shepherd tending the flock is rooted in the
Old Testament understanding of God as shepherd of the people,
a role entrusted to the good shepherd, the new David, the messianic shepherd-king. In the Infancy Narrative, laden with
Davidic imagery, the prophecy of Micah concerning the birth of
the shepherd-king says: 'From you shall come a ruler who is to
shepherd my people Israel' (Mt 2:6; Mic 5:2). In his ministry
Jesus had compassion on the crowds 'because they were harassed and helpless, like sheep without a shepherd' (Mt 9:36). He

---

of 'peoples' without signifying their being pagan Gentiles, as in giving
the vineyard to a nation bearing its fruits (Mt 21:43); nation rising
against nation (Mt 24:7); hated by all nations (Mt 24:9); proclamation of
the good news to all nations (Mt 24:14) and making disciples of all nations
(Mt 28:19).

spoke of the caring shepherd leaving the ninety-nine to seek the lost sheep (Mt 18:12). In the immediate onslaught of his arrest and passion and death he will quote the prophecy: 'I will strike the shepherd and the flock will be scattered' (Mt 26:31).

The reader may ask: 'Why does the shepherd separate the sheep and goats?' In the Palestine of Jesus' day the sheep and goats were herded together during the day. At night the goats suffered the cold and had to be put into shelter, the sheep preferred the open air. Furthermore, some species of sheep and goats looked somewhat alike and a definite act of separation was needed. The sheep were the more valuable animal and so got the preferential treatment.

Who are 'the least of my brethren?' The 'least', *elachistoi*, is the superlative of the *mikroi*, the 'little ones'. Earlier in the gospel the prophet, the righteous one, the disciple of Christ (vulnerable in their mission endeavours) are called 'these little ones' and 'whoever gives one such a cup of cold water will not go without his reward' (Mt 10:41-42). The vulnerable member of the community who may be led into sin is also called 'one of these little ones' and the one who causes one of these to be scandalised would be better if a millstone were fastened round his neck and he were drowned in the depth of the sea (Mt 18:6). The term 'brother' (used inclusively for brother and sister), here combined with *elachistos*, is found also in Mt 18:15, 17, 21, 35; 23:8; 28:10 where it undoubtedly refers to members of the Christian community. Other references to brother (sister) probably have the same meaning (Mt 5:22, 23, 24, 47; 7:3, 4, 5),

One understanding of 'the least of my brothers/sisters' is to see them as the missionaries and the ordinary followers of Jesus. The nations are judged according to their treatment of the Christians and especially their missionaries. The Son of Man identifies himself with these followers: 'You did it/you did it not to me.' In this line of thought the criteria of the judgement arise from the treatment of Jesus' missionaries and followers.

However, many scholars broaden the interpretation to see 'the least of my brethren' as referring to everyone who is vulner-

able and in need. J. P. Meier makes the case for the broader interpretation:

> The stunning universalism of this revelation must not be
> blunted by restricting 'the least of my brethren' to Christians,
> to poor or insignificant Christians, or to Christian missionar-
> ies. The phrases used in such passages as 10:42 ('little ones'...
> 'because he is a disciple') and 18:6 ('these little ones who be-
> lieve in me') are different, and the context in such places is
> clearly ecclesiastical; they lack the sweeping universalism of
> this scene.[37]

Meier's assessment highlights an aspect of the gospel that
makes extremely uncomfortable reading for everyone who lives
a comfortable life without thought for and action in favour of
the poor and suffering of the world, locally and internationally.

Conclusion of the Discourse (Mt 26:1)
At the conclusion of the other four major discourses there is a
statement that Jesus had finished what he wanted to say (Mt
7:28), had completed his instruction (Mt 11:1), completed his
parables (Mt 13:53) and had finished these sayings (Mt 19:1).
Now at the end of the fifth and final major discourse the narrator
says he had finished *all these words* (Mt 26:1). This statement of
completion covers all the major discourses and, as in the other
cases, leads into the ongoing narrative.

---

37. J. P. Meier, *Matthew*, 304.

The Passion Narrative
Mt 26-28

Transition: Mt 26:1

As in the case of the other major discourses, the narrator closes the discourse with the remark that Jesus finished what he had to say. In this case, however, there is a note of finality as Jesus is described as having finished all his teaching, 'all the words (*pantas tous logous*) he wanted to say'. There is a certain reminiscence of the end of Moses' journey with the people as he ends his ministry on the brink of the Promised Land, and addresses the people, encouraging them to observe the Law in the land they are crossing the Jordan to possess as he himself faces his own death (Deut 32:45-47).

The Passion Narrative

In dealing with the formation of the Passion Narrative some scholars point to the emergence of a shorter Passion Narrative beginning in Gethsemane which was then developed into a longer narrative beginning with the betrayal and the anointing of Jesus in Bethany. In effect this means that the Passion Narrative falls into two distinct parts, the introduction leading up to the arrest in Gethsemane and the passion account proper describing the events from Gethsemane to the grave. The entire narrative is made up of material that has been woven into a single piece and the dramatic effect and movement are aided by the changes of place and the indications of the passage of time.[1]

1. BETRAYAL AND ANOINTING MT 26:1-16

a. The plot to kill Jesus Mt 26:1-5//Mk 14:1-2

Jesus himself now announces to the disciples that the Passover is just two days away and that the Son of Man will be handed over

---

1. See comments on pp 593-4 concerning approaches to the Passion Narrative'.

to be crucified.[2] This, the fourth prediction of his passion and death associates his passion with the Passover and for the second time mentions crucifixion as the method of execution.[3] Mentioning the Passover gives a context and creates a mood, but also introduces the feast as an interpretative backdrop for the unfolding events. Jesus will invest the feast with a new meaning, bringing to completion the older promise of the feast and opening it onto a new future, springing from the gift of new life in his death and resurrection, a (new) covenant established in his blood.

'Handed over' strikes the keynote of the narrative. It ultimately signifies the plan of God to which Jesus responds obediently by allowing himself to be handed over. It also represents the series of actions of 'handing over' on a human level. Judas hands him over to the Jewish authorities, they hand him over to Pilate and Pilate hands him over to crucifixion.

The first 'unit' in the larger passion account is an intercalation, or sandwich in which one story is inserted into another. The story of the official plot against Jesus and the co-operation of Judas is divided into two parts (Mt 26:3-5 and 26:14-16) and inserted into the middle is the story of the anointing at Bethany, creating a contrast between scenes of hostility and betrayal on the one hand and faithful love and service on the other.

The plot against Jesus comes as no surprise to the reader. Throughout the ministry Jesus encountered determined critics and hostile opponents and now the chief priests and the elders take the initiative in conspiring against him as they assemble in

---

2. 'Two days before the Passover and the feast of Unleavened Bread' in the Semitic way of counting the days probably refers to the 13th, the day before the eve of the feast, the 14th Nisan, which will be the next time indicator when Jesus sends the disciples to prepare the Passover Meal (to take place in the evening as the 14th becomes the 15th at sunset). John follows a different chronology, having Jesus crucified on the day before the feast (the 14th).

3. Unlike Mark and Luke, Matthew makes no mention at this point of the feast of Unleavened Bread even though the two feasts were celebrated as one great pilgrimage, combining the spring agricultural festival with the remembrance of the Exodus.

the palace courtyard of the high priest Caiaphas. Although the conspirators are trying to carry out their lethal plan in secret, (*dolô* has all the overtones of secrecy and underhandedness), their hostility and lethal intentions towards Jesus are already well known. After his action in the Temple the chief priests and the elders challenged him and questioned his authority but he silenced them with his question about the authority of the Baptist (Mt 21:23-27) and followed it up with the parables of the two sons, the wicked tenants and the wedding feast. The chief priests and the scribes would have arrested him after he told the parable of the wicked tenants but they were afraid of the crowds who regarded him as a prophet (Mt 21:45-46). In the first of the passion predictions the elders, the chief priests and the scribes in Jerusalem are portrayed as the main agents of Jesus' downfall (Mt 16:21) and in the third prediction the chief priests and scribes in Jerusalem are named (Mt 20 18).[4] Jesus' popularity with the crowd is the very reason they now give for needing to 'get hold of him (*kratêsôsin*) by stealth (*dolô*) in order to kill him'[5] but *mê en tê heortê*, a phrase that could be translated as either 'not during the festival', or 'not among the festal crowd' lest there be a disturbance among the people who were present and in enthusiastic mood about Jesus and the hopes they had pinned on him.[6]

---

4. The priesthood was hereditary through male membership of a priestly family and as the numbers of priests increased a hierarchy of authority and influence emerged. Some were poor and powerless while others were very wealthy, powerful in their own circle and influential with the Romans. The chief priest in the 'hierarchy' was the High Priest, supposedly chosen for life, but the Romans gained control of the office, kept the ornamental vestments in the Antonia fortress and released them for specific occasions. The Romans used the High Priest and his council as their 'go-between' with the Jews and were prepared to dismiss him if he did not co-operate. This accounts for the stinging remark in Jn 11:49, 'Caiaphas was High Priest that year', though it was an office for life! The family of Annas and Caiaphas were highly political and several of them held the office of High Priest.

5. *Kratêsantes* signifies more than a legal process of 'arrest'. It could be translated 'get the better of him', 'take hold of him', 'capture him'.

6. In St John's gospel there is a parallel and even more pointed repetition of the desire of the authorities or others to arrest or stone him: Jn 5:16; 7:20, 30, 32; 10:39; 11:49-54, 57.

The element of secrecy and plotting heightens the tension in the narrative and throws even more bad light on the conspirators and the betrayer.

Popularity of a prophetic or messianic figure always posed a problem for the Jewish authorities who feared the Roman reaction against themselves if they seemed to lose control of the situation. As seen earlier, this was the reason Josephus gives for the arrest of the Baptist. It was also the reason for the concern of Caiaphas in Jn 11:48-50 when he said it was better for one man to die for the people than that the whole nation should perish. It is now a similar situation here in Matthew's gospel as they plot the arrest of Jesus. The pilgrimage feasts, especially Passover, were highly charged with religious and national fervour and messianic expectations. As the population of the city multiplied during the festal period the festivities and the presence of the crowd could provide opportunity and cover for revolutionary activity against the Roman administration.[7] The authorities dared not risk a riot that could easily ensue if they arrested him in public. To operate by stealth they needed an 'inside' collaborator.

b. Jesus anointed for burial Mt 26:6-13//Mk 14:3-9; Jn 12:1-8

In this classic use of an intercalation Matthew (like Mark) places the story of the anointing of Jesus by an unnamed woman in Bethany, in the house of Simon, a leper, between the two parts of the account of the plot to arrest and kill Jesus and his betrayal by one of his closest associates, Judas Iscariot.[8]

Sandwiched between the scheming of the (male) authorities and the betrayal by a (male) disciple, the noble action of the woman stands out as a gesture of faithful love, service and discipleship. Having already said the gospel will be preached to all

---

7. Josephus, *Antiquities of the Jews*, 17.213-218; 20.105-112; *Jewish War* 2.255; 2.280f; 5, 244.

8. Historically there has been an amount of confusion between the accounts of the anointing by the woman in Bethany (named Mary in Jn 12:3) and the story of the woman with the bad reputation in Lk 7, who has been mistakenly named as Mary Magdalene, though Luke gives no name.

nations (Mt 24:14), Jesus will now go on to say that wherever the gospel is preached the action of this woman will be told in memory of her. The Matthean/Markan and Johannine settings of the anointing seem to reflect an early tradition in which a dark frame or context highlights the noble action of the woman.[9] John alone gives the woman's name as Mary.

In contrast to the plotting of the authorities and the treachery of Judas, there stands out in high profile the striking action of the woman who invades the male space at the banquet, bringing an alabaster jar of precious ointment that she pours over the head of Jesus as he reclined at table.[10] For the woman of Bethany it was the sacrificing of something very precious, the action of a devoted disciple demonstrating her faith in, and love for, Christ. Whether she realised it or not, her action mirrors the anointing on the head of a Messiah or King. The note of messianic kingship had been struck at the birth of Jesus, repeated during his healing ministry when he was addressed as Son of David and proclaimed at his triumphal entry into Jerusalem. Earlier in the gospel at Caesarea Philippi Peter had confessed his belief that Jesus was the Messiah (Christ). The title is now symbolically conferred in the anointing by the woman of Bethany.

The disciples react angrily, calling the woman's action a waste, and pointing out that the ointment could have been sold for a high price and the money given to the poor. In responding to the disciples' criticism of her action Jesus reprimands them

---

9. In John's gospel Judas is introduced into the anointing scene as the one who voices criticism of the anointing and is also described there as the one who was to betray Jesus (Jn 12:1-8).

10. Mark describes the ointment as pure nard, an extremely expensive perfume, made from a plant grown in northern India, and costing in this case three hundred *denarii*, a year's wages. He also says that she broke the jar, probably the long slender neck of the jar, to facilitate the pouring of the ointment, a gesture to show she was not being sparing with it and that she clearly intended to pour the whole amount. A denarius a day was the usual pay at the time. Taking Sabbath days and holy days into account there were approximately three hundred working days in the year. Women sometimes wore small flasks of nard around their necks with which to freshen up.

for upsetting/harassing the woman and points out how 'she has done a beautiful deed, a noble action (*ergon kalon*) for me.'

The disciples who saw her action as a waste of precious ointment couched their criticism in false concern for the poor, a bluff called immediately by Jesus who reminded them that the poor were always present and in need of help, a remark very likely charged with the implied question and reprimand: 'What have you done for them before, and what will you do for them in the future? Don't be using them as an excuse!' Matthew (like Mark) describes Jesus' reprimand and states in addition that Jesus said the woman had done a good work. The Jews divided good works into almsgiving and charitable deeds, the latter including among other pious works the fitting burial of the dead. Then he explained that she had prepared him for burial. He said that they will always have the poor present, but will not always have him. This is a reminder of Jesus' earlier comment: 'The days will come when the bridegroom will be taken away and then they will fast' (Mt 9:15).

Jesus then points out what he meant by 'doing a noble action for me'. 'She has anointed my body beforehand for burial.' He sets her action in the context of his forthcoming death. The 'noble action' is in fact 'one of the good works', that is, the fitting burial of the dead. Her silent proclamation-in-action is in line with Jesus' own predictions of his passion that were first spoken as a corrective to mistaken notions of Messiahship. As Jesus moves forward towards death from this point in the narrative his anointed kingly status emerges more and more clearly. Jesus' words about his forthcoming death link the story of the anointing to its dark frame and at the same time they inform the reader that the plotting and treachery will succeed.

Jesus has already said that the gospel will be preached to all nations and now as he praises the action of the woman he states that: 'Wherever the good news is preached in the whole world, what she has done will be told in memory of her' (Mt 26:13// Mk 14:9).[11]

---

11. John reflects a similar understanding as he points out that the aroma

Anticipating the burial of Jesus, she becomes the first disciple to understand the significance of his death.[12] She does beforehand what the disciples of John had done for their murdered master (Mt 14:12), and what the 'official' male disciples of Jesus will fail to do for him, as they will already have left him and fled. She prepared him for a fitting burial, and interestingly Matthew will not say the women's purpose in going to the tomb was to anoint the body with spices. For Matthew that anointing has already taken place symbolically.

c. Judas facilitates the Plot Mt 26:14-16//Mk 14:10-11//Lk 22:3-6

The narrator emphasises the nature of the betrayal by identifying Judas Iscariot as one of the Twelve, and going on to say that he went to the chief priests and said: 'What are you willing to give me if I hand him over to you?' They paid him thirty pieces of silver. From then on he is watching the opportune moment to hand Jesus over.

Only Matthew mentions the thirty pieces of silver. It is a highly symbolic sum. It is the value placed on a slave in Exod 21:32. Zechariah spoke about the shepherd whose wages were valued at thirty pieces of silver and whom YHWH told to 'throw it into the treasury, this princely sum at which they have valued me' (Zech 11:12-14), the implication being that valuing the shepherd of God's people at this sum amounts to valuing God and God's care for his flock at this same sum. Whether the thirty pieces of silver is to be taken literally or whether the actual sum is symbolic, highlighting by way of biblical allusions the heinous nature of the reward, does not alter the character of the betrayal involved.

---

filled the house (Jn 12:3). The reference to the aroma may reflect the same tradition as that in *Midrash Rabbah* on Eccles 7:1 which says: 'The fragrance of a good perfume spreads from the bedroom to the dining room; so does a good name spread from one end of the world to the other.' This parallels the saying, 'Wherever the gospel is preached in the whole world, what she has done will be told in memory of her' (Mt 26:13//Mk 14:9).

12. W. J. Harrington, *op. cit.*, 64.

Matthew says Judas asked for the money. Mark and Luke say the chief priests tempted Judas with the offer of money. John further develops this money loving weakness in terms of stealing from the common fund in his charge (Mt 26:15; Mk 14:11; Lk 22:5; Jn 12:4-6). This interpretation portrays Judas' weakness in terms of what is often seen as the root of all evil, love of money. However, Luke and John also see a greater force at work, the Prince of Evil, at the root of Judas' actions. Both say that Satan entered into Judas, and John also says that Judas was a devil (Lk 22:3; Jn 13:27; cf 13:2; 6:70). The mind and motives of Judas have continued to be a subject of discussion throughout history. Since New Testament times historians, priests, poets, playwrights, writers of popular fiction and many others have continued to speculate on his motives. What can be said, however, is that he is a failed disciple, one called 'to be with Jesus' who joins with those who are not only against him but in fact violently opposed to him, and Judas will arrive 'with them' to betray and arrest him. He is a vital link in the chain of people involved in the 'handing over' of Jesus. At the same time he functions as a human instrument in the great design of God, 'as it is written'.

2. PASSOVER/BETRAYAL/EUCHARIST MT 26:17-30

a. Jesus prepares the Passover Meal Mt 26:17-19//Mk 14:12-16

Matthew now speaks of the feast of Unleavened Bread stating that it was 'the first day of Unleavened Bread.' The first day of the feast was in fact due to begin that evening at sunset. This 'inaccuracy' in referring to the first day before the official beginning of the feast in the evening was probably a 'concession' to a non-Jewish audience/readership for whom the day already began in the early morning. The Paschal Meal with the Paschal Lamb would have been eaten that evening, when the new day (15th Nisan) began.

The disciples approached Jesus and asked him where he wished them to make preparations for him to eat the Passover. In the original legislation, which had the extended family celebration in mind, it was prescribed that the sacrifice should take place between the two evenings, that is, in the twilight between sundown and darkness (Exod 12:6).[13] In Jesus' time, however, following various reform movements, Passover was a pilgrimage feast and the sacrifices took place in the Temple. The huge numbers attending the feast necessitated the slaughtering / sacrificing of the lambs from noon onwards.

The disciples asked Jesus where he wished them to go to make preparations 'for you' to eat the Passover.[14] 'For you to eat' (*soi phagein*) emphasises the fact that it is Jesus' Passover meal and so the others would join him in his Passover meal, Jesus being the *paterfamilias*, the head of the group / family. In Mark the same point is made by the use of the singular verb (*phagês*), 'that you may eat.' Unlike the account in Mark, however, Jesus does not send the disciples to ask about the location of the room, instead he tells them to announce: 'The Teacher says: "My time is near; I will keep the Passover at your house with my disciples".' Jesus' statement: 'My time is near' is a theologically loaded expression. The word for time, *kairos*, in the context of salvation history means the appropriate time, the time appointed by God.[15] Saying that it is near, *eggus estin/eggizein*, is also a well used expression for the approach of some divinely ordered event, and in particular for the end time and the coming of the Son of Man.[16] Jesus now proclaims: 'My time is near.' The great plan of God is about to come to fruition.

---

13. For the biblical background to the legislation and customs see Exod 12:1-20; Lev 23:5-8; Num 28:16-25.

14. Because the pilgrims were expected to eat the Passover meal in the city, the inhabitants were expected to make available their suitable spare rooms and accommodation for the many pilgrims. Furthermore, the night of the Passover was to be spent within the city boundaries and because of the crowds of pilgrims the boundary had been extended to include the Mount of Olives.

15. Other examples are the Gadarene demoniacs' appeal not to be destroyed before their time (Mt 8:29); gathering the weeds at the time of the harvest (Mt 13:30); not knowing the signs of the times (Mt 16:3); the time for fruit (Mt 21:34).

16. The Baptist, Jesus and the Twelve proclaim that the kingdom of heaven is near at hand (Mt 3:2; 4:17; 10:7); in the parable of the tenants

The deliberate act of sending the disciples to the city to make preparations recalls Jesus' sending the disciples to acquire the donkey and colt and his deliberate preparations for entering the city.[17] Jesus is master of the situation as he prepares to respond to God's will, though the unfolding events will appear to master him. F. J. Moloney puts it succinctly:

> The events that are about to happen transcend the expected, and Jesus goes into them knowing what lies ahead, and makes suitable arrangements for the first of the events of his passion.[18]

b. Jesus predicts Judas' betrayal Mt 26:20-25//Mk 14:17-21

The disciples did as Jesus ordered and prepared the Passover. The Twelve are said to form the company of Jesus for the meal. 'When it was evening he reclined with the Twelve.' From now on they will be seen in increasingly negative light, one betraying him to his enemies, another denying him, and all leaving him in the garden and fleeing. The meal is overshadowed by the prophecy of Judas' betrayal, followed shortly afterwards by the prophecy of the disciples' desertion and Peter's denials, a dark shadow of negativity on the part of the disciples shrouding the

---

the time for fruit was near (Mt 21:34) and when the fig tree puts out its leaves you know that summer/harvest is near (Mt 24:32-33).

17. The similarity is more obvious in Mark where there is a more detailed account of their instructions as Jesus now sends two disciples to acquire the room for the supper. In Mark his prophetic words about seeing a man carrying a jar of water are fulfilled to the letter. This is striking because it was unusual for a man to carry water in a jar. Women drew the water in jugs and jars for domestic purposes, and men carrying water for a journey or into the fields would do so in a leather bottle. His predictions about entering a house where they will find 'a large room well decked out and ready' are also fulfilled. Describing the room as *anagaion mega* points to its being 'a large upper room,' *coenaculum magnum*, above a shop or other business along the street front. Describing it as 'decked out/well furnished', *estrômenon*, refers to its being well furnished with coverings such as carpets, cloths/drapes.

18. F. J. Moloney, *op. cit.*, 283.

meal which will come to symbolise the total self-giving of Jesus when he reclined with the Twelve (*anekeito meta tôn dôdeka*).

In the evening Jesus reclined with the Twelve (disciples) to eat the meal. The Passover meal was begun between official sundown and the onset of darkness. Though originally it was eaten standing up in the manner of persons in a hurry, staff in hand and dressed for flight (Exod 12:11), by Jesus' time it was celebrated in the manner of a Greco-Roman banquet with the guests reclining on mats, leaning on one elbow. This may also have had the significance of emphasising their status as free people after liberation from the slavery of Egypt, since slaves did not recline to eat.

As they are eating, *esthiontôn autôn*, Jesus shocked the Twelve with a revelation of something known to the reader since Judas was introduced as the traitor when the Twelve were chosen and named, and again clearly revealed to the reader in his dealings with the enemies of Jesus who were seeking a way to capture him away from the crowd. Now the Twelve are confronted with the shocking revelation, proclaimed in a solemn 'amen I say to you' formula by Jesus. 'Amen, I say to you, one of you will betray me/hand me over.'

The shock of the Twelve is described in terms of their great distress and sorrow that one of them should behave thus towards Jesus, and their anxiety articulates itself in a chorus of dissociation from the heinous act as one after another they protest: 'Not I, Lord!' The Greek *mêti* emphasizes the fact that they expected a negative answer. It could be paraphrased: 'Surely, it is not I?' expecting the answer, 'Of course not!' Maybe they protest too much. Do they realise their own vulnerability and potential for betrayal? Or are they still hoping that Jesus may even be mistaken?

The heinous nature of betrayal is highlighted by the multiple references to table-fellowship: 'he reclined with them', 'while they were eating', 'one of you', and 'one who has dipped his hand into the dish with me'. The sense would be well rendered into English if the word *you* were emphasised and the sentences read as: 'Amen I say to *you*, one of *you*, yes, one of *you*, one of *you* who is actually here and now dipping into the dish and eating with me, will betray me.'

Jesus responds to their initial reaction with a reaffirmation: 'One who has dipped his hand with me into the dish, this one will betray me.' In doing so he emphasises the close bond of table fellowship, the betrayal of which is seen in biblical eyes as one of the greatest of all forms of betrayal. One psalmist laments: 'even my bosom friend in whom I trusted, who ate my bread, has lifted the heel against me' (Ps 41:9), and another laments: 'It is not enemies who taunt me – I could bear that ... but it is you, my equal, my companion, my familiar friend, with whom I kept pleasant company ...'(Ps 55:12-14).

Jesus now proclaims: 'The Son of Man goes forth as it is written of him.' This is almost like a summary and recapitulation of the earlier predictions of the passion to be endured by the Son of Man, the first of which was introduced with *dei*, the statement of divine necessity or decree, 'It is necessary that the Son of Man should suffer many things ...'(Mt 16:21). The divine necessity or decree is represented here by the authoritative word of scripture, 'as it is written of him'. The willing obedience of the Son of Man to that divine plan is emphasised in the choice of words 'he goes forth' (*hypagei*). He is not captured, constrained or dragged along. He goes forth willingly.

From early on in their Christian lives, the first followers of Jesus 'searched the scriptures' (Acts 17:11) and found in them the passages that enabled them to see and accept the divine will and economy at work in the events surrounding the death and resurrection of Jesus. Paul could write to the Corinthians that he was handing on to them what he himself had received, 'that the Lord Jesus died for our sins *according to the scriptures* ... that he rose on the third day *according to the scriptures*' (1 Cor 15:3-5). By the time the Acts of the Apostles was written the words *foretold, foreseen, foreknowledge, predetermined* were the stock in trade vocabulary for showing the divine plan in Jesus' suffering and death (Acts 2:23; 3:18, 24; 13:27-29).[19] Matthew, however, like the other evangelists, does not excuse Judas' deliberate action in cutting himself off from Jesus and plotting his downfall, even though it fits into this overall plan of God. Matthew (like Mark 14:21) reports Jesus' prophetic style lamentation: 'Woe to one by whom the Son of Man is handed over; it would be better for him that he had never been born' (Mk 14:21).

The 'woe' (*ouai*) recalls the warnings of the prophets and Jesus' condemnation of the scribes and the Pharisees (Hos 7:12-14; Amos 5:17-19; 6:3-5; Mic 2:1-2; Isa 5:7-23; 28:1-2; Mt 23:13-32; Lk 6:24-26). Here in typical prophetic style the activity of the betrayer is condemned and lamented. The woe points like a lamentation to the total failure to grasp what Jesus had done and taught, a total closing off from what he offered. It is like the one who has gained everything and lost his life (Mt 10:39; 16:24-26). In prophetic words, it resembles a saying about those who deny the Lord of Spirits, 'It were better had he never been born' (1 Enoch 38:2).

Finally, the reaction of Judas to Jesus' remark is singled out. He says the same words as the other disciples but adds the address, 'Master (Rabbi)', a title that usually designates a lack or absence of faith in Jesus. It is the address he will use as he betrays him to his captors in the garden (Mt 26:49). He said: 'Surely it is not I, Master?' Jesus said to him: 'You have said it.' Jesus will use the same expression (*su eipas, su legeis*) to the High Priest (Mt 26:64) and to Pilate (27:11) to confirm the truth of the words they have spoken.

c. Jesus shares the Passover Meal/the Eucharist Mt 26:25-30
The phrase 'as they were eating' introduces the institution of the Eucharist, repeating the phrase in Mt 26:21 which introduced the dialogue about his betrayal. Maybe the repetition is a pointer to the fact that the two accounts were originally handed on separately and Matthew wishes to keep both of them intact.[20] This is

---

19. The Acts of the Apostles was probably written in the early eighties.
20. cf D. J. Harrington, *op. cit.*, 367, n 26.

another intercalation, setting the story of the betrayal in the context of the Passover/Eucharist.

Matthew, Mark and Luke seem to present the meal as the Passover Meal though there is no detailed account of the overall ritual and there is no mention of the principal dish, the lamb. By implication Jesus is the lamb and the emphasis on his blood brings out his significance as the Passover Lamb. The sharing of the cup and the mention of 'covenant' emphasise the Passover dimension, as does the hymn singing at the conclusion of the meal. The reference to the blood is a reminder of the escape from the slavery of Egypt when the blood of the lamb was sprinkled on the doorposts in Egypt marking out the Israelites as the children of God (Exod 12:1-14), and of the blood of the sacrificial animals, half of which was poured on the altar and half sprinkled on the people as a sign of the sealing of the covenant at Sinai between God and the recently liberated chosen people (Ex 24:6-8).

The reader was informed in the story of Jesus' birth that he was given his divinely appointed name, 'Jesus', because 'he is the one who will save his people from their sins' (Mt 1:21). Here now he is anticipating his saving death in sharing the cup of his blood given as 'the blood of the covenant which is to be poured out for many for the forgiveness of sins'.

During the meal, literally, 'as they were eating', having taken bread, and having said the blessing, Jesus broke (it) and having given (it) to the disciples, said: 'Take (and) eat. This is my body.' Taking the cup and having given thanks he gave (it) to them saying: 'All of you drink from this, for this is my blood of the covenant which is poured out for many for the forgiveness of sins.' (Mark puts it in the narrative form 'They all drank'). Some manuscripts have 'the *new* covenant',[21] but with or without the word 'new' the concept of something new taking place is obvious from the context. (In practice there would have been an in-

---

21. Important mss like Vaticanus and Sinaiticus just say ' covenant'. The addition of the word 'new' in some mss may be under the influence of the parallel Lukan text (Lk 22:20) and/or the Eucharistic text in Paul's First Letter to the Corinthians (1 Cor 11:25).

terval between the eating of the bread and the drinking of the wine (cf 1 Cor 11:25).

At one level the ritual of taking the bread and the cup, saying a blessing or giving thanks, then breaking and distributing the bread, and handing around the cup of wine reflects the action of the *paterfamilias* at a festal meal.[22] On another level it reflects the stylised ritual action and language of the early Christian Eucharistic celebration, a ritual reflected already in the two accounts of the multiplication of the loaves (Mt 14:19; 15:16//Mk 6:41; 8:6; Lk 9:16).[23] A similar ritualised formula is used with the cup.[24] Though the bread was probably unleavened bread, *azymos*, and the reference to the Feast of Unleavened Bread has already been made in the pericope, still the term *artos*, a loaf of ordinary leavened bread, is used, again a reflection of Eucharistic language.

The Jewish custom of praising God and giving thanks at the beginning of the meal is reflected in the use of *eulogêsas* ('having said the blessing') and *eucharistêsas*, ('having given thanks'), again two terms that became established ritual expressions in the Eucharistic celebration. Matthew and Mark have both terms but Luke and Paul kept to *eucharistêsas*, giving thanks, probably because it was better suited to the language of their Gentile audiences.[25] However, Matthew and Mark, unlike Luke and Paul, do not include Jesus' injunction to repeat the action in his mem-

---

22. The monumental work of J. Jeremias, *The Eucharistic Words of Jesus*, New York: Scribner's, 1966, has been of huge influence in reconstructing the historical ritual and language of the Passover Meal and examining its setting and interpretation in the New Testament. However, scholars have pointed out that the information drawn from the Mishnah and Talmud on which it relies sometimes reflects a situation somewhat later than the New Testament, when significant changes had been brought about by the dramatic events of 66-70AD and their aftermath. See also M. Casey, 'The Original Aramaic Form of Jesus' Interpretation of the Cup,' *JTS* 41 (1990) 1-12; D. B. Smith, 'The More Original Form of the Words of Institution,' *ZNW* 83 (1992) 166-86; G. Ossom-Batsa, *The Institution of the Eucharist in the Gospel of Mark*, Bern-Frankfurt: Lang, 2001.

23. *labôn arton, eulogêsas, eklasen, dous, eipen, labete, phagete.*

24. *labôn potêrion, eucharistêsas, edôken, legôn, piete.*

25. Mt 26:26-28; Mk 14:22-24; Lk 22:19-20; 1 Cor 11:23-26.

ory (Lk 22:19; 1 Cor 11:24f) as Matthew's focus at this point in the narrative is not on showing the beginning of the church's eucharistic practice but rather on emphasising the salvific nature of the total self gift of Jesus' body and blood, 'the blood of the covenant which is poured out for many for the forgiveness of sins.' The 'self-giving' of Jesus, represented in the giving of his body and blood, is significantly juxtaposed to the 'handing over' of Jesus by Judas.

'My body' (*to soma mou*) and 'my blood' (*to haima mou*) are two parallel, rather than complementary, ways of saying 'myself' or 'my life', each pointing to the fullness of the identity and life of Jesus in his gift of himself/his life.[26] 'The many', in Hebrew *rabim*, means 'the multitude', 'a number beyond counting', 'all and sundry', an all-inclusive term, rendered in Greek by *hyper pollôn*, (but losing some of its all inclusive import in the English translation 'for many'). Jesus already spoke of giving his life as 'a ransom for many', *lytron anti pollôn*, (Mt 20:28). Paul emphasises this vicarious/salvific theme in several letters. In addition to his handing on the tradition of the Last Supper and the Institution of the Eucharist in First Corinthians (1 Cor 11:24), he wrote to the Romans that: 'Christ died for us while we were still sinners', and 'God did not spare his own Son but gave him up for the benefit of us all' (Rom 5:8; 8:32). To the Galatians he wrote: 'Christ ... sacrificed himself for our sins', and 'the Son of God sacrificed himself for my sake' (Gal 1:4; 2:20). 'For many' is a Semitic equivalent of this universal language of Paul.

Passing the cup (*potêrion*) around for all of them to drink has the triple significance of sharing the wine in fellowship, entering the (new) covenant in his blood for the forgiveness of sins and accepting the cup of suffering. The blood is the blood of the covenant, established in his name. 'The cup' has overtones of the fate of Jesus, his suffering and death. Jesus' prayer in Gethsemane for the cup to be taken away from him will emphasise

26. John, on the other hand, in the Eucharistic section of his Bread of Life treatise uses *sarx* and *haima*, the flesh and blood as separated in sacrificial rituals, and therefore complementary (Jn 6:53-56).

this. Those who are about to betray, deny and flee from him are all invited to participate in the meal, in the suffering and in the covenant. The salvific death of Jesus is for all. St Paul brings out the significance: 'The cup of blessing that we bless, is it not a sharing in the blood of Christ? The bread that we break is it not a sharing in the body of Christ? Because there is one bread, we who are many are one body, for we all partake of one bread' (1 Cor 10:16-17).

'Covenant' is central to the experience of Israel. The covenant with Abraham established *YHWH* as the patron God of Abraham and promised a future for his offspring and for all nations who would be blessed in his name (Gen 17:1-27). The covenant with Moses and the people at Sinai established God as the suzerain God of a newborn nation bound to God by covenant as they were reminded of God's historical acts of kindness and benevolence on their behalf (Exod 19:1-9). The covenant with David made God the patron of a dynasty charged with shepherding the people (2 Sam 7:1-29). The prophets Jeremiah and Ezekiel looked to the future to a new covenant, not written on stone for the people in general but written on the heart of every individual (Jer 31:29-34; Ezek 18:2; 36:22-28). Jesus now speaks of his blood that is to be poured out as the blood of the (new) covenant. A whole new relationship of God 'with the many' is being established in his blood. The blood of Jesus ratifies this (new) covenant just as the blood of the sacrificial lambs at the first Passover was sprinkled on the doorposts, marking out the children of Israel as the firstborn of God in contradistinction to the first-born of the Egyptians (Exod 12:7,13). At Sinai the sacrificial blood was sprinkled on the people to ratify the covenant whereby they became the chosen people of God: 'You will be my people and I will be your God' (Exod 24:1-8; cf Heb 9:19ff; 10:28ff). Zechariah later spoke of God setting the captives free from the waterless pit 'because of the blood of my covenant with you' (Zech 9:11). Now Jesus' blood establishes the covenant 'with the many' for the forgiveness of sins.

'For the forgiveness of sins' is Matthew's unique contribution to the institution formula. It brings to the fore the emphasis on forgiveness of sins that has been present throughout the gospel. The Davidic child was named 'Jesus', a name interpreted as signifying his role in saving the people from their sins (Mt 1:21). Forgiveness of sins and one's own willingness to forgive the sins of others are emphasised in the Lord's Prayer and in its 'appendix' in the Sermon on the Mount (Mt 6:12, 14, 15). Jesus drew the ire of the scribes and was accused of blasphemy when he proclaimed to the paralytic that his sins were forgiven (Mt 9:6). He reinforced his teaching about forgiving one another in his instructions about dealing with the erring members of the community (Mt 18:21-35). The entire meaning of his life and death and the new relationship they establish with the Father are now summed up in terms of 'my blood of the covenant poured out for the remission of sins'. The *peri pollôn*, 'for the multitude', recalls also the vicarious suffering of the Servant in Isa 52:13–53:12 where the Suffering Servant who takes on himself the sins of us all, prays all the time for sinners. For Matthew, Jesus is replacing the atonement rituals of the temple.

The imminence of Jesus' death, symbolised by his broken body and spilled blood, seems to mark the end of his mission, of his coming to announce the arrival of the kingdom of heaven. His mission appears to have been thwarted, his project defeated, his task a failure. But all is far from lost. Immediately following the words and actions over the bread and cup in Matthew and Mark, and immediately before them in Luke, Jesus looks to the final triumph of the kingdom. The earthly table-fellowship may be over, but as he announces a fast he speaks the final words of hope in the face of his earthly failure and death. He will not drink of this fruit of the vine until that day when he will drink the new wine 'in the kingdom of my Father with you' (Mt 26:29; Mk 14:25; Lk 22:18).[27] His last earthly supper anticipates the banquet that he will share with them in the kingdom of his Father. A

---

27. Matthew adds 'with you' to the tradition found in Mark, to emphasise their sharing with him, and 'from this moment on' (*ap' arti*) emphasising the significance of what is taking place.

defining moment has been reached, a new era dawns *ap' arti*, 'from this moment on'.

Earlier in the gospel when he was challenged because the disciples of John and the disciples of the Pharisees were fasting but his disciples were not, Jesus responded that it would not be right for them to fast while the bridegroom was still with them, but the days would come when the bridegroom would be taken away, and then they would fast (Mt 9:15). Now the bridegroom is about to be taken away and it is the bridegroom himself who will fast. Speaking of a fast from the fruit of the vine that will come to an end when he drinks new wine in the kingdom of his Father points forward to the eschatological, heavenly messianic banquet. Coming after the solemn predictions of Judas' betrayal and followed closely by the prediction of the denials by Peter and the flight of the disciples, all of which are fulfilled within the immediate context of the gospel itself, this prediction/prophecy gains a profile of credibility for its fulfilment, even though it points to a context beyond the bleak horizon of the gospel. Only God can bring that about. J. P. Meier comments on the prophecy:

> The prophecy … is thus a final cry of hope from Jesus, expressing his trust in the God who will make his kingdom come, despite Jesus' death. To the end, what is central to Jesus' faith and thought is not Jesus himself but the final triumph of God as he comes to rule his rebellious creation and people – in short, what is central is the kingdom of God.[28]

Fasting was done as an act of repentance, as an expression of mourning, as an accompaniment for prayer of petition (often in sackcloth and ashes), as a preparation for contact with the holy or as a preparation for the Day of the Lord. The reader may see Jesus here as fulfilling the role of the obedient, faithful servant suffering on behalf of the many and praying all the time for sinners (Isa 52:13–53:12). If so, then the fasting can be seen as an accompaniment to his prayer on behalf of the people, of the many for whom his blood has been poured out (Mt 26:28), of the many

---

28. J. P. Meier, *A Marginal Jew*, vol 2, 308.

for whom his life is given in ransom (Mt 20:28) at this critical moment (cf Isa 53:12) as he places his own fate in the hands of God. In his moment of failure and rejection Jesus stands in solidarity with humanity and places his hope in God.

The reference to 'the kingdom of my Father' here at the end of his ministry forms an inclusion with his initial call to 'repent for the kingdom of heaven is close at hand' (Mt 4:17). It emphasises that it is an 'already but not yet' presence of the kingdom. As Jesus speaks of the coming kingdom of his Father (rather than the more usual kingdom of heaven or kingdom of God), the reader remembers the prayer he taught his disciples: 'Our Father in heaven ... may your kingdom come ...'(Mt 6:10).

From here on the gloom of isolation and imminent catastrophe will engulf the scene and thicken until Jesus' death next day. Meanwhile he will be betrayed by a table companion, deserted by his disciples, denied by Peter, rejected by the Jewish authorities, executed by the foreigners, cast out from the holy city and people, and finally die by crucifixion, the cruelest and most dreaded method of execution.

3. GETHSEMANE MT 26:31-56

a. Jesus predicts the Disciples' Flight and Peter's Denials Mt 26:31-35
After they had sung the hymns (*hymnêsantes*) they set out for the Mount of Olives, a ridge stretching for about three miles from north to south on the eastern side of the city. *Hymns* is probably a better translation than the usual 'having sung *a hymn*', as it very likely refers to the Hallel Psalms 113 to 118 which recall God's saving power and his leading Israel from slavery to freedom. These hymns 'the great Hallel' were sung on festal occasions.

Human crisis and divine judgement are very much associated with the area they traverse between the supper room and the Mount of Olives. Heading for the Mount of Olives, they had to cross the Kidron Valley. Jesus' crossing to the Mount of Olives re-echoes the story of David. The reader remembers David's sense of abandonment crossing this same valley when his son Absalom had betrayed him and raised a rebellion against his authority. On hearing of the rebellion David fled from the city and made his way across the Kidron. He arrived at the Mount of Olives weeping and praying only to discover that he had been betrayed also by his close personal adviser and friend Ahitophel who later took his own life, the only suicide in the Old Testament apart from soldiers in battle not wishing to be taken by the enemy (2 Sam 15:13-31; 17:23). The reader now sees Jesus and hears his words in similar circumstances.

Retracing this historic and tragic journey of David, Jesus, Son of David, shepherd king, tells his disciples: 'You will all be scandalised in me this night' and goes on to say that it is written, 'I will strike the shepherd and the sheep of the flock will be scattered.' This is a loose quotation from Zechariah. The original text in Zechariah states: 'Strike the shepherd so that the sheep will be scattered' (Zech 13:7). Here in Matthew (as in Mark) it is: 'I will strike the shepherd and (as a result) the sheep will be scattered.' The Greek word *skandalon* means 'a trap, a snare, a stumbling block that causes one to fall, to lose faith and be lost.' 'You will fall away/lose faith/desert' are better translations of *skandalisthêsthe* than 'you will be scandalised'. It was used of the seed that fell away and produced no harvest because trials and persecutions proved to be a 'scandal' or stumbling block (Mt 13:21). It was used of Peter himself when he refused to accept Jesus' first prediction of his passion and death and Jesus described him as a 'scandal to me', a stumbling block in his way (Mt 16:23).

However, as in the passion predictions there is a note of hope, a promise of resurrection. As Jesus led them on the journey from Galilee to Jerusalem, so too after his resurrection he will go before them, that is, he will, as a shepherd, lead the scattered sheep back to Galilee, not only to the geographic location, their home place, but also to their spiritual home, the place where they left everything to follow him when the arrival of the kingdom was proclaimed, and mighty words and deeds accompanied its proclamation. Even there the heavy hand of the Jerusalem authorities had made itself felt but now Jesus has come to the centre of opposition and the final struggle is about to take place. After his vindication, his resurrection, he promises to go ahead of them, to lead them back as his disciples following him, to Galilee.

Jesus predicts the scattering of the sheep when the shepherd is struck down and Peter responds as on previous occasions in the gospel when he speaks either for the group, or for himself. His response here is rather ironic. 'Even if all are scandalised in you (fall away from you), I will never be scandalised in you.'[29] Here again Jesus has to correct his well-meaning impetuosity and add a note of caution to his optimism. With a solemn 'amen' pronouncement Jesus says to him: 'Amen, I say to you that in this very night before the cock crows you will deny me three times.' Peter responded very forcefully about his willingness to die with Jesus: 'Even if I must die with you, I will never deny you.' And *all the disciples said the same*. Ironically the scene is set for *all the disciples* (*mathêtai pantes*) to flee the scene and for Peter to deny that he was a disciple and then to deny on oath that he ever knew him! However, *all of them* had drunk from the cup of Jesus' blood of the covenant, 'poured out for many for the forgiveness of sins', and ironically 'the many' for whom it was poured out included themselves.

As the story unfolds and Jesus' prophecy is fulfilled, Peter will make the most emphatic denial of Jesus, a denial that will be a major factor in the story whenever it is told. 'This very night, before the cock crows' emphasises how quickly and unexpectedly (from Peter's point of view) it will happen. Furthermore, the triple denial emphasises the deliberate nature of the denial. From putting himself forward as the leader of the followers he will emerge as the leader of the renegades! In John's gospel Jesus tells him: 'You cannot follow me now, but you will follow me later' just before he predicts his denials (Jn 13:36f). In fairness to

---

29. Mark at this point emphasises Peter's self-confidence. The grammar of Mark's sentence emphasises Peter's self assurance which could be translated as, 'Not I, of all people!' The use of *ephê* rather than the more frequent *elegen* brings out the idea of a boastful pronouncement as though to illustrate the point that Jesus and the others spoke but Peter announced or declared (Mk 14:30).

Peter, however, it should be said that the others had already run away so the storyteller's spotlight had been removed from them. As on the occasion when Peter stepped out of the boat and onto the storm tossed waves, while the others remained in the relative safety of the boat, Peter on this occasion followed Jesus until he was overcome by his own frailty. The others were by now well away from the scene in relative safety.

In the post-resurrection scene at the Sea of Tiberias (Jn 21:15-17) Peter is given three opportunities to undo his triple denials as he responds to Jesus' question: 'Do you love me' and he is told to 'feed my lambs, feed my sheep' and then told how when he grows old he will be bound and led to where he would rather not go (to martyrdom) (Jn 21:18). This Johannine emphasis, sixty or so years after the event, shows how high a profile Peter's denials continued to have in the early church and how they may well have been used as a high profile example of denial, repentance and restoration for the *lapsi*, those who had fallen away during the persecutions of Nero or Domitian.[30] In this way Peter's denials became a great source of hope and reassurance to those who had fallen away during persecution and had subsequently come to regret their failure. Some time later Pliny the Younger wrote about the Christians being given three opportunities to affirm or deny whether they were Christians, a practice that was probably in use even before Pliny's time in the reign of Trajan (c 110 AD).[31]

b. Jesus in Gethsemane Mt 26:36-46//Mk 14:32-42//Lk 22:40-46

Then Jesus came with them to the place called Gethsemane (a name which means 'the oil press'), a spot on the Mount of Olives opposite the temple and city where the cultivation of oil has been well attested.[32] Central to the scene in Gethsemane is the

---

30. For a study of Peter's denials and their function and importance in the gospel as a whole see A. Burrell, *The Good News of Peter's Denial. A Narrative and Rhetorical Reading of Mark 14:54, 66-72,* Atlanta: Scholars, 1998.

31. Pliny, *Epistles,* 10.96:2,3.

32. R. E. Brown, *The Death of the Messiah,* 1:148f.

prayer of Jesus, highlighted against the failure of the three 'special' disciples to 'keep watch', the inner group of disciples who had accompanied him to the Mount of Transfiguration (Mt 17:1-8),[33] and the fear that caused all the disciples, those chosen 'to be with him' to 'flee from him'.[34] The alternating scenes highlight the contrast between Jesus' watching and praying and the disciples' sleeping and failing to watch and pray.

Jesus seeks comfort from Peter, James and John

On arrival, Jesus removes himself from the body of disciples, instructing them to 'sit here while I go yonder and pray.' Bringing Peter and the two sons of Zebedee (James and John) with him he began to be sorrowful and distressed. As he now began (*êrxato*) to be sorrowful (*lupeisthai*)[35] and distressed/troubled (*adêmonein*) he confides in them: 'My soul is sorrowful (*perilypos*) even unto death.' The use of *êrxato*, 'he began', seems to emphasise the moment of his embarking on the suffering of his passion and death. The calm, determined 'spiritual' and 'cerebral' quality of his predictions of his own suffering at various points so far in the story and his foretelling of the betrayal by Judas, of the flight of the disciples and of the denial by Peter, all under the rubric of God's great design, now gives way to a 'gut reaction' in the face of impending death and the reaction of the heart in the need for companionship. The reader thinks of the prayer of the Psalmist: 'Fear and trembling come upon me, and the terror of death overwhelms me' (Ps 55:5-6).

Scholars have discussed what exactly 'unto death' means. It

33. Mark further emphasises their special position by pointing out how they were given special names when Jesus called them (Mk 3:16f), how they accompanied Jesus to the house of Jairus (Mk 5:37), and how, together with Andrew, they were the ones to whom he spoke close to this very spot about the coming disaster on the city and temple and the end of the world as we know it (Mk 13).

34. See the extensive treatment in R. E. Brown, *The Death of the Messiah*, Vol I and also D. M. Stanley, *Jesus in Gethsemane*, New York, Paulist, 1980. See also the article by J. Murphy-O'Connor, 'What Really Happened at Gethsemane?' *Bible Review* 14/2 (1998) 28-39,52.

35. Mark uses a stronger verb, *ekthambeisthai*, 'a shuddering horror', R. E. Brown, *The Death of the Messiah*, Vol 1, 153.

could mean sorrow at the onset of death, or sorrow so great that it could kill, or such sorrow that makes one wish to die. R. E. Brown seems closest to Matthew's and Mark's context when he assesses the various conjectures and draws the conclusion:

> In the context of being surrounded on all sides by enemies, Sirach 51:6 affirms, 'My soul has been close to death; my life has gone down to the brink of Sheol.' If Jesus is the weary prophet in Mk/Mt, in part it is because he foresees his disciples scandalised and scattered by his arrest and death, after they have betrayed and denied him. The very thought of this is enough to kill him, and he will ask God to be delivered from such a fate.[36]

He instructs the three disciples to 'remain here and watch with me'. 'With me' emphasises the role of the disciple with the master. From the tone and distressed attitude of Jesus, so uncharacteristic of his previous predictions of his suffering, it is obvious that something is about to happen this night and at this critical moment Jesus exhorts them to 'stay here and watch with me'. 'Watching' is not simply staying awake physically and being ready for danger through the various watches of this night, but also a command to maintain spiritual alertness, an awareness of what is really taking place at a level beyond the immediately perceptible events.

Jesus prays to the Father Mt 26:39-46//Mk 14: 35-36 Lk 22:39-46

Going on a little further he fell on his face, praying and saying: 'My Father, if it be possible, let this cup pass from me, but not as I, but as you wish.' Doing what the Father wishes, carrying out the plan of the Father is the great mark of righteousness. This prayer is almost a paraphrase of Jesus' remark to the Baptist about fulfilling all righteousness (Mt 3:15). Instead of Mark's description of Jesus falling on the ground to pray, Matthew describes Jesus' posture as 'falling on his face', the

36. Ibid, 155f.

most respectful posture of someone making an intense petition
to God or to some very important person. The proviso in Jesus'
prayer, 'if it be possible' sets the petition in the context of acceptance of God's design, even if it entails God's refusal of the petition. 'The cup (or chalice), *potêrion*, is a traditional image regularly used for 'the cup of suffering' or the outpouring of the
wrath of God by way of punishment.[37]

The reader is reminded of the psalms of lament, where the
just one pours out spontaneous sentiments of sorrow and distress to God. Jesus' lament is 'at once fearful and yet trusting
God'.[38] D. Senior's comment on the prayer as described in Mark
is equally relevant for Matthew:

> With stunning boldness Mark presents Jesus as engulfed in
> the prayer of lament. In the tradition of the just ones of Israel
> – anguished before death, tormented by the betrayal of
> friends, vulnerable to enemies – Jesus clings to the one thread
> that gives ultimate meaning to his existence, his faith in the
> God of Israel.[39]

F. J. Moloney comments in similar vein. Speaking of the
psalms of lamentation he points out how they come from

> ... someone in a situation of suffering, abandonment, hope-
> lessness, and violated innocence. But through all the expres-
> sions of fear, suffering, and hopelessness and the questions
> put to God, a profound trust is expressed in the ultimate vic-
> tory of God over the source of evil ... The passion has begun,
> and these words of lament and anxiety point forward to the
> horror of the events that will follow. Jesus' sudden change of
> attitude indicates the unrelenting nature of the suffering that
> he is about to endure. However, it does not take away from
> him the trust that – whatever may happen to him – God will
> have the last word.[40]

---

37. Isa 51:17, 22; Jer 25:15-6; 49:12; 51:7; Lam 4:21; 23:31f; Ezek 23:23; Hab
2:16; Ps 75:8-9. It is sometimes for good fortune, God's favour (Ps 23:5).
38. F. J. Moloney, *op. cit*, 290.
39. D. Senior, *The Passion of Jesus in the Gospel of Mark*, 70.
40. F. J. Moloney, *op. cit.*, 291f.

The Father-Son relationship acknowledged by the Father from the region of heaven at the baptism and from the midst of the cloud of the Divine Presence at the transfiguration is now witnessed from the other side of the relationship. From the depths of human isolation and suffering the Son acknowledges the Father: 'My Father, not as I, but as you, wish.'

Jesus comes to the three disciples he had singled out from the group and brought forward to be *with him* on this occasion. Having told them to 'remain and watch with me,' he finds them sleeping and challenges them. These are people who had specifically stated their intention and assured him of their resolve and ability to be with him in spite of anything that might happen. James and John had assured him they could drink the cup he had to drink (Mt 20:22). Peter had protested that even if all lost faith he would not, and would be willing to die with him rather than disown him (Mt 26:33). Jesus now says to Peter: 'Were you not able to watch one hour with me?' (Again he says, 'with me', as the disciple should be 'with the master'.) Again he issues the instruction: 'Watch and pray lest you enter into temptation (i.e. lest you are put in a situation of severe testing, *eis peirasmon*).'

Watching and praying are very important in the face of the *peirasmos*, the 'testing' that lay ahead. Jesus reminds them that the *peirasmos*, in this case the reaction of the hostile world under Satan's influence about to break upon them, will pose a real threat to their frail humanity, even in spite of their 'spiritual' commitment to Jesus as his disciples. He points out that 'the spirit is willing, but the flesh is weak' and already this is being proved true in their failure to keep watch.

Jesus returns and prays for the second time: 'My Father, if it is not possible for this to pass unless I drink it, let your will be done.' Jesus again returns to the disciples and his sense of isolation is further increased by finding the disciples still sleeping. The 'weakness of the flesh' is now highlighted by the statement that 'their eyes were heavy'. Then leaving them again he went and prayed for the third time, saying the same word(s).

Jesus returns to the sleeping disciples a third time. Three is a number of completion. Three prayers and three failures to watch match each other as complete demonstrations of Jesus' attitude and the failure of the disciples. Peter will later deny Jesus three times, again showing a completeness of attitude and action (Mt 26:69-74). As he says to them: 'Sleep on and take your rest' he announces: 'Behold the hour is at hand, and the Son of Man is betrayed into the hands of sinners.' Resolutely facing the crisis Jesus says: 'Arise, let us go. Behold, the one handing me over is close at hand / draws near.'

As the betrayer and his company approach, far from cowering or running away, Jesus rises up and moves towards his great moment of resolve. He takes a definite initiative as he proclaims:[41] 'Arise! Let us go!'[42] His final invitation to the disciples to accompany him, 'Arise, let us go,' will be too much for them as they have not 'watched and prayed'. The verb 'arise' has connotations of rising up from sleep resolved to do the will of God (as Joseph did (Mt 1:24; 2-13,21) or rising from sleep in strength and power to confront a threatening power as when Jesus rose from

---

41. Mark at this point has Jesus saying *apechei* which is almost impossible to translate and scholars have made many suggestions. In Greek the verb *apechein* usually has a commercial or financial meaning, as in the receipt of payment or settling of a debt. In this context it would refer to the payment of the traitor, the making of the deal. See R. E. Brown, *Death of the Messiah*, vol 2, appendix III, 1379-83. He summarises the many different approaches to a translation and suggests as a translation: 'The money is paid.' Other approaches have been influential, but are not very clear or convincing. The Vulgate translates *apechei* as '*sufficit*', 'it is enough', and this translation has been widely used. But to what does it refer? Enough of Jesus' reprimand? Enough watching and prayer? Enough talk of sorrow and the *peirasmos*? The verb *apechei* can also mean 'it is far off' (or 'is it far off?'). In this sense Jesus' statement would read: 'Is it far off? The hour has come!' Some have suggested it is a mistranslation of the Aramaic *kaddu* which means 'already'. Some mss like Codex Bezae and Old Latin mss have variant readings.

42. This resolve of Jesus is presented in a dramatic fashion and high christology in John's gospel where Jesus astounds the arresting party with his question 'Whom do you seek?' and presents himself for arrest with the '*ego eimi*' response to their seeking of 'Jesus of Nazareth'. Underlying the very different accounts of Matthew / Mark and John is the firm resolve of Jesus.

sleeping in the boat and rebuked the elements of wind and sea (Mt 8:26).

It is *the hour*, the opportunity for the apparent triumph of evil, of the power of Satan over the Son of Man, the apparent frustration of the promise of the arrival of the kingdom and the fulfilment of God's design. 'The Son of Man is handed over (*paradidotai*) into the hands of sinners.' Jesus' first proclamation in the gospel, after the handing over of John the Baptist was, 'the kingdom of heaven is close at hand'. Now at the end of his ministry he proclaims: 'The one handing me over is close at hand.'

c. Jesus' arrest and the disciples' flight (Mt 26:47-56//Mk 14:43-53//Lk 22:47-53//Jn 18:1-11

'While he was still speaking' Judas came. It was as though his 'Arise, let us go, behold the betrayer is at hand' had set the action in motion. The betrayer is immediately identified as 'one of the Twelve', not however, any longer described as a disciple 'with him (Jesus)', but as one who is now in very different company. '*With him* there was a great crowd with swords, and clubs, sent by the chief priests and the elders of the people',[43] the very group of officials who challenged Jesus' authority and lost out in his counter question about the Baptist's authority (Mt 21:23). He aimed the parables of the two sons, the wicked tenants and the murderous invitees to the banquet at these authority figures, and now they are adding another victim to the list of rejected messengers! Now their response comes in terms of violent arrest under cover of darkness away from the crowd who supported Jesus and saw through their lack of authority when confronted by him.

Again the term 'betrayer', *ho paradidous*, is used for Judas as

---

43. Mark describes them as: 'sent by the chief priests, the scribes and the elders' (Mk 14:43). Luke speaks of 'a number of men', and subsequently Jesus addresses 'the chief priests and captains of the temple guard and elders who had come for him' (Lk 22:47, 52). John speaks of 'the cohort, together with a detachment of guards sent by the chief priests and the Pharisees' and he is led away by the cohort and its commander (*chiliarchos*) and the Jewish guards (Jn 18:3, 12).

the narrator relates how he arranged a sign, 'the one I shall kiss,' for the arresting party to know whom to seize. Some commentators wonder why it was necessary to point out Jesus since he was well known to the crowds and authorities in the city and temple area where he preached and disputed openly in the sight of all and in the full light of day. Maybe it was rather difficult to spring a surprise arrest on one of a group gathered in the darkness and in the shade of the olive trees. Maybe 'kissing or embracing' Jesus brought Judas close enough to take hold of him in the event of an attempted escape while the arresting party approached. John's gospel speaks of a company of Roman soldiers (*speira*) coming with the arresting party. If they had been drafted into the city for the feast they may well need to have Jesus pointed out to them. The Mount of Olives was regarded as part of the city for the purpose of the pilgrims who were supposed to spend the night of Passover within the city limits. Therefore, there may have been various groups camped in the area. It is quite possible that the greeting 'Rabbi' and a Mediterranean or Oriental style kiss would have been a customary way for a disciple to greet a teacher. The address, 'Rabbi', on the one hand, highlights the heinous nature of the deed and illustrates the treachery and poignancy of the moment, and on the other hand, at the level of Matthew's redaction, it shows the lack of faith on the part of Judas as he uses this non-believer's address for Jesus. The action and the word are said to take place 'immediately', *eutheôs*. 'And immediately approaching him, he said 'Greetings, Rabbi'[44] and he kissed him, thus writing the betrayer's kiss into the record of humanity's darkest moments, as it became the sign to 'lay hold of him'. The word 'immediately' signifies the inexorable unfolding of God's design. The predictions/prophecies of Jesus throughout the gospel are now being fulfilled. Then Jesus responds to Judas with the words: 'Friend, why are you here?'

---

44. Translating '*Chaire*' is difficult. 'Hail' is a bit too dramatic and solemn in the context which is meant to be a (pseudo-) friendly encounter, and 'Hello' is too informal for the disciple to the master. 'Greetings' seems to strike the right note.

which, according to some commentators imply: 'Do what you are here for!'[45] The latter would fit in with the overall context of Jesus' control of the situation in Matthew and would correspond also to a parallel statement of Jesus' control in John: 'What you do, do quickly' (Jn 13:27).

'Then approaching, they laid hands on Jesus and seized him.' Their violent action provoked a violent reaction. Matthew states that one of those who were with Jesus (i.e. a disciple) stretched out his hand, drew his sword and struck the slave of the High Priest and cut off his ear.[46] Mark says 'one of the bystanders' drew his sword. Luke says 'those who were around him' (*hoi peri auton*) asked if they should strike with the sword, and one of them struck the High Priest's servant and cut off his right ear (Lk 48-51). Later John's gospel names the person who struck the servant as Peter and names the servant as Malchus, a servant of the High Priest. Luke alone states that Jesus healed him (Lk 22:51).

Jesus reacts to the display of violence with a command to desist and a saying about violence. 'Put your sword back in its place, for all who resort to the sword will perish by the sword.' His command and his comment about violence (which may reflect a proverb since a similar statement turns up in Rev 13:10) are directly in line with his teaching in the Sermon on the Mount about offering the wicked man no resistance, turning the other cheek (Mt 5:38-42), loving one's enemies and praying for one's persecutors (Mt 5:43-48).

Jesus then points out how the unfolding events are in the plan of 'my Father', who otherwise would send more than twelve legions of angels to defend him. The language of the twelve legions of angels reflects the current apocalyptic expectations of the eschatological battle between good and evil where the angels of holiness will fight with the armies of the just, as seen, for exam-

---

45. See D. J. Harrington, *The Gospel of Matthew*, 374, n 50.
46. John uses the diminutive *ōtarion* probably meaning 'earlobe'. John and Luke mention the 'right' ear(lobe). See the article by B. T. Viviano, 'The High Priest's Servant's Ear: Mark 14:47,' *RB* (1989) 71-80.

ple, in the Qumran War Scroll (1 QM 7:6). Jesus states that it must be so (*houtôs dei genesthai*) for how else could the scriptures, i.e. God's will/plan be fulfilled?

At that hour, Jesus addressed the crowds (his captors). 'At that hour' is more than a reference to the time of the night. It is a reference to 'his hour', the *peirasmos*, a moment of great trial and eschatological significance. He asked them if they had come to arrest him with swords and clubs as if he were a robber/bandit (*lêstes*), though he had been seated (the official teaching position) teaching in the temple day after day and they never arrested him. The implication is clear. Their deed is foul and needs the cover of darkness. Jesus accepts his fate as a fulfilment of the scriptures of the prophets: 'in order that the scriptures of the prophets might be fulfilled'. Fulfilling the scriptures is fulfilling God's will. In spite of the apparent evil in all that is happening, God has a grand design for his people and for the world. No specific scriptural passage is quoted. The widespread presence in scripture of passages dealing with the ill treatment of God's servants, the just ones and the Suffering Servant come to mind in a general way but a verse that immediately springs to mind is the verse from Zechariah quoted by Jesus on his way to Gethsemane about striking the shepherd and the sheep being scattered (Zech 13:7; Mt 26:31) because as the arresting party laid hands on Jesus to arrest him, the disciples, instead of 'rising up and going with him' as he had asked them to do moments before, all left him and fled. 'All' (*pantes*), recalls Jesus' prediction on the way to the garden that 'all' would fall away, repeated in Peter's protests (Mt 26:31, 33). Jesus' prophecy about striking the shepherd and the sheep being scattered is already fulfilled.[47]

The flight of the disciples not only leaves Jesus to face his terrible ordeal alone but it seems to signify the undoing of his mis-

---

47. Matthew, Luke and John do not have the final scene of the naked youth fleeing from the garden described in Mark's account (Mk 14:51-52). It is as evocative as it is puzzling. Instead of ' following with Jesus' he follows with the disciples in their flight as he leaves everything, even the clothes that covered his nakedness, to get away from him.

sion and the wiping out of his standing as a significant person who drew disciples to himself. Greco-Roman society highly prized philosophers and holy men who drew a following. Jewish society inherited the tradition of the prophets and the Wisdom teachers with their schools of followers and the Rabbis drew followers in accordance with their reputations. The last word on the Baptist's life in the gospel described how his disciples had come to give him fitting burial. But in the case of Jesus, his known disciples have left him and fled.

4. THE JEWISH 'TRIAL', PETER'S DENIALS, JUDAS' REMORSE MT 26:57-75
a. Peter follows at a distance

The Jewish 'trial' of Jesus is framed by the story of Peter's following him 'at a distance' to the High Priest's house where he subsequently denied him three times, setting up a stark contrast between the formal 'trial' or questioning of Jesus and the informal questioning or 'trial' of Peter.

Though we were told that all the disciples had left Jesus in the garden and fled, we now read that Peter 'followed him' but *apo makrothen*, 'at a long distance,' 'at quite a distance', or to use the English idiom, 'at a safe distance', as far as the courtyard of the high priest. The play on 'followed', the technical term for the allegiance of a disciple to his master, is not missed on the reader, and neither is the cautious, even cowardly, 'followed at a (safe) distance.' The disciple who is called to be 'with the master' now takes his place with the attendants of his enemies as he sat with them, 'to see the outcome'.[48]

Matthew says that those who had seized Jesus led him to Caiaphas the high priest, where the scribes and the elders were gathered. Mark and Luke do not name the high priest. Mark does not give the name of the High Priest anywhere in the gospel.[49] John says they first brought him to Annas, a former

---

48. Mark is even a bit cynical as he ascribes a purely personal motive for sitting with the enemies, 'warming himself at the light of the fire' (Mk 14:54).

49. R. Pesch, *Das Markus Evangelium*, 2.425 suggests that this is because he was still reigning and his name was known as the gospel story was formed.

high priest, and he in turn subsequently sent him to Caiaphas
(Jn 18:13,24). Jesus is now in the power of the forces that op-
posed him all along. They gather under cover of darkness.
Matthew describes those who gathered as 'the scribes and the
elders' (Mt 26:57) and 'the chief priests and the whole sanhedrin'
(Mt 26:59). Mark describes them as 'all the chief priests, the elders
and the scribes' and 'the chief priests and the whole Sanhedrin'
(Mk 14:53,55). They now have their opportunity.

b. Jesus before the High Priest: The Jewish 'Trial'

Matthew (like Mark) conveys the idea that Jesus was tried by
'the chief priests and the whole Sanhedrin' during the night.[50] It
may well be the case historically that the term *synedrion* is loosely
used and best understood here as an *ad hoc* 'assembly' rather
than a formally convened meeting of the complete Sanhedrin.
Matthew, like Mark, is building up a picture of the quiet, even
silent, dignity of Jesus in the face of the forces massed against
him. In doing so he describes how, in spite of 'the chief priests
and the whole Sanhedrin' and the false witnesses, Jesus still
maintains his dignity, as he did in the garden when facing arrest.[51] The parallel account of the trial in Luke is set in the early
morning. John, who is probably the most accurate historically,
does not have a trial of Jesus before the Sanhedrin as such but an
interrogation before the former High Priest Annas, who then
sends him bound to Caiaphas (Jn 18:12-24). The exact nature of
the session appears to be more accurately remembered by John

---

50. Some important studies of the trial of Jesus prior to the works of R.
E. Brown and D. Senior, already mentioned, were: J. Blinzer, *The Trial of
Jesus. The Jewish and Roman Proceedings Against Jesus Christ Described and
Assessed from the Oldest Accounts*, Westminster, Md: Newman, 1959; S.
G. F. Brandon, *The Trial of Jesus of Nazareth*, London: Batsford, 1968 and
E. Bammel (ed), *The Trial of Jesus*, Studies in Biblical Theology, Second
Series 13, London, SCM Press, 1970; J. R. Donahue, *Are You the Christ?
The Trial Narrative in the Gospel of Mark*, Missoula: Scholars 1973; D. Juel,
Messiah and Temple: The Trial of Jesus in the Gospel of Mark, Missoula:
Scholars, 1977.
51. cf R. H. Gundry, *op. cit.*, 12.

as an interrogation for the purpose of presenting a case to the official (Jewish? and) Roman court. Legally a trial should have been in the presence of the high priest, Caiaphas, and it is very unlikely that the Sanhedrin, which must have contained many rigorously legal-minded members, would have been formally convened in haste for a night session with all the appearances of a kangaroo court. Also the remark of Pilate, as reported by John 'Take him yourself and try him by your own law' (Jn 18:31) seems to point to there not having been an official court trial. R. E. Brown comments:

> John may be more accurate in describing on this night before Jesus died only an interrogation by the high priest that would quite plausibly be held at 'the court (palace) of the high priest'.[52]

The night session was deeply embedded in the tradition(s) because of the double 'trial', that of Jesus and that of Peter, both of which took place simultaneously during the night. As Jesus is led before the assembly of chief priests, scribes and elders, 'the whole Sanhedrin,' Peter follows him into the High Priest's courtyard and sits there awaiting the outcome. The two 'trials' follow. Jesus holds his ground before the important and power-ful people in spite of the *false testimony* against him. Peter loses his nerve before the unimportant maidservants and the by-standers and denied their *true testimony* in relation to his disci-pleship and his association with Jesus.

The chief priests and all those assembled were seeking false testimony against Jesus in order to put him to death but found none, though many false witnesses came forward. The verb 'seek', *zêtein*, has connotations of hostile activity or intention against Jesus. The narrator tells us that many bore false testimony, and, by implication, their testimonies did not match (a fact stated explicitly by Mark). The prescription in the Torah against bear-ing false witness is being flagrantly violated (Exod 20:16; Deut 5:20). According to the Torah two or three witnesses are re-

---

52. R. E. Brown, *Death of the Messiah*, vol I, 404.

quired to gain a conviction. Nobody is to be convicted on the
testimony of one witness (Deut 17:6; 19:15). Jesus' innocence
should now be acknowledged, but the 'seeking' continues and
finally the required number of two witnesses came forward and
said: 'This man said "I am able to destroy the temple of God and
to build it in three days".'

Worse than an outright lie, which is easily contradicted, is a
verisimilitude, something that has an aspect and appearance of
the truth but is presented with an untrue slant. Such is the case
with the statement about the temple. Sticking strictly to
Matthew's narrative, what Jesus said on the occasion of his action in the temple was: 'It is written, my house shall be called a
house of prayer but you are making it a den of thieves' (Mt
21:13). Jesus never spoke of destroying the temple or rebuilding
it on that occasion. The statements about destroying and rebuilding the temple are heard on the lips of false accusers and
mocking enemies.[53] In the apocalyptic discourse, when he
speaks privately to the disciples about the coming destruction of
the temple, he does not say he will destroy or rebuild it. Looking
at the broader New Testament tradition one sees that in John's

---

53. In St John's gospel, however, these statements are not heard on the
lips of opponents, but form the basis for a high christological statement,
or *logion*, on the lips of Jesus himself, and they serve the purpose of raising the issue onto another plane (Jn 2:19-22). As seen earlier in the
gospel, Matthew uses another *logion* in the context of the dispute about
breaking the Sabbath. Having pointed out that the temple priests are
blameless in 'breaking' the Sabbath by carrying on their ministry, Jesus
makes a profound christological statement in the *logion* 'something
greater than the temple is here', and then goes on in true prophetic style
to quote the text: 'What I want is mercy not sacrifice', before making a
second christological statement in the *logion* 'The Son of Man is master
of the Sabbath' (Mt 12:5-8). The synoptics thus portray Jesus breaking
the mould and transcending the institutions and practices of Israel's
past. In all the gospels his attitude to Temple, Torah and Sabbath is of
central significance and displays his greatest claims to divine authority.
The many variations on the statement about the temple point to a widespread diffusion of the theme and to its having sprung from historical
reminiscence rather than from the creation of a midrashic style commentator.

gospel Jesus does not say 'I will destroy this Temple and in three days build it up,' but rather: 'Destroy (i.e. if you, or anyone, destroy) this temple and in three days I will build it up' and the narrator adds that he was speaking of the temple of his body (Jn 2:19-22). Subtleties of Jesus' position, lost, misunderstood or deliberately misrepresented in transmission, lent themselves to false accusation.

To the false testimony Jesus made no reply and the high priest, in the presence of the whole assembly, intervened and asked him had he nothing to say to the accusation.[54] Given the ongoing hostility towards Jesus by the priestly group throughout the story so far, one is most likely correct in assuming that the high priest's intervention at this point is motivated by the desire to make Jesus incriminate himself.

He stood up and questioned Jesus, saying: 'Have you no answer? What do these witness against you?' By law Jesus was not required to answer contradictory and transparently false witness. He was silent. The reader is reminded of the suffering servant of Deutero-Isaiah or 'the just one' in the Psalms and the Book of Lamentations who offers no resistance, opens not his mouth and in whose mouth there are no rebukes, suffering blows and insults in silence. The Fourth Song of the Suffering Servant comes immediately to mind where the servant is silent like the lamb led to the slaughter, having been taken by force and by law, and with nobody to plead his cause (Isa 53:7). So too do the passages in the Psalms such as Ps 38:13-15 which reads: 'But I am like the deaf, I do not hear, like the mute who cannot speak. Truly, I am like one who does not hear, and in whose mouth is no retort. But it is for you, O Lord that I wait; it is you, O Lord, my God, who will answer.' Lam 3:28-30 speaks of the good man sitting in silence and offering his neck to the striker and enduring insults.[55] R. E. Brown says that Jesus is now re-

---

54. Mark has the high priest dramatically, and intimidatingly, standing out in the middle of the assembly.
55. The silence of Jesus is quoted in 1 Peter 2: 21, 23 as an example to be followed by 'fellow sufferers', the persecuted Christians of Asia Minor to whom the letter was written.

signed to his fate and knows that nothing he says will change the outcome of the proceedings. His silence is therefore a sign of his contempt for the hostile proceedings.[56] His silence is also in keeping with Jesus' regal bearing throughout the Passion Narrative.

The central point of the passage now follows. The high priest puts a leading question to Jesus, using an oath formula: 'I adjure you by the Living God that you tell us if you are the Christ, the Son of God?'[57] The reader knows the truth of Jesus' identity and can therefore see the irony in the high priest's question. However, he asks the question against the background of a very narrow, traditional, politico-social understanding which the reader has already seen to be quite inadequate.

Jesus is now forced into the situation of admitting that this is who he really is. Up until now he had been very careful to avoid messianic acclaim and enthusiasm. He ordered Peter and the disciples 'not to tell anybody' on the occasion of Peter's proclamation of faith in his being the Christ/Messiah and Son of the living God (Mt 16:20; Mk 8:28-30). He had carefully prepared his approach to Jerusalem as a countersign to popular messianic expectations (Mt 21:1-5). He openly challenged the teaching (and by implication the popular misunderstanding) that the Messiah was 'merely' a Son of David and set the role in a whole new dimension of 'Lord'. On former occasions when his identity, authority and destiny were in question he referred to himself in terms of the Son of Man and so the reader already knows that the Son of Man not only has power/authority on earth to forgive sins (Mt 9:1-8), and to declare himself master of the Sabbath (Mt 12;8), but that he is destined to suffer grievously and be put to death and that he will rise from the dead (Mt 17:22-23; 20:18-19). Furthermore he has come not to be served but to serve and to

---

56. R. E. Brown, *Death of the Messiah*, Vol 1, 464.
57. Mark at this point has 'the Son of the Blessed', and Luke simply has 'the Christ'. John says they questioned him about his disciples and his teaching (Mt 18:19, 20) but later they say to Pilate that 'he has made himself Son of God' (Jn 19:7).

give his life as a ransom for many (Mt 20:28) and he will come in the glory of his Father and his angels (Mt 16-27).

Now under the spotlight of the High Priest's leading question, Jesus himself admits to what the reader has already been told in the gospel concerning his being Christ and Son of God. However, he does so by saying to Caiaphas: 'You have said it.' This both affirms the truth of the statement and also shifts responsibility for any false messianic understandings on to the high priest who has formulated his question in these terms that Jesus would have avoided using of himself in public and would have understood quite differently. Then he returns to the title he prefers for himself, Son of Man. He looks beyond the present crisis and imminent disaster to his future coming in glory as Son of Man.[58] He proclaims that 'Hereafter you will see the Son of Man, sitting at the right hand of the Power and coming on the clouds of heaven.' Now that Jesus' passion has begun, the process is set in motion whereby he will be established as the glorified Son of Man, at the right hand of the Power, that is, enjoying all authority and from there he will 'come on the clouds of heaven' (Dan 7:13).[59]

In response to Jesus' reply to his question, the high priest circumvents due legal process in his action and in his words. He tore his garments and declared Jesus' statement a blasphemy. Tearing one's garments was a gesture indicating indescribable grief. There is a long history of the gesture in the Old Testament as a reaction on hearing the news of the death of a leader or a loved one. Jacob tore his clothes on hearing of the death of Joseph (Gen 37:34). Joshua tore his clothes and prostrated him-

---

58. In Mark, he responds with a statement of self-revelation and identity 'I am'. The simple affirmation 'I am', *egô eimi*, is primarily a statement of self identification in this context but the reader cannot avoid the overtones of 'I am' as a phrase occurring in theophanies, a self designation of the divine, and a phrase used already by Jesus when he calmed the fear of the disciples as he came to them over the water (Mt 14:27//Mk 6:50).

59. In the persecution of the holy people by Antiochus IV, Epiphanes, of Syria, Daniel was promised that final authority would be given to 'one like a Son of Man' (Dan 7:13).

self before the altar as he pleaded with God to spare the people from the Amorites (Jos 7:6). David did likewise on hearing of the deaths of Saul and Jonathan (2 Sam 1:11-12). Elisha tore his clothes as he lamented the departure of Elijah (2 Kings 2:12). The practice was known in the broader Greco-Roman world. R. E. Brown quotes the examples of Licinius Regulus tearing his clothes in the Roman Senate when he was omitted from the list of selected members and of the emperor Augustus who tore his clothes on hearing of the defeat of Varus in Germany.[60] In the world of the Jews the practice of tearing one's garments was long established as a response to blasphemy. The messengers of King Hezekiah, on hearing the blasphemous remarks of the commander of the Assyrian armies, tore their clothes. The Assyrian cup-bearer-in-chief stood on the city wall and taunted them in the hearing of the people of Jerusalem in their own Judean language that their God could not save them, their king or their city any more than the gods of the other subject peoples saved theirs. The messengers tore their clothes on hearing the blasphemy and when they reported the matter to Hezekiah he responded by tearing his own (2 Kings 18:30, 37; 19:1). The law, later enshrined in the Mishnah, stating that the judges in a blasphemy trial should tear their clothes on hearing the blasphemy, may have been in force at the time of Jesus. If not, at least the general understanding of the gesture, which eventually was enshrined into law, was well established.

What garments did he tear? Was he wearing the formal ceremonial, liturgical robes of the High Priest that were not supposed to be worn outside the temple area, and were guarded by the Romans in the Antonia fortress and only released by them for solemn festivals? Did he usually wear them at Sanhedrin meetings? One can only speculate, and, as already noted, one has to ask whether it was a formal meeting, and whether the Romans would have released the vestments for a hastily convened night meeting (though they may have already been re-

---

60. R. E. Brown, *Death of the Messiah*, Vol 1, 517.

leased for the celebration of the feast). Whatever clothes he tore, the gesture was clear.

The high priest goes on to state/ask: 'What further need have we of witnesses? You have now heard the blasphemy!' On previous occasions they sought to trap Jesus in his speech. They now seem to have succeeded. The understanding that nobody can incriminate himself, later incorporated in the Talmud,[61] may already have operated as a principle. If so it points further to the fact that this was not a legally convened and official meeting of the Sanhedrin, but an assembly of powerful members of the Sanhedrin opposed to Jesus and/or clients of the very powerful house of Caiaphas and Annas.

Then the High Priest put the question to the assembly: 'What is your opinion?' They answered and said: 'He is deserving of death.' No examination of the meaning of blasphemy or how Jesus may have been guilty of it follows. There is no account of individual opinions given by the members or of votes taken. The major question that remains is whether Jesus was officially condemned by a formal meeting of the Sanhedrin or by a powerful lobby group preparing for a trial.

In Matthew's gospel, from earlier in his ministry when Jesus was accused of blasphemy because of his words pronouncing the forgiveness of sins (Mt 9:1-8), through to his trial, when he answered affirmatively to the question about his being the Christ/Messiah, the Son of God, and his adding of the remark about the Son of Man sitting at the right hand of the power and coming on the clouds, the suspicion is that he is 'arrogantly claiming what belongs to God alone'.[62]

His condemnation is followed by physical abuse, as they spat in his face, struck him, and some beating him said: 'Prophesy to us, Christ, who is it that struck you?' They thus mocked his prophetic/messianic role. One is reminded of the fate of the

---

61. *b. Sanhedrin*, 9b. It is, however, difficult to know for certain how closely the actual procedures at the time of Jesus correspond to those later contained in the Talmud.

62. So R. E. Brown concludes a lengthy discourse on the various uses of blasphemy/blaspheming/blasphemer, *Death of the Messiah*, Vol 1, 524.

righteous one in the Book of Wisdom who is 'tested with insult and torture' and 'condemned to a shameful death' because he claims to have knowledge of God and to have God as his father (Wis 2:12-20). In fact one could apply the term 'blasphemy' to the abuse inflicted on Jesus. Luke actually describes his treatment at the hands of the guards as blasphemy against him (Lk 22:65).

Simultaneously with their mockery of his prophetic role, a recent prophecy of Jesus is actually being fulfilled in the triple denial of Peter, who has already taken his place, not with Jesus, as a disciple should, but *meta tôn hypêretôn*, 'with the attendants/guards', the servants and companions of those mocking and inflicting blows on Jesus.

c. Peter denies knowing Jesus and being a disciple Mt 26:69-75

Peter was sitting outside in the courtyard and all four gospels agree that the first person to challenge him was a 'servant girl'.[63] She approached Peter, saying: 'You, too, were with Jesus the Galilean.' This could be paraphrased: 'You too were a disciple of Jesus the Galilean.' (Mark says 'Nazarene'.) It is most unlikely that she simply meant 'You were with him in the garden' as a young servant girl would never have been in that armed band at night on such an errand. He denied it before all, saying: 'I do not know what you are saying.'[64] The verb, 'denied', *êrnêsato* here is in the aorist tense, so a single denial is meant. After this first denial in which he refused to acknowledge that he was 'with Jesus' he was making his way out through the gateway and was thus removing himself to a distance from the threat of further recognition, but not leaving the property completely. He was still

---

63. See the article by N. J. McEleney, 'Peter's Denials – How Many? To Whom?' *CBQ* 52 (1990) 467-72.

64. Mark has: 'I neither know nor understand.' Though some scholars comment on the inelegance or inaccuracy of the use of *'oute ... oute'* ('neither know nor understand') as negativing particles on two verbs which are in fact virtually synonymous, in fact the immediacy of anxious repetitive speech comes through, as Peter at first pretends not to know what she is saying or of what she is accusing him.

holding on to something of his discipleship and his boast never
to abandon Jesus when another maidservant[65] said: 'This one
was with Jesus the Nazarene.' Again he denied it, this time with
an oath, saying 'I do not know the man' (Mark reports this second denial in the imperfect tense, conveying the idea that it was
a repeated denial). The third recognition comes a little later from
the bystanders who say to Peter,' Truly (*alêthôs*) you are (one) of
them, for even your speech/accent/dialect reveals you.' There
is a great irony in the fact that the bystanders recognise Peter as
being ' truly' a disciple in spite of his denials. The only other use
of 'truly' (*alêthôs*) will be in an even more ironic situation when
the centurion and those with him guarding Jesus, on seeing the
earthquake and the signs that took place as he died, proclaim
that Jesus is 'truly (*alêthôs*) the Son of God' (Mt 27:54).

The recognition and challenge to Peter are more serious now.
It is no longer the relatively unimportant young maidservants
who recognise him, but a group, possibly made up of various elements. Also they are convinced of the accuracy of their recognition: 'Truly, *alêthôs*, you are one of them.' They can see, or rather,
hear that he is a Galilean. This piles the pressure on Peter who
now makes a much stronger denial: 'He began to call down a
curse and to swear (an oath): 'I do not know the man.' Was he
cursing Jesus or, the more likely possibility, calling down a curse
on himself if he was lying?[66]

The prophecy of Jesus explodes into his consciousness as 'immediately a cock crew' and Peter remembered the word Jesus
had spoken to him: 'Before the cock crows you will have dis-
owned me three times.' As Peter remembers he is overcome
with grief and, having gone outside, he wept bitterly.

d. The Morning Assembly Mt 27:1-2//Mk 15:1 cf Lk 22:66-23:1
Matthew and Mark describe a 'consultation' of the Jewish leaders in the morning. Matthew mentions the chief priests and the

65. Mark says: ' the same maidservant'.
66. He is not respecting Jesus' teaching on swearing oaths in the
Sermon on the Mount (Mt 5:33-37) or heeding his warning to the
Pharisees about swearing in the 'woes' against them (Mt 23:16-22).

elders of the people taking council together in order to put him to death. Mark mentions the chief priests, the elders and the scribes taking part.[67] 'Taking council together' (*symboulion elabon*) in the gospel so far has sinister overtones of plotting against Jesus. The Pharisees 'took council together' how to destroy Jesus after he healed the man on the Sabbath (Mt 12:14) and again 'took counsel together' to work out a plan to trap him in his speech (Mt 22:15). The chief priests will 'take council together' on buying the potter's field and, they will 'take counsel together' with the elders, on bribing the guards to say the disciples stole the body of Jesus (Mt 27:7; 28:12).

No details are given in Matthew or Mark of what took place on the fateful morning of Jesus' last day alive when the chief priests and elders of the people 'took counsel together' in order to put him to death. In Matthew's account of the night session the assembly answered the high priest's pointed question about what ought to be done saying: 'He deserves to die', *enochos thanatou estin*, but no explicit death sentence seems to have been passed. For Matthew the morning session completes the business of condemnation. If he had been formally condemned already why would it have been necessary to hold another court?[68] However, Mark's rendering of the decision taken during the night session is more explicit: 'They condemned him as deserving to die', *katekrinan auton enochon einai thanatou* (Mk 14:64). Luke gives no account of a session during the night and gives an account of the morning session more or less reflecting what Matthew and Mark say about the night session (Lk 22:66-23:1). John makes no mention of a morning session.

In all four accounts Jesus is brought to Pilate. Matthew says: 'They bound him and led him away and *handed him over* to Pilate.' Jesus' predictions of his passion are being fulfilled. He

---

67. Was it because the law required a second hearing, on the following day, before passing judgement in capital cases? Technically, in the Jewish way of reckoning the day from sunset to sunset, it would have been the same day.

68. It may be reminiscent of the rabbinic custom of allowing a day's lapse between two sessions of a trial on a capital offence.

has been rejected, suffered grievously, been condemned and is *being handed* over to the pagans.

e. The Remorse of Judas Mt 27:3-10

Peter has wept bitterly and now Matthew alone tells us that Judas, on seeing that Jesus was condemned, had a change of mind. Significantly the usual New Testament word for repentance *metanoia* or its verbal form *metanoein*, already used in the gospel by Matthew (Mt 3:2, 9, 11; 4:17) are not used. The verb *metamelêtheis*, is used for his change of mind. It is the same verb that was used for the son who refused to go into the vineyard to work for his father but then changed his mind (Mt 21:30). Was it genuine repentance on Judas' part or remorseful and guilty unease? Did Judas on hearing of Jesus' condemnation (which he may not have expected) remember the curse in Deuteronomy: 'Cursed be the one who takes a bribe to slay an innocent person' (Deut 27:25). He returned the thirty pieces of silver to the chief priests and the elders, saying; 'I have sinned in handing over innocent blood.' They rebuffed him with the comment: 'What is that to us? You see to it!' Their remark might be paraphrased: 'You did the dirt on him. You can live with it now! We are only doing our duty.'

According to Matthew, Judas threw back the money into the temple and then withdrew. He went out and hanged himself. The reader sees a parallel with the betrayal of David. When David withdrew from Jerusalem and ascended the Mount of Olives, grief stricken that his son Absalom had rebelled against him, he was greeted with the further shocking news that his close associate and adviser Ahitophel had betrayed him. Later, Ahitophel went and hanged himself (2 Sam 15:30-31; 17:23). The 'Son of David' has now been betrayed by a close associate who, in the story as told by Matthew, also hangs himself.

However, the chief priests realised that, though they had given the money themselves, (and so shared in the 'crime'), it was blood money and could not be put into the temple treasury, so 'taking counsel together' they decided to buy the potter's field with it as a burial ground for foreigners. The narrator adds: 'Therefore it has been called *field of blood* till this day.'[69]

True to his style, Matthew sees in the whole sordid affair the fulfilment of scripture. The betrayal by Judas, the evil machinations and deeds of the chief priests and elders and the resulting condemnation and fate of Jesus are therefore encompassed by the will and plan of God, though this does not excuse their evil deeds. In a quotation ascribed to Jeremiah, which is in fact a pastiche of allusions to Jeremiah and Zechariah, the narrator states: 'Then was fulfilled what was spoken by the prophet Jeremiah: "And they took the thirty pieces of silver, the price of the one for whom the price was set, on whom they had set a price from the sons of Israel, and they gave them for the potter's field, as the Lord directed me".'

A possible play on the Hebrew words *oser* (treasury) and *yoser* (potter), together with the reference to buying a field, and the field being used as a graveyard, and being called the potter's field opens up a series of allusions to Jeremiah whose visiting the potter (Jer 18), proclaiming that Tophet would become a burial ground for want of space (Jer 19:12), and buying the field (Jer 32:7), all conjure up the prophetic words and deeds of Jeremiah whose ministry and whose words against Jerusalem and the temple put him in danger of his life, foreshadowing the ministry and fate of Jesus. Matthew has already quoted Jeremiah by name (also in a mixed citation) in relation to the violent activity already directed at Jesus by the authorities at his birth (Mt 2:17). He is the major prophetic figure under whose umbrella other prophetic voices are gathered by Matthew.

---

69. The Acts of the Apostles, however, in the account of the meeting of the apostles to fill the vacancy left by Judas' departure, gives a different account of the death of Judas and of the origin of the name 'field of blood' (*Hakeldama* in Aramaic). The account says Judas bought the field with the money he got for his crime, that he 'fell forward' and his entrails scattered on the field and since everyone in Jerusalem heard of it, therefore it came to be known as *Hakeldama* (because of the 'blood money' paid for it, or because of the bloody end of its owner, or both?) (Acts 1:8-20).

5. THE ROMAN TRIAL BEFORE PILATE MT 27:11-31//MK 15:1-15 //LK 23:1-7, 13-25//JN 18:28-19:16

'Jesus stood before the governor.' The change of location from the house of the High Priest to the court of Pilate signals another major step in the story of Jesus' passion.[70] The sequence of events is following the third prediction of the passion: 'The Son of Man will be *handed over* to the chief priests and the scribes, and they will condemn him to death, and *hand him over* to the pagans to be mocked and scourged and crucified...' (Mt 20:18-19).

Matthew, Mark or Luke do not state why they did not execute him themselves (by stoning?) but took him to Pilate.[71] Neither do they describe any real surprise on Pilate's part at being presented with Jesus for trial. Does this reflect the fact that the Romans were already involved, as is implied by John in the reference to the 'cohort' of soldiers (*speira*) present at the arrest (Jn 18:12)?

The Roman trial is composed of three short episodes, each highlighting the theme of Jesus' 'political' kingship or his royal, messianic status, depending on one's point of view, whether it reflects the secular-political view of the Romans or the religious-political view of the Jews.

a. Pilate asks Jesus if he is the King of the Jews (a political term in Pilate's Gentile vocabulary) (Mt 27:11-14).

b. The hostile mob rejects 'Jesus called the Messiah' in favour of Barabbas, a 'notorious prisoner', *desmion episêmon*, (Mt 27:15-23).

c. Pilate hands Jesus over for crucifixion and the soldiers mock 'the King of the Jews' (Mt 27:27-31).

---

70. For recent studies on Pontius Pilate see H. K. Bond, *Pontius Pilate in History and Interpretation*, Cambridge and New York: CUP, 1998; and B. C. McGing, 'Pontius Pilate and the Sources,' *CBQ* 53 (1991) 416-38.

71. John, however, gives a reason: 'It is not permitted to us to put anyone to death'. Does this 'not permitted' refer to Roman or Mosaic Law? Scholars debate whether it is a pointer to their inability to secure a legitimate death sentence on Jesus in Jewish law or to the fact that the Romans had removed the power of capital punishment from them some time before the Jewish War. It is known that they lost the power of capital punishment some time before the Roman War in 66AD but exactly when is not known.

a. 'Are you the King of the Jews?' Mt 27:11-14

The governor (*hêgemôn*) immediately addresses Jesus on the matter that would have concerned his authority as Roman governor: 'Are you the King of the Jews?' a title that has a completely secular ring on the lips of Pilate, a Gentile.'[72] 'King of Israel', the title used later in mockery at the crucifixion is a more religious, messianic designation, on the lips of Jews (Mt 27:42 / / Mk 15:32). Jesus' response: *su legeis*, 'It is you who say it', parallels his response to the High Priest, *su eipas*. It functions on two levels. It does not deny his kingship, but it is a somewhat indirect way of affirming it without accepting the political overtones that he would rather avoid. It also says equivalently: 'Don't put words in my mouth to my legal detriment' or as a modern lawyer might say by way of objection: 'Don't lead the witness or the accused.' It implies that the question should not have been asked. However, the question and Jesus' response are central to his life and death since he has been described at his birth as King of the Jews by the magi (Mt 2:2), called Son of David throughout his ministry and his official death notice (*titulus*), displayed on the cross, will describe him as 'King of the Jews' (Mt 27:37).[73]

Another parallel to the Jewish trial follows as Jesus, to

---

72. Here again, Matthew reflects a tradition found in John. After the raising of Lazarus, when the Sanhedrin met, they were confronted with the question: 'What will we do, because this man does many signs? If we let him continue thus, everyone will believe in him' (Jn 11:47f). It was then Caiaphas had moved from the 'religious' concern to a 'political' one, presenting the danger that the Romans would come and destroy the holy place and the nation (Jn 11:48). After the triumphal entry into the city the Pharisees lamented to each other, 'Look, there is nothing you can do about it. The world has gone after him' (Jn 12:19). The Jews were primarily concerned with the religious implications of Jesus' activity, but they realised that these matters were of interest to the Romans only in so far as they had possible political implications and repercussions.

73. The death notice may well be the historical bedrock beneath the tradition of the trial. R. E. Brown, *The Death of the Messiah*, 1:729-32, suggests the Roman question about Jesus' claim to royal status may well be the oldest stratum in the Passion Narrative; similarly, J. Painter, *Mark's Gospel*, 199; cf N. A. Dahl, *The Crucified Messiah and Other Essays*, Minneapolis: Augsburg, 1974, 10-36.

Pilate's great amazement, again makes no reply and remains silent before the accusations of the chief priests and the elders, answering not even one of the charges. In this he is like the lamb dumb before the shearers, the Suffering Servant (Isa 53:7) and the just one abandoned by friends and surrounded by lying accusers (Ps 109:2-3). Throughout the litany of mockery that will surround him from here on until he expires on the cross, Jesus will remain silent until his final prayer of abandonment and the loud cry he utters as he dies (Mt 27:46, 50). Jesus' silence leaves Pilate completely perplexed at this point. Matthew (like Mark) does not elaborate on the accusations made by the Jewish authorities at this point.[74]

b. Jesus or Barabbas[75] *Mt 27:15-23//Mk 15:6-15//Jn 18:38-40; cf Lk 23:18-20*

All the gospels speak of the custom of releasing a prisoner of their choice to the crowd at the festival. Matthew says they held a *desmion episêmon*, a notorious prisoner, called Barabbas.[76] Matthew now mentions the crowd gathered for the customary release of a prisoner and Pilate sees it as an opportunity to release Jesus (lawfully according to custom) at the behest of the people (and so without leaving himself open to the charge of not punishing a criminal/rebel). He puts the question to the crowd: 'Whom do you want me to release to you, Barabbas or Jesus who is called Christ?' Pilate appears now not only to be non-condemnatory, but convinced of Jesus' innocence, aware of the motive of

---

74. Pilate's failure to condemn Jesus there and then in spite of the accusations brought by the Jewish authorities leaves the reader to wonder if they used their 'religious' arguments or switched to political ones, accusing him of aspiring to political or revolutionary power. Luke says they accused him of 'perverting our nation, and forbidding us to give tribute to Caesar, and saying that he himself is Christ, a king' and 'he stirs up the people' (Lk 23:2; 23:5). John says they accused him of claiming to be the Son of God, a fact that unnerved Pilate (Jn 19:7).

75. See the Appendix for a historical note on the Barabbas incident.

76. Some mss call him Jesus Barabbas, but the mss evidence is weak and the parallel seems somewhat forced as the people choose between Jesus Barabbas or Jesus called Christ.

those who handed him over (Mt 27:18). He knows they handed him over through *phthonos*, jealousy breeding malicious spitefulness, a vice described in the Book of Wisdom as the devil's motivation for bringing death into the world (Wis 2:24).[77]

At this juncture a story told only by Matthew tells of the message sent to Pilate sitting on the judgement seat,[78] from his wife, telling him that he should have nothing to do with 'that just man' because she had suffered much over him in a dream on that day. The account of this intervention is very typical of Matthew as it describes an action in response to a 'revelation' in a dream and also describes Jesus in Matthew's favourite phrase, *dikaios*, 'a just man'. Like the woman who anointed Jesus in Bethany, this woman shines out also in the midst of the story of lethal plotting and intrigue, and in this case the woman was a Gentile. By way of contrast, the chief priests and the elders persuade the crowds to ask for Barabbas and so destroy Jesus.

However, the pressure from the chief priests and the elders that failed to convince Pilate is successful in turning the crowd against Jesus and in favour of Barabbas. When the governor puts the choice of the two before the crowd they ask for (Jesus) Barabbas. Pilate asked: 'What then shall I do with Jesus who is called Christ?' They all said: 'Let him be crucified!' Pilate responded: 'What evil has he done?' But they shouted all the more 'Let him be crucified!'

Only Matthew tells us that at this point, when he realised he was not making any headway with the crowd, and that a riot was breaking out, Pilate took water and washed his hands before the crowd saying: 'I am innocent of the blood of this man.[79]

---

77. See A. C. Hagedorn and J. H. Neyrey, 'It Was Out of Envy that They Handed Jesus Over (Mark 15:10): The Anatomy of Envy and the Gospel of Mark,' *JSNT* 69 (1998),15-56.

78. The judgement seat was set up in front of the palace where Pilate was lodging in Jerusalem. Traditionally it was believed to be at the Antonia Fortress beside the Temple area. Recent scholarly opinion is inclined to suggest that Pilate in fact lodged at Herod's palace, the citadel beside the modern Jaffa Gate.

79. Some mss have Matthew's favourite word *dikaios*, 'this *righteous* man's blood'.

See to it yourselves.' The same phrase 'See to it yourself' was used by the Jewish authorities when Judas wanted to give back the money saying he had betrayed innocent blood. It signifies 'It is your responsibility and your guilt.' Washing one's hands, as a sign of innocence in the case of bloodshed, is a custom testified to in the Old Testament (Deut 21:6-9; Ps 26:6-10; Isa 1:15-16).

In response to Pilate's protestation of innocence 'all the people' answered: 'Let his blood be upon us and upon our children.' Matthew's remark, 'They all said: "Let him be crucified"' and the cry of all the people: 'His blood be on us and on our children' need to be put in historical context. Who are the 'all'? Up to this point in the narrative the spotlight has been on the chief priests, the elders and the scribes and their urging on of the crowds. Now there is a significant shift from 'the crowds' (*hoi ochloi*) to 'the whole people' (*pas ho laos*), meaning Israel as a whole. Matthew is here reflecting on the fulfilment of the warning to 'Jerusalem that kills the prophets' that 'upon you may come all the righteous blood shed on earth '(Mt 23:35). The parable of the wedding feast had described the violent reaction of the king to the murder of the messengers in terms of the destruction of the murderers and the burning of their city (Mt 22:7). Matthew is viewing the situation from the perspective of the horrific blood-shed and destruction of the Roman War, the destruction of Jerusalem and the burning of its temple. As the Deuteronomistic historian(s), commenting on the Exile after the destruction of the temple and city in 587BC, pointed out how the people had brought the punishment on themselves by doing what was displeasing to *YHWH* and not listening to and ill treating the prophets and messengers, so too in Matthew's view it is the people who have brought this latest disaster on themselves.

Pilate, then released Barabbas to them and having had Jesus scourged, *handed him over* to be crucified (Mt 27:26).

c. Mocking the King of the Jews Mt 27:27-31

Having been scourged, Jesus was *handed over* to be crucified. The customary scourging was a preliminary to crucifixion, starting

the flow of blood and weakening the victim so that the crucifixion would not drag on too long.[80] The physical abuse was followed by what the bible portrays as the greatest personal abuse,
mockery, which aims to destroy the person's self worth and
identity and, in the religious context, to ridicule the person's
faith and hope in the God who saves. Mockery is the backdrop
to his unjust condemnation and execution. It will be the dominant note struck throughout Jesus' final hours. In the biblical
tradition mocking the good man's faith and hope is the ultimate
weapon in the attempted destruction of the victim. The passion
and death of Jesus are steeped in a context of mockery. The attendants of the high priest mock him as a false prophet (Mt
26:67-68). The Roman soldiers mock him in political terms as a
pathetic pretender to the status of King of the Jews (Mt 27:27-31).
His Jewish opponents and passers-by mock him in religious
terms parodying his messianic identity and his saving work, his
relationship with God and his standing as King of Israel (Mt
27:39-44).

The soldiers of the governor took Jesus into the Praetorium
(the governor's residence when he was in Jerusalem) and gathered the whole cohort (*holên tên speiran*). They stripped him, put
a scarlet robe/cloak around him, and having plaited a crown of
thorns they put it on his head and a reed in his right hand.
Kneeling before him they mocked him, saying, 'Hail, King of the
Jews!' They thus mocked his kingship, a political model of kingship he never claimed. They spat on him and took the reed and
struck him on the head. In the third prediction of the passion
(Mt 20:18-19) Jesus had foretold how he would be handed over

---

80. The placing of the scourging and mockery of kingship in the middle
of the Roman trial in John (Jn 19:1-3) seems to be for literary and theological reasons as the central position in a chiasm (a concentric arrangement of the elements in a pericope) highlights the theme, in this case the
theme of kingship which dominates all four gospel accounts. The synoptic account which places the scourging (and accompanying mockery)
at the end of the Roman trial is more in keeping with the historical facts
where scourging was a preliminary to crucifixion, carried out after the
passing of the death sentence.

to the pagans and mocked and scourged and crucified. Just as he was mocked as prophet and Messiah at the High Priest's palace, so too here the mockery revolves around the charges and their (mis)understanding of his identity as 'King of the Jews'. When they had finished mocking him they removed the purple cloak, put on his own clothes and led him away to crucifixion.

The Passion Narratives in the gospels all pick up on this theme of mockery that is so dominant in the psalms of lamentation. In his response to the mockery, the true nature of Jesus' kingship is highlighted in the calm dignity he displays in the face of the mock coronation, robing, royal salute and acts of obeisance. He thus turns the trappings of blind power and kingship without principle back on themselves in the countersigns of a crown of thorns, a purple robe stained with blood, and a mocking salutation. The unjust torture of the one already declared innocent places Jesus at the epicentre of human suffering and the mockery highlights his kingship of the servants of God and of all suffering humanity.

The crowning with thorns as depicted in art emphasises the suffering from the thorns piercing the skin and causing blood to flow, with accompanying discomfort and pain. However, this is not the main emphasis of the gospel and in fact it misses the real point of the exercise. Mockery is the motive. Statues and pictures of gods, heroes and 'divinised' emperors showed them not only with a crown of various designs, but even more strikingly a halo of radiating beams of light around their heads. The plaited large thorn bough imitated this 'radiating' image or halo and was a blatant mockery of kingship and divinity. It was accompanied by the purple cloak and reed in the hand, symbols of imperial dignity and office, and by the mock obsequiousness of the soldiers' salutation of the emperor. This is as ironic as it is significant. The first readers of the gospels would have been very familiar with the role of the military in making and unmaking emperors. The ultimate power rested with them especially since the murder of Caligula by the Praetorian Guard and their forcing the Senate to accept Claudius as emperor (41AD). Their power and influence had been very much in evidence ever afterwards in the unmaking and making of a series of emperors from the suicide of Nero, because of a military threat, to the accession of Vespasian in the year of the four emperors, all created by the military in 68-69AD.[81] Their king-making power is displayed here in the mock coronation and salutation of Jesus.

The reader knows that the divine source of all power is revealed through Jesus and the apparently all-powerful mocker is ultimately powerless. The irony is striking. The one who is in a position to mock a victim appears to be all-powerful in dealing with him. The two powers are here placed side by side, the worldly power represented by the might of Rome, apparently omnipotent, the other, the power of the kingdom proclaimed by Jesus, apparently impotent and defeated. The unfolding story will reverse them and, just as the Roman military mocked the 'King of the Jews', their commander and representative, the centurion, together with the others guarding Jesus, will be the first to acknowledge the status of the one they have mocked as 'truly Son of God' (Mt 27:54).

The striking of his head places Jesus in the company of all those represented by the Songs of the Suffering Servant of (Deutero-)Isaiah[82] and the persecuted righteous one of the Wisdom tradition whose enemies 'test him with insult and torture' and 'test what will happen at the end of his life' (Wis 2:17-20). In Matthew, as in Mark, Jesus is stripped of his 'kingly' attire after the mock ceremony and led to crucifixion.[83]

Jesus has now been *handed over* by a disciple, *handed over* by the Jewish 'court', *handed over* by the Roman court and is crucified. All shared in the guilt of his judicial execution. R. E. Brown puts it succinctly:

For neither Jew nor Roman was it enough that Jesus die; his

---

81. Galba, Otho, Vitellius and Vespasian.
82. Isa 42:1-9; 49:1-6; 50:4-9; 52:13–53:12.
83. In Luke's gospel the mockery takes place in Herod's court and he is sent back to Pilate in the robe Herod bestowed on him in mockery. In John's gospel he goes to his death robed and crowned as a king.

claims had to be derided. In a sequence where Judas hands Jesus over to the chief priests, and the chief priests hand Jesus over to Pilate, and Pilate hands Jesus over to be crucified, it becomes clear that disciple, Jewish leader, and Roman leader all have a share of guilt.[84]

Theological and Political Apologetics

Matthew does not show an agonising or dithering Pilate, just a calculating business-like official who asks, in response to the call of the mob for his crucifixion, 'What evil has he done?' and then without scruple in spite of his own implicit judgement of innocence (and the pleading of his wife), hands Jesus over, under pressure from the mob, in spite of the fact that there seemed to be no case against him. He did so in order to placate the hostile crowd who, under pressure from the Jewish authorities, had rejected Jesus in favour of Barabbas. In this way Matthew continues to emphasise the role of the Jewish authorities. The gospels, for apologetic and theological reasons, put emphasis on Pilate's predicament in order to show that he was placed in a no-win situation by pressure from the Jewish authorities and the crowd, (and under threat of a report being sent to the emperor according to Jn 19:12). From a theological point of view the rejection of Jesus and his claims by the legitimate Jewish authorities and their scholars/legal experts was of great religious significance, just as Pilate's confirmation of Jesus' innocence was of great political significance for Jesus' followers, particularly in the succeeding decades when they were under suspicion and suffered persecution and hostility from the officials of the empire and society at large.[85]

6. AT THE PLACE OF THE SKULL (GOLGOTHA) MT 27:31-56

'When they had mocked him, they stripped him of the robe, and put his own clothes on him, and led him away to crucify him' (Mt 27:31). The change of location from the Praetorium to the

---

84. R. E. Brown, *A Crucified Christ in Holy Week*, 29.
85. See the appendix on Pilate at the end of the commentary for a historical note on his character and period in office.

place of crucifixion marks the beginning of the final dramatic episode in Jesus' life.[86] The accounts of the crucifixion, while avoiding any concentration on the physical cruelty involved, are laden with allusions to Psalms 22 and 69, prayers of lamentation on the lips of the suffering just one. R. E. Brown makes a very important point in the introduction to his book, *A Crucified Christ in Holy Week*:

> ... we should reflect on what Jesus' passion meant to Christians of the NT period, using the gospels as a guide. It is noteworthy that many features depicted by later artists and writers have no place in the gospel accounts, for instance elements of pathos and emotion, and a concentration on pain and suffering. On Calvary, the evangelists report laconically 'they crucified him' without reference to the manner. Strikingly, however, they pay attention to the division of his garments and to the exact placement of the criminals crucified with him. Such details were important to the early Christians because they found them anticipated in OT psalms and prophets. Not biography but theology dominated the choice of events to be narrated, and the OT was the theological source book at the time. (This approach is far more likely than the skeptical contention that the Christians created the details of the passion in order to fulfil the OT.)[87]

a. The King of the Jews is Crucified Mt 27:31-38
As they led him out to crucify him they came upon a man of Cyrene, Simon by name, and enlisted him to carry his cross.[88]

---

86. For a study of crucifixion in the ancient world, see J. A. Fitzmyer, 'Crucifixion in Ancient Palestine, Qumran Literature, and the New Testament,' *CBQ* 40 (1979) 493-513 and M. Hengel, *Crucifixion in the Ancient World and the Folly of the Message of the Cross*, Philadelphia: Fortress, 1977. See also T. E. Schmidt, 'Mark 15:16-32: The Crucifixion Narrative and the Roman Triumphal Procession,' *NTS* 41 (1995) 1-18; and E. Bammel, 'Crucifixion as a Punishment in Palestine,' in E. Bammel (ed), *The Trial of Jesus*, 162-165.
87. R. E. Brown, *A Crucified Christ in Holy Week*, 18.
88. Only Mark tells us that he was father of Alexander and Rufus, two persons probably known to the intended readers of Mark's gospel.

Cyrene is in North Africa and so Simon may have been a pilgrim from the Diaspora for the Passover. Willingly or not, Simon found himself in a role that identifies the true disciple, 'taking up his cross.'[89] As the cross of Jesus becomes his to carry he has also become, in the broader Christian tradition, a model of Christian service to those in need.[90]

At the scene of the crucifixion, Golgotha, they offered Jesus wine mixed with gall which, on tasting, he refused to drink. This is the only compassionate action in the cruel scenario. As Matthew and Mark tell the story, it appears to be the Roman soldiers who offered the drink. It may, however, be a reminiscence in the tradition of an action usually done by compassionate women from Jerusalem, perhaps like those lamenting Jesus' treatment in Luke's account (Lk 23:27f). The tradition of offering a drink to kill the pain is mentioned in the Talmud, reflecting Prov 31:6f.[91] However, as it stands in Matthew and Mark it appears to be the action of the soldiers. Refusing the drink emphasises Jesus' willingness to accept in full consciousness the suffering laid down for him by the will of, and in the design of, the

---

Mark's description of Simon as 'coming from the country', has sometimes been used in arguments about whether he was coming from work in the fields, and therefore a pointer to the fact that it was not the day of the Passover Feast. The reference, however, may simply be a statement of the direction he was following. It may even be pointing out that 'coming from the country' meant he was a pilgrim approaching the city *en route* to the Passover Festival and was unaware of the commotion in the city surrounding the impending executions, and happened upon them suddenly. It may also be the case that able-bodied men avoided these occasions lest they find themselves dragooned into a situation like Simon was and so the information in Mark that he was coming from the country and unaware of what was happening may be an explanation of how he got involved.

89. Luke adds, 'behind Jesus' (Lk 23:26), a further emphasis on the imagery of a disciple 'taking up his cross and following Jesus'.

90. The Johannine tradition does not mention Simon or his involvement. It emphasises Jesus' control and independence throughout the Passion Narrative. M. D. Hooker, *op. cit.*, 372, points out that John may also have been reacting against Gnostic assertions that it was Simon and not Jesus who was crucified.

91. *b. Sanh.* 43a, reflecting Prov 31:6-7.

Father. Psalm 69:21 comes to mind as one reads of his being offered wine mixed with gall.[92] They divided his garments by casting lots, and then sat down and kept watch over him there.
Personal effects such as clothing were seen as the property of the
executioners. Ps 22:18 comes to mind when lots are cast for his
clothes. Ps 22 will be quoted when he calls out 'My God, my
God, why have you forsaken me?' These biblical allusions put
Jesus' suffering in the context of the just person making lamentation to God in the psalms.

Over his head they placed the *titulus*, the charge against him
which stated: 'This is Jesus, the King of the Jews.' This brings the
royal acclamations to an ironic climax now in Jesus' being raised
up in the view of all with the notice of his crime, 'This is Jesus,
King of the Jews' above his head, pointing to the crime for which
he is being crucified. It is an ironic statement of truth. Matthew,
Mark and Luke note how the two crucified with Jesus were put
one on his right and the other on his left. John states that he was
crucified with two others, one on either side, with Jesus in the
middle' (Jn 19:18). The mother of the sons of Zebedee had
sought for her sons the positions at his right and left (Mt 20:20-
23), not realising the nature of Jesus' kingdom and kingship!
Now she will figure in Matthew's list of the women who
watched the crucifixion from a distance (Mt 27:56). Jesus is now
reckoned with the unrighteous, with two robbers/bandits.[93]
When they had come to arrest him in the garden, Jesus had
asked: 'Have you come out as against a robber/brigand with
swords and clubs to arrest me?'(Mt 26:55). Significantly he now
ends his life in the midst of brigands.

The reference to the actual crucifixion is brief, stark and to

---

92. Mk 15:23 says the wine was mixed with myrrh. Matthew is aligning
the statement with 'wine mixed with gall' in Ps 69:13.
93. *Lêstai*, means robbers or bandits (Mt 27:38,44//Mk 15:27) with connotations of activity of a revolutionary nature; *kakourgoi*, 'evildoers' is
used in Lk 23:33; John just says 'two others' (Jn 19:18). *Lêstai* was used of
the buyers and sellers in the Temple in calling it a 'den of robbers' (Mt
21:13), and when Jesus was arrested he asked: 'Have you come out as
against a *lêstês*?'(Mt 26:55).

the point. It was probably not necessary to elaborate on it in any ancient document since it was widely practised, and therefore well known and feared as a form of execution in the ancient world. The Romans used it for slaves, serious criminals and those who rebelled against Roman rule. The victim was fixed naked to the cross to die slowly, possibly over a number of days, struggling for breath in a constant action of raising the body to breathe against the pressure of the ropes and/or nails keeping the body fixed to the cross. In addition there was the excruciating pain from the preliminary flogging and the crucifixion itself, and the torment from sun, thirst, insects and the taunts of whoever wished to express a mocking opinion. That nails were used to affix Jesus to the cross is known from the reference to the marks of the nails in Jn 20:25 (and by implication from the references to his hands and feet in Lk 24:39f). Several ancient writers commented on the horror of crucifixion. Josephus called it 'the most pitiable of deaths'[94] and Cicero the Roman philosopher and orator spoke of it as 'a most cruel and disgusting penalty' and 'the extreme and ultimate penalty for a slave.'[95] It was a form of execution designed not only to inflict physical pain, but also to humiliate and shame the victim and thus obliterate his memory and eliminate any possible following he may have gathered in life. This was a very important consideration in a society that put such emphasis on honour and shame, and particularly on honourable death as the final crowning of the honourable life of a teacher of wisdom, philosophy or religion. It is no wonder that Jesus' death was to prove, in the words of Paul to the Corinthians 'a stumbling block to the Jews and foolishness to the Gentiles' (1 Cor 1:23). The crucifixion was usually carried out in a public place as a deterrent to other malefactors. The Aramaic name, Golgotha, is interpreted as 'the place of the skull', probably indicating the shape of a low lying mound of earth near the roadway approaching the city gates, a place of maximum exposure and most effective deterrent.

---

94. Josephus, *War*, 7.203.
95. Cicero, *In Verrem*, 2.5.64, 66.

b. Mockery of the crucified Mt 27:39-44

The passers-by 'blaspheme' him, bowing their heads. Ironically Matthew uses the verb 'blaspheme'. Jesus had been accused of blasphemy. Now as he himself is 'blasphemed', the two charges levelled against him during his Jewish and Roman trials will be used against him in mockery. The passers-by, reflecting the two charges at the Jewish trial say: 'You who would destroy the temple and build it in three days, save yourself' and 'If you are the Son of God come down from the cross.' The officials who opposed Jesus, the chief priests, the scribes and the elders, also have their mocking say: 'He saved others, he cannot save himself.' Ironically their mocking comment at the same time bears testimony to the fact of Jesus' saving work! They, too, challenge him to come down from the cross as a proof of his claims: 'He is the King of Israel; let him come down now from the cross and we will believe in him. He trusts in God; let God deliver him now, if he wants him; for he said: "I am the Son of God".' The robber/bandits crucified with him also insulted/reproached him.

As noted already one of the very dominant aspects of the suffering encountered by the just one in the Psalms of lamentation is mockery. The gesture of wagging their heads recalls the words of Ps 22:7: 'All who see me mock at me, they make mouths at me, they wag their heads', and of Lam 2:15: 'All who pass along the way clap their hands at you; They hiss and wag their heads at daughter Jerusalem.' The scoffing exclamation recalls Ps 35:21: 'They open wide their mouths against me; they say "Aha! Aha! Our eyes have seen it".' Similar sentiments are found in Pss 40:15 and 70:4.

The triple mockery, by passers-by, by the chief priests, scribes and elders and by those crucified with him, is skilfully used to embrace the full theological canvas of the gospel story. The passers-by mock him in the terms of the charge brought against him at the Jewish trial about threatening to destroy the temple and to rebuild it in three days, claiming to be the Son of

God, and they challenge him to save himself and come down from the cross.[96]

The chief priests, the scribes and the elders mocked him saying: 'He saved others, he cannot save himself!'[97] Ironically their mockery is a testimony to the 'saving work' of Jesus during his ministry and how he fulfilled his claim that he had come to serve others rather than to be served himself, and eventually to give his life 'as a ransom for many'. Their mockery continued with: 'He is the King of Israel. Let him come down from the cross now so that we can see and believe.' In suggesting that he come down from the cross, they are suggesting that he vacate the place where he is King of the Jews, the King of Israel. Here his enemies are demanding that 'seeing and believing' be facilitated on their own terms and that he come down from the cross so that they would see and believe. Matthew and Luke, in their accounts of the temptations in the desert, proleptically presenting the temptations that would surface in his ministry, spoke of the 'religious sign', throwing himself from the pinnacle of the temple so that the angels, in keeping with the promise of Psalm 91, would protect him and by implication people would see and believe (Mt 4:5-6//Lk 4:9-12). Here, in the very real circumstances of the crucifixion, Jesus encounters a very similar temptation on the mocking lips of his enemies.

The real sting, however, comes in Matthew's account of the mockery of the foundations of Jesus' faith and hope: 'He trusts in God; let God deliver him now, if he wants him, for he said: "I am the Son of God".' The echoes of Psalm 22 are heard also in the mocking comment about God coming to save him: 'Let him rescue the one in whom he delights' (Ps 22:8). Ironically their blasphemy is a proclamation of the truth of Jesus' kingship, and

---

96. Ironically it is precisely in dying on the cross that he is establishing the temple not made by hands, built on the rejected cornerstone. His teaching to those who would follow him as disciples had emphasised the fact that to save one's life one must lose it, and in losing one's life one saves it (Mt 16:25; 10:39).

97. Mark says they mocked him 'among themselves', probably at a safe and dignified distance from what was happening!

significantly it is articulated in the more 'religious' term, 'King of Israel,' rather than the more secular 'King of the Jews'.

To round off this 'cascade of abuse'[98] Matthew (like Mark) refers back to the opening of this scene with the reference to those crucified with him and points out that even those sharing his terrible suffering and death mock him. Jesus is now isolated to the point of not even sharing the company and mutual fellow feeling of those executed with him. He will die alone and in agony with the mockery of enemies resounding in his ears.

c. Darkness over the earth and the cry of Jesus Mt 27:45-49

The death of Jesus is set between the great cosmic sign (the darkened sun) accompanied by the cry of Jesus and the great sign in Israel (the torn veil of the Temple and the earthquake with the appearance of the dead) accompanied by the cry/confession of the centurion and those with him guarding Jesus.[99]

Matthew, Mark and Luke describe the apocalyptic darkness over the whole land/the whole earth from the sixth to the ninth hour, that is from noon to 3 pm, when the sun is normally at its brightest. It is reminiscent of the prophecy of Amos about the Day of the Lord when the land will be visited by the judgement of God: 'It will mean darkness, not light' and on the day of punishment God 'will make the sun go down at noon and darken the earth in broad daylight' (Amos 5:18; 8:9). Jesus had spoken to the disciples in his apocalyptic discourse about the frightening portents that would herald the end time: 'In those days the sun will be darkened, and the moon will not give its light' (Mt 24:29, quoting Isa 13:10). Now the death of Jesus is heralded by such a sign. This darkness is more than a literary 'pathetic fallacy' or alignment of natural phenomena with a terrible event. It is more than the ancient belief in signs and portents heralding the deaths of great people and the approach of significant tragic events.[100] It

---

98. D. Senior. *The Passion of Jesus in the Gospel of Mark,* 117.
99. See D. Ulansey, 'The Heavenly Veil Torn: Mark's Cosmic Inclusio,' *JBL* 110 (1991) 123-125.
100. It was common belief that the deaths of great people were marked by signs and wonders.

is the harbinger of an eschatological event in the history of salvation. The reader is being made aware that the moment of God's definitive intervention into the human story has arrived.[101] The darkness 'covers the whole earth'. 'Covering the whole earth' is not just a 'geographic' reference, but also a theological statement of the universal nature of the eschatological event taking place and of its significance for all nations.[102]

'The solemn marking of the hours is perhaps intended to remind us that what is taking place is in accordance with God's plan and is the fulfilment of his purpose.'[103] 'The reader is led up to the death of Jesus through a foreboding tunnel of gloom.'[104] The darkness comes about during the time of the day when the sun should be at its brightest. The mention of the hours, from the sixth to the ninth hour (12 noon to 3 pm) highlights the divine nature of the sign, as in the prophecy of Amos that describes the day of darkness when the sun goes down at noon (Amos 5:18; 8:9).

About the ninth hour Jesus pierces the eschatological darkness as he breaks his silence and screams (*aneboêsen*) with a loud cry (*phônê megalê*). 'The lament of Jesus issues from the darkness leading up to the fateful ninth hour'.[105] His lament: 'My God, my God, why have you forsaken me?'(Mt 27:46) is the opening verse of Psalm 22 and it is here quoted by Matthew in Hebrew: *Eli, Eli, lama sabachthani* and then translated into Greek for the readers. (Mark quotes the psalm in Jesus' mother tongue, Aramaic, (*Eloi, Eloi, lama sabachthani*). Quoting the psalm, Jesus addresses his Father, not with the familiar 'my Father', but as 'my God', and in so doing is completely identified with all those who address God in lamentation from a situation of total isolation and appar-

---

101. F. J. Moloney, *op. cit.*, 325.
102. R. E. Brown, *Death of the Messiah*, 2:1036.
103. M. D. Hooker, *op. cit.*, 373.
104. D. Senior, *The Passion of Jesus according to Mark*, 122; See also V. Taylor, *op. cit.*, 593; R. E. Brown, *Death of the Messiah*, Vol 2, 1035f traces the allusions to the theme of light and darkness right through the Old Testament.
105. D. Senior, *The Passion of Jesus in the Gospel of Mark*, 124.

ent abandonment. It is a cry of faith, a prayer when all supports
are taken away, an address to God when all that is left is naked
faith in the face of torment and abandonment, when even God
appears to have turned away. Though the psalm goes on to develop the themes of faith and hope in God's deliverance and
thanksgiving for that deliverance, the sense of the citation in
Matthew (and Mark) is that of the opening description of utter
desolation of the one who calls out to God in the words 'I cry by
day and you give no reply, I cry by night and find no peace' (Ps
22:2). Jesus has denied himself everything, even the sense of
closeness to the Father as his intimate 'my Father' address in
prayer has been replaced with the anguished cry to a 'distant'
God. Paul describes Jesus' humility in taking on the human condition as an 'emptying of self' in his obedience 'unto death, even
death on a cross' (Phil 2:8), which Paul elsewhere describes as
'becoming a curse' (Gal 3:13) or 'being made sin' (2 Cor 5:21),
both emphasising the total oneness of Jesus with the human situation of being alienated from God and under judgement of the
Law.

However, as F. J. Moloney points out so succinctly, 'Jesus'
focus is entirely upon God, however desperate his cry.'[106] As he
cries out in abandonment some of the bystanders think he is calling Elijah and one ran, took a sponge full of sour wine, placed it
on a reed and offered it to him to drink. The others mockingly
said: 'Leave it! Let us see if Elijah comes to rescue him.' It was
widely believed that Elijah would come to the aid of the righteous in their need and there are many accounts in rabbinic literature of such appearances of Elijah.[107]

All four gospels speak of the offer of the drink, but in different ways. Luke portrays it as a deliberately mocking gesture on
the part of the soldiers, offering him cheap wine and saying:
'Save yourself if you are the King of the Jews' (Lk 23:36), a
provocation which calls to mind Ps 69:21 with its mocking of the

106. F. J. Moloney, op.cit., 327.
107. The expectation had it roots in 1 Kings 17:1-24 and was developed
in rabbinic literature. F. J. Moloney, op. cit., 327, n 270, lists several examples.

just one with poison for food and vinegar for drink. In Jn 19:29 the drink of cheap wine is offered in response to Jesus' cry, 'I thirst'. It seems to be offered by a soldier. In Matthew and Mark the drink is offered when Jesus calls out the first line of Ps 22. The offer of the drink and the reference to Elijah are linked together in Matthew and Mark, though it is more likely the wine (*oxos*) was the cheap wine drunk by the soldiers (as in Jn 19:29), whereas the comment about Elijah was more likely from a Jewish onlooker. Both reactions, offering the drink and the saying about Elijah, seem to have been fused together in the tradition. Matthew quotes the verse in Hebrew, '*Eli, Eli ...*' which scholars believe is more likely to have been original since it is more easily mistaken for a call to Elijah, than the Aramaic '*Elôi, Elôi ...*'[108]

d. The Death of Jesus Mt 27:50; Mk 15:37; Lk 23:46; Jn 19:30

Jesus, having cried out again in a loud voice, the implication being that he repeats the sentiments of Psalm 22, gave up the spirit (*aphêken to pneuma*). This is a deliberate act of returning the breath of life to the Father (rather than a reference to the Holy Spirit as in Jn 19:30). It is close to the account in Luke where Jesus' cites Psalm 31, 'Father into your hands I commend my spirit' and then 'expired' (*exepneusen*). In Mark's account Jesus 'screams and expires' (*exepneusen*) (Mk 15:37). In John Jesus leans his head forward and hands over the Spirit to the representative group, the incipient messianic community around the cross and dies with a statement of completion and deliberateness, of having fulfilled all the Father gave him to do, 'it is finished' (*tetelesthai*) (Jn 19:30).

e. Signs and Portents. The Romans' Reaction Mt 27:51-54

As Jesus died, the veil of the temple was torn in two from top to

---

108. It was widely believed that Elijah, who was taken up into heaven (2 Kings 2:11f) would come to inaugurate the time of the Messiah. But, as the reader knows, Matthew and Mark have already described the coming of Elijah to prepare the way in the person of John the Baptist, and he too had been put to death!

bottom.'[109] For all the evangelists, the death of Jesus was intimately linked to the destruction of the temple and the emergence of a new temple. Matthew has consistently shown the temple and Jerusalem in negative light in his gospel. The action of Jesus in the temple, combined with the parabolic words/action of the withering of the fig tree sounded a loud prophetic-style condemnation of the temple and a clear prediction of its demise (Mt 21:18-19). His words re-echoed the threat of Jeremiah against the temple when he called it a den of thieves and predicted it would share the destructive fate of Shiloh (Mt 21:13; Jer 7:8-15). At the conclusion of the parable of the wicked tenants Jesus spoke about the stone rejected by the builders and its destiny to be the cornerstone, understood in terms of the cornerstone of a new temple (Mt 21:42). As he left the temple for the last time he predicted that 'not one stone would be left upon another' (Mt 24:2). During his Jewish trial (Mt 26:61) the false witnesses accused him of threatening to destroy the temple and in three days to build it up. As he hung on the cross he was taunted by the passers-by with his reported sayings about the temple (Mt 27:40). Now as he dies the first reported result is the very significant happening right at the heart of the temple as the veil of the temple is torn in two from top to bottom.

There were two veils both described as *to katapetasma* (Exod 26:33,37; LXX) and the text does not specify which is meant. One veil covered the outer entrance and door and so could be seen by all, even by Gentiles who were forbidden to enter the sanctuary. The other veil (without an accompanying door) covered the entrance to the Holy of Holies, the most sacred part of the temple, where the High Priest entered the Divine Presence once a year on the Day of Atonement, *Yom Kippur*, to make reparation for the sins of the people.[110] It is the opinion of most scholars that

---

109. Scholars debate whether the veil mentioned is the veil dividing the outer and inner part of the temple or the veil enclosing the Holy of Holies. Probably the evangelists are not thinking of the distinction, but in a general way of the veiling of God's presence.

110. Josephus similarly describes them, *Ant* 8:3.3.

this is the veil intended by the evangelists. However, symbolically, the tearing of either or both provides a powerful symbol of the judgement of God at the very core of the most holy centre of Israel.[111] Matthew and Mark see the tearing of the veil primarily in terms of divine judgement, but another, positive, dimension must also be remembered. The tearing of the veil signifies the opening up to all and sundry of the previously hidden presence of God and of the approach to the mercy seat.[112] 'A new temple is built on the destroyed body of Jesus as privileged access to the old temple comes to an end.'[113]

The tearing of the veil of the temple is followed by a series of portents, described only by Matthew, that happen at the death and resurrection of Jesus.

The description of the earthquake with the shaking of the earth and the splitting of the rocks[114] is reminiscent of the theophany of the Day of *YHWH* as the great apocalyptic judgement approached (cf Amos 1:2). The opening of the tombs and the appearance in the holy city of the risen bodies of the saints who had fallen asleep is a graphic presentation, very likely drawn from Ezekiel's vision of the graveyard where the dry bones were brought back to life (Ezek 37:1-14), of the same truth which Paul described in 1 Cor 15:20-23, namely, that Jesus 'is the first fruits of all who have fallen asleep ... as all die in Adam all are brought to life in Christ.' Matthew somewhat awkwardly inserts the 'after his resurrection' into the middle of the events accompanying Jesus' death.

In response to the portents taking place the centurion and

111. Matthew and Mark share a negative view of Jerusalem and the temple, but Luke has a very positive view throughout, and in this instance sees the tearing of the veil as an 'opening', the revelation to all nations of the inner sanctum with its mercy seat (Lk 23:45).
112. This is the primary emphasis of Luke who has a positive attitude to the temple throughout the gospel (Lk 23:45).
113. F. J. Moloney, *op. cit.*, 330.
114. Christian art has imaginatively portrayed the skull of Adam underneath the place of the cross, and portrayed the blood of Jesus flowing onto the skull of Adam through a fissure in the rock, symbolising the universality of salvation for all humankind.

those with him guarding Jesus were greatly afraid and said: 'Truly this man was the Son of God.'[115] The centurion's confession 'on seeing how he died' in Mark becomes in Matthew a chorus of voices affirming belief in this man on seeing such signs accompanying his death.

Exactly how they understood their profession of faith at that moment can only be a matter of speculation. In a Roman's religious vocabulary, to proclaim someone son of a God or of a divine being was the greatest accolade possible as, for example, when Augustus was proclaimed *Filius Divi Julii*. The soldiers were here presented with a whole new religious scenario focused on the person of Jesus and, on seeing the portents, professed their belief in him and what he stood for by using their 'holiest' vocabulary.

Jesus' own people had taunted him, saying he had claimed to be Son of God, with the challenge to come down from the cross so that they would believe. In this great twist of irony at the end of the gospel, the centurion and the soldiers who were pagans and representatives of the greatest power in the world, whose cohort had mocked Jesus as King of the Jews with royal apparel and imperial salute, are now moved to faith in him precisely as 'Son of God'.

Their confession reflects the words of the Father at the Baptism and Transfiguration and the confession of some believers during the ministry. These foreigners, 'outsiders', acknowledge the crucified one as the Son of God. They become a sign of the community's future mission to the nations and they take their place alongside other 'outsiders' who had been magnetised by Jesus' presence while the family of Jesus, the leaders of Israel,

---

115. The Greek expression *huios theou* does not have the definite article and so has at times been translated as 'a son of God'. The Semitic construct case does not use the article and a very direct translation from a Hebrew or Aramaic idiom in the earliest tradition would probably not have the article either. Furthermore, if the centurion spoke Latin, there is no definite article and Filius *Dei/Dei* Filius would be translated exactly as *theou huios*.

and at times the disciples had remained dull and uncomprehending.[116]

Their words are the words used in the confession of Christian faith, and they are found on the lips of Gentiles at the moment of Jesus' death.[117] The representatives of the military might of Rome, whose soldiers earlier mocked Jesus with the trappings of earthly kingship and imperial power, now witness to the reversal of status and roles as earthly power gives way to the divine power shining through apparent human weakness, folly and failure.[118]

f. The Watching Women Mt 27:55-56//Mk 15:40-41

'There were many women watching the crucifixion from a distance (*apo makrothen*).' The same phrase is used of Peter 'following from a distance' to the courtyard of the High Priest (Mt 26:58). In the case of Peter it was a cautious following, in a state of fear that was to result in the denial of his master and of his own discipleship and to end up in his running away in tears. The women watch from a distance because they would have been kept at a distance from the scene of an execution. Their presence throughout the crucifixion, their observation of the deposition and disposal of the body and their coming to the tomb on the first day of the week demonstrate the loyalty and tenacity of these women who had followed him from Galilee and cared for him during his ministry. Their presence stands out in contrast to the murderous intent and injustice of the male establishment figures who brought about his condemnation, the political expediency of Pilate, the cold cruel efficiency of the military in

---

116. D. Senior, *The Passion of Jesus in the Gospel of Mark*, 131.

117. M. D. Hooker, *op. cit.*, 379.

118. See J. Pobee, 'The Cry of the Centurion – a Cry of Defeat,' in E. Bammel (ed), *The Trial of Jesus*, 91-102; T. H. Kim, 'The Anarthous *hyios theou* in Mark 15:39 and the Roman Imperial Cult,' *Bib* 79 (1998) 221-41; E. S. Johnson, 'Mark 15:39 and the So-Called Confession of the Roman Centurion,' *Bib* 81 (2000) 406-13 and T. W. Shiner, 'The Ambiguous Pronouncement of the Centurion and the Shrouding of Meaning in Mark,' *JSNT* 78 (2000) 3-22.

carrying out the crucifixion, the cowardly flight of the disciples and the falling to pieces of their leader Peter. The presence of the women, introduced with an adversative *de*, is a counterbalance to all that has taken place: 'But (*de*) there were also the women watching from a distance' (*êsan de ekei gynaikes pollai apo makrothen theôrousai*).[119]

Matthew (like Mark and Luke) mentions the presence of these women from Galilee. In speaking of them he uses terms associated with discipleship to describe their relationship with Jesus: 'they *followed him*', 'they *ministered to him*', and Mark adds, 'they came up *with him* to Jerusalem.' Matthew gives their names as Mary Magdalene, Mary the mother of James and Joseph and the mother of the sons of Zebedee (quite possibly the woman named Salome in Mk 16:1).

Their presence in the gospel fulfils a further important function. Their observation of the death, deposition and burial of Jesus (they were sitting opposite the tomb) is a prelude to their going to the tomb, which they have carefully observed, and finding it empty. They are therefore the immediate witnesses and living link between the living, dead and risen Jesus. They fulfill this function in the canonical and also in the apocryphal gospels.

7. The Deposition and Burial of Jesus Mt 27:57-61 // Mk 15:42-47 // Lk 23:50-56

a. The Deposition

Matthew's description of Joseph and of the deposition is sparser than Mark's. He does not give details about Joseph of Arimathaea's seeking the kingdom and his courage in approaching Pilate. He simply says that he was a rich man and a disciple of Jesus.[120] He does not at this point mention the

---

119. John has a highly symbolic and theological presence of the mother of Jesus, her sister Mary, the wife of Clopas, Mary Magdalene and the beloved disciple at the foot of the cross (Jn 19:25-27).

120. Unlike the rich young man in Mt 19:16-22, Joseph had become a disciple.

Preparation Day, the day before the Sabbath nor does he mention Pilate's summoning the centurion to ascertain that Jesus was in fact dead. Matthew simply states that Joseph went to Pilate to ask for the body. It was evening when Jesus died and so in keeping with the custom of burying the dead on the day of death it was necessary to obtain the body and bury it forthwith. Though the Romans were wont to leave the bodies of crucified criminals hanging on their crosses till they decayed, as a warning to other evildoers, they were known to respond to Jewish requests in line with the prescription of Deut 21:23 that the bodies of criminals should not be left overnight at the place of execution.[121]

When the Baptist was murdered, his disciples came and took the body away for proper burial. In the absence of his chief male disciples, Joseph of Arimathaea,[122] described by Matthew as a rich man, a disciple, comes to render this service to Jesus. Again a 'minor' character, a hitherto unheard of disciple, exhibits the qualities one would have expected in the chief disciples. Mark describes him as an influential member of the council (most likely the Sanhedrin) and a man 'seeking the kingdom of God' (Mk 15:43). Describing him in this way would probably point to his openness to Jesus and what he stood for, and his desire to do what was seen as one of the good works, to provide fitting burial for someone who had nobody to provide such a service. He associates himself with the executed Jew. John describes him as a disciple, though a secret one, through fear of the Jews (Jn 19:38), and Luke points out how he had nothing to do with the plan and action of the Sanhedrin against Jesus (Lk 23:50f).

Joseph went to Pilate, asked for the body of Jesus and Pilate ordered it to be given to him. He took the body, wrapped it in a clean linen shroud, and laid it in his own new tomb, which he had hewn in the rock, rolled a great stone to the door of the tomb, and departed. The description is one of a hurried burial. A

---

121. Josephus, *War*, IV, 5.2.
122. Usually identified as Ramathaim, a village about twenty miles from Jerusalem.

tomb hewn from the rock was a sign of an important and wealthy person.[123] Matthew states that it was Joseph's own new tomb (Mt 27:59-60). Mark does not actually say that the tomb belonged to Joseph but it is a reasonable assumption (Mk 15:46) and Luke says it was a tomb hewn in the rock, where no one had ever yet lain (Lk 23:5). The piety and courage of a man of standing, the wrapping of the body in linen and the use of a tomb hewn from rock rendered honour to the corpse. The stone rolled to the mouth of the tomb protected the corpse from predatory beasts and preying birds, and spared it the public shame to which executed criminals were usually exposed.[124]

Seeking the body of a crucified rebel could put one in danger, or at least cause uncomfortable questions to be raised about association with the deceased, especially if the person asking for the body was not a relative. Joseph therefore showed courage in making the request, a fact pointed out in Mk 15:43, for those condemned in Jewish courts were not allowed honourable burial.[125] Those crucified by the Romans were usually left to decay at the place of execution. Joseph's request could have been refused and the refusal could have been accompanied by hostile questioning.

---

123. The steward Shebna is condemned as a self promoting official with ideas of grandeur for carving himself such a tomb in Isa 22:15-19.

124. F. J. Moloney, *The Gospel of Mark*, 334, n 304 looks at the traditions of the burial and differences of opinion among scholars as to whether historically Jesus had an honourable burial, even though a hurried one, or the burial of a common criminal. Mark's position is that he was buried with honour and his tomb was well known. cf R. H. Gundry, *Mark: A Commentary on his Apology for the Cross*, 13, who sets the burial in the ongoing glory-suffering equation of the gospel. John's gospel describes the burial in terms of the burial of a king with linen and a lavish amount of spices (Jn 19:38-42).

125. R. E. Brown, *The Death of the Messiah*, 2:1209-10).

b. The women watching the burial Mt 27:61//Mk 15:47//Lk 23:55

After the account of the burial Matthew states pointedly that two of the women, Mary Magdalene and the other Mary[126] were sitting opposite the sepulchre. These are the same persons who, according to Matthew, go to the tomb early in the morning on the first day of the week. They have first hand knowledge of the location of the tomb and the body. Mark says the women saw where he was laid (Mk 15:47) and Luke says the women who had come from Galilee took note of the tomb and the position of the body (Lk 23:55).

c. The Guard at the Tomb Mt 27:62-66

The chief priests and the Pharisees came together and approached Pilate after the day of Preparation saying that 'that imposter' had said while he was still alive: 'After three days I will rise again.' They asked to have the tomb sealed until the third day lest his disciples go and steal the body and tell the people, 'He has risen from the dead.' They added that this latest deception would be worse than the first. Pilate gave them a guard of soldiers[127] and told them to go and make the tomb as secure as they were able. So they went and secured the sepulchre, sealing the stone and placing a guard.

Having brought about his death, Jesus' enemies pursued him beyond the grave. The story of the placing of the guard and the sealing of the tomb, recounted only by Matthew, is an obvious apologetic response to false claims that the disciples had stolen the body of Jesus and proclaimed him risen from the dead. Mark's strong emphasis on the fact that he had really died, as seen in Pilate's questioning of the centurion to make sure he was dead, may be an apologetic response to another anti-resurrection statement claiming that Jesus had not really died before he was taken down from the cross (Mk 15:44-45).[128]

126. Mark identifies her as Mary of Joses.
127. Note the Latinism *koustôdia*, for the Latin *custodia*.
128. Mark points out that Pilate was amazed to hear that Jesus had died so quickly, as death by crucifixion could drag on for days. The centurion was questioned and confirmed the death. The emphasis on Pilate's

Who killed Jesus? A final word on the Passion Narrative

In the light of the terrible history of anti-Semitism any writing, teaching or preaching on the Passion Narrative should include a very clear caution against a facile blaming of 'the Jews' for the death of Jesus. Jesus' story is a universal story and the factors that happened to manifest themselves in a Jewish and Roman context would have manifested themselves in any human society. Jesus was handed over by a faithless disciple and friend turned enemy, a jealous, manipulating, religious authority, a judge who failed to administer justice and a hostile mob. The failure of discipleship, the abuse of friendship, the jealous protection of religious status, the ignoring of justice, the mindless hatred of a mob, the political expediency of an occupying power and the dutiful obeying of orders by the military, all contributed to the handing over of 'the King of the Jews' to a horrible and shameful death. All human life was there just as it has been in all societies throughout history. Sinful humanity through its representatives on that specific occasion crucified 'the King of the Jews'. But theirs was neither the last word nor the last act in the drama. Very soon Jesus' followers would be proclaiming: 'You put him to death, but God raised him to life'(Acts 2:23).

---

amazement and his questioning of the centurion (the executioner) who gives explicit witness to the death may reflect an apologetic in Markan circles against rumours that Jesus had not actually died before he was taken down from the cross. The likelihood that Pilate's question and the centurion's response were included and emphasised for this apologetic reason in Mark's gospel is highlighted by the fact that these two verses (Mk 15:44,45) do not appear in Matthew and Luke.

The Risen Jesus
Mt 28:1-20

1. THE EMPTY TOMB

a. The Women and the Empty Tomb Mt 28:1-7

The women who saw Jesus crucified were the same women who saw him buried and discovered the empty tomb. Their witness to the death, burial and resurrection is most likely the evangelists' primary reason for referring to their presence at the crucifixion. The close similarity of all three synoptic accounts seems to point to an ancient, well rehearsed *apologia* for the Resurrection, emphasising the fact that the same people had witnessed Jesus' death, had seen him placed in a clearly identifiable tomb and had later found that the tomb was empty. The story of these women and their presence on Calvary/Golgotha focuses on them as witnesses to the truth of the underlying facts surrounding the death, burial and resurrection which found expression in the early *kerygma* learned by Paul and repeated in his First Letter to the Corinthians: 'I handed on to you what I had received myself, that Christ died for our sins according to the scriptures; that he was buried; and that he was raised to life on the third day in accordance with the scriptures'(1 Cor15:3f).

'As the Sabbath faded[1] into the dawn of the first day of the week' Mary Magdalene and the other Mary went to see (to visit) the sepulchre.[2] The first day of the week is in fact, in the Jewish manner of counting, three days after or the third day after the crucifixion, the day foretold by Jesus as the day of the resurrection in the various passion predictions throughout the gospel

---

1. The word *opse* is regularly used as an adverb meaning 'late in the day' and it is sometimes used as a preposition with the genitive case meaning 'after'.
2. The verb *theôrêsai* has a fuller meaning than simply 'seeing'. It means 'seeing with a purpose', 'inspecting', 'visiting'.

(Mt 16:21; 17:22-23; 20:18-19).[3] Mark and Luke say they were
going to the tomb with spices (Mk 16:1; Lk 24:1). Some commentators point to the unlikelihood of anointing a body so long
dead, when decomposition may already have set in. Matthew
may have that in mind when he says they were going there to
'see the tomb' (Mt 28:1) and John says Mary Magdalene (mentioning her alone) 'came to the tomb' (Jn 20:1), both cases pointing to a visit 'to pay one's respects', 'to mourn' or 'to see everything was in order' at the first opportunity after the Sabbath.

The apocalyptic tone of the portents surrounding Jesus'
death re-emerges with the reference to the earthquake and the
angel descending from heaven coming to roll back the stone and
sit on it. His appearance was like lightning and his garment
white as snow and for fear of him the guards trembled and became like dead men.

This 'apocalyptic' scenario in Matthew is very different in
tone to the more down to earth account in Mark where the
women are approaching the tomb wondering how they will remove the stone, and arrive to find it rolled back

Matthew speaks of 'an angel of the Lord', recalling the angel
of the Lord who functioned in the Infancy Narrative announcing
to Joseph the divine origin of the child, warning the magi about
Herod's murderous intentions and sending Joseph to Egypt and
then back to the land of Israel. Since the time of Zechariah the
angel has been the interpreter of divine messages in the apocalyptic tradition. Whereas Matthew employs the apocalyptic imagery and language, Mark simply says they entered the tomb
and saw a young man (*neaniskos*, youth) sitting at the right hand
side dressed in a white garment.[4]

As in all biblical accounts of 'divine encounters' or theophanies,
the recipients of the 'vision' are reassured by the divine visitor.

---

3. 'Three days' also reflects the theme of rebuilding the destroyed temple, an allusion to Jesus as the new temple.
4. The angelic formula/announcement differs in the accounts, highlighting the individual approaches of the synoptics, but also, by contrast, emphasising the uniformity of the underlying tradition of the fact
of the women's witness to the empty tomb.

The angel responds (to the fear of the women) and says: 'Do not be afraid!' (*mê phobeisthe*) and goes on to say, in a statement that has the ring of a liturgical formula or summary proclamation: 'I know you seek Jesus who has been crucified. He is not here. He has been raised as he said. Come see the place where he lay.' The announcement of the Resurrection is followed by the commission to proclaim it to his disciples: 'Go quickly and tell his disciples that he has been raised from the dead and is going before you into Galilee. There you will see him. Behold, I have told you.' From a grammatical point of view, *êgerthê* can be translated as 'He has been raised' or 'He is risen'.[5] In this context it seems best to emphasise the activity of God in line with the passion predictions and in response to the final cry of Jesus: 'My God, my God, why have you forsaken me?' God has not forsaken his Son. He has been raised, that is, God has raised him.

The mockers were saying they would believe if they 'saw' him come down from the cross, and some were waiting 'to see' if Elijah would come to save him. Now, the women who were faithful to the last are invited to '*come and see*' the place where he lay and the angel commissions the women to go and say to the disciples: 'He goes before you into Galilee. There *you will see* him.' On the way to Gethsemane Jesus had foretold them that, as it was written, they would all desert him: 'I will strike the shepherd and the sheep will be scattered. But after I am raised up I will go ahead of you to Galilee' (Mt 26:32). 'Go ahead' in this context means 'lead' rather than simply 'precede'. M. D.

---

5. The three passion predictions, (Mt 16:21; 17:23; 20:19), the command to the disciples not to speak of the Transfiguration until after he is risen/raised on the third day (Mt 17:9), the promise to precede the disciples into Galilee after he is risen/raised (Mt 26:32) and the angel's announcement of the resurrection (Mt 28:6) all use the verb *egerthênai*. Mark on the other hand uses the verb *anistêmi* in the predictions of the Passion (Mk 8:31; 9:31; 10:34), as he does for the warning at the end of the Transfiguration (Mk 9:9). In the promise to go ahead of them into Galilee after the resurrection he uses the verb *egeirein* (Mk 14:28) and uses it also in the message of the young man in the tomb (Mk 16:6). It is also the verb used in the healings when Jesus 'raises' people or tells them to 'rise up' from their sickness (e.g. Mk 13:1; 5:41).

Hooker, commenting on the parallel verse in Mark puts it very clearly:

> Mark…is certainly saying something far more significant than that Jesus will arrive in Galilee before the disciples. This is no mere rendezvous but a call to the disciples to follow Jesus once again. On the way to Jerusalem, Jesus had gone ahead…, and the disciples had seen him and followed. Now they are called to follow him, even though they cannot see him. What looks like an inconsistency in Mark may be a deliberate attempt on his part to underline that this is what discipleship means, now that Jesus has been raised from the dead.[6]

Galilee was the native place of the disciples, the place where they were first called and left everything to follow Jesus. It was the area of their first mission and would again be the starting point for a whole new mission, to Jew and Gentile, since it was Galilee of the Gentiles, where Jew and Gentile lived in close proximity and from where they would be sent to 'make disciples of all nations' (Mt 28:19).

b. The Women and the Risen Jesus Mt 28:8-10

The women departed quickly from the tomb with fear (awe) and great joy, and ran to tell his disciples. 'And, behold Jesus met them and said: "Greetings".' Their response is a headline for the Christian community's attitude to the Risen Lord. 'They came up and took hold of his feet and did homage to him.'[7] Jesus basically repeats the message of the angel. He tells them not to be afraid and he commissions them to go and 'tell my brothers to go to Galilee and there they will see me.' The meeting in Galilee is again mentioned. The gospel story is building up to the climactic moment of the meeting in Galilee.

---

6. M. D. Hooker, *op. cit.*, 385f.
7. This is like an alternative version of the account in John, which focuses on Mary Magdalene. The fourth gospel tends to focus on individuals as representative types.

c. The Reaction of the Guards Mt 28:11-15

Meanwhile, as they were departing, some of the guards went into the city, reported to the chief priests all that had happened and they in turn 'took counsel' with the elders. They paid the guards a handsome sum of money to say that while they were asleep the disciples came and stole the body and promised to keep them out of trouble if the matter came to the ears of the governor. They took the money and did as they were instructed. Matthew emphasises the fact that this story had been spread among the Jews 'until this day', that is until Matthew wrote the gospel about fifty years later. Not only was the story false. It purported to be based on the testimony of sleeping men!

The empty tomb in itself is not a proof of, but a pointer to, the resurrection. The appearances of Jesus the Risen Lord and the words of the angelic visitor(s) explain the meaning of the empty tomb.

d. A Historical Note

The earliest written witness to the resurrection is in Paul's First Letter to the Corinthians (1 Cor 15:3-8). It mentions the burial, but does not mention the empty tomb or the account of the women finding it. Paul's interest is in the reality of the Risen Christ and his ongoing presence in the community, arising from his own experience of the Risen Christ. Some writers cast doubt on the story of the empty tomb because of this 'omission' on Paul's part. In so doing they overlook two vital factors. Paul's interest is not in the 'pre-Paschal' or 'historical Jesus'. He has little or no interest in telling the story of Jesus and his associates prior to his resurrection and glorification, except perhaps for his reflection on the institution of the Eucharist which he does to correct abuses in Corinth (1 Cor 11:23-33). His interest is in the risen Christ, not in the empty tomb or the women's experience. Furthermore there is a sound legal and logical principle that states that absence of evidence is not evidence of absence. The fact that Paul does not mention something does not mean it did not happen. Secondly it should be kept in mind that if, as appears to be the case from Matthew's explicit account, there were rumours about disciples stealing the body (Mt 28:11-15), the story of the women's visit in the early hours before sunrise may have been kept quiet for a long time for apologetic reasons. Stories of followers going under cover of darkness to the tomb would serve to reinforce suspicions of their having stolen the body. This silence and the resulting lack of knowledge about the women's visit to the tomb may have also been a factor in prompting Mark to emphasise the fact that they told nobody (Mk 16:8).

2. THE MOUNTAIN APPEARANCE IN GALILEE MT 28:16-20

No specific mountain is mentioned, but, as usual, the mountain setting is full of biblical significance as the place of God's presence, manifestation, revelation, law and covenant. It is associated with the characters of Moses and Elijah and with the central events of the Sermon on the Mount and the Transfiguration in the ministry of Jesus. It recalls the story of Moses looking from the mountain into the Promised Land as he directed the people to cross and instructed them how to live and behave in their new land and way of life. The Risen Jesus here instructs his disciples how to behave in the new situation into which he is sending them as his representatives in the whole world

The eleven (Judas has departed the scene) came to the mountain in Galilee to which Jesus had directed them. On seeing him they paid homage, but some doubted. Paying homage is the proper attitude towards the Risen Lord. This 'condensed' appearance account reflects the fact spelled out in other appearance accounts in the gospels that the disciples had difficulty in recognising Jesus. John, typically, focuses on Thomas' doubt, portraying an individual as representative of all the apostles (Jn 20:24-29). In emphasising their doubts and difficulties the gospel writers are anxious to show that the disciples were not gullible or over enthusiastic to see a prophecy of resurrection fulfilled.

'Jesus approached them', though usually in the gospel others approach Jesus. This too is very possibly part of the apologetic emphasising the fact that the initiative in the appearance accounts is entirely with Jesus, and not a product of wishful fulfilment or hallucination on their part.

When Jesus approached them he first announced his authority in his glorified state, then gave them a universal commission and finally promised to be with them till the end of the age.

Announcing his authority he says: 'All authority in heaven and earth has been given to me.' This description recalls the commissioning by the Ancient of Days of 'one like a Son of Man' who is given dominion and glory and kingdom, that all peoples and nations and languages should serve him' (Dan 7:14).

Jesus' final commission to the disciples is to make disciples of all nations. The noun 'disciple' (*mathêthês*) is here made into a verb, 'make disciples of' all the nations. The commission is a universal commission, reflecting the universal dominion of the Son of Man and in this sense 'all nations' is a universal designation rather than a reference to the Gentiles as distinct from the Jews.

'Making disciples' is spelled out in definite terms. Baptising them in the name of the Father and of the Son and of the Holy Spirit is a reflection of the developing Trinitarian theology of Matthew, very probably a developed baptismal formula (a development akin to that in the *Didachê* 7:1-3). For the first time now in the gospel of Matthew the disciples are told to 'teach'. Matthew's gospel is the great gospel of teaching with its lengthy discourses. However, it is only when they have heard all the discourses and experienced the glorification of the Son that they are in a position to teach. What are they to teach? They are to teach the nations 'to observe all that I have commanded you'. This means not only teaching the content, but also teaching the importance of observing/practising what they have learned in Jesus' authentic interpretation of the Law and the Prophets, not like the scribes and Pharisees who teach and extol the Law but do not practise what they preach (Mt 23:3).

Finally, Jesus makes a promise, already foreshadowed in the name Emmanuel, 'God with us' in the Infancy Narrative. He promises to be with the disciples (all Christians) all days until the end of the age, the familiar apocalyptic theme of the present age giving way to the age to come. The reader is again reminded of the Son of Man whose 'dominion is an everlasting dominion which will not pass away, and his kingdom a kingdom that shall not be destroyed.'(Dan 7:14).

A Historical Note on Pilate[1]

The reader wonders how accurately the evangelists portray the historical character of Pilate, since literary, theological and apologetic considerations abound in the narratives.[2] Pilate was appointed Prefect (not Procurator) of Judaea in 26AD, a position he held until he was removed, following complaints, in 37AD.[3] His appointment may have owed a good deal to the recommendation of his friend Seianus, the regional Roman official, a known anti-Semite. Pilate himself also pursued policies which offended Jewish sensibilities. He wanted to place Roman standards with the image of the emperor Tiberius in Jerusalem in spite of serious objections and only stopped when he realised that people were ready to die rather than have the Holy City so profaned. He took Corban money (funds dedicated to Temple use) to build an aqueduct and clubbed to death those who protested at his action.[4] Luke speaks of his murder of Galileans while they were sacrificing in Jerusalem (Lk 13:1). Eventually he was removed after his mishandling of religiously motivated trouble between Jews and Samaritans.[5] His fall may have been facilitated by the fact that he no longer had a powerful ally in Seianus, whose removal from office in 31AD had left him (Pilate) vulnerable in a changed, or changing, relationship with the authorities, and in particular with the emperor himself in Rome. This fact is borne out in John's gospel by his fear of a neg-

1. See the article by B. C. McGing, 'Pontius Pilate and the Sources,' *CBQ* 53 (1991) 416-38.
2. See the studies by H. K. Bond, *Pontius Pilate in History and Interpretation*, Cambridge and New York: CUP, 1998 and W. Carter, *Pontius Pilate: Portraits of a Roman Governor*, Collegeville, Minn: Liturgical Press, 2003.
3. A contemporary inscription in Caesarea, the seat of his administration, calls him Prefect.
4. Josephus, *Ant*, 18.3.1; *War*, 2.9.2-3.
5. The trouble arose at a Samaritan religious procession in 35A.D.

ative report about him reaching the emperor's ears and losing his standing as *amicus Caesaris*, friend of Caesar (Jn 19:12).[6] Philo of Alexandria, in *De Legatione ad Gaium*, an appeal to Gaius (Caligula) against anti-Semitism, speaks of Pilate as 'naturally inflexible, a blend of self-will and relentlessness' who governed by bribery, insults, robberies, executions without trial and great cruelty.[7] Allowing for exaggeration and even some fabrication in the process of making his impassioned appeal, Philo still paints a very unflattering portrait of Pilate and his methods of government. The evangelists, living in the Roman Empire at difficult times, would not want to be too outspoken about Pilate, since he had been such a high ranking official, and so he was 'whitewashed' somewhat, shown to be trapped or vacillating (Mark) rather than unjust, basically favourable to Jesus, and played upon by the Jewish authorities and the mob.[8] For apologetic reasons it was highly desirable that he be shown not to have believed the charges against Jesus, especially the political charge of claiming to be a rival king.

A note on the Barabbas incident

Whatever the exact historical details, the evangelists use the offer of an amnesty to great effect. Matthew shifts the call for Jesus' execution away from Pilate, thus clearing Jesus together with his contemporary and subsequent followers in dangerous times of any charge of sedition or seditious intentions against the Romans. Matthew also brings into play what was probably an important element in the remembered story of Jesus, the hostility of an element of the crowd. Their call for Barabbas probably points to the strong presence of a zealot presence among the crowd which could be easily manipulated. The tradition as it appears in the various accounts is pointing in that direction. Mark

---

6. Tacitus, *Annals*, 6, 8. Tacitus states that anyone who was a close friend of Seianus was a friend of Caesar (Tiberius).
7. Philo, *Legatio ad Gaium*, 301f.
8. See the portrait of Pilate in R. E. Brown, *Death of the Messiah*, Vol 1, 698-705.

says Barabbas was imprisoned for murder *during the uprising* (Mk 15:7). Luke says he was imprisoned for *rioting and murder* (Lk 22:19). John speaks of Barabbas as *lêstês* which seems to brand him as a bandit in the sense of a guerrilla (Jn 18:40). His supporters were probably very disappointed with, and consequently hostile to Jesus for not allowing himself and his popularity with the crowds to be manipulated politically. With the rejection by this vocal mob Jesus is left without any support. His entire movement seems now to have been wiped out. Matthew places the blame squarely on the shoulders of the chief priests and the elders who worked on the crowd.

Probably the historical reality lying behind the Barabbas incident is more complex than the impression given by the account in the Passion Narratives. The gospel accounts serve to make the point that disciple, Jewish authority, Roman authority and hostile crowd all played a part in the 'handing over' of Jesus to death, thereby fulfilling the scriptures and the divine plan. Throughout the ministry the crowd in the synoptic tradition(s) shows no hostility to Jesus. In fact the enthusiasm of the crowd is highlighted in response to Jesus' teaching and miracles, and on the occasion of his triumphal approach to and entry into the city. As in many other cases, the Johannine tradition throws another light on events, particularly in Jerusalem. There the crowd during the ministry when Jesus visited the city, was divided into those who were favourable or willing to listen and learn and those who were hostile to the point of wanting to arrest him (Jn 7:40-44) or stone him for blasphemy for his teaching in the temple from which he escaped with his life (Jn 10:31) and the disciples thought his return to Judea to the dying Lazarus would cost him, and them, their lives (Jn 11:8). After the raising of Lazarus an element of the crowd went to report the matter to the authorities (Jn 11:46). It is quite possible also that the already mentioned more militant element, possibly Galileans with zealot tendencies, were disappointed with Jesus' non-militant approach, and saw him as undermining their influence with the broader crowd, a block on their revolutionary path. This combination of a Jerusalem crowd who played up to the Jewish authorities and wanted to facilitate their desired outcome and the dangerously disgruntled Galilean zealot types would not take much persuasion to reject Jesus and request the release of Barabbas, a rebel with blood on his hands from a previous (unspecified) outbreak of rebellion (Mk 15:7). Whatever their motive or mixture of motives, the Jewish authorities were able to manipulate them for their purposes and Pilate was able to use them for his purpose, avoiding the explosive situation of a foreign governor executing a prominent native and risking a violent reaction.

All four gospels speak of the custom of freeing a prisoner at Passover. Therefore the custom cannot be easily dismissed, though it has come under severe scrutiny from historians. They point out that outside the New Testament no other record of such a custom at Passover has been found. However, similar customs are recorded. It may have been an application of the Jewish practice of buying the freedom of a prisoner on the occasion of Passover as a practical way to commemorate their liberation from the slavery of Egypt.[9] It could equally have been an application to this specific time and place of the broader custom of offering an amnesty on Roman festivals and special occasions such as the emperor's birthday. If so it was probably one of those half official local customs that are often used to bring about a compromise with a nod and a wink, and probably not officially recorded for posterity. D. Senior, drawing attention to the discussion by R. Pesch, sums up the position very well:

> It is unlikely, however that such an unusual event would have been fabricated by the tradition. Release of a prisoner fits into the liberation motif of the Jewish Passover and may have been a concession on the part of the Roman administration of Judea.[10]

---

9. E. Bammel, 'The Trial before Pilate', in *Jesus and the Politics of His Day*, ed. E. Bammel and C. F. D. Moule. 427; reflecting the practice in *m. Pesah*, 8.6.

10. D. Senior, *op. cit.*, 110; R. Pesch, *Das Markusevangelium II*, 462.

Scholars also point out the extraordinary nature of the co-incidence of the arrival of the crowd at the Praetorium just at the appropriate moment when Pilate is in a difficult position. It does not seem so unlikely if one considers the possibility of a crowd carefully 'stirred up' or 'rented' either to put pressure on Pilate or to provide opposition to the Jewish authorities in Pilate's interest, or a crowd simply gathered out of curiosity as news of the arrest spread through the festal crowd. Plenty of disgruntled persons and zealots could be present in the festal crowd waiting for just such an incident to vent anger, further sedition or simply relieve boredom and provide distraction.

The presence of the hostile crowd in the scene highlights, perhaps in a simple and dramatic way, the complexities of the situation which Pilate manipulated in his own interest and which the evangelists were able to exploit for their apologetic and theological interests.[11] In a very real way, however, Pilate was governed by those he was appointed to govern.

---

11. John develops it in line with his theology throughout the gospel where Jesus has been repeatedly described as Son, Son of God and Son of Man. In his discourses in John, Jesus had contrasted his paternity with that of his critics. He is now accused of blasphemy for calling himself God's Son. He is put up beside Barabbas, a name which means in Aramaic, 'Son of the Father'. The reader naturally asks, 'Who is his father and what does he stand for?' John's account is highly symbolic and theological, but the irony is equally striking in Matthew.

ABD	Anchor Bible Dictionary
ABRL	Anchor Bible Reference Library
Ant	Josephus: Antiquities of the Jews
b.	Babylonian Talmud
Bib	Biblica
BVC	Bible et Vie Chrétienne
BZ	Biblische Zeitschrift
CBQ	Catholic Biblical Quarterly
de Ben	Seneca: *De Beneficiis*
ÉtB	Études Bibliques
ETL	Ephemerides Theologicae Lovaniensis
ExpTim	Expository Times
Hist Eccl	Eusebius: *Ecclesiastical History*
HTR	Harvard Theological Review
IDB	The Interpreter's Dictionary of the Bible,
j.	Jerusalem Talmud
JB	Jerusalem Bible
JBC	Jerome Biblical Commentary
JBL	Journal of Biblical Literature
JSNT	Journal for the Study of the New Testament
JSOT	Journal for the Study of the Old Testament
JTS	Journal of Theological Studies
Ketub.	*Ketubot*
LXX	Septuagint
Ned.	*Nedarim*
NRSV	New Revised Standard Version
NTS	New Testament Studies
OCD	Oxford Classical Dictionary
PIBA	Proceedings of the Irish Biblical Association
IQH	Qumran Hymns (from cave I)
IQM	Qumran War Scroll (from cave I)
4QF	Qumran Florilegium (from cave 4)
4QT	Qumran Testimonia (from cave 4)

IQS	Qumran Manual of Discipline (from cave I)
RB	Revue Biblique
m.	*Mishnah*
MT	Masoretic Text
NRSV	New Revised Standard Version
SBLDS	Society of Biblical Literature Dissertation Series
SBLMS	Society of Biblical Literature Monograph Series
SNTSMS	Society of New Testament Studies Monograph Series
StB	H. L. Strack and P. Billerbeck, Kommentar zum Neuen Testamentum aus Talmud und Midrasch (vols 1-5, Munich: Beck,1922-55)
TS	Theological Studies
TDNT	Theological Dictionary of the New Testament, G.Kittel and G.Friedrick. Vols 1-10, Grand Rapids: Eerdmans, 1964-76.
TS	Theological Studies
War	Josephus: *The Wars of the Jews*
ZNW	Zeitschrift für die neutestamentlichen Wissenschaft

Bibliography

OVERVIEWS OF SCHOLARSHIP

Burgess, J. A., *A History of the Exegesis of Matthew 16: 17-19 from 1781 to 1965*, Ann Arbor: Edwards, 1976.

Senior, D., *What Are They Saying about Matthew*? Ramsey: N.J: Paulist, 1983.

Stanton, G., 'The Origin and Purpose of Matthew's Gospel: Matthean Scholarship from 1945 to 1980.' *Aufstieg und Niedergang der romischen Welt*, 25/3, ed. W. Haase. Berlin-New York: de Gruyter, 1985, 1889-1951.

Wagner, G., ed, *An Exegetical Bibliography of the New Testament. Matthew and Mark*, Macon, Ga: Mercer University Press, 1983.

COMMENTARIES

Albright, W. F., and C. S. Mann, *Matthew*, Anchor Bible, Garden City, New York: Doubleday. 1971.

Allen, WC., *A Critical and Exegetical Commentary on the Gospel according to St Matthew*, Edinburgh: Clark, 1912.

Beare, F. W., *The Gospel according to Matthew*, San Francisco: Harper and Row, 1981.

Boring, M. E., 'The Gospel and Letters of Matthew,' in *The New Interpreter's Bible*, ed. L. E. Keck *et al*, Vol 8, Nashville: Abingdon, 1995, 87-505.

Brown, R. E., 'The Gospel According to Matthew' in *An Introduction to the New Testament*, 171-227, New York: Doubleday, 1997.

Davies, W. D., and D. C. Allison, *A Critical and Exegetical Commentary on Matthew*, ICC, 3 Vols, Edinburgh: T&T Clark, 1988-2000.

Didier, M. ed, *L'Evangile selon Matthieu. Rédaction et théologie*, Gembloux: Duculot, 1972.

Ellis, P. F., *Matthew: His Mind and His Message*, Collegeville: The Liturgical Press, 1974.

Fenton, J. C., *St Matthew*, Philadelphia: Westminster, 1978.

France, R. T., *The Gospel according to Matthew: An Introduction and Commentary*, Grand Rapids: Eerdmans, 1985.

Garland, D. E., *Reading Matthew: A Literary and Theological Commentary on the First Gospel*, New York: Crossroad, 1993.

Gnilka, J., *Das Matthäusevangelium*, Freiburg–Basel-Vienna: Herder 1986, 1988.

Gundry, R. H., *Matthew: A Commentary on his Literary and Theological Art*, Grand Rapids: Eerdmans, 1982.

Gundry, R. H., *Matthew: A Commentary on His Handbook for a Mixed Church Under Persecution*, Grand Rapids, Md: Eerdmans, 2nd ed. 1994.

Hagner, D., *Matthew 1-13*. World Biblical Commentary 33a. Dallas: Word, 1993.

Hare, D. R. A., *Matthew, Interpretation*, Louisville: John Knox. 1993.

Harrington, D. J. SJ, *The Gospel of Matthew*. Sacra Pagina. Collegeville: Liturgical Press, 1991.

Hill, D., *The Gospel of Matthew*, Grand Rapids: Eerdmans; London: Oliphants, 1972.

Jones, A., *The Gospel According To St Matthew: A Text and Commentary for Students*, London: Chapman, 1965.

Kingsbury, J. D., *Matthew. Proclamation Commentaries*, Philadelphia: Fortress. 1986.

Lagrange, M. J., *Evangile selon Saint Matthieu*, Paris: Gabalda, 1948.

Lange, J., *Das Matthäus-Evangelium*, Darmstadt: Wissenschaftliche Buchgesellschaft, 1980.

Limbeck, M., *Matthaus-Evangelium*, Stuttgart: Katholisches Bibelwerk, 1986.

Lohmeyer, E., *Das Evangelium des Matthäus*, 4th ed.,Göttingen: Vandenhoeck & Ruprecht, 1956.

Luz, U., *Matthew 1-7. A Commentary*, Minneapolis: Augsburg, 1989.

McNeile, A. H., *The Gospel according to St. Matthew, The Greek Text with Introduction and Notes*, Grand Rapids: Baker, 1980.

Meier, J. P., *Matthew,* New Testament Message 3, Wilmington, Del: Glazier, 1980.

Patte, D., *The Gospel according to Matthew: A Structural Commentary on Matthew's Faith,* Philadelphia: Fortress, 1987.

Perlewitz, M., *The Gospel of Matthew,* Wilmington: Glazier, 1998.

Plummer, A., *An Exegetical Commentary on the Gospel according to Matthew,* London: Scott, 1909.

Sabourin, L., *The Gospel according to St Matthew,* 2 vols. Bombay: St Paul Publications, 1982.

Sand, A., *Das Evangelium nach Matthäus,* Regensburg: Pustet, 1986.

Schweizer, E., *The Good News according to Matthew,* Atlanta: John Knox, 1975.

Senior, D., *The Gospel of Matthew,* Nashville: Abingdon Press, 1997.

Smith, R. H., *Matthew,* Minneapolis: Augsburg, 1989.

Staunton, G. N., *A Gospel for a New People. Studies in Matthew,* Edinburgh: T&T Clark, 1992.

Stock, A., *The Method and Message of Matthew,* Collegeville: The Liturgical Press, 1994.

Trilling, D. W., *The Gospel According to St Matthew, New Testament for Spiritual Reading,* ed. J. L. McKenzie, London: Burns and Oates,1969.

Wainright, E. M., 'The Gospel of Matthew' in *Searching the Scriptures: A Feminist Commentary,* ed. Elizabeth Schlüssler Fiorenza, 2:635-77. New York: Crossroad 1995.

SELECT BIBLIOGRAPHY (GENERAL AND SPECIFIC)

Abrahams, I., 'The Greatest Commandment' in *Studies in Pharisaism and the Gospels,* First Series, Cambridge: CUP, 1917.

Allison, D. C., Jr., *The New Moses: A Matthean Typology,* Minneapolis: Augsburg / Fortress, 1993.

Alter, R., *The Art of Biblical Narrative,* New York: Basic Books, 1981.

Aune, D., 'Greco-Roman Biography', in *Greco-Roman Literature and the New Testament: Selected Forms and Genres,* Society of

Biblical Literature Sources for Biblical Study 21, ed. D. Aune, Atlanta: Scholars Press, 1988.

Bacon, B. W., *Studies in Matthew*, New York: Holt; London: Constable, 1930.

Balabanski,V., *Eschatology in the Making: Mark, Matthew and the Didache*, SNTS Monograph Series 97, Cambridge: CUP, 1997.

Balch, D., *Social History of The Matthean Community: Cross-Disciplinary Approaches*, Minneapolis: Fortress, 1991.

Bammel, E., (ed), *The Trial of Jesus*, Cambridge Studies in Honour of C. F. D. Moule, Studies in Biblical Theology, Second Series 13, SCM Press, London, 1970.

Bammel, E., 'Crucifixion as a Punishment in Palestine,' in E. Bammel (ed), *The Trial of Jesus*, Cambridge Studies in Honour of CFD Moule, Studies in Biblical Theology, Second Series 13, SCM Press, London, 1970, 162-165.

Barton, S., *Discipleship and Family Ties in Mark and Matthew*, SNTSMS 80, Cambridge: CUP, 1994.

Bauckham, R., 'The Brothers and Sisters of Jesus: An Epiphanian Response', *CBQ* (1994), 686-7000.

Baudoz, J-F., *Les Miettes de la table. Étude synoptique et socio-religieuse de Mt 15:21-28 et Mc 7:24-30*, Paris: Gabalda, 1995.

Bauer, D. R., 'The Kingship of Jesus in the Matthean Infancy Narrative: A Literary Analysis', *CBQ* 57:306-23, 1995.

Bauer, D. R., *The Structure of Matthew's Gospel. A Study in Literary Design*, Sheffield: Almond, 1998.

Bayer, H. F., *Jesus' Predictions of Vindication and Resurrection*, Tübingen: J. C. Mohr (Paul Siebeck), 1986.

Beasley-Murray, G. R., *Jesus and the Last Days: The Interpretation of the Olivet Discourse*, Peabody: Hendrickson, 1993.

Bellinzoni, A. J., ed, *The Two Source Hypothesis*, Macon, Ga: Mercer University Press, 1985.

Betz, H. D., *The Sermon on the Mount*, Hermeneia. Minneapolis: Fortress, 1975.

Blinzer, J., *The Trial of Jesus. The Jewish and Roman Proceedings Against Jesus Christ Described and Assessed from the Oldest Accounts*, Westminster: Newman, 1959.

Bond, H. K., *Pontius Pilate in History and Interpretation*, Cambridge and New York: CUP, 1998.

Bonnard, P. L., *L'Evangile selon Saint Matthieu*, 2nd revised edition, Neuchâtel: Delachaux & Niestlé, 1970.

Bornkamm, G., Barth, G. and Held, H. J., *Tradition and Interpretation in Matthew*, 2nd revised edition, London: SCM, 1982.

Bornkamm, G., 'The Stilling of the Storm in Matthew' in G. Bornkamm, G. Barth and H. J. Held, *Tradition and Interpretation in Matthew*, Philadelphia: Westminster/London: SCM,1963.

Borrell, A., *The Good News of Peter's Denial. A Narrative and Rhetorical Reading of Mark 14:54, 66-72*, trs S. Conlon, Univ. of South Florida International Studies in Formative Christianity and Judaism, Atlanta: Scholars Press, 1998.

Boucher, M. I., *The Mysterious Parable. A Literary Study*, Washington DC: Catholic Biblical Association, 1977.

Brandon, S., *The Trial of Jesus of Nazareth*, London: Paladin, 1968.

Brodie, T. L., *The Crucial Bridge. The Elijah-Elisha Narrative as Interpretative Synthesis of Genesis-Kings and a Literary Model for the Gospels*, Collegeville: The Liturgical Press, 2000.

Brooks, S. H., *Matthew's Community: The Evidence of His Special Sayings Material*, JSNT Sup 16, Sheffield: JSOT, 1987.

Brown, R. E., 'The Pater Noster as an Eschatological Prayer', in *New Testament Essays*, 217-253, New York: Doubleday, 1965.

Brown, R. E., K. Donfried, and J, Reumann, eds, *Peter in the New Testament: A Collaborative Assessment by Protestant and Roman Catholic Scholars*, Minneapolis: Augsburg/New York: Paulist, 1973.

Brown, R. E., *The Birth of the Messiah*, Garden City: Doubleday, 1977.

Brown, R. E., and J. P. Meier, *Antioch and Rome*, New York: Paulist, 1983.

Brown, R. E., *The Churches the Apostles Left Behind*, New York: Paulist, 1984.

Brown, R. E., A *Crucified Christ in Holy Week, Essays on the Four Gospel Passion Narratives*, Collegeville: The Liturgical Press, 1986.

Brown, R. E., *The Death of the Messiah: From Gethsemane to the Grave*, Anchor Bible Reference Library, New York: Doubleday, 1994.

Bultmann, R., *History of the Synoptic Tradition*, trs John Marsh, Oxford: Basil Blackwell,1968.

Burridge, R. A., *What Are the Gospels? A Comparison with Graeco-Roman Biography*, Society for New Testament Studies Monograph Series 70, Cambridge: CUP, 1992.

Cahill, L. S., *The Ethical Implications of the Sermon on the Mount*, Interpretation 41:144-56.

Caird, G. B., *The Revelation of St John the Divine*, London: A& C Black, 1966.

Carroll, J. T., and J. B. Green, *The Death of Jesus in Early Christianity*, Peabody: Hendrickson, 1995.

Carter, W., *What Are They Saying About Matthew's Sermon On The Mount?* New York: Paulist, 1994.

Carter, W., 'The Crowds in Matthew's Gospel', *CBQ* 55: 54-67, 1993.

Carter, W., 'Kernels and Narrative Blocks: The Structure of Matthew's Gospel', *CBQ* 54:463-81, 1992.

Carter, W., *Pontius Pilate: Portraits of a Roman Governor*, Collegeville: The Liturgical Press, 2003.

Carter, W., *Households and Discipleship: A Study of Matthew 19-20*, *JSNT* Sup 103, Sheffield: JSOT, 1994.

Carter, W., *Matthew: Storyteller, Interpreter, Evangelist*, Peabody: Hendrickson, 2004.

Carter, W., 'Recalling the Lord's Prayer: The Authorial Audience and Matthew's Prayer as Familiar Liturgical Experience,' *CBQ* 57: 514-30, 1995.

Carter, W., '"To See the Tomb." A Note on Matthew's Women at the Tomb (28:1).' *Expository Times* 107:201-5, 1996.

Carter, W., and J. P. Heil, *Matthew's Parables: Audience-Oriented Perspectives*, *CBQ* Monograph Series 30, Washington DC: CBA, 1998.

Casey, M., 'The Original Aramaic Form of Jesus' Interpretation of the Cup,' *JTS* 41 1-12, 1990.

Casey, M., *Son of Man: The Interpretation and Influence of Daniel 7*, London: SPCK, 1979.

Catchpole, D. R., *The Trial of Jesus: A Study in the Gospels and Jewish Historiography from 1770 to the Present Day*, Leiden: Brill, 1971.

Charlesworth, J. H., *The Lord's Prayer and Other Prayer Texts from the Greco-Roman Era*, Valley Forge: Trinity Press International, 1994.

Charlesworth, J. H. (ed): *The Messiah: Developments in Earliest Judaism and Christianity*, The First Princeton Symposium on Judaism and Christian Origins, Minneapolis: Fortress, 1992.

Claudel, G., *La confession de Pierre, trajectoire d'une péricope évangelique*, Paris: Gabalda, 1988.

Collins, A. Y., 'The Genre of the Passion Narrative,' *Studia Theologica* 47 (1993) 3-28.

Collins, A. Y., 'The Signification of Mark 10:45 among Gentile Christians', *HTR* 90 (1997), 371-82.

Collins, J. J., *The Sceptre and the Star: The Messiahs of the Dead Sea Scrolls and Other Ancient Literature*, ABRL, New York: Doubleday, 1995.

Collins, J. J., 'The Nature of Messianism in the Light of the Dead Sea Scrolls' in *The Dead Sea Scrolls in their Historical Context*, (eds, T. H. Kim, L. W. Hurtado, A. Graeme Auld, and Alison Jack), Edinburgh: T&T Clark, 2000, 199-219.

Collins, R. F., *Divorce in the New Testament*, Collegeville: The Liturgical Press, Michael Glazier, 1992.

Collins, R. F., *Sexual Ethics and the New Testament: Behaviour and Belief*, New York: Crossroads, 2000.

Coloe, M. L., *God Dwell With Us: Temple Symbolism in the Fourth Gospel*, Collegeville: The Liturgical Press, Michael Glazier, 2001.

Cook, M. J., ' Interpreting "Pro-Jewish" Passages in Matthew,' in *Hebrew Union College Annual* 53:135-46, 1984.

Cope, O. L., *Matthew, A Scribe Trained for the Kingdom of Heaven*, Washington DC: Catholic Biblical Association, 1976.

Corley, K. E., 'Women and the Crucifixion and Burial of Jesus. "He Was Buried: On the Third Day He was Raised,"' *Forum* 1 181-225, 1998.

Cox, P., *Biography in Late Antiquity: A Quest for the Holy Man*, Berkeley: University of California Press, 1983.

Crosby, M., *House of Disciples: Church, Economics, Justice*, Maryknoll: Orbis, 1998.

Crossan, J.D., *In Parables. The Challenge of the Historical Jesus*, New York: Harper & Row, 1973.

Cullman, O., *Peter, Disciple, Apostle Martyr: A Historical Study*, English trs, SCM, 1966.

Dahl, N. A., *The Crucified Messiah and Other Essays*, Minneapolis: Augsburg, 10-36, 1974.

Dahl, N. A., *Jesus in the Memory of the Early Church*, Minneapolis: Augsburg, 1976.

Dahl, N. A., 'The Passion Narrative in Matthew' in *The Interpretation of Matthew*, ed. G. Stanton, Philadelphia and London: Fortress and SPCK, 1983, 42-55.

Daube, D., *The New Testament and Rabbinic Judaism*, London: Athlone, 1956/Peabody: Hendrickson 1994.

Davies, W. D., *The Setting of the Sermon on the Mount*, New York/London: CUP, 1964, 1966.

De Lubac, H., *The Motherhood of the Church*, San Francisco: Ignatius Press, 1982.

Deming, W., 'Mark 9:42-10:12, Matthew 5:27-32 and *B. Nid* 13b: A First-Century Discussion of Male Sexuality,' *NTS* 36, (1990).

Dibelius, M., *From Tradition to Gospel*, trs B. L. Woolf, Library of Theological Translations, Cambridge and London: James Clarke, 1971.

Dillon, R. J., '"As One Having Authority" (Mk 1:22): The Controversial Distinction of Jesus' Teaching,' *CBQ* 57:92-113, 1995.

Dodd, C. H., *The Parables of the Kingdom*, London: Collins 1936/New York: Scribners, 1965.

Donahue, J. R. SJ, *Are You the Christ? The Trial Narrative in the Gospel of Mark*, SBLDS 10, Missoula: University of Montana Press, 1973.

Donahue, J. R., 'Recent Studies on the Origin of "Son of Man" in the Gospels.' *CBQ* 48:484-98, 1986.

Donahue, J. R., *The Gospel in Parable. Metaphor, Narrative, and Theology in the Synoptic Gospels*, Philadelphia: Fortress, 1988.

Donahue, J. R., and D. J. Harrington, *The Gospel of Mark*, Sacra Pagina 2, Collegeville: The Liturgical Press, Michael Glazier, 2002.

Donaldson, J., '"Called to Follow," A Twofold Experience of Discipleship', *Biblical Theology Bulletin* 5 (1975), 67-77.

Donaldson, T., *Jesus on the Mountain: A Study in Matthean Theology*, JSNT, Supplement Series 8, Sheffield: JSOT Press, 1985.

Donfried, K., 'The Allegory of the Ten Virgins (Matt 25:1-13) as a summary of Matthean Theology', *JBL* 93:415-28, 1974.

Drury, J., *The Parables in the Gospels*, New York: Crossroads, 1985.

Duling, D., 'The Therapeutic Son of David: An element in Matthew's Christological Apologetic', *New Testament Studies* 24: 392-410, 1977-1978.

Dunn, J, D. G., *Jesus and the Spirit: A Study of the Religious and Charismatic Experience of Jesus and the First Christians as Reflected in the New Testament*, London: SCM Press, 1975.

Dunn, J, D. G., *The Partings of the Ways Between Christianity and Judaism and Their Significance for the Character of Christianity*, Philadelphia: Trinity Press International, 1991.

Evans, C. A., *To See and Not Perceive: Isaiah 6:9-11 in Early Jewish and Christian Interpretation*, JSOT Sup 64. Sheffield: JSOT, 1989.

Evans, C. A., 'Jesus and the "Cave of Robbers": Toward a Jewish Context for the Temple Action,' *Bulletin of Biblical Research* 3, 93-110, 1993.

Filson, F. V., *The Gospel according to St Matthew*, London: A & C Black, 1960.

Fischer, G., and M. Hasitschka, *The Call of the Disciple. The Bible on Following Christ*, New York: Paulist, 1999.

Fitzmyer, J. A., 'Anti-semitism and the Cry of "All the People" (Mt 27:25)', *TS* 26:667-71, 1965.

Fitzmyer, J. A.,' Crucifixion in Ancient Palestine, Qumran Literature, and the New Testament,' *CBQ* 40 (1979) 493-513.

France, R. T., *Matthew: Evangelist and Teacher*, Grand Rapids: Zondervan, 1989.

Freed, E. D., 'The Women in Matthew's Genealogy', *JSNT*, 29:3-19, 1987.

Frei, H. W., *The Eclipse of Biblical Narrative: A Study in Eighteenth and Nineteenth Century Hermeneutics*, New Haven: Yale University Press, 1974.

Freund, E., *The Return of the Reader: Reader Response Criticism*, New Accents, London: Methuen, 1987.

Freyne, S., *The Twelve: Disciples and Apostles. A Study in the Theology of the First Three Gospels*, London: Sheed and Ward, 1969.

Freyne, S., 'Jesus a Jewish Galilean: A New Reading of the Jesus Story', *PIBA*, No 28, 2005, 106-123.

Furnish,V. P., *The Love Command in the New Testament*, Nashville: Abingdon, 1972.

Gager, J. G., 'Religion and Social Class in the Early Roman Empire,' in *The Catacombs and the Colosseum*, ed. S. Benko and J. J. O'Rourk, Valley Forge: Judson, 1971.

Garland, D., *The Intention of Matthew 23*, Supplements to *Novum Testamentum* 52, Leiden: E. J. Brill, 1979.

Gaston, L., *No Stone on Another: Studies in the significance of the Fall of Jerusalem in the Synoptic Gospels*, *NovT*, Sup 23, Leiden: 1970.

Gerhardsson, B., *The Mighty Acts of Jesus according to Matthew*, Lund: Gleerup, 1979.

Gerhardsson, B., *The Testing of God's Son (Matt 4:1-11& //s)*, Coniectanea Biblica New Testament Series 2:1, Lund: CWK Gleerup, 1966.

Giblin, C. H., 'The "Things of God" in the Question Concerning Tribute to Caesar (Lk 20:25; Mk 12:17; Mt 22:21)', *CBQ* 33:510 -27, 1971.

Goulder, M., *Midrash and Lection in Matthew*, London: SPCK, 1974.

Grassi, J. A., *The Hidden Heroes of the Gospels: Female Counterparts of Jesus*, Collegeville: The Liturgical Press, 1989.

Grassi, J. A., *Loaves and Fishes: The Gospel Feeding Narratives*, Collegeville: The Liturgical Press, 1991.

Gray, S. W., *The Least of My Brothers: Matthew 25:31-46: A History of Interpretation*, SBLDS 114, Atlanta: Scholars Press, 1989.

Guelich, R., 'The Matthean Beatitudes: "Entrance Requirements" or Eschatological Blessings?' *Journal of Biblical Literature*, 95:415-34, 1976.

Guelich, R., *The Sermon on The Mount*, Dallas: Word, 1982.

Gundry, R. H., *The Use of the Old Testament in Matthew's Gospel*, Leiden: Brill, 1967.

Gundry, R. H., *Matthew: A Commentary on his Literary and Theological Art*, Grand Rapids: Eerdmans, 1982.

Gundry, R. H., *Mark. A Commentary on his Apology for the Cross*, Grand Rapids: Eerdmans, 1993, 2000.

Hagedorn, A. C. and J. H. Neyrey, '"It Was Out of Envy that They Handed Jesus Over" (Mark 15:10): The Anatomy of Envy and the Gospel of Mark', *JSNT* 69 (1998)15-56.

Hare, D. R. A., *The Theme of Jewish Persecution of Christians in the Gospel of Matthew*, New York/London: CUP, 1967.

Hare, D. R. A. and D. J. Harrington, '"Make Disciples of all the Gentiles" (Mt 28:19),' *CBQ* 37:359-69, 1975.

Hare, D. R. A., *The Son of Man Tradition*, Minneapolis: Fortress Press, 1990.

Harner, P. B., *Understanding the Lord's Prayer*, Philadelphia: Fortress, 1975.

Harrington, W. J. OP, *Matthew: Sage Theologian: The Jesus of Matthew*, Dublin: The Columba Press, 1998.

Hay, D. M., *Glory at the Right Hand. Psalm 110 in Early Christianity*, SBLMS 18, Nashville: Abingdon, 1973.

Hedrick, C. W., 'On Moving Mountains. Mark 11:22b-23/Matt 21:21 and Parallels,' *Forum* 6: 219-37, 1990.

Heil, J. P., 'Significant Aspects of the Healing Miracles in Matthew', *CBQ* 41: 276-287, 1979.

Heil, J. P., *Jesus Walking on the Sea. Meaning and Gospel Functions of Matthew14:22-33, Mark 6:45-52 and John 6:15b-21*, Rome: Biblical Institute Press, 1981.

Heil, J. P., *The Death and Resurrection of Jesus: A Narrative-Critical Reading of Matthew 26-28*, Minneapolis: Fortress, 1991.

Heil, J. P., *The Transfiguration of Jesus: Narrative Meaning and Function of Mark 9:2-8, Matthew 17:1-8 and Luke 9:28-36*, Rome: Biblical Institute Press, 2000.

Hengel, M., *Crucifixion in the Ancient World and the Folly of the Message of the Cross*, Philadelphia: Fortress, 1977.

Hogan, M., *Seeking Jesus of Nazareth: An Introduction to the Christology of the Four Gospels*, The Columba Press, Dublin, 2001.

Holman, C. L., *Till Jesus Comes: Origins of Christian Apocalyptic Expectation*, Peabody: Hendrickson, 1996.

Hooker, M. D., *Jesus and the Servant: The Influence of the Servant Concept of Deutero-Isaiah in the New Testament*, London: SPCK, 1959.

Horsley, R. A. and J. H. Hanson, *Bandits, Prophets and Messiahs. Popular Movements at the Time of Jesus*, San Francisco: Harper and Row, 1985.

Howell, D. B., *Matthew's Inclusive Story: A Study in the Narrative Rhetoric of the First Gospel*, JSNT Sup 42, Sheffield: Sheffield Academic Press, 1990.

Hubbard, B. J., *The Matthean Redaction of a Primitive Apostolic Commissioning: An Exegesis of Matthew 28:16-20*, SBLDS 19, Missoula: Society of Biblical Literature and Scholars Press, 1974.

Jeremias, J., *The Parables of Jesus*, revised edition, London: SCM Press, 1972.

Jeremias, J., *The Eucharistic Words of Jesus*, London: SCM Press 1966.

Jeremias, J., *Jerusalem in the Time of Jesus. An Investigation into Economic and Social Conditions during the New Testament Period*, London: SCM Press, 1969.

Juel, D., *Messiah and Temple: The Trial of Jesus in the Gospel of Mark*, SBLDS 31, Missoula: Scholars Press, 1977.

Johnson, E. S., 'Mark 15:39 and the So-Called Confession of the Roman Centurion', *Bib* 81 (2000) 406-13.

Johnson, L. T., 'The New Testament's Anti-Jewish Slander and the Conventions of Ancient Rhetoric', *JBL* 108: 419-41, 1989.

Johnson, M. D., *The Purpose of Biblical Genealogies*, Society for New Testament Studies Monograph Series 8, Cambridge: CUP, 1969.

Katz, S., 'Issues in the Separation of Judaism and Christianity after 70 C.E.: A Reconsideration', *JBL* 103:43-76, 1984.

Keck, L. E., 'Ethics in the Gospel According to Matthew', *Iliff Review*, 40:39-56, 1984.

Kermode, F., *The Genesis of Secrecy. On the Interpretation of Narrative*, Cambridge, Mass/London: Harvard University Press, 1979.

Kim, T. H., 'The Anarthous *hyios theou* in Mark 15:39 and the Roman Imperial Cult,' *Bib* 79 (1998) 221-41.

Kingsbury, J. D., *The Parables of Jesus in Matthew 13: A Study in Redaction Criticism*, Oxford: Clarendon, 1969.

Kingsbury, J. D., *Matthew: Structure, Christology, Kingdom*, Philadelphia: Fortress, 1975.

Kingsbury, J. D., 'Observations on the "Miracle Chapters" of Matthew 8-9.' *CBQ* 40:559-573, 1978.

Kingsbury, J. D., 'The Figure of Peter in Matthew's Gospel as a Theological Problem', *JBL* 98:67-83, 1979.

Kingsbury, J. D., 'The Figure of Jesus in Matthew's Story: A Literary-Critical Probe.' *JSNT* 21:3-36, 1984.

Kingsbury, J. D., 'The Parable of the Wicked Husbandmen and the Secret of Jesus' Divine Sonship in Matthew: Some Literary Critical Observations', *JBL,* 105:643-655, 1986.

Kingsbury, J. D., 'The Place, Structure, and Meaning of the Sermon on the Mount within Matthew', *Interpretation* 41:131-143, 1987.

Kingsbury, J. D., 'The Plot of Matthew's Story', *Interpretation* 46: 347-56, 1992.

Kingsbury, J. D., 'The Title "Son of David" in Matthew's Gospel', *JBL* 95: 591-602, 1976.

Kingsbury, J. D., 'The Developing Conflict between Jesus and the Jewish Leaders in Matthew's Gospel: A Literary Critical Study.' *CBQ* 49: 57-73, 1987.

Kingsbury, J. D., *Matthew as Story*, Philadelphia: Fortress, 1988.

Klassen, W., *Love of Enemies: The Way to Peace*, OBT, Philadelphia: Fortress, 1984.

Knowles, M., *Jeremiah in Matthew's Gospel: The Rejected-Prophet Motif in Matthean Redaction*, JSNTS Sup 68, Sheffield: JSOT, 1993.

Kodell, J., *The Eucharist in the New Testament*, Zacchaeus Studies, Wilmington: Michael Glazier, 1988.

Kudasiewicz, J., *The Synoptic Gospels Today*, New York: Alba House, 1996 (E.T. of original in Polish, 1986).

Lachs S. T., *A Rabbinic Commentary on the New Testament. The Gospels of Matthew, Mark and Luke*, Hoboken NJ: Ktav, 1987.

Levine, A. J., *The Social and Ethnic Dimensions of Matthean Social History. 'Go nowhere among the Gentiles...' (Matt 10:5b)*, Lewiston NY: Mellen, 1998.

Lightfoot, R. H., *The Gospel Message of St Mark*, Oxford, Clarendon, 1950.

Lindars, B., *New Testament Apologetic: The Doctrinal Significance of the Old Testament Quotations*, London: SCM Press, 1961.

Lindars, B., 'Salvation Proclaimed. VII. Mark 10:45: A Ransom for Many,' *Exp Tim* 93 (1981-82), 292-95.

Lindars, B., *Jesus Son of Man: A Fresh Examination of the Son of Man Sayings in the Gospels*, London: SPCK, 1983.

Lischer, R., 'The Sermon on the Mount as Radical Pastoral Care,' *Interpretation* 41:1987, 157-169.

Loader, W. R. G., 'Christ at the Right Hand. Ps CX.1 in the New Testament', *NTS* 21: 81-108, 1974/1975.

Loader, W. R. G., 'Son of David, Blindness, Possession and Duality in Matthew', *CBQ* 44:570-585, 1982.

Lohr, C., 'Oral Techniques in the Gospel of Matthew', *CBQ* 23: 403-435, 1961.

Lohse, E., *History of the Suffering and Death of Jesus Christ*, Philadelphia: Fortress, 1967.

Luz, U., 'The Disciples in the Gospel According To Matthew', in *The Interpretation of Matthew*, ed. G. Stanton, Philadelphia: Fortress, 1983, 98-128.

Luz, U., 'The Son of Man in Matthew: Heavenly Judge or Human Christ', *JSNT* 48:3-21, 1992.

Luz, U., *Matthew in History: Intrerpretation, Influence, and Effects*, Minneapolis: Fortress, 1994.

Luz, U., *The Theology of the Gospel of Matthew*, New Testament Theology, Cambridge: CUP, 1995.

Luz, U., *Studies in Matthew*, Grand Rapids: Eerdmans, 2005.

Main, E., 'Les Sadducéens et la résurrection des morts: comparaison entre Mc 12:18-27 et Luc 27-37,' *RB* 103 (1996) 411-32.

Malina, B. J., *The New Testament World. Insights from Cultural Anthropology*, Louisville KY: W/JKP, 2001.

Malina, B. J., *The Social History of Jesus. The Kingdom of God in Mediterranean Perspective*, Minneapolis: Fortress, 2001.

Manek, J., 'Fishers of Men', *Novum Testamentum*, 2 (1957-58), 138-41

Manson, T. W., *The Sayings of Jesus*, London: SCM, 1949.

Manson, T. W., *The Teaching of Jesus*, Cambridge: CUP, 1967.

Marcus, J., 'The Jewish War and the *Sitz im Leben* of Mark,' *JBL* 111 (1992), 446-48.

Marcus, J., *The Mystery of the Kingdom of God*, SBLDS 90, Atlanta: Scholars Press, 1986.

Matera, F. J., *Passion Narratives and Gospel Theologies: Interpreting the Synoptics Through Their Passion Stories*, Theological Inquiries, New York: Paulist Press, 1986.

Matera, F. J., 'The Plot of Matthew's Gospel', *CBQ* 49:233-253, 1987.

McConnell, R. S., *Law and Prophecy in Matthew's Gospel: The Authority and Use of the Old Testament in the Gospel of St Matthew*, Basel: Reinhardt, 1969.

McEleney, N. J., 'Peter's Denials – How Many? To Whom?', *CBQ*

52: 467-72, 1990.

McGing, B. C., 'Pontius Pilate and the Sources', *CBQ* 53 (1991) 416-38.

Meier, J. P., 'Salvation History in Matthew: In Search of a Starting Point', *CBQ* 37:203-215.

Meier, J. P., *Law and History in Matthew's Gospel. A Redactional Study of Mt 5:17-48*, Rome: Biblical Institute Press, 1976.

Meier, J. P., 'Nations or Gentiles in Matthew 28:19?', *CBQ* 39:94-102, 1977.

Meier, J. P., *The Vision of Matthew: Christ, Church and Morality in the First Gospel*, New York: Paulist 1979; Crossroads 1991.

Meier, J. P., *A Marginal Jew: Rethinking the Historical Jesus*, 3 vols, New York: Doubleday, 1991, 1994, 2001.

Meier, J. P., 'The Brothers and Sisters of Jesus in Ecumenical Perspective', *CBQ* 54 (1992) 1-28.

Meier, J. P., 'The Debate on the Resurrection of the Dead: An Incident from the Ministry of the Historical Jesus?' *JSNT* 77: 3-24, 2000.

Moloney, F. J., *The Gospel of Mark: A Commentary*, Peabody: Hendrickson, 2002.

Mullins, M., *Called To Be Saints: Christian Living in First Century Rome*, Dublin, Veritas, 1991.

Mullins, M., *The Gospel of John, A Commentary*, Dublin: Columba Press, 2003.

Mullins, M., *The Gospel of Mark, A Commentary*, Dublin: Columba Press, 2005.

Murphy-O'Connor, J., 'Fishers of Fish, Fishers of Men,', *Bible Review* 15/3, 1999.

Murphy-O'Connor, J., 'What Really happened at the Transfiguration?', *Bible Review*, 3/3, 8-21, 1987.

Murphy-O'Connor, J., 'What Really Happened at Gethsemane?' *Bible Review* 14 /2: 28-39, 52, 1998.

Neusner, J., *From Politics to Piety: The Emergence of Pharisaic Judaism*, Englewood Cliffs NJ: Prentice Hall, 1973.

Neusner, J., *Judaism. The Evidence of the Mishnah*, 2nd ed., Atlanta: Scholars Press, 1988.

Neyrey, J., 'The Thematic Use of Isa 42:1-4 in Matthew 12', *Biblica* 63: 457-473, 1982.

Nickelsburg, G. W. E., *Resurrection, Immortality, and Eternal Life in Intertestamental Judaism*, Cambridge, Mass: Harvard University Press, 1972.

Nolan, B. M., *The Royal Son of God: The Christology of Matthew 1-2 in the Setting of the Gospel*, Göttingen: Vandenhoeck & Ruprecht, 1979.

O'Connell, S., 'Towards the First Gospel', *PIBA*, 26, 66-87, 2003.

O'Leary, A. M., *Matthew's Judaization of Mark: Examined in the Context of the Use of Sources in Graeco-Roman Antiquity*, New York/London: T&T Clark, 2006.

O' Neill, J. C., ' "Good Master" and the "Good" Sayings in the Teaching of Jesus', *Irish Biblical Studies* 15 (1993).

O'Rourke, J. J., 'Roman Law and the Early Church', in *The Catacombs and the Colosseum*, ed. S. Benko and J. J. O'Rourke, Valley Forge: Judson, 1971.

Orton, D. E., *The Understanding Scribe. Matthew and the Apocalyptic Ideal*, Sheffield: JSOT, 1989.

Osiek, C., *What Are They Saying About The Social Setting of the New Testament?*, New York: Paulist, 1992.

Overman, J. A., *Matthew's Gospel and Formative Judaism. The Social World of the Matthean Community*, Minneapolis: Fortress, 1990.

Overman, J. A., *Church and Community in Crisis: The Gospel According to Matthew*, The New Testament in Context, Valley Forge: Trinity Press International, 1996.

Painter, J., *Mark's Gospel: Worlds in Conflict*, New Testament Readings, London: Routledge, 1997.

Perkins, P., *Love Commands in the New Testament*, New York: Paulist, 1982.

Perkins, P., *Peter: Apostle for the Whole Church*, Columbia: University of South Carolina Press, 1994.

Perrin, N., *A Modern Pilgrimage in New Testament Christology*, Philadelphia: Fortress, 1974.

Pesch, R., *Das Markusevangelium*, 2 vols, Herders theologischer Kommentar zum Neuen Testament, 2, Freiburg: Herder, 1976.

Petrie, C. S., 'The Authorship of "The Gospel According to Matthew": A Reconsideration of the External Evidence', *NTS* 14:15-33, 1967-1968.

Petuchowski, J. J., and M. Brocke, *The Lord's Prayer and Jewish Liturgy*, New York: Seabury, 1978.

Piper, J., '"Love Your Enemies": Jesus' Love Command in the Synoptic Gospels and the early Christian Paraenesis', *SNTSMS* 38, Cambridge: CUP, 1979.

Pobee, J., 'The Cry of the Centurion – a Cry of Defeat,' in E. Bammel (ed), *The Trial of Jesus*, Cambridge Studies in Honour of C. F. D. Moule, Studies in Biblical Theology, Second Series 13, London: SCM Press, 1970, 91-102.

Powell, M. A., 'The Plot and Subplots of Matthew's Gospel', *NTS* 38:187-204, 1992.

Powell, M. A., 'Towards a Narrative-Critical Understanding of Matthew', *Interpretation* 46:341-46, 1992.

Powell, M. A., 'Do and Keep What Moses Says (Matthew 23:2-7)', *JBL* 114:419-35, 1995.

Przybylski, B., *Righteousness in Matthew and His World of Thought*, Cambridge: CUP, 1980.

Radermakers, J., *La bonne nouvelle de Jesús selon Marc*, 2 vols, Bruxelles, 1974.

Richardson, A., *The Miracle-Stories of the Gospels*, London: SCM, 1941.

Richardson, P., *Herod*, Columbia: University of South Carolina Press, 1996.

Riesenfeld, H., *The Gospel Tradition*, Philadelphia: Fortress, 1970.

Rohrbaugh, R., (ed), *The Social Sciences and New Testament Interpretation*, Peabody: Hendrickson, 1996.

Saldarini, A. J., *Jesus and Passover*, New York: Paulist, 1984.

Saldarini, A. J., *Pharisees , Scribes and Sadducees in Palestinian Society. A Sociological Approach*, Wilmington: Michael Glazier, 1988.

Saldarini, A. J., *Matthew's Christian-Jewish Community*, Chicago: University of Chicago Press, 1994.

Sand, A., *Das Gesetz und die Propheten*, Regensburg: Pustet, 1974.

Sanders, E. P., *Jesus and Judaism*, Philadelphia: Fortress, 1985.

Schams, C., *Jewish Scribes in the Second-Temple Period*, Sheffield: Sheffield Academic Press, 1998.

Schenk, W., *Die Sprache des Matthäus*, Göttingen: Vandenhoeck & Ruprecht, 1987.

Schmidt, T. E., 'Mark 15:16-32: The Crucifixion Narrative and the Roman Triumphal Procession,' *NTS* 41:1-18, 1995.

Schneiders, S. M., *The Revelatory Text. Interpreting the New Testament as Sacred Scripture*, San Francisco: Harper,1991.

Schrage, W., *The Ethics of the New Testament*, Edinburgh: T.& T. Clark, 1988.

Schuler, P.L., *A Genre for the Gospels. The Biographical Character of Matthew*, Philadelphia: Fortress, 1982.

Scott, B. B., *Jesus, Symbol-Maker for the Kingdom*, Philadelphia: Fortress,1981.

Seely, D., 'Jesus' Temple Act,' *CBQ* 55 (1993) 263-83.

Senior, D., 'The Death of Jesus and the Resurrection of the Holy Ones (Mt 27:51-53)', *CBQ* 38:312-29, 1976.

Senior, D., *The Passion of Jesus in the Gospel of Mark*, Wilmington: Michael Glazier, 1984.

Senior, D., *The Passion of Jesus in the Gospel of Matthew*, Wilmington: Michael Glazier, 1985.

Senior, D., 'Matthew's Special Material in the Passion Story', *ETL*, 63: 272-94, 1987.

Senior, D., 'Matthew's Account of the Burial of Jesus Mt 27:57-61' in *The Four Gospels 1992: Festschrift Frans Neirynck*, eds. F. Van Segbroeck, C. M. Tuckett, G. Van Belle, and J. Verheyden, Leuven: Leuven University Press, 1992, 1433-48.

Senior, D., *What Are They Saying About Matthew?* New York: Paulist, 1983.

Sherwin-White, A. N., *Roman Society and Roman Law in the New Testament*, Oxford: Clarendon, 1963.

Sigal, P., *The Halakah of Jesus of Nazareth according to the Gospel of Matthew*, Lanham Md: University Press of America, 1986.

Sloyan, G. S., *Jesus on Trial. The Development of the Passion Narratives and Their Historical and Ecumenical Implications*, Philadelphia: Fortress, 1973.

Smith, D. B., 'The More Original Form of the Words of Institution,' *ZNW* 83 (1992) 166-86.

Snodgrass, K., 'Recent Research on the Parable of the Wicked Tenants: An Assessment,' *Bulletin of Biblical Research* 8: 187-215, 1998.

Stanton, G., *The Interpretation of Matthew*, Philadelphia: Fortress, 1983.

Stanton, G., *A Gospel for a New People: Studies in Matthew*, Edinburgh: T&T Clark, 1992.

Stendahl, K., *The School of St Matthew and Its Use of the Old Testament*, Philadelphia: Fortress, 1968.

Strecker, G., *Der weg der Gerechtikeit. Untersuchungen zur Theologie des Matthäus*, Göttingen: Vandenhoeck & Ruprecht, 1962.

Streeter, B. H., *The Four Gospels: A Study of Origins*, New York: Macmillan, 1925.

Suggs, M. J., *Wisdom, Christology and Law in Matthew's Gospel*, Cambridge, Mass: Harvard University Press, 1970.

Swartley, Wilard M., ed, *The Love of Enemy and Nonretaliation in the New Testament*, Louisville: Westminster John Knox, 1992.

Talbert, C. H., *What Is a Gospel? The Genre of the Canonical Gospels*, Macon GA: Mercer University Press, 2nd ed, 1985.

Taylor, N. H., ' Palestinian Christianity and the Caligula Crisis', Part 1: *JSNT* 61:101-24; 1996; Part 2: *JSNT* 62; 13-41, 1996.

Travis, S., *The Revival of the Griesbach Hypothesis*, Cambridge: CUP, 1983.

Twelftree, G. H., *Jesus the Miracle Worker. A Historical and Theological Study*, Downers Grove, Ill: Intervarsity, 1999.

Van Tilborg, S., *The Jewish Leaders in Matthew*, Leiden: Brill, 1972.

Viviano, B. T., 'Where was the Gospel According to St Matthew Written?' *CBQ* 41:533-546, 1979.

Viviano, B. T., *The Kingdom of God in History*, Collegeville: The Liturgical Press, 1991.

von Balthasar, H. U., 'Theology and Aesthetic', *Communio*, 1, 1981.

von Balthasar, H. U., *The Office of Peter in the Church*, San Francisco: Ignatius Press, 1989.

Yee, G. A., *Jewish Feasts and the Gospel of John*, Zacchaeus Studies: New Testament, Wilmington: Michael Glazier, 1989.

Wainright, E. M., *Towards a Feminist Critical Reading of the Gospel According to Matthew*, Beihefte zur Zeitschrift fur die Neutestamentliche Wissenschaft 60, New York: de Gruyter, 1991.

Walker, P. W. L., *Jesus and the Holy City: New Testament Perspectives on Jerusalem*, Grand Rapids: Eerdmans, 1996.

Walker, R., *Die Heilsgeschichte im ersten Evangelium*, Göttingen: Vandenhoeck & Ruprecht, 1962.

Weaver, D. J., *Matthew's Missionary Discourse. A Literary Critical Analysis*, JSNT Sup 38, Sheffield: JSOT, 1990.

Wehnam, D, and C. Blomberg, eds, *Gospel Perspectives 6: The Miracles of Jesus*, Sheffield, 1986.

Weren, W. J. C., 'The Use of Isaiah 5:1-7 in the Parable of the Tenants (Mark 12:1-12; Matthew 21:33-46)', *Biblica* 79: 1-26, 1998.

Weren, W. J. C., 'The Macrostructure of Matthew's Gospel: A New Proposal', *Biblica* 87 (2006) 171-200.

Wheeler, S. E. *Wealth as Peril and Obligation: The New Testament on Possessions*, Grand Rapids: Eerdmans, 1995.

White, K. D., 'The Parable of the Sower,' *JTS* 15: 300-307, 1964.

White, L., 'Grid and Group in Matthew's Community: The Righteousness/Honor Code in the Sermon on the Mount', *Semeia* 35:61-90, 1986.

Wilkins, M. J., *The Concept of Disciple in Matthew's Gospel*, Leiden: Brill, 1988.

Wilkins, M. J., *Discipleship in the Ancient World and Matthew's Gospel*, Grand Rapids: Baker, 1995.

Wilson, W. R., *The Execution of Jesus. A Judicial, Literary and Historical Investigation*, New York: Scribners, 1970.

Wink, W., *John the Baptist in the Gospel Tradition*, Cambridge: CUP, 1969.

Wink, W., 'Beyond Just War and Pacifism: Jesus' Nonviolent Way.' *Review and Expositor* 68: 197-214, 1992.

Wrede, W., *The Messianic Secret*, London: Clarke, 1971 (E. T. by J. C. G. Grieg of *Das Messiasgeheimnis in den Evangelien*, Göttingen 1901).

Select General Index

Index of Modern Authors